I0754854

Pavilion
An imprint of HarperCollins*Publishers* Ltd
1 London Bridge Street
London SE1 9GF

www.harpercollins.co.uk

HarperCollinsPublishers
Macken House
39/40 Mayor Street Upper
Dublin 1
D01 C9W8
Ireland

10 9 8 7 6 5 4 3 2 1

First published in Great Britain by Pavilion
An imprint of HarperCollins*Publishers* 2026

ISBN 978-0-00-874151-8

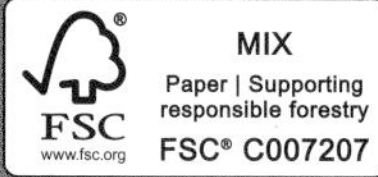

Publishing Director: Laura Russell
Commissioning Editor: Shamar Gunning
Design Manager: Alice Kennedy-Owen
Designer: Cara Rogers
Production Controller: Louis Harvey
Proofreader: Sarah Epton
Indexer: Ruth Ellis

Printed and bound by Papercraft in Malaysia

DEDICATION
For Augustine Tadeu Hopkinson, my first American grandson and a very distant relation of Francis Hopkinson of New Jersey, who signed the Declaration of Independence in 1776.

ACKNOWLEDGMENTS
The publishers would like to thank the authors of the following *Then and Now* and *Lost* books for their picture research/text extracts.

Old West Then and Now, Vaughan Grylls: *San Diego Then and Now*, Nancy Hendrickson: *Charleston Then and Now*, Leigh Jones Handal: *Philadelphia Then and Now*, Ed Mauger and Bob Skiba: *Boston Then and Now*, Patrick Kennedy: *San Antonio Then and Now*, Paula Allen: *Washington, DC, Then and Now*, Emma Tanner: *New Orleans Then and Now*, Sharon Keating: *New England Then and Now*, Derek Strahan: *Lost New Orleans*, Richard Campanella: *Lost San Francisco*, Dennis Evanosky and Eric J. Kos: *Lost Washington*, Paul Kelseu Williams: *Cincinnati Then and Now*, Jeff Suess: *St Louis Then and Now*, Maureen Kavanaugh: *Mark Twain's America Then and Now*, Laura DeMarco: *Salt Lake City Then and Now*, Kirk Huffaker: *Civil War Battlefields Then and Now*, Jim Campi Jr: *New York Then and Now*, Marcia Reiss: *Chicago Then and Now*, Kathleen Maguire: *Detroit Then and Now*, Cheri Gay: *Milwaukee Then and Now*, Sandra Ackerman: *San Francisco Then and Now*, Dennis Evanosky and Eric J. Kos: *Savannah Then and Now*, Polly Cooper and Ted Eldridge: *New York Then and Now* (Compact), Hetty Hopkinson and Karl Mondon: *Houston Then and Now*, William Dylan Powell: *Route 66 Then and Now*, Joe Sonderman: *Seattle Then and Now*, Benjamin Lukoff: *Los Angeles Then and Now*, Rosemary Lord: *Indianapolis Then and Now*, Nelson Price and Joan Hostetler: *Memphis Then and Now*, Russell Johnson: *Hollywood Then and Now*, Rosemary Lord: *Las Vegas Then and Now*, Su Kim Chung.

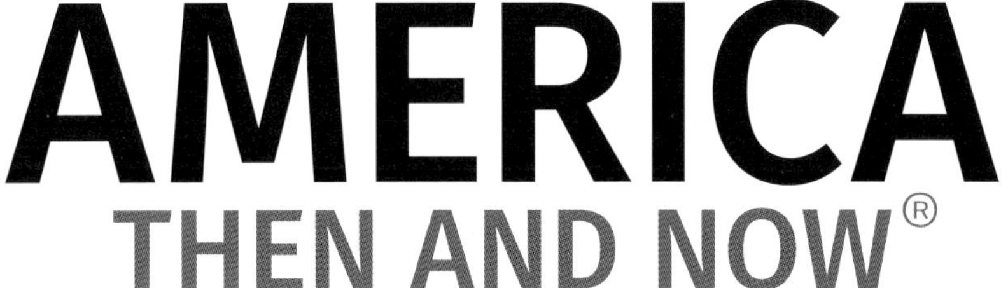

Frank Hopkinson

PAVILION

CONTENTS

INTRODUCTION

America's history is thousands of years in the making, ever since the land bridge of "Beringia" allowed tribes to migrate from Asia and populate the Americas. There are few tangible relics of those migratory tribes, but buildings inserted high on the cliff face in Canyon de Chelly remind historians that at one point the Pueblo Indians stopped roaming the land to practice agriculture while the climate allowed.

The Spanish, venturing north from "New Spain," explored and then exploited the land in the Southwest, while in the north, French explorers and fur trappers ventured deep into the interior. But modern America sprung from the Thirteen Colonies on the Atlantic seaboard, largely from English and Dutch colonists who sought freedom from religious persecution, or a grant of land to make their fortune, or were criminals transported at his majesty's pleasure.

The rigors of emigration and the natural qualities needed to survive in a strange environment, often with hostile natives unwilling to cede land, created a breed of settler unwilling to be pushed around by the "mother country." One hundred and fifty years after the first settlers had alighted at Plymouth Rock, the Thirteen Colonies began to push back against taxes, restrictions on taking Native land, and a lack of representation. It fostered a grinding Revolutionary War, finally ended by the Treaty of Ghent in 1783, a conflict from which emerged a titan of American politics, George Washington.

Getting rid of the British was one thing, founding a new nation was almost as troublesome, especially with factions in the South making it clear their aims were at odds with politicians in the North. Alexander Hamilton wanted to emulate the economies of Northern Europe, not the plantation economies of the West Indies— from which he'd immigrated—and their reliance on slave labor. Jefferson saw the country's future in agriculture.

He struck a deal with the embattled French, the nation for which he had been American ambassador until 1789, to purchase the Louisiana territories in return for $15 million. Sam Houston, on the other hand, took Texas by force and the Mexican army's capitulation in 1848 gained the nation New Mexico, Utah, Nevada, Northern Arizona and California. It was now truly a nation from sea to shining sea, rich in natural resources and rife for expansion into the newly acquired lands.

The discovery of gold in California hastened its elevation into a full state, which only served to ratchet up existing tensions about new territories joining the union and their attitude to slavery. This toxic problem ultimately led to the secession of the southern states and the Civil War that followed. General Robert E. Lee led an under-provisioned and poorly armed force to the brink of victory at Gettysburg but fell short. As the smoke cleared in 1865, over 600,000 soldiers had perished, more than the combined totals of World War I and II, Korea and Vietnam.

Warfare is often the catalyst to innovation and a spur to industry and in the postwar years the economy roared. The generation that had been lost were replaced by immigrants keen to build a new life in the land of opportunity (many arriving at Ellis Island as pictured right). The boom took America into what Mark Twain described as the "Gilded Age," a time when leisure and travel were discovered, when the growth of railroads made fortunes for a selected few, and Standard Oil cornered the market. World's fairs in Philadelphia, Chicago, Omaha, and San Francisco showcased America's industrial power while Pennsylvania steel became the new architectural backbone for skyscrapers that had been limited in height by weight of stone but were now set free by the Chicago School.

Soon the nation had the resources to place some of the great landscapes under protection of national park status—Yellowstone, Yosemite, and Crater Lake were all examples of jaw-dropping natural beauty preserved for the future. To these have been added battlefield sites, famous landmarks, and monuments.

America Then and Now is a series of historical snapshots that mark some of the key moments in the development of the nation. It singularly focuses on events that have taken place on American shores. Compiled and curated over 300 pages, it tells the story of the most dynamic nation in the world, which, within 250 years of passing its Declaration of Independence, has placed men on a different planet (a feat still not matched 60 years later). The remarkable achievements featured in these pages show what has happened to many of these sites where history was made in the intervening years. Viewed together they form a compelling narrative about the unstoppable trajectory of the United States.

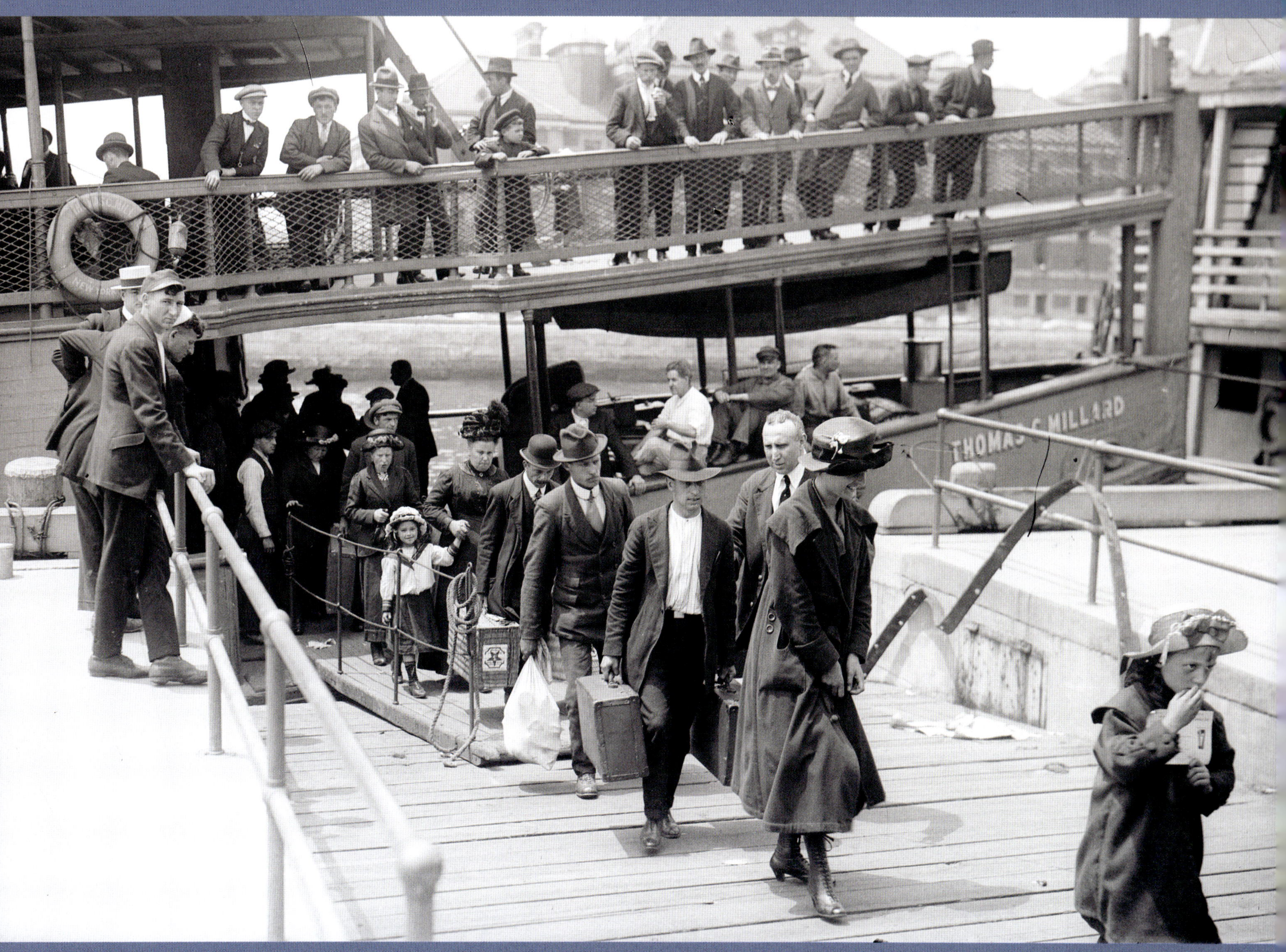
THOMAS C MILLARD

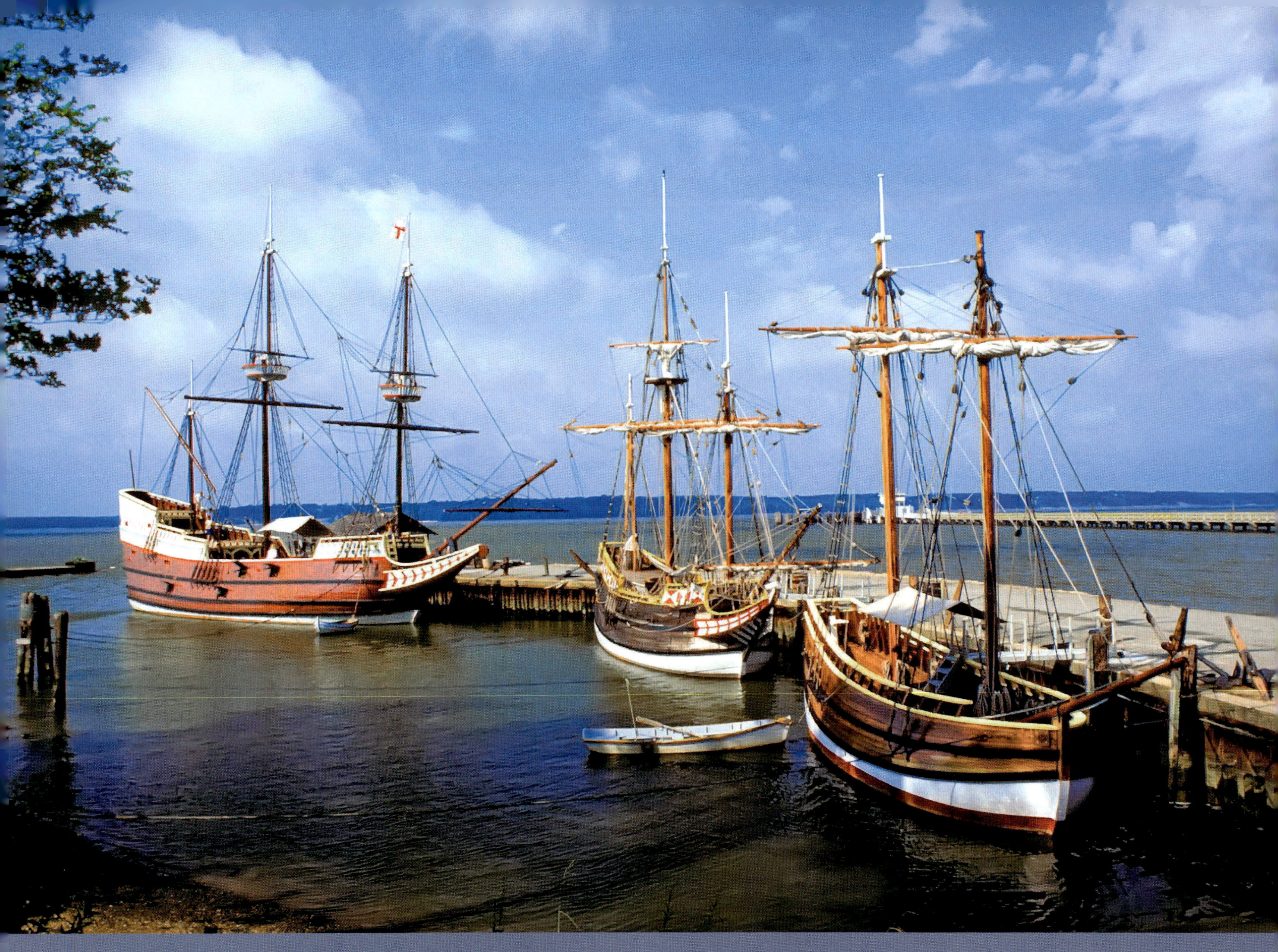

THE ROOTS OF SETTLEMENT

Long before European colonists arrived on the North American shores, indigenous peoples had established complex societies and settlements. It is estimated that there were over a thousand distinct Native American tribes residing within what is now the United States during the pre-Columbian era.

They had arrived from Asia via a land bridge between Asia and America (present-day Alaska) that existed during the ice ages more than 15,000 years ago. Scientists have found that Native American populations—from Canada down to the southern tip of Chile—have DNA sequences that link them to the first great migration and two subsequent migrations.

The majority became migratory tribes which moved around through the seasons and left no long-lasting trace of their presence on the land, bar a few petroglyphs, or inscriptions carved into rock. But there were some early settlements that have survived. One of the most remarkable of these is in Canyon de Chelly, located in present-day northeastern Arizona. By around 1000 CE, the Ancestral Puebloans (also known as the Anasazi) had built a network of cliff dwellings and stone structures within the canyon's walls, some of which are still visible today.

These communities, which included multiroom complexes, *kivas* (ceremonial rooms), and sophisticated irrigation systems, thrived on agriculture, particularly corn, beans, and squash. Over time, as climate patterns shifted, they were forced to move on. However, their descendants—including the Hopi, Zuni, and other Pueblo peoples—have carried on their cultural traditions.

The Hopi people, considered among the oldest continuous residents of North America, maintained village life atop easily defendable mesas in the high desert. Hopi society was structured around matrilineal clans and ceremonial calendars. They had a strong spiritual connection to the land, which involved their famous snake dance.

SPANISH ARRIVAL AND THE MISSION SYSTEM

Spanish missionaries ventured north into this territory following the Spanish conquest of the Aztec Empire. Present-day Mexico was officially named New Spain by Hernán Cortés in 1521 after the conquest, and the Viceroyalty of New Spain was established in 1535.

By the 1600s, the Spanish had established a mission system throughout New Mexico and parts of Texas and California. Missions were religious and economic centers designed to convert indigenous populations to Christianity and often brutally exploit them. This system brought about massive cultural disruption, along with diseases against which the native population had no natural immunity. However, armed resistance persisted, most notably in the Pueblo Revolt of 1680, in which a coalition of Pueblo peoples drove the Spanish out of the region for over a decade.

ENGLISH SETTLEMENTS ON THE ATLANTIC COAST

While Spanish colonization dominated the southwest, English settlers began establishing colonies along the Atlantic coast. The first permanent English settlement in North America was founded in 1607 at Jamestown in what is now Virginia. Sponsored by the Virginia Company, the settlement faced immense hardship—disease, starvation, and conflict with the local Powhatan Confederacy. It was not until the introduction of tobacco cultivation by John Rolfe that Jamestown became economically viable. Tobacco became a cash crop, and with it came the first enslaved Africans, brought over in 1619, marking the beginning of a system of slavery that would shape American society for centuries.

PLYMOUTH ROCK, 1620

In 1620, a group of English religious separatists known as the Pilgrims landed at (a place which would be renamed) Plymouth Rock in present-day Massachusetts. Fleeing religious persecution in England, they had initially planned a move to Virginia but settled farther north. The Mayflower Compact, signed aboard their ship, established a rudimentary form of self-government. With assistance from local indigenous peoples—especially Squanto of the Patuxet tribe—the Pilgrims survived their first winter. The Wampanoag Confederacy, led by Massasoit, formed an uneasy alliance with the settlers, commemorated in the First Thanksgiving.

MASSACHUSETTS BAY AND RELIGIOUS MIGRATION

In 1630, a larger wave of Puritan settlers arrived in New England, founding the Massachusetts Bay Colony under the leadership of John Winthrop, who famously envisioned the colony as a "city upon a hill." Unlike the profit-driven Virginia settlers, these Puritans sought to build a religious utopia based on strict moral codes and communal responsibility. They established towns, schools, and churches, fostering a literate and organized society that still have strong echoes to this day. Tensions over religious doctrine would lead to the founding of other colonies, such as Rhode Island by Roger Williams and Connecticut by Thomas Hooker.

CHARLES TOWN AND THE SOUTHERN COLONIES

Charles Town (now Charleston, South Carolina) was founded in 1670 by English settlers from Barbados. This colony quickly adopted a plantation-based economy, growing rice and indigo using enslaved African labor. Unlike the family-based colonies of New England, the Carolinas developed a more hierarchical and aristocratic society, heavily influenced by Caribbean plantation culture. By the late 1600s, slavery had become deeply entrenched in the southern economy, and the demographic makeup increasingly included a large African-descended population.

THE GROWTH OF EDUCATION

As the English and Dutch colonies stabilized, they began investing in education, particularly in New England, where religious life demanded a literate population. In 1636, just six years after the founding of the Massachusetts Bay Colony, settlers established Harvard College in Cambridge, Massachusetts. It was originally intended to train Puritan ministers, emphasizing classical education in Latin, Greek, theology, and philosophy. By the 1720s, Harvard had become the intellectual beating heart of the colonies, shaping future leaders and promoting a distinctly American academic tradition.

By the early eighteenth century, the foundations of the United States were in place. European settlers had arrived and negotiated a foothold on the land. Often there was conflict with native tribes, sometimes harmonious integration (Savannah in Georgia was just such a model), religious migrations, and the beginning of a complex society that would evolve into a new nation.

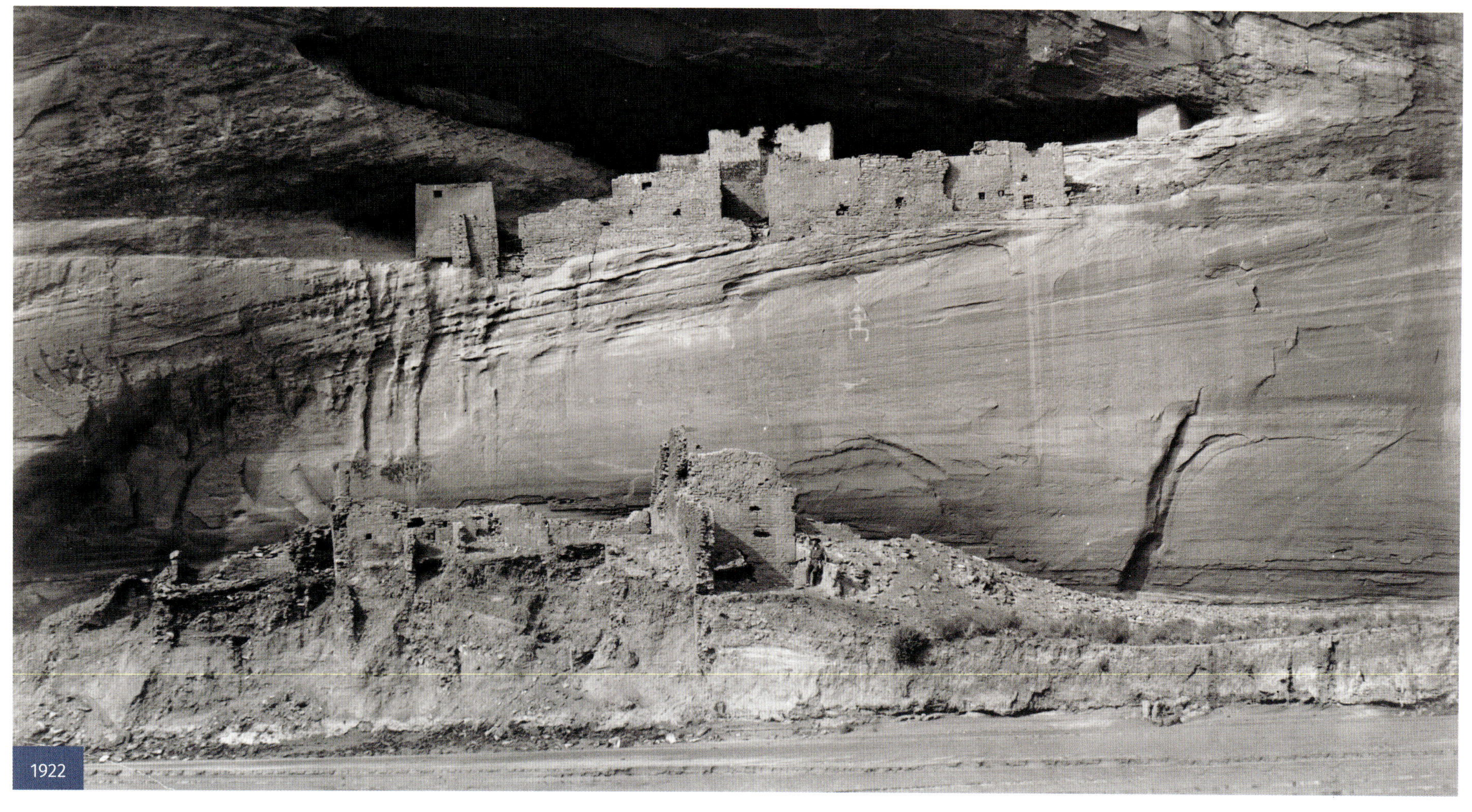
1922

WHITE HOUSE, CANYON DE CHELLY, ARIZONA

These early pueblos were abandoned when the land could not be farmed

The ruined White House in Canyon de Chelly, Arizona, was built by Ancestral Puebloans (or Anasazi), who lived in the present-day Four Corners region comprising southeastern Utah, northeastern Arizona, northwestern New Mexico, and southwestern Colorado. Their presence in the region has been dated as far back as the twelfth century BCE, stretching through to around 1350 CE when climate change, most likely a lack of rainfall for crops, forced them to move on. They left behind what the Spanish colonists labeled "pueblos," a collection of structures that included small pit houses, larger structures for extended families, along with the best-preserved relics—cliff dwellings—which were impermeable to rain and ideal for defense. These feats of building ingenuity were often only accessible by rope or ladders. The White House was so-named because of a prominent section of upper wall still coated with fading white plaster. After the Anasazi—a Navajo word meaning "enemy ancestor"—moved away, Hopi Indians periodically occupied the land until the 1700s, when Navajo tribes from New Mexico took control. The Navajo farmed the land until 1863, but in the bitter winter of 1863–64 Colonel Kit Carson was obliged to pursue the tribe with any hostile means. Canyon de Chelly was their last refuge, but seeing the damage

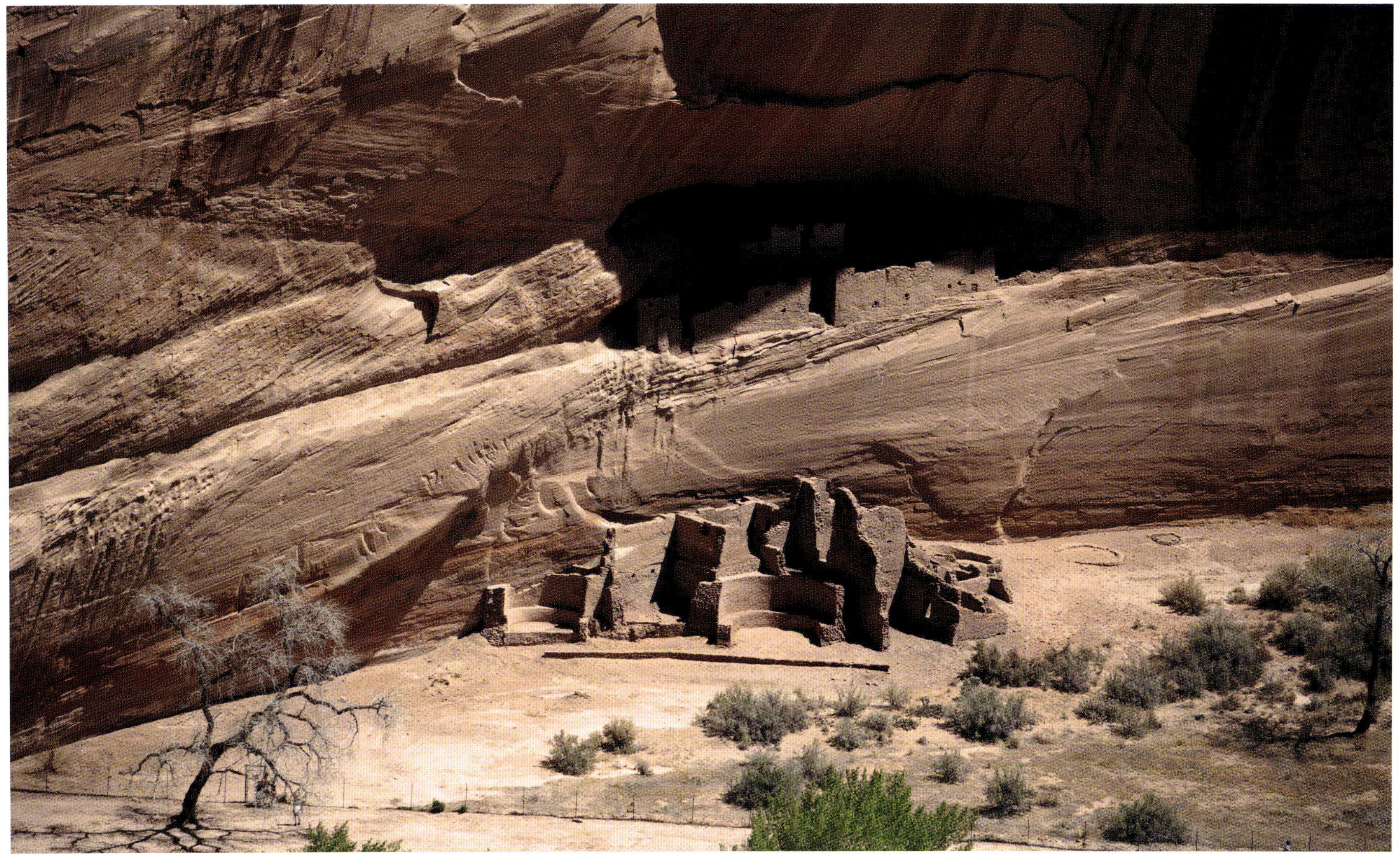

inflicted upon their homes and peach orchards by the US troops, they surrendered. Nearly 8,000 were moved to Fort Sumner's desolate Bosque Redondo reservation in New Mexico, many dying along the way, including stragglers who were often shot. This eviction became known as the "Long Walk."

After four years, those Navajo still alive were allowed to return. Today, the Canyon is part of the Navajo Indian Reservation, managed by the National Park Service on behalf of the Navajo. Having closed to visitors during Covid 19, the White House trail was reopened in 2025.

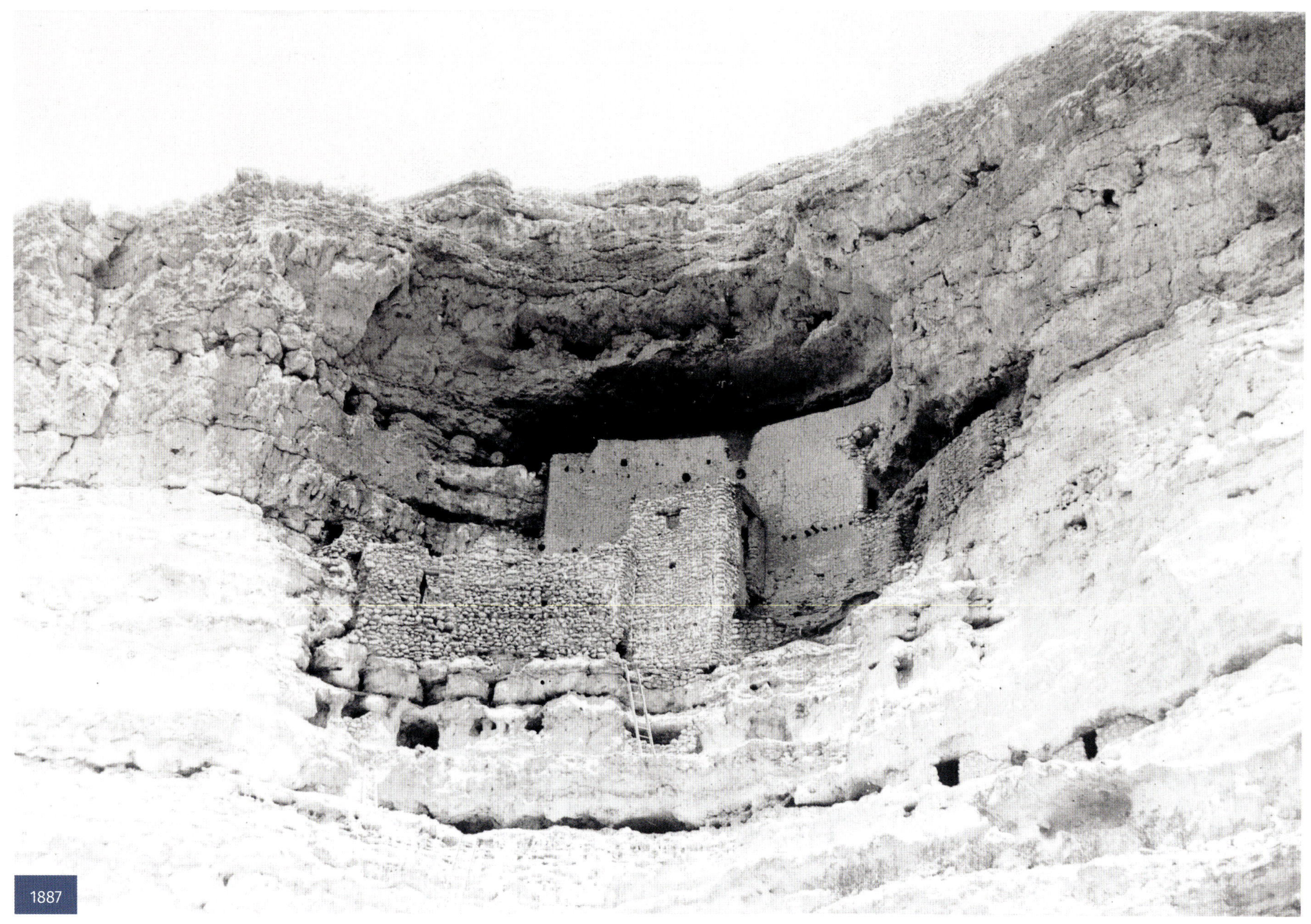

1887

"MONTEZUMA'S CASTLE," BEAVER CREEK, ARIZONA

Wrongly attributed to Montezuma, the Sinagua people made their homes highly defensible

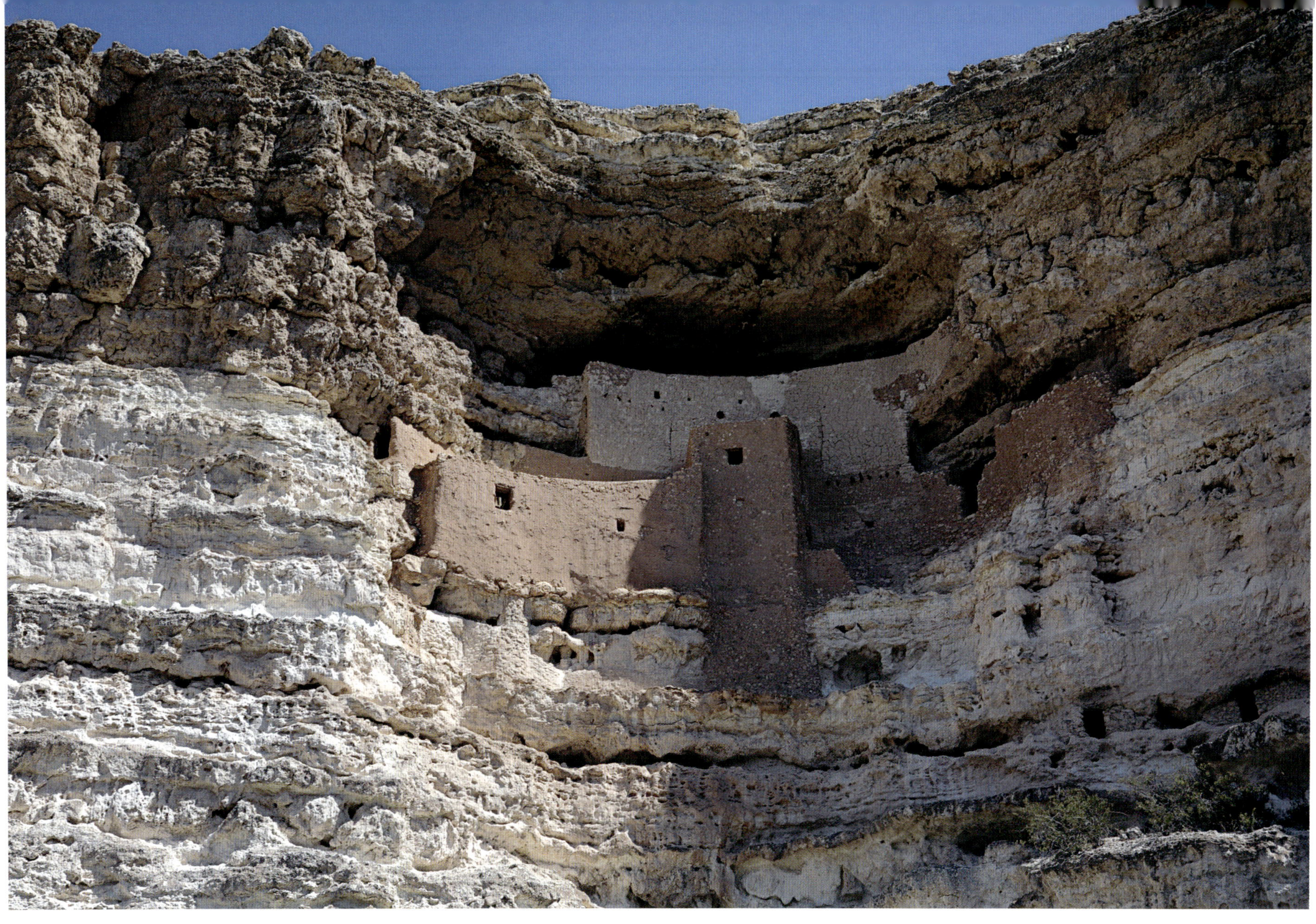

American Indians were regarded by white settlers as a universally nomadic people, the principal reason for confrontation between the cultures. It hadn't always been the case, as evidenced by the Ancestral Pueblo buildings in Canyon de Chelly. This astonishing cliff dwelling overlooking Beaver Creek (three miles from the US fort at Camp Verde) was dubbed "Montezuma's Castle" by European Americans in the 1860s. It was probably because the Aztec emperor of Mexico—killed by the Spanish in 1520—was thought the only person in the New World capable of organizing such an impressive structure. It was actually built by the Sinagua people as early as the twelfth century CE. This 1887 photograph is one of the earliest taken. The 20-odd rooms, each capable of holding 30–50 people, would have been designed to be reached by at least three separate ladders from the valley floor.

Sadly much of the structure and its remaining artifacts were looted in the late nineteenth century. So in 1906, Theodore Roosevelt, when choosing four sites in the US as national monuments, identified Montezuma's Castle as being "of the greatest ethnological value and scientific interest." Now part of the National Park Services's inventory, it attracts over 350,000 visitors a year. Constructed from limestone blocks and adobe, the builders' fingerprints are still visible on the adobe bricks, and the structure's sycamore roof beams are still intact, although tourist access to the buildings ended in 1951. There is a museum which explains thoroughly the Sinagua's achievement and the cultural background which gave rise to such a formidable structure.

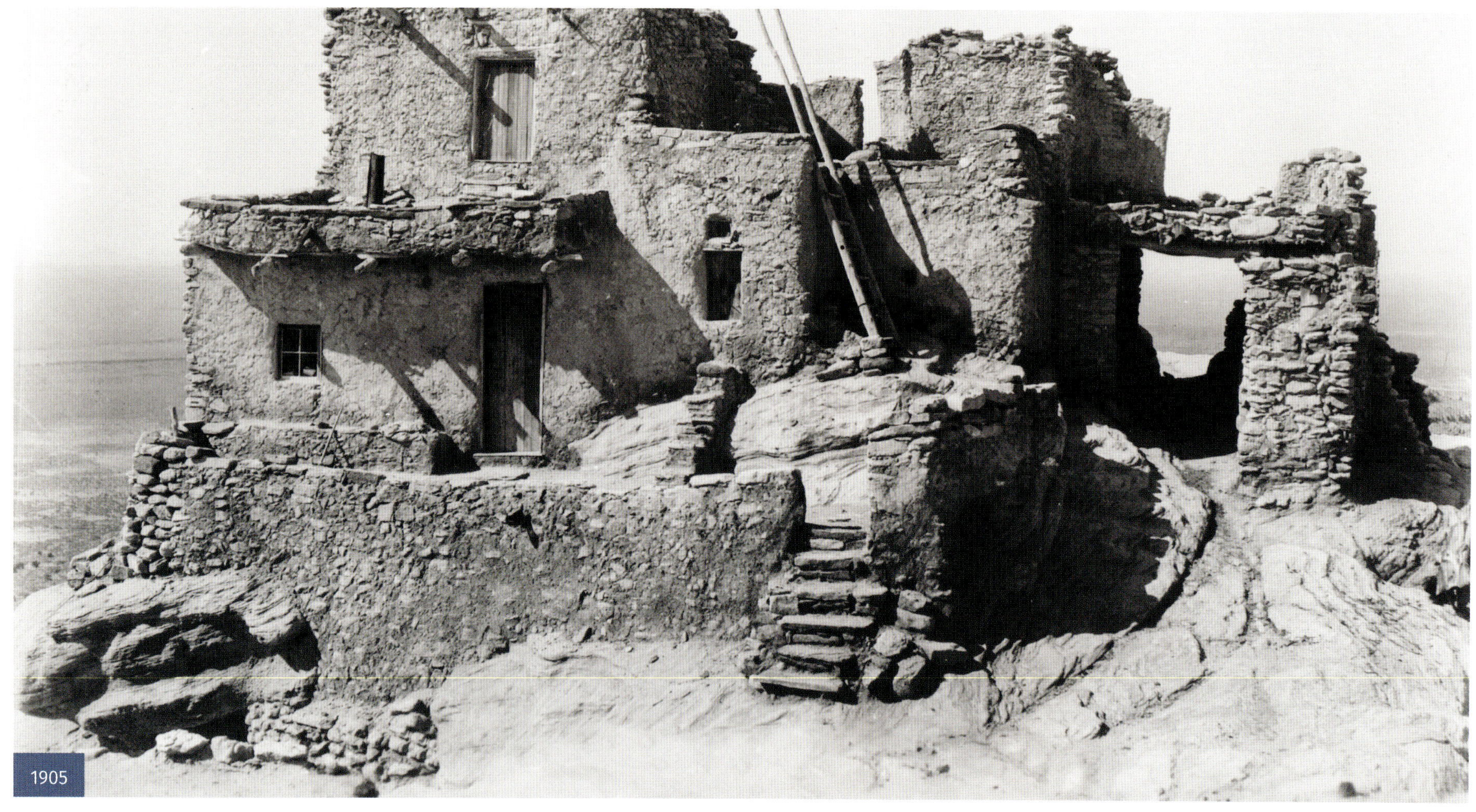

1905

HOPI VILLAGES, ARIZONA

The Hopi Indians were a peaceful tribe—until the arrival of the Spanish...

The Spanish referred to the Hopi Indians as "Pueblo people," because they lived in villages similar to those in Canyon de Chelly and the tribe is thought to be descended from the Ancestral Pueblo, or Anasazi, people who lived along the Mogollon Rim of northern Arizona. The Hopi originally settled near the foot of the Arizona mesas but to protect themselves from Utes, Apaches, and Spanish, moved their settlements to the top in villages such as Walpi. One meaning of the word Hopi can be described as "behaving one, one who is mannered, civilized, peaceable, polite, who adheres to the Hopi Way," which is in sharp contrast to many warring tribes of the region.

Although the Spanish tried to enslave the Hopi in the mission system, taking their crops and their labor, the Pueblo Revolt of 1680 put an end to it. The Spanish treatment of Hopi Indians led them to abandon their "peaceable" aspect as diverse Pueblo groups converged on the principal mission at Awatovi and dismantled it stone by stone, killing the New World occupants. The Spanish returned twenty years later and suffered the same fate, effectively putting an end to Spain's interest in the area. Under US rule, the Hopi Reservation was established in 1882 by President Chester A. Arthur, but it remains entirely surrounded by the much larger Navajo Reservation,

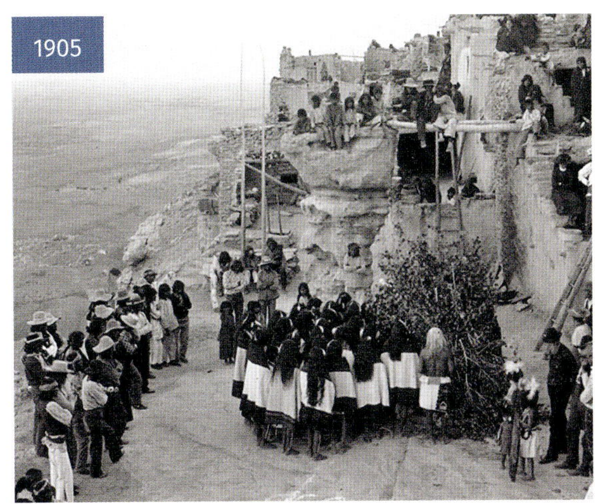

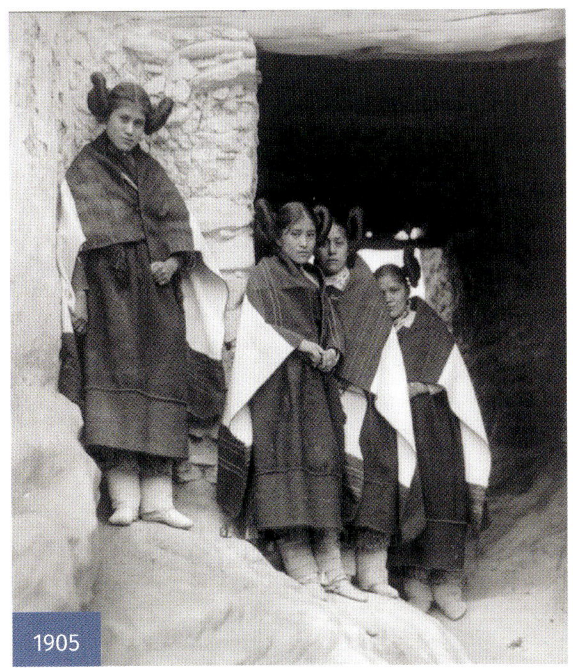

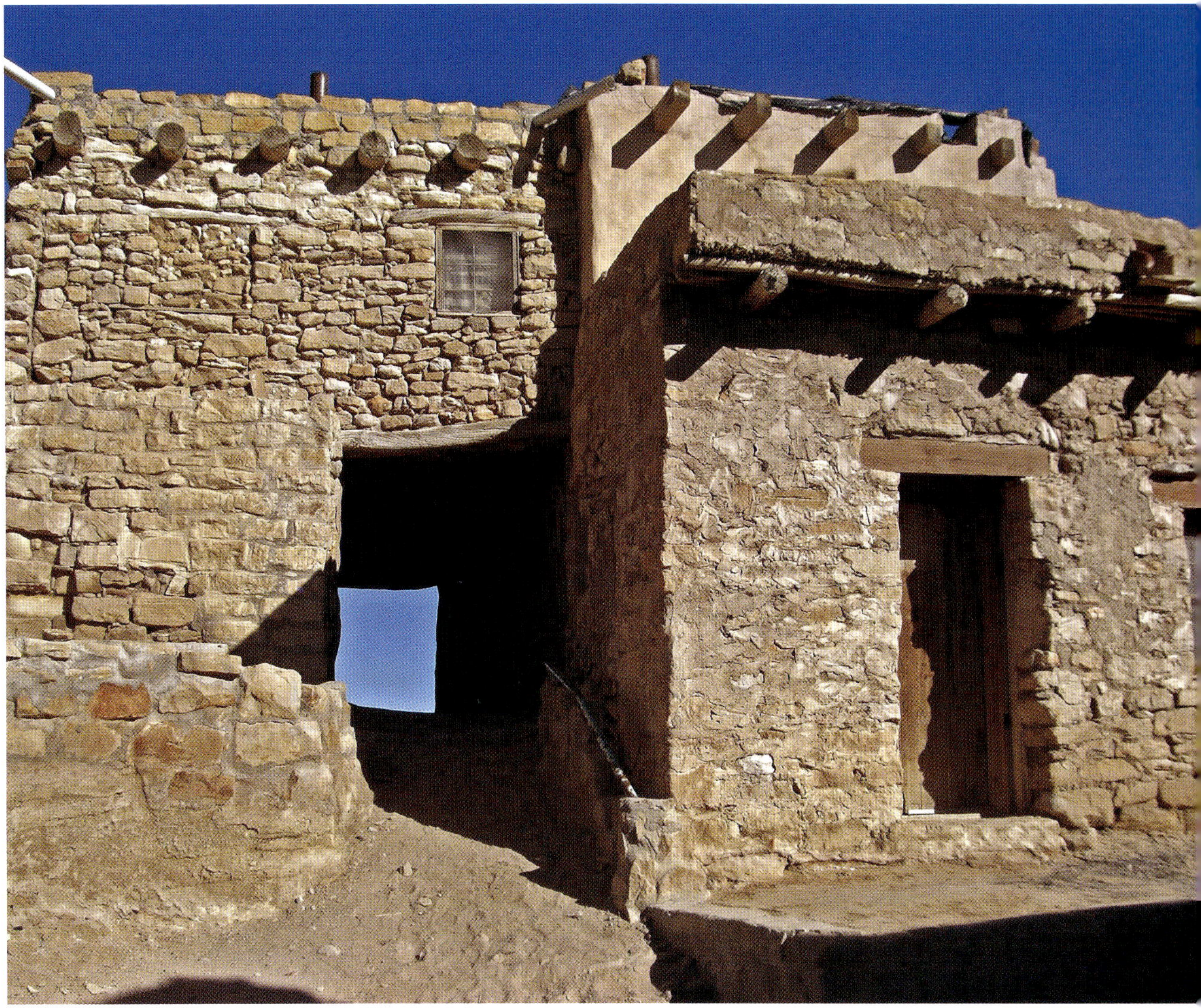

ABOVE: Two of Edward S. Curtis's turn-of-the-century photographs documenting Hopi traditional dress and culture.

ABOVE RIGHT: Walpi as it looks today.

a source of conflict to this day. An example of Hopi building outside of Walpi can be found in the Grand Canyon National Park.

The historic (but faux) Hopi House, located right on the southern rim of the Grand Canyon, has been offering authentic American Indian arts and crafts for over 100 years. It was designed by Mary Colter to resemble a Hopi dwelling similar to those at Oraibi, Arizona. Its purpose was to showcase souvenirs from Fred Harvey Indian Arts, an offshoot of the historic restaurant chain. Indeed, the Hopi House is just yards from the Grand Canyon Village station running trains from Williams, and tourists can still buy a decorated *olla*, or ceramic jar.

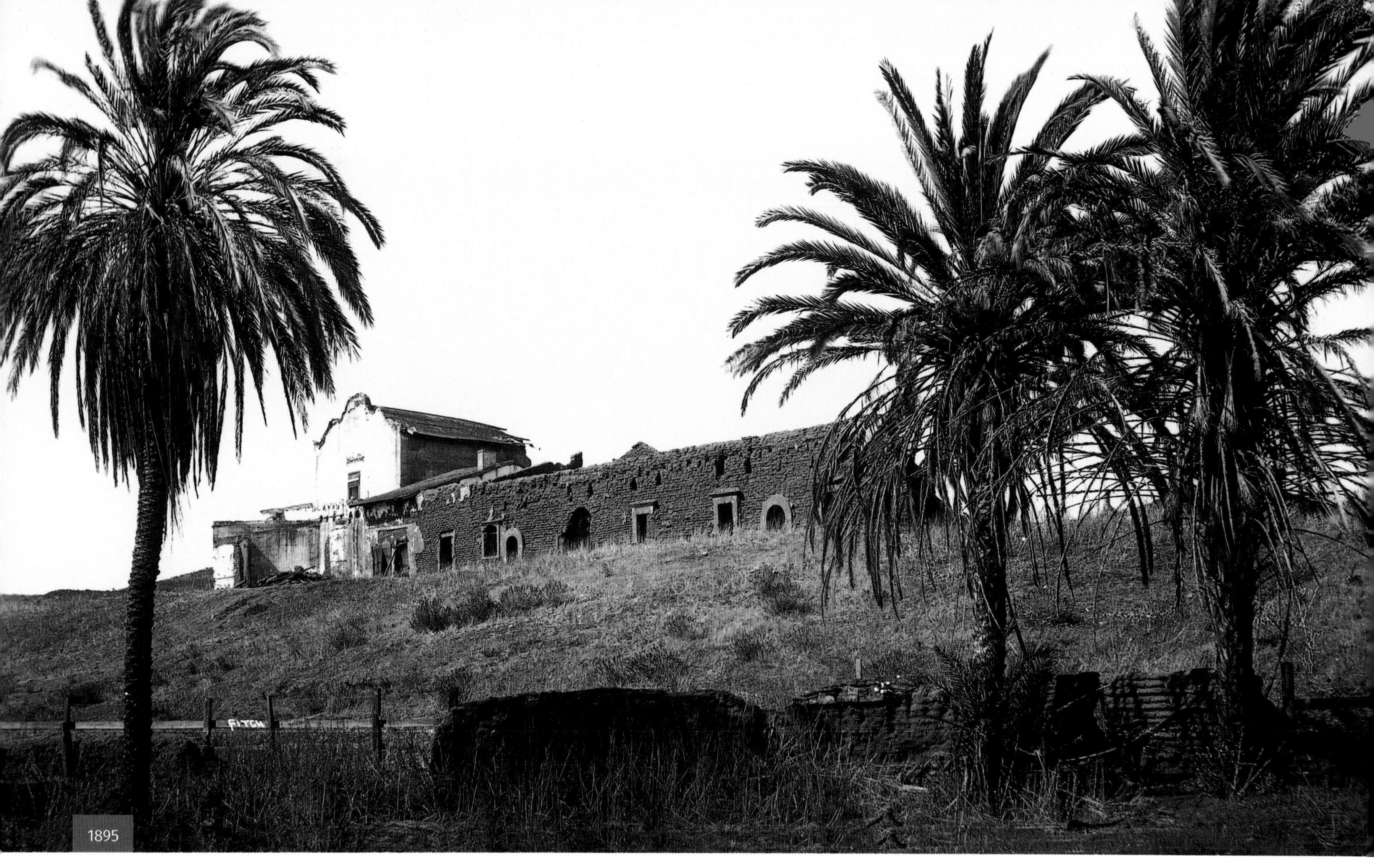

1895

MISSION SAN DIEGO DE ALCALA, CALIFORNIA

Spain's ruthless exploitation of American Indians still has repercussions today

Known as the "Mother of the Missions," San Diego de Alcala was the first of the twenty-one California missions set up by the Spanish. Founded on July 16, 1769, by Father Junipero Serra, the mission was originally located on a hill overlooking the bay. Because of poor soil and scarce water supply, the mission remained on this site for just five years. A new location was chosen six miles to the east, in what is now Mission Valley, to spread the Catholic faith. In 1775, though, hundreds of local Tipai Indians ruthlessly subjugated by the Spanish colonizers stormed the new mission. Indians taken into the missions had been put to work on agricultural projects and not allowed to leave. They were packed into overcrowded living quarters, frequently picked up European diseases, and were poorly fed. If they tried to leave they were severely beaten and shackled.

A Majorcan by birth, Father Luis Jayme became the first Christian martyr in California when he was killed in the uprising. Fearing there would be another such raid, Father Serra returned to oversee the rebuilding of the mission, this time built

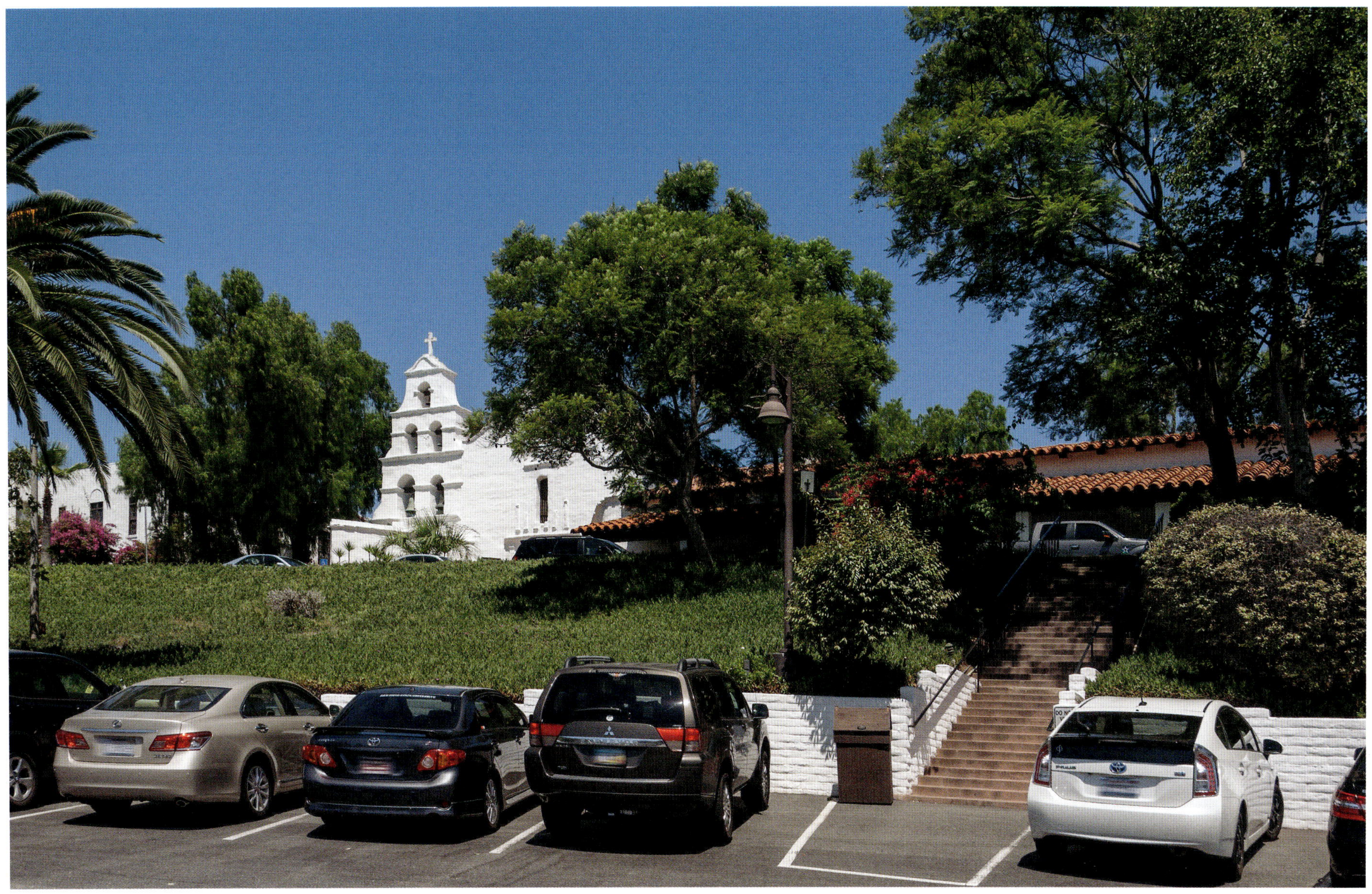

to the specification of an army fort. Serra's work in what was then Spanish-occupied Alta California in the Province of Las Californias, New Spain, has proven highly controversial and his canonization by Pope Francis was protested by representatives of California's last surviving Native American populations.

The Franciscans departed the site in 1834 while the American military occupation of the mission began in 1846 and lasted sixteen years. Abraham Lincoln returned it to the Catholic Church in 1862. In 1931 the mission was rebuilt to mirror the 1813 church; remarkably the new building was the fifth church on this site. The pope bestowed the honor of naming the Mission San Diego de Alcala as a basilica in 1976. It is just one of four in California. In the Catholic Church a basilica is a church with historical significance, and the murdered priest, Father Jayme, remains to this day buried underneath the altar.

MISSION SAN XAVIER DEL BAC, ARIZONA

The missions of New Spain were not immune from religious schisms

A mission was established here by Jesuit Father Eusebio Kino in 1692. The site was a village of the native O'odham tribe, named "W:ac." The word translates to "submerge," as this was where the Santa Cruz River submerged into the ground. The Spanish renamed it as "Bac." Father Kino died long before the first Jesuit church was built in 1756 by Father Espinosa. However, the Jesuits were expelled from New Spain in 1767 and the Franciscans took control of converting the local tribes to the Catholic faith. It was the Franciscans who built the grand Ignacio Gaona-designed Baroque church between 1783 and 1797. After Mexico gained independence from Spain in 1821 with the Treaty of Córdoba, the Franciscans left and the mission fell into decline and disuse. After the Gadsen Purchase of 1859, it fell under the jurisdiction of the

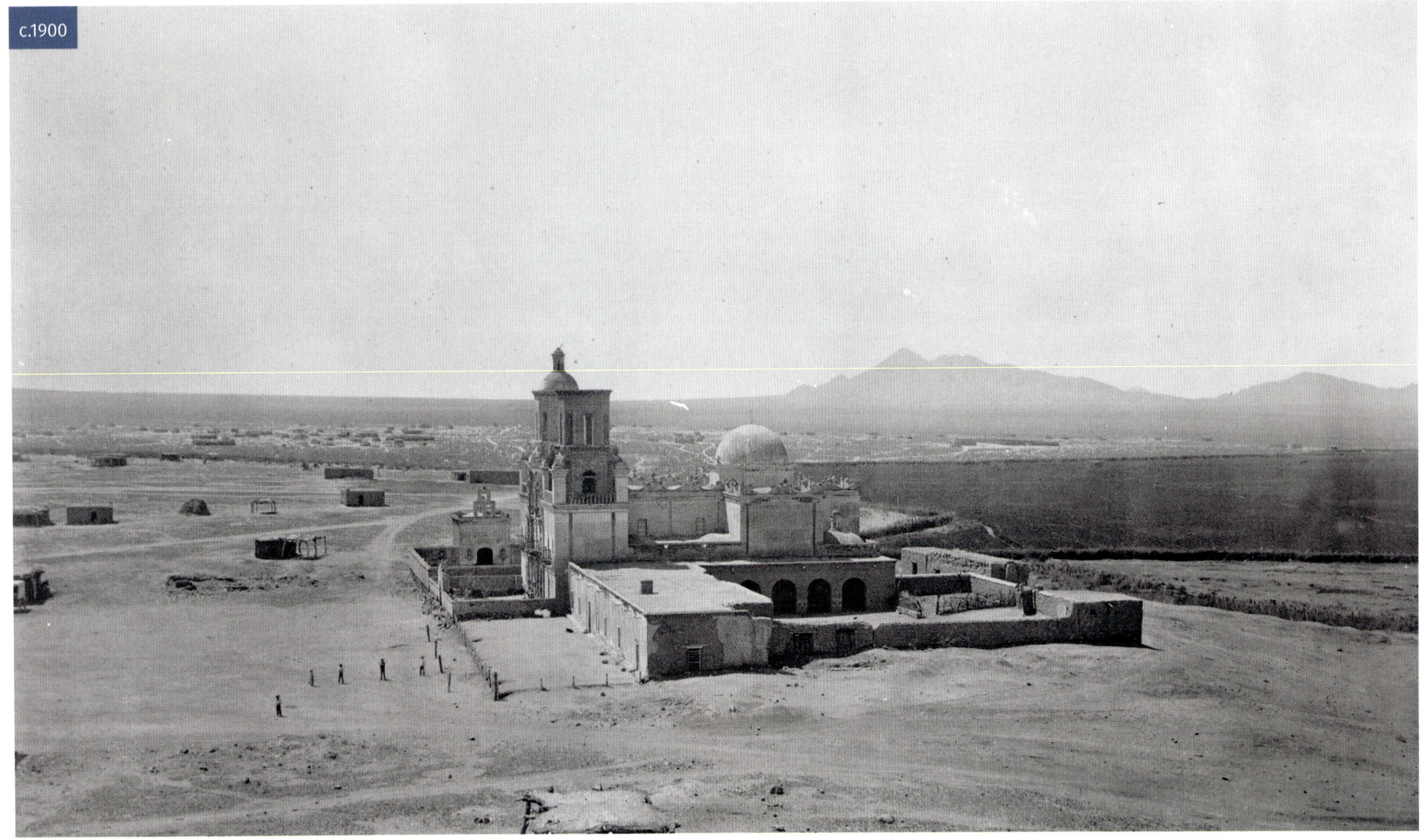
c.1900

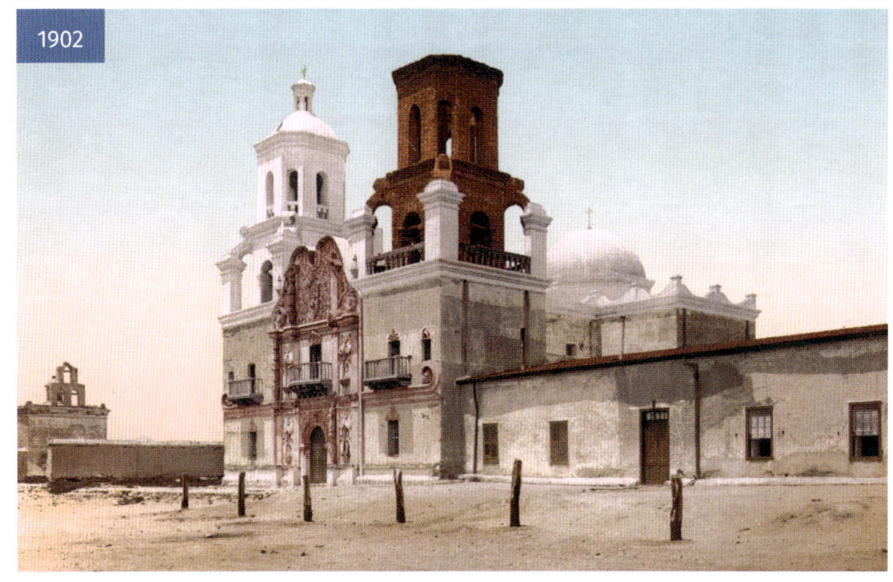

US and the Diocese of Santa Fe. The diocese recommissioned the church, ordering essential repairs, and once more it opened for worship. Seen here in 1900 the compound remains the oldest group of European buildings in Arizona. In the 1980s more extensive restoration work took place on the exterior walls, which over time had been subject to earthquake damage. Unfortunately the modern rendering damaged the lavish interior decoration through excess humidity, as the stucco used did not breathe. In recent years this has been rectified by removing the render and replacing it with traditional mud plaster.

Today, this large complex known as the White Dove of the Desert receives many tourist visitors, lying as it does just ten miles south of Tucson.

LEFT: A colorized view of the mission produced by the Detroit Photographic Company.

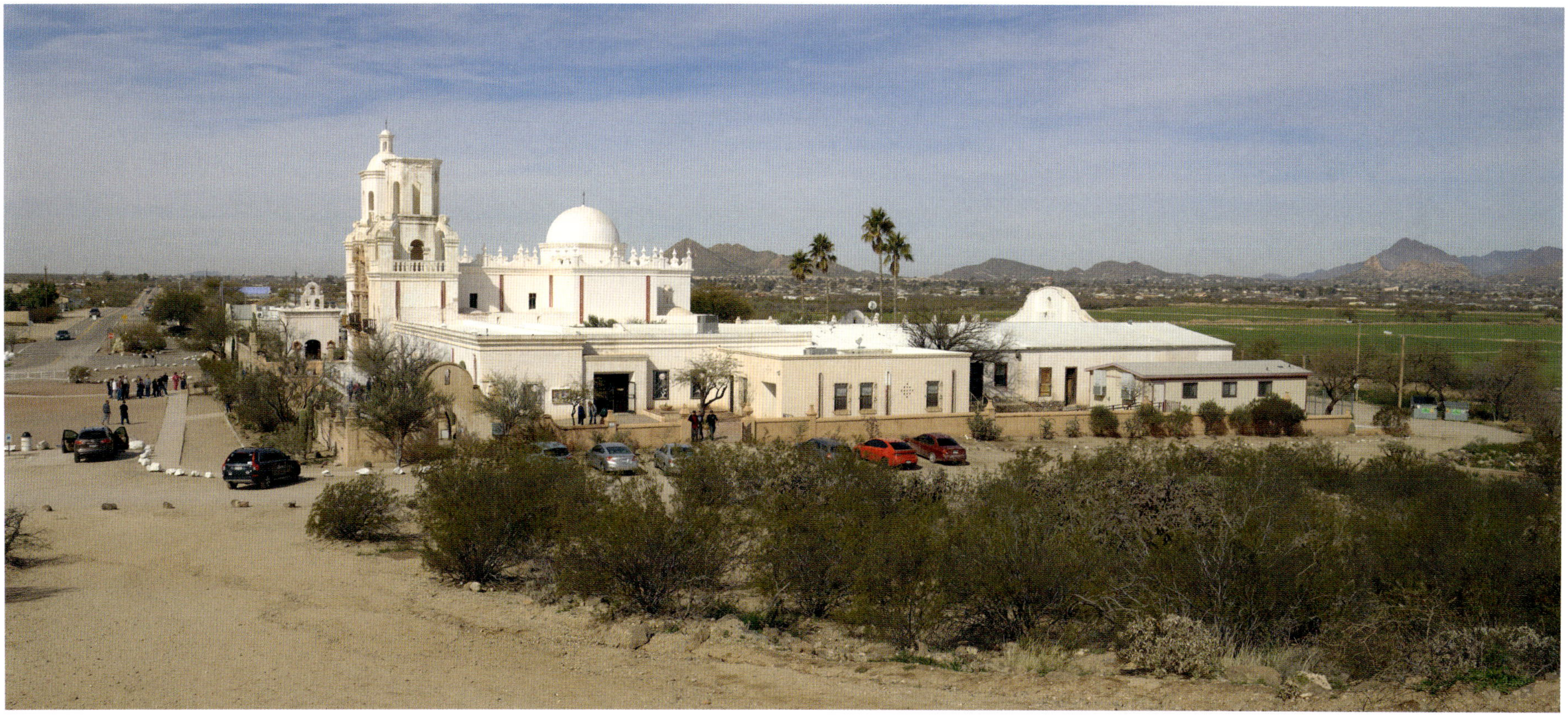

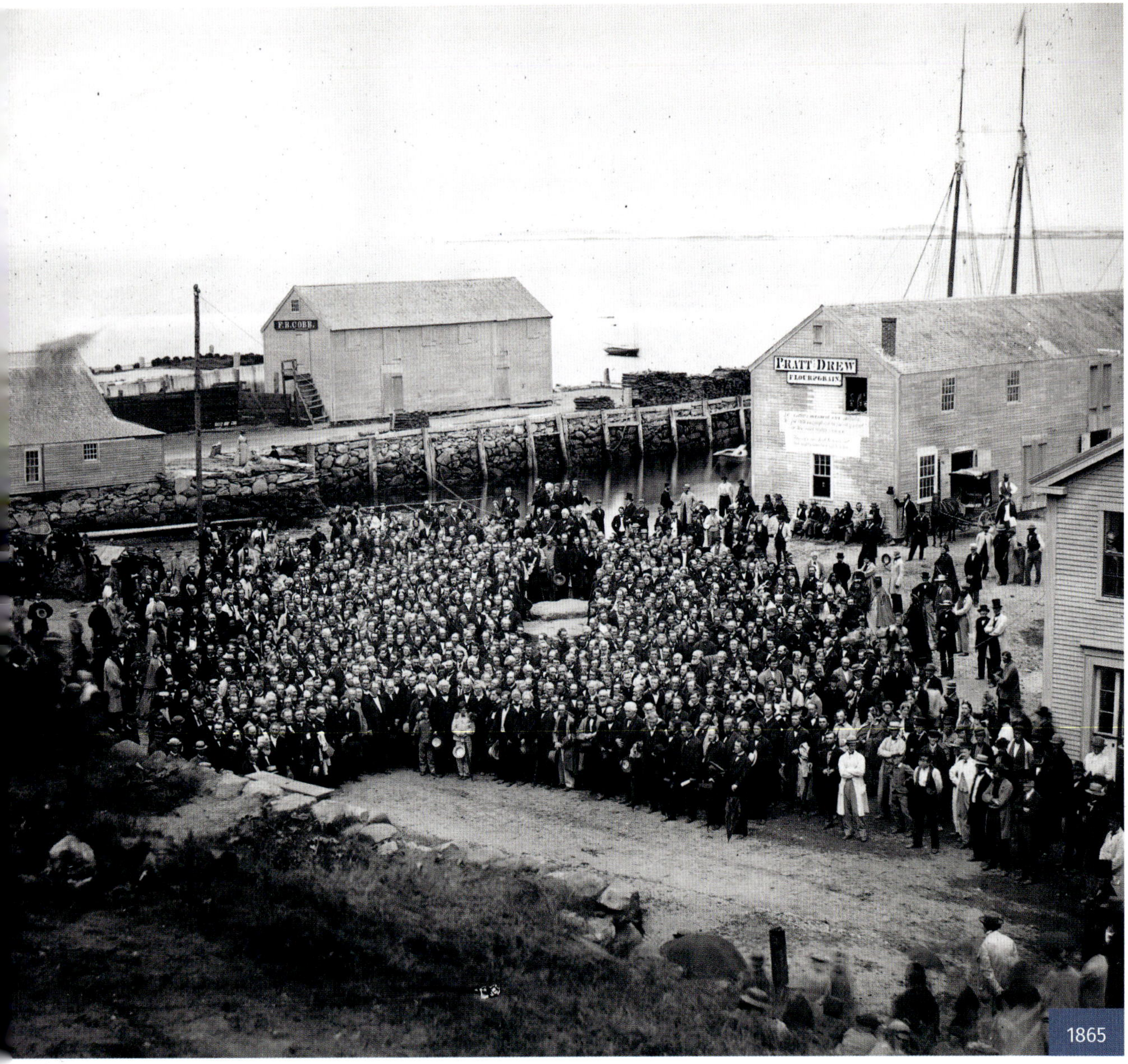

1865

PLYMOUTH ROCK, PLYMOUTH, MASSACHUSETTS

The plain "boundary stone" was elevated into an object of great historical significance

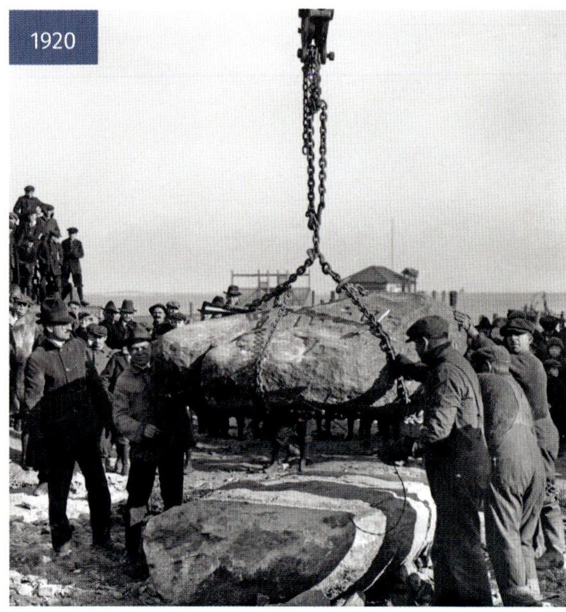

1920

The Plymouth Rock in Plymouth, Massachusetts, marks the ceremonial spot where the *Mayflower* Pilgrims, who founded Plymouth Colony, landed in December 1620. The fact that the Pilgrim Fathers arrived in Plymouth is unquestioned, but the site of the rock and its presence where the thankful passengers finally reached land is less certain. The prominent shoreline rock first drew public note in 1741 after a plan was unveiled to build a wharf that would bury it.

Thomas Faunce, a 94-year-old church elder, stepped forward to declare that it was the rock marking the site of the pilgrims' arrival. Faunce's father had arrived in "New Plymouth" aboard the ship *Anne* three years after the *Mayflower* landing. In 1623, *Anne* and *Little James* were the third and fourth ships financed by the London-based Company of Merchant Adventurers to travel to North America in support of the Plymouth Colony, following *Mayflower* in 1620 and *Fortune* in 1621. Thomas Faunce was born in 1647, when many of the Mayflower Pilgrims were still alive, and identified the place under Cole's Hill that had received the weary travelers.

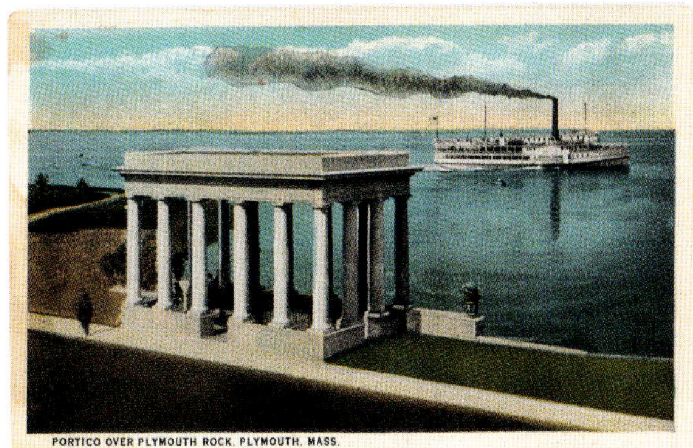

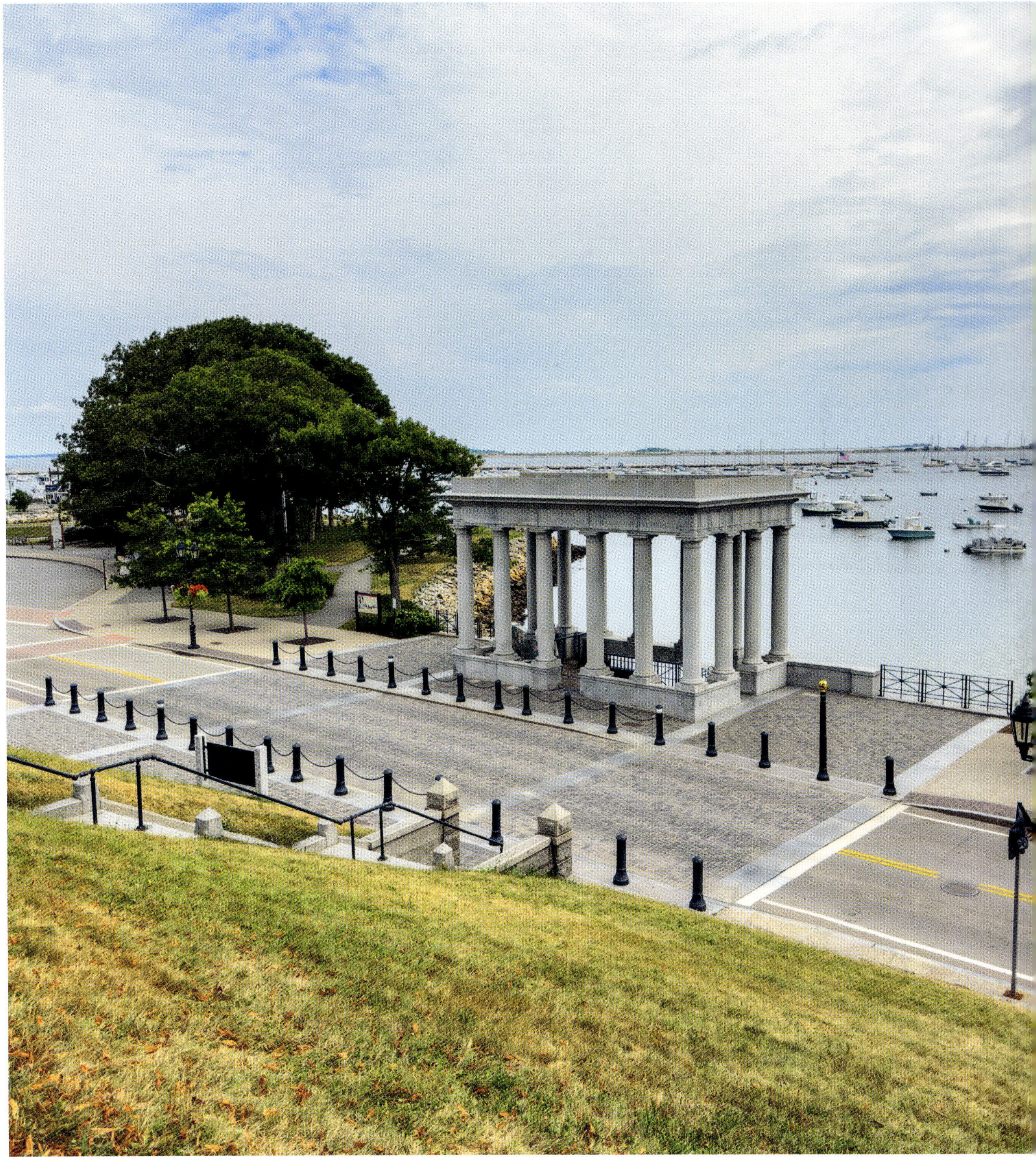

Thus began many moves for what the town records simply described up until that time as a boundary stone or "a great rock." It was hauled to the town square in 1774 and broke in half on the way. Half was returned to the coast, while the other half took its place in the town square before being made safe from souvenir hunters intent on chipping bits off (a tendency hilariously recorded in Mark Twain's book debut, *The Innocents Abroad*, where he observes American tourists determined to chisel off historic parts of the Holy Land) and moved to the Pilgrim Hall museum in 1834.

The shoreline rock has been housed in different structures, including an ornate Victorian canopy in 1867 sponsored by the Pilgrim Society. The two halves of the rock were reunited in 1880 and then again in 1920, on the occasion of the 300-year anniversary, when the wharf was removed and the waterfront landscaped. The Plymouth Rock was reinstalled at sea level beneath a Roman portico designed by McKim, Mead & White, where it remains to this day.

OPPOSITE: A meeting of the National Congregational Council at Plymouth Rock, June 22, 1865.

OPPOSITE TOP: The two halves of the rock were reunited on the shoreline in 1920.

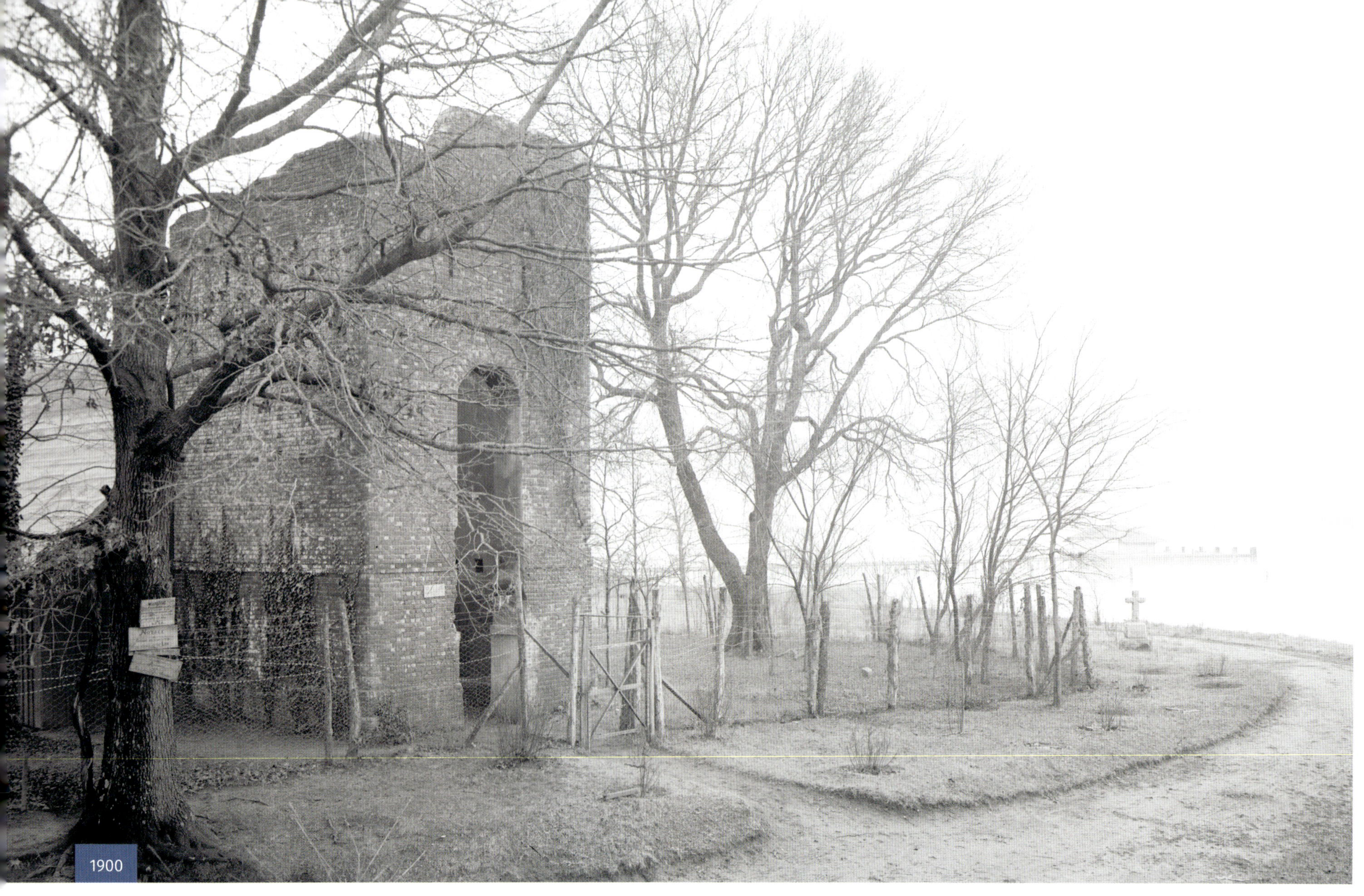
1900

JAMESTOWN, VIRGINIA

There were grave fears Jamestown would suffer the same fate as the abandoned Roanoke

Jamestown was the first permanent English settlement in the Americas. It was established by the London Company on the James River, about 2.5 miles southwest of present-day Williamsburg, from May 1607. Gaining a foothold in the New World was not easy. The Roanoke Colony was a bid by Sir Walter Raleigh in 1585 to found a settlement on Roanoke Island in present-day North Carolina, but the mission was fraught with supply problems and friction with local tribes. When a delayed resupply vessel arrived at the Roanoke fort they found it abandoned with no trace of the 100-plus settlers. Jamestown was almost abandoned in 1610 after the "Starving Time" of 1609 reduced the colonists from 214 to 60, but the evacuees met a resupply convoy in the James River.

Jamestown served as the colonial capital of Virginia from 1616 through to 1699. It survived Bacon's Rebellion but suffered the fate of being burned to the ground in 1767. Presaging what would happen in the north a hundred years later, between 1676 and 1677 Nathaniel Bacon led an armed rebellion by Virginia settlers against

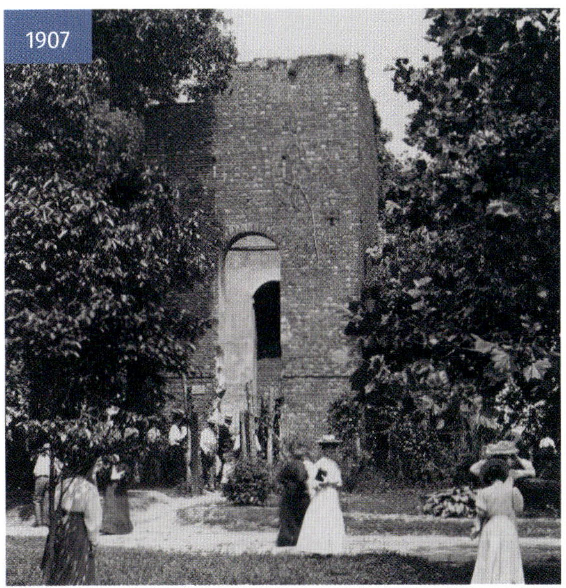

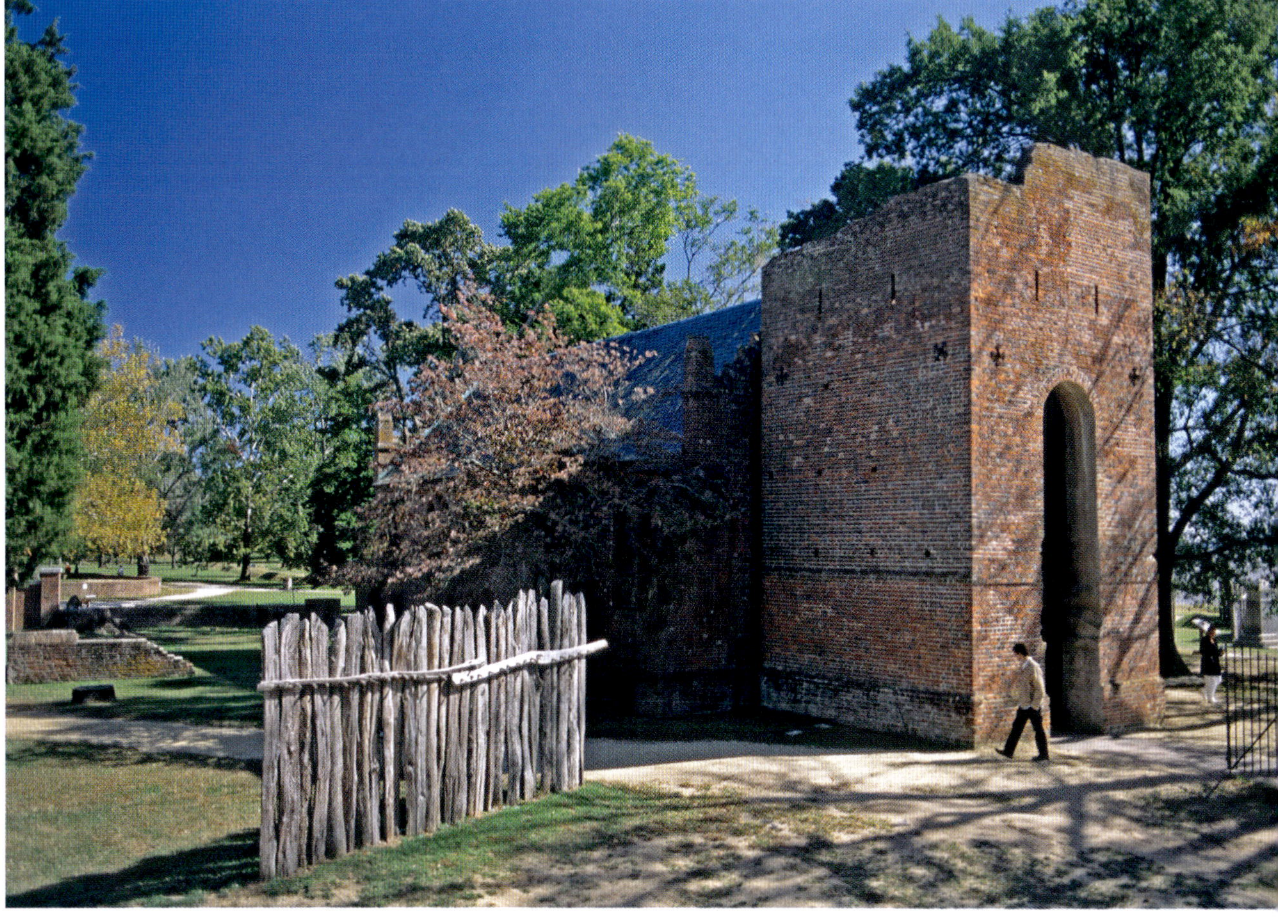

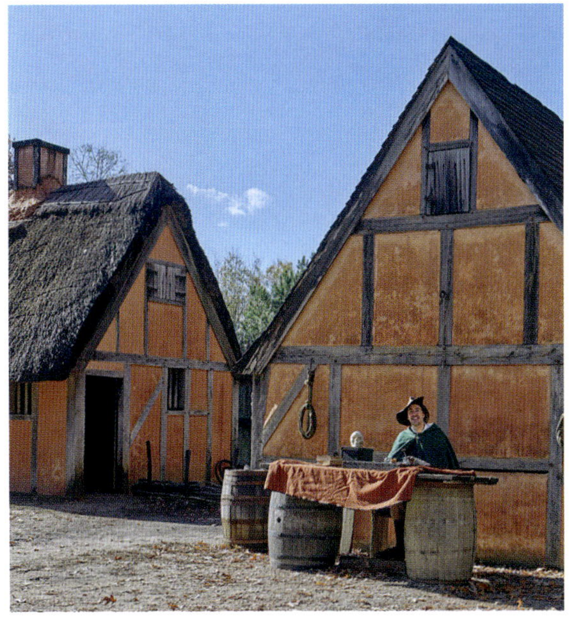

TOP: There was renewed interest in visiting the site during the Jamestown Exposition of 1907 held in Norfolk, Virginia.

ABOVE: A docent displaying craft skills at the restored site.

Colonial Governor William Berkeley, after he refused Bacon's request to drive Native American Indians out of Virginia. Fertile land was at a premium and farmers would quickly exhaust the nutrients in the land and need to move on to more virgin ground. Although Jamestown was eventually rebuilt, the temporary move of state business to Berkeley's Green Spring Plantation, and then to Middle Plantation was a sign of things to come. When Jamestown's state house caught fire again in 1698, this time accidentally, legislators were able to meet in the new facilities of the College of William & Mary, established by royal charter in 1693. Middle Plantation was duly renamed Williamsburg to honor the reigning monarch, King William III. In the eighteenth century the town dwindled to nothing, anchored till around 1750 by Jamestown's church, the ruins of which still remain.

Today it is one part of the triangle of Colonial Virginia encompassing Williamsburg and Yorktown. Jamestown Settlement is a living history interpretive site, administered by the Jamestown Yorktown Foundation, a state agency of the Commonwealth of Virginia.

MANHATTAN ISLAND, NEW YORK

The Dutch found the perfect location for their New Holland colony

As European powers raced to establish colonies and exploit the resources of the New World, the Dutch established a settlement and subsequently built Fort Amsterdam on the southern tip of Manhattan Island. It proved to be an excellent staging post for the lucrative fur trade, particularly beaver pelts, which were traded with native tribes farther up the Hudson River.

The fort was built on the western side of the island, so that its guns could protect this valuable commerce coming up and down the river—particularly from the English and French. The colony of New Netherland had been chartered by the Dutch West India Company in 1621 and by 1626 governor Peter Minuit had bought New Amsterdam from the local Algonquin tribe, the Manhattans, for sixty guilders. Manhattan Island at this time was not rich agricultural ground but covered by marshes and scrub woodland where bears roamed and which, in the early 1640s, concealed Indians intent on robbing the settlers after relations with the native tribes had soured.

As can be seen from the seventeenth-century map of Manhattan (opposite), a defensive palisade, or wall, was established and gave name to the modern Wall Street. Conditions at the "edge of empire" were very different for the Dutch expats from

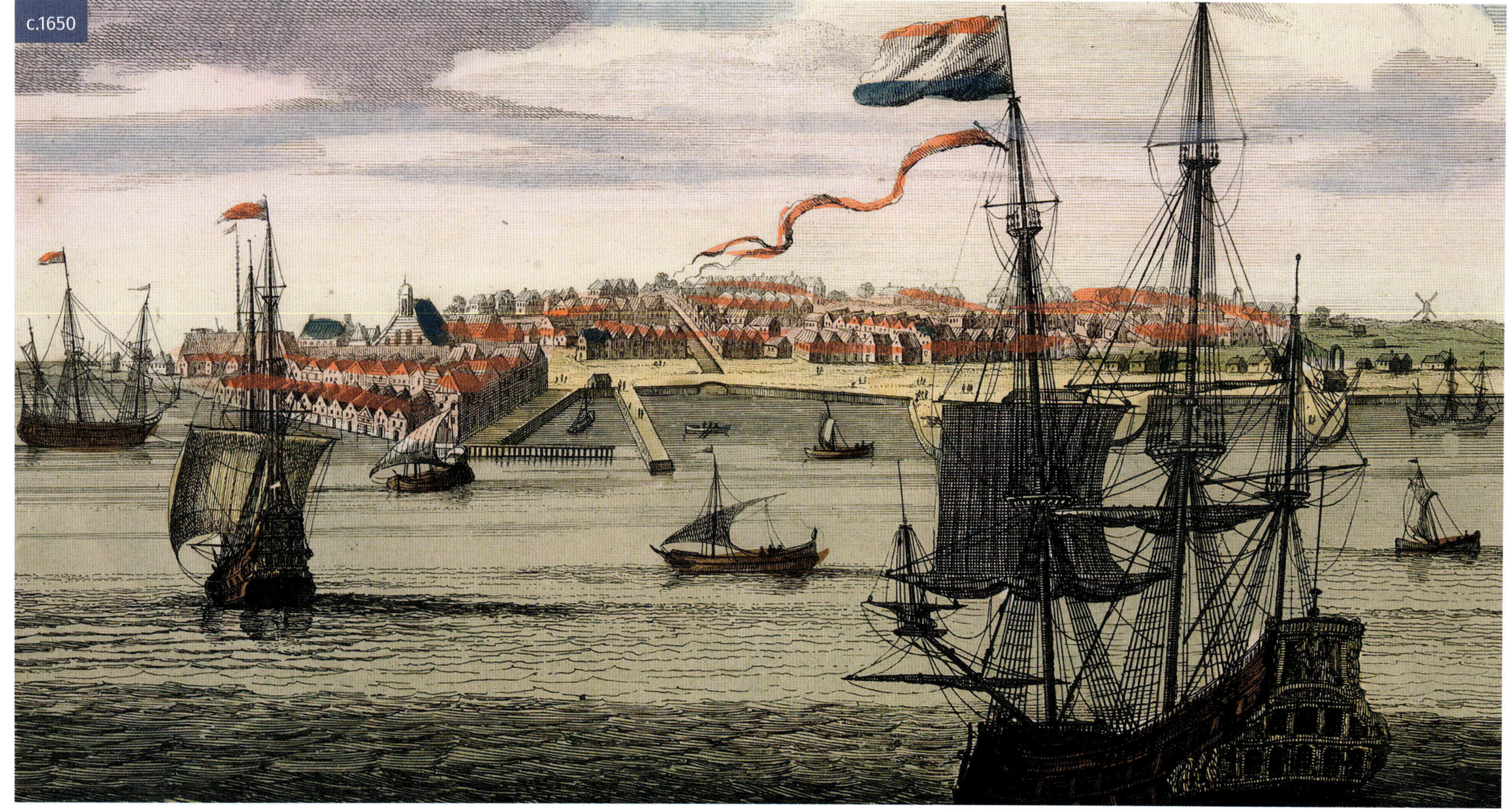
c.1650

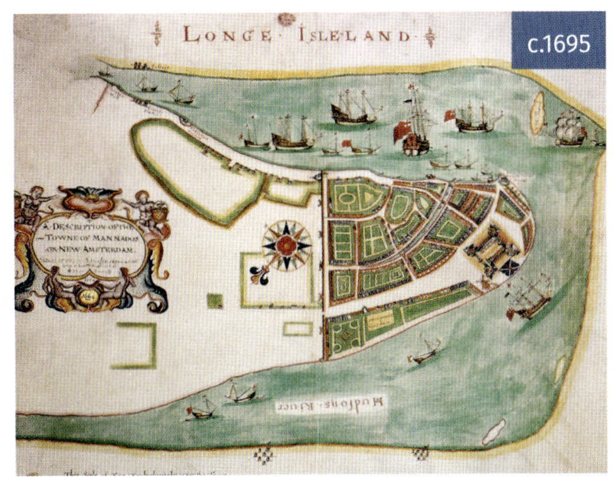

c.1695

the metropolitan life they had left behind in bustling Amsterdam, and drunkenness among soldiers and administrators ensured the imposition of strict discipline and the replacement of several governors. Governor Peter Stuyvesant was of a different mold, but by 1664 the English, realizing the advantages of the outpost, set about claiming it for Charles II. On August 29, 1664, four English warships commanded by Colonel Richard Nicolls, carrying 450 marines and bearing 120 heavy guns, arrived in New Amsterdam's harbor. Stuyvesant was prepared to fight, but the residents of the colony, faced with overwhelming odds, persuaded him that a peaceful transition might be best. England and the Netherlands were two protestant countries on reasonable terms—Charles II had spent his period in exile there.

Thus New Amsterdam became New York, and the Dutch colony became an English one, until Revolution came. Today, the sixty guilders Peter Minuit paid for Manhattan would not buy one night at the Algonquin Hotel.

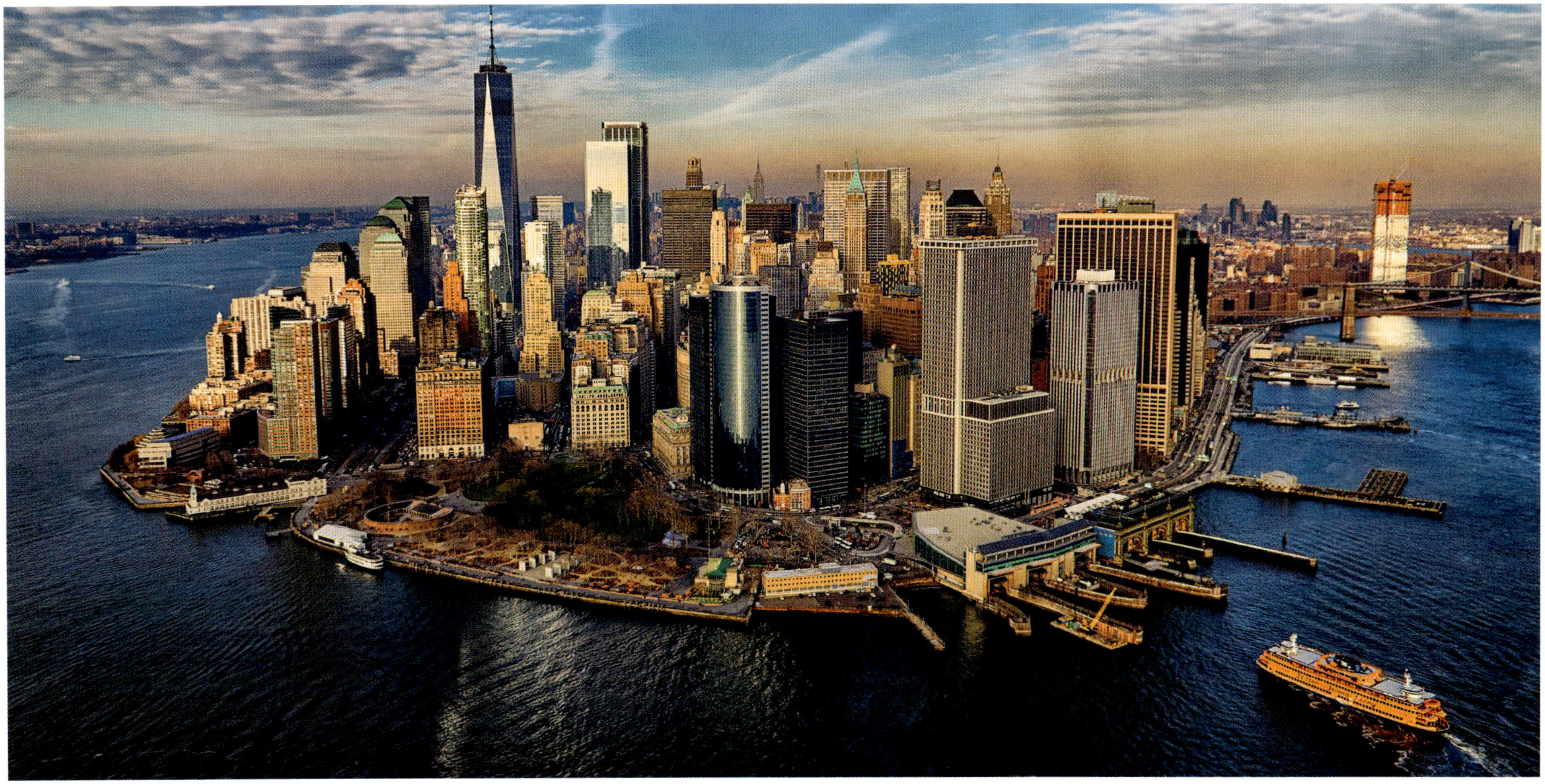

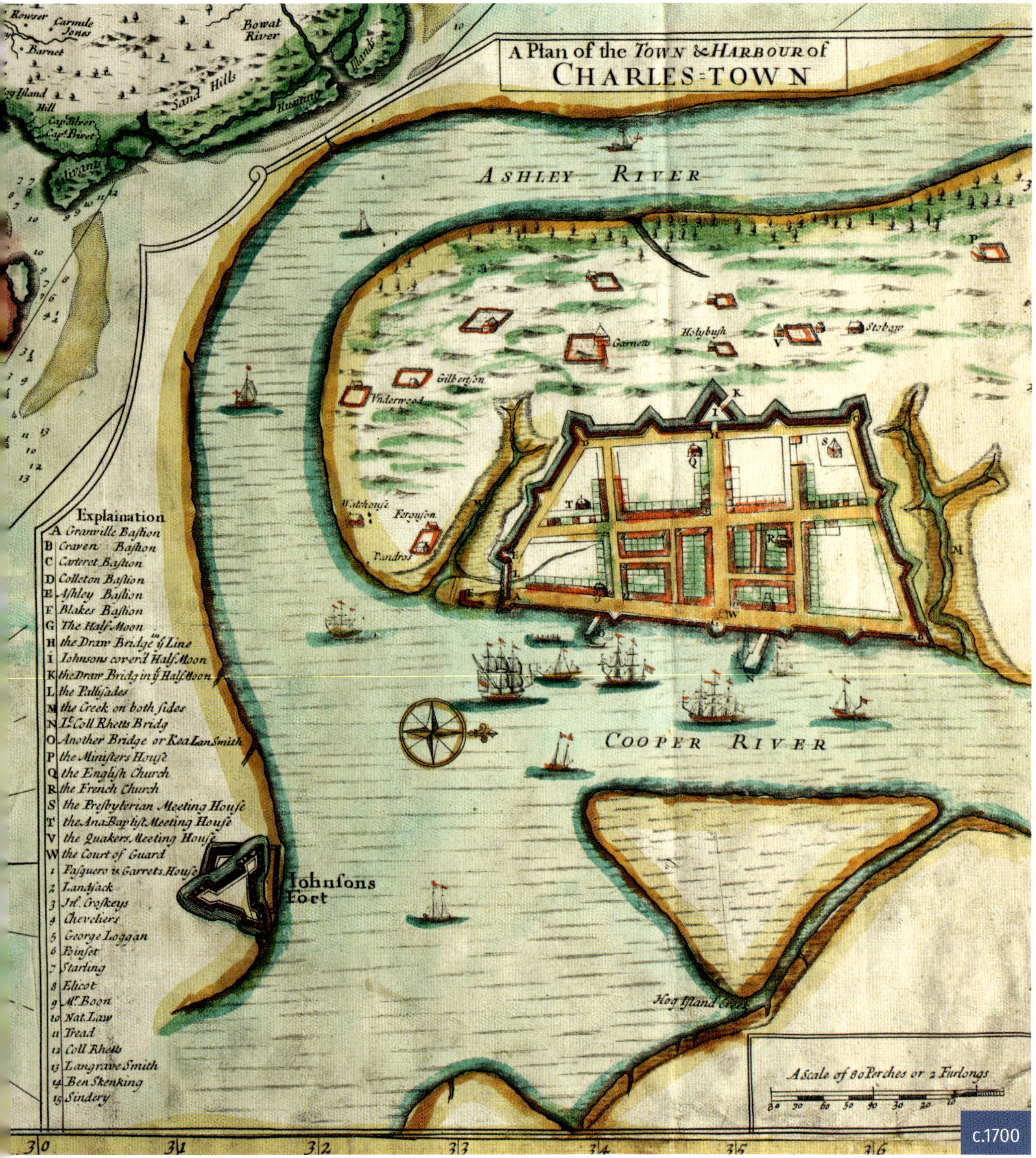

c.1700

CHARLES TOWN, SOUTH CAROLINA

The most treacherous environment in all the Thirteen Colonies

The question of who controlled the huge swathe of land south of Virginia and north of St. Augustine in Spanish La Florida was hotly debated when the first English settlers arrived aboard the *Carolina* in 1670. Settlers had to be wary of many enemies both on land and at sea. The Spanish in St. Augustine perennially

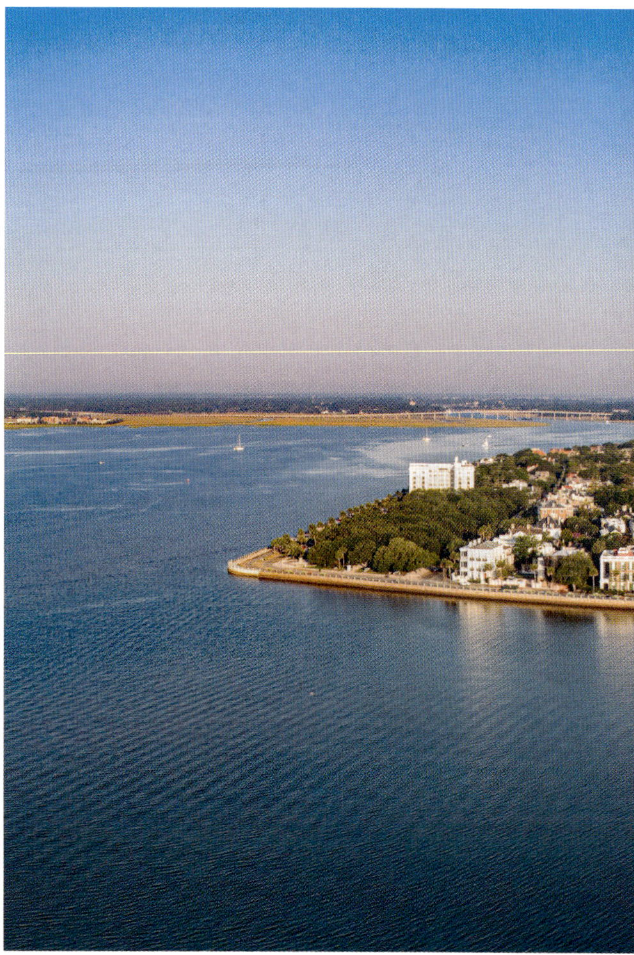

raided the area, making life difficult for Native Americans who they attempted to enslave. For that reason some local tribes, though not all, welcomed the English and their advanced weaponry. Meanwhile, the French continued looking for their chance to claim land along America's eastern seaboard and pirates established havens along the Charles Town coast. Charles Town was besieged by the notorious pirate Blackbeard for several days in May 1718 and only released hostages in exchange for a chest of medicine from Governor Robert Johnson.

Though they first settled about ten miles up the Ashley River, by 1680 early colonists had begun to relocate the settlement to the peninsula we know today as Charleston, feeling it was a more defensible position. The sea breeze helped mitigate the hordes of mosquitos which were a problem. The town developed a reputation as one of the least healthy locations in the Thirteen Colonies for ethnic Europeans. Malaria was endemic.

Charles Town was carefully planned. Known as the "Grand Modell" the plan designated civic spaces and residential lots, all protected by a wall which included defensive fortifications made of wood, earth, brick, and stone. With its walls, moats, and drawbridges, Charles Town became the only English walled city in America. Using alliances with the Cherokee and Creek peoples to hunt deer, the early economy developed around the deerskin trade. In time, rice became the major crop, as the climate did not suit tobacco. Plantation owners often sought slaves from the "Rice Coast"—Senegal and Sierra Leone in West Africa—who were skilled in its cultivation. Thus business boomed and the lowcountry around Savannah and Charleston became home to many ethnic Gullah, whose traditions and cultural heritage live on to this day. Like its Georgia counterpart, Savannah, modern Charleston has largely been bypassed by corporate America, making the preserved city a tourist destination of note.

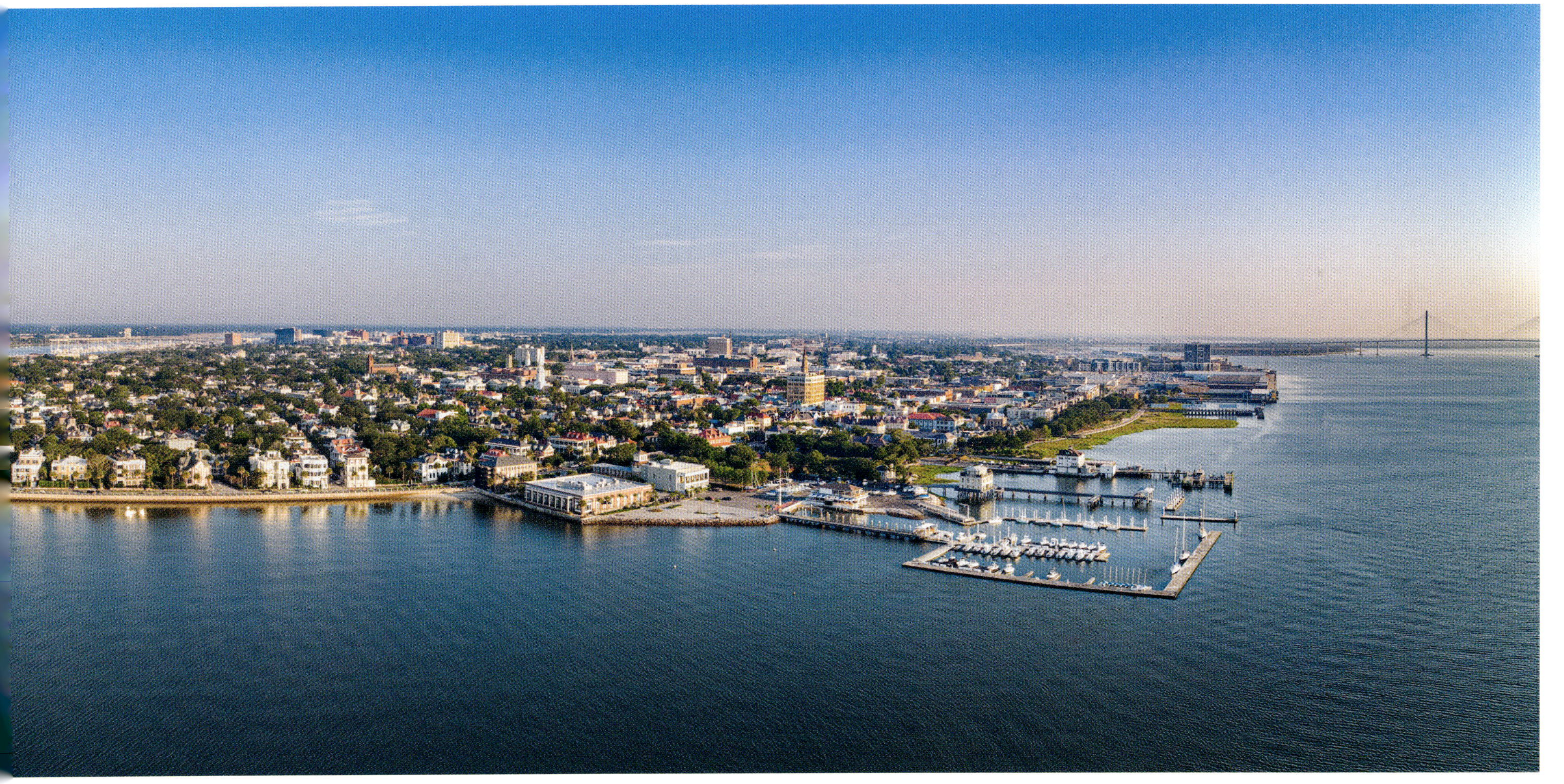

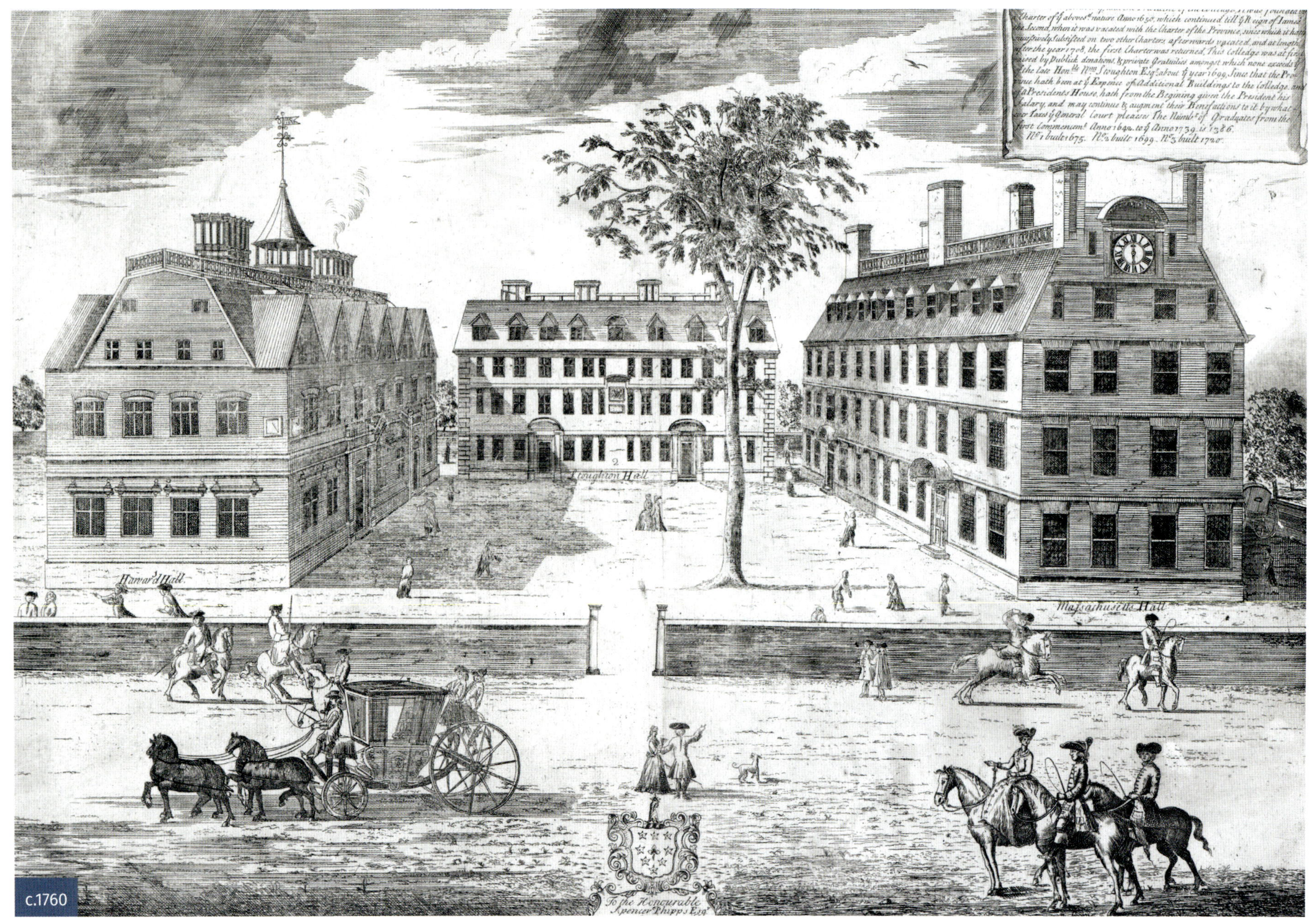

c.1760

HARVARD COLLEGE, CAMBRIDGE, MASSACHUSETTS

Originally established to train clergymen for the New World colonists

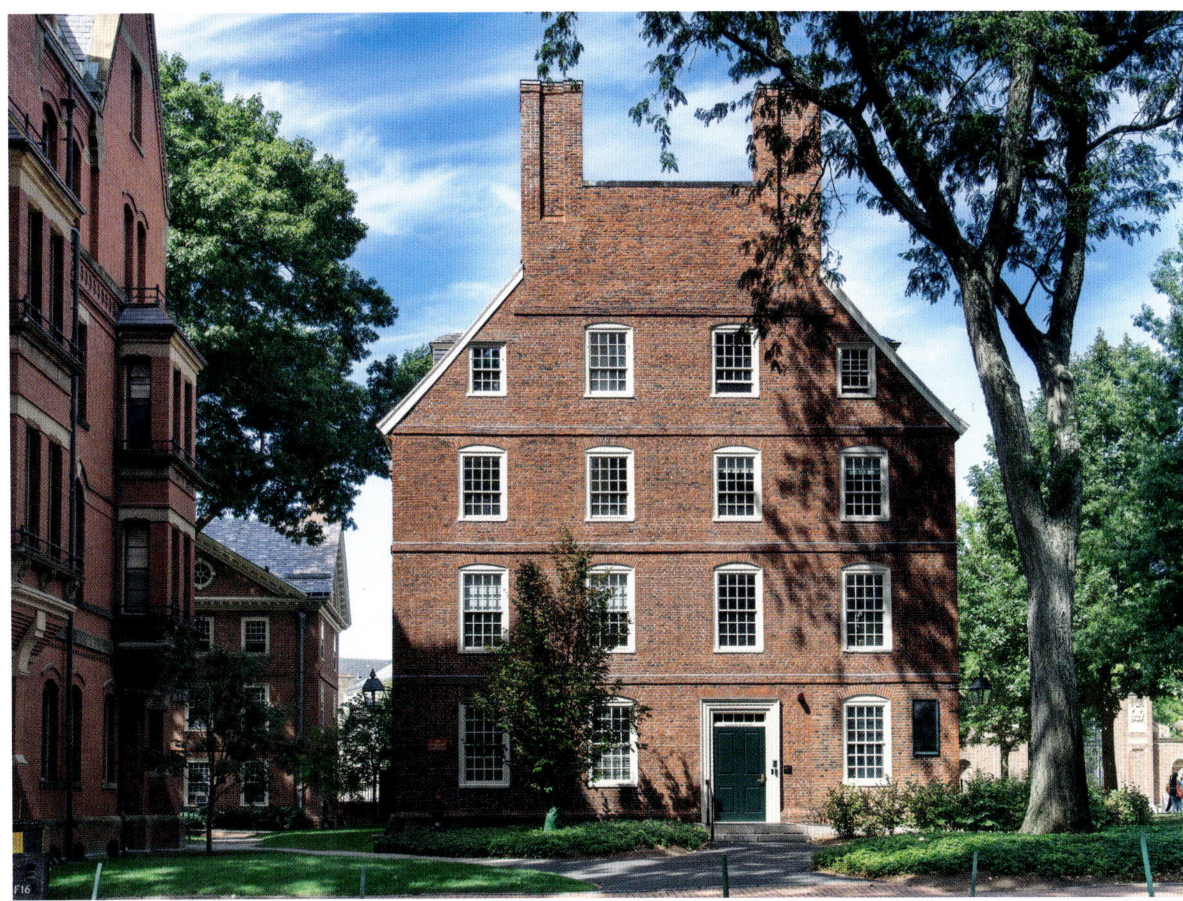

Though historians shrink at the term "first university," Harvard was certainly the first institute of higher education in America. The college was set up in 1636 by the Massachusetts General Court to train clergymen and was given the name of its great benefactor, John Harvard. Harvard was a Puritan clergyman who emigrated to the colony from England and bequeathed the emerging college £780 and his considerable library of some 320 books. By the eighteenth century the curriculum had broadened to include more secular, classical subjects, often taught by Cambridge-educated scholars. This drift away from its ecclesiastical focus enraged Harvard's sixth president, Increase Mather, who viewed the rest of the Harvard clergy as "Latitudinarians"—that is, broad church and failing to adhere to the strict Puritan orthodoxy of the protestant faith. The feud caused Mather and his son Cotton to champion the collegiate school that would eventually become Yale University (pictured in the insets below), in the hope that they would steer a more Puritan course.

Massachusetts Hall (pictured opposite), built from 1718 to 1720, is the oldest surviving building at Harvard and the second-oldest US academic building after the Wren Building at the College of William & Mary. The building initially was a dormitory made up of 32 bedrooms and 64 small private studies for 64 male students (the companion Radcliffe College for female undergraduates would not open until 1879). During the Siege of Boston in the Revolutionary War, 600 American soldiers crammed into the hall. It was noted that much of the interior woodwork and hardware, including brass doorknobs, went missing at this time.

After the American Civil War, Harvard president Charles William Eliot oversaw the development of the private college—one of the "Ancient Eight," later to become the "Ivy League"—into a modern research university. Today it is a world-leading academic institution and after three centuries of use, during which time the Massachusetts Hall has been used as a physics lab, lecture rooms, and an observatory, the hall is once again a dormitory for freshmen and houses the administrative offices of the President, Provost, and Treasurer.

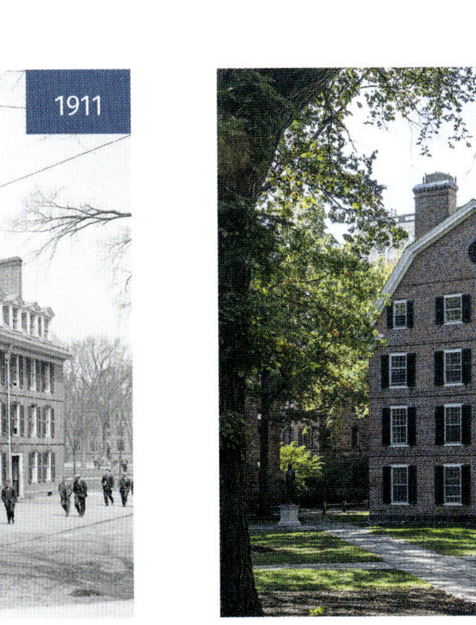

1911

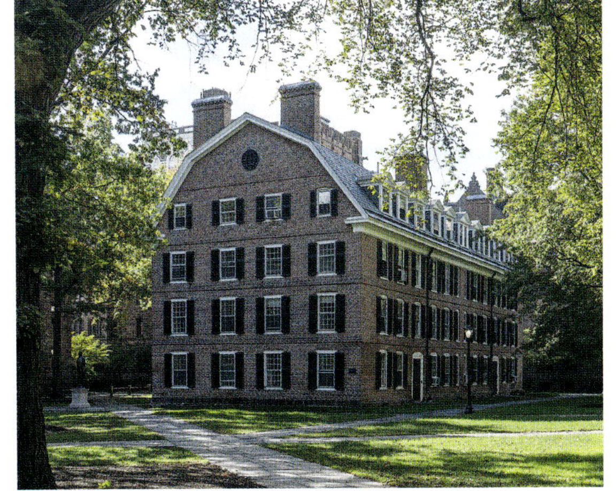

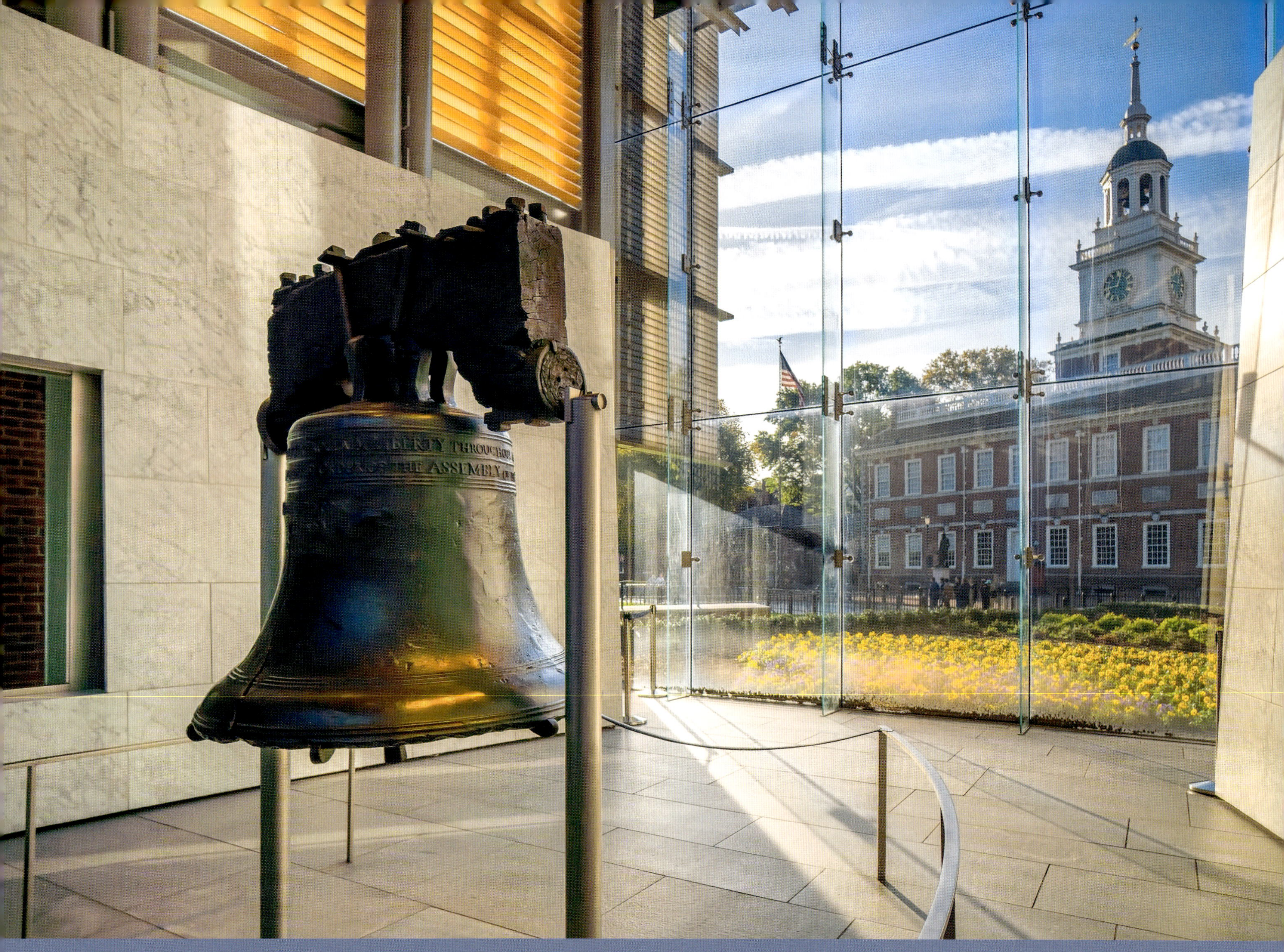

REVOLUTION AND INDEPENDENCE

REVOLUTION!

By the mid-eighteenth century, tensions between the American colonies and the British Crown were reaching boiling point. Though colonists considered themselves loyal subjects of the British Empire, the imposition of tax and a lack of colonial representation in Parliament spurred growing dissent, particularly among the land-owning classes.

FEDERAL HALL AND THE STATE HOUSE

Federal Hall, located in New York City, was the site of early colonial resistance. Originally built as New York's City Hall in 1700, it hosted important meetings of the colonial assembly. In the pre-revolutionary years, it became a space where grievances against British policies—especially the Stamp Act of 1765—were aired. It later gained prominence after independence as the site of the first US Congress and George Washington's inauguration, but even in the revolutionary years, its role as a center of political discussion was vital.

More pivotal still was the Pennsylvania State House in Philadelphia, now known as Independence Hall. This building became the heart of revolutionary activity. Here, the First Continental Congress met in 1774 to respond to the Coercive Acts, and in 1775, the Second Continental Congress convened, eventually adopting the Declaration of Independence in 1776. Virginia plantation owner Thomas Jefferson drafted the initial document which was then revised by the Committee of Five, including John Adams, Benjamin Franklin, Jefferson, Robert R. Livingston, and Roger Sherman. It formally severed political ties with Britain and declared the colonies to be free and independent states.

THE LIBERTY BELL AND THE CALL TO ARMS

The Liberty Bell, now housed in a pavilion near Independence Hall, became a symbol of American independence. Though cracked and not rung for the Declaration itself, the bell was originally used to call legislators to session and mark important events. Its inscribed words—"Proclaim Liberty Throughout All the Land Unto All the Inhabitants Thereof"—taken from Leviticus, had been dedicated to Englishman William Penn, who wanted those qualities preserved in his own colony, Pennsylvania, but it became emblematic of the American ideals of freedom and self-determination.

Skirmishes at Lexington and Concord in April 1775 marked the outbreak of war. The colonial militias had begun to organize and figures such as Paul Revere played crucial roles in rallying resistance. Revere, a Boston silversmith, was one of several riders sent out to alert colonial militias of British troop movements—a story later immortalized by poet Henry Wadsworth Longfellow.

Paul Revere's home in Boston still stands as a monument to the early revolutionary movement. It was a gathering place for the Sons of Liberty, an underground resistance group opposed to British rule. Their acts of protest, including the Boston Tea Party in 1773, showed the growing frustration of ordinary colonists—not just the landed gentry who stood most to gain.

Another enduring icon of the Revolution is Betsy Ross, a Philadelphia seamstress long credited with sewing the first American flag at the request of George Washington and other leaders. Though the historical evidence is debated, the Betsy Ross House remains a symbol of the civilian contribution to the war effort.

A HARD-FOUGHT WAR

The early years of the war were difficult for the Continental Army. General George Washington, commanding a poorly equipped and loosely organized force, suffered losses in New York but achieved surprise victories at Trenton and Princeton during the winter of 1776–77.

In 1777, a turning point came at the Battle of Saratoga in New York. American forces, under General Horatio Gates, defeated a major British army led by General Burgoyne. This victory convinced France to enter the war on the American side, providing much-needed military and financial support.

After years of grueling warfare across the colonies, the war culminated at the Siege of Yorktown in Virginia in 1781. British General Charles Cornwallis had moved his troops to the Yorktown peninsula, expecting resupply by sea. Instead, he was trapped by a combined American and French force—Washington advancing from the north, and French troops under Rochambeau, with French naval support under Admiral de Grasse, blocking the coast.

After weeks of bombardment, Cornwallis surrendered on October 19, 1781. This decisive victory effectively ended major combat in the American Revolutionary War, though the Treaty of Paris would not be signed until 1783, formally recognizing the United States' independence.

A NEW NATION AND A NEW FRONTIER

With independence won, the fledgling nation turned to the monumental task of forming a government for the Thirteen Colonies, each with their own agenda. Resistance to the British had been a unifying force; now that had disappeared. The Articles of Confederation proved weak, leading to the Constitutional Convention in 1787, again held at the Pennsylvania State House. Here, the US Constitution was drafted, creating a stronger federal structure and establishing the enduring principles of American democracy. Freed from British-imposed restraint on expansion west into tribal lands, the western frontier became the next great stage of conflict.

THE ALAMO AND THE SPIRIT OF TEXAS

Fast-forward a few decades to the 1830s, and a new struggle for independence was underway—not against Britain, but Mexico. American settlers, known as Texians, had been moving into the Mexican territory of Tejas under agreements that soon fell apart over issues like governance, religion, and slavery.

In 1836, Texian and Tejano forces declared independence from Mexico, forming the Republic of Texas. The most dramatic episode in this conflict was the Battle of the Alamo, where a small band of defenders held out for thirteen days against the vastly larger Mexican army led by General Santa Anna.

The decisive victory came on April 21, 1836, at the Battle of San Jacinto. Under the leadership of General Sam Houston, Texian forces launched a surprise attack on Santa Anna's army near modern-day Houston. The battle lasted just eighteen minutes. Santa Anna was captured and forced to recognize Texan independence.

Thus, the Republic of Texas was born—an independent nation that would exist until it joined the United States in 1845, reigniting sectional tensions over slavery and pushing the country toward the Mexican–American War that would ultimately see the addition of California, Arizona and New Mexico.

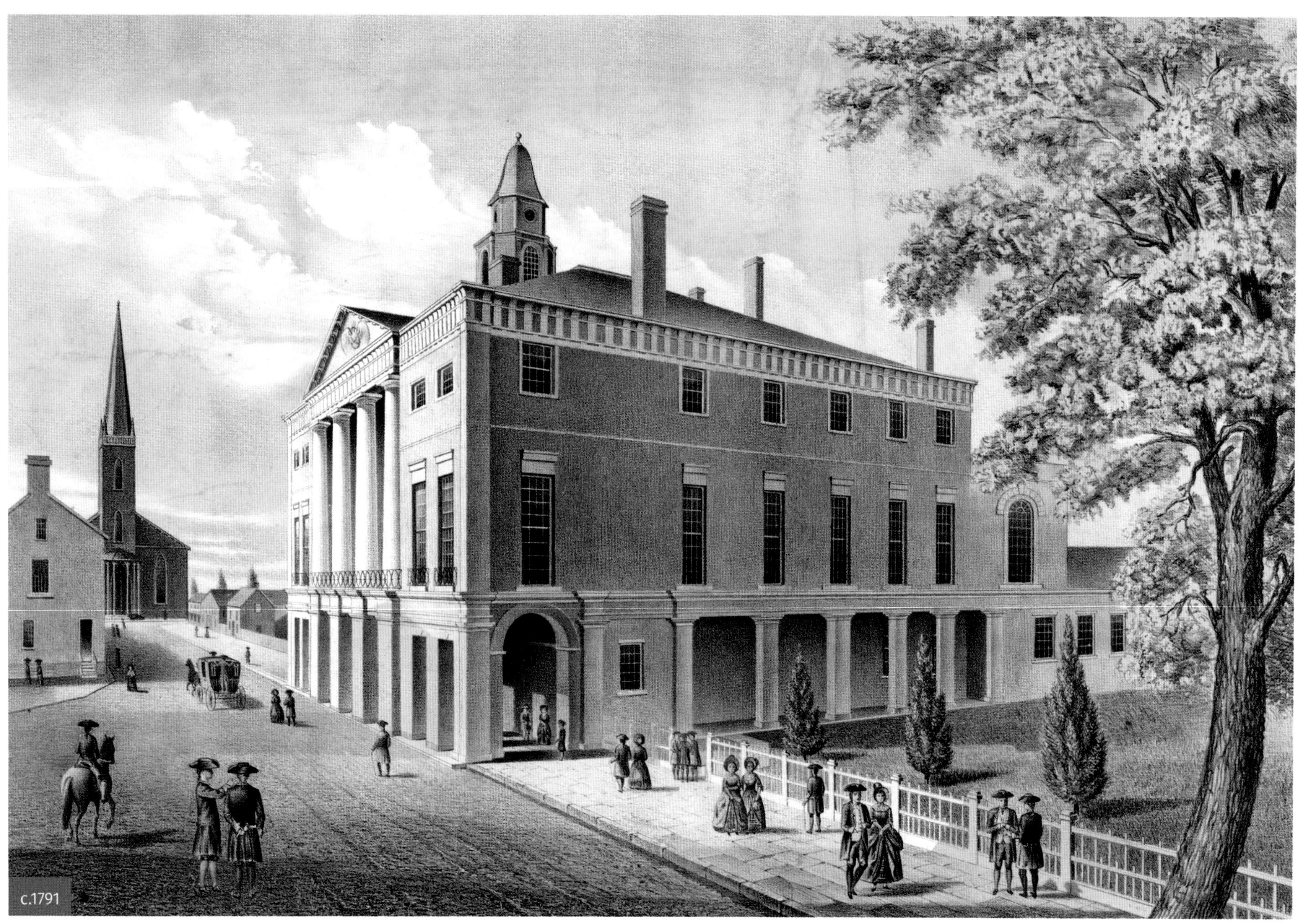

FEDERAL HALL, NEW YORK

Agitation around the Stamp Act came to a head at Federal Hall

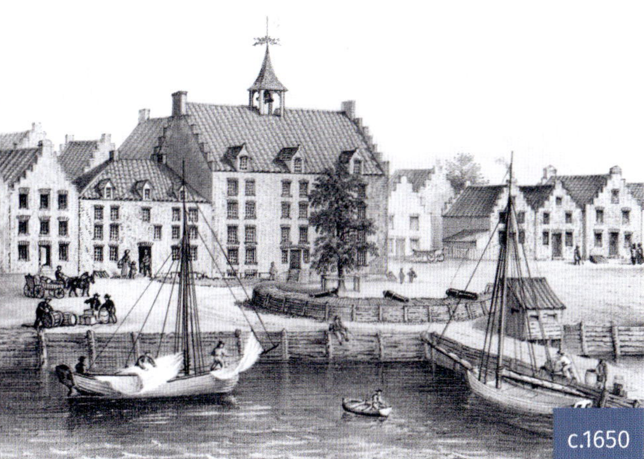

c.1650

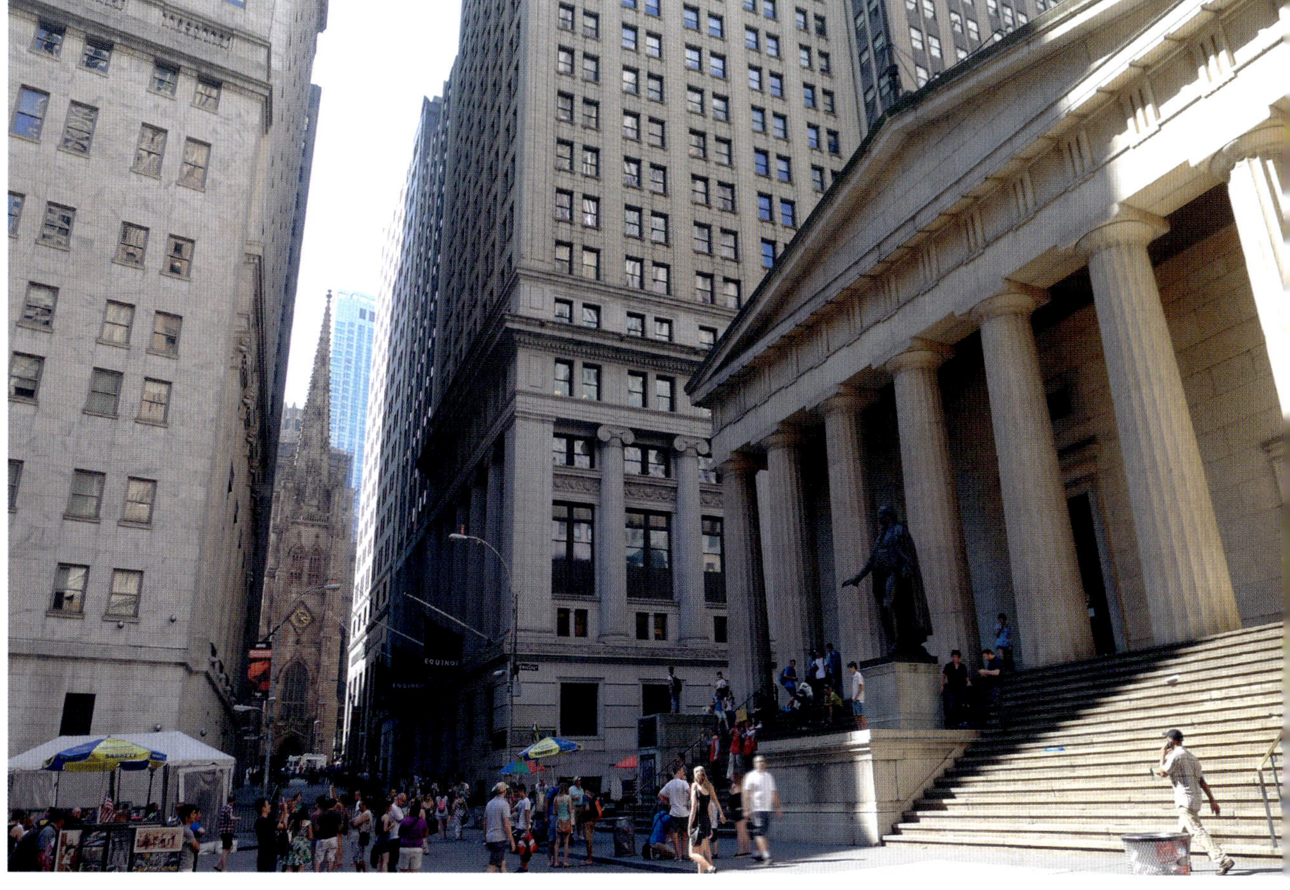

The original building on this site in Wall Street would serve New York as its city hall from 1699. It was designed by James Evetts to replace Stadt Huys, the Dutch administrative center (pictured above) built in 1642 much closer to the water's edge. The replacement included a public library and acted as a fire station, equipped with two fire engines shipped from London. It served as a courthouse and also a debtors' prison. In 1735, newspaper publisher John Peter Zenger was arrested on a charge of committing a gross libel against the royal governor and was imprisoned and tried there. He was acquitted on the grounds that his allegations were true, which established an important precedent for freedom of the press within the colony.

In 1765 a third story was added, around the time of increased resistance to the Stamp Act. Delegates from the Thirteen Colonies met for the first time to present their grievances at being taxed by a British parliament in which they were not represented (England had joined with Scotland in 1707 to become Britain after the Scots' near-bankruptcy through the failed Darien scheme in Panama).

After the successful Revolutionary War and the reoccupation of New York, the patriots set about remodeling the building to their own specification. Pierre Charles L'Enfant, the French architect responsible for Washington, DC's masterplan, was employed to transform the building with four grand Doric columns fronting the street and a pediment that depicted an American eagle with thirteen arrows. It was in this building—illustrated with Trinity Church visible at one end of Wall Street—that George Washington was inaugurated as the first President of the United States in 1789. It was also here where the first Bill of Rights was proposed.

In 1790, the United States capital moved to Philadelphia and the Federal Hall's place in history passed. It survived the New York fire of 1804 but with a new City Hall opening in 1812 it was demolished. It was replaced with a Greek Revival structure acting as both the US Custom House and a place of political intrigue. After the US Custom House moved out it became a Subtreasury building, at one time holding $519 million worth of bullion. It was used as an assay office in the 1920s before the United States Post Office Department suggested replacing the building with a replica of Federal Hall as it appeared in 1789 and using it as post office. The plan never came to fruition and it continued to be used as a passport office while historical and patriotic societies argued about its future use. On May 26, 1939 the building was designated as Federal Hall Memorial National Historic Site and the National Park Service took custody of one of America's most historic locations.

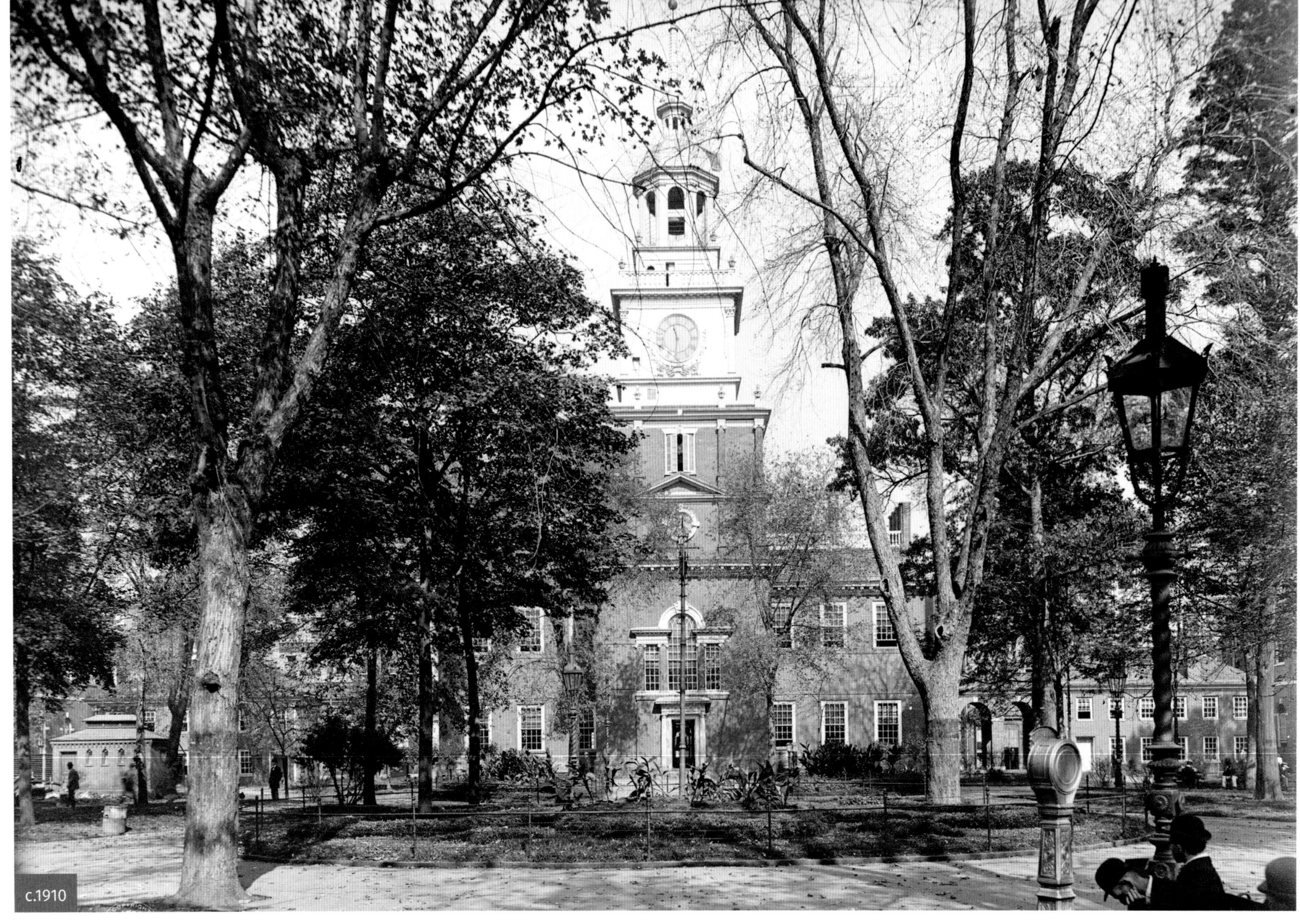
c.1910

INDEPENDENCE HALL, PHILADELPHIA

It started life as the Pennsylvania State House, but then received a higher calling

The construction of the Pennsylvania State House was completed in 1753. It served as the first capitol of the Province of Pennsylvania and, following American independence, the nation's first capitol building. As early as 1729, there had been proposals to build a state house in Philadelphia, and a committee was formed to look at sites and designs. It soon became a dispute. John Kearsley wanted to have it constructed on High Street, present-day Market Street, and Andrew Hamilton believed Chestnut Street the better location. Kearsley had drawn up plans for the design, as had Hamilton. When presented to the full committee they chose Hamilton's interpretation, thus the great Georgian building resides on the south side of Chestnut Street between Fifth and Sixth Streets.

It would witness the formative moments of the United States. From May 1775 to 1783, the Pennsylvania State House served as the principal meeting place of the

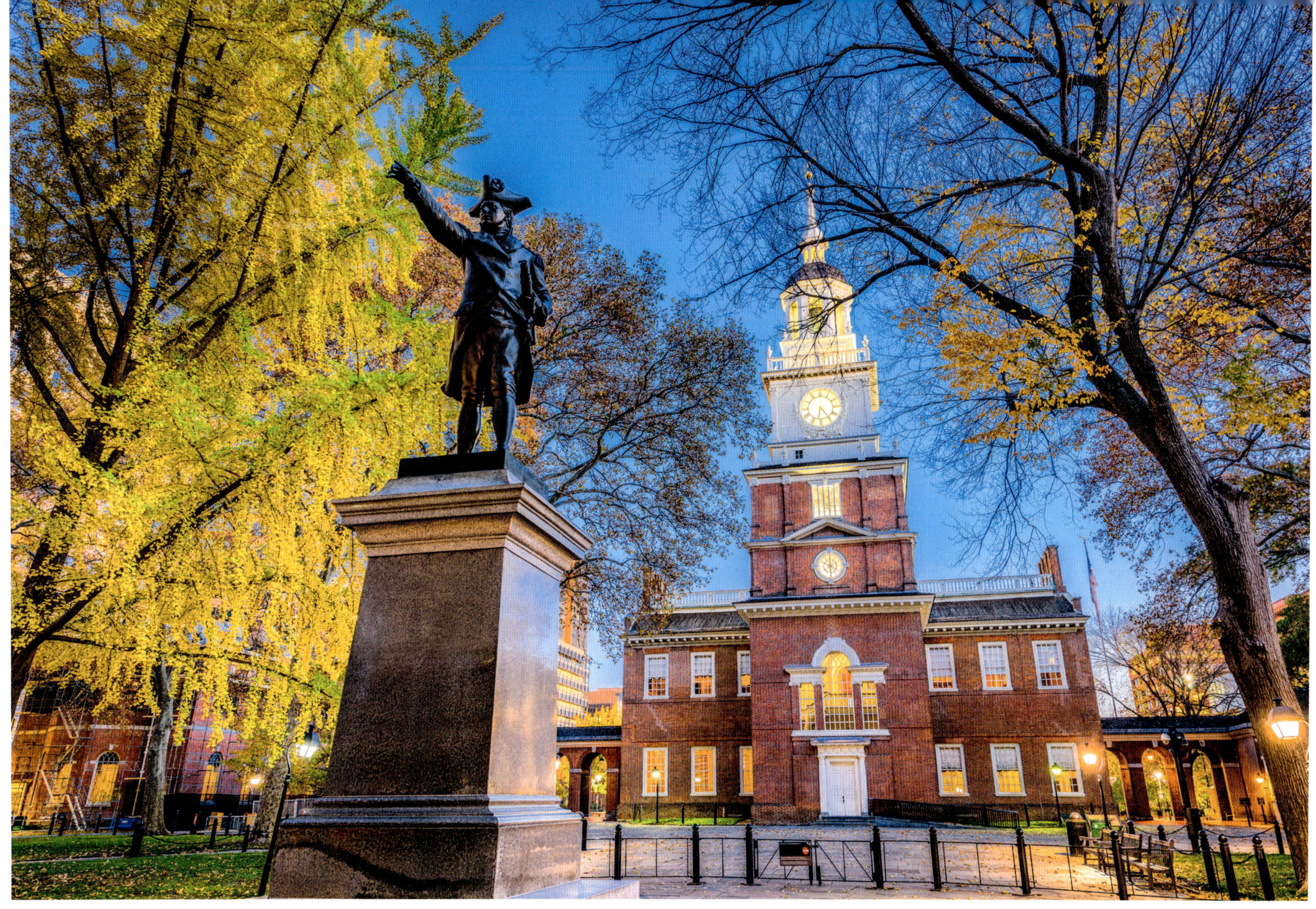

Second Continental Congress, a body of representatives from each of the Thirteen Colonies. In June 1775 George Washington was nominated as commander-in-chief of the Continental Army in the Assembly Room. Later that year Benjamin Franklin would be appointed the first Postmaster General of the United States Post Office.

However it was on July 4, 1776 that the Declaration of Independence was read aloud to the public in what has become Independence Square. The document officially unified the colonies of North America who declared themselves independent of Great Britain and explained their justifications for doing so. There were 56 signatures, including Francis Hopkinson of New Jersey and John Hancock of Massachusetts, who signed first and in such prominent letters that the term "John Hancock" has become an alternative term for "signature."

The central building in the story of the nation has been modified and reconstructed many times. Because its construction by Edmund Wooley was funded by the Pennsylvania colonial legislature, it was finished piecemeal, as and when the finance became available. The exterior of the central portion of the building is original, but the wings, steeple and much of the interior were reconfigured much later. Only twenty years after the building was deemed finished, the wooden steeple had rotted through and was eventually removed in 1781. The wings were replaced in 1812 and a replacement steeple, designed by William Strickland, topped the building again in 1828. The replacement wings were replaced themselves in 1898 but the steeple remains. Today it is a UNESCO World Heritage Site, part of the Independence National Historic Park.

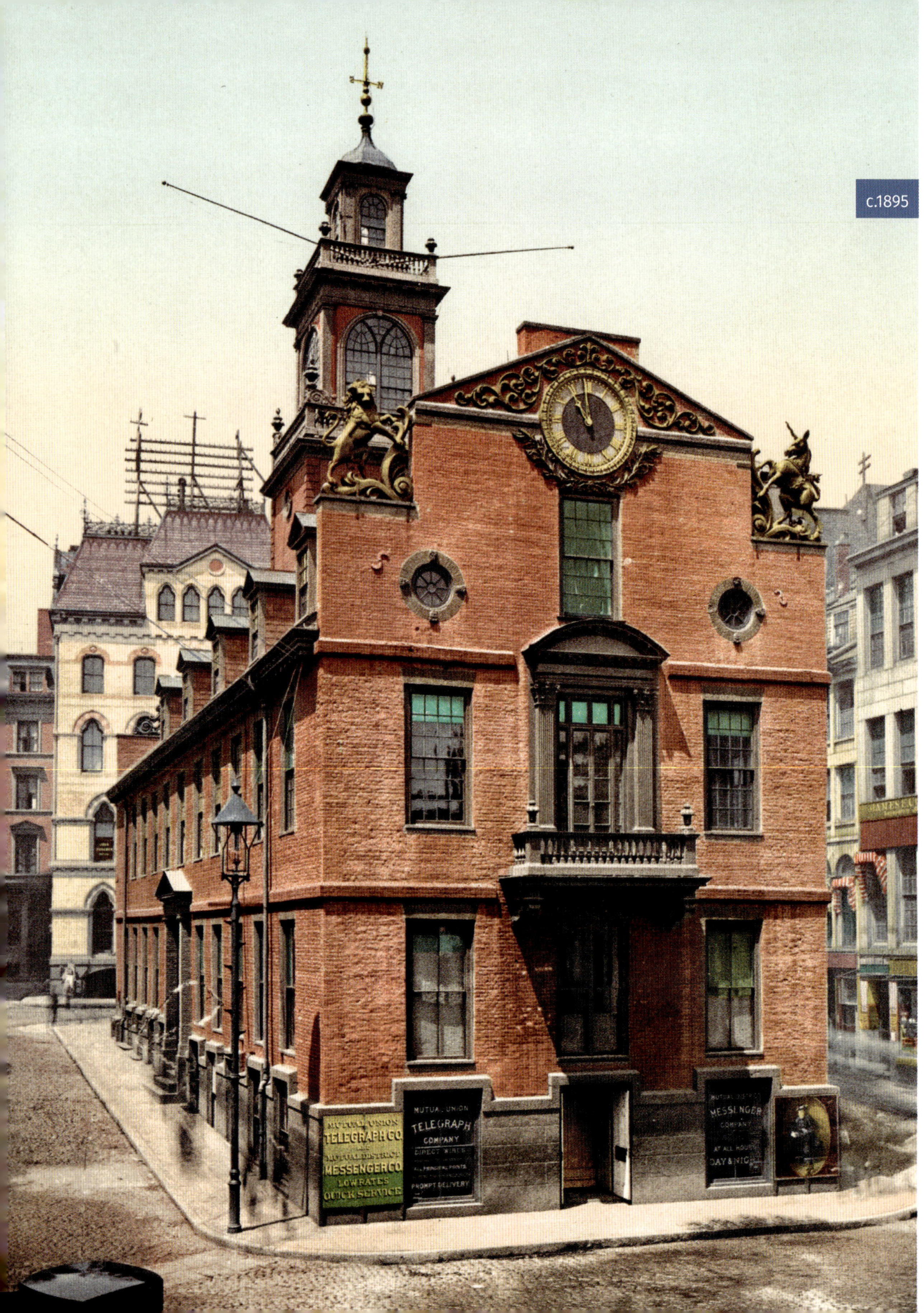

c.1895

OLD STATE HOUSE, BOSTON

Once slated for demolition to ease Boston's traffic flow...

Although it was the seat of British power in the Massachusetts Bay Colony, the 1713 edifice at the head of then King Street was paradoxically also where "the child independence was born," as John Adams wrote. Besides the royal governor's office, it held the Massachusetts Assembly where colonists aired grievances against the crown. In 1770 crowds protesting against the Townsend Acts (which imposed duties on certain goods, including tea, and led to the Boston Tea Party) were taunting soldiers outside the State House. When objects started to get lobbed at the Redcoats from the crowd, they opened fire, killing five people in what became known as the Boston Massacre.

Captain Thomas Preston and eight soldiers were charged and tried for murder. Their defense was led by future second President John Adams, a respected Boston lawyer at the time, who argued that they acted in self defense. The trial resulted in six soldiers being acquitted, while two were convicted of manslaughter. Adams' decision to defend Redcoats was politically risky, but he later said it was one of the most important and honorable acts of his life because it upheld the rule of law.

In 1776 the Declaration of Independence was read from the second-floor balcony, at which point the building became the Massachusetts State House and its address changed to State Street. After the Revolutionary War the state government moved to Beacon Hill, in 1798, and the Old State House became a gaudy commercial building. When some suggested to demolish it to improve traffic flow, the Bostonian Society formed in 1881 to preserve and restore the historic structure. Twentieth-century buildings now form a canyon around little Old State House, while the subway station built underneath in 1903 can be accessed through a portal in its ancient brick exterior.

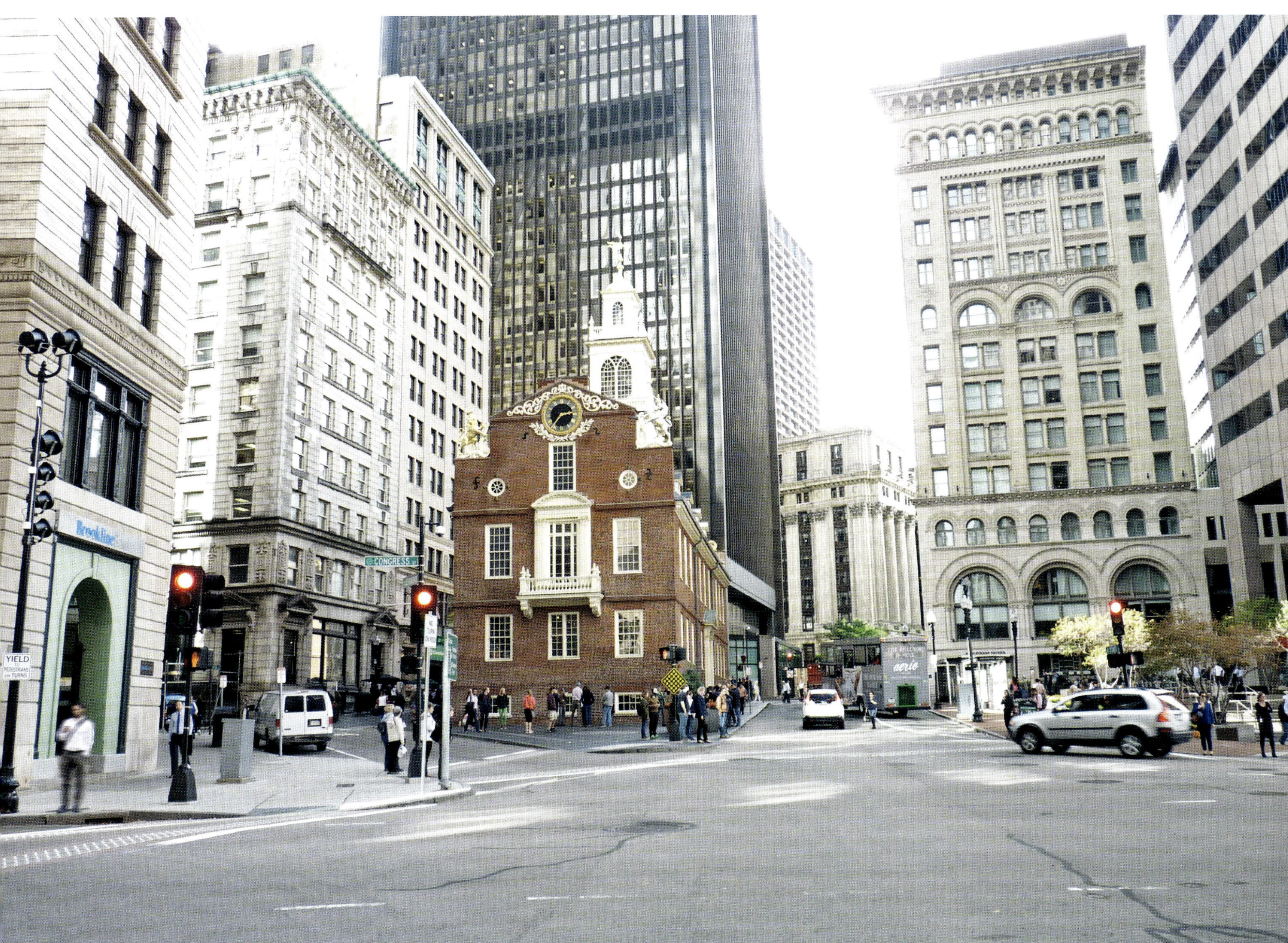
Brookline
CONGRESS
YIELD
aerie

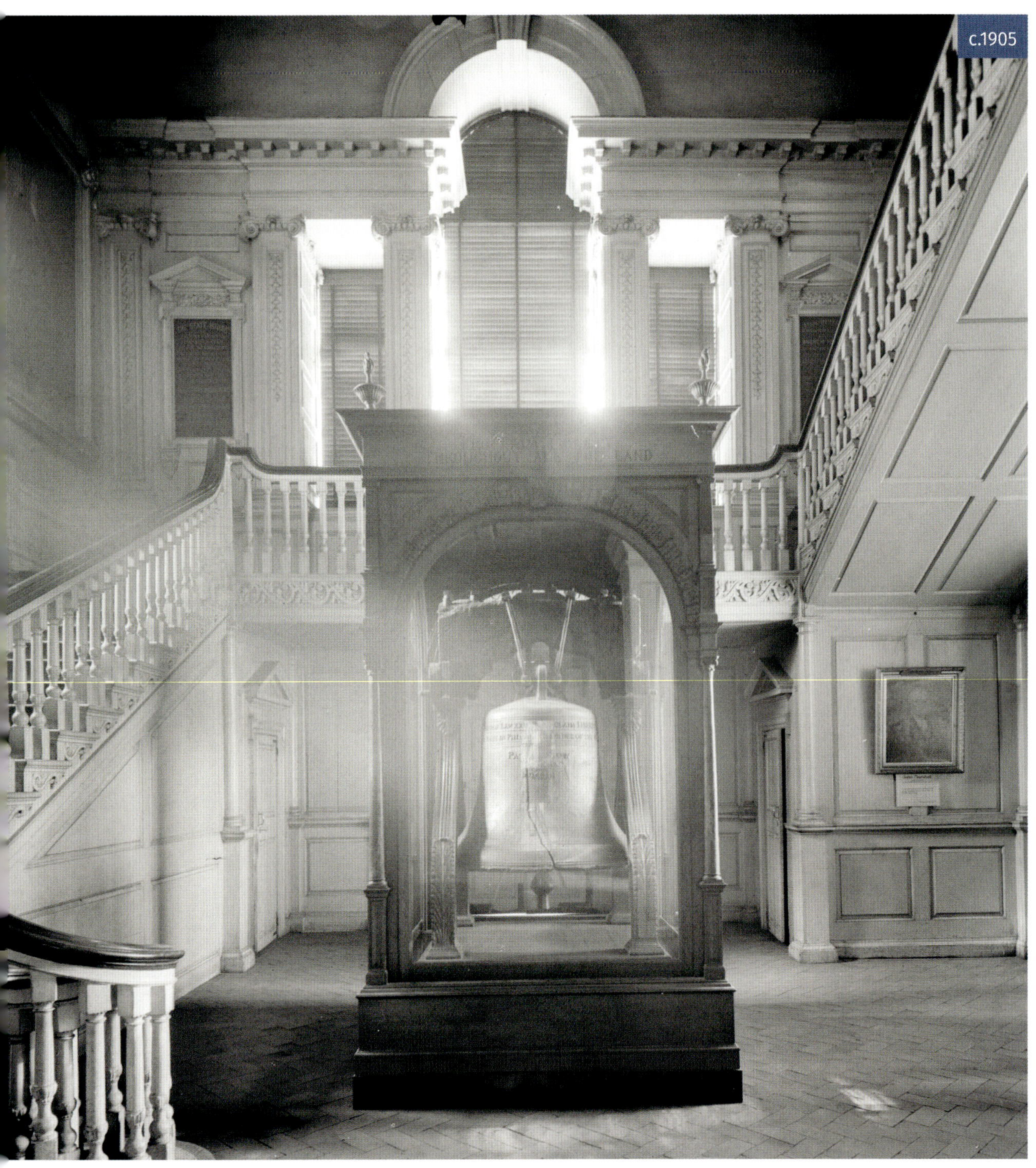

c.1905

LIBERTY BELL, PHILADELPHIA

Celebrating lines taken from the King James Bible

Isaac Norris, speaker of the Pennsylvania Assembly, first ordered a bell for the State House bell tower in 1751 from the Whitechapel Foundry in London. It was Norris's tribute to William Penn to celebrate the 50th anniversary of Penn's 1701 Charter of Privileges, which granted religious liberties and political self-government to the people of Pennsylvania. The bell arrived in 1752 carrying the inscription from the King James Bible: "Proclaim Liberty Throughout All the Land Unto All the Inhabitants Thereof."

Bells had been cast in Whitechapel since Geoffrey Chaucer's time and the foundry dated to 1420 (Big Ben is their most famous bell), so it was with dismay that the colonists found a crack in the bell on first ringing. Whitechapel believed either it had been dropped or the clapper had been struck on the rim, not the solid wall of the bell. It was recast in 1753 by Pass and Stow, a Philadelphia company founded by John Pass, who was an immigrant Maltese bell founder. The bell they produced was not of good tone, one listener at a test ringing described it as "similar to the sound of two coal scuttles being banged together!" Pass and Stow hastily took the bell away to recast it again. In June 1753, the recasting was completed, and the sound was deemed acceptable, though Norris indicated that he did not personally like it.

During the Revolutionary War the State House bell, along with others in the city, were evacuated to prevent them falling into British hands and then being cast as munitions. It was sent under heavily guarded wagon train to Bethlehem and then to the Zion German Reformed Church in Allentown, where it was hidden. After Washington and the Continental Army were defeated in the Battle of Brandywine, the British occupied the city until June 1778. When it was safe to return, though, the State House steeple was in poor condition and so the bell was placed on an upper floor,

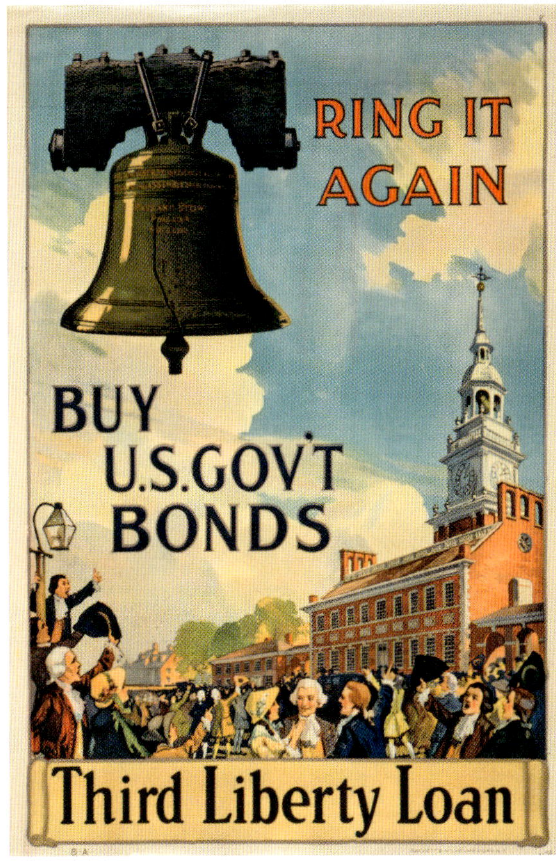

where it was rung on Independence Day, Washington's Birthday, and on election day to remind voters to hand in their ballots.

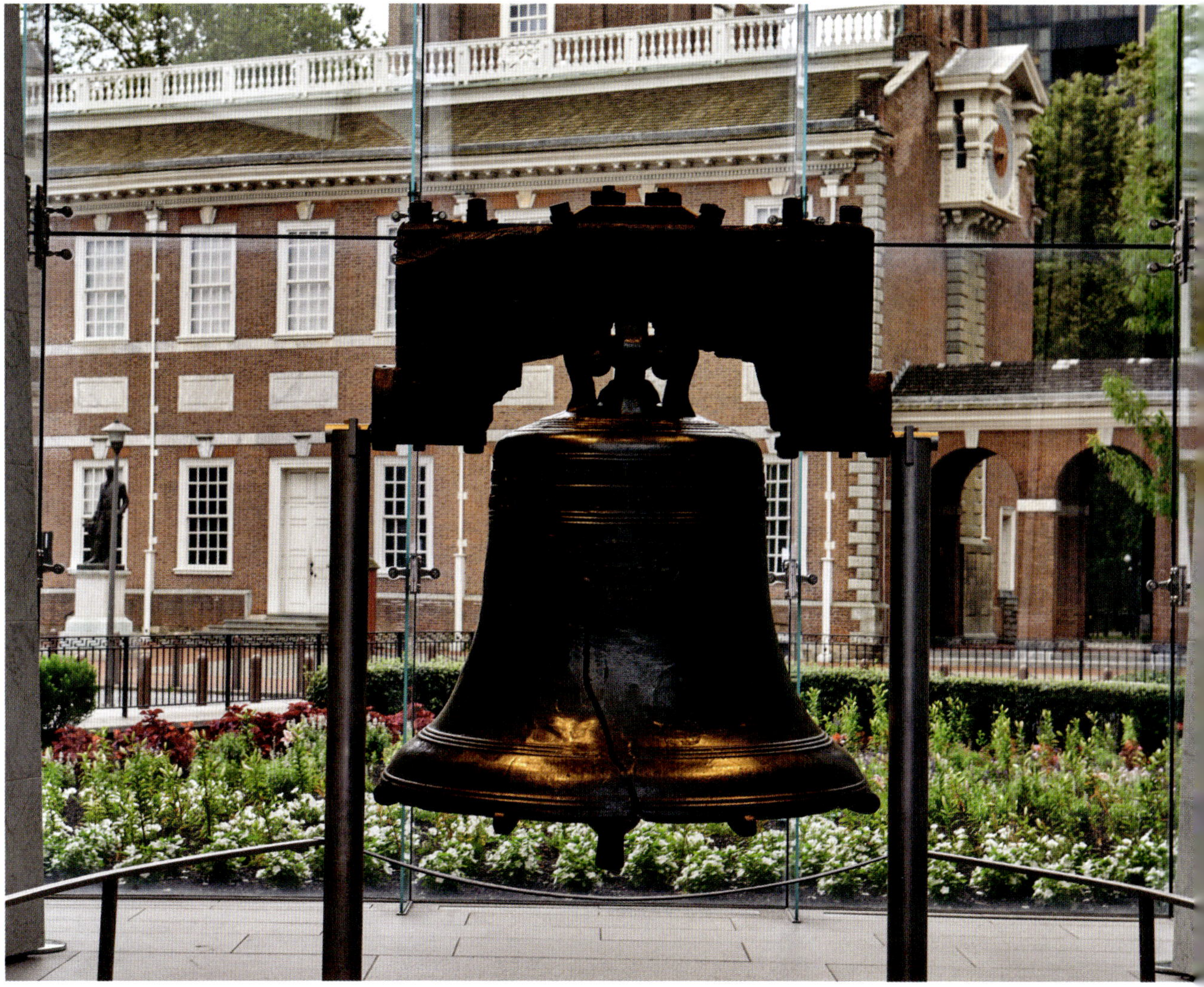

It is not known exactly when the third Liberty bell cracked between 1817 and 1846. In an attempt to repair the damage, metal workers widened the thin crack to prevent its further spread and restore the tone of the bell using a technique called "stop drilling"—making a large hole at each end of the crack; the only problem with this method is that the crack visible to the naked eye is not usually its end point. Despite its imperfections, the bell has gone on tour, also appearing at world's fairs as a prestige exhibit. Now installed in its own building in Philadelphia, it may not be rung, but the bell's inscription of liberty first envisioned by Isaac Norris is a powerful and unifying message.

ABOVE: The Liberty Bell has often been used as a symbol of American independence and a rallying cry during times of war. *Anti-Slavery Record*, an abolitionist publication, first referred to the State House bell as the Liberty Bell in 1835, but that name was not widely adopted until many years later.

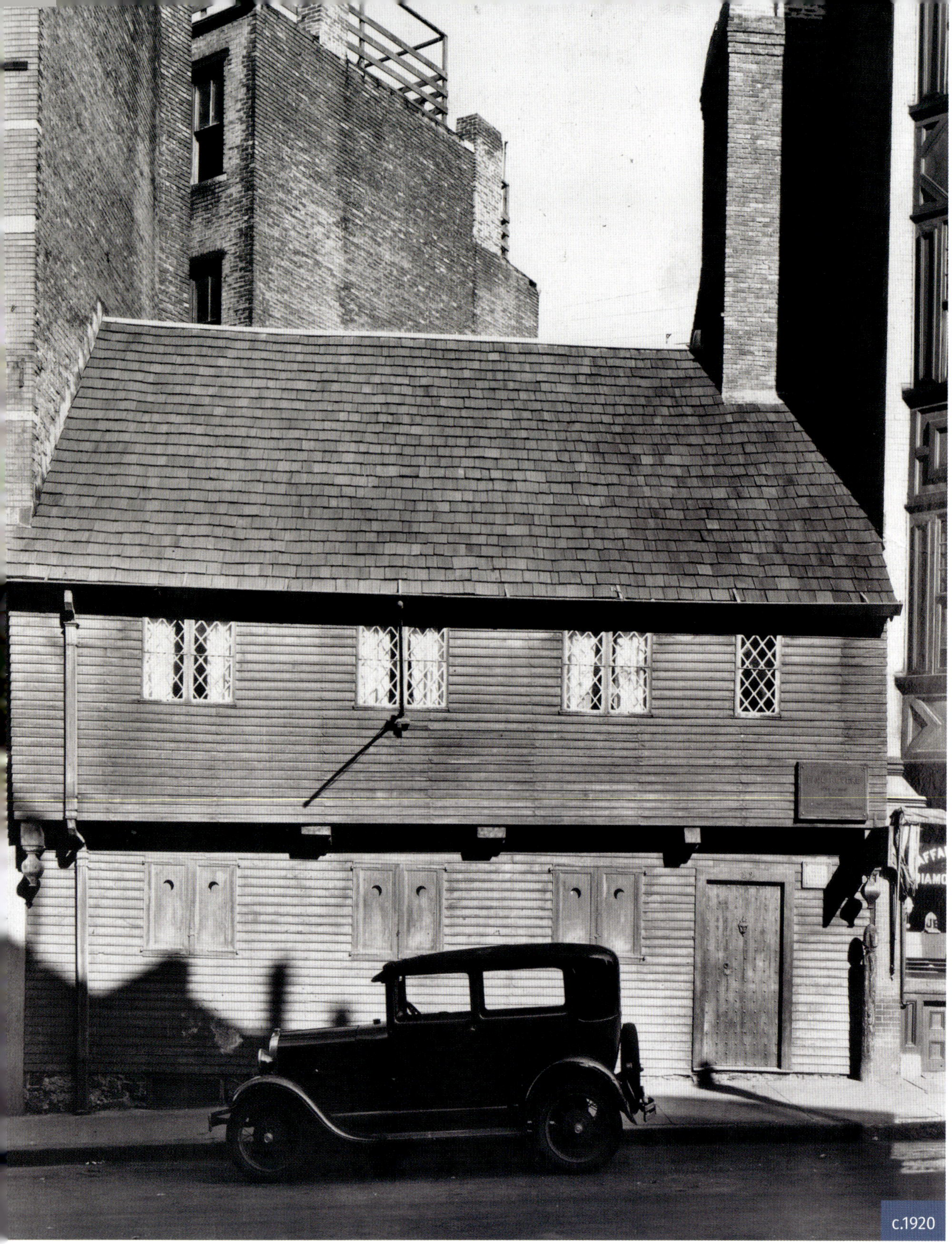

c.1920

PAUL REVERE HOUSE, BOSTON

Revere's house has had many incarnations over the years

Puritan minister Increase Mather, one of the driving forces for the foundation of Yale College and the father of Cotton Mather, a participant in the Salem witch trials, lived on this spot in North Square. Mather's house burned down in 1676 and four years later merchant Robert Howard built what is now the oldest house in Boston, albeit one that has been vastly altered across the years. Silversmith Paul Revere bought the house in 1770. There he lived for more than twenty years, raising fourteen children. It was a stone's toss from his cousin Nathaniel Hichborn's home, and a short walk to his workshop.

After his famous ride of 1775 he moved to Charter Street in 1790, but didn't sell this house till 1800. Over the course of the next century, waves of immigrants washed through Boston's North End and Paul Revere's former home was put to use as tenement apartments, a candy factory, a cigar factory, Banca Italiana, and by 1895, when the photo below was taken, a Hebrew grocery store.

In 1905 preservation-minded citizens formed the Paul Revere Memorial Association, bought the property and commissioned architect Joseph Everett-Chandler

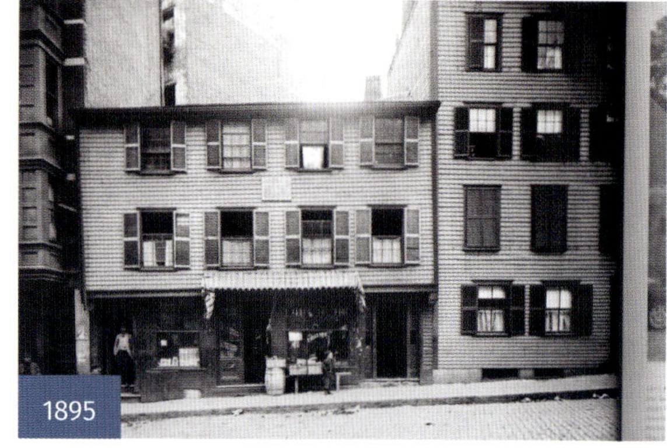

1895

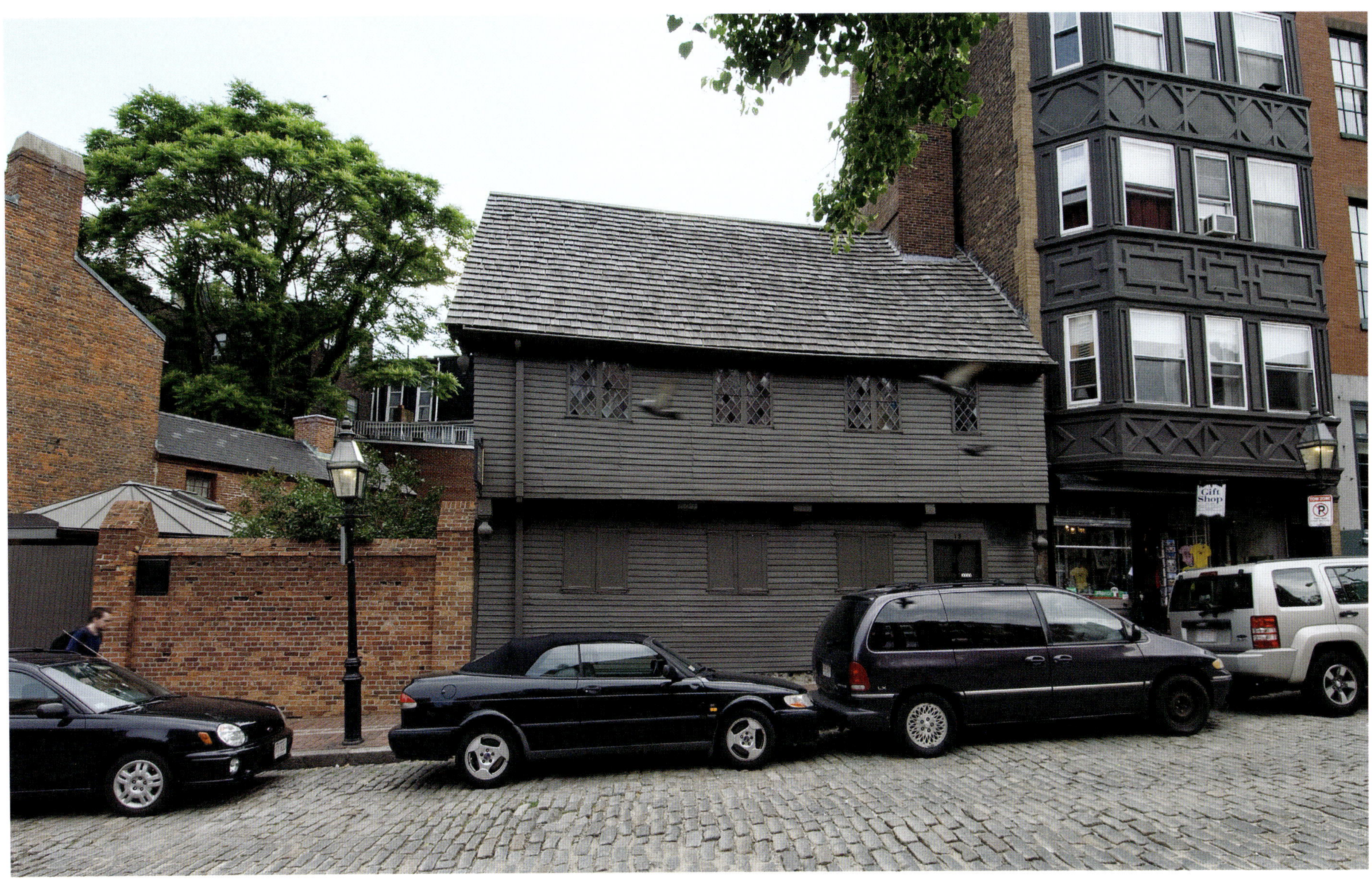

to restore the house to its colonial appearance, which included the removal of the third-floor additions as well as refitting the building with a steep overhanging roof, clapboard siding, and diamond-paned casement windows. The association opened the house as a museum in 1908 and it is pictured around 1920. The Revere House today contains fine samples of the silversmith's work plus the saddlebags from his "midnight ride" in April 1775. Revere was not the only courier that night but Longfellow's poem placed the Bostonian at center stage.

The poem was published in the *Atlantic Monthly* magazine in 1861 at the start of the Civil War and intended to inspire Northerners. One of the less discussed elements of the poem was its anti-slavery sentiment. There are several allusions, such as to a burial ground for enslaved people and the use of the name "Somerset" at the beginning of the poem. The Somerset Case of 1772 was a landmark legal action that limited slavery in Britain, a move which added to the fears of the Virginian plantation owners and accelerated their need to rid themselves of colonial shackles.

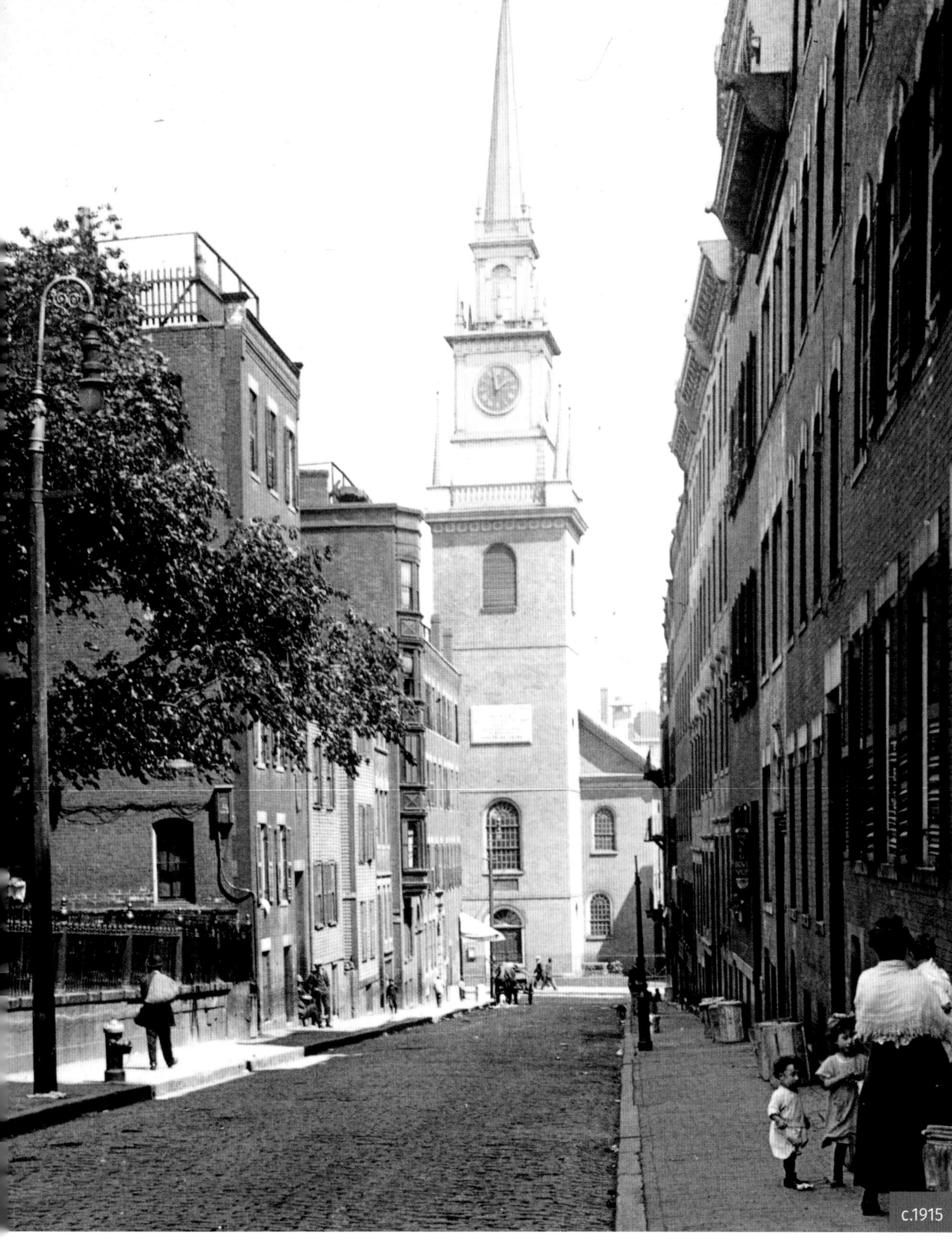
c.1915

OLD NORTH CHURCH, BOSTON

Paul Revere once rang the bells in this local church

Figuring prominently in Henry Wadsworth Longfellow's poem *Paul Revere's Ride*, the Old North Church was built in 1723 as Puritan power waned and Boston's Anglican congregation outgrew King's Chapel on School Street. Its official name is Christ Church, and the landmark 197-foot steeple wasn't added until 1740; its bells were imported from England four years later. A suspected smuggler with a god-fearing conscience donated some of the church's interior decorations—angel statues intended for a Catholic convent in Canada, stolen from a French ship. In 1750 a second-generation French Protestant teenage Paul Revere was a bell-ringer for Old North Church. Twenty-five years later, church sexton Robert Newman famously placed two lanterns in its steeple to warn colonists of British troop movements so that couriers from the Sons of Liberty, including William Dawes, Samuel Prescott, Martin Herrick, and Paul Revere, could ride through the countryside and deliver the message. Dawes took a different route to Lexington than Revere so that he was less likely to be stopped. Prescott was the only rider to make it to Concord in time to warn the militia.

In 1806 a hurricane toppled the wooden steeple, which was replaced by a shorter brick tower, seen in the archive photo taken over a century later. A renewed awareness of their colonial history took hold of Bostonians in the early twentieth century and

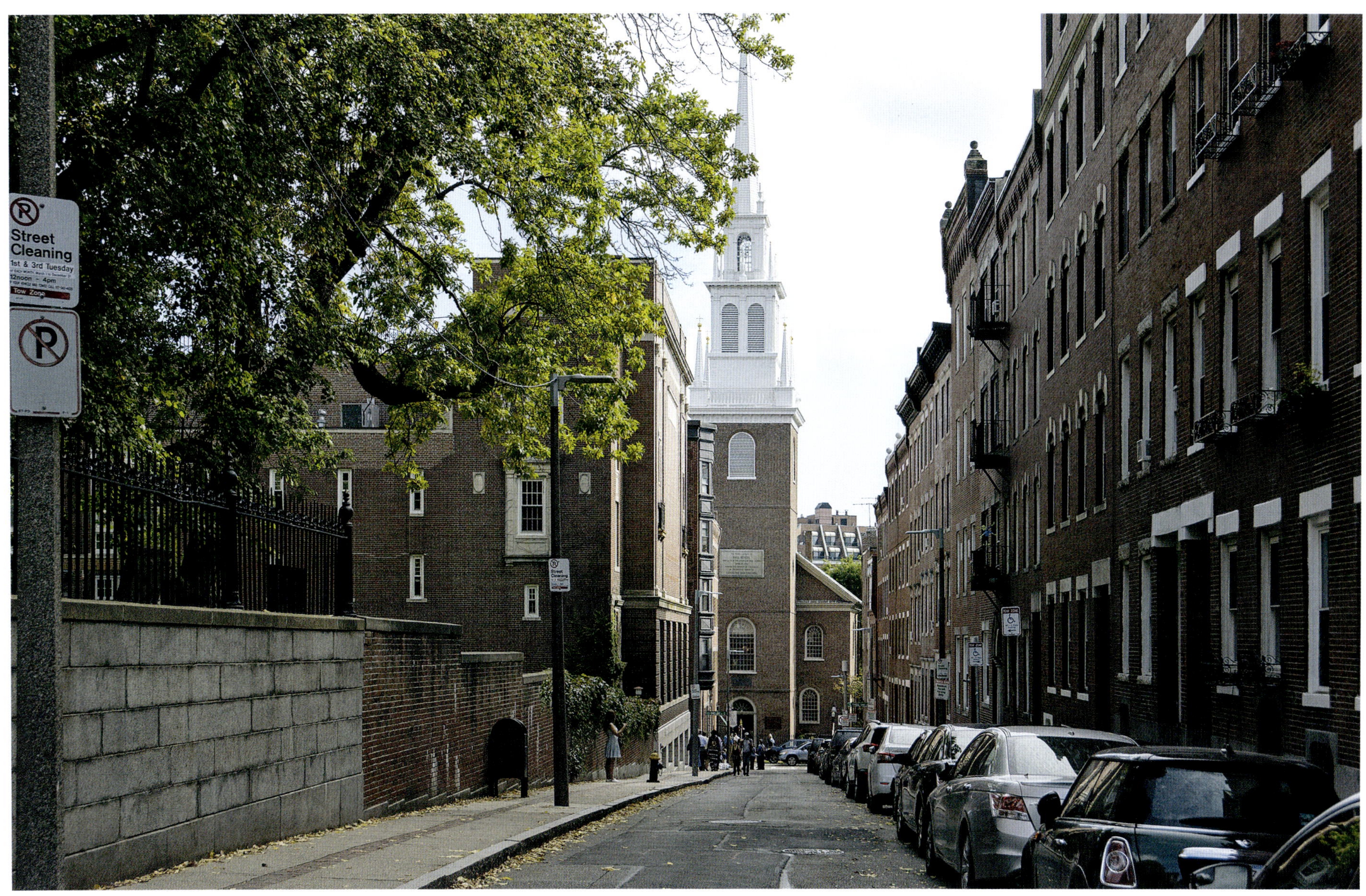

in 1912 the Old North Church's interior was repainted white and its pews reverted to the old box style. In 1954, Hurricane Carol blew down the church's second steeple and a wooden replica of the first steeple was raised in its place. Boston's oldest place of worship is not only a popular tourist attraction but is still an active Episcopal church in continuous operation—only interrupted by a Revolution and a coronavirus pandemic.

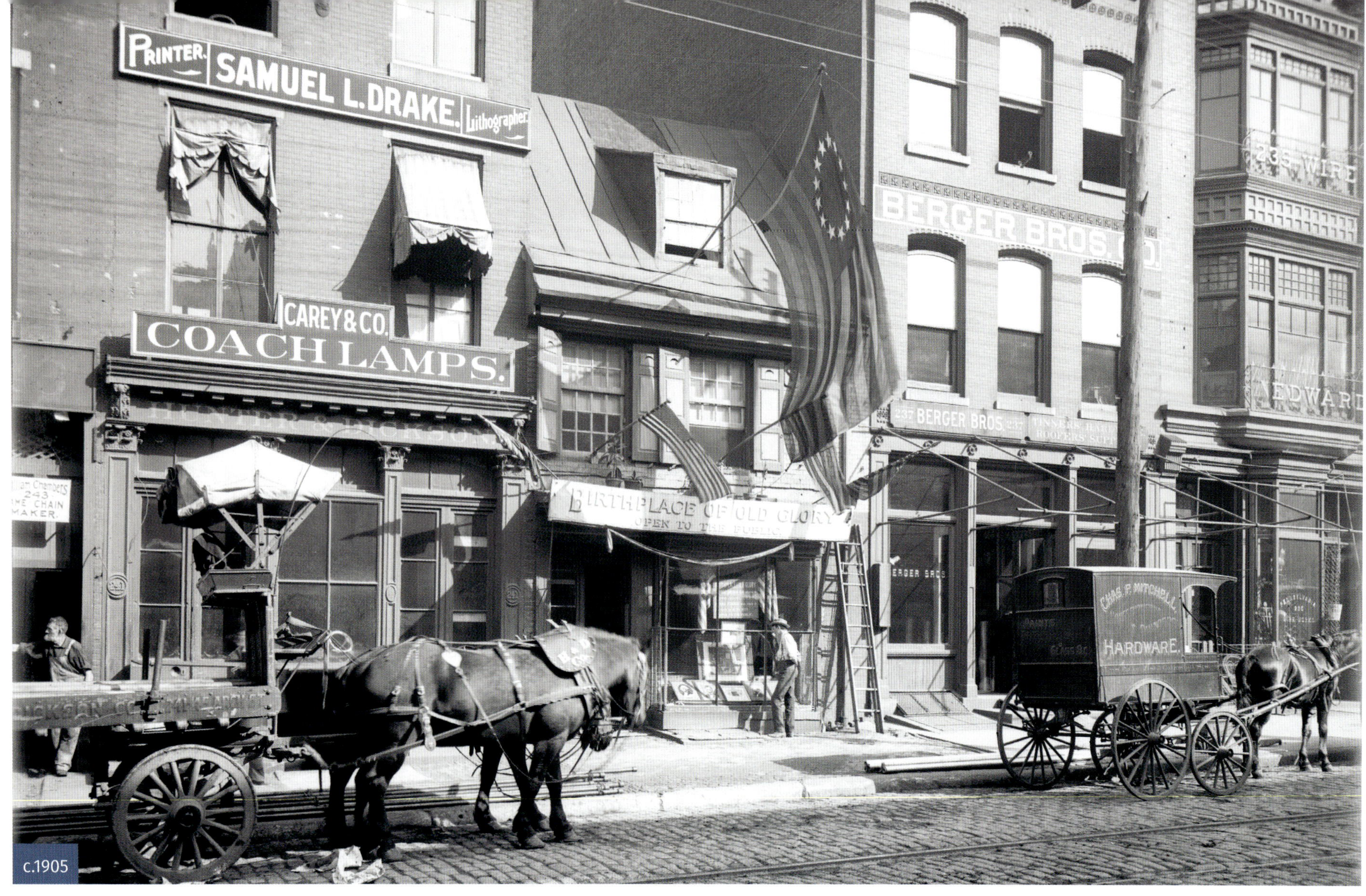

c.1905

BETSY ROSS HOUSE, PHILADELPHIA

The seamstress of the Stars and Stripes once lived here

A question that has vexed Philadelphia historians for over a century is, which was the Betsy Ross House? It is believed she lived in one of these twin houses on Arch Street (both pictured in the inset photo of 1859), several blocks from Independence Hall and the Liberty Bell. The front part of the original building was constructed around 1740, in the Pennsylvania colonial style, with a bakery on the left and a tailor on the right. Twenty years later and the bakery had been demolished and replaced with a four-story building, leaving the tailor's shop as the surviving twin (the lower inset retains the tree out front). And because Ross was an upholsterer and flag maker, this was surmised as her residence.

In 1895, Charles Weisgerber, who had immortalized Betsy Ross in his life-sized painting at the 1893 Chicago World's Fair, led a campaign to save the remaining house from demolition. One million children purchased ten-cent certificates to save the Betsy Ross House.

There is also doubt as to whether Ross actually sewed the first flag. The story of her involvement was promoted by her grandson, William Canby, nearly a hundred years after the event, and long after Betsy Ross was dead. Canby's only source for the story was from family members. However, there certainly is written evidence that she was hired to make flags for the Pennsylvania fleet. An entry in the naval records of

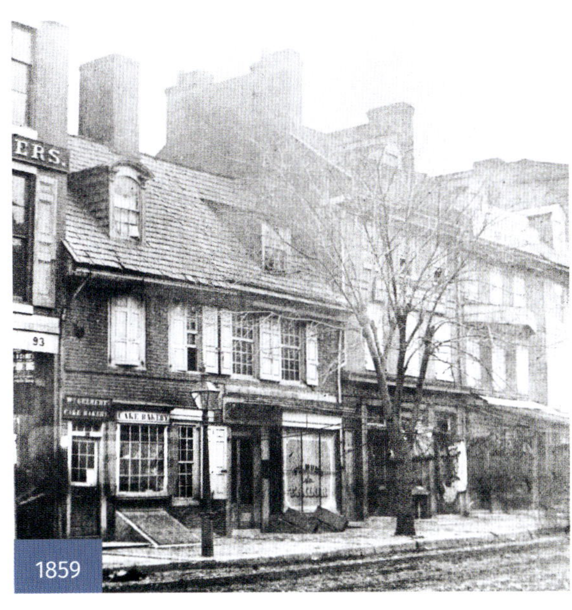
1859

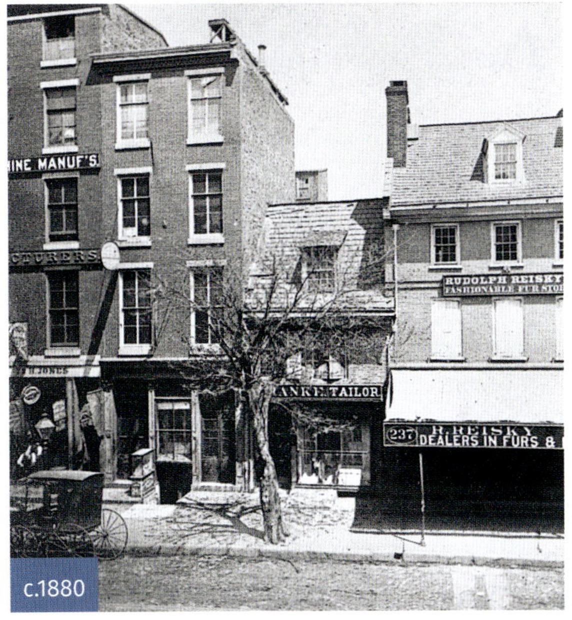

c.1880

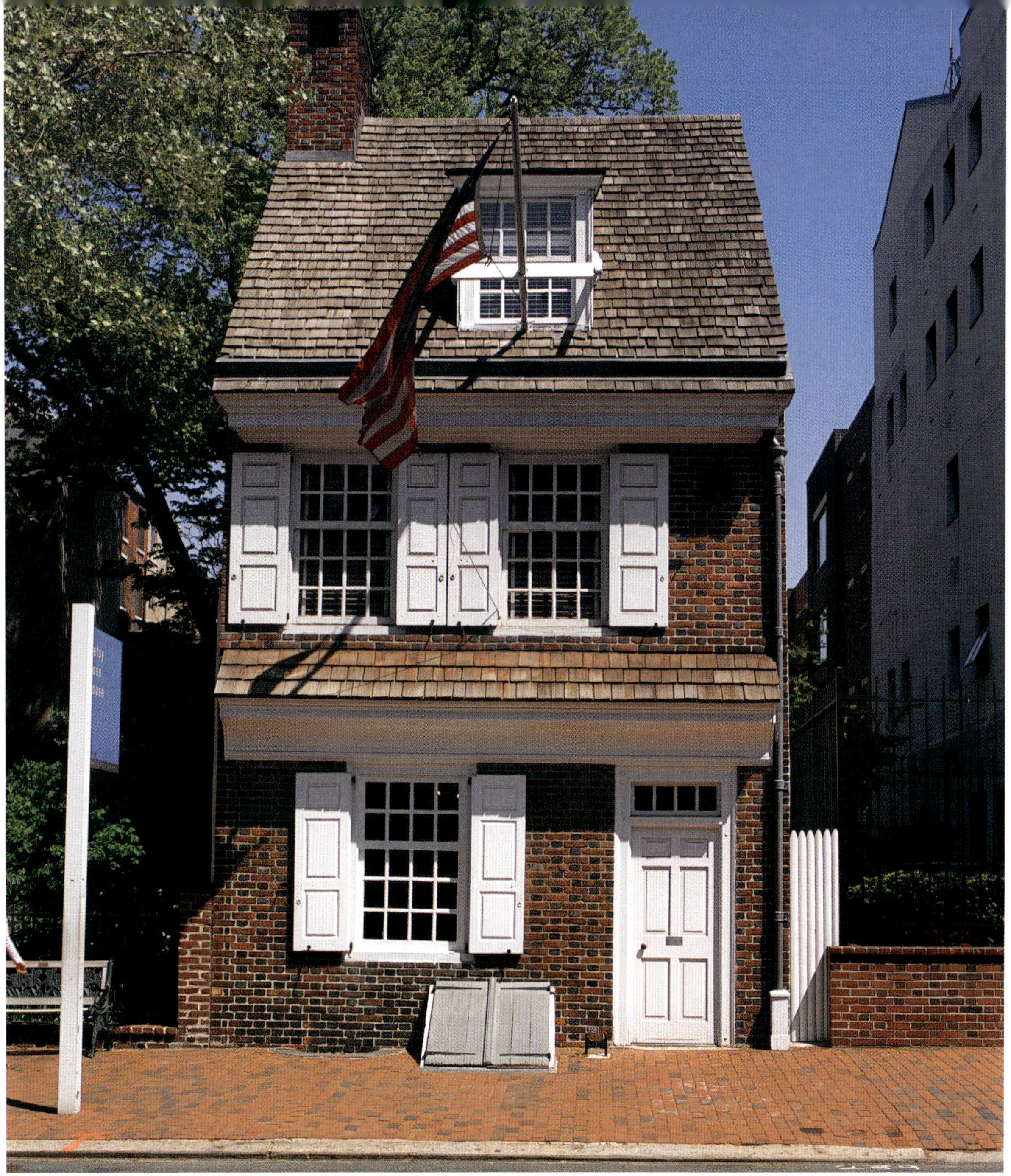

the Pennsylvania Navy Board, dated May 29, 1777, includes a document to pay her for her work: "An order on William Webb to Elizabeth Ross for fourteen pounds, twelve shillings and two pence for Making Ships Colors."

Now millions of children visit this house to honor one of the few women ranked in the Revolutionary pantheon. Not quite the sweet matronly seamstress painted by Weisgerber, Betsy was a fiercely independent twentysomething spitfire during the Revolution who went on to make flags for 50 years before her death in 1836.

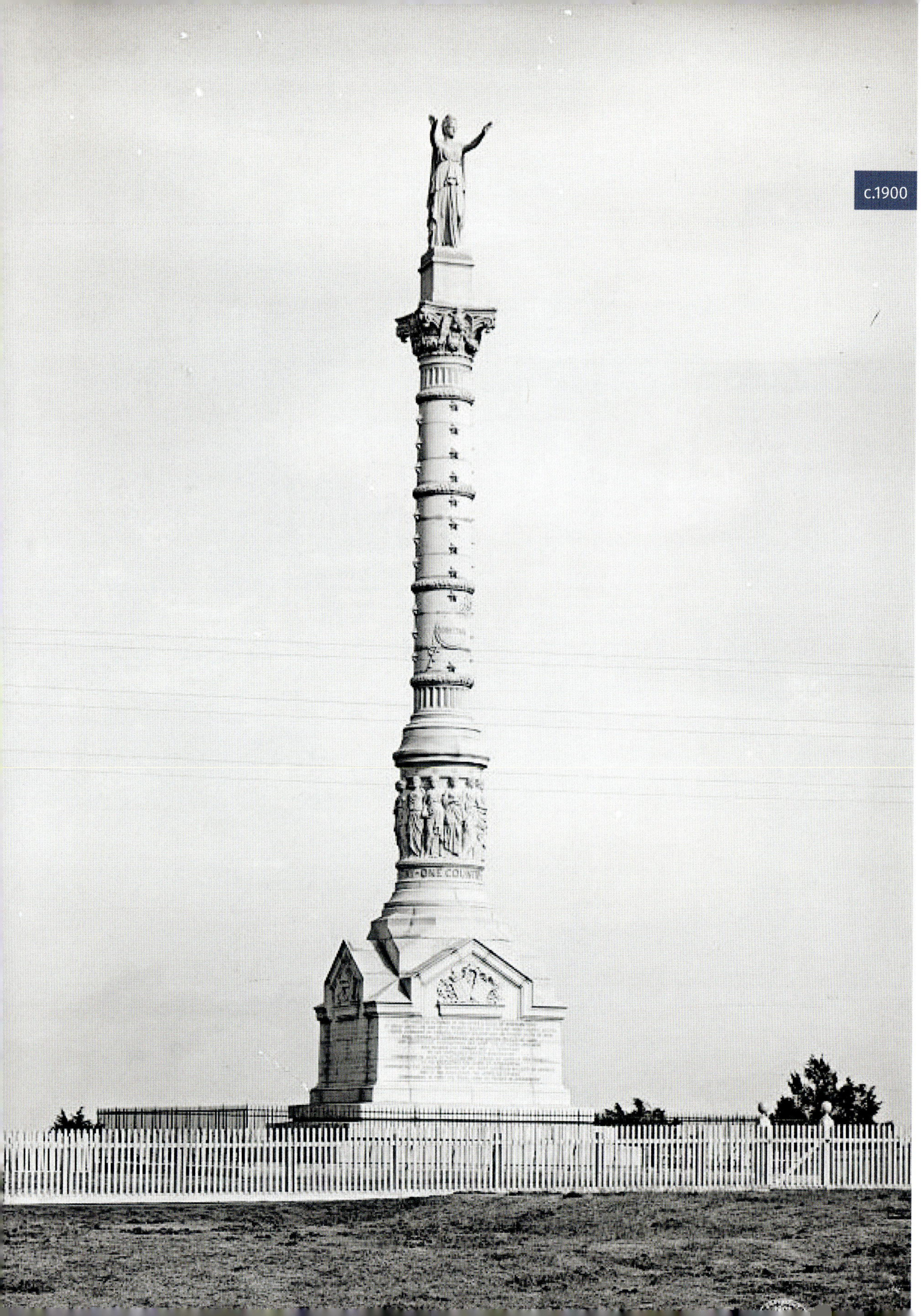

c.1900

YORKTOWN, VIRGINIA

The Continental Army forced a humiliating defeat on Lord Cornwallis

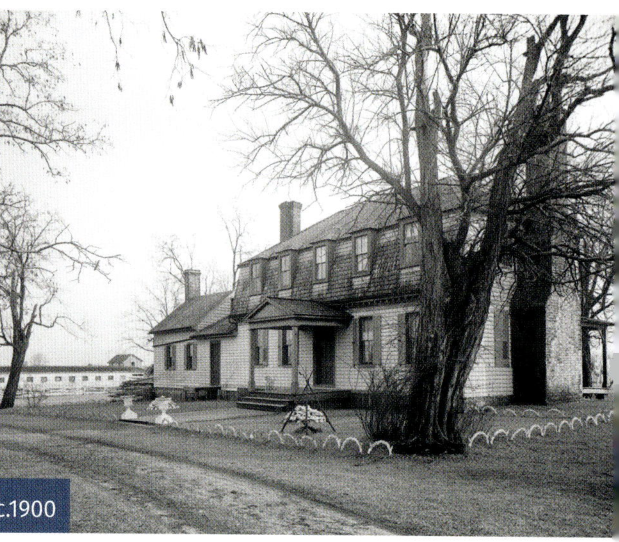

c.1900

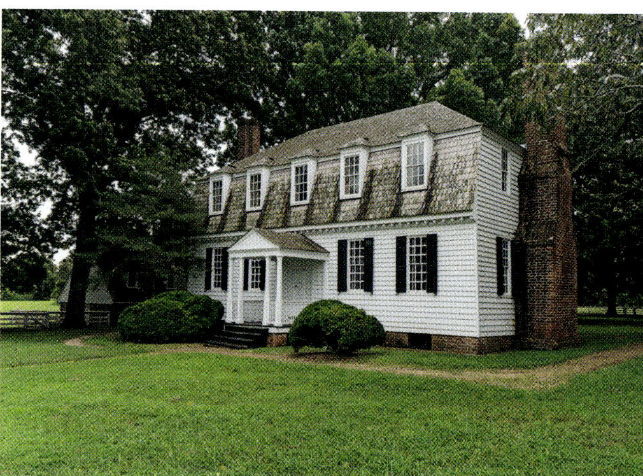

ABOVE: The surrender negotiations for Lord Cornwallis's army took place at the Moore House. While the surrender ceremony itself was held elsewhere, the formal surrender documents were drafted and signed at this house located within the Colonial National Historical Park in Yorktown,

The Battle of Yorktown, fought in the autumn of 1781, was the final major military engagement of the American Revolutionary War and marked a decisive turning point that led to American independence. The battle took place in Yorktown, Virginia, and pitted the combined American and French forces under General George Washington and French General Comte de Rochambeau against the British army commanded by General Charles Cornwallis.

Cornwallis had successfully campaigned through the Carolinas and then moved into Virginia to consolidate British control. In response, Washington saw an opportunity to trap the English general's forces. With French support—both military and naval—the Americans devised a plan to encircle the British in Yorktown.

Crucial to the plan was a French naval blockade. Admiral François de Grasse led a larger French fleet to Chesapeake Bay, defeating a British fleet at the Battle of the Virginia Capes in early September 1781. This victory ensured that Cornwallis could not be resupplied or evacuated by sea to continue the fight. Meanwhile, Washington and Rochambeau marched their armies south from New York, covering more than 400 miles in six weeks.

By late September, American and French forces had Cornwallis completely surrounded. The siege of Yorktown began on September 28, 1781. Over the following weeks, the Allies constructed siege lines and conducted a relentless bombardment of the British positions. The turning point in the siege came on October 14, when American and French forces stormed and captured two key British redoubts. Recognizing the hopelessness of his situation, Cornwallis surrendered his entire army of about 8,000 men on October 19, 1781.

A century later the Yorktown Monument was erected to commemorate the key siege. The original figure of *Liberty* that topped the column, sculpted by John Quincy Adams Ward (sculptor of George Washington outside Federal Hall in New York), was destroyed by lightning in 1942 and has since been replaced.

Yorktown also figured prominently in the American Civil War, serving as a major port on the York River to supply both Northern and Southern towns, depending upon who held the port at the time. Today, Yorktown is one of three sites of the Historic Triangle, which also includes Jamestown and Williamsburg as important colonial-era settlements. Cornwallis is remembered in the naming of the small cove below the monument.

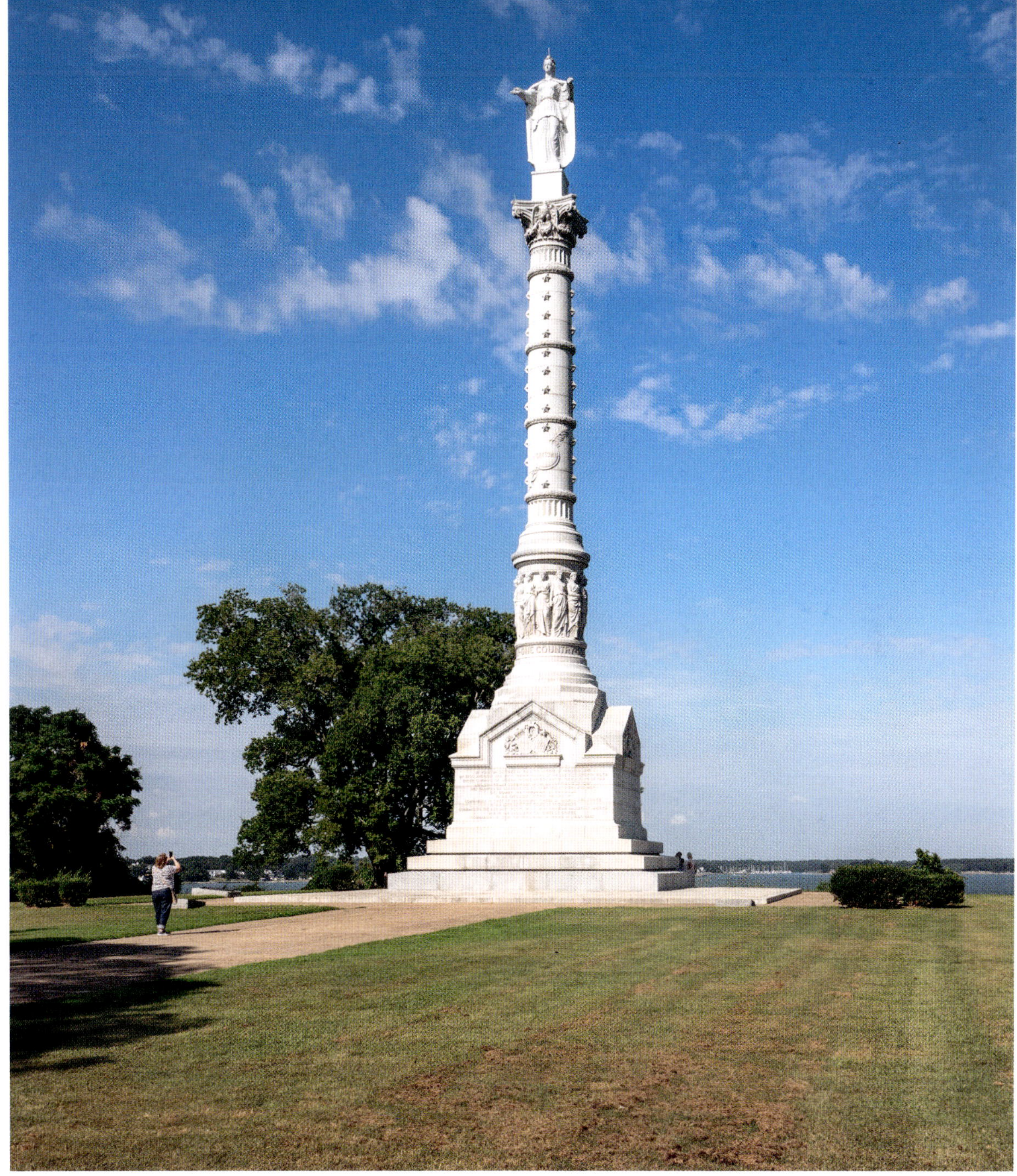

THE ALAMO, SAN ANTONIO

William Travis was trapped in the old mission building by the advancing Mexican army

The Alamo came to national prominence after the 1836 siege in which the advancing Mexican forces of General Santa Anna assaulted the stronghold of rebel Texas citizens. What is known as the Alamo today was originally the San Antonio de Valero mission, chartered by the Mexican viceroy in 1716 to educate local natives and convert them to Christianity. Alamo is Spanish for cottonwood, which is found in nearby groves. Santa Anna mounted a massive assault and slaughtered the Texian rebels after a thirteen-day siege.

The Alamo wasn't a strategically important location for either side—there was no critical bridge, vital port, meeting of roads or cache of resources. For the Mexican military, it was about controlling a rebellion. And for the Texians (many of whom were ethnic Mexicans), it was about the ability to exploit the land. Stephen F. Austin, the "Father of Texas," spent years corresponding with the Mexico City bureaucracy over the necessity of enslaved labor to the Texas economy, particularly the cotton crop.

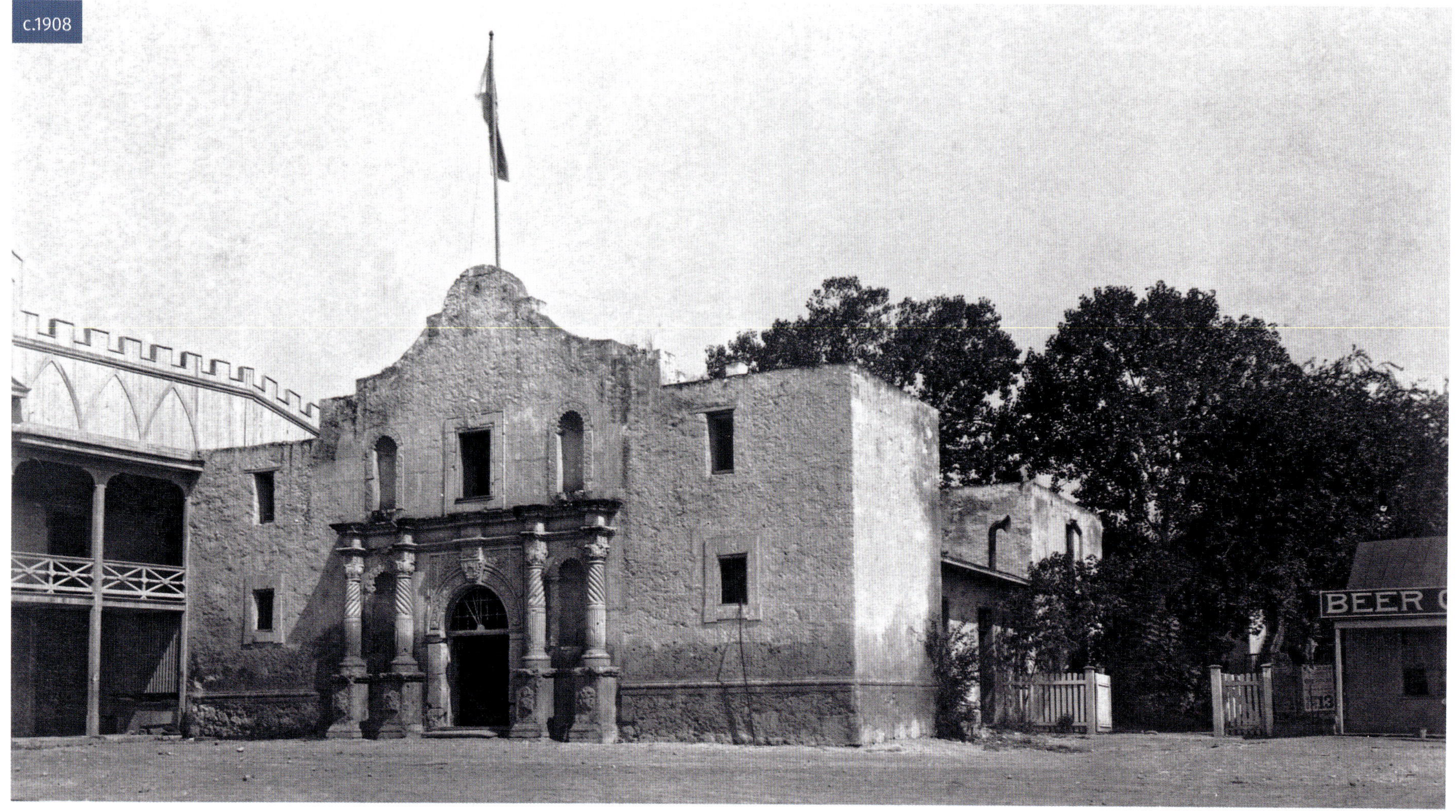

c.1908

Some historians believe the battle should never have been fought. Travis ignored multiple warnings of Santa Anna's approach and was simply trapped in the Alamo when the Mexican army arrived. His famous last stand, along with Jim Bowie and Davy Crockett, was out of necessity. Those who surrendered were slaughtered by the uncompromising Santa Anna. It was a powerful incentive for those fighting weeks later at the Battle of San Jacinto, who were urged to "Remember the Alamo."

After the Battle of the Alamo, the Republic of Texas passed an act returning the grounds to the church in 1841. When the United States annexed Texas, it demanded ownership—then turned around and leased it to the church. In 1905 the state legislature granted ownership to the Daughters of the Republic of Texas. It is now a popular tourist spot, with 2.5 million visitors annually, the state's biggest draw. Part museum, part monument, and part cultural icon—visiting the Alamo is always free of charge. The site includes a shrine, as well as multiple educational exhibits on the Texas Revolution and Texas history.

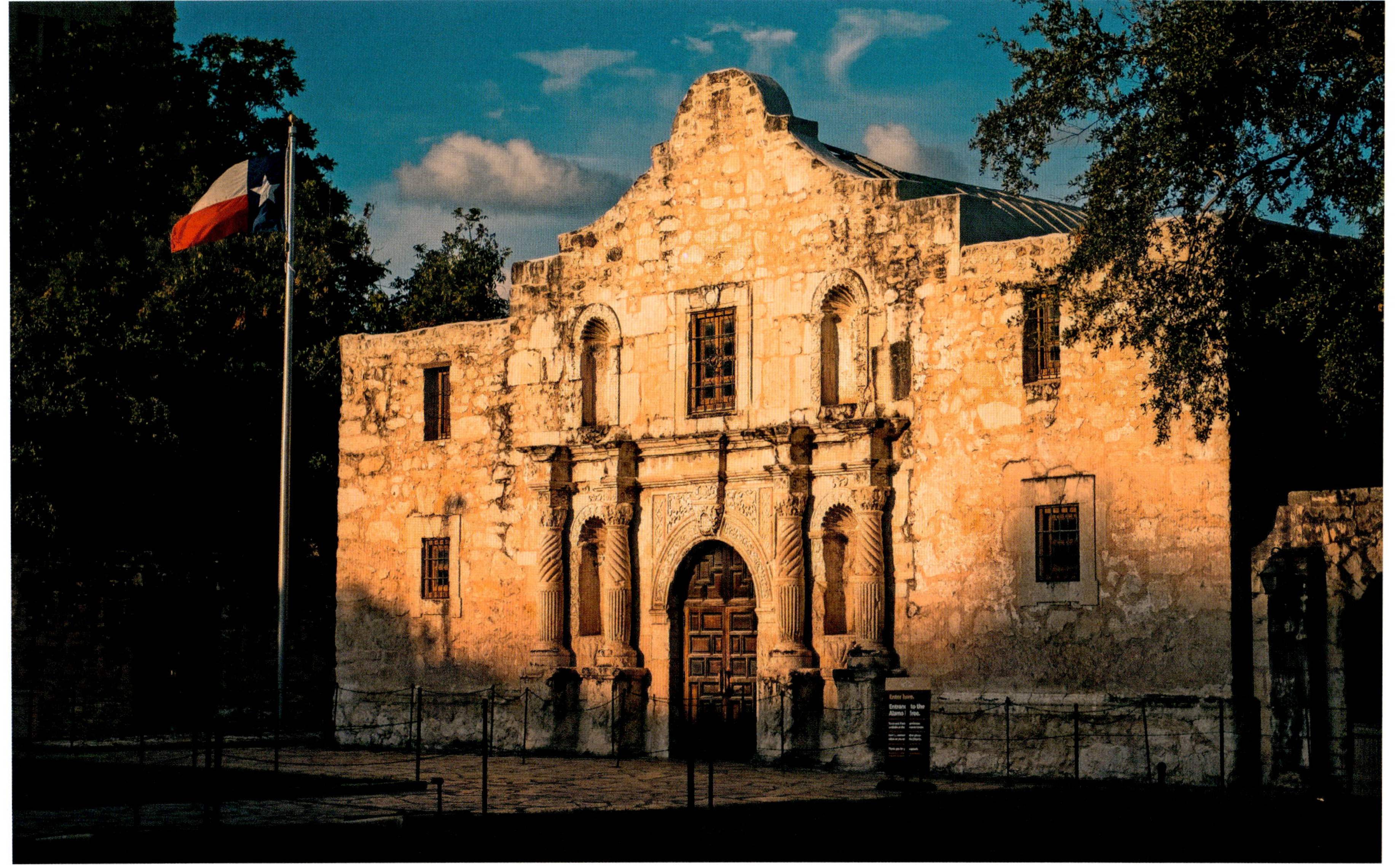

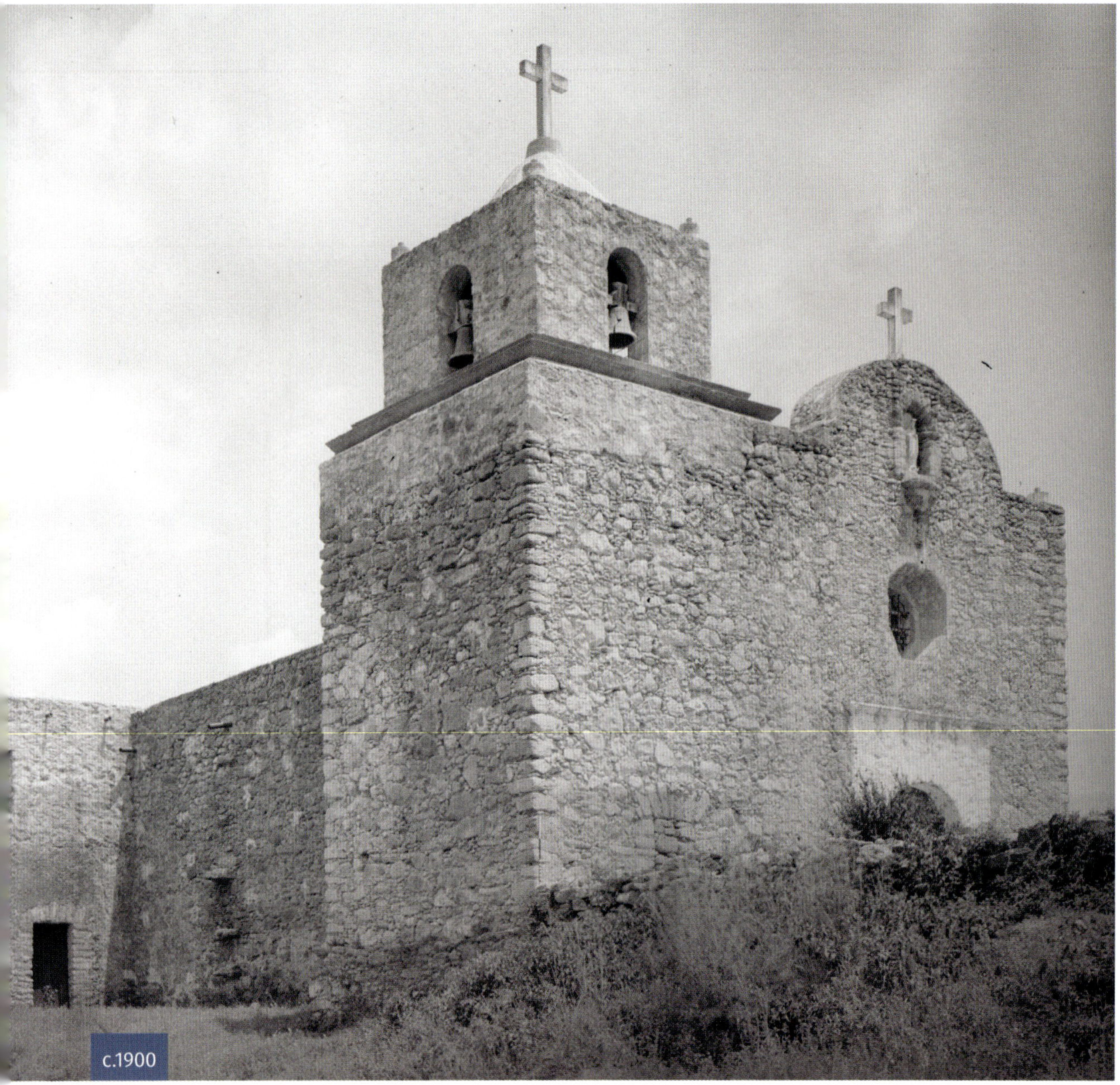

c.1900

OUTRAGE AT GOLIAD, TEXAS

Mexican leader Antonio López de Santa Anna strengthened the Texians' resolve at Goliad

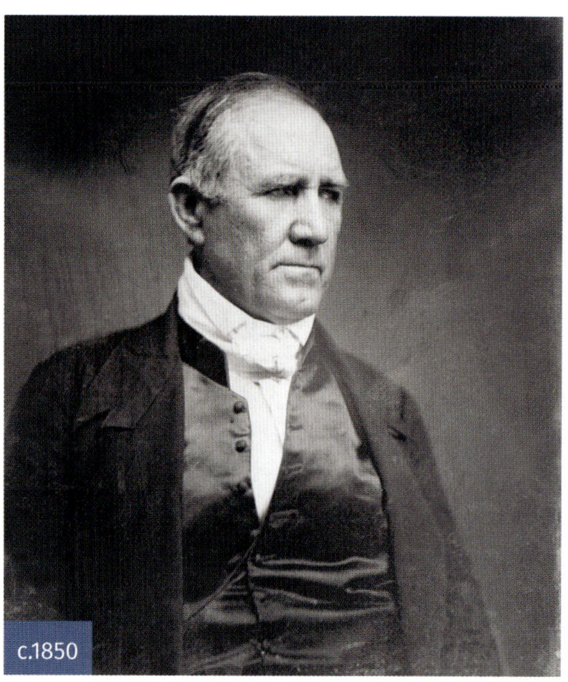
c.1850

After Mexico gained independence from Spain in 1821, it inherited the vast and sparsely populated territory of Texas. To stabilize the region and counter Native American resistance, the Mexican government encouraged American settlers to move in under the empresario system, with Stephen F. Austin leading the first major colonization. Thousands of Anglo-Americans settled in Texas, bringing with them different cultural and political values—particularly on issues such as slavery and governance.

Tensions grew as Mexico, under President Antonio López de Santa Anna, shifted toward centralization, revoking the 1824 Constitution that had granted Mexican states considerable autonomy. Texas settlers, both Anglo and Tejano (Texans of Mexican descent), resisted this change, leading to a growing push for independence.

The conflict escalated in 1835, when Texians seized control of local garrisons, beginning the Texas Revolution. One key moment came with the Battle of the Alamo in March 1836, when Texian defenders, including Jim Bowie, William Travis, and

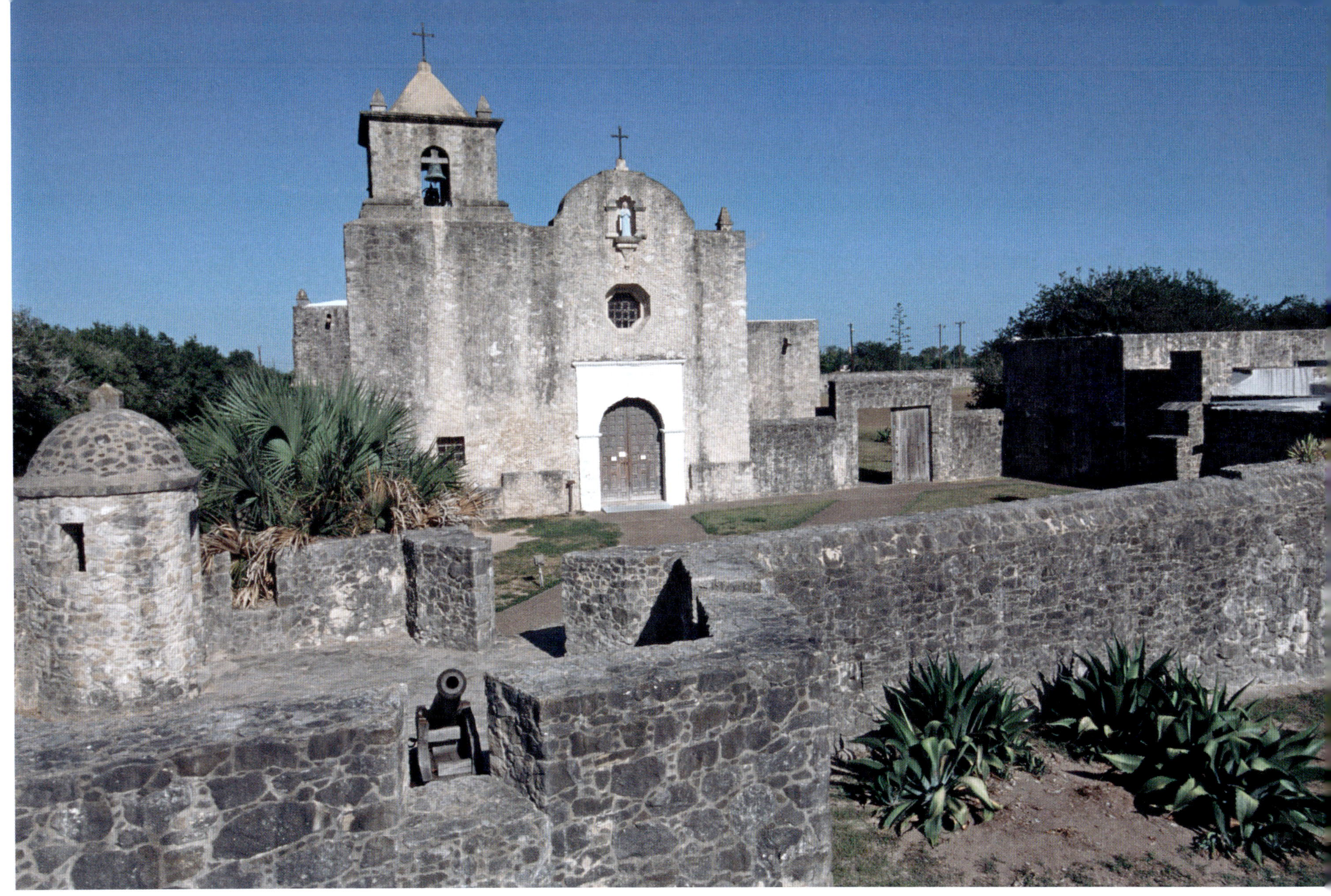

Davy Crockett, held out for thirteen days against Santa Anna's vastly superior force in San Antonio.

Just weeks later, another tragedy struck. After the Battle of Coleto, Texian forces under Colonel James Fannin surrendered to Mexican troops near Goliad. Despite promises of fair treatment, Santa Anna ordered the execution of the captured troops. On March 27, 1836, around 350 Texian prisoners were massacred in what became known as the Goliad Massacre.

Herman Ehrenberg was among 28 men who feigned death and escaped and later wrote an account of the massacre; William Lockhart Hunter survived despite being bayoneted and clubbed with a musket; and because of the intervention of Francita Alavez (known as the "Angel of Goliad"), 20 more men were spared to act as doctors, interpreters, or workers. Also spared were the 75 soldiers of the Miller and Nashville Battalion, who were given white armbands. However, among those killed was Colonel James Fannin.

These brutal events outraged Texians and fueled their resolve. Whereas the Alamo had been a clear-cut skirmish, this was military treachery. On April 21, 1836, under General Sam Houston (pictured opposite), Texian forces defeated Santa Anna at the Battle of San Jacinto, securing Texas' independence and marking a dramatic turning point in North American history.

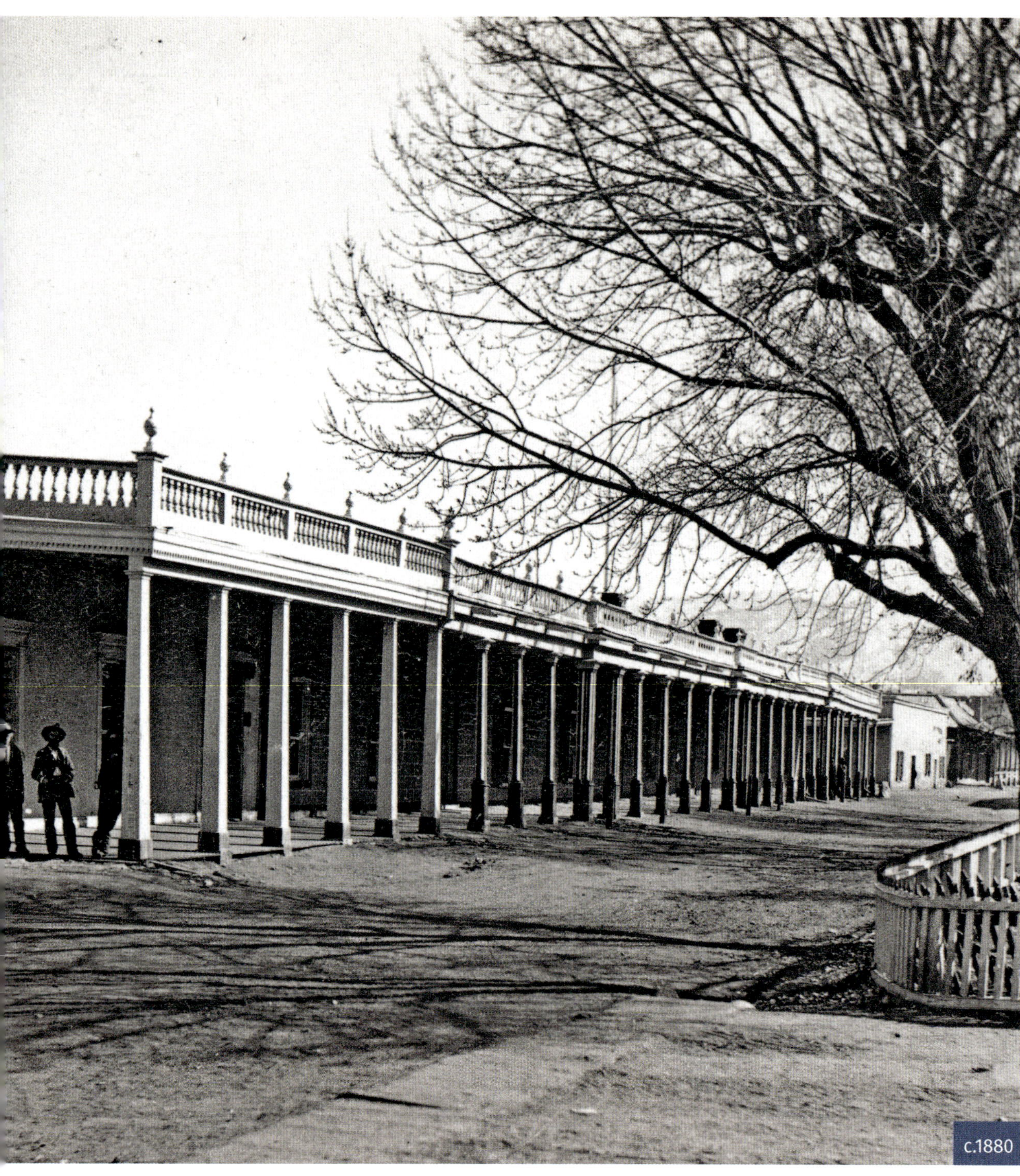

PALACE OF THE GOVERNORS, SANTA FE, NEW MEXICO

The oldest constitutional building in the United States

In 1598, Spanish conquistador Don Juan de Oñate led a group of settlers north from what is now Mexico into the Rio Grande Valley. They established the first permanent European settlement at San Juan de los Caballeros. Oñate claimed the territory for Spain and named it "La Nueva México."

In 1610, Santa Fe—officially known as La Villa Real de la Santa Fe de San Francisco de Asís (the Royal Town of the Holy Faith of Saint Francis of Assisi)—became the provincial capital replacing San Gabriel. Pedro de Peralta, the newly appointed governor of Santa Fe, oversaw the construction of the Palace of the Governors from 1618. It was from here that the vast territory, including modern-day Texas, Arizona, Utah, Colorado, Nevada, and New Mexico, was administered. Like the fluctuating control of New Orleans (also, once a Spanish possession) Santa Fe has had many masters. During the Pueblo Revolt of 1680, the Spanish lost control of Santa Fe to the Pueblo Indians led by a Tewa religious leader named Popé. The Pueblos were reacting to decades of Spanish oppression. On August 10, 1680, the revolt began, and within days, the Pueblo forces had killed around 400 Spaniards, including 21 missionaries, and driven the rest, including the governor, out of Santa Fe. The Spanish retreated to El Paso del Norte (modern-day El Paso, Texas).

The Spanish were back in the Palace by 1692, ruling until Mexico gained its independence from Spain in 1821. The Mexican-American war of 1848 settled the land in America's favor, while statehood in the form of a vastly diminished New Mexico (compared to its original size when under Spanish control) beckoned in 1912.

The Palace is the oldest public building in continuous occupation constructed by European settlers in the continental United States. In 1909 it became the Museum of New Mexico and its low profile has ensured that nearby buildings don't rise above it. Although the historic La Fonda Hotel rises to four stories farther across the Plaza, it was built before the planning rule was applied.

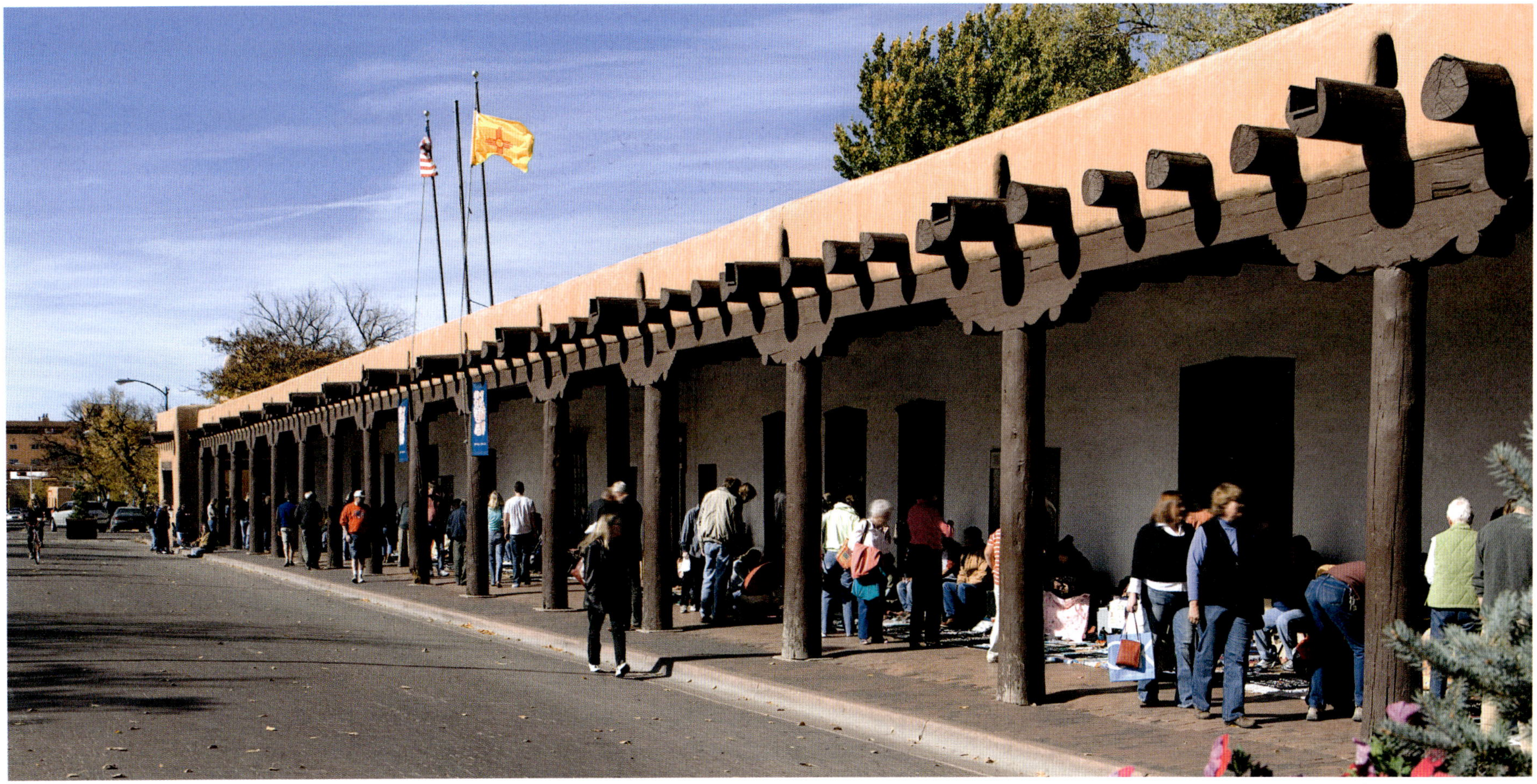

Today the city is celebrated for its artistic community. An estimated 10% of the employment is dedicated to cultural activities, whether museums or the 200-plus art galleries—with much activity revolving around three annual art events: the Santa Fe International Folk Art Market; the Spanish Colonial Market, and the Indian Market. The porch of the Palace of the Governors is traditionally where Native Americans sell their arts and crafts on a year-round basis.

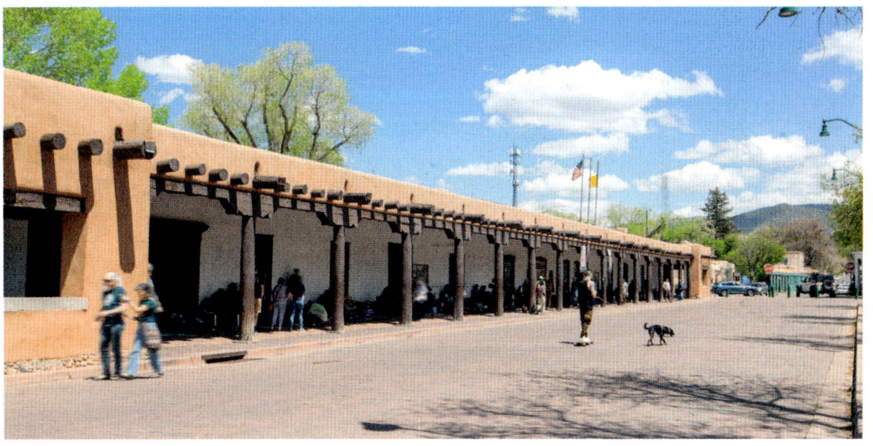

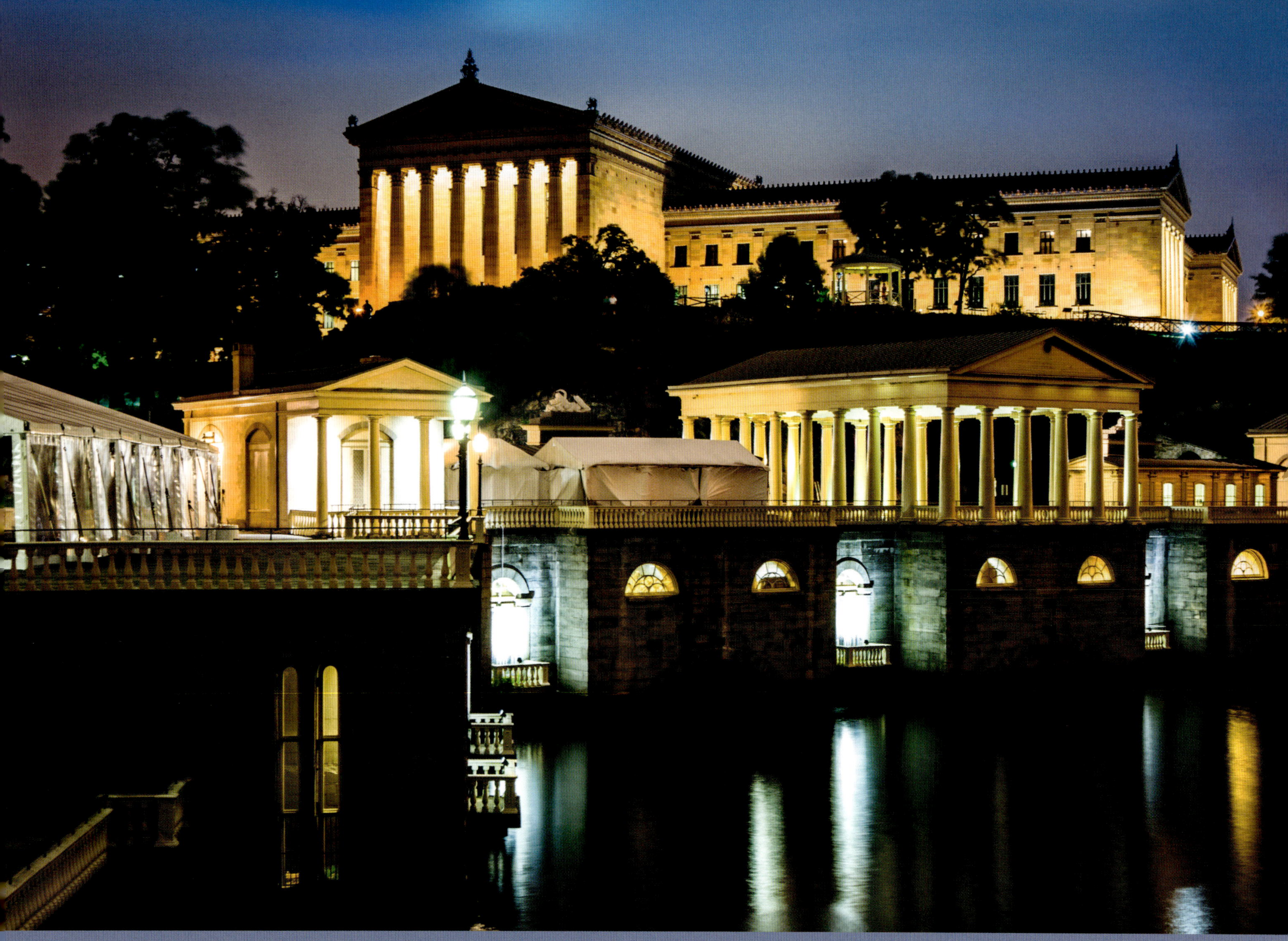

A NATION IS BORN

The Constitutional Convention convened in Philadelphia in 1787, where delegates debated a new framework for government. The resulting US Constitution, ratified by 1789, established a stronger federal government with separate executive, legislative, and judicial branches. It also included mechanisms for amendments and important checks and balances.

To address concerns about individual liberties, the first ten amendments—the Bill of Rights—were adopted in 1791. These guaranteed freedoms such as speech, religion, and due process. George Washington, already a national hero, was unanimously elected the first President of the United States in 1789. His presidency (1789–1797) helped stabilize the fledgling nation. Washington set crucial precedents, including forming a cabinet and limiting himself to two terms. He issued a farewell address warning against political factions and foreign entanglements.

ESTABLISHING THE CAPITAL: WASHINGTON, DC

One early controversy was the location of the national capital. Northern and southern states debated its placement until a compromise was struck in 1790: the federal government would assume state war debts (a northern priority), and in return, the capital would move to a location on the Potomac River, between Maryland and Virginia.

When the city was first established, the surrounding area was largely undeveloped with dense forests and mosquito-infested swamps. In its early years, Washington, DC was often described as a "skeleton city," "wilderness," or "romantic but wild." Visitors noted the large open spaces, dirt roads, and the city's underdeveloped character. Some described it as having "more streets than houses." But grandeur would come.

Designed by Pierre Charles L'Enfant, the new District of Columbia became the official capital in 1800, though construction of key buildings—like the Capitol and White House—continued for years. The city, later named Washington, DC, symbolized a new federal authority, set apart from any individual state.

PARTISAN POLITICS AND EXPANDING BOUNDARIES

By the 1790s, political factions had solidified into the first American parties. Federalists, led by Alexander Hamilton, favored a strong central government, financial probity, and close ties to Britain. Democratic-Republicans, led by Thomas Jefferson, championed states' rights and sympathy for revolutionary France.

In 1801, Jefferson took over the presidency in a peaceful transfer of power between rival parties—an important test for the young republic. With anarchy reigning in France, in 1803 he opted to pay the French $15m for the Louisiana territories when critics pointed out it could be gotten for nothing. Nevertheless, it doubled the size of the United States and Jefferson celebrated by sending off explorers Meriwether Lewis and William Clark to find out just exactly what the country had spent their money on.

Lewis and Clark were commissioned to map this new territory, journeying to the Pacific from 1804 to 1806. Their expedition helped shape American ideas of westward expansion—known as Manifest Destiny, the belief that the US was destined to expand across the continent.

WAR AND NATIONALISM: THE WAR OF 1812

Despite growth, the US remained vulnerable internationally. Ongoing trade disputes with Britain and the British Navy's impressment of sailors from American-flagged vessels led to President James Madison's invasion of Canada in 1812. Though the conflict had mixed military results—including the burning of the US capital in retaliation for the burning of government buildings in York (now Toronto)—it ended in a draw, with the Treaty of Ghent of 1815 and the Battle of New Orleans, fought unknowingly, after the treaty had been signed.

MARKET REVOLUTION

The early nineteenth century saw dramatic changes to American society. The Market Revolution—spurred by transportation innovations like canals, roads, and railroads—transformed the economy. The Erie Canal (1825) connected the Great Lakes to the Atlantic, turning New York City into a commercial hub.

Industrialization, especially in the North and promoted by Alexander Hamilton, who wanted to emulate the industrial success of Britain, led to the creation of the Slater Mill in New England. In the South, cotton became king, fueled by the invention of the cotton gin (1793) and entrenched slavery. This economic divergence between North and South would define much of the country's political strife in the coming decades.

In 1828, Andrew Jackson, a war hero and populist, was elected president. His victory marked the rise of Jacksonian Democracy, which expanded voting rights for white men (by eliminating property requirements) and emphasized the will of the "common man." Jackson's presidency was controversial. Most notoriously, he signed the Indian Removal Act (1830), leading to the Trail of Tears during which thousands of Native Americans—especially the Cherokee—were forcibly relocated west of the Mississippi, often at great human cost.

TEXAS, EXPANSION, AND THE ROAD TO WAR

Meanwhile, American settlers pushed westward into new territories. By 1846, the Mexican–American War had begun. US forces, led by generals Zachary Taylor and Winfield Scott, invaded Mexican territory. Meanwhile, settlers in California—some inspired by John C. Frémont—rose up in what became the Bear Flag Revolt, asserting independence from Mexico.

By 1847, the US military had captured key cities, including Monterrey and Mexico City, and the war was drawing to a close. The eventual Treaty of Guadalupe Hidalgo (signed in 1848) would grant the US vast new territories—including California, Arizona, New Mexico, and parts of Colorado and Utah—cementing American dominance across the continent.

Between 1783 and 1847, the United States transformed from a fragile confederation into an expansive and increasingly assertive nation. Canals were built that would be an immediate boost to trade but were soon superseded by the railroads. Riverboats plied goods up and down the Ohio, Missouri, and Mississippi as the economy boomed. Washington, DC rose as the symbolic and political heart; wars tested and confirmed American sovereignty—witnessing the blockade of Baltimore, Francis Scott Key wrote the poem that would become the national anthem—and territorial expansion redefined the country's geography and ambitions.

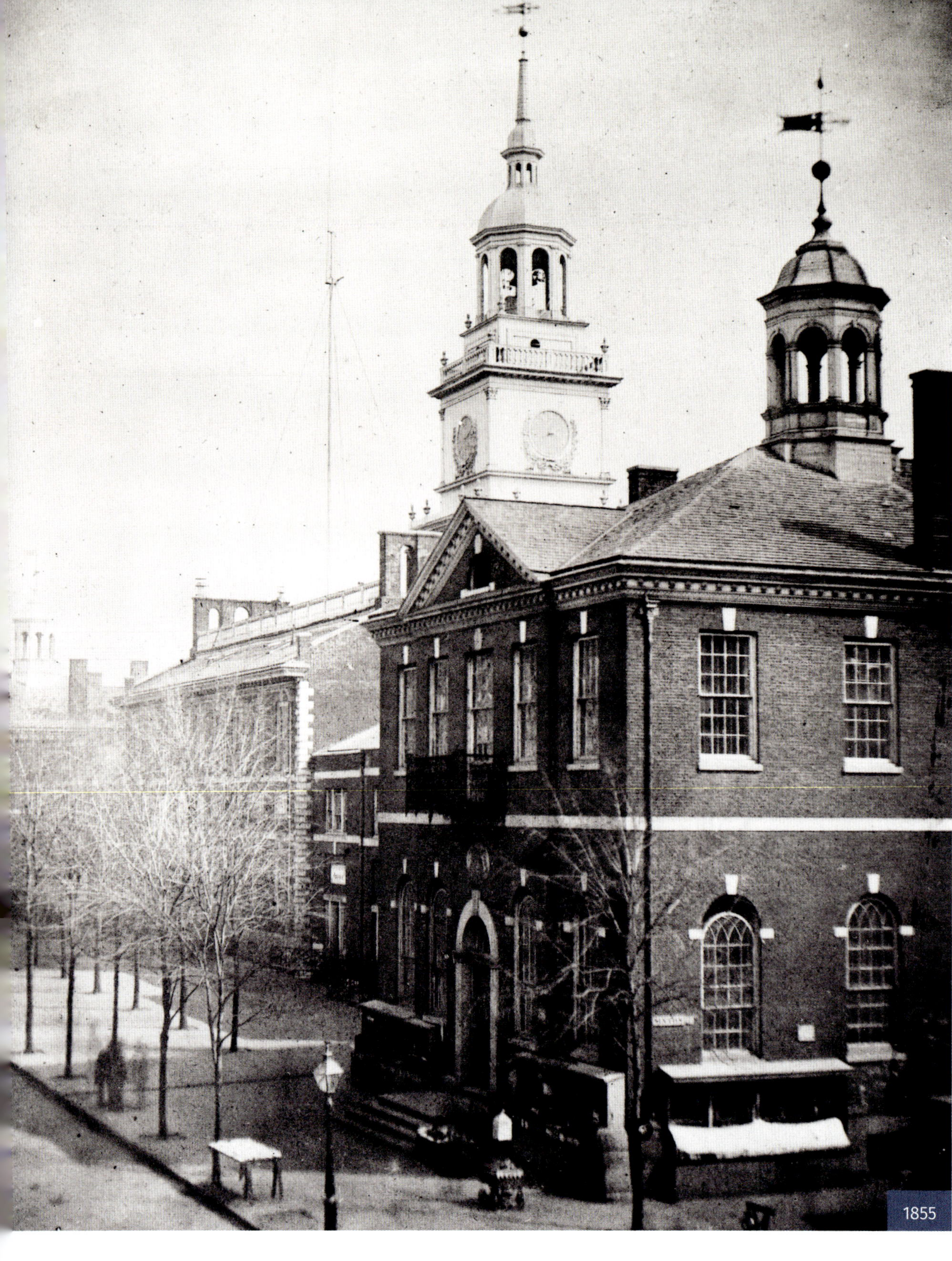

CONGRESS HALL, PHILADELPHIA

The building in which George Washington dared Congress to impeach him...

This 1855 photograph shows a bookseller's stall attached to America's oldest congressional building. During its first decade, Congress cut its legislative teeth here, creating the Bill of Rights, admitting the first new states: Vermont, Kentucky and Tennessee, mandating the first census and reapportioning delegates. A bristling President Washington clashed with Congress here and dared them to impeach him over the Jay Treaty. The US and Great Britain had signed the (John) Jay Treaty in 1794 to resolve lingering issues from the Revolutionary War and prevent renewed conflict. It secured British withdrawal from frontier forts and also resolved pre-war debts owed to British creditors. Many Jeffersonian Republicans had seen the Revolution as an excuse not to pay British banks and merchants.

The treaty was highly controversial because many Americans believed it was too conciliatory to Britain and betrayed the revolutionary spirit. In 1796, the House of Representatives, led by anti-treaty Republicans (such as James Madison), demanded that President Washington turn over all documents relating to the negotiation of the Jay Treaty. However, Washington refused, asserting that the House had no constitutional role in treaty-making, which was the domain of the President and the Senate. He claimed that turning over the documents would set a dangerous precedent and undermine executive authority. Washington invoked "executive privilege," one of the first times a US president had done so. He sent a strongly worded message to Congress, essentially saying: If you believe I've overstepped my authority, impeach me.

The building was constructed as the Philadelphia County Courthouse in 1789, but served as the meeting place for Congress from 1790 to 1800, when the national capital moved to Washington, DC. George Washington's second inauguration was held in the hall.

This building, along with Independence Hall next door, are where the most critical debates of the eighteenth century still echo. It has been faithfully restored. The interior of Congress Hall now looks as much as possible as it did in the 1790s.

Downstairs, visitors can view the restored meeting space of the House of Representatives, with rows of reproduction mahogany desks and leather-covered chairs. Upstairs, visitors will find the more elaborate chambers of the smaller Senate, decorated with red velvet drapes and forest green walls. In the adjoining committee rooms hang portraits of Marie Antoinette and Louis XVI, allies during the Revolutionary War who were later beheaded by the people of France.

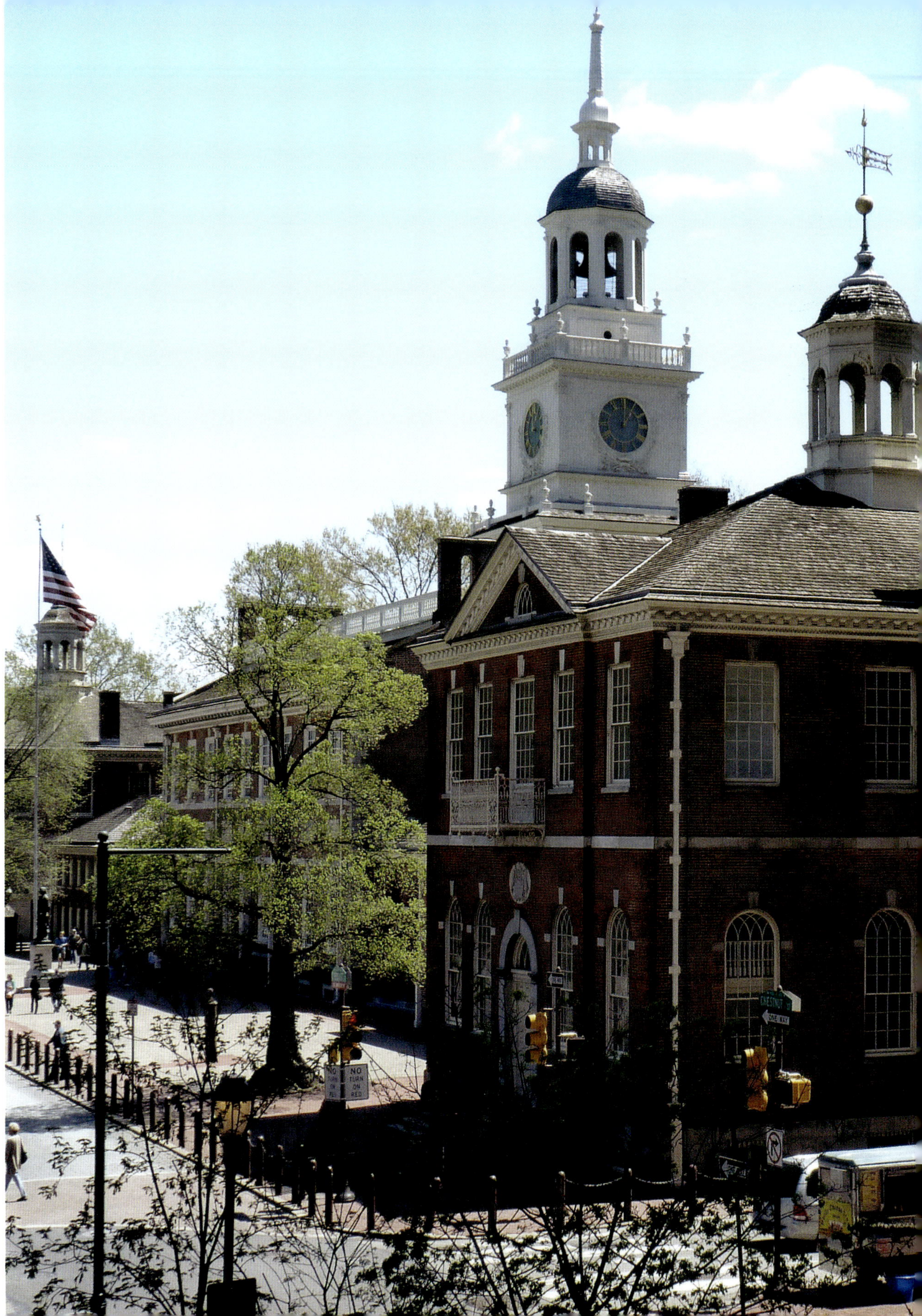

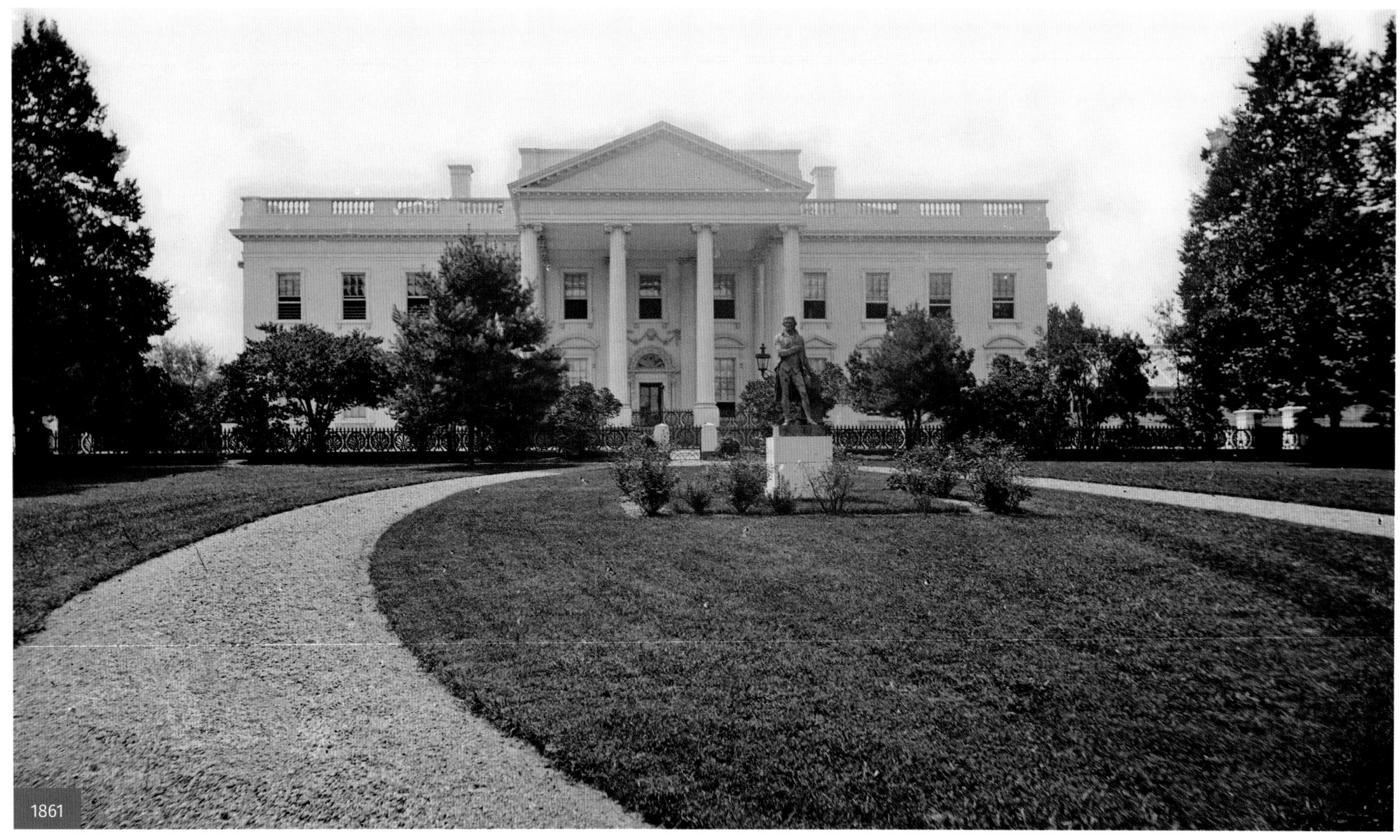
1861

THE EXECUTIVE MANSION, WASHINGTON, DC

A chance meeting in Charleston introduced George Washington to the building's architect

In Pierre Charles L'Enfant's 1791 plan for Washington, he detailed wide avenues and the location of important federal buildings. One of the most recognizable is the White House. There was still a decade before Washington would officially become the capital city in 1800. However, the city wanted to be ready for its new government and leadership, and began construction on the Executive Mansion only a year after L'Enfant announced his plan. Despite his overview of the project, President George Washington would never live in the mansion himself, as it was only completed in 1800, a year after his death. It was designed by James Hoban, an architect Washington had met after his week-long stay in Charleston, South Carolina. Eager to live in the Executive Estate, President John Adams and his wife moved into the unfinished

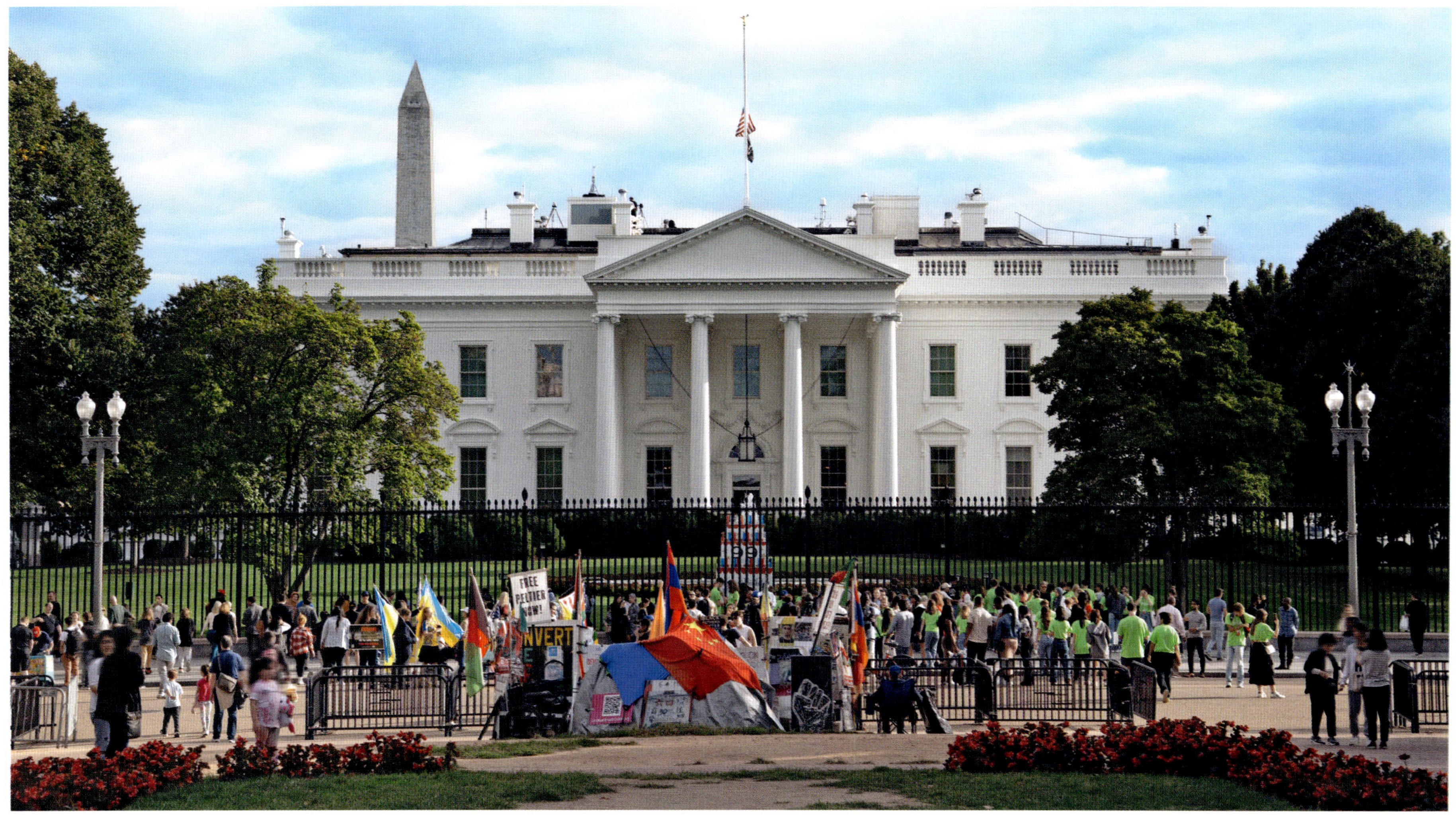

building in 1800. The President's House finally had its first resident and federal work in Washington could now begin in earnest.

The work of the executive came to a halt in 1814. America had launched an ill-advised invasion of Canada in 1812 in an attempt to seize territory as a bargaining chip in a maritime dispute with Britain. Most Americans assumed that the conquest of Canada would be, in the words of former president Thomas Jefferson, "a mere matter of marching." Badly paid and under-prepared militias invaded at three points, but all three campaigns ended in failure. The burning of public buildings in York, Upper Canada's capital, by American forces in April 1813 led to retaliation in 1814. The British invaded the young capital city, attempting to burn all buildings of significance; including the White House. President James Madison and his wife Dolley were forced to flee the building. As one of the oldest federal buildings in Washington, the White House required frequent maintenance and updates.

The archive photo from 1861, around the time of Lincoln's inauguration, is believed to be the first. During President Theodore Roosevelt's time in office he constructed the West Wing, where White House staffers work. It was also during Roosevelt's presidency that the building garnered its current name, The White House. Today, the site continues to host visitors attempting to catch a glimpse of the President, as well as foreign dignitaries on state visits. On any given day, visitors may see staffers walking to their offices, reporters using the Executive Mansion as a backdrop for their stories, and eighth graders learning about one of the most contentious and famed branches of the United States government.

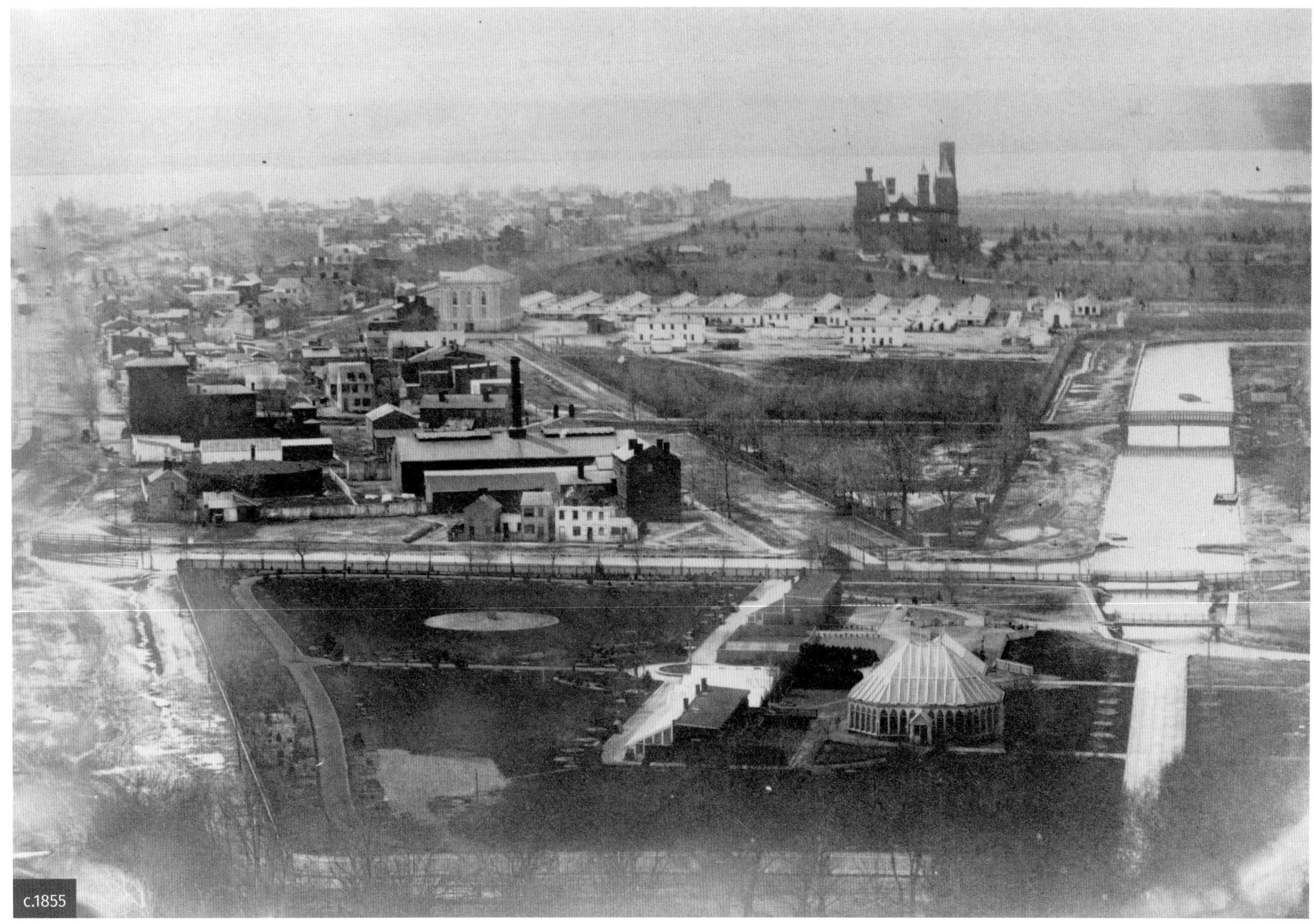
c.1855

THE L'ENFANT PLAN, WASHINGTON, DC

The visionary planner established the capital's revolutionary street grid

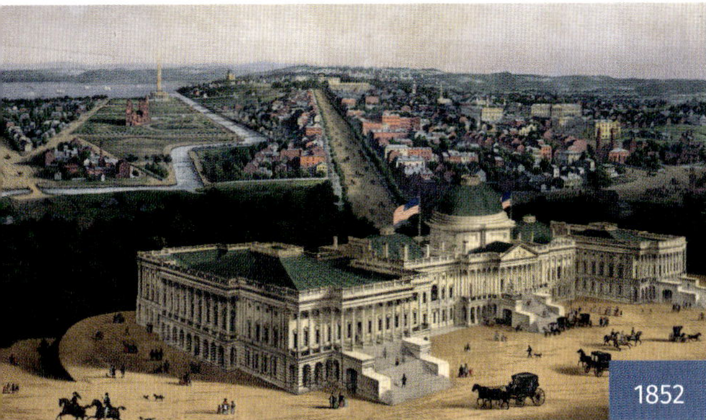

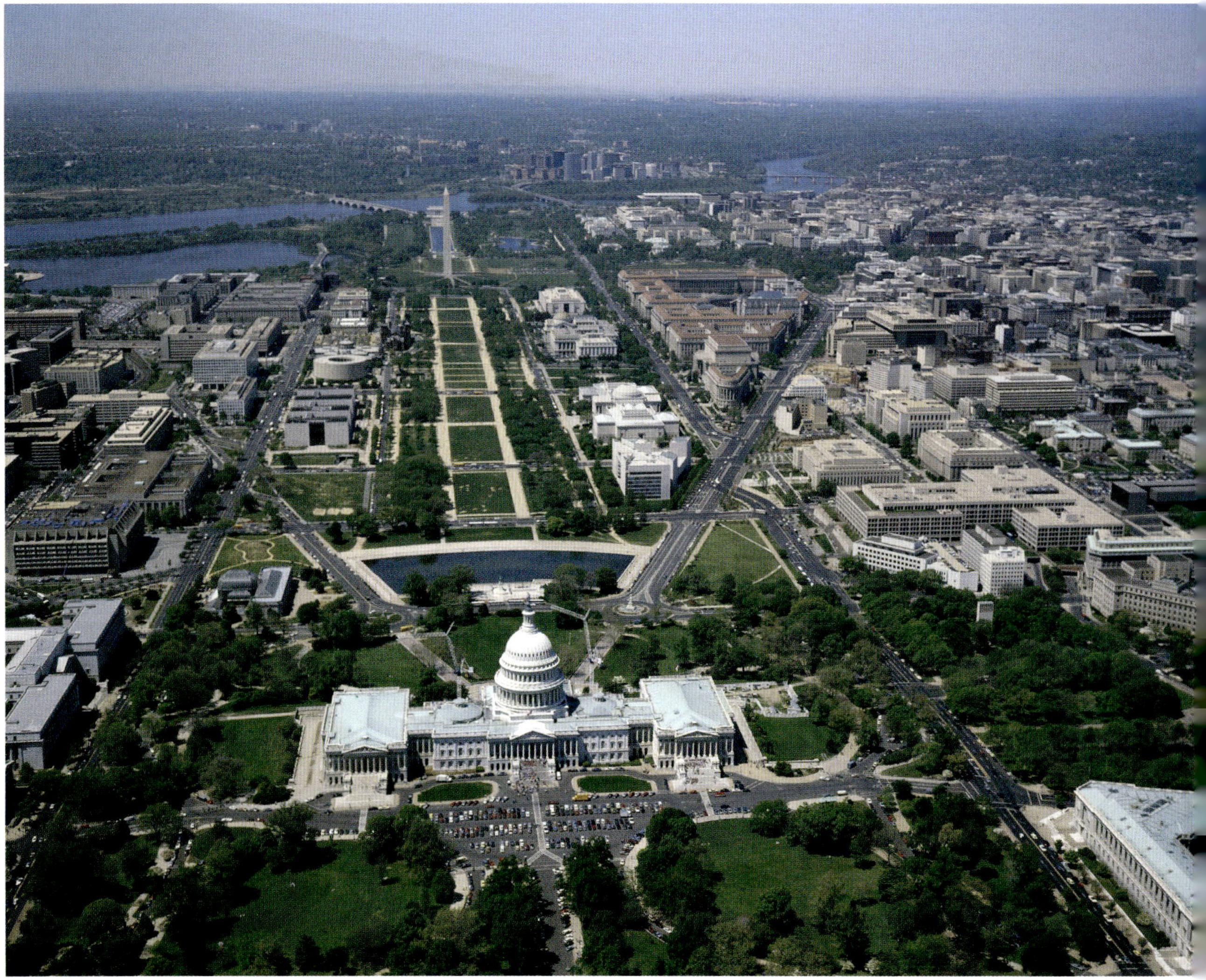

TOP: Looming in the distance, to the right of the Smithsonian Castle (1849) and close to the water's edge, is the intended Washington Monument in its original planned form, with a colonnade at the base which was never built.

Pierre Charles L'Enfant, a French-American architect and civil engineer, was commissioned by President George Washington in 1791 to design the layout of the nation's capital city, which, to avoid allegations of favoritism, would lie outside any existing state. Born in Paris, L'Enfant had arrived in 1777 at the age of 23, to serve as a military engineer in the Continental Army with Major General Lafayette and served on General George Washington's staff at Valley Forge. L'Enfant envisioned a grand capital that would rival the great cities of Europe in beauty and function. The most defining feature of the plan was its combination of a grid system with diagonal avenues that radiated from key points—such as the Capitol and the President's House—forming circles and squares at intersections.

The National Mall, now a central feature of Washington, DC, was part of L'Enfant's original vision with a canal skirting its northern side. He placed the "Congress House" (now the Capitol) on Jenkins Hill and established it as the city's focal point. A long, open public space extended westward from it, offering a symbolic and visual link to the "President's House" (the White House).

In the early years of the nascent state there was great interest in creating canals within cities to aid commerce. L'Enfant included one which was intended to connect the Anacostia River (then known as the Eastern Branch), which was navigable into Maryland, with the Potomac, which was seen to be the gateway to the west. Ultimately the canal suffered from a lack of investment, and constant silting limited barges to those with a depth of three feet.

L'Enfant also designed the city with civic grandeur in mind. Public buildings were to be monumental and set amid open spaces with geometric harmony and spatial relationships intended to inspire national unity and pride. However, the architect's uncompromising personality and clashes with landowners and government officials led to his dismissal before the plan was fully implemented.

Although the canal was eventually paved over, a lock keeper's cottage, built at the eastern terminus of the C&O (Chesapeake and Ohio) canal, where it emptied into Tiber Creek and the Potomac River, still stands at the southwest corner of Constitution Avenue and 17th Street NW.

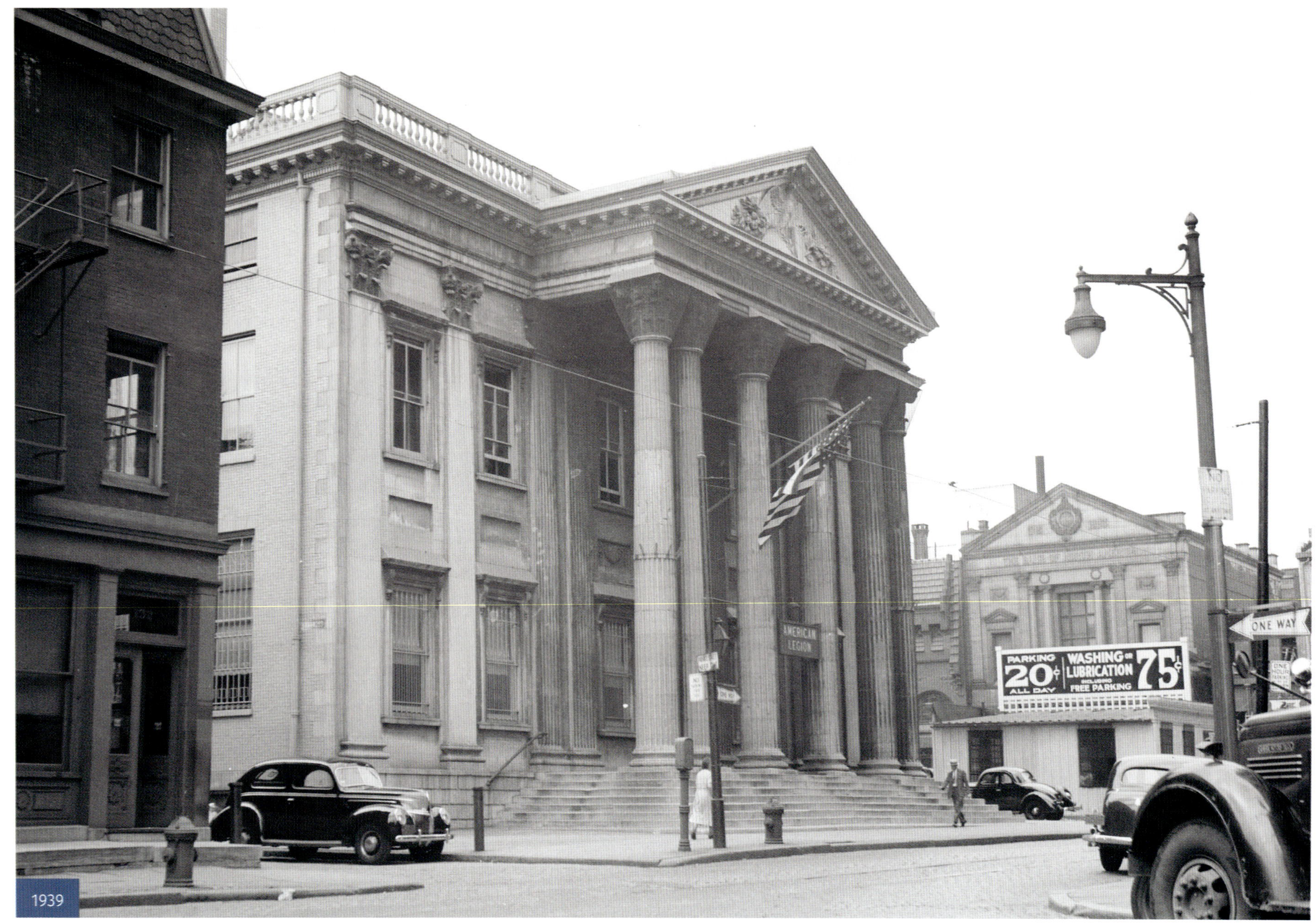

1939

FIRST BANK, PHILADELPHIA

Alexander Hamilton's pioneering bank was central to his economic plan

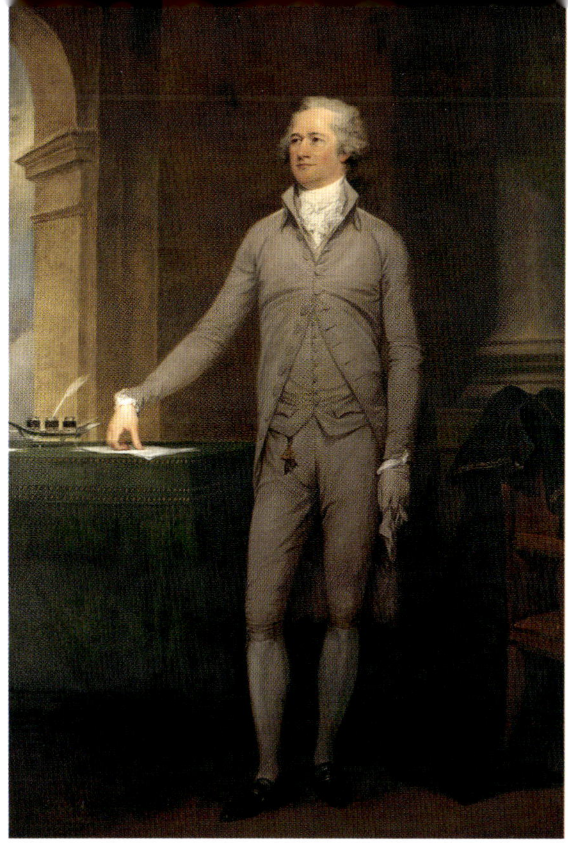

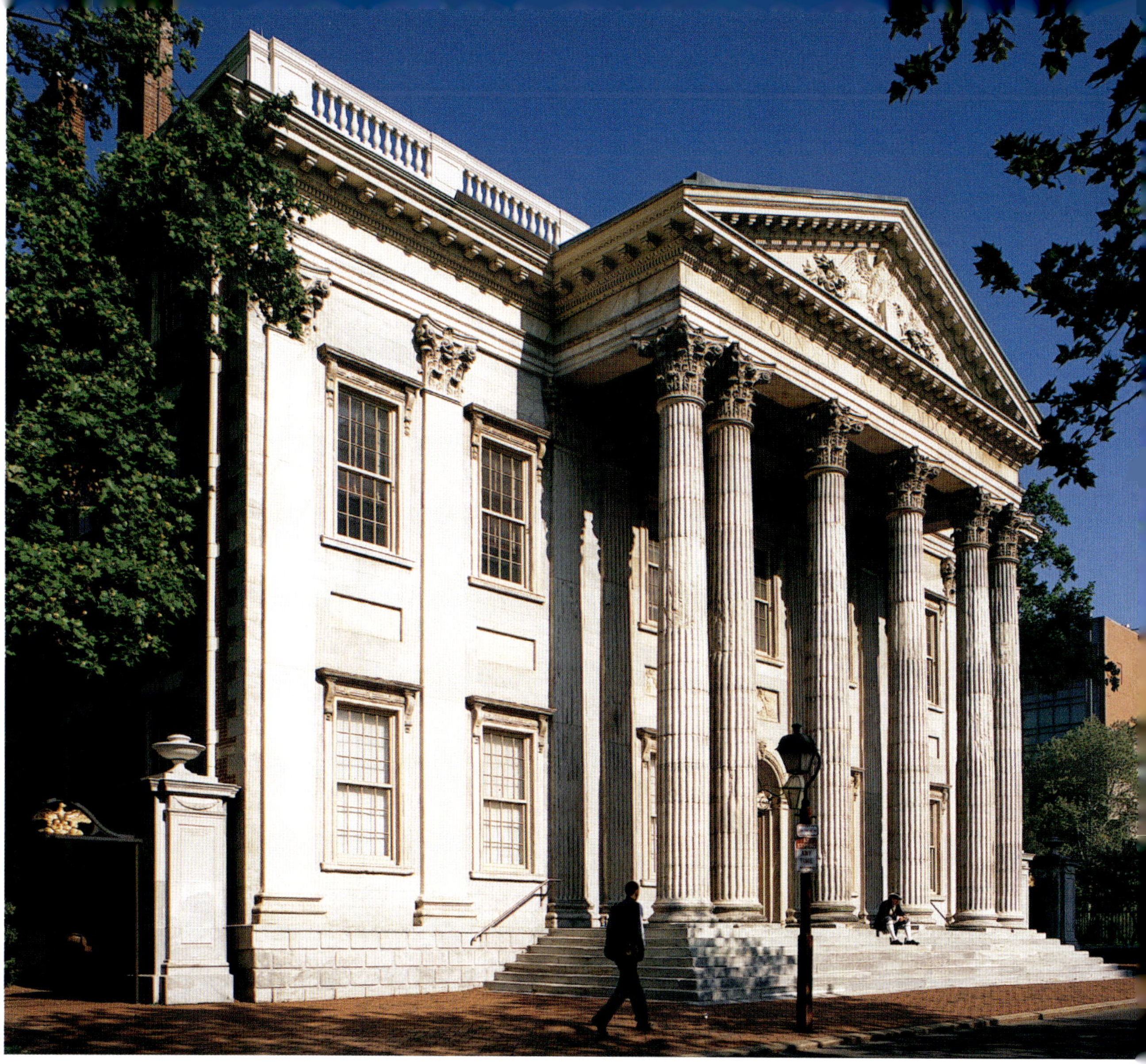

One of the four members of George Washington's cabinet, Treasurer Alexander Hamilton, built up a Federal bureaucracy of three hundred employees on Third Street. As a leading proponent of big government, he hired more staff than the other three cabinet members combined. Hamilton understood the role of money better than the other founders: "Power without revenue is only a name," he opined. The First Bank of the United States became the centerpiece of his fiscal program, despite the fact that the Constitution never explicitly mentioned giving the government the power to establish a bank.

Secretary of State Thomas Jefferson was a vocal opponent. Hamilton argued that the Constitution also didn't prohibit the formation of such a bank. Even after both the House and the Senate approved the bill, Jefferson urged President Washington to veto the plan. Washington gave his former aid-de-camp a week to address Jefferson's arguments. Hamilton delivered a 15,000-word rebuttal that won the argument. However, when the bank's charter expired in 1811, Stephen Girard bought the building for his own Girard Bank. It continued to operate under that name until 1929. Like many important buildings in Independence Park, the building lay vacant until it was purchased by the Park Service in 1955. Throughout the 1970s the Park Service worked at restoring the classical exterior while retaining its 1902 interior.

The National Park Service now uses the First Bank for offices and storage. Completed in 1795, it was one of America's first Greek Revival buildings, with marble-clad walls and Corinthian columns. It was hailed as a masterpiece. Since other buildings encroached on either side when the building was constructed, the classical and marble ornamentation were limited to its Third Street facade to save expenses. The American bald eagle over the portico is carved from mahogany but painted to look like stone. The cornucopia to its right represents abundance, a fitting symbol for a bank. This is one of the first times the national symbol, complete with arrows and olive branches, appeared on a public building.

ABOVE: A portrait of Alexander Hamilton, who was killed in a duel with Aaron Burr in 1804. Now famously the inspiration for a musical, Hamilton was, according to historian Paul Johnson, a "genius—the only one of the Founding Fathers fully entitled to that accolade."

SLATER'S MILL, RHODE ISLAND

Birthplace of the American industrial revolution

The American Industrial Age started with a bit of manufacturing espionage courtesy of Samuel Slater. The Englishman had been apprenticed as a young man to mill owner Jedediah Strutt in Belper, Derbyshire. Strutt's Mill used the revolutionary, water-powered cotton spinning machines first developed by Richard Arkwright, which were strictly embargoed for export from England. Slater had memorized the machinery for carding, drawing, and spinning cotton and took his knowledge across the Atlantic to Moses Brown of Providence, Rhode Island. Together they produced a working set of machines necessary to spin cotton yarn using water power. Construction of the machines was completed in 1793, and a mill was set up on the banks of the Blackstone River in Pawtucket, Rhode Island, along with a dam, waterway, and waterwheel. This innovation allowed for mass production of cotton yarn and laid the groundwork for factory-based manufacturing in the United States. Unlike traditional cottage-industry or artisan

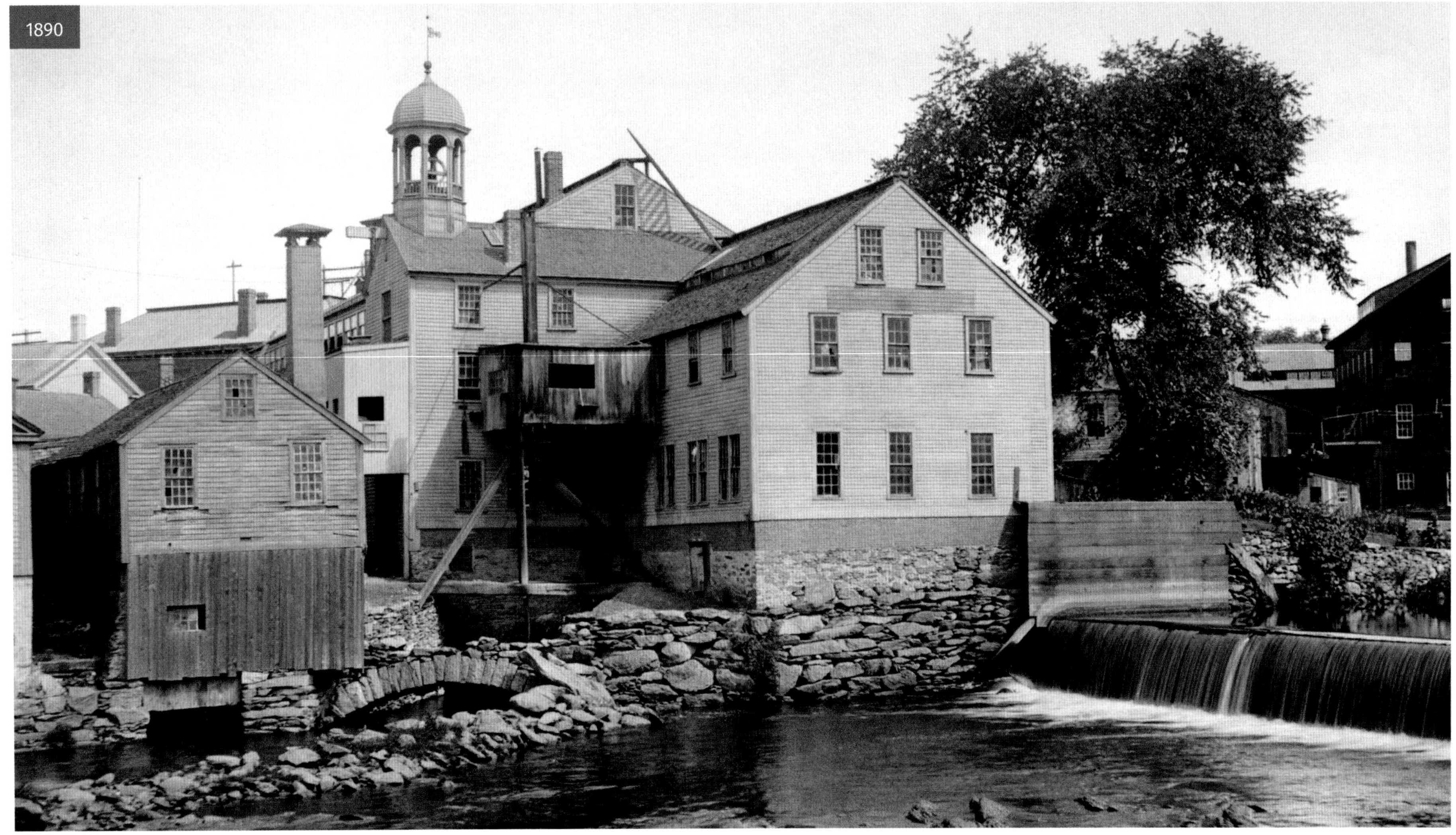
1890

production, Slater's system centralized labor and mechanization, increasing efficiency and lowering costs, thus the perfect model for moving away from the agrarian economy.

The success of Slater's Mill demonstrated the viability of mechanized industry in America, something Alexander Hamilton had actively promoted. It spurred the rapid growth of textile mills across New England. It also set precedents for the use of child and family labor. Workers at Slater's Mill in the early 1800s—especially children and women—were typically expected to work 12 to 14 hours a day, six days a week. The workday usually began around 5:00 a.m. and ended after 7:00 p.m., with only short breaks for meals. Children, some as young as seven or eight years old, were employed for low wages and often lived in boarding houses near the mill. These long hours and difficult conditions eventually fueled unrest, leading to the first US labor protest and strike in 1824 at Slater's Mill.

Cotton spinning continued until 1895, by which time production had largely shifted to the American South and the buildings were used for other business purposes. Industrial heritage is often overlooked, but in 1921 the Old Slater Mill Association was founded to save and preserve the historic mill. It opened as a museum in 1955 and now serves as a museum, educational center, and music venue. It includes five acres of land on both sides of the Blackstone River, a dam on the river and two historic mills (the Slater Mill and Wilkinson Mill). The Old Slater Mill Historic District was acquired by the National Park Service in 2021 as part of a new national park championing the nation's industrial past.

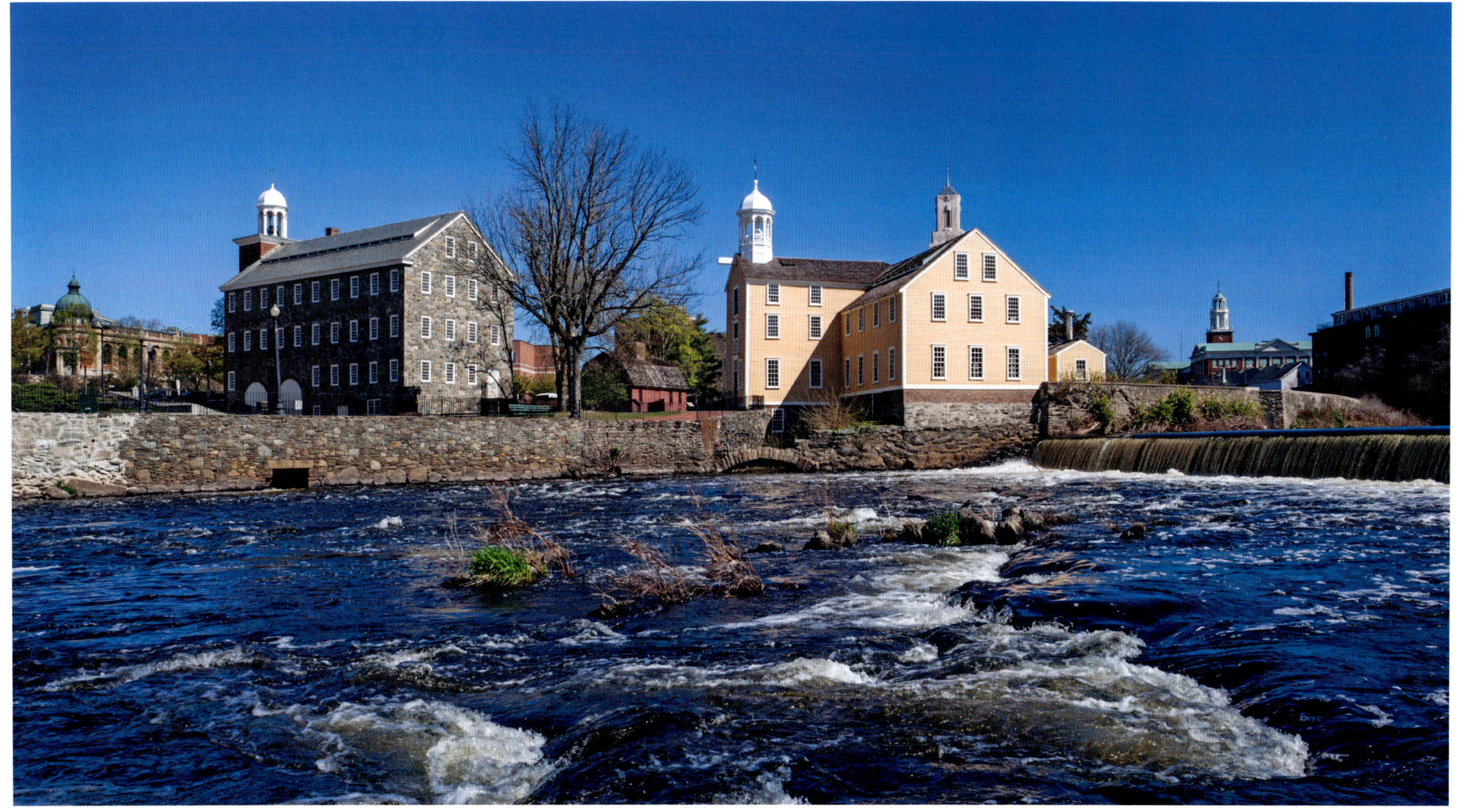

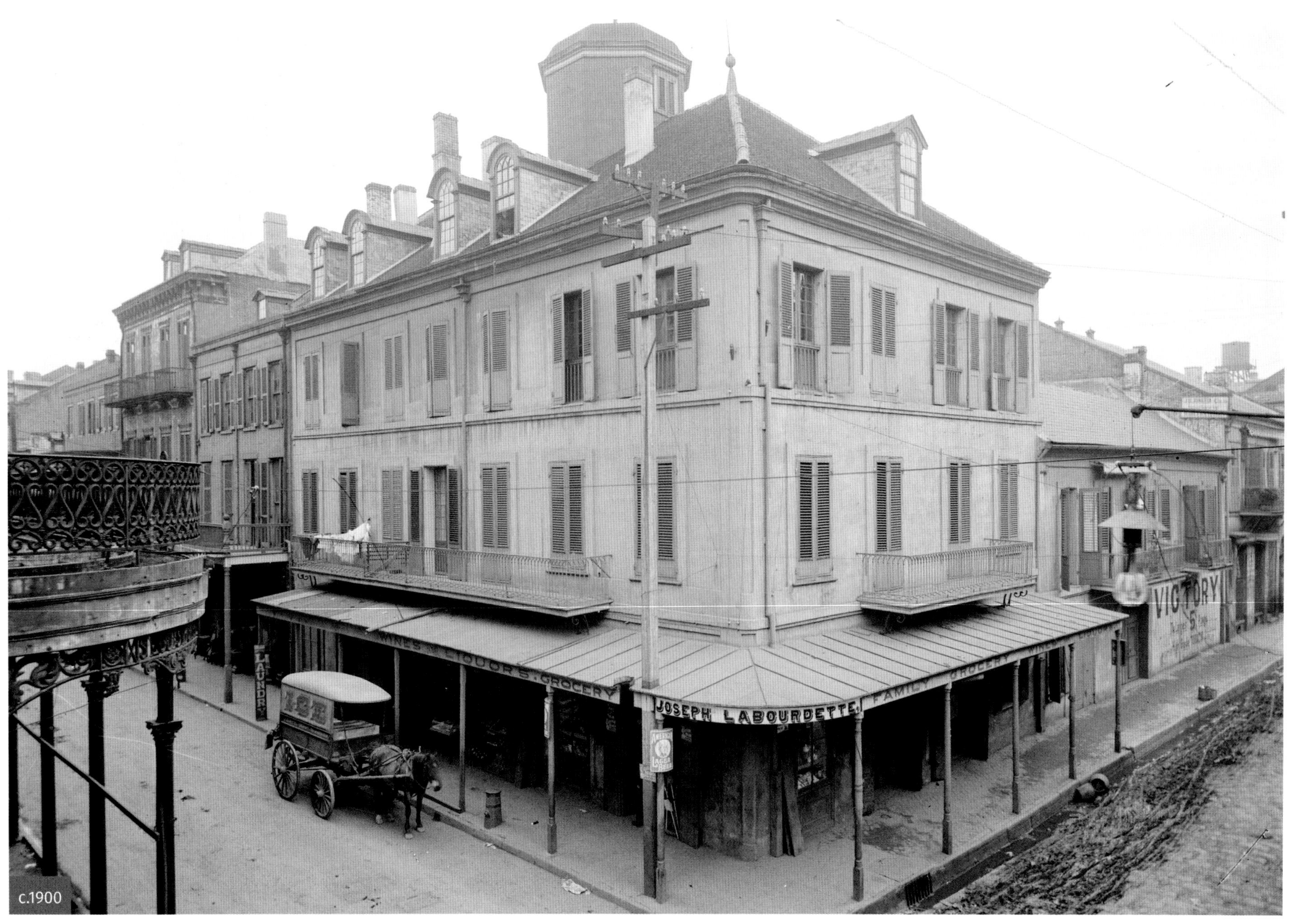

c.1900

NAPOLEON HOUSE, NEW ORLEANS

Waiting in vain for the release of the exiled French emperor

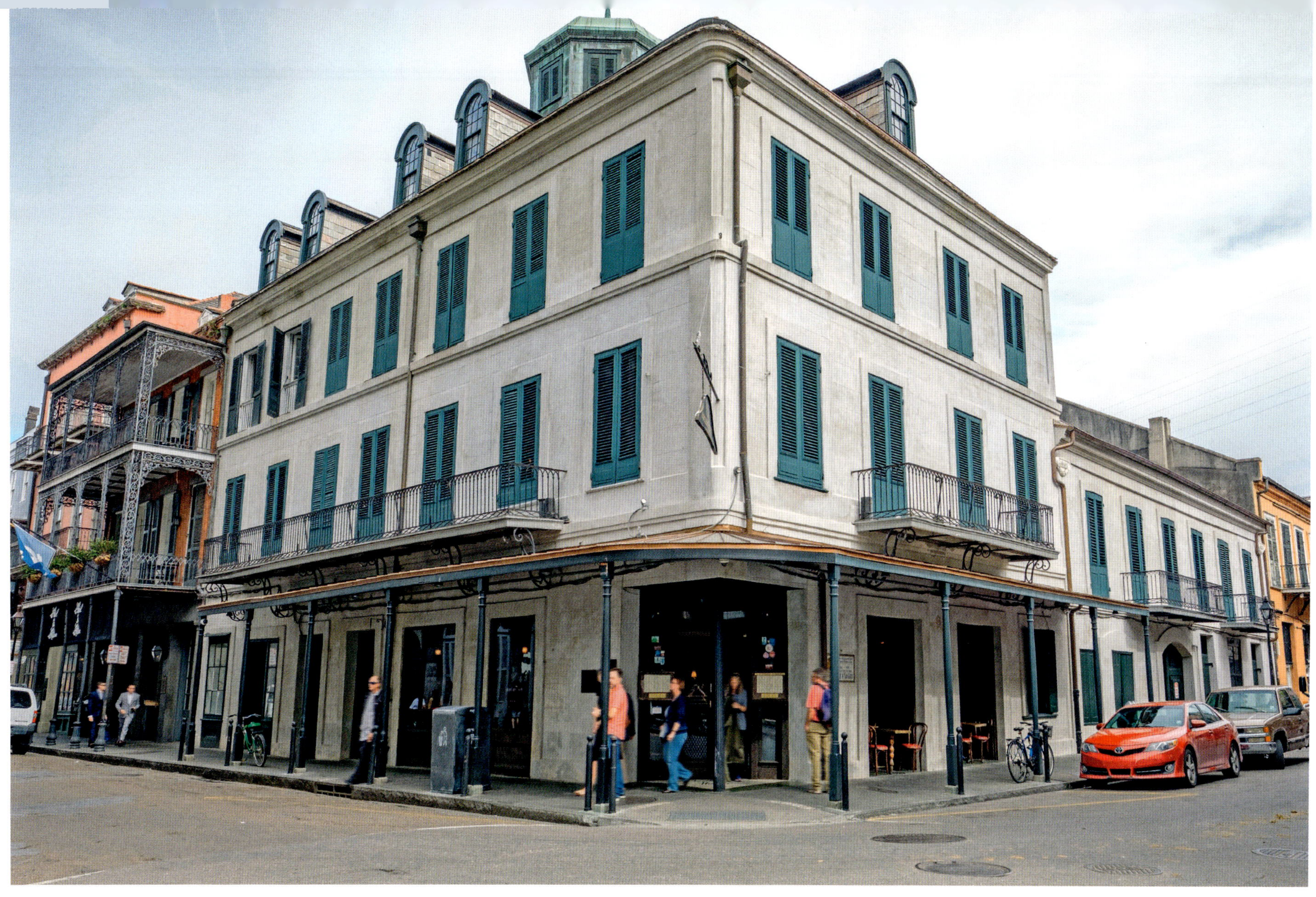

Founded by Frenchman Jean-Baptiste Le Moyne de Bienville in 1718, New Orleans changed nationalities several times in 100 years. It was platted into 80 blocks by French military engineers and in 1722 became the capital of French Louisiana. Following the Seven Years' War, France secretly ceded Louisiana, including New Orleans, to Spain in 1762 via the Treaty of Fontainebleau. Spain controlled the heavily French-influenced city until 1800, when Napoleon pressured Spain to return the territory. France's repossession was short-lived. Facing military setbacks and financial strain, Napoleon sold the Louisiana Territory to the United States in 1803 through the Louisiana Purchase.

The Napoleon House was constructed in 1794 at 500 Chartres Street in the French Quarter of New Orleans. It was originally owned by Claude Girod, and Claude and his brother Nicolas conducted business on the first floor. Nicolas Girod, who became mayor of New Orleans, built the cupola on top so he could watch the Mississippi River for his ships coming into port. The legend of this house is that when Napoleon was exiled, Mayor Girod planned to launch a rescue mission and build a refuge for Napoleon in this house should it succeed. The legend has never been proven as historically accurate but it was sufficient to change the name of the house. At the turn of the twentieth century it was home to Joseph Labourdette and his family grocery—subsequently the "Napoleon Grocery."

The Napoleon House is considered to be one of the best surviving examples of French architecture in the Vieux Carré, and in 1970 was designated as a National Historic Landmark. The Impastato family bought the Napoleon House in 1914 and since then it has operated a world-famous restaurant and bar which has graced the pages of *Esquire* magazine and its list of the Top 100 bars in America.

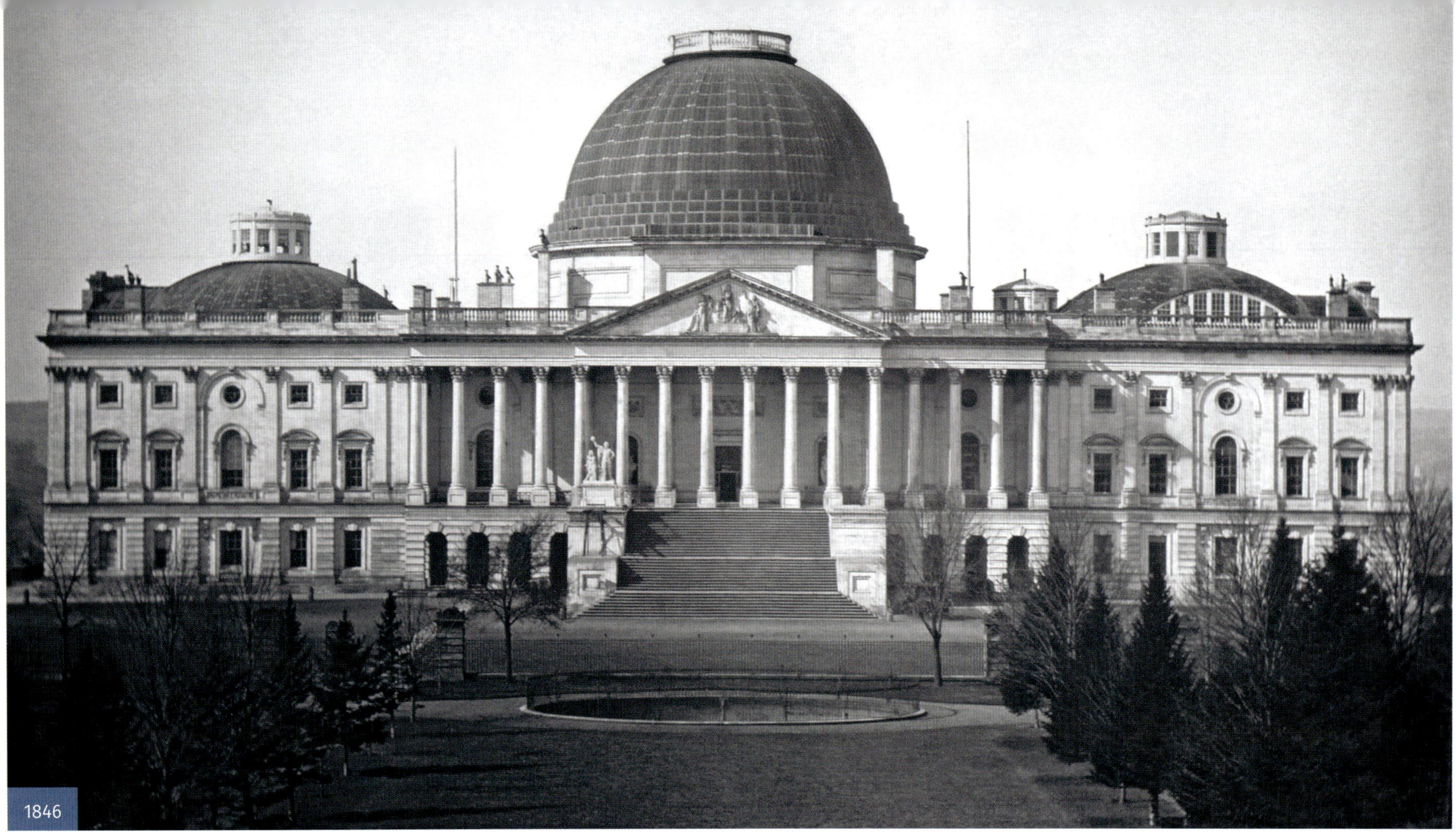

US CAPITOL, WASHINGTON, DC

Setting the blueprint for many state capitols around the nation

When city planners began work on the new capital of the United States, they needed a home for Congress. As early as 1793 the location was selected and President George Washington laid its cornerstone on the southeast corner of the Capitol Building's eventual foundation. Unsure of who to hire for the job, the new United States Congress held a competition for the best architectural design, which was won by William Thornton, a relatively new architect in Washington, DC. The expected move-in date for the new legislative branch was 1800 but the architectural plans proved to be overly ambitious. By the time Congress arrived in Washington from Philadelphia, only the Senate wing had been completed. Construction continued to face early challenges throughout the nineteenth century when, in 1814, British troops burned it in reprisal for American raids on the Canadian capital. A rainstorm prevented the structure's complete destruction, but the building ultimately required improvements.

As the country expanded westward into Indian territory, more senators and representatives were needed for the growing number of seats, which meant the initial chambers constructed in the Capitol Building became overly crowded. The building was

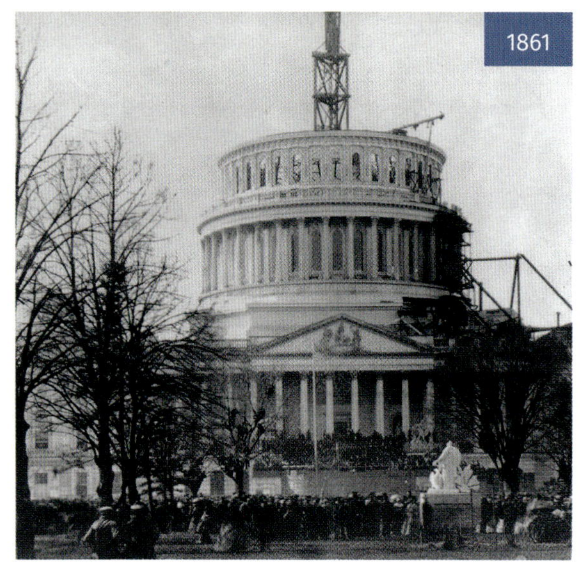

RIGHT: A view of the Capitol at the time of Abraham Lincoln's inaugural address in 1861.

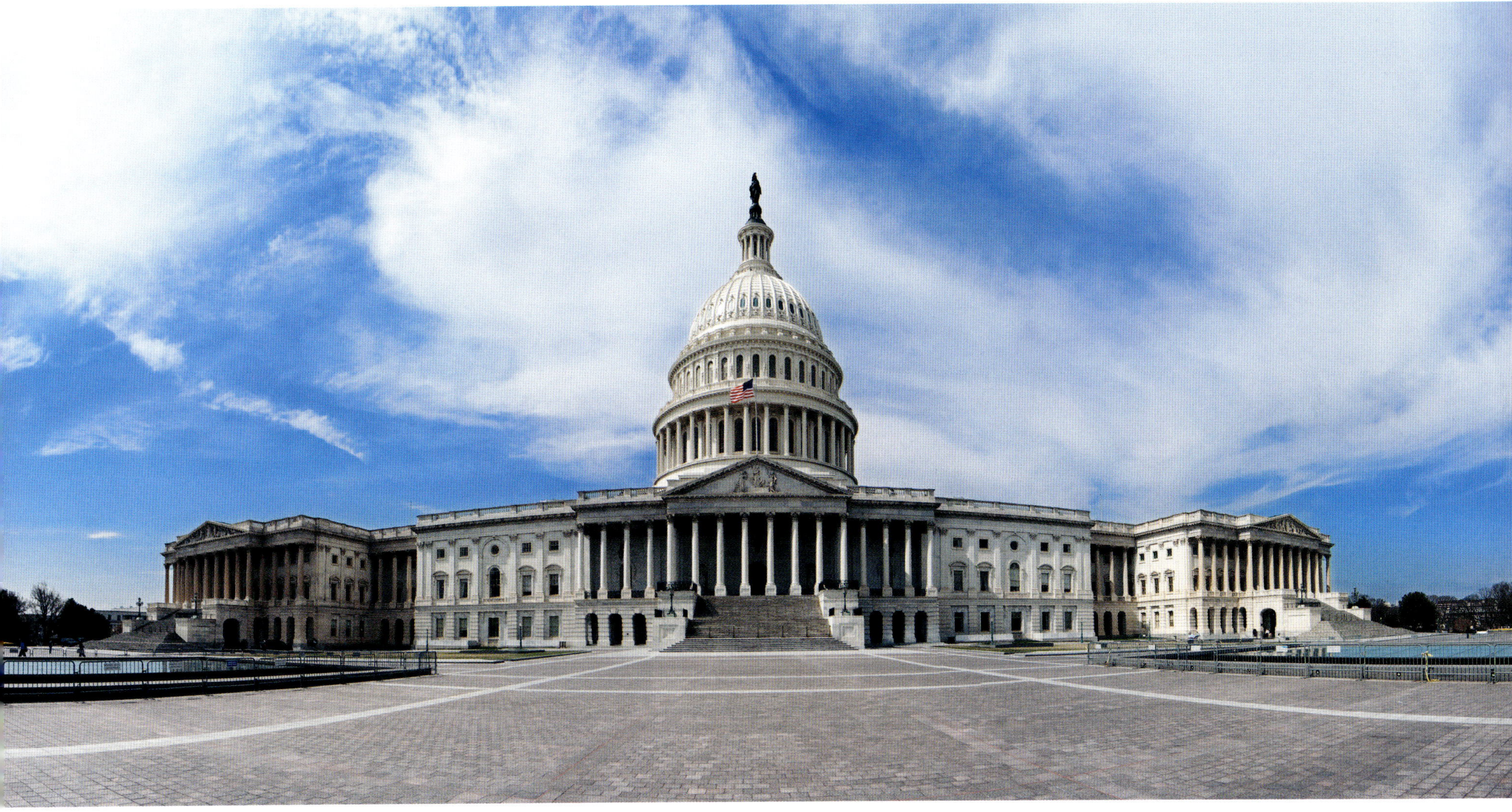

already packing in its reference library—the Library of Congress—and the third branch of the American government, the Supreme Court.

Construction stopped during the Civil War to provide support for the Federal cause. It was used as military barracks, a hospital, and, at one point, a bakery. The Capitol Building had been a relatively flat building with no distinguishable top feature but finally gained its iron dome in 1863.

The Library of Congress was eventually granted its own building to free up space for Congress, and in 1935 the Supreme Court left the legislative branch for a building of its own, right behind it. The Capitol's congressional steps have seen presidential inaugurations, influential speeches, and moments of protest. In recent memory, on January 6, 2021, the Capitol Building was beset by a group of politically motivated individuals whose actions led to a breach of Capitol security and several related deaths, which continue to affect Washington and the US political landscape.

Thornton's design has set the template for state capitols around the country. More than 30 of the 50 state capitol buildings incorporate neoclassical elements or are directly modeled after the US Capitol's domed design and overall classical revival style, including Colorado (Denver) Texas (Austin), Wisconsin (Madison) and Iowa (Des Moines).

THE KEY MANSION, GEORGETOWN

Francis Scott Key's home and law office was once open as a free museum

The house that Francis Scott Key purchased on M Street in Georgetown in 1805 was home to the lawyer and his wife, Mary Taylor Lord, for 20 years. Key was a native of Frederick, Maryland, and attended law school at St. John's College before moving to Georgetown to become a partner in his uncle's law firm. In this rather humble Federal-style house, high on a bluff overlooking the Potomac River, Key and his wife would raise a family of six children. He also built a one-story addition to the house on the west side to serve as his law office.

In September 1814, during the War of 1812, Key came to the defense of Dr. William Beanes who had inflated a story about three British officers disturbing the peace. Beanes was held as a noncombatant prisoner of war on the British admiral's flagship. Key visited him via the American cutter *Minden* for negotiations during a truce period on the Chesapeake Bay and succeeded in having Beanes released. They were put aboard a small boat just outside Baltimore Harbor. The British officers would not allow them to return for fear they might reveal the plans for an attack on Fort McHenry, which guarded Baltimore.

The commandant of Fort McHenry was flying an enormous Stars and Stripes. He raised the flag in front of the looming British fleet and both Key and Beanes witnessed the failed assault on the fort from their boat on September 12. Key began to pen his

c.1900

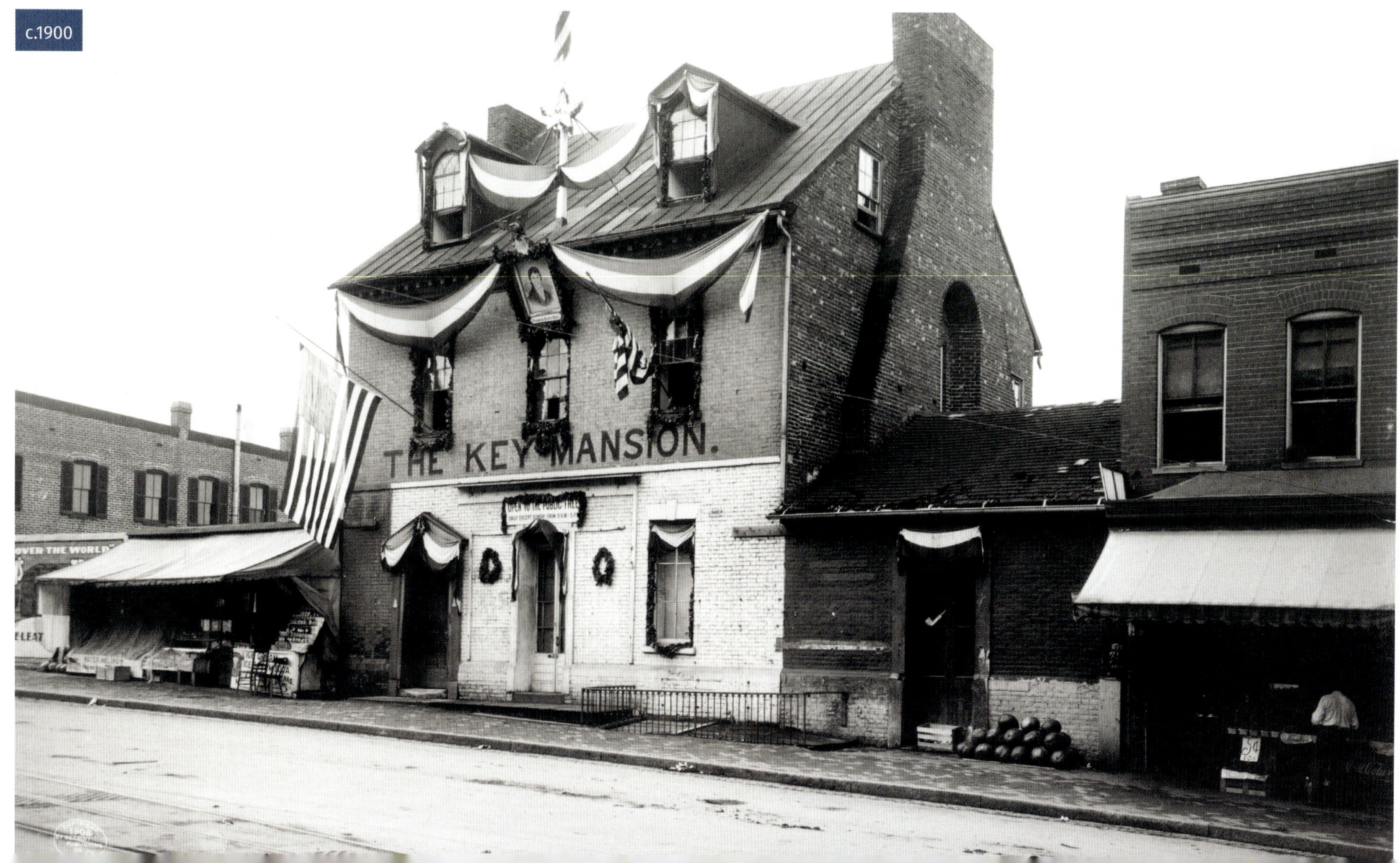

c.1890

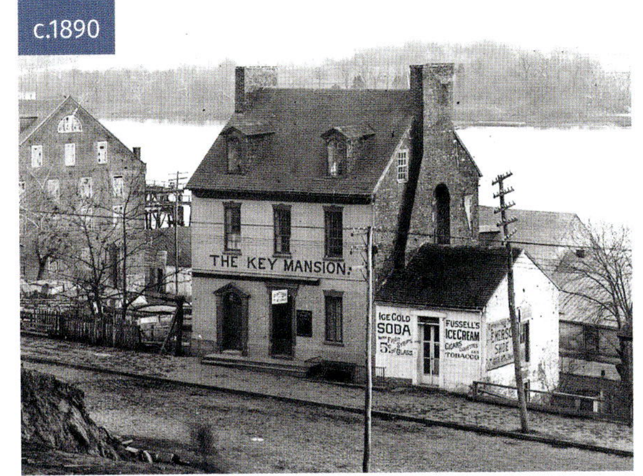

epic poem *The Defense of Fort McHenry*, for what would become the national anthem, while he was still on the boat. Married to the tune of "The Anacreontic Song," a drinking song by English composer John Stafford Smith (son of Gloucester Cathedral's director of music), it would become "The Star Spangled Banner."

Key eventually became the District Attorney for Georgetown from 1833 to 1841 and was known as a staunch supporter of slavery. He was active in prosecuting individuals for possessing and distributing abolitionist pamphlets, regularly represented slave owners in cases involving runaway slaves, and promoted the repatriation to Africa of freed slaves.

The Key Mansion was purchased by attorney Hugh Taggert and opened as museum in 1907. It languished afterward—his office being used for many years as a grocery store. It was purchased by the National Park Service in 1931, but plans for the Whitehurst Freeway and Key Highway called for its removal. Attempts to relocate it failed and it was eventually razed in 1948. Today there is a small park dedicated to his memory, not far from its original site.

BELOW: Looking back at Georgetown from the Francis Scott Key Bridge over the Potomac. Key's house was located just to the right of the clock tower building at right of frame.

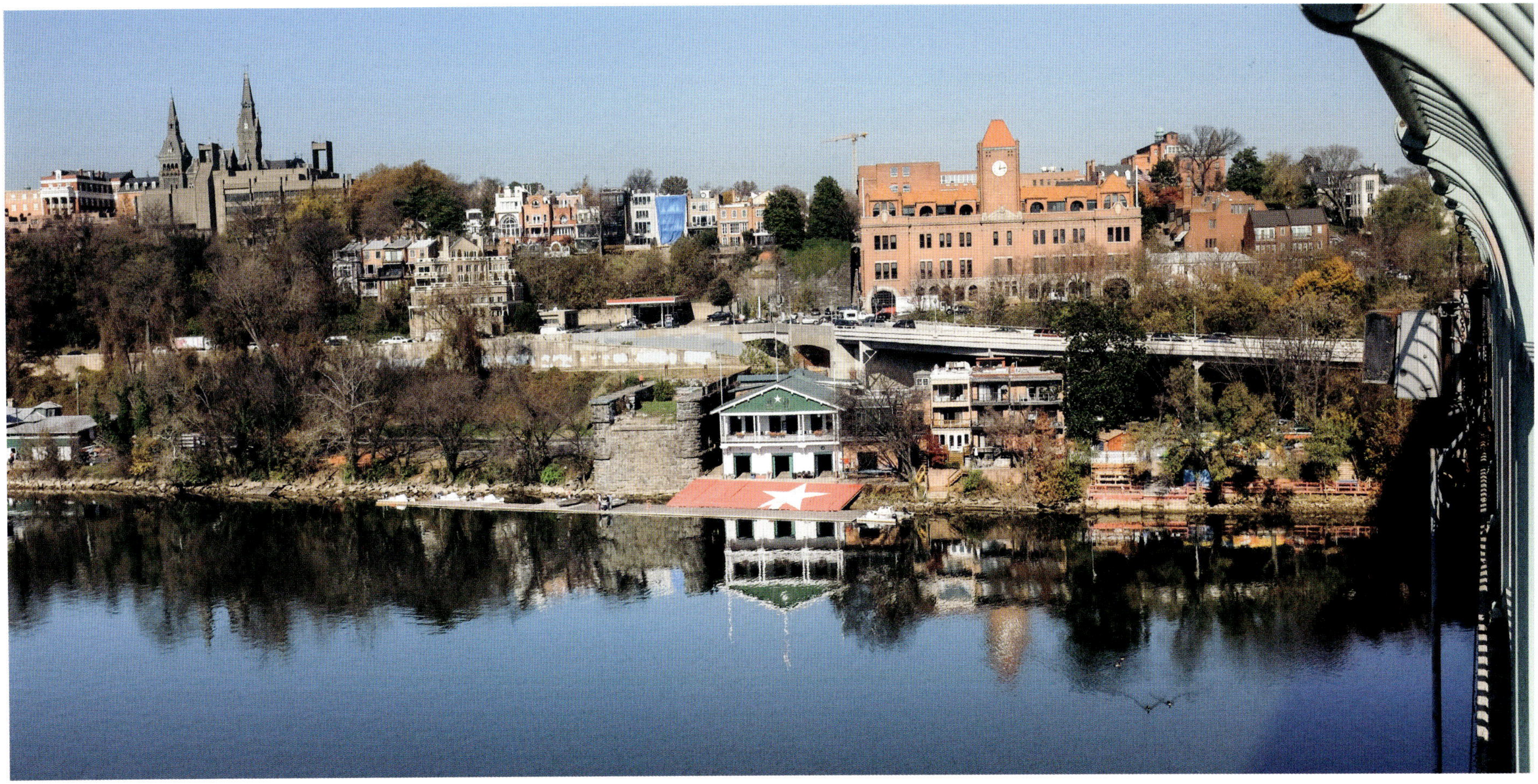

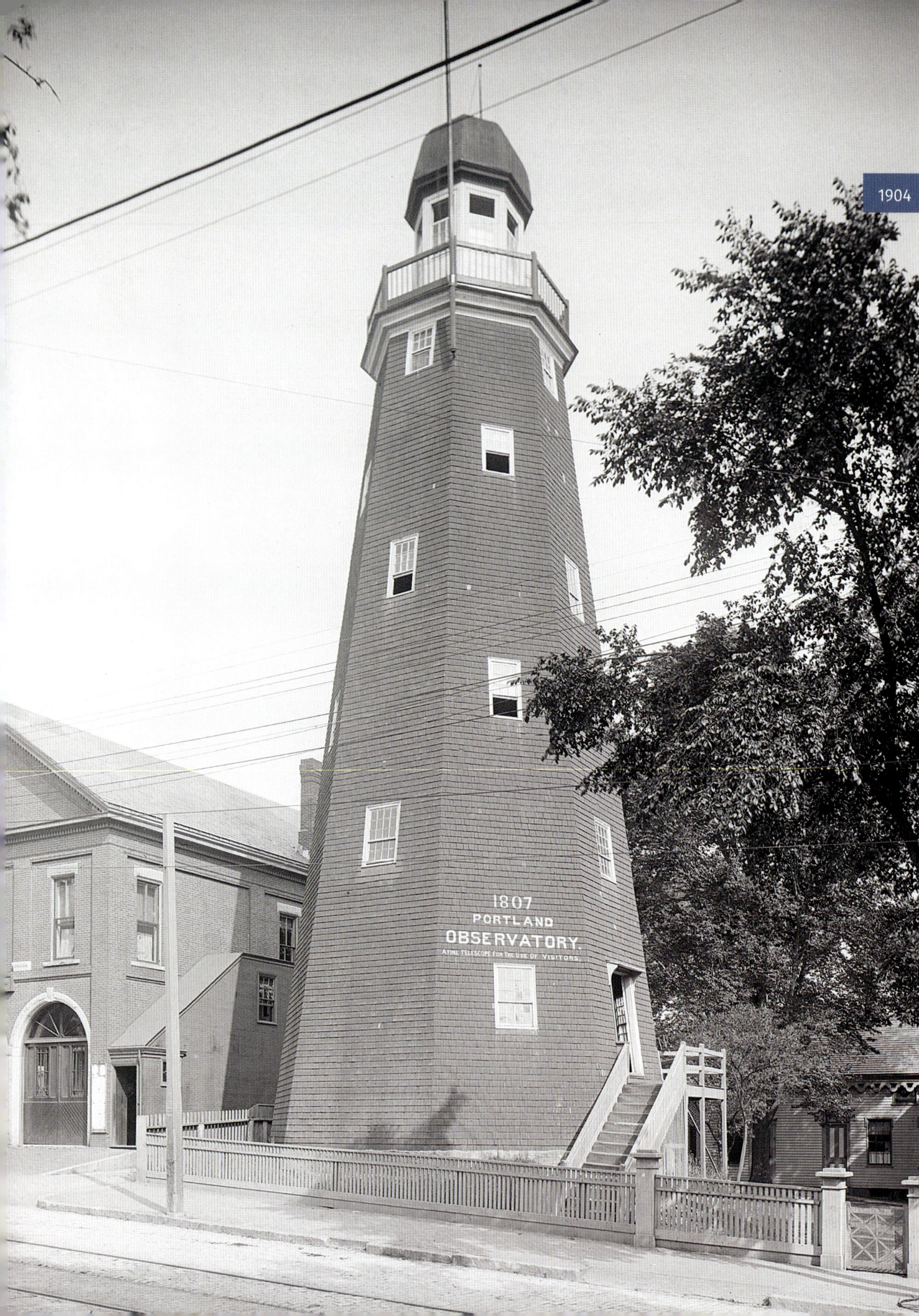

1904

PORTLAND OBSERVATORY, MAINE

The only surviving signal tower of its type in the country

After the American Revolution, Portland, then part of Massachusetts, was among the busiest ports in the country. However, with its jagged, rocky coastline and many islands, it was often treacherous for mariners entering and leaving the port. As a result, in 1791 Portland Head Light was completed here, marking the southern edge of the main shipping channel into Portland. It was the first of many lighthouses to be built in present-day Maine, and the first to be completed by the United States government.

In the days before ship-to-shore communication, timing the arrival of ships was essentially guesswork. This was particularly problematic for merchant ship owners, who had little advance notice to prepare the wharves for unloading their cargo. In a busy port like Portland, that meant time and valuable wharf space was lost while the cargo sat in the ships before unloading. To solve this problem, Lemuel Moody built his observatory in 1807, in a cow pasture at the top of Munjoy Hill. This 86-foot, lighthouse-like tower, when equipped with a good telescope, allowed ships to be recognized up to 30 miles away. The observer would then raise signal flags, notifying the wharves, where merchants would now have several hours to prepare before the ship's arrival. Aside from observing, Moody also kept detailed weather records here, and published the average temperatures.

Although built during the age of sail, the Portland Observatory functioned well into the steamship era. Communications to the wharves were modernized with the installation of a telephone in 1879, but visual signals remained the only practical way of communicating from a ship until the turn of the twentieth century. With the invention of the radio, though, the observatory was soon obsolete. It closed in 1923, and for the next fifteen years it deteriorated, until Moody's great-granddaughter donated it to the city in 1938. It was restored and reopened in 1939. Much of the tower still consists of original wood, and it still stands as the only surviving signal tower of its type in the country. Just as it was two centuries ago when Lemuel Moody operated it, the tower is open to the public, and in 2006 it was designated as a National Historic Landmark.

Today, along with lobsters and pine trees, Maine's most defining feature is probably the nearby Portland Head Light, which still warns mariners more than 225 years after George Washington appointed its first keeper. Over the years, it has been the subject of a poem by Longfellow, a painting by Edward Hopper, and countless photographs by tourists who visit the lighthouse every day.

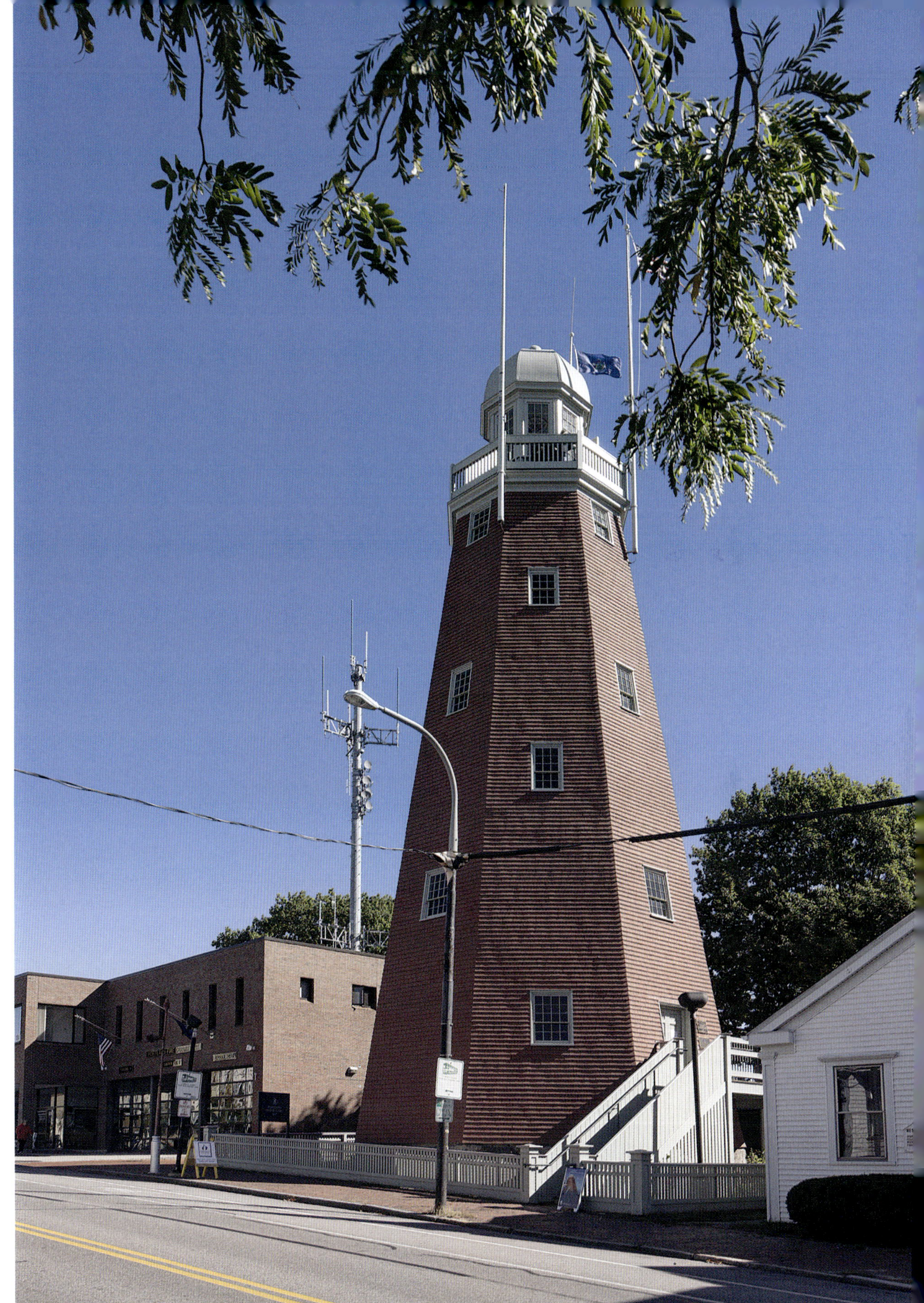

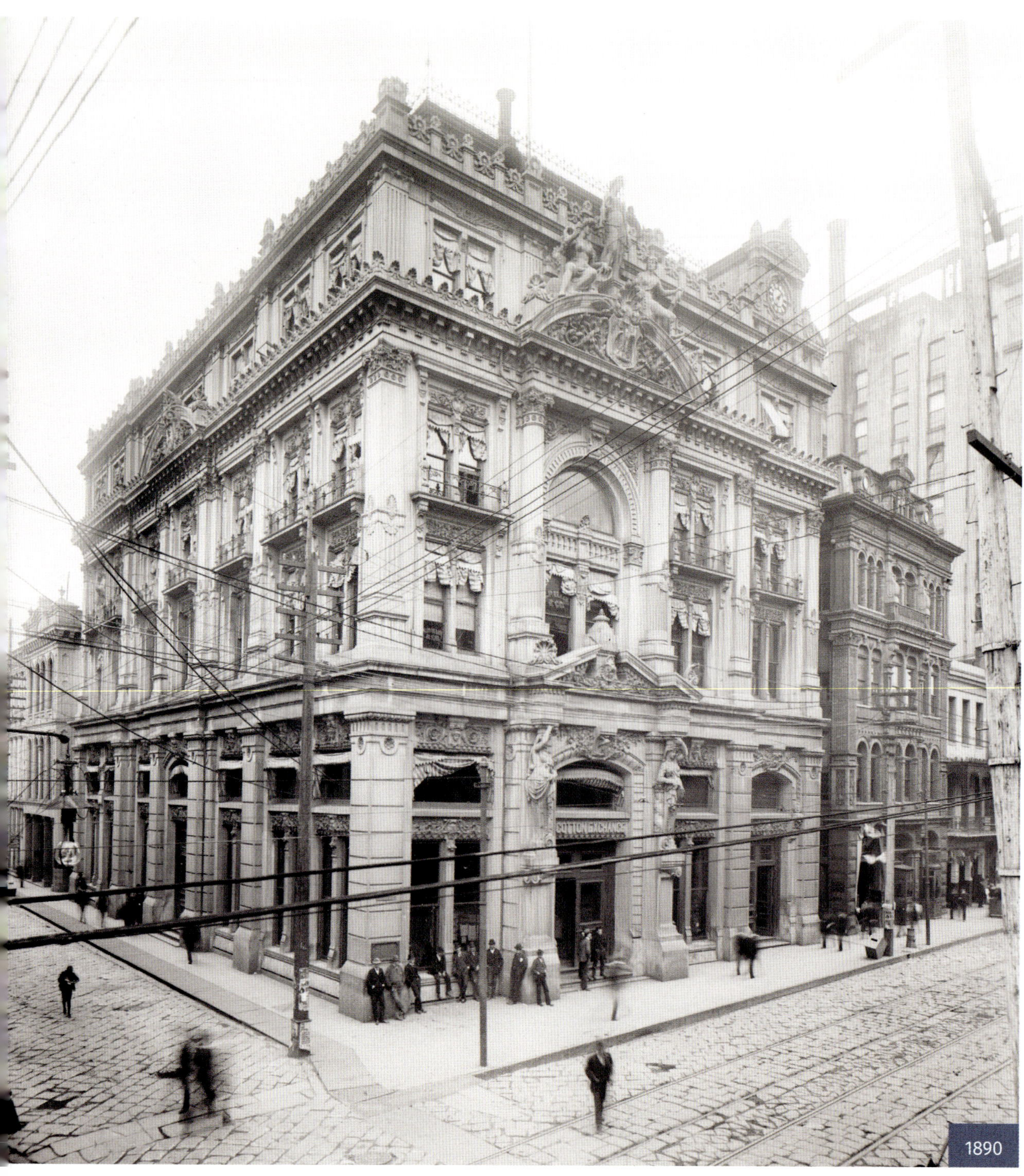

1890

THE COTTON EXCHANGE, NEW ORLEANS

King Cotton ruled New Orleans—except during Mardi Gras when King Rex ruled for one day

In the United States, the introduction of Eli Whitney's "cotton engine" or "gin" (1793) enabled a ten-fold saving of time to remove seeds and debris from lint. Within a few years, cotton rose from a minor regional crop in the lower Mississippi Valley to a major export. The two million pounds of cotton raised in Louisiana in 1811 had become 38 million pounds by 1826. In 1834, the harvest was over 62 million pounds. For decades to come, New Orleans would serve as the key city for "King Cotton." Central to the industry were cotton brokers, merchants, agents, and cotton factors.

Factors accepted cotton on consignment from planters and sold it at the highest prices obtainable. The nature of trading a commodity like cotton entailed a great deal of information-sharing and market awareness. This was aided by firms clustering together. Of the 147 cotton firms listed in 1854 in New Orleans, 46 had addresses on Carondelet, and another 24 operated on Gravier Street in the American sector. The draw of the district was so strong that even dealers in cotton gins and other accessories set up shop nearby.

In February 1871 a hundred industry leaders organized the New Orleans Cotton Exchange, chartering the organization to provide meeting space, arbitrate disputes, establish standards, and serve as an information center. The Cotton Exchange commissioned a three-story building on Gravier at Theater Alley, but soon outgrew the space. A decade later, the organization decided to erect a larger, grandiose building on the corner of Carondelet and Gravier. Costing an enormous $380,000 it opened in 1883, an ornate mix of Second Empire, Renaissance, and Italian-style architecture.

World War I drove demand for lint used in military uniforms. The South produced its first billion-dollar crop during these years, and doubled it in 1919. Counting on a rosy future, the New Orleans Cotton Exchange had its now unfashionable and structurally unstable building replaced in 1921. But foreign competition lowered prices and the boll weevil devastated crops. By the mid-1920s, it had spread to all US cotton-growing regions.

Cotton acreage in Louisiana has declined to little over 100,000 acres today and only two companies keep cotton moving through New Orleans, from warehouses at the Napoleon Avenue Container Terminal.

In 1962 the New Orleans Cotton Exchange organization sold its landmark building and rented the space. The Exchange finally closed on July 9, 1964. The building was renovated into a hotel in the 2000s, and the corner space at Carondelet and Gravier now hosts a bank.

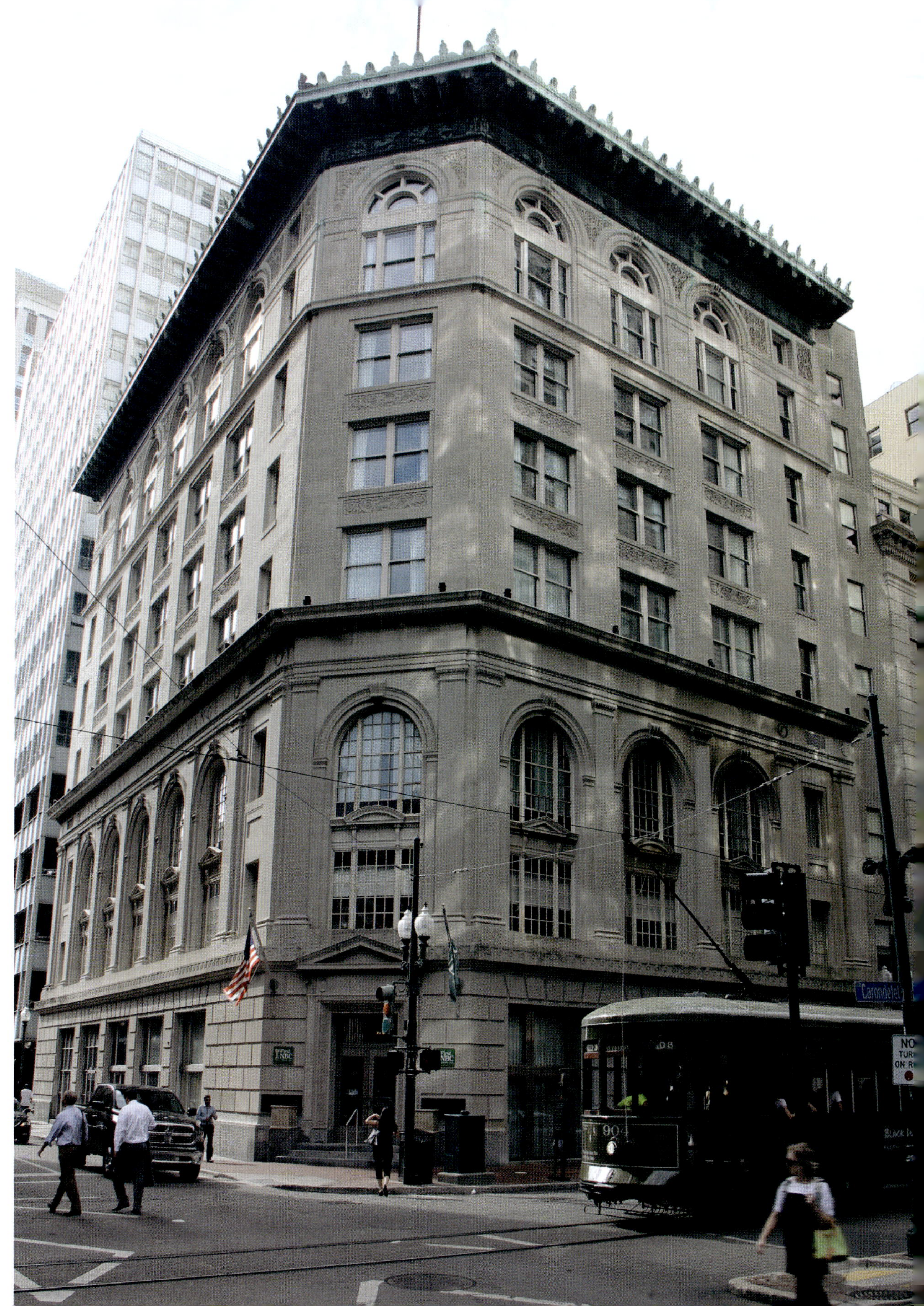

ERIE CANAL, NEW YORK

America's first superhighway

Linking the Hudson River to Lake Erie in upstate New York, the Erie Canal was a pioneering waterway connecting the Atlantic to the Great Lakes. A similar canal from the Hudson River to the Great Lakes was first proposed in the 1780s, but a formal survey was not conducted until 1808. The New York State legislature authorized construction in 1817.

Political opponents of the canal (referencing its lead supporter, New York Governor DeWitt Clinton) labeled the project as "Clinton's Folly" and "Clinton's Big Ditch." They were proven wrong immediately. Opening on October 26, 1825—the toll revenue in its first year covered the state's construction debt. The westward connection gave New York City a strong advantage over major East Coast US ports such as Boston, Baltimore, and Philadelphia and brought major growth to canal cities such as Albany, Utica, Syracuse, Rochester, and Buffalo.

Construction of the canal was a landmark in American civil engineering. When completed, the 363-mile canal was the second longest in the world after the Grand Canal in China. Initially 40 feet wide and 4 feet deep, the canal was expanded several times, most notably from 1905 to 1918 when the "Barge Canal" was built and over half the original route was abandoned.

The Erie's peak year was 1855, when 33,000 commercial shipments took place. It continued to be competitive with railroads until about 1902, when tolls were abolished. Commercial traffic declined heavily in the latter half of the twentieth century due to competition from trucking and the 1959 opening of the larger St. Lawrence Seaway.

Today, the Erie Canal is mainly used by recreational watercraft. The canal has also become a tourist attraction in its own right—several parks and museums are

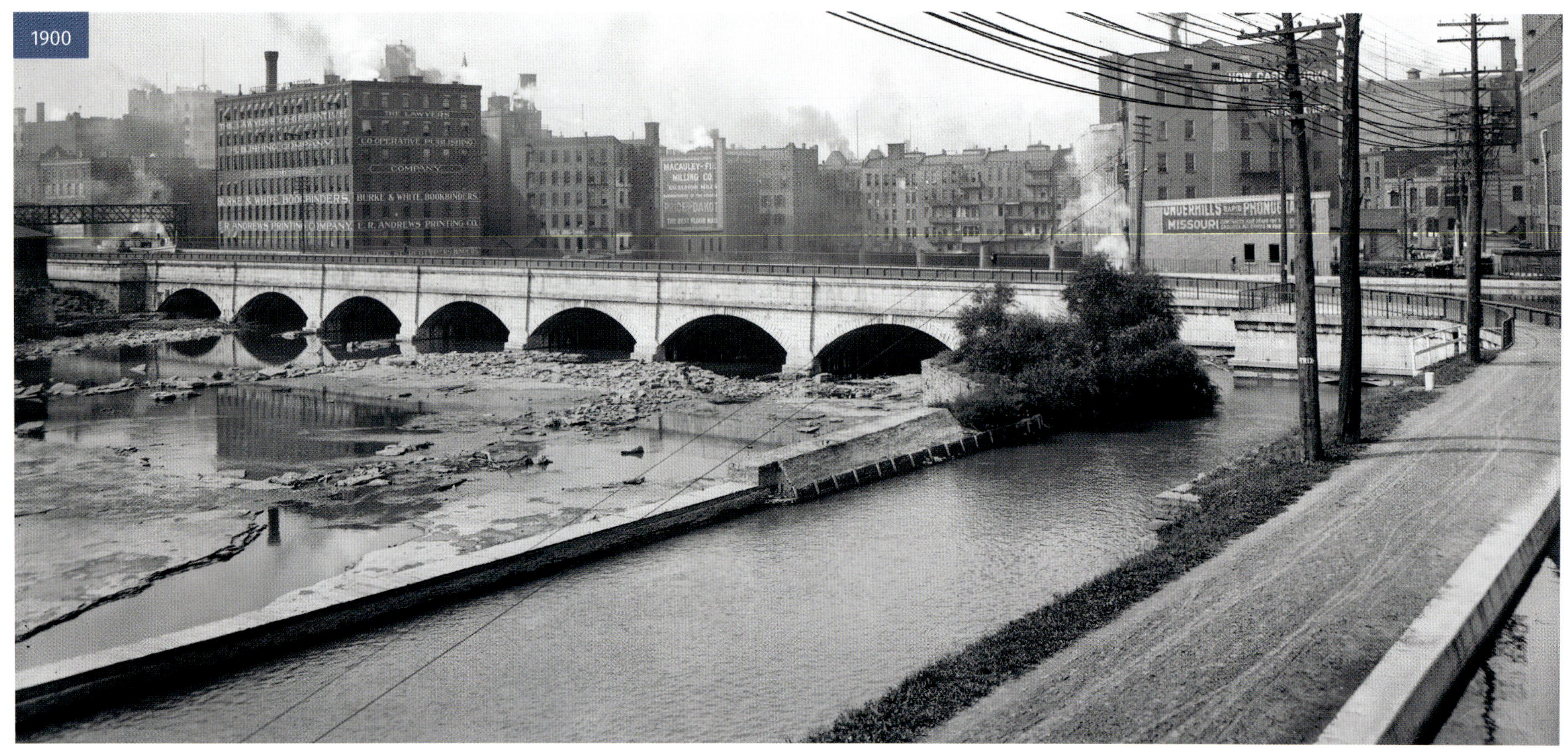

1900

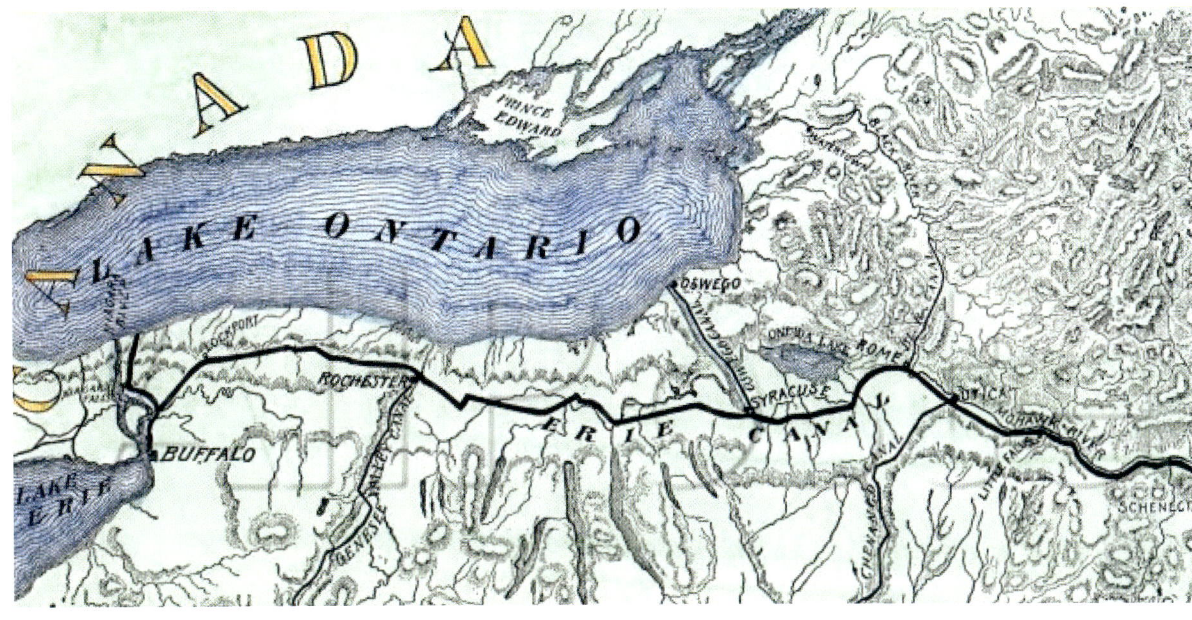

dedicated to its history. The New York State Canalway Trail is a popular cycling path that follows the canal across the state. In 2000, Congress designated it the Erie Canalway National Heritage Corridor to protect and promote the system.

The Erie Canal no longer runs through Rochester, NY, over the Broad Street Bridge. The canal (seen opposite at extreme right) was rerouted in 1918 as part of the New York State Barge Canal project. It now crosses the Genesee River at Genesee Valley Park. The original stone aqueduct that once carried the Erie Canal over the Genesee River was repurposed in the 1920s to accommodate the Rochester Subway system, and later, the Broad Street roadway was constructed on top.

LEFT: An early map of the canal route.

BELOW LEFT: New York Governor DeWitt Clinton.

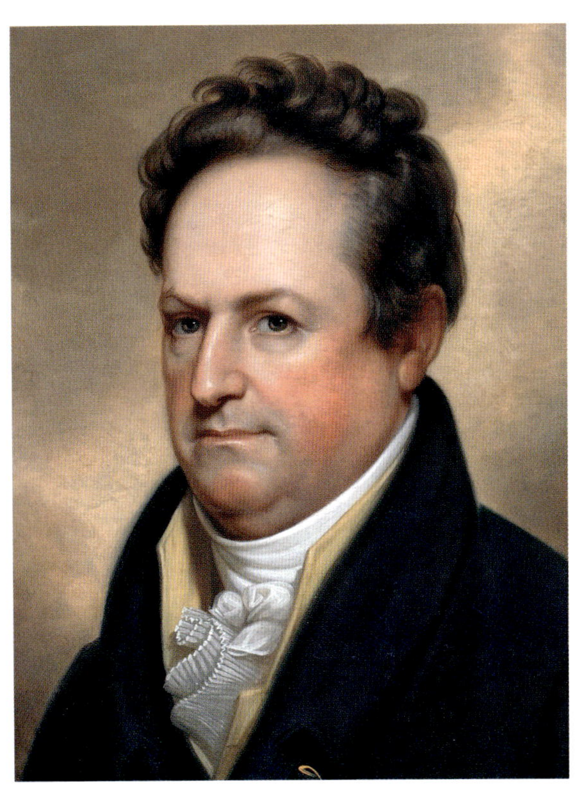

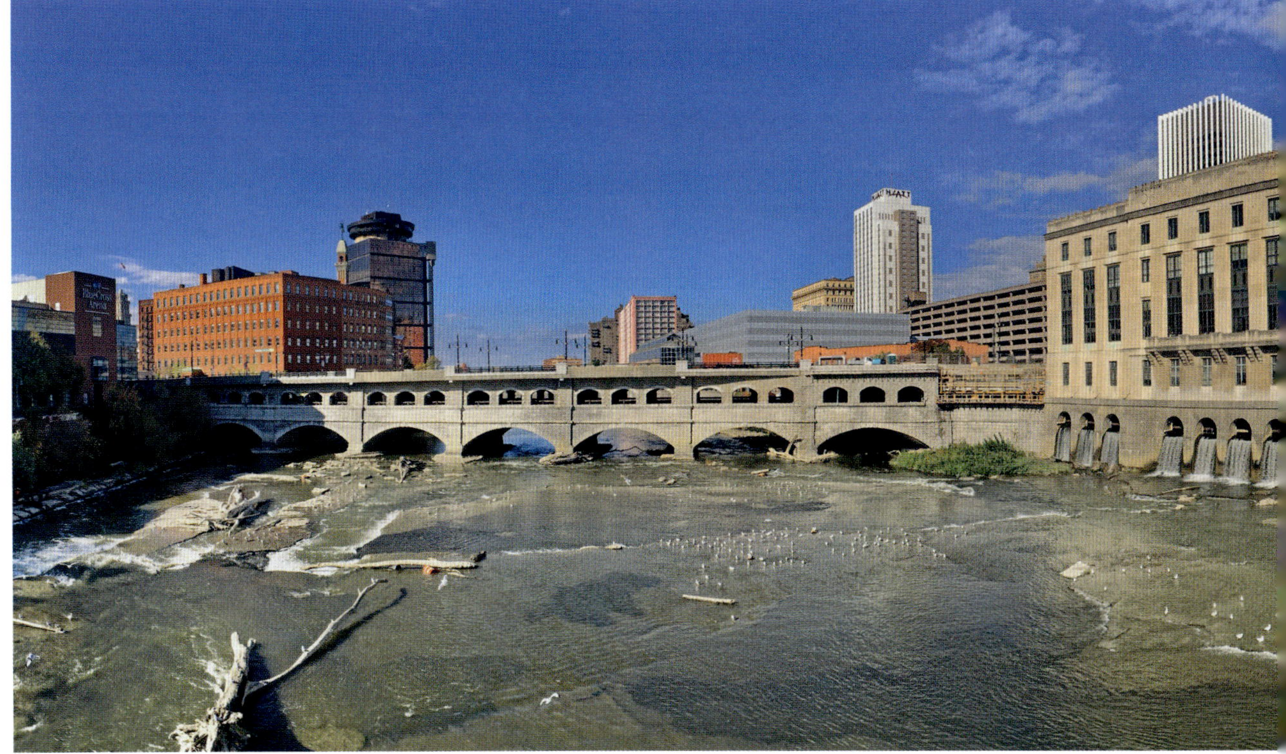

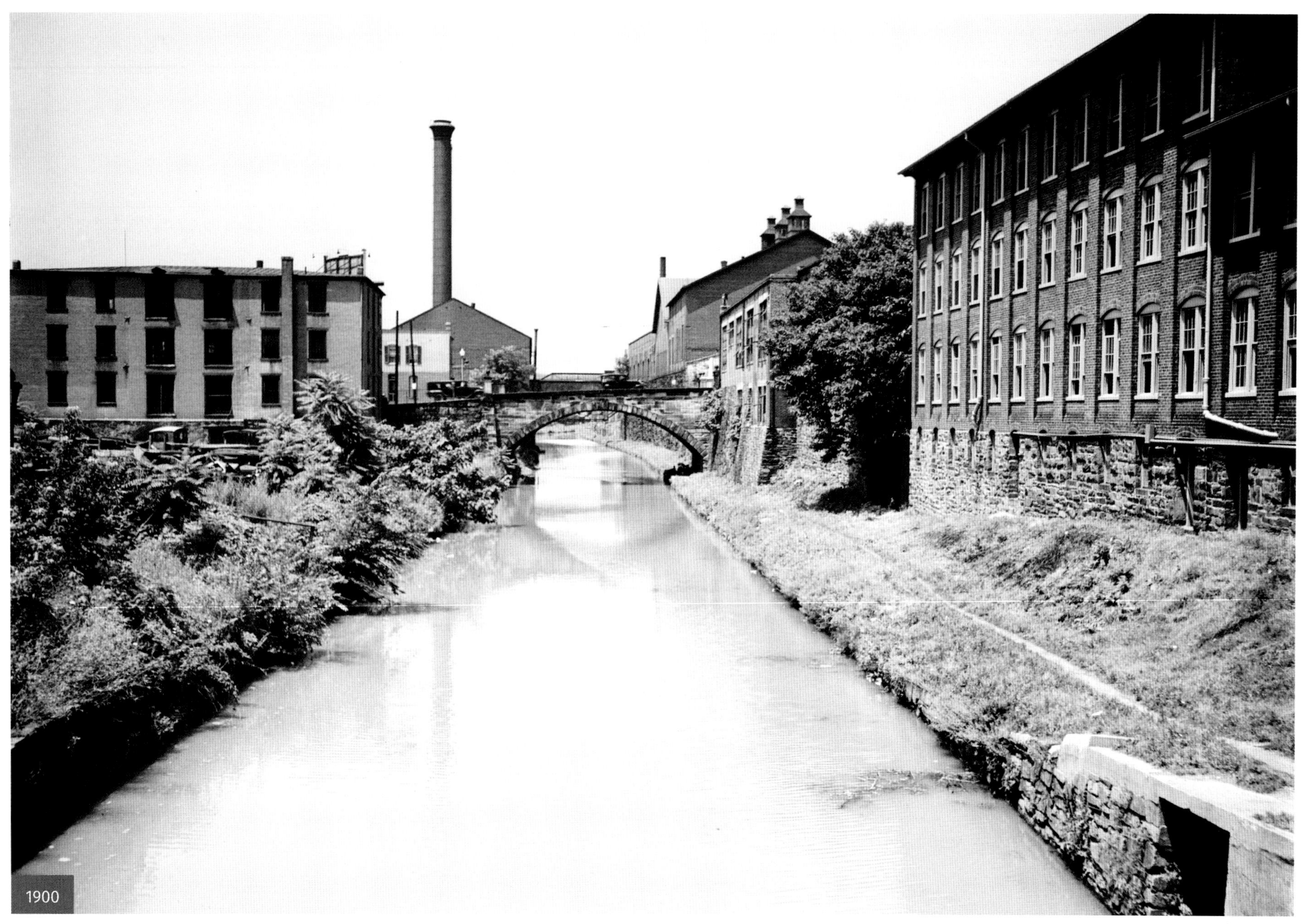

1900

CHESAPEAKE AND OHIO CANAL, WASHINGTON, DC

An important canal which played an economic role for half a century

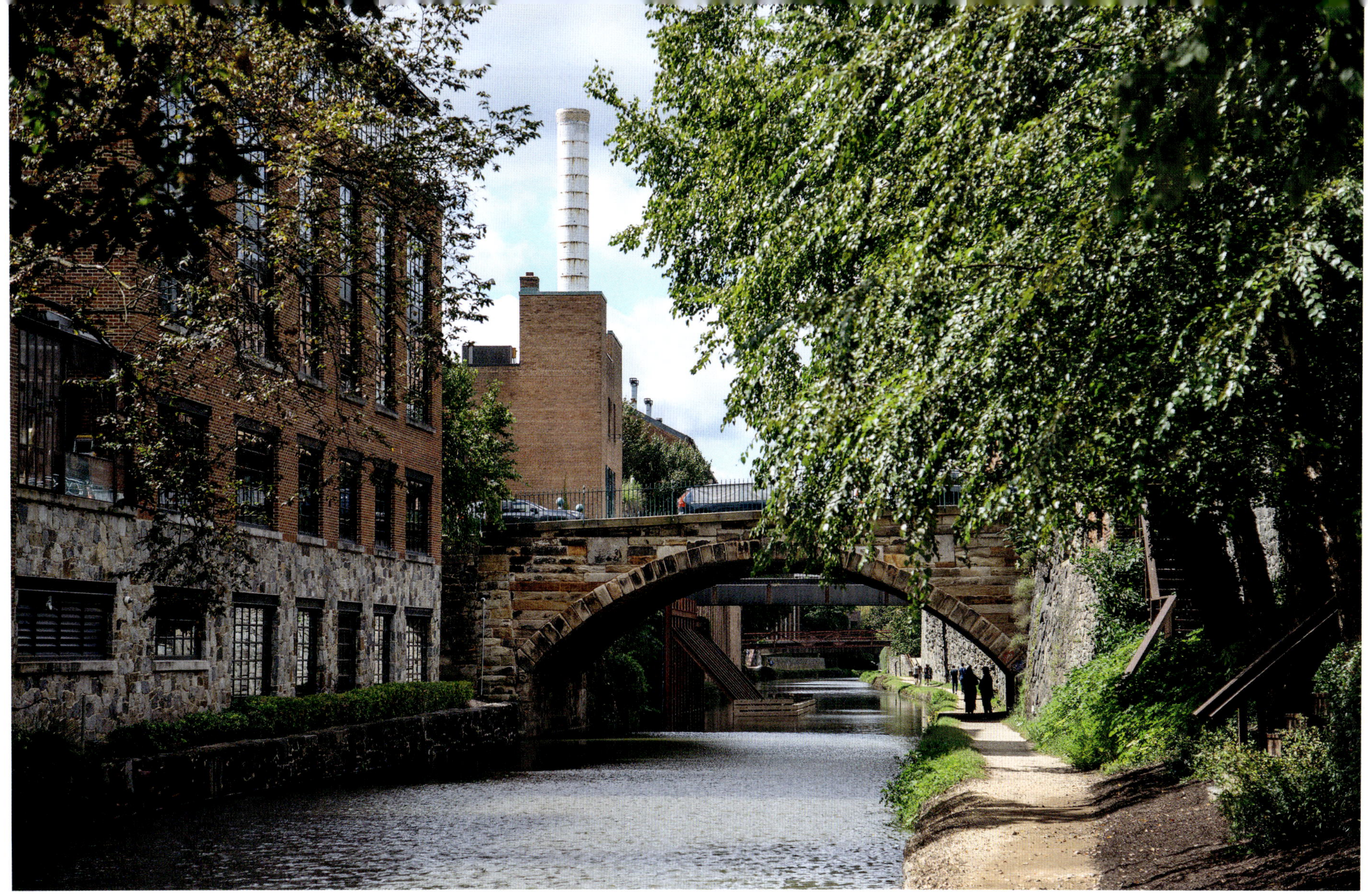

While Washington always had the benefit of being surrounded by two major rivers with access to the Bay, it was decided in 1825 that the city should have a new canal. The district already had one canal that ran downtown, known as the Washington City Canal, which connected to the Eastern Branch, now known as the Anacostia River, yet DC was looking to further connect this downtown canal to the natural resources of Maryland. In one of his last acts of Presidency, James Monroe signed a bill chartering this great feat of transportation: the Chesapeake and Ohio (C&O) Canal. With the first groundbreaking of the C&O Canal in 1828, construction was officially underway. The canal was completed in sections, working its way up to Cumberland in Maryland, a town on the northern border of the state.

The majority of workers on the canal were Irish immigrants, alongside some German and Native-born Americans. Workers were paid very little and toiled up to fifteen hours a day, many digging the primary canal prism with rudimentary tools such as shovels and picks. These workers would travel with their families, moving the entire unit as the canal progressed. After 20 years of construction, the completed canal arrived in Cumberland, Maryland in 1850. In Georgetown, four sandstone locks were constructed, as well as a watermill for power and a large boat incline for lowering barges. Like the Erie Canal, the C&O Canal proved its worth almost instantly, as it brought food, commercial goods, and building materials into the city. Georgetown, one of Washington's oldest and most established neighborhoods, saw increased commercial success as well as new businesses that were able to open along the accessible waterway.

Even until the early twentieth century, the C&O Canal was an important point of access for many traders and locals, but it could not keep up with the rise of railroads and, eventually, its career serving Washington came to an end.

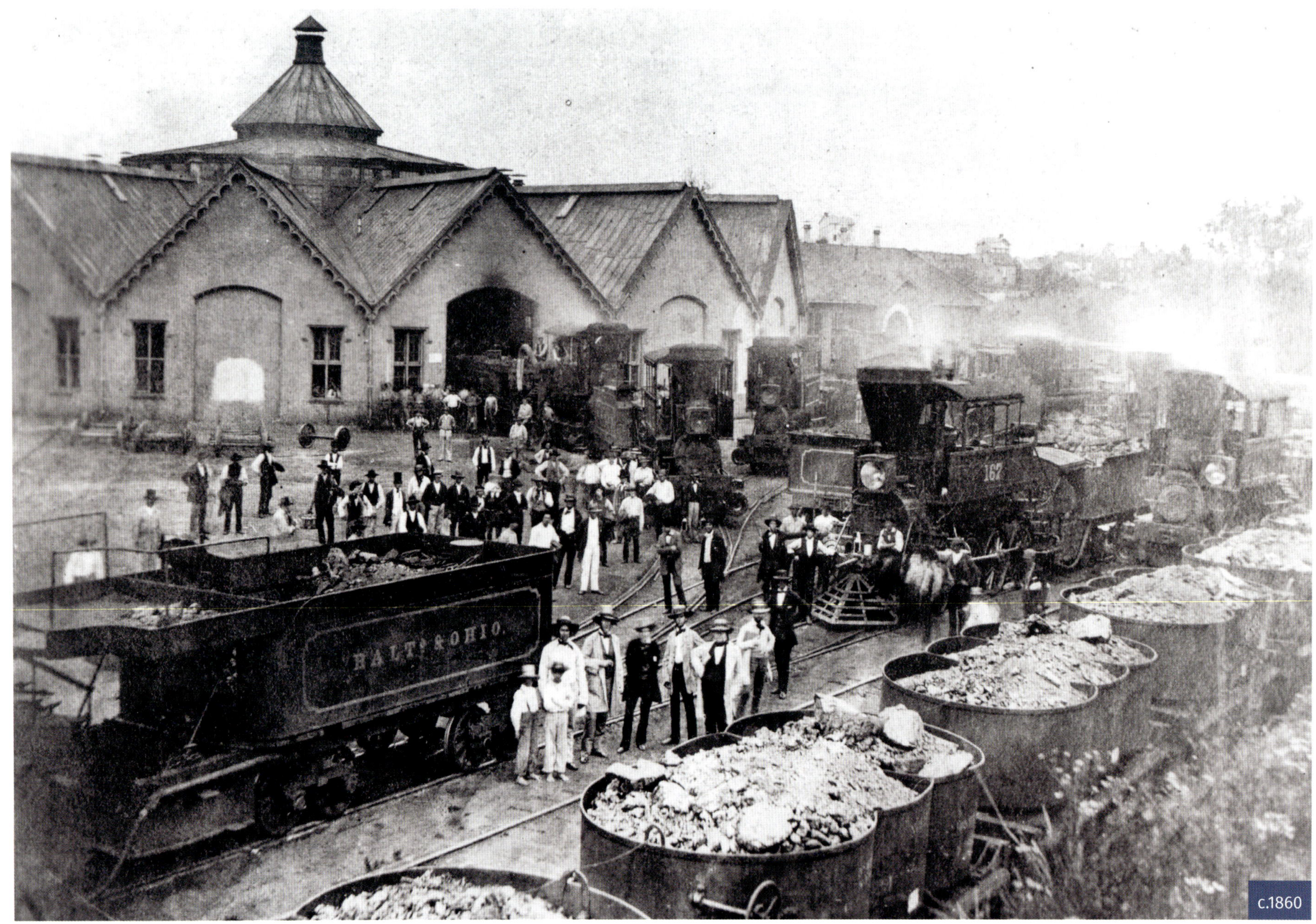

c.1860

BALTIMORE AND OHIO RAILROAD, MARYLAND

The first railroads aimed to steal a march on the canals

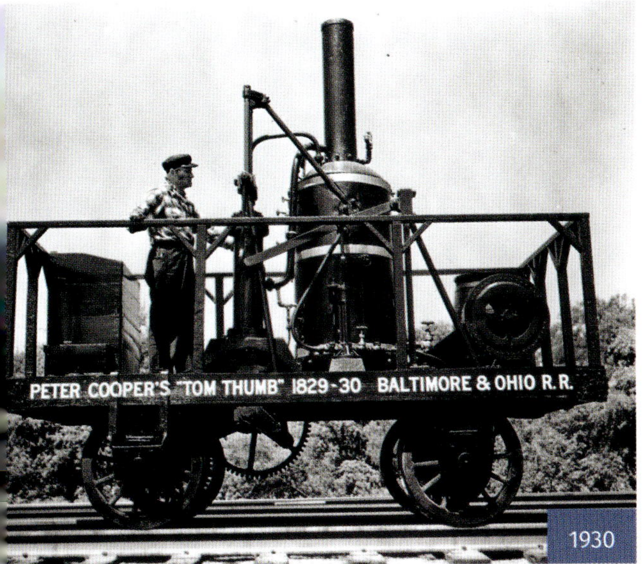

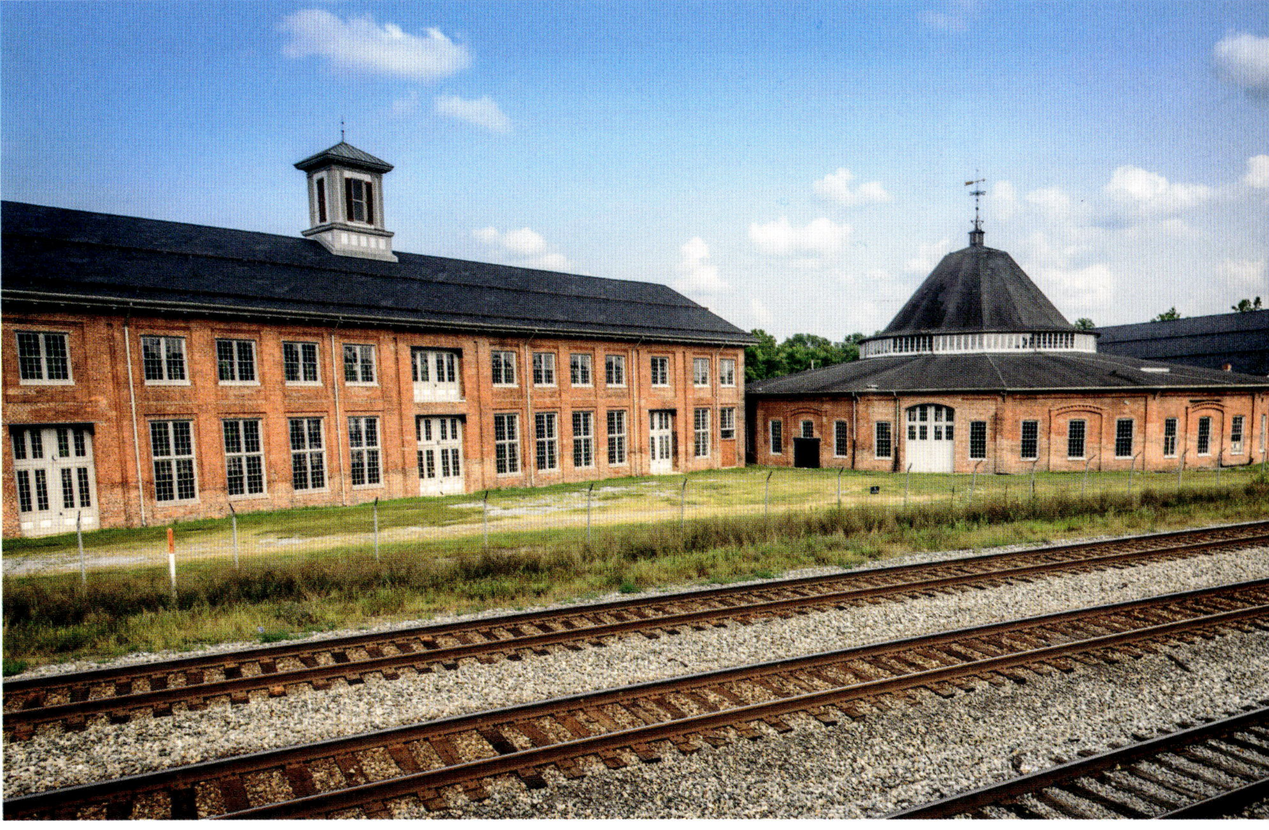

On February 28, 1827, the Baltimore and Ohio Railroad (B&O), chartered to become the first commercial railroad in the United States. It was established by Baltimore merchants and civic leaders who were alarmed by the rise of the port of New York City after the opening of the Erie Canal. Baltimore considered building a canal westward to the Ohio River to match this—but the Appalachian Mountains posed a huge engineering challenge. The railway era had already begun in Britain with the Stockton and Darlington Railway opening on September 27, 1825, marking the first public railway to use steam locomotives. Railroads—though still experimental in the 1820s—offered a promising new way to bypass geographical obstacles like steep grades and winding rivers.

Construction began in 1828, and the B&O's ceremonial first stone was laid by Charles Carroll, the last surviving signer of the Declaration of Independence. The first section of track opened in 1830 and the B&O introduced Tom Thumb (pictured above), a pioneering American-built steam locomotive designed by Peter Cooper.

The B&O had to overcome political problems from rival railroads. Only the Pennsylvania Railroad was allowed to build in its home state, requiring the B&O to skirt around a corner of the state, but still the railroad was able to expand steadily westward. In 1852 it reached the Ohio River at Wheeling, Virginia (now West Virginia), fulfilling its original charter. The company later extended to Cincinnati, St. Louis, and Chicago, becoming a major east-west route and linking the Atlantic coast to the American Midwest.

The B&O played a pivotal role during the American Civil War, as its routes were of strategic importance to the Union. The railroad transported troops and supplies and was frequently targeted by raiding Confederate forces.

Pictured here circa 1860, the Martinsburg (West Virginia) roundhouse and engine shops were built in the 1840s to provide a maintenance and repair hub for the B&O. It was a strategic target during the Civil War due to the railroad's importance to Union logistics. In 1861, Confederate forces under Stonewall Jackson destroyed parts of the facility to disrupt Union operations. After the war, the shops were rebuilt and expanded. Martinsburg is also historically famous as the starting point of the Great Railroad Strike of 1877. Today, the Roundhouse Complex is preserved as a historic site and is listed on the National Register of Historic Places.

Though the B&O Railroad no longer exists as an independent entity, its legacy endures. Its headquarters in Baltimore and its old lines remain symbols of the early railroad era. The B&O Railroad Museum in Baltimore, located on the site of the original Mount Clare Station and shops, preserves its remarkable history for future generations.

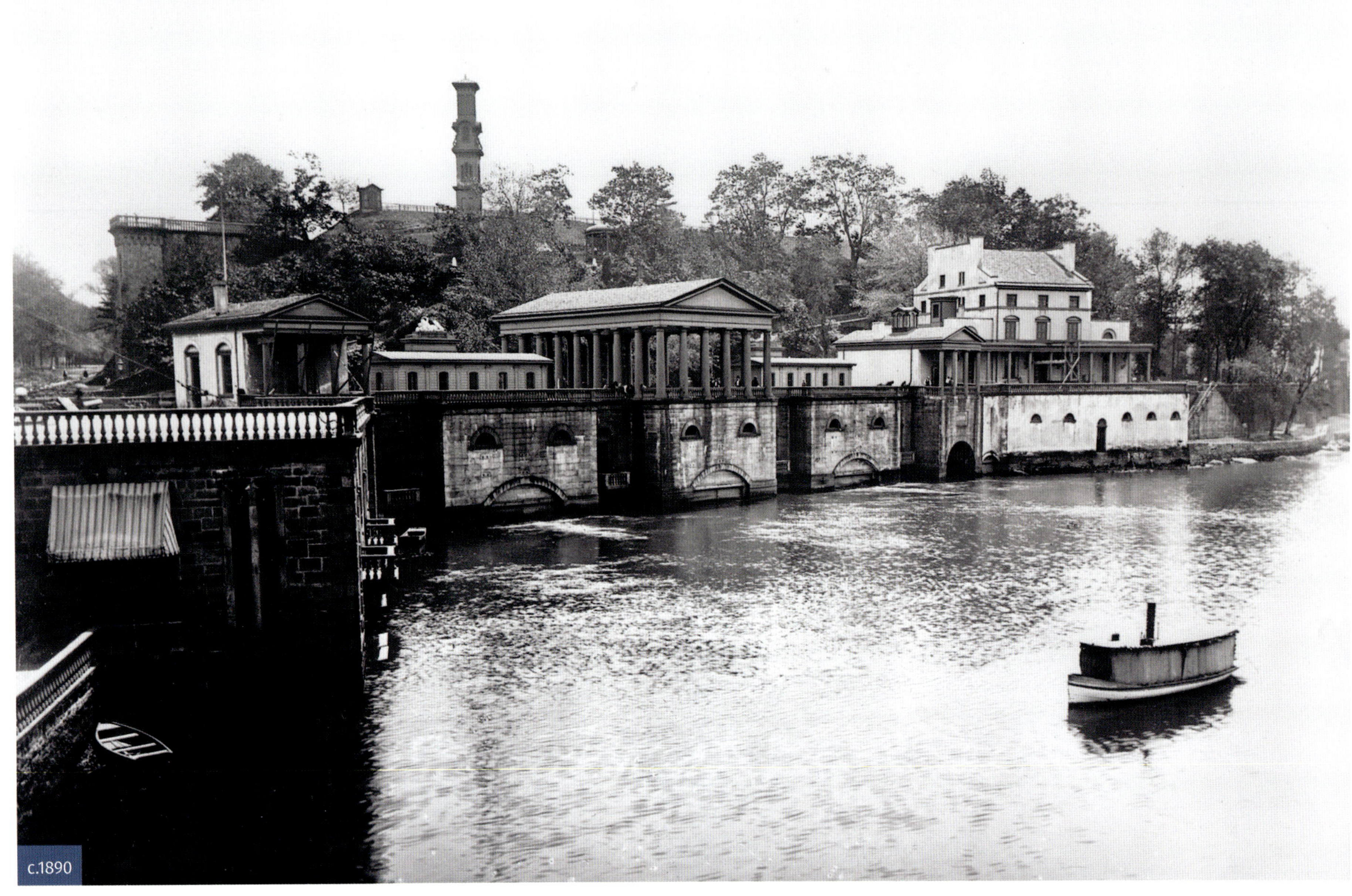
c.1890

PHILADELPHIA WATER WORKS, PENNSYLVANIA

The city's new water works became a top tourist attraction

In the early nineteenth century, Philadelphia was one of the most crowded cities in the United States with all the attendant health problems—contaminated wells and frequent outbreaks of yellow fever. The Philadelphia Water Works was one of the earliest public health initiatives that would highlight American engineering ingenuity at its best. Water was pumped by steam engines from the Schuylkill River and distributed from a reservoir.

Though innovative, the steam engines were costly and unreliable, prompting the city to consider alternatives. Under the guidance of engineer Frederick Graff, construction began on what would become the Fairmount Water Works, starting in 1815. This facility was located on the east bank of the Schuylkill River and marked a major shift: instead of steam, it would rely on water power, using the river's own flow to drive massive water wheels and pumps. Four million gallons a day was raised to a reservoir on Fairmount Hill from where gravity distributed it to the city's homes, businesses, and fire hydrants.

The Philadelphia Water Works was a top tourist destination as soon as it opened. Paved courts, canals, gardens, and handsome Roman temples designed by Benjamin

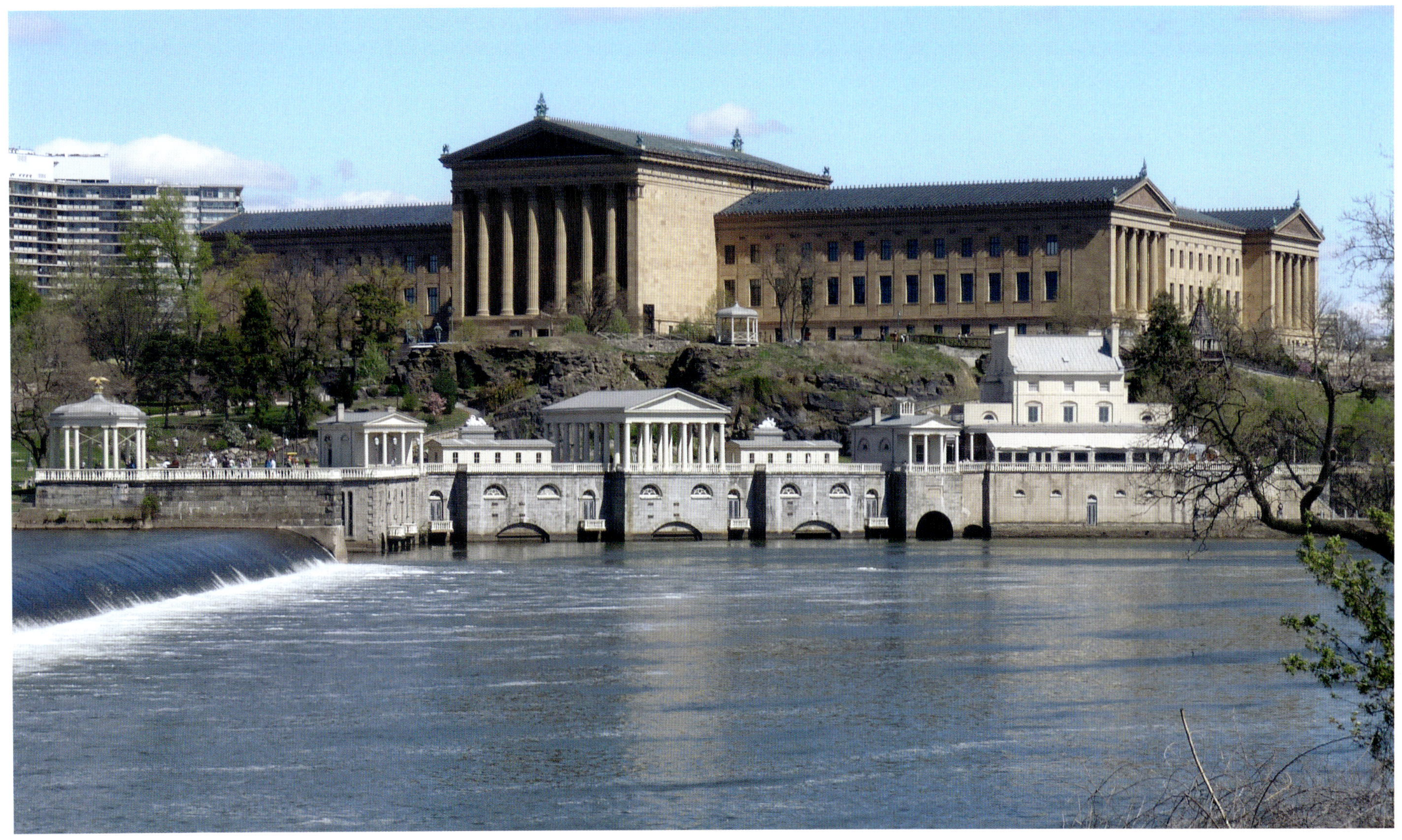

Latrobe provided a grand promenade for the thousands who came to see one of the great accomplishments of the industrial age.

Charles Dickens was mightily impressed and wrote about it on his 1842 American tour: "Philadelphia is most bountifully provided with fresh water, which is showered and jerked about, and turned on, and poured off, everywhere. The Waterworks, which are on a height near the city, are no less ornamental than useful, being tastefully laid out as a public garden, and kept in the best and neatest order. The river is dammed at this point, and forced by its own power into certain high tanks or reservoirs, whence the whole city, to the top stories of the houses, is supplied at a very trifling expense."

Today the site is overlooked by the massive Philadelphia Museum of Art (built between 1895 and 1933). In 1909, the Water Works was decommissioned as a pumping station. From 1911 up until 1962, it was home to the Philadelphia Aquarium. For the next ten years, the site was used as a practice pool for competitive swimmers and city school district students. The cluster of classical Roman temples that architect Benjamin Latrobe designed to house the water works machinery have been beautifully restored. The main building now serves as a romantic riverside restaurant, and the center building is home to the below-ground-level Water Works Interpretive Center, a permanent educational facility that is open free to the public.

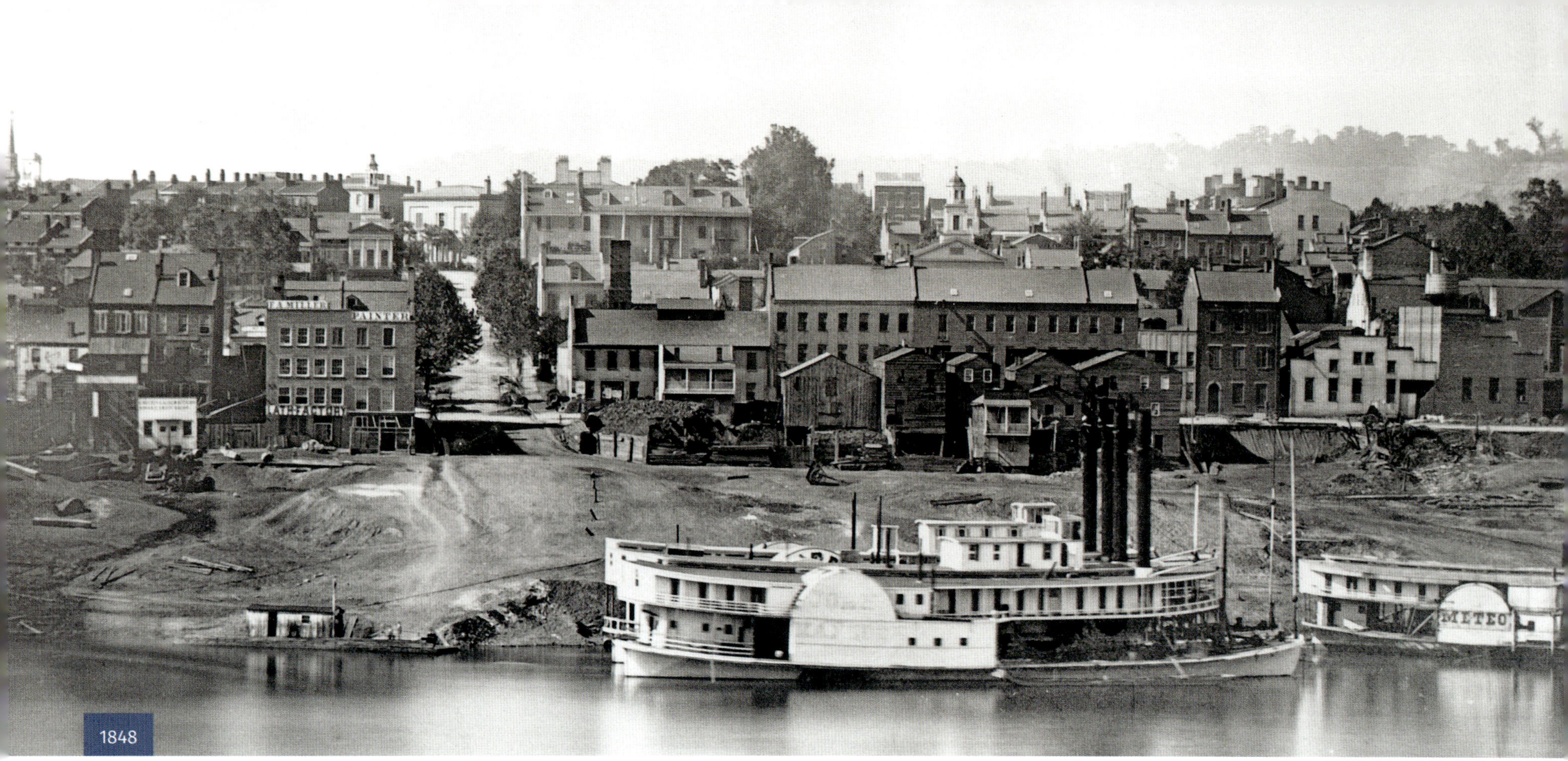

1848

CINCINNATI, OHIO

Riverboat transport helped Cincinnati become "Porkopolis"

Cincinnati—originally platted in 1789—can lay claim to be the first all-American city, the first founded after the Revolutionary War. By 1811 steamboats were traveling to Cincinnati on the Ohio River and within a few years, thanks to the Miami and Erie Canal connecting Lake Erie to the Ohio, Cincinnati was a bustling trading port and a leader in shipbuilding.

It was the prodigious meatpacking operations that earned Cincinnati the unwelcome nickname of Porkopolis. Drivers herded pigs through the streets on the way to the many slaughterhouses. The river systems of the Mississippi, Ohio, and Missouri were key to the agricultural exploitation of America's vast interior and, thanks to its connections, Cincinnati's population doubled every ten years. By 1850, Cincinnati was the sixth largest in the United States.

The vintage daguerreotype photo from 1848, taken from across the river in Newport, Kentucky, shows the public landing just about the time that Samuel Clemens (Mark Twain) came to work in the city as a typesetter for T. Wrightson and Company, at 167 Walnut Street. Cincinnati had major commercial ties with both St. Louis and New Orleans, and the steamboat-loving Clemens left Cincinnati for good in the February of 1857, heading southbound toward New Orleans on the riverboat *Paul Jones*.

When the railroads stretched the country farther west, the vast plains for raising livestock were closer

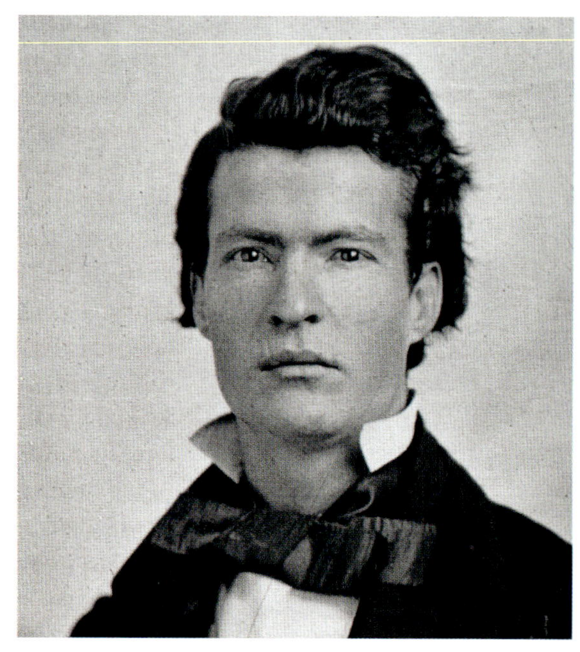

RIGHT: Samuel Clemens was around 21 years of age when he set out from Cincinnati to make his fortune in South America.

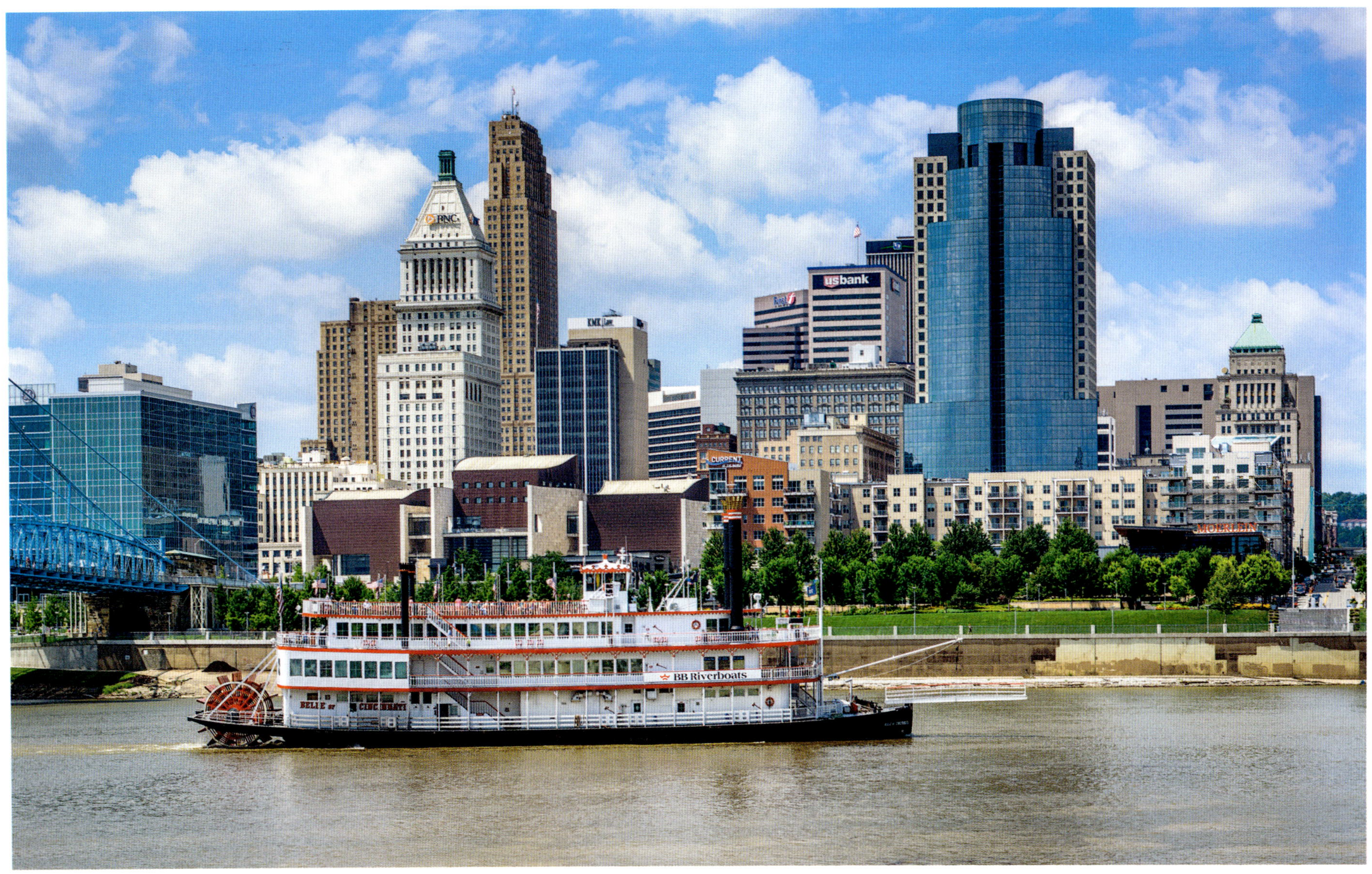

to meatpacking facilities in Chicago, and the original West became the Midwest. When river trade died out, the Public Landing that had been the pivot of the city for a hundred years was turned to other uses. In 1967 it was appropriated to build Riverfront Stadium as part of an effort to revitalize the area. Today, there is a giant paddle wheel monument above the landing outside Great American Ballpark to commemorate its role in the development of the city.

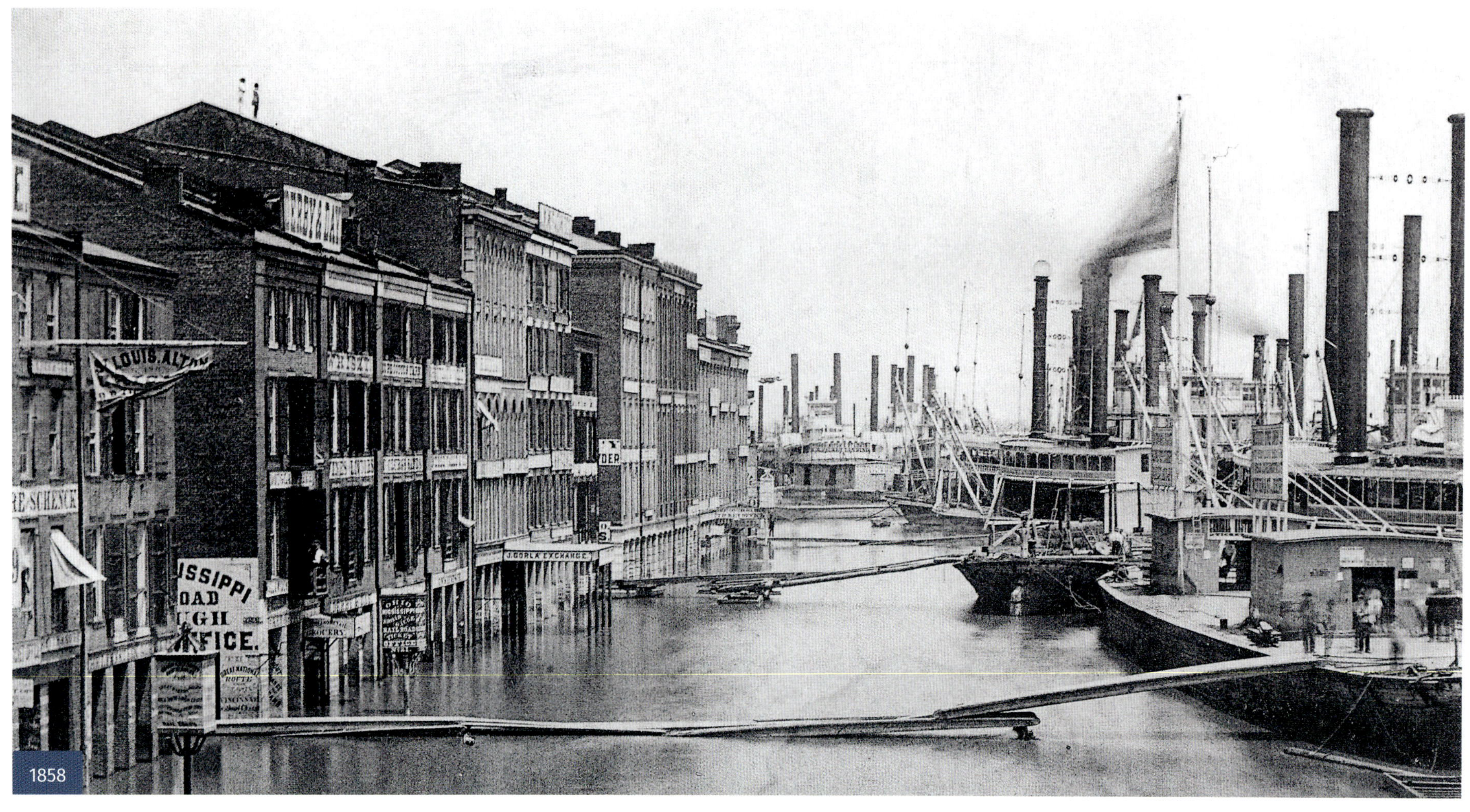

1858

RIVERBOATS AT ST. LOUIS, MISSOURI

In the early nineteenth century, Mississippi riverboats were key to the Midwest economy

For pioneers looking for a new life in the West, St. Louis was an important place to start. Established by the French in 1764 as a fur-trapper trading post, it lay on the west bank of the Mississippi near the confluence with the Missouri. By the end of the Civil War it was the largest city between these mighty rivers and San Francisco. Before the introduction of the railroads; guides, wagons, and provisions for the long journey west could be procured in St. Louis. This photo of Laclede's Landing in St. Louis, dates from around the time that Samuel Clemens passed through with riverboat pilot Horace Bixby. He had plans to travel to South America and make his fortune growing coca, but his journey on the *Paul Jones* convinced him his future lay in guiding steamboats up and down the Mississippi. Twain was around 21 years old and persuaded Bixby to take him on as an apprentice, or "cub." Bixby agreed (famously, Twain later said he offered to pay $500 for the training, though Bixby replied that he wouldn't take money until Twain proved he could learn).

Although the river was the most important artery for trade, flooding was an annual problem. The city's limestone bluffs at St. Louis initially afforded some measure of protection; however, by the mid-1800s, the bluffs had been cut away to form a more

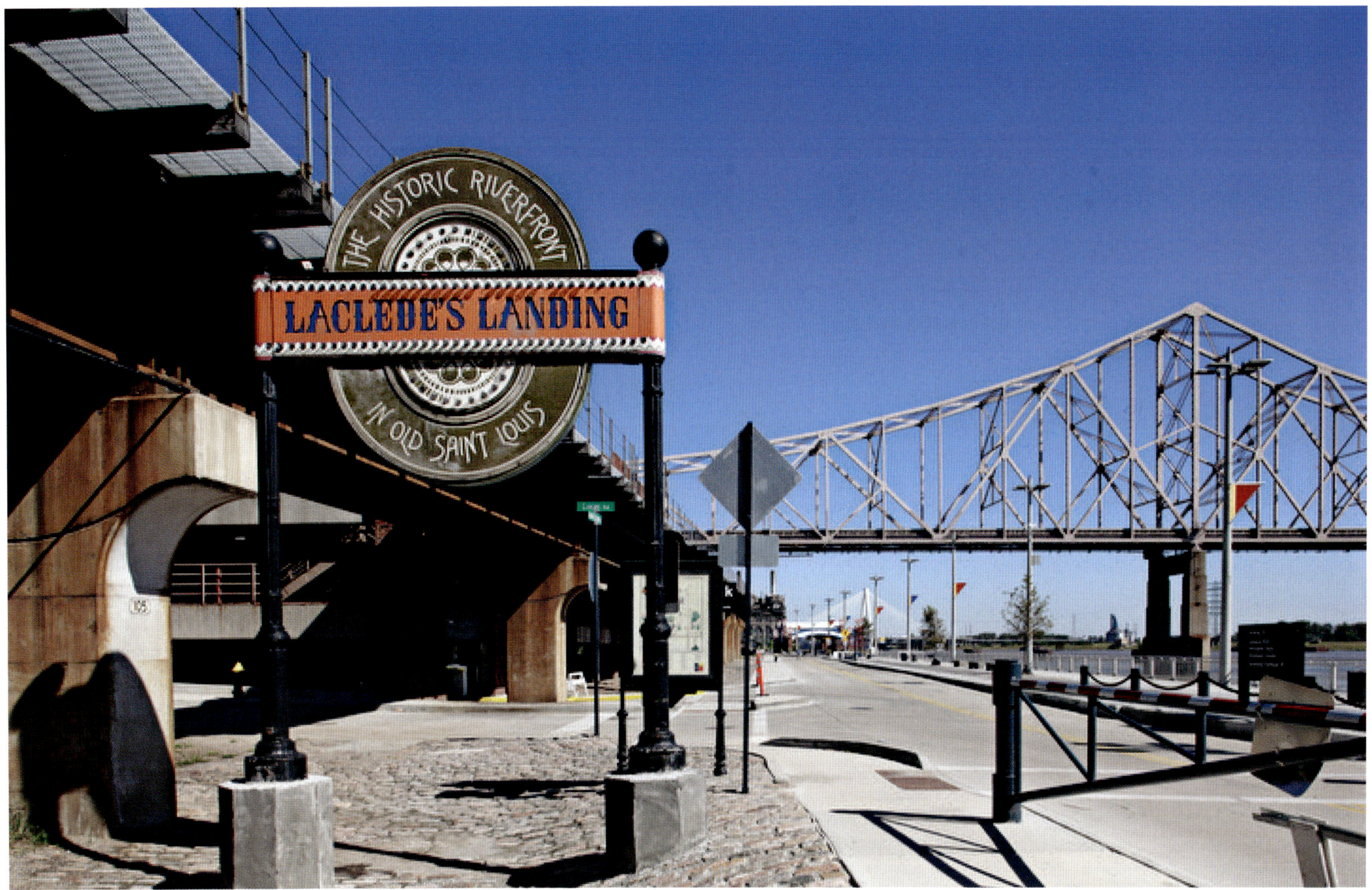

accessible levee. Here, in the photograph opposite, the steamers are practically tying up to the buildings on First Street (well above the levee) at Laclede's Landing. Fourteen years earlier, during the Great Flood of 1844, the river created something of a≈freshwater sea stretching twelve miles wide and rising even beyond Second Street.

The Civil War ended Clemens' career prospects on the river, just as railroads reduced the need for river transport for all but the most bulky of raw materials. The St. Louis warehouse buildings on First and Second Streets were eventually cleared after a scheme for their removal was first proposed in 1915, resurrected in the 1930s, and voted through in a flurry of lawsuits that uncovered much political skulduggery. It would eventually result in Eero Saarinen's magnificent $13 million Gateway Arch, to celebrate the Louisiana Purchase and St. Louis's role as the gateway to American expansion west into the former Indian territories.

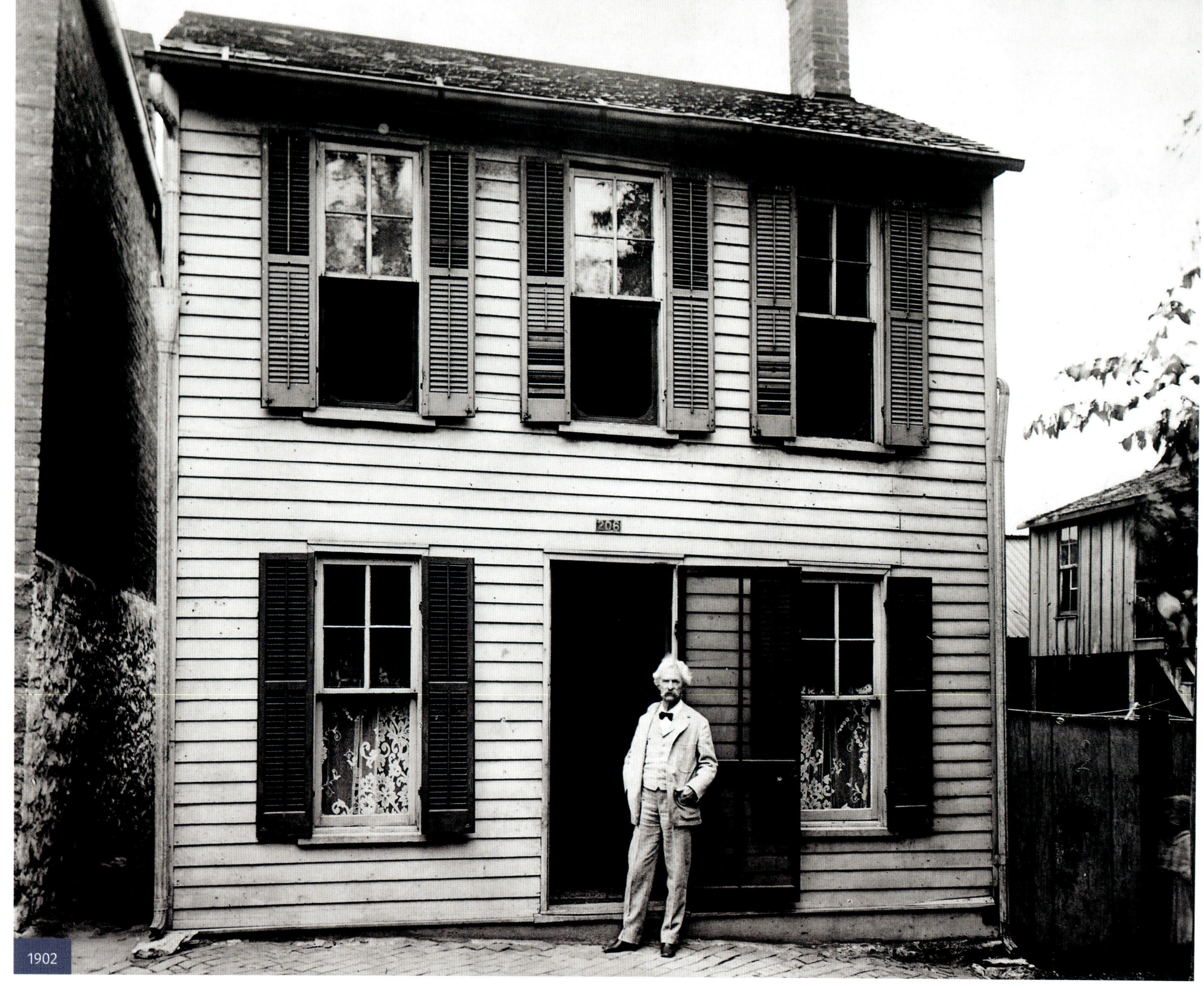

MARK TWAIN CHILDHOOD HOUSE, HANNIBAL, MISSOURI

Where Tom Sawyer almost painted a fence...

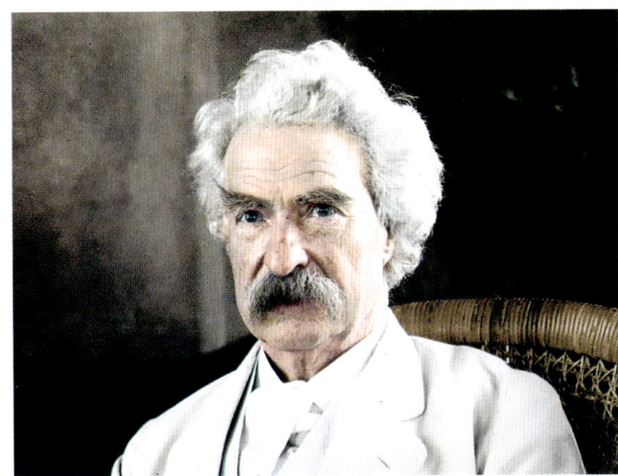

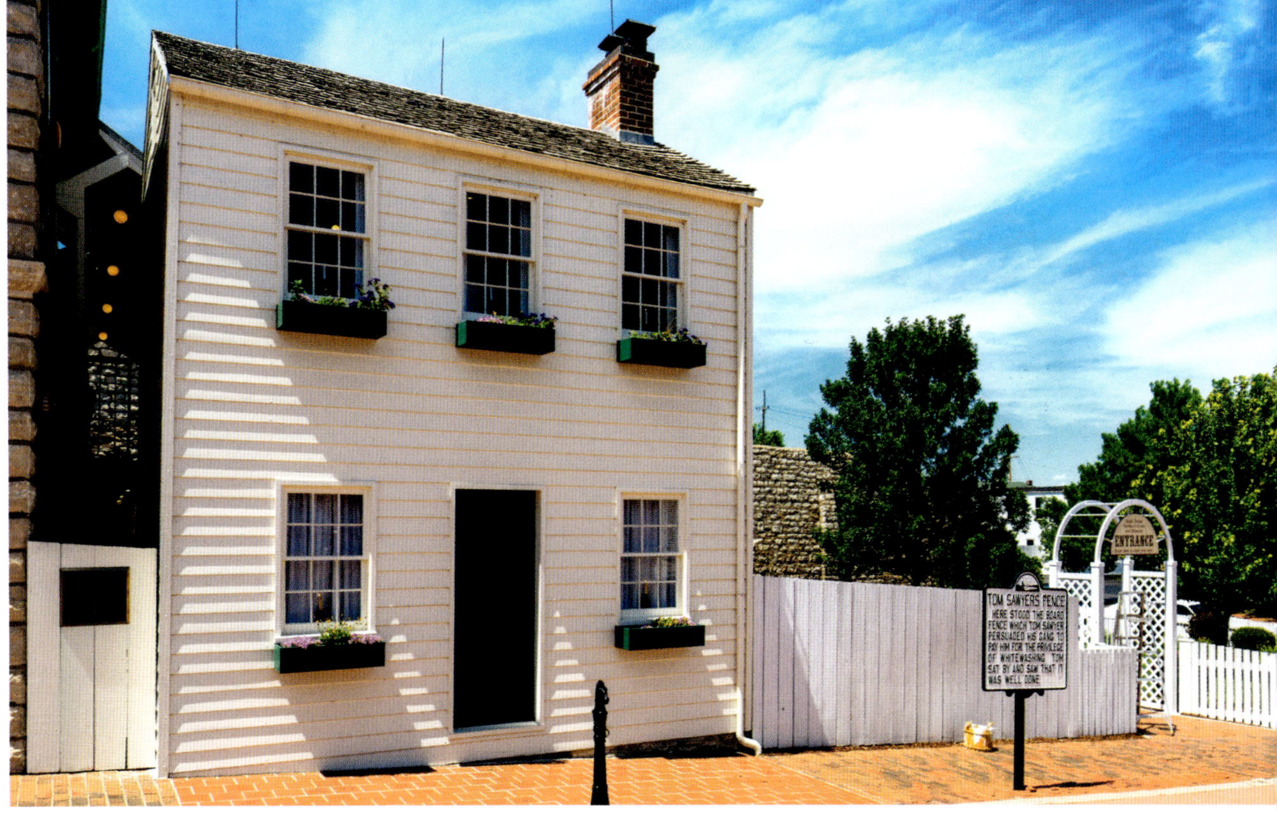

The boyhood home at 206 Hill Street would become known around the world. And if the boyhood home is arguably the most famous house in American literature, Hannibal is the most famous small town. It was in this antebellum river town of 2,000 that Samuel Clemens developed the distinctly American voice that would define the writings of Mark Twain. It was here that the writer found the inspiration for Tom Sawyer, Huckleberry Finn, Becky Thatcher and so many more characters and stories. It was here that Clemens led what has come to be seen as the quintessential early-American childhood. Ninety miles north of St. Louis on the Mississippi, modern Hannibal predates the Clemens family's arrival by just 20 years. It became part of the United States in the 1803 Louisiana Purchase and was surveyed in 1819. Prior to that, it had been home to many Native American tribes, including the Chickasaw, Illini, and Iowa.

By the time John Clemens relocated to Hannibal, it was Missouri's third largest settlement. Its main industries were logging, a limestone quarry, hog farming, and meat-packing. The river hub was fertile ground for John Marshall Clemens' ventures, which ranged from running a general store to establishing the Hannibal and St. Joseph Railroad. He also served as a steamboat commissioner. Though John's business ventures were never successful, he was elected Justice of the Peace and was a prominent figure in the town. His office on Bird Street (now relocated to 205 Hill Street) also provided inspiration for his inquisitive young son. Afraid to return home one late night, Samuel snuck into his father's office to sleep, only to literally stumble upon a dead body awaiting investigation by the judge. This was just one of many Hannibal adventures—and misadventures—that stuck in the mind of the writer-to-be. The late 1840s were not easy for the Clemens family. They lost their house at one point and, tragically, John died from pneumonia in 1847. Though just 11, Sam's mother forced her son to stand by his father's dead body and promise to be a better boy, a moment that would long haunt him. That same year, Sam would witness a man shot to death on the street, and come across the mutilated body of an escaped slave on the Mississippi. This was the end of Samuel Clemens' innocent boyhood, though he would remain in Hannibal for several more years.

Sam Clemens returned to Hannibal on several occasions and he would invariably run into characters known from his childhood. This vintage photo shows his final visit, a lifetime away, in 1902.

Today, Mark Twain's and Hannibal's glory days live on at the Mark Twain Boyhood Home & Museum complex, which also includes John M. Clemens' restored office. Hannibal, home to 17,000, has become a tourist destination for travelers from around the world seeking to experience this iconic Midwest American town. Those carefree days of hiding in caves and playing by the river were overtaken by work and the concerns of the adult world—until decades later when Sam Clemens revived his childhood upon the page.

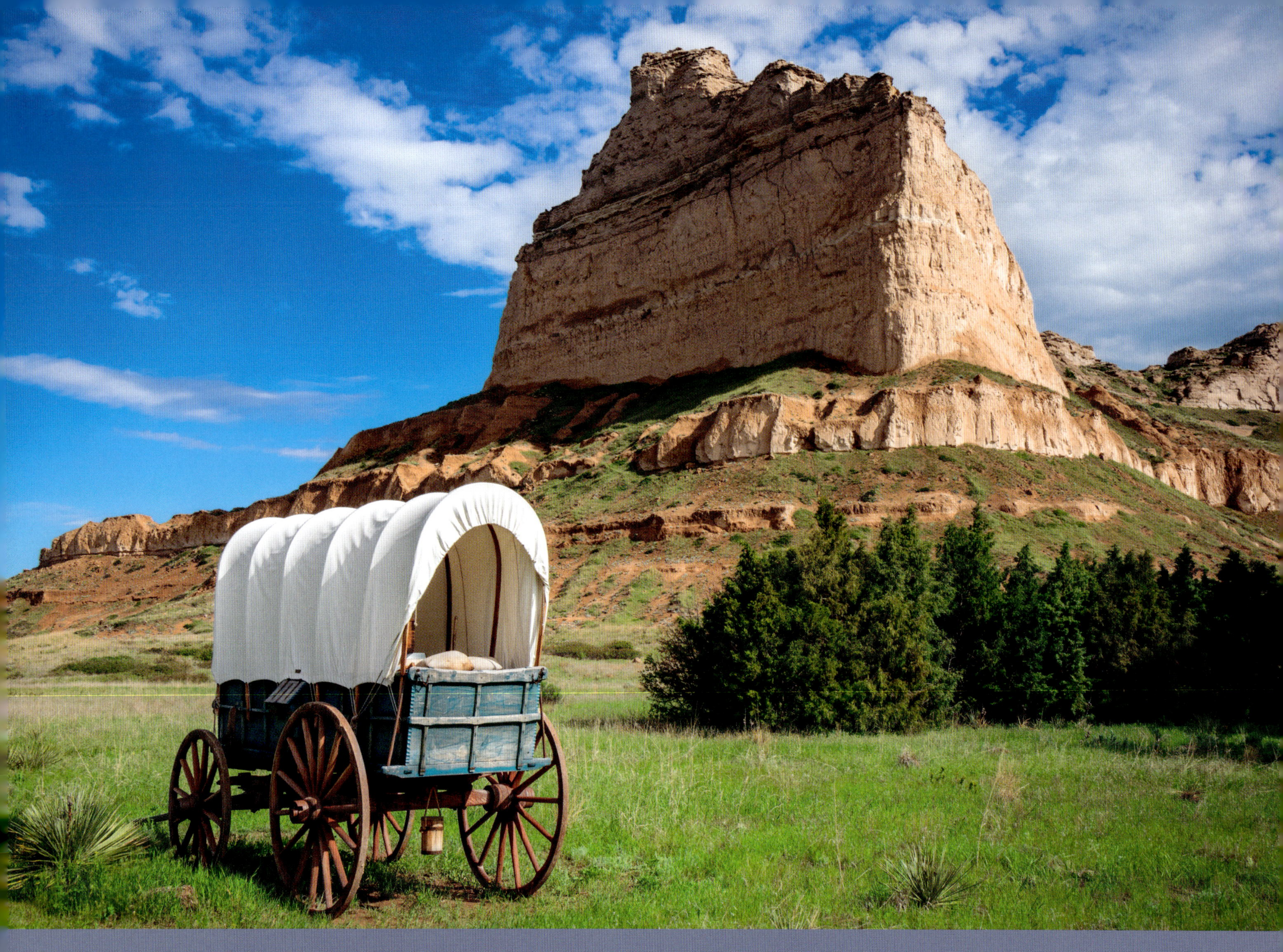

JOURNEYS WEST AND GOLD RUSH

By the mid-1800s, the United States was gripped by the powerful idea of Manifest Destiny—the belief that Americans should expand across the North American continent. This belief spurred millions to head west. Some went in wagons with families and dreams of a better, if more precarious life; others pursued the get-rich-quick approach of mining gold or silver. Together, their journeys reshaped the physical and cultural map of America.

THE MORMON EXODUS: A JOURNEY OF FAITH

Among the earliest large-scale migrations west were the Mormons, members of the Church of Jesus Christ of Latter-day Saints. Founded in upstate New York in the 1830s by Joseph Smith, the church faced hostility for its doctrines and communal lifestyle. After Smith was killed by a mob in Illinois in 1844, leadership passed to Brigham Young. In 1847, under increasing persecution, Young led thousands of Mormons westward in search of religious freedom. Their journey, beginning in Nauvoo, Illinois, spanned over a thousand miles across the Great Plains and the Rocky Mountains, following what would become the Mormon Trail to Salt Lake Valley, then part of Mexico.

THE CALIFORNIA GOLD RUSH: FORTUNE AND FRENZY (1848–1855)

Just a year after the Mormons arrived in Utah, gold was discovered at Sutter's Mill near Coloma, California, in 1848. Though the news spread slowly at first, by 1849, the Gold Rush was in full swing. Tens of thousands of people—nicknamed "Forty-niners"—flooded into California from across the US, Latin America, Europe, and Asia. Boomtowns like San Francisco, which had a population of 1,000 in 1848, exploded to over 25,000 within two years. Other settlements sprang up overnight wherever gold was found. While some miners struck it rich, most found modest success—or nothing at all.

The Gold Rush accelerated California's path to statehood, which it achieved in 1850, bypassing the typical territorial process due to its sudden and massive population boom. It also intensified debates over slavery, with the admission of California as a free state.

THE OREGON TRAIL AND OVERLAND MIGRATION

Even as gold fever took hold, many settlers journeyed west with quieter ambitions: farmland, space, and a fresh start. The Oregon Trail, a roughly 2,000-mile route from Missouri to the Pacific Northwest, became a major artery of westward expansion.

Between the 1840s and 1860s, more than 300,000 people traveled this path. The journey was treacherous—disease, accidents, violence, starvation, and extreme weather were constant threats. The Donner Party were famously stranded when the snows blocked their route, while Olive Oatman's family set off alone and were attacked by Native Americans. Yet families pressed forward in wagons pulled by oxen, driven by hope and stories of rich farming land in places like the Willamette Valley. The success of these settlers helped solidify American claims to Oregon and other territories and established critical footholds in the Pacific Northwest.

THE TRANSCONTINENTAL RAILROAD: BINDING THE NATION (1863–1869)

Though wagon trains and stagecoaches had carried pioneers westward for decades, the task was long, perilous, and slow—often the hazardous journey would take six months or more. That changed dramatically with the completion of the first transcontinental railroad.

Authorized by the Pacific Railway Act of 1862, two companies undertook the task: the Union Pacific, building west from Omaha, Nebraska; and the Central Pacific, building east from Sacramento, California.

The Central Pacific faced mountainous terrain and snowbound passes and its progress depended heavily on the labor of thousands of Chinese immigrants, who worked under brutal conditions. The Union Pacific, crossing the plains, employed many Irish immigrants, Civil War veterans, and former enslaved people.

On May 10, 1869, the two lines met at Promontory Summit, Utah. The ceremonial "Golden Spike" was driven into the final tie, uniting the coasts and heralding a new era in American history.

BOOMTOWNS AND THE WILD FRONTIER

With migration and transportation came explosive growth—and chaos. Towns near mining regions or along the rail lines sprouted seemingly overnight. These boomtowns were often rough, lawless places where fortunes were made and lost, and the life expectancy of sheriffs was short.

In places like Deadwood, South Dakota (gold), Virginia City, Nevada (silver), and Tombstone, Arizona (silver), wealth flowed freely—and so did whiskey and gambling. Saloons, brothels, and gambling halls dominated the main streets, and shootouts were not uncommon. Law enforcement was sparse or corrupt, and justice often came through vigilantism.

Notorious figures emerged from this era: Wild Bill Hickok, Billy the Kid, Jesse James, and Wyatt Earp became legends, blurring the lines between outlaw and hero. Some of the towns, such as Tombstone and Virginia City, lingered on; while others, such as Bodie in California, faded off the map.

Westward expansion came at a high cost—especially to Native American tribes. As settlers and railroads encroached on Ancestral lands, conflict was inevitable. Forced treaties, broken promises, and outright warfare led to the removal and suffering of Indigenous peoples across the Plains and the West. The US Army waged campaigns to suppress Native resistance to many broken treaties, resulting in tragic episodes such as the Sand Creek Massacre (1864) and later the Battle of the Little Bighorn (1876).

By 1870, the American West had been irreversibly transformed. The combined forces of religious migration, gold and silver rushes, railroads, and land policies had brought millions to new frontiers. New Territories were transformed into States while the frontier was rapidly being absorbed.

The myth of the West—its promise, danger, and opportunity—would live on in American memory. It has been recreated in movies for the last century, though seldom bringing home the true, brutal reality of how tough it was to survive on the edge of America.

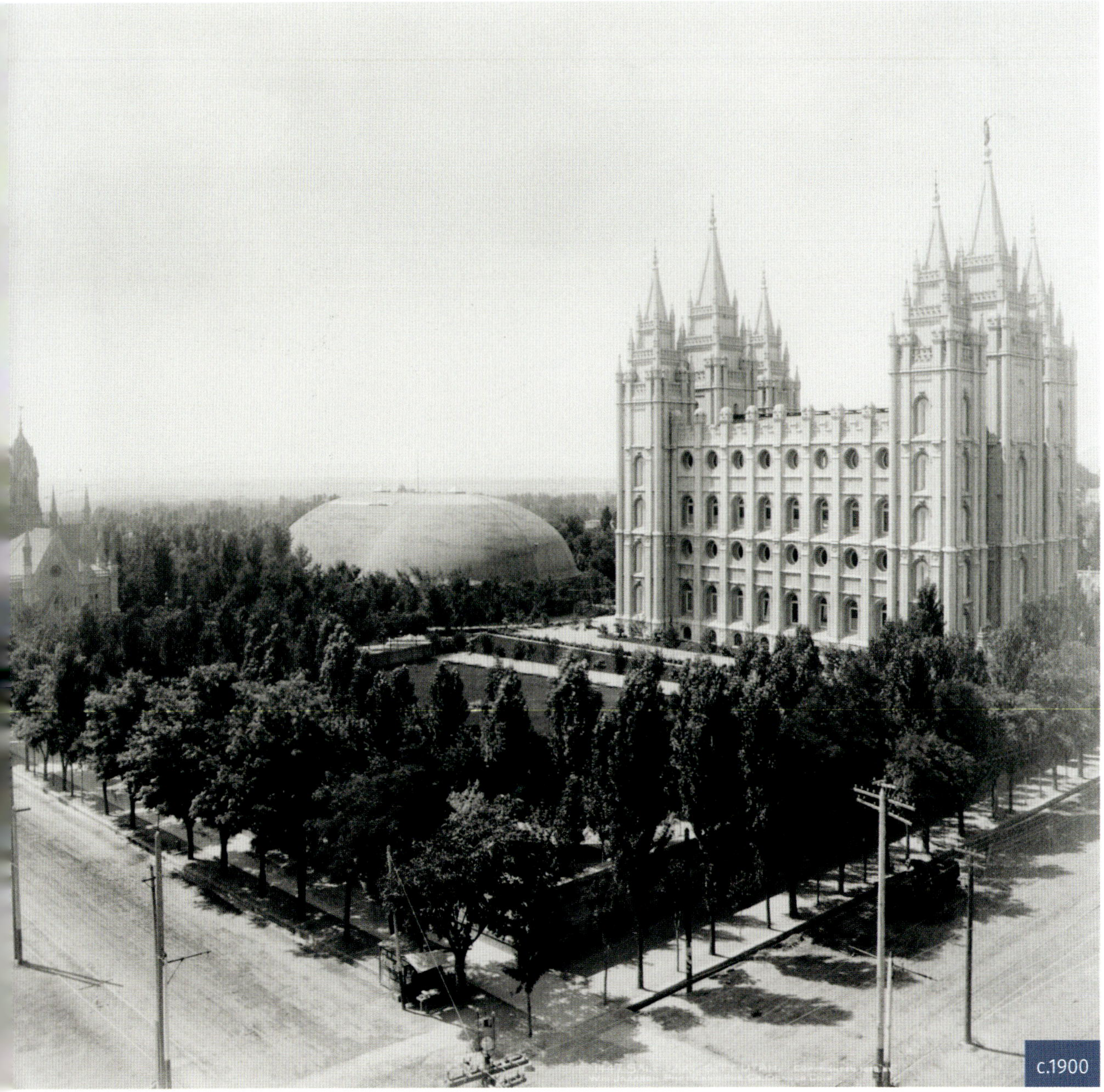

c.1900

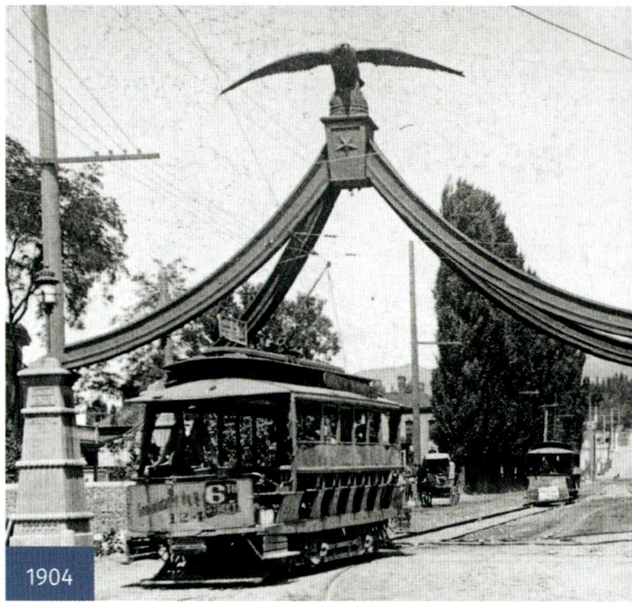

SALT LAKE CITY, UTAH

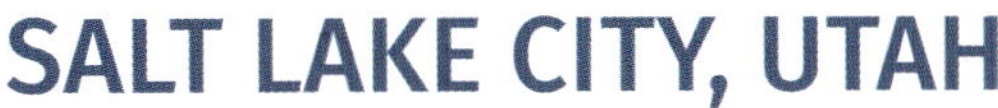

Mormon pioneers finally found a home free from persecution

Most of the "Journeys West" undertaken in the nineteenth century were either to settle land or reach the gold fields of California. The settlement of Salt Lake City by the Mormons was done out of necessity following relentless religious persecution. The search for a "promised land" for the Church of Jesus Christ of Latter-day Saints (LDS) had begun in the 1830s, when the religion was founded by Joseph Smith in upstate New York. The new religious movement quickly gained followers but also provoked hostility for its unorthodox beliefs and practices. Driven from New York, the Mormons moved to Ohio, Missouri, and then Nauvoo, Illinois. After the 1844 murder of Joseph Smith and his brother Hyrum by a mob, leadership passed to Brigham Young, a determined and pragmatic leader who believed that the only way for the church to survive was to find a remote location where they could live free from persecution. In July 1847, the first group of Mormon pioneers reached the Salt Lake Valley in what was then northern Mexico, just before the end

ABOVE: The Eagle Gate is a replica of Brigham Young's original 1859 Eagle Gate, which served as an entrance to his property and the City Creek Canyon road.

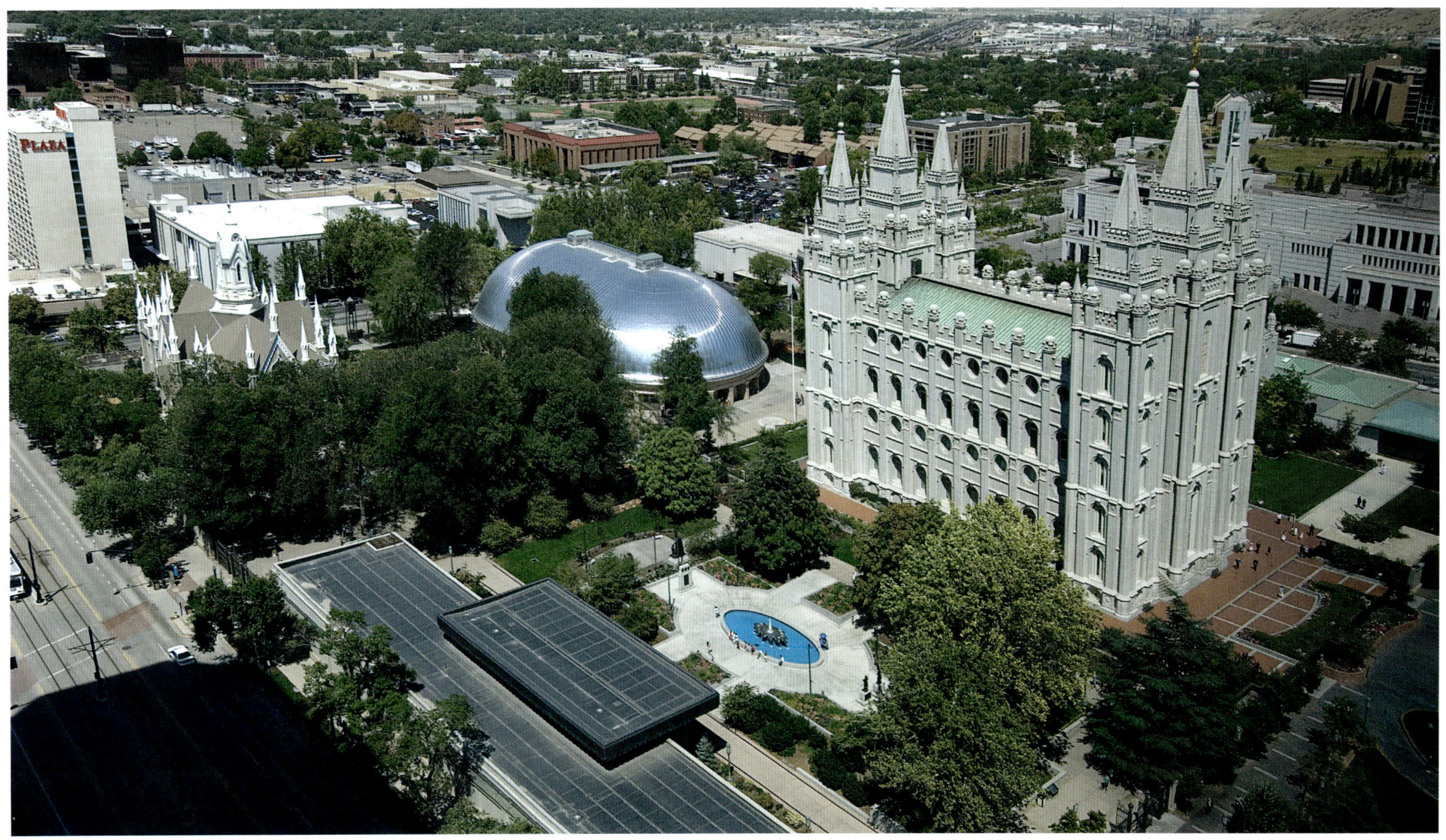

of the Mexican–American War. When Brigham Young arrived and looked out over the arid valley, he reportedly said, “This is the right place. Drive on.” The valley was dry and largely uninhabited, but it offered isolation from critical neighbors and most important of all, the potential for self-sufficiency.

The settlers immediately began building a city and a new life. They implemented a communal and highly organized approach to agriculture, digging extensive irrigation systems to bring water from mountain streams to their fields. This innovative irrigation enabled them to grow crops in the desert and support a growing population. Salt Lake City was laid out in a grid system, with wide streets and designated areas for homes, businesses, and public buildings, including the iconic Salt Lake Temple.

The Salt Lake Temple and the domed Salt Lake Tabernacle are iconic symbols of the LDS Church. The soaring Temple, begun in 1853 and completed in 1893, was designed by Truman Osborn Angell, the brother-in-law of Brigham Young, who served many years as the official architect of the LDS. He was part of the first wave of Mormon settlers and helped perfect the acoustics for which the building is famous. Owing to its proximity to the Great Salt Lake, the city was originally named Great Salt Lake City, but in 1868 “Great” was dropped from the name. Today the city, nicknamed “The Crossroads of the West,” part of the Salt Lake City–Ogden–Provo area, has a population in excess of a million, the 22nd largest in the US.

SUTTER'S MILL, CALIFORNIA

The discovery of gold transformed the new territory of California

John Sutter, a German-Swiss settler, arrived with other Europeans in Mexican-administered Alta California in 1839. He established an agricultural and trading colony near the confluence of the Sacramento River and American River and called it Nueva Helvetia (New Switzerland). The site was just a few miles east of where his son, John Sutter Jr., would establish Sacramento.

A peace treaty for the Mexico-America war of 1848 had yet to be concluded when Sutter decided to begin construction of a sawmill in the forest about 30 miles northeast of his existing colony near present-day Coloma, California. Sutter partnered with a carpenter and millwright named James W. Marshall to build a sawmill along the American River, in order to supply lumber for his growing settlement.

On January 24, 1848, while inspecting the mill's tailrace—a trench carrying water away from the waterwheel—Marshall spotted shiny flakes in the riverbed. After conducting simple tests, such as smashing the flakes with a rock to see if they flattened rather than shattered, he became convinced he had found gold.

1848

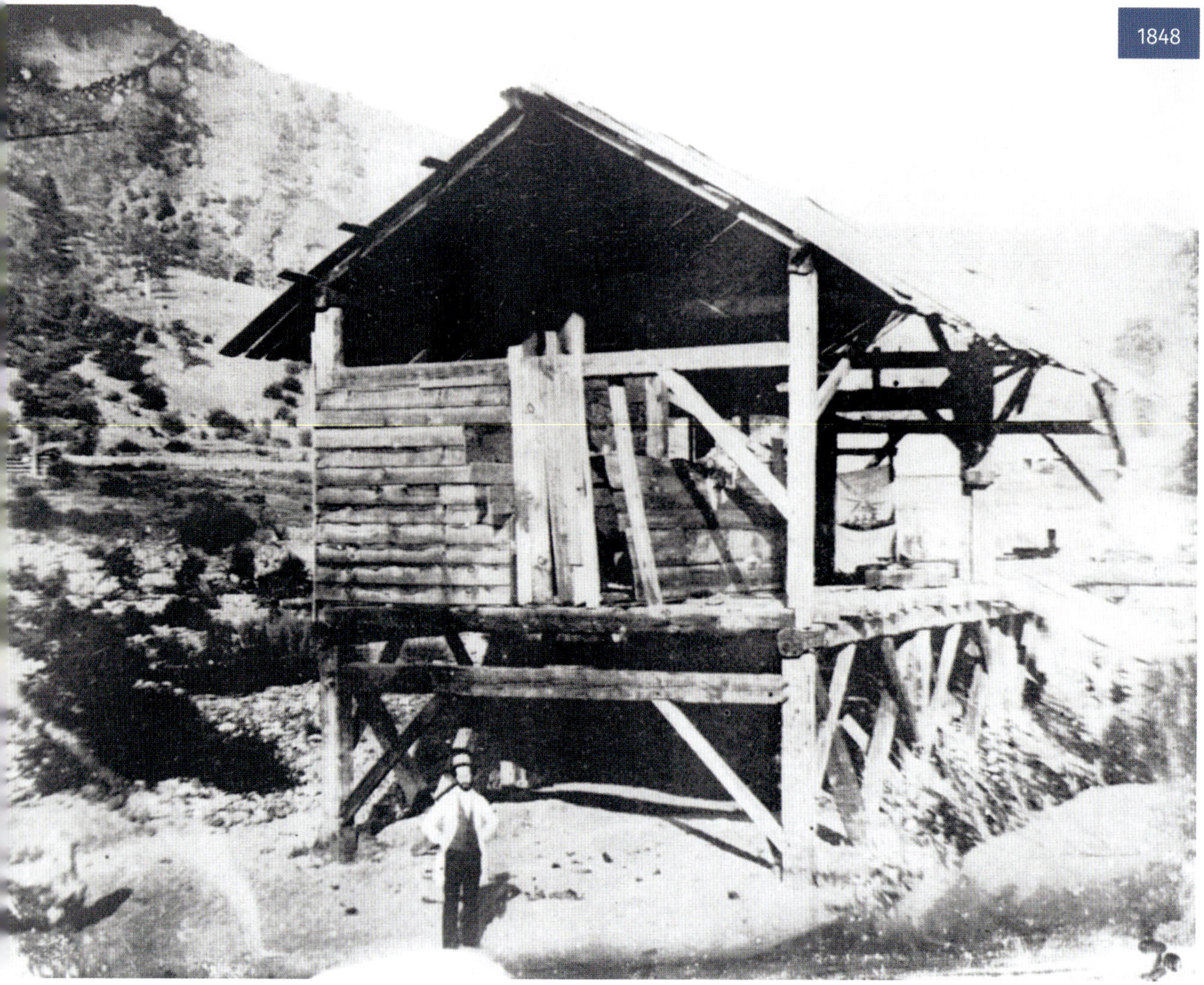

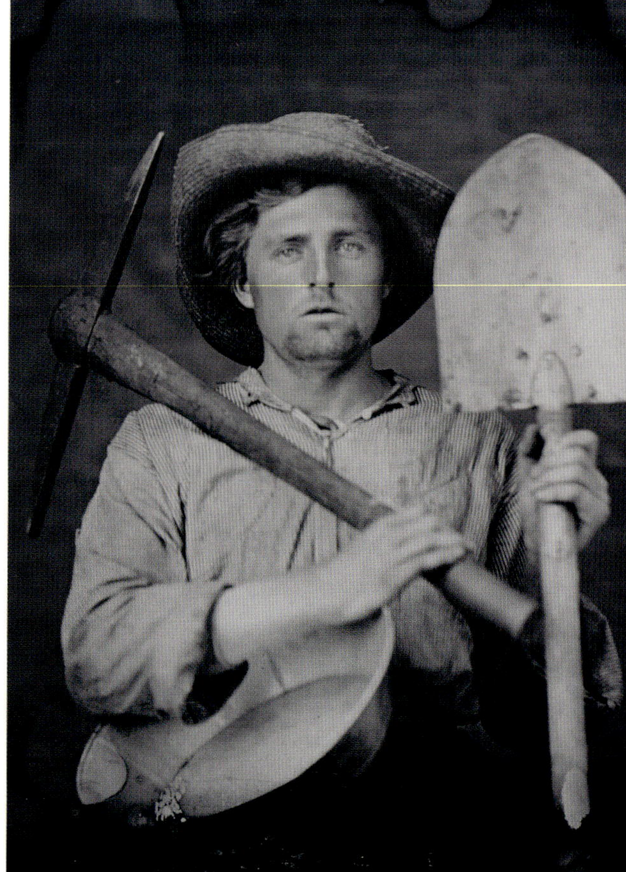

Marshall rushed to inform Sutter, who confirmed the discovery and hoped to keep the find a secret to protect his land and business interests. However, word soon spread. Workers at the mill talked, and soon rumors reached San Francisco and beyond. The discovery was confirmed by US Army officer and explorer John C. Frémont and the Gold Rush was on.

Ironically, neither John Sutter nor James Marshall profited from the gold discovery. The Rush overwhelmed Sutter's land, which was overrun by squatters and prospectors. Marshall, too, struggled financially and lived much of his life in poverty. Despite this, both men became enduring figures in American folklore.

The site of the mill is now part of the Marshall Gold Discovery State Historic Park, registered as California Historical Landmark number 530. Since 1848 the stream has changed course—an original replica (taken from Marshall's initial plans) from 1965 was replaced in 2014 by one closer to the original site.

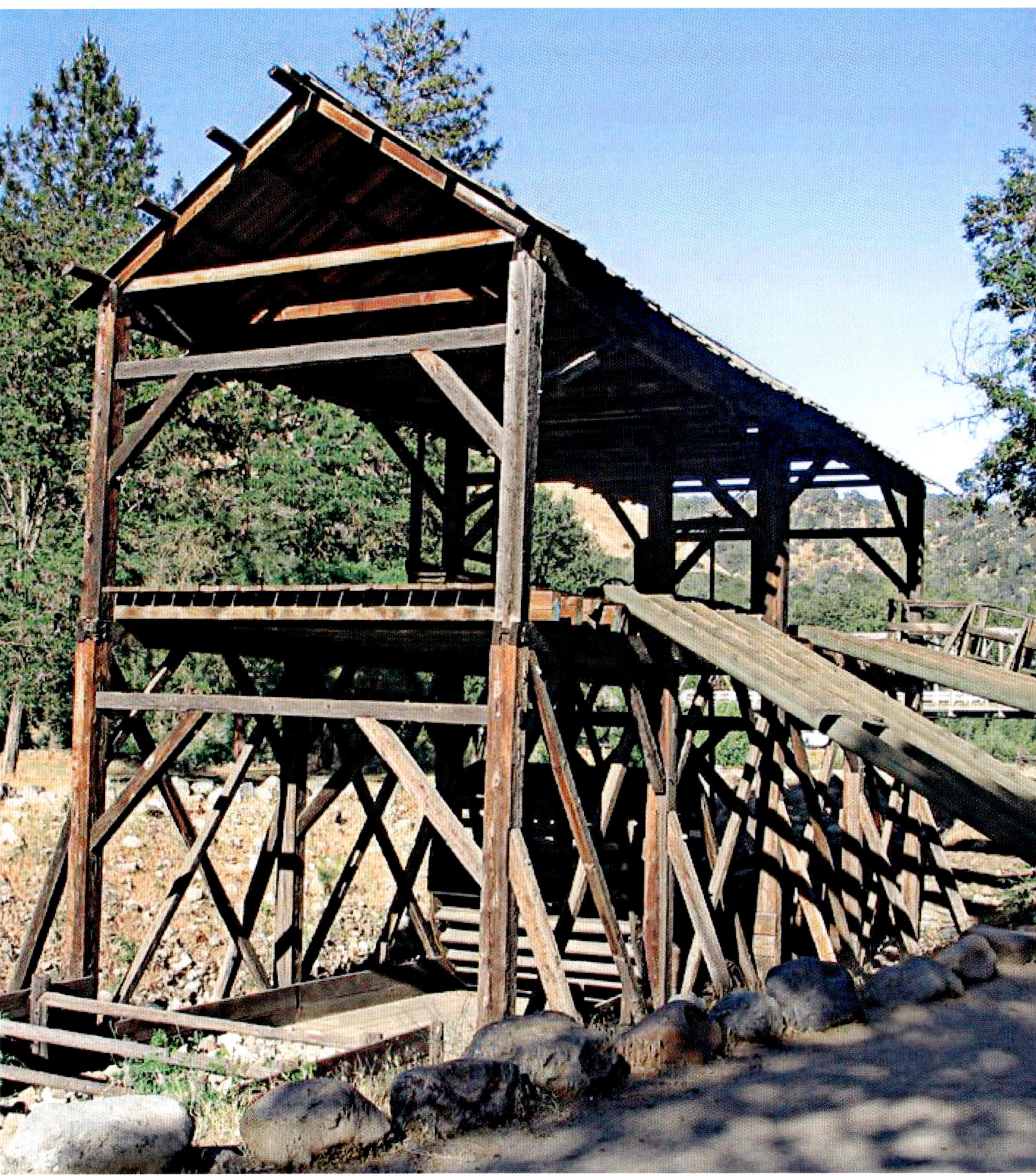

OPPOSITE RIGHT: Photographers set up shop in the gold fields to take advantage of "49ers" who wanted to send photos to loved ones back East and convince them they were prospering.

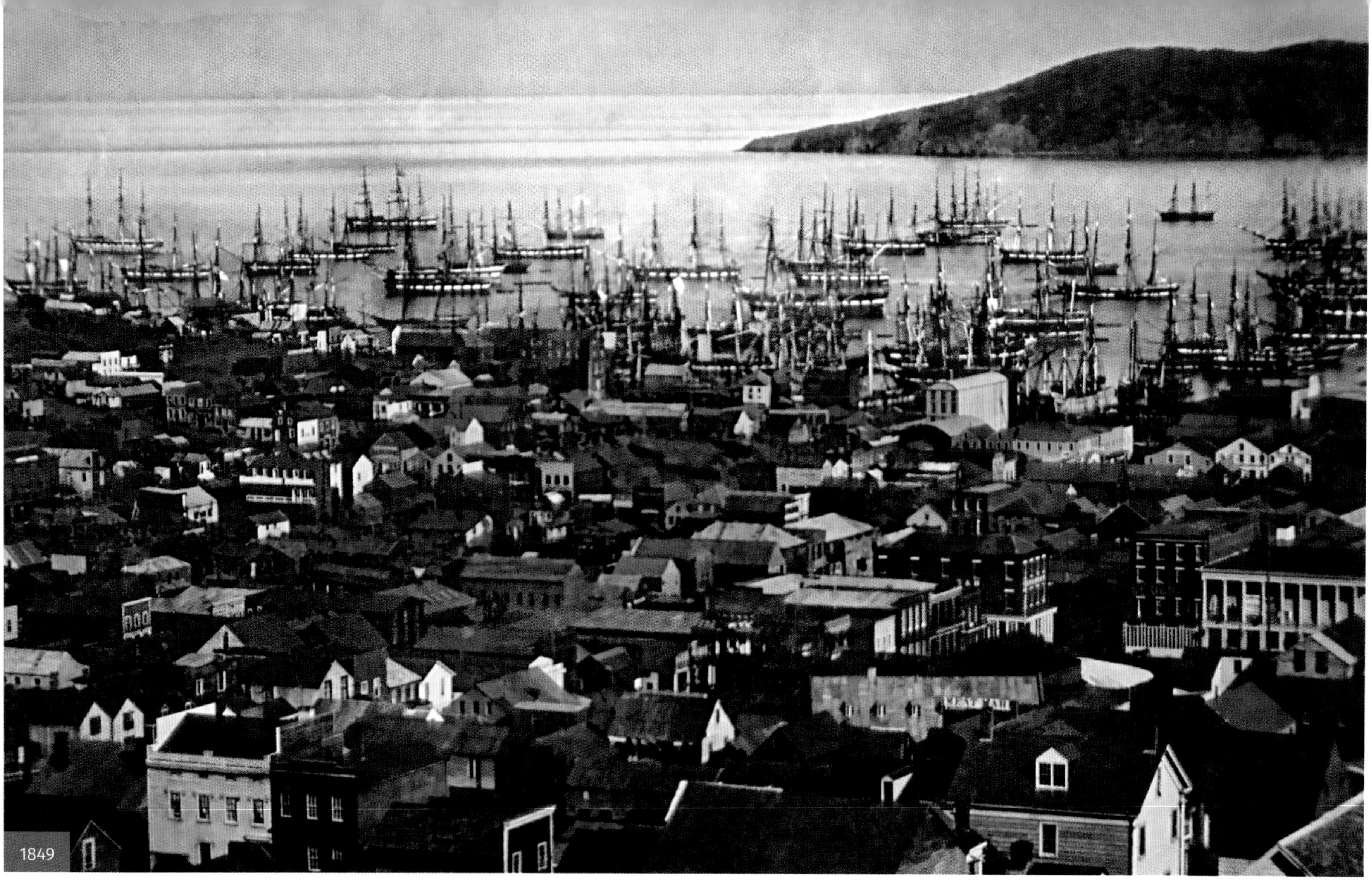

1849

SAN FRANCISCO, CALIFORNIA

The Gold Rush turned a small harbor town into a city

As news of the gold discovery spread to the East Coast and around the world, settlers flocked to the new US territory of California. Prior to the Gold Rush, San Francisco—then called Yerba Buena—was a modest settlement with fewer than 1,000 residents, mostly traders, Native Americans, and Californios (Mexican settlers). However, within a few years, it would become the fastest-growing city in America, propelled by waves of immigrants and booming commerce.

In 1849 alone, San Francisco's population skyrocketed from around 1,000 to over 25,000. By 1852, the population had surpassed 36,000, transforming the quiet port of a few streets into a chaotic boomtown. The main vintage photo of 1849 shows numerous ships moored off the shoreline today occupied by the Ferry Building; while the inset

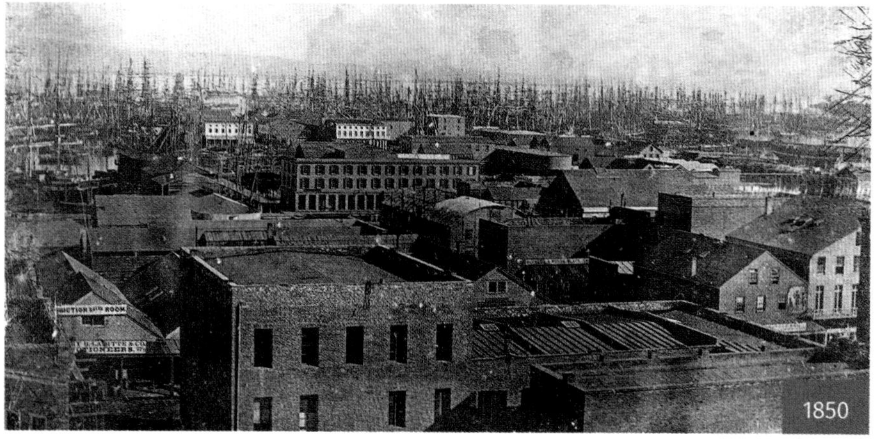

1850

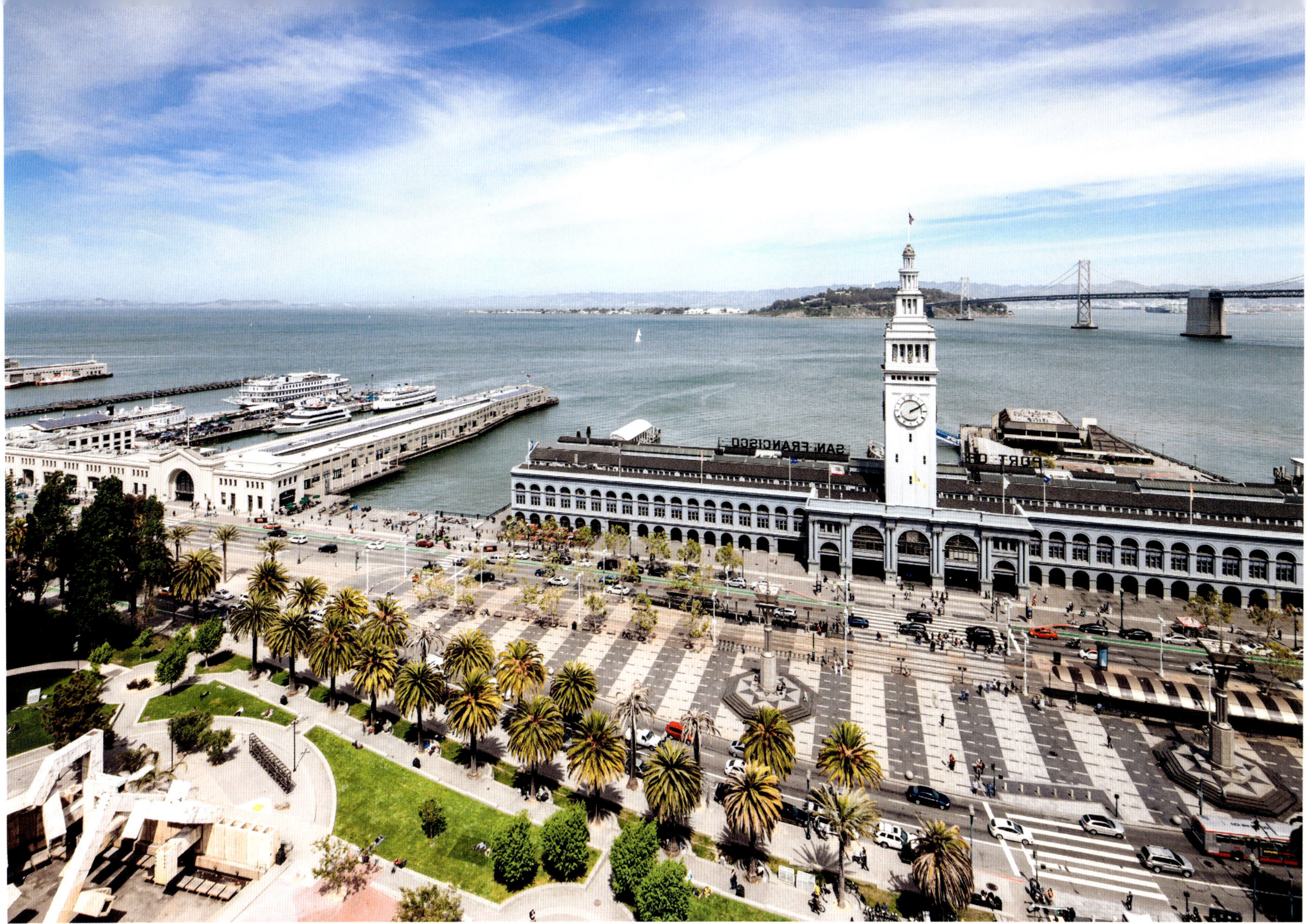

photo reveals how many ships had been moored and abandoned there by 1850.

Hastily built wooden structures lined the muddy streets, and with little planning the city expanded rapidly, often haphazardly. Crime and lawlessness were rampant; gambling halls, saloons, and brothels flourished. Fires were a constant threat, and between 1849 and 1851, the city experienced at least seven major fires that destroyed large portions of the downtown area.

Despite these early struggles, the Gold Rush spurred tremendous economic growth. San Francisco quickly developed a thriving port economy. Goods, mining supplies, and people flowed through its docks. Entrepreneurs and merchants made fortunes by selling tools, clothing, and food to miners at jacked-up prices.

The shipping industry boomed. So many abandoned ships crowded the bay—left behind by crews who deserted to search for gold—that some were repurposed as warehouses, hotels, and even prisons. The hulks were later sunk and used to create the base for land reclamation. Financial institutions like Wells Fargo and the Bank of California were founded to serve the growing economy, while real estate speculation soared as land values rose.

The Gold Rush also brought immense cultural change. Immigrants from around the world poured into the city, especially the industrious Chinese, creating one of the most diverse urban populations. This led to the development of vibrant ethnic communities, including Chinatown, which remains a central part of the city today.

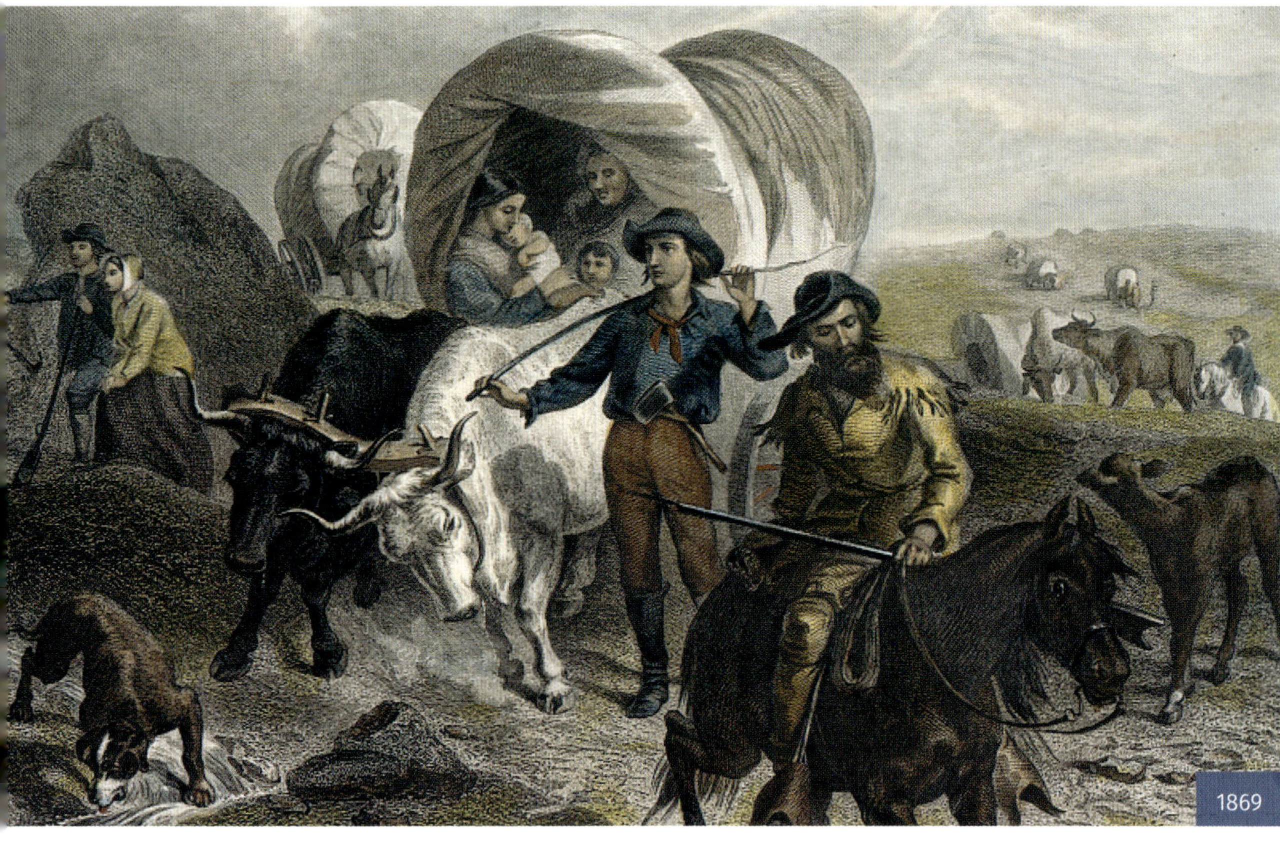

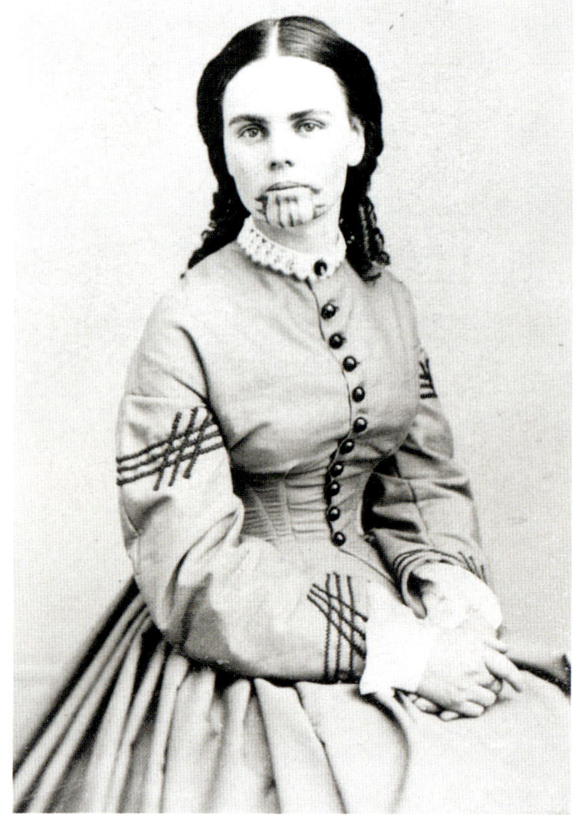

OATMAN, ARIZONA

Like the Donner Party, Olive Oatman represented a journey west with fatal consequences

Olive Oatman was the sole survivor of a family heading west. She was one of seven children in a former Mormon family that had joined a breakaway sect led by James Brewster. In 1850, the Brewsterites set out for California, seeking religious freedom and a new start.

But as the group traveled west, disagreements splintered the party. Olive's family, the Oatmans, broke off and attempted to reach California alone. In 1851, near the Gila River in present-day Arizona, the family was attacked by a group of Native Americans, likely Yavapai. The attack killed most of the family, leaving only 14-year-old Olive and her younger sister, Mary Ann, alive.

The group held the sisters in brutal conditions, treating them more as slaves than adopted members of the tribe. After about a year, the girls were traded to a group of Mojave people. The Mojave treated them much better, and according to many accounts, the girls were adopted into the tribe. Olive and Mary Ann were given tattoos on their chins—traditional Mojave markings for tribal identification and beliefs about the afterlife.

Mary Ann died of starvation during a severe drought, but Olive, now the only survivor, remained with the Mojave for several years. By 1856, word had reached American officials that a white girl was living with a Mojave tribe. Through negotiations and pressure from authorities, the Mojave ultimately agreed to release her. Olive, then about 19 years old, was brought to Fort Yuma, where she was recognized and eventually reunited with surviving relatives.

Her return to white society was a national sensation. In 1857, with the help of a Methodist minister, Royal B. Stratton, Olive's story was published in a bestselling book, *Life Among the Indians*.

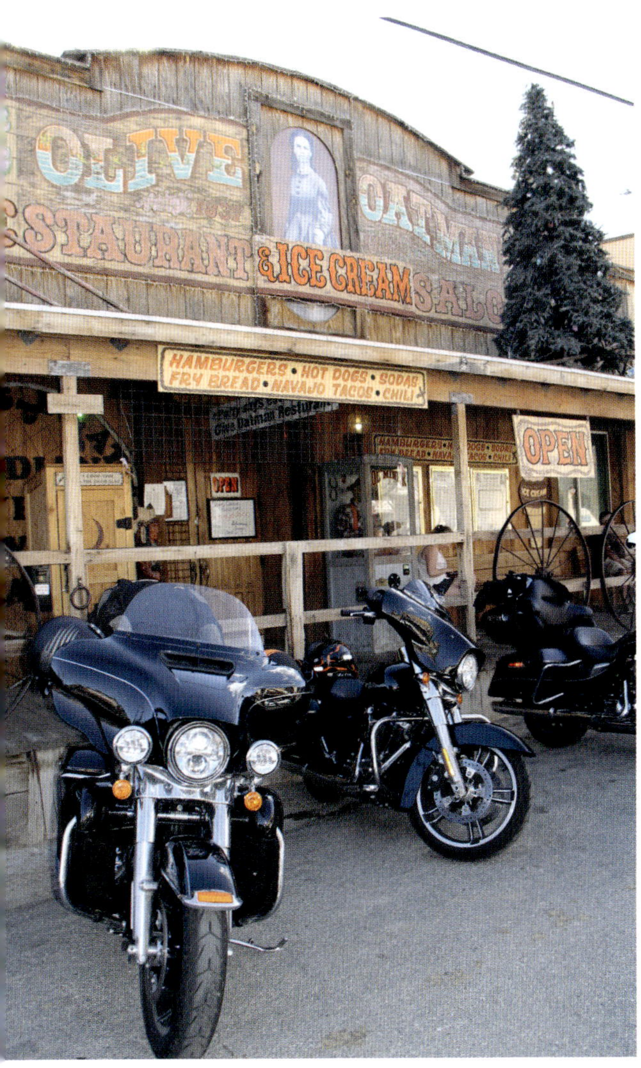

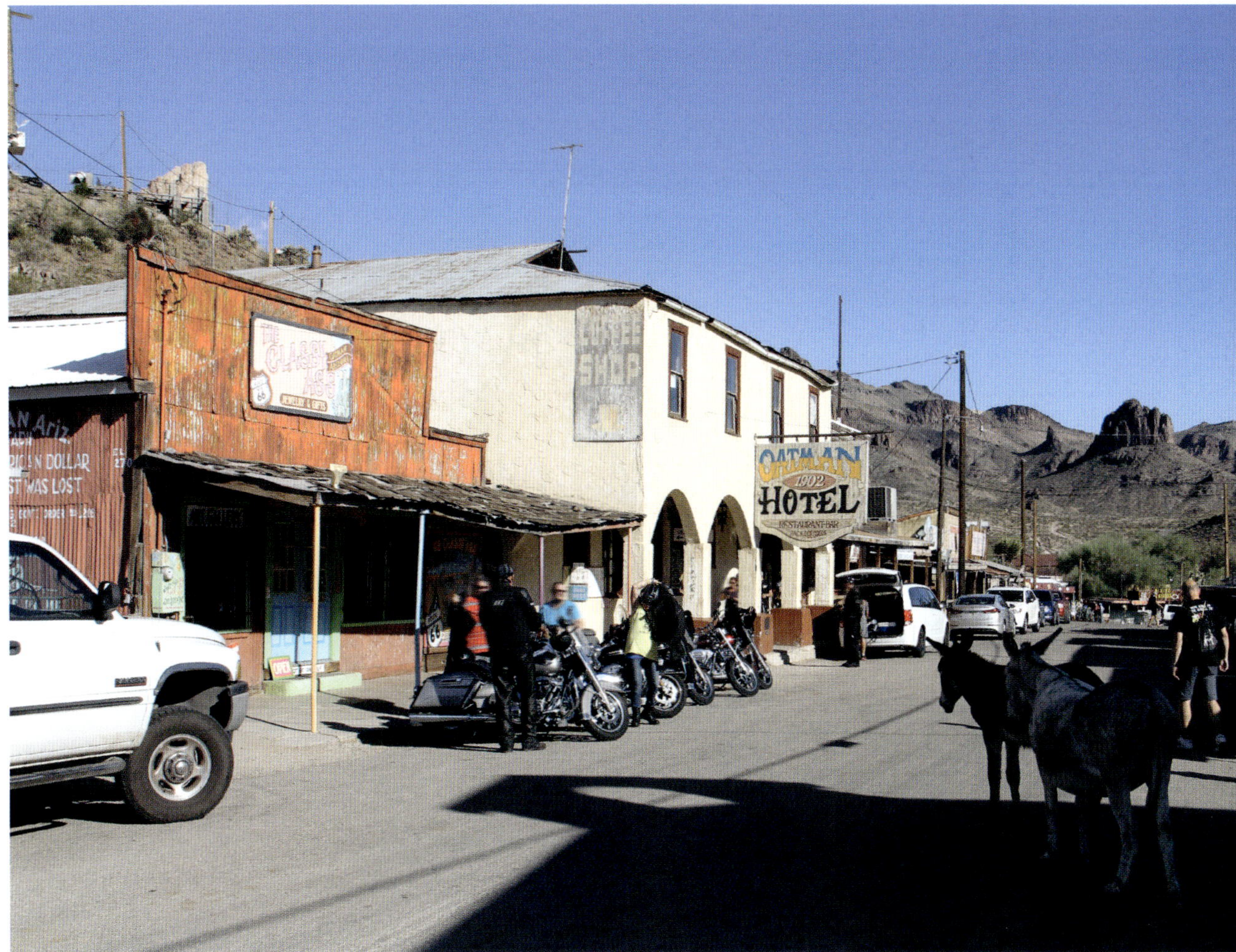

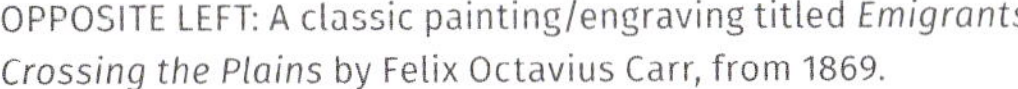

OPPOSITE LEFT: A classic painting/engraving titled *Emigrants Crossing the Plains* by Felix Octavius Carr, from 1869.

OPPOSITE RIGHT: Olive Oatman photographed around 1863. The historic town of Olive City, in Arizona, is also named in her honor.

ABOVE AND RIGHT: Two images from modern-day Oatman. The town's boardwalk was added for the movie *How the West Was Won*.

A mine near where Olive was released was named in her honor and a boomtown sprang up after huge deposits of gold were discovered in 1908 and again in 1915. The population of Oatman peaked at over 10,000 before the mines closed. The population dropped but Oatman could still depend on the steady traffic on Route 66—until September 17, 1952.

Twenty-four hours after Oatman was bypassed in 1952, six of the seven gas stations in town had closed. The population plummeted to about 60 people. But Oatman found gold in Route 66 tourism. About 500,000 tourists a year are drawn to the Wild West atmosphere (part of the town was rebuilt for the movie *How the West Was Won*). When the mines closed, the prospectors turned their burros loose, and their descendants still rule the street, nuzzling tourists for handouts and decorating the wooden sidewalks. A saloon bears the portrait of Olive Oatman, an extraordinary survivor.

SOD HOUSES, NEBRASKA

There were few natural resources to build a home on the great plains

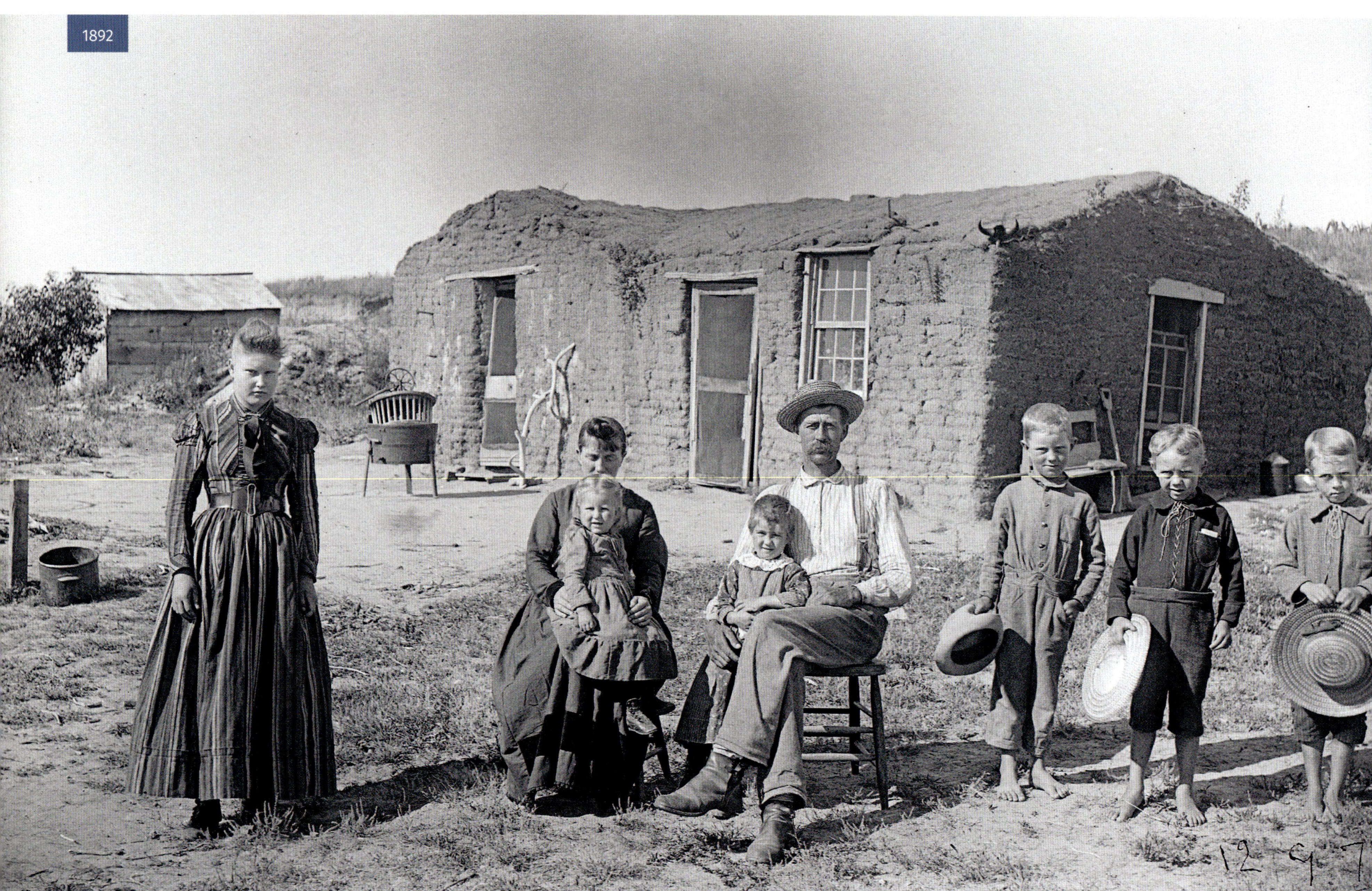

1892

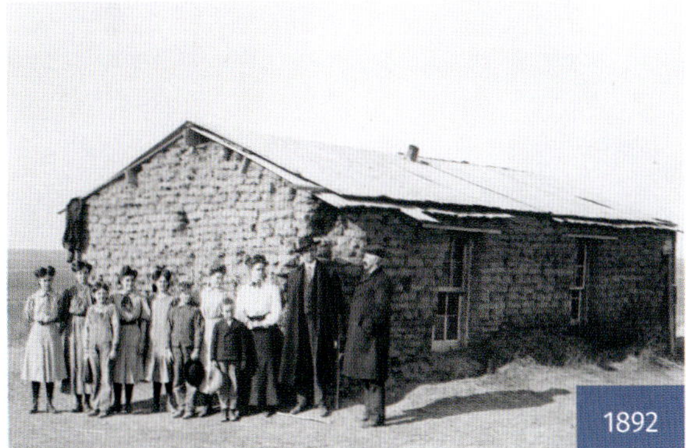

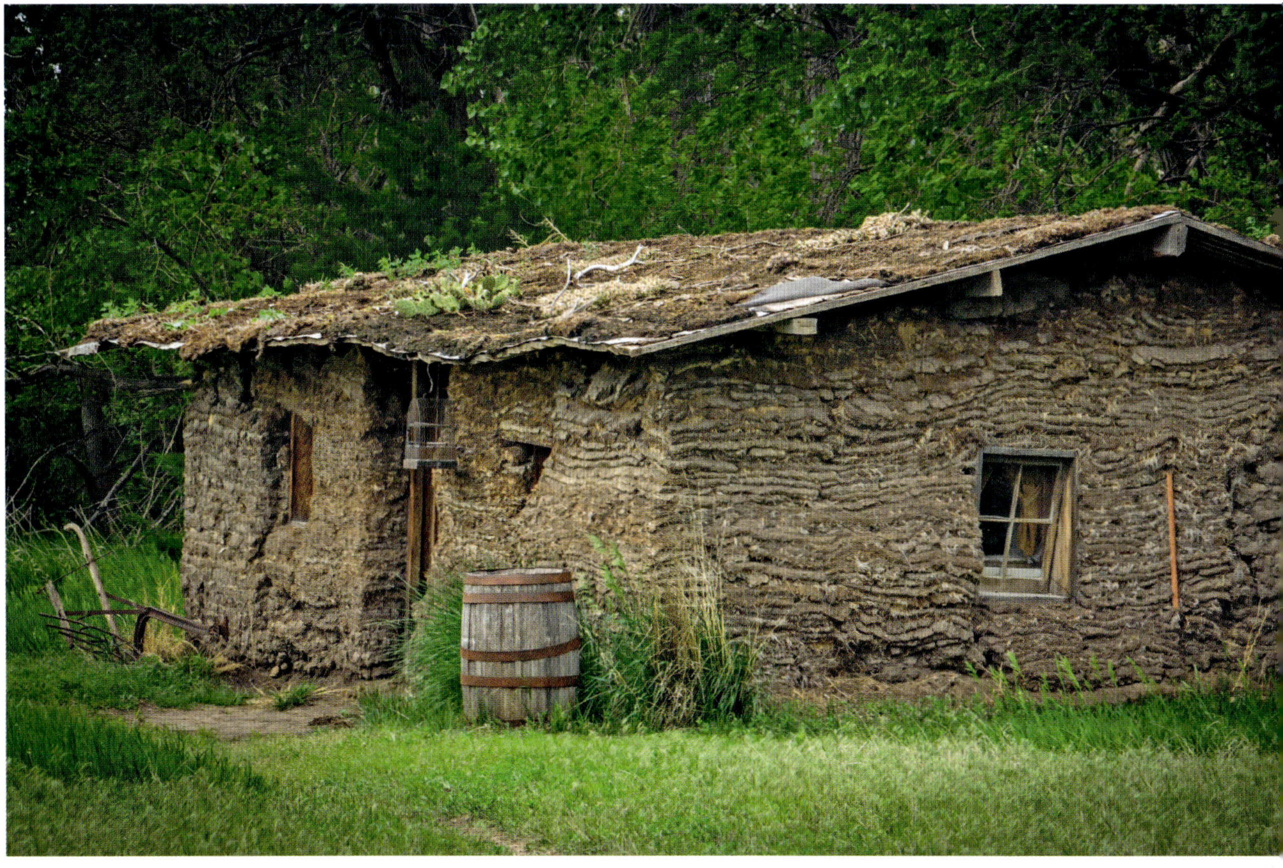

The Homestead Act of 1862 granted to any US citizen 160 acres of land in the West to settle and farm for at least five years. There had been opposition to the idea of homesteaders from slave-owning Southern plantation owners. They also feared that increasing the voter eligibility, based as it was on property ownership, could directly undermine their political dominance. But the outcome of the Civil War put paid to plantation power and so the homesteading pioneers prospered. However, the central and western regions of Nebraska, covered in vast stretches of grassland, posed a problem: there were few trees for lumber. In response settlers adapted by cutting sod bricks from the earth. These bricks, typically about two feet long, one foot wide, and four inches thick, were made by slicing into the dense, root-bound prairie grass with special plows known as "breaking plows." The strong grass roots held the soil together, making it surprisingly durable for construction. Those in Nebraska who lived in sod houses (or "soddys") were called "sodders."

Building a sod house was labor intensive but cost effective. Walls were laid like bricks, overlapping and sometimes reinforced with wooden posts or willows when available. Roofs were often made of wooden frames (when wood could be found) covered with layers of sod or canvas. Their thick walls provided excellent protection against the prairie's blistering summer heat and bitter winter cold. Not surprisingly few sod houses have survived

After the first five years of farming a homestead, the homesteader could apply for a "patent" or deed of official ownership, of the land. They needed to prove that they had lived there for five years, built a dwelling, and cultivated and improved the land (usually by farming part of it).

The main sod house image with the trio of barefoot boys was taken eight miles north and one mile east of Mason City in Custer County, Nebraska. It belonged to Edward Marsh, and the portrait of the homesteader and his family taken in 1892 by Solomon D. Butcher is one of a fascinating series held by the Library of Congress and by the Nebraska state library.

Homesteading continued into the early twentieth century. The Kinkaid Act (1904) increased homestead claims from 160 to 640 acres, recognizing that the arid sandhills of Nebraska required more land for sustainable ranching.

Today, few original sod houses remain, as most eventually deteriorated or were dismantled. However, historical reconstructions and preserved sites, such as those at the Sod House Museum in Gothenburg, Nebraska, keep the memory of this architectural tradition alive.

ABOVE: Raising a family of eight children in a one-roomed cabin was not easy. Laura Ingalls Wilder depicted a romanticized view of the life in *Little House on the Prairie*, but her own memoir, *Pioneer Girl*, reveals a more down-to-earth reality that was often omitted from the children's books.

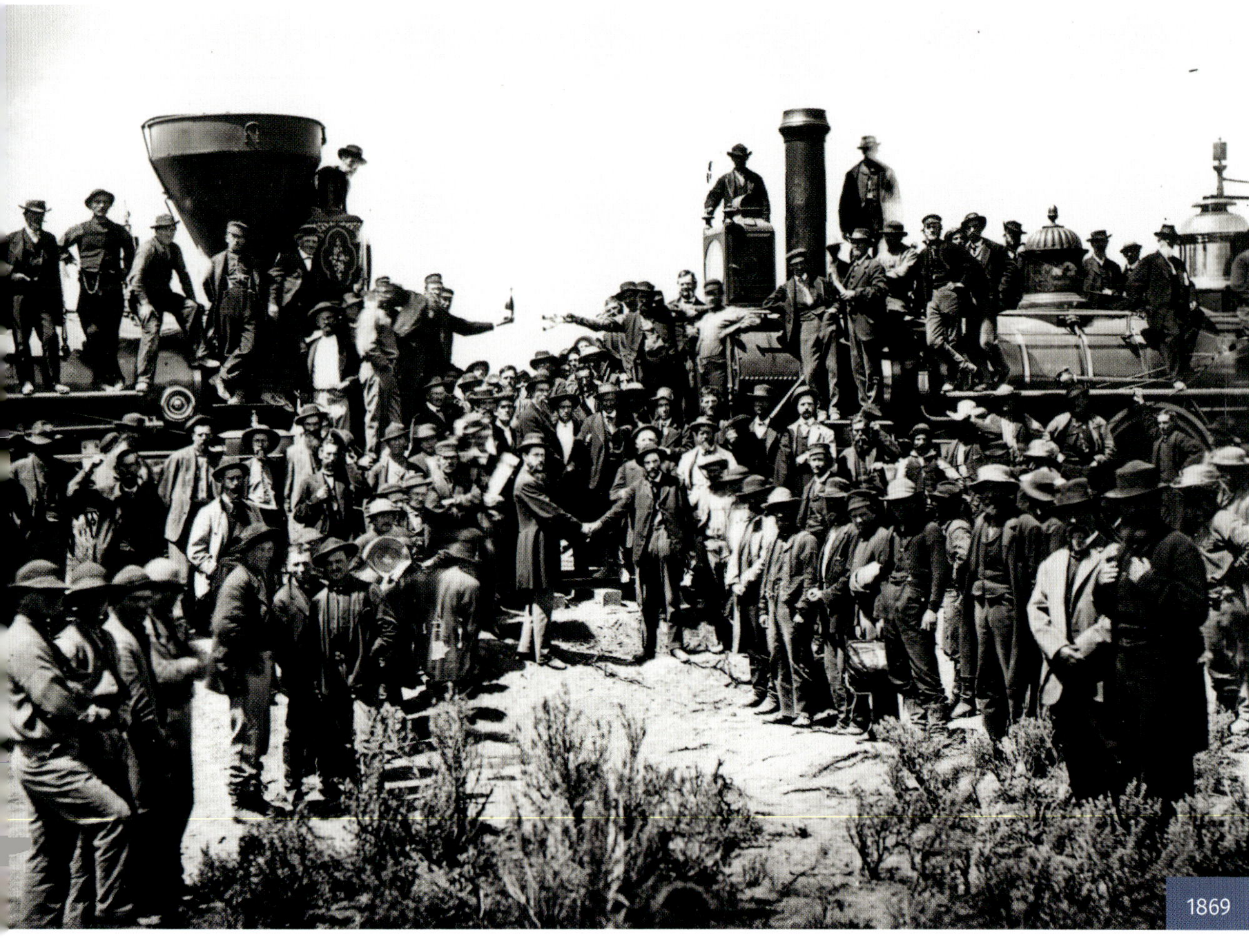
1869

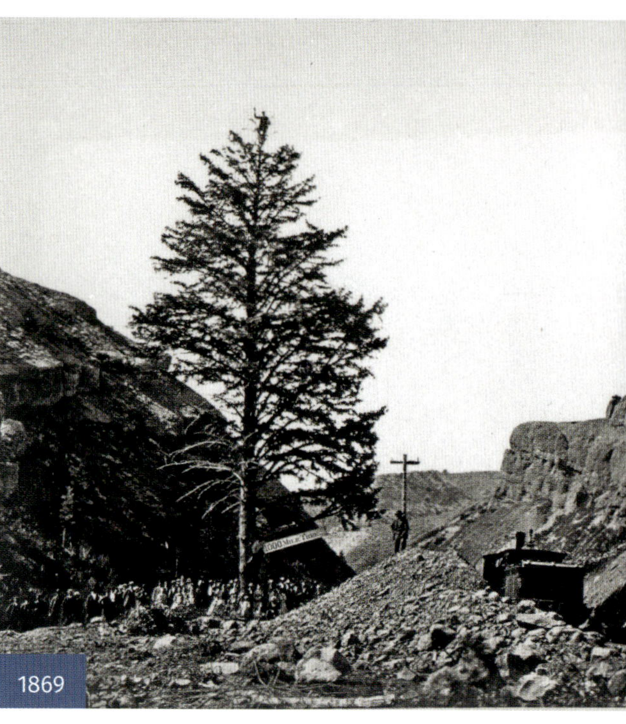
1869

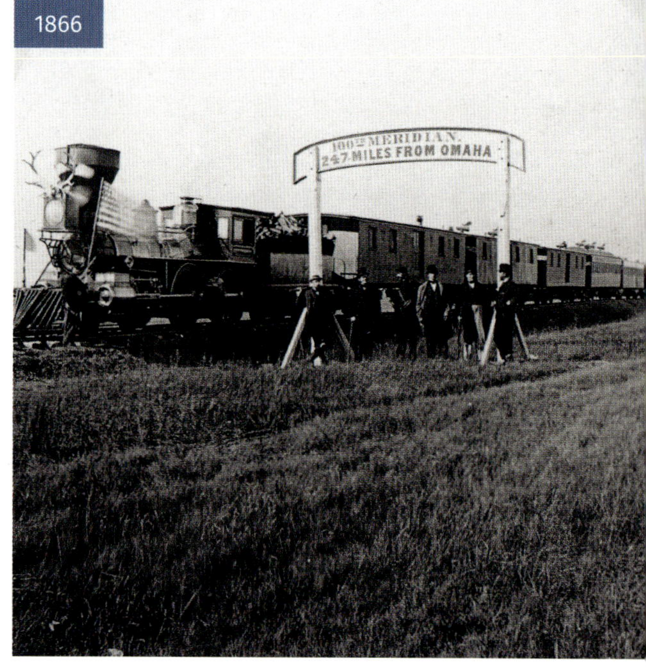

1866

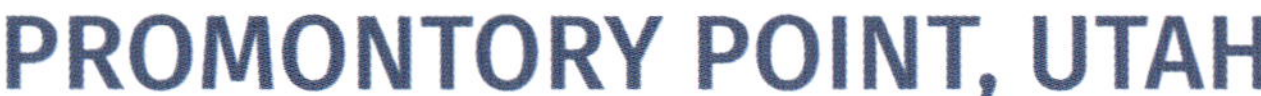

PROMONTORY POINT, UTAH

Where the Union Pacific met the Central Pacific Railroad

As the railroads headed west, so the commemorative photos needed to be taken. On October 6, 1866, out on the prairie, 247 miles west of Omaha, the directors of the Union Pacific Railroad collected under a sign they had erected that announced proudly that their railroad had reached the 100th Meridian west of Greenwich. This was an important occasion as it signified the nominal boundary between the eastern and western United States. Ahead lay the Great Plains and an indigenous population hostile to the arrival of the "iron horse."

In January 1869, at an elevation of over 5,000 feet and exactly 1,000 miles from where they had set out at Council Bluffs, Iowa, the builders of the Union Pacific Railroad came across an isolated 90-foot tree in the Wilhelmina Pass of Weber Canyon. This would be known as the 1000-mile tree. When the passenger trains went into operation, riders were given the opportunity to

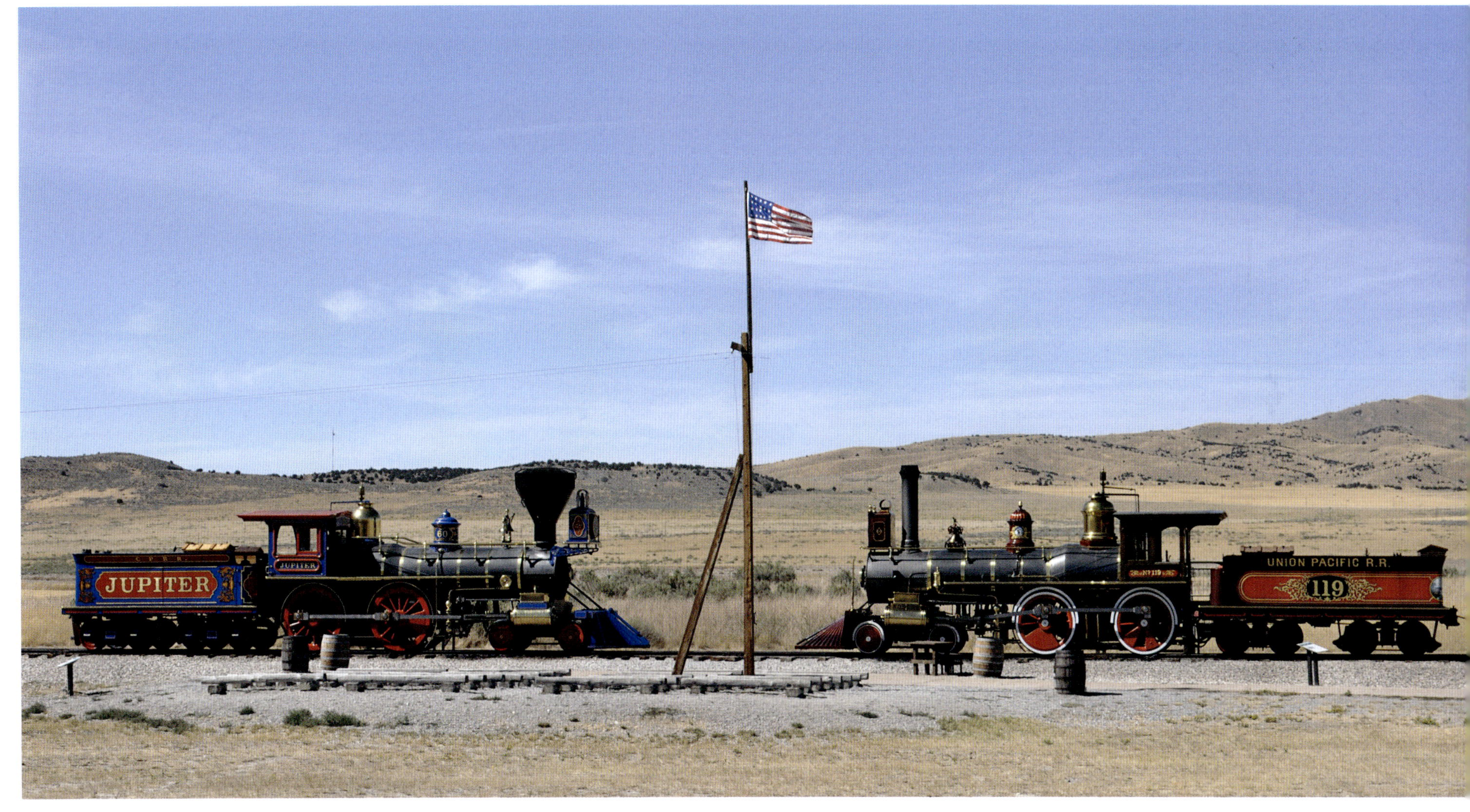

view it up close. The engineer stopped the train allowing them to get out and inspect it. The tree lasted only thirty years before dying, and Union Pacific planted a replacement in 1982—though trains no longer stop to view the successor—and technically it is now the 960-mile tree, after 40 miles were shortened from the original route.

The main photo opposite, from Promontory Summit, Utah, was taken soon afterward on May 10, 1869. It shows the joining of the transcontinental railroad: the Union Pacific arriving from the east and the Central Pacific from the west. This momentous event involved driving in three spikes—one silver, one gold and one an alloy of gold, silver, and iron. It was officiated by Reverend John Todt who called it the "Wedding of the Rails" ceremony. Though it is often referred to as the "Golden Spike"' ceremony.

Although the line has subsequently been rerouted, the Golden Spike National Historic Site maintains 1.7 miles of track on which have been placed two replicas of the engines involved in the original ceremony—Jupiter and 119. The original Jupiter is on display at the Smithsonian National Museum of American History in Washington, DC.

OPPOSITE TOP: The 1000-mile tree.

OPPOSITE BOTTOM: Celebrating the railroad's arrival at the 100th Meridian, 247 miles from Omaha.

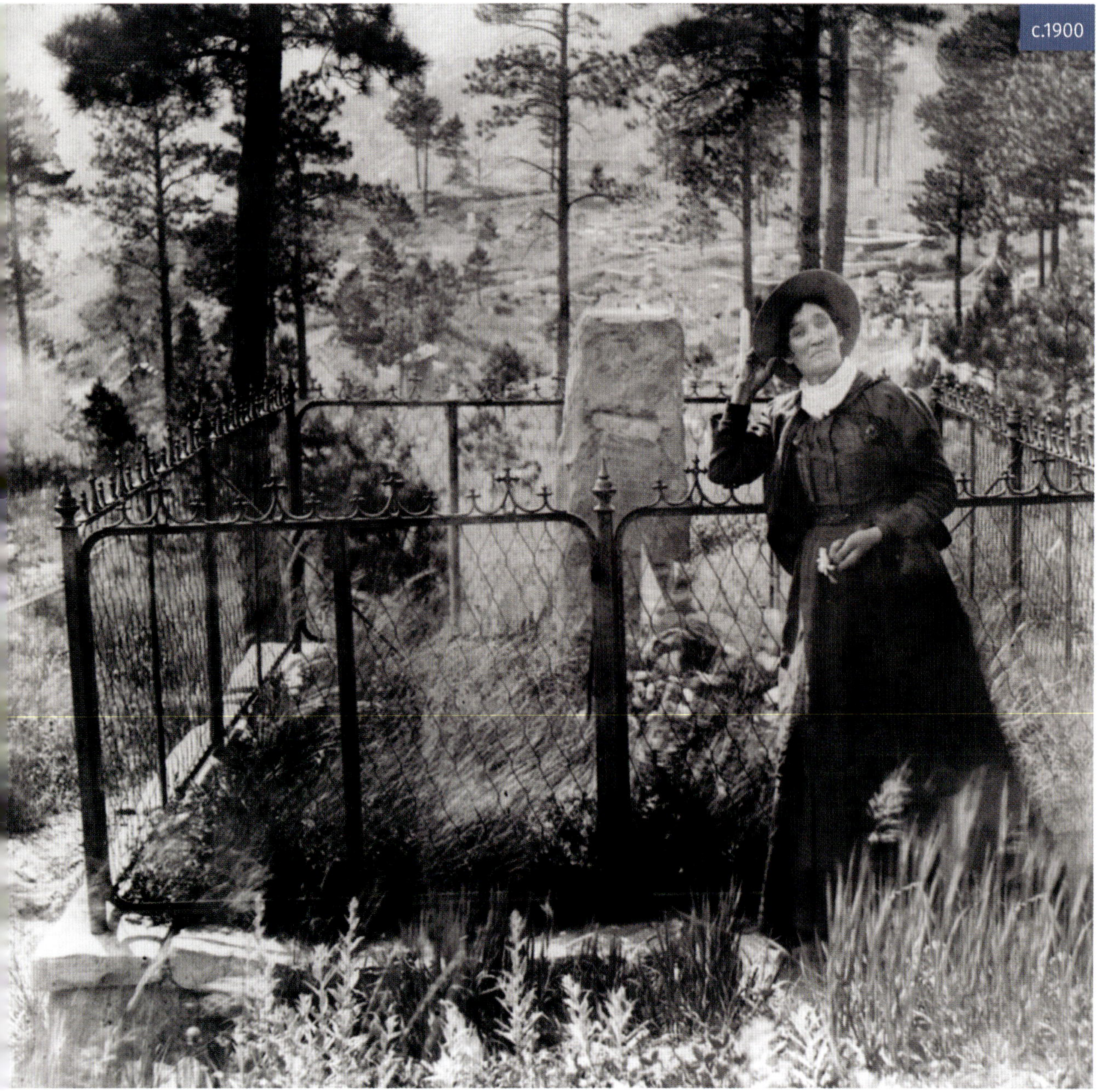

c.1900

WILD BILL HICKOK, DEADWOOD, SOUTH DAKOTA

Frontier scout, lawman, gambler, and holder of the "dead man's hand"

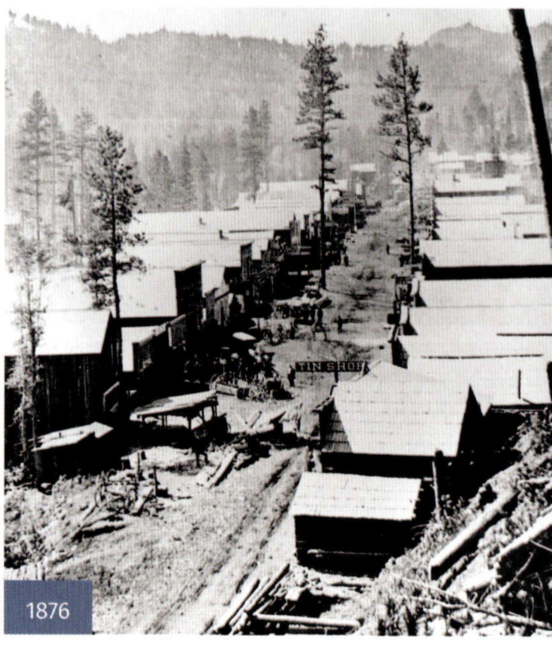

1876

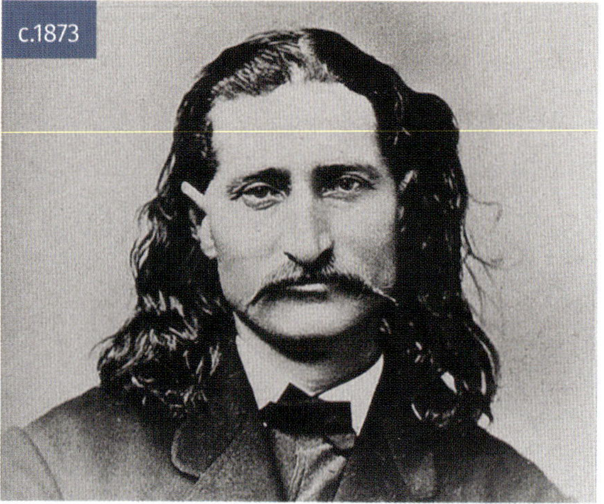

c.1873

ABOVE: Hickok was not shy about being photographed, and in his time appeared with Buffalo Bill Cody, both dressed in city duds.

TOP: Deadwood in South Dakota was a typical Gold Rush town. This photo is from the year in which Wild Bill was shot.

James Butler "Wild Bill" Hickok was a legendary figure of the Old West, known for his reputation as a lawman, gambler, gunslinger, and scout. Born in Troy Grove, Illinois, Hickok left home in his late teens to work as a stagecoach driver and later as a lawman. His early adult years were marked by various frontier occupations, but his fame began to rise after the Civil War in which he served as a Union scout and spy.

Hickok's reputation as a gunslinger was ensured in 1865 when he killed Davis Tutt in a quick-draw, public duel in Springfield, Missouri. Newspapers exaggerated the story, making Hickok a household name. Although his name was often misspelled as Hitchcock.

Over time he served as a US marshal in various frontier towns, including Hays and Abilene, Kansas. A skilled gambler, Hickok spent much of his later life at poker tables, though his vision deteriorated in his final years, contributing to his downfall. He was shot in the back of the head while playing poker in Deadwood, Dakota Territory, in 1876 by Jack McCall. At the time of his death, Hickok was holding a pair of aces and a pair of eights, forever known as the "dead man's hand."

Calamity Jane (Martha Jane Cannary), herself a frontierswoman and scout, is often romantically linked to Hickok, though the true nature of their relationship remains unclear. The two were contemporaries and both spent time in Deadwood. Jane herself claimed they were close and even asserted that they were married—a claim most historians dismiss due to lack of evidence.

The turn-of-the-century photo opposite shows Jane at Hickok's gravesite in Mount Moriah Cemetery, Deadwood, and she requested to be buried next to him, a wish that was honored when she died in 1903. Whether their relationship was romantic or platonic, it was certainly close enough for them to spend eternity together.

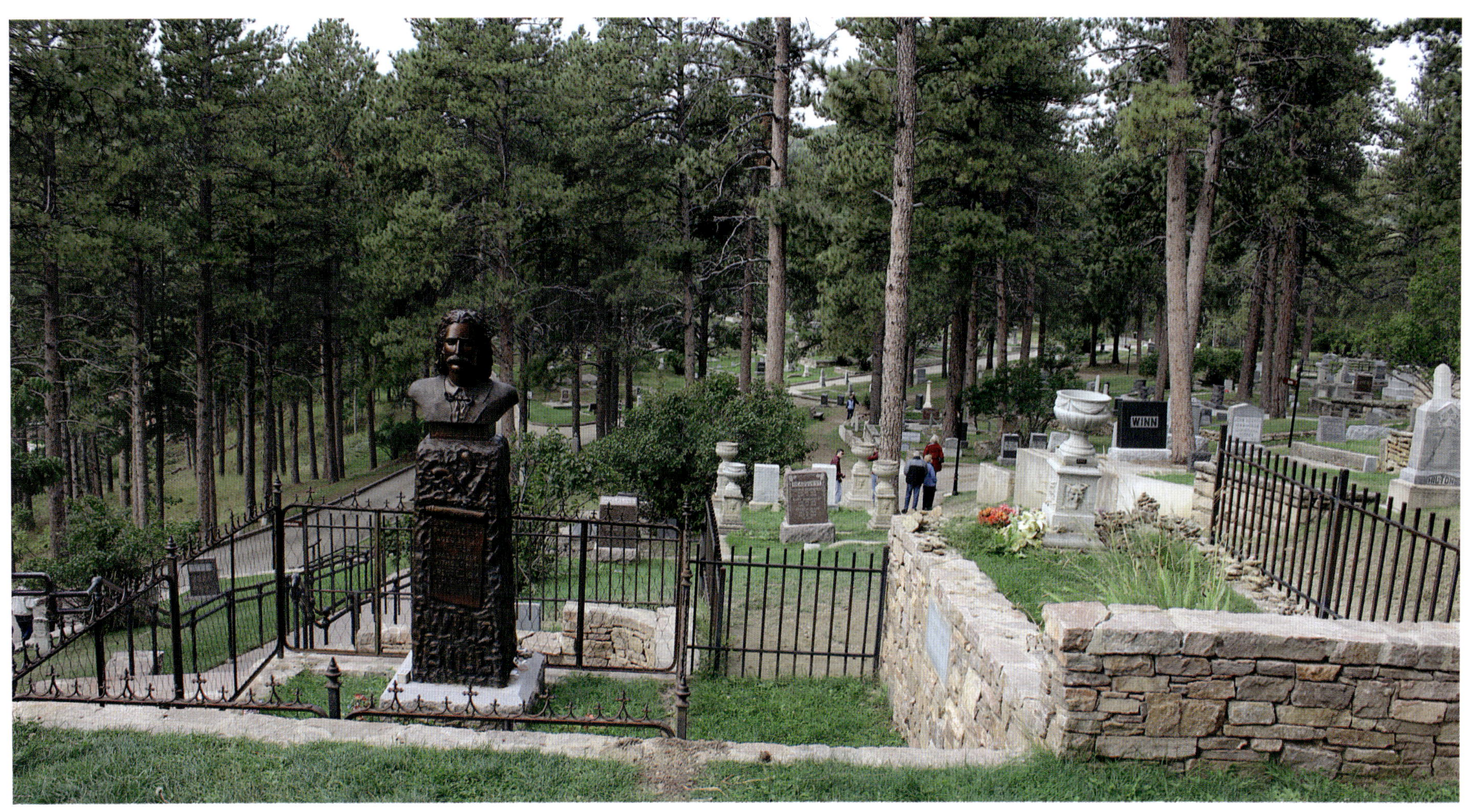

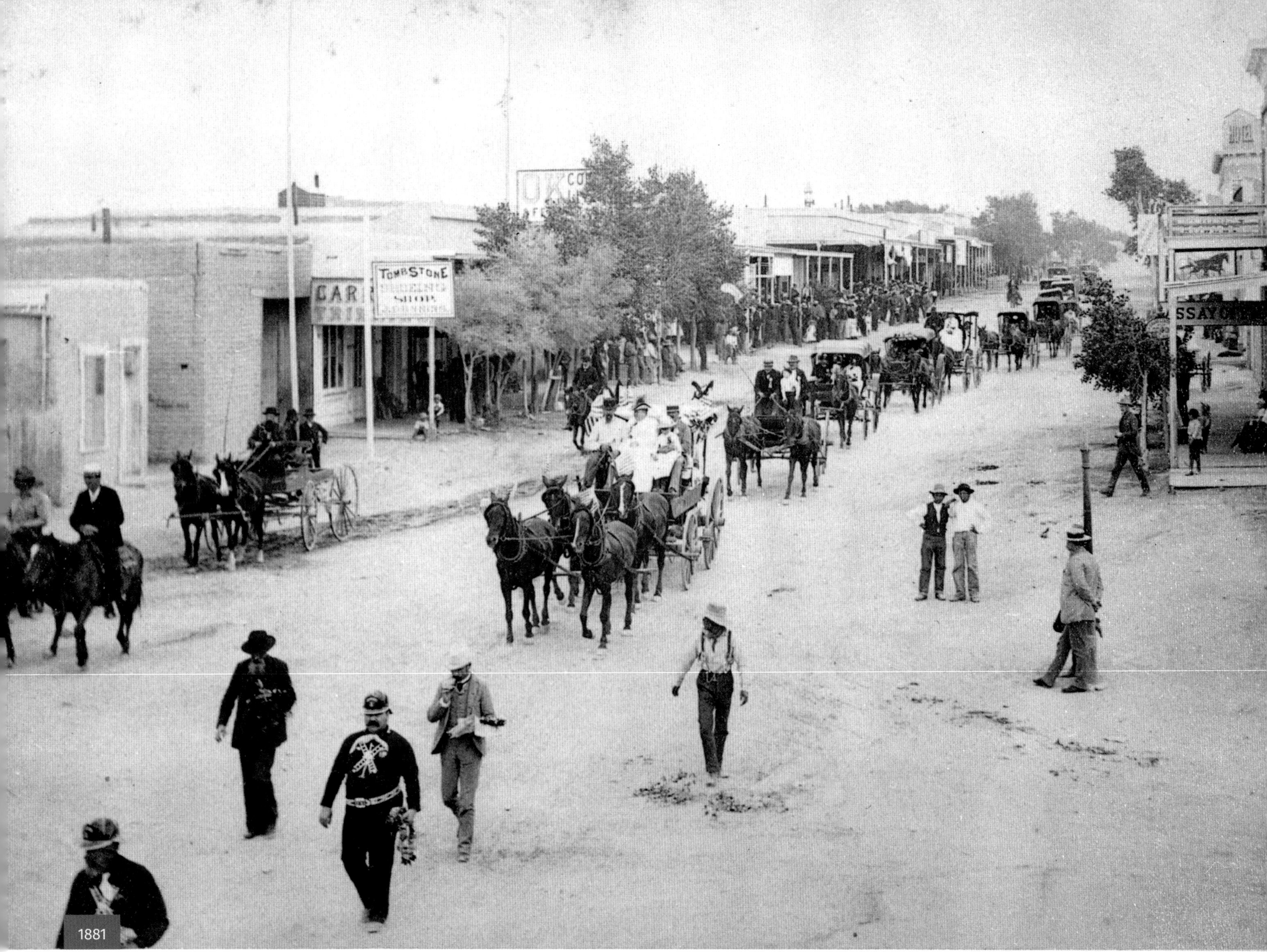

1881

TOMBSTONE, ARIZONA

Law and order was always a problem in mining boomtowns

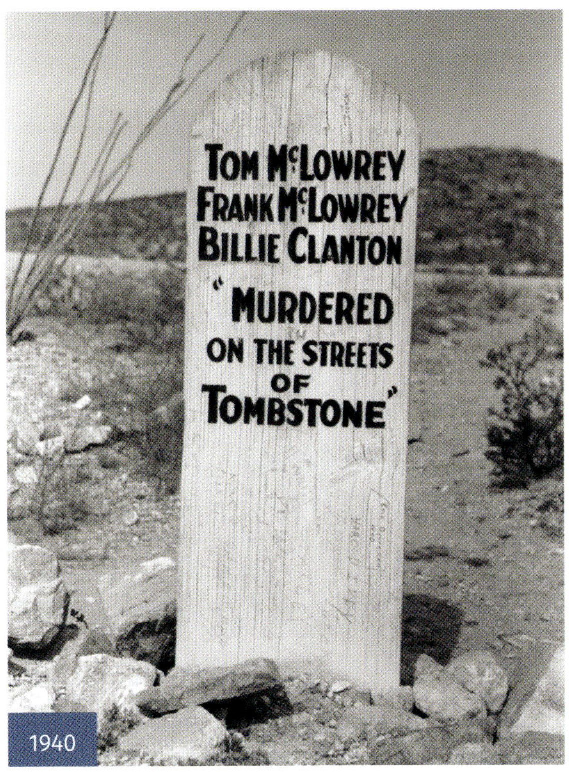

ABOVE: Wooden tombstones in Boot Hill Cemetery have been replaced over the years, but the spelling remains uncorrected...

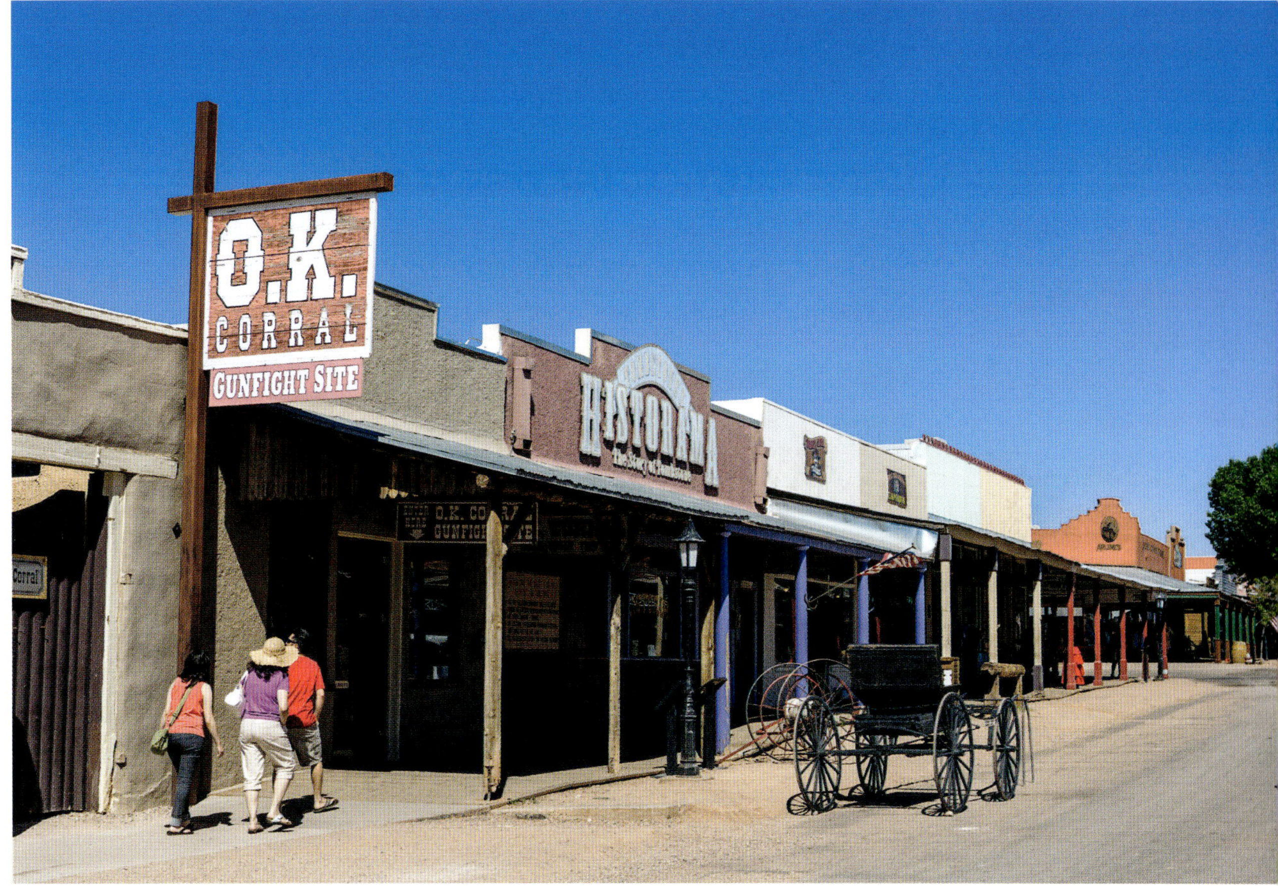

If the name of one town can conjure up images of the Old West at its wildest, that name has to be Tombstone. Wyatt Earp and his brothers and their shootout with the Clantons is one of the main reasons. The underlying reason that Tombstone became synonymous with the Old West is probably because it was one of the last boomtowns. Founded in 1879 by silver prospector Ed Schieffelin, the new mines boosted the population to around 10,000 in Tombstone's first five years. The fact that the Mexican border was only 30 miles away encouraged smuggling and lawlessness

The shootout at the O.K. Corral took place on October 26, 1881, and was a conflict rooted in long-standing tensions between two groups: the lawmen—Wyatt Earp, his brothers Virgil and Morgan, and their friend Doc Holliday—and a group of outlaws and cowboys, notably the Clantons (Ike and Billy) and the McLaury brothers (Tom and Frank).

The Clantons were suspected of cattle rustling, stagecoach robbery, and the general lawlessness of throwing their weight around. The cowboys arrived in Tombstone, armed and threatening violence. Around 3:00 p.m., near the O.K. Corral (the shootout actually occurred in a nearby vacant lot), the two sides met. The gunfight lasted only about 30 seconds.

Billy Clanton and both McLaury brothers were killed. Virgil and Morgan Earp were wounded, and Doc Holliday received a minor injury. Wyatt Earp emerged unscathed. The event triggered a cycle of revenge, including the assassination of Morgan Earp, and Wyatt's subsequent vendetta ride.

This photo of a procession from 1881, the year of the gunfight, shows the O.K. Corral sign on the left of Main Street. When the water table was breached, the silver mines flooded, the railroad bypassed Tombstone, and it boomed no more. Tombstone risked becoming a ghost town. But in 1929 "the town too tough to die" started Helldorado Days, a yearly festival celebrating its hell-raising history. Tombstone pulled through.

Now the historic town receives half a million visitors a year, keen to see fight reenactments, push through the batwing doors of the Crystal Palace saloon, drink a shot of red eye, and visit the cemetery at Boot Hill, where they will find Billy Clanton and the McLaury Bothers.

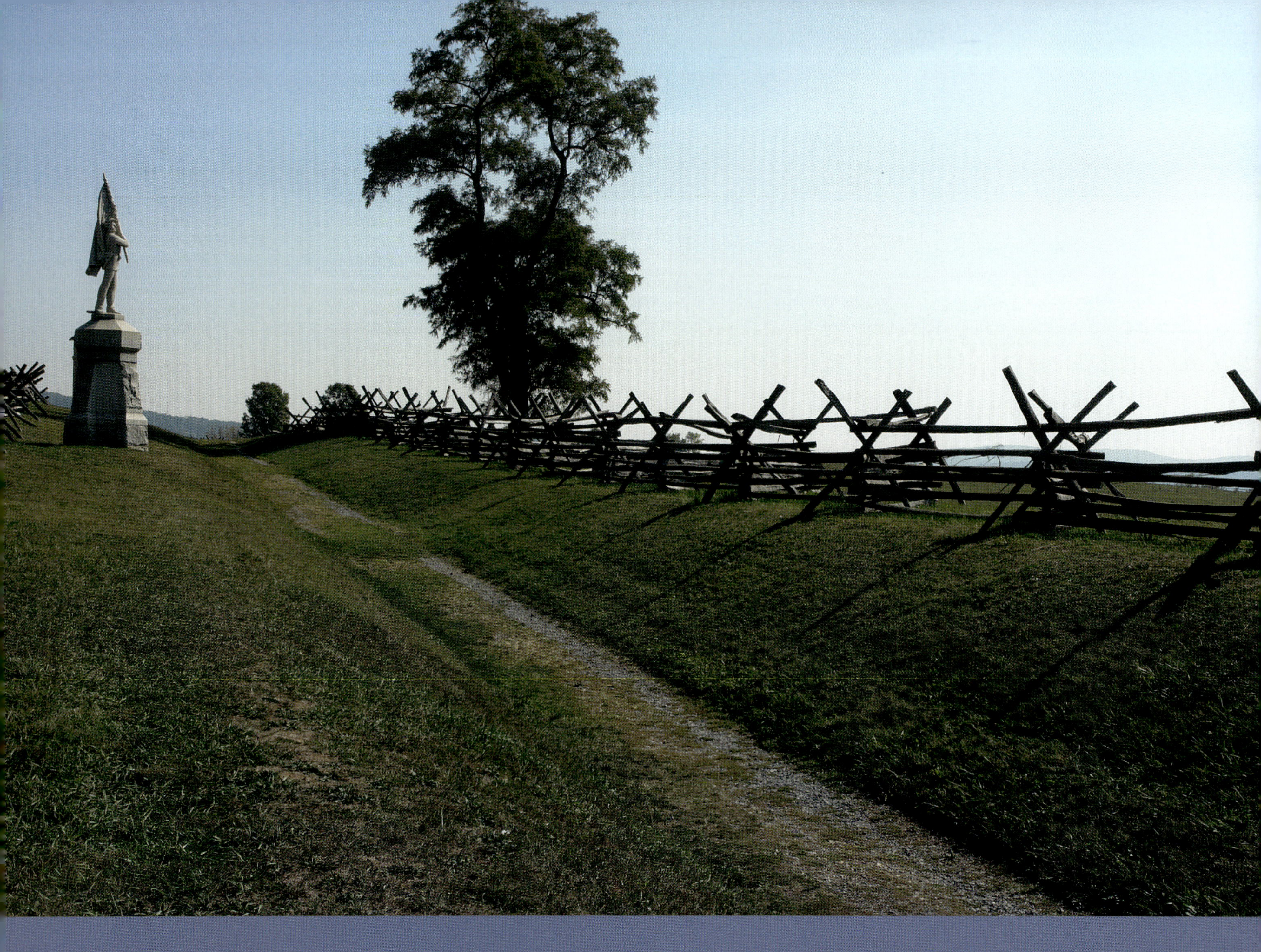

A NATION TORN APART AND REBUILT

By 1860, the United States was bitterly divided over slavery. The Northern states, increasingly industrial and abolitionist, clashed with the Southern states, whose agricultural economies relied heavily on enslaved labor. The debate over whether slavery should expand into the new western territories only further entrenched sectional tensions.

The election of Abraham Lincoln in November 1860 was the breaking point for many in the South. Lincoln, a Republican, opposed the expansion of slavery, though he did not call for its immediate abolition. Indeed, in an August 1862 letter to newspaper editor Horace Greely, he wrote: "If I could save the Union without freeing any slave I would do it." Even so, Southern leaders feared his presidency would spell the end of their way of life.

Before Lincoln even took office, seven Southern states—led by South Carolina—seceded from the Union. In February 1861, they formed the Confederate States of America and elected Jefferson Davis as president. Four more states would later join them after the war began.

THE CIVIL WAR BEGINS

On April 12, 1861, Confederate forces opened fire on Fort Sumter in Charleston Harbor, South Carolina, marking the official start of the American Civil War. Lincoln responded by calling for volunteers to suppress the rebellion and they came forward in droves. The war was fought on multiple fronts. The Union, or the North, enjoyed superior industry, infrastructure, and population, while the Confederacy, or the South, had strong military leadership and the advantage of fighting a defensive war on familiar terrain.

At the Battle of First Bull Run in July 1861 a Confederate victory shattered Northern hopes of a quick war. Antietam (September 1862) the bloodiest single day in American history, gave Lincoln the opportunity to issue the Emancipation Proclamation. On January 1, 1863, Lincoln issued the proclamation, declaring all enslaved people in Confederate territory free. While it did not immediately free all slaves, it transformed the war's purpose—from preserving the Union to ending slavery—and allowed Black Americans to enlist in the Union Army.

GETTYSBURG AND VICKSBURG

Gettysburg in July 1863 proved to be the high water mark of Confederate ambitions. A three-day battle in Pennsylvania, just 80 miles north of Washington, DC, ended Confederate general Robert E. Lee's invasion of the North.

Victory at Vicksburg, one day later on July 4, handed control of the Mississippi River to Union forces led by General Ulysses S. Grant. It had been a long siege and earmarked Grant for the future command of the Union armies.

Lincoln, who had been under immense political pressure, used these victories to rally the Union. In November 1863, he delivered the Gettysburg Address, a brief but powerful speech that redefined the war as a struggle for a "new birth of freedom."

THE WAR'S END

In 1864, General Grant launched a relentless campaign against Lee in Virginia, while General William Tecumseh Sherman conducted his "March to the Sea," devastating Georgia's infrastructure and economy.

By April 1865, Lee's army was surrounded. On April 9, he surrendered to Grant at Appomattox Court House in Virginia, effectively ending the war. Over 620,000 Americans had died, but the greatest single loss was still to come. Just five days later, on April 14, 1865, Lincoln was assassinated by John Wilkes Booth, a Southern sympathizer, while attending a play at Ford's Theatre in Washington. Lincoln died the next morning, plunging the nation into mourning.

Lincoln's assassination complicated the postwar process of Reconstruction—the effort to reintegrate the Southern states and secure rights for newly freed African Americans. His successor, Andrew Johnson, lacked Lincoln's political skill and vision. While slavery had ended, the South resisted racial equality in any way they could.

WESTWARD EXPANSION AND NATIVE RESISTANCE

Even as the nation healed from civil war, its expansion westward continued. The US government signed treaties with Native American tribes yet still pushed settlers, railroads, and the military into Ancestral lands. This sparked a series of armed conflicts, known collectively as the Indian Wars, which intensified in the 1870s as resistance to US expansion grew.

One of the most famous clashes came at the Battle of the Little Bighorn in June 1876. In violation of treaties, gold prospectors had invaded the Black Hills, sacred to the Lakota Sioux. The US Army was sent to force Native tribes back onto reservations.

Led by General George Armstrong Custer, a detachment of the 7th Cavalry encountered a large encampment of Lakota Sioux, Northern Cheyenne, and Arapaho warriors under leaders including Sitting Bull and Crazy Horse near the Little Bighorn River in Montana.

Custer, underestimating the strength of the Native forces, launched a foolhardy attack and his troops were swiftly overwhelmed. Custer and over 200 of his men were killed. While the battle was a victory for the Native Americans, it prompted national outrage. The US Army redoubled its efforts, eventually forcing the tribes into submission. Sitting Bull would later surrender in 1881, take part in Buffalo Bill's Wild West shows and, was then killed resisting arrest in 1890; in custody, Crazy Horse was bayoneted by a guard in 1877.

TRAGEDY AT WOUNDED KNEE

By the late 1880s, Native resistance had been largely crushed and tribes confined to reservations. But a new spiritual movement—the Ghost Dance—offered hope. It prophesied that Native peoples would regain their lands, the buffalo would return, and white settlers would vanish.

The US government, fearing the Ghost Dance might spark an uprising, moved to suppress it. In December 1890, the Army attempted to disarm a band of Lakota Sioux near Wounded Knee Creek in South Dakota.

On December 29, a shot was fired—by whom remains unclear—and soldiers opened fire on the encampment using a new form of Hotchkiss machine gun. Over 250 Native Americans, including many women and children, were killed. It was not a battle but a massacre.

Wounded Knee marked the end of armed Native resistance in the continental United States and symbolized the brutal consequences of American expansion. Though the Ghost Dance faded, its message of spiritual resistance echoed in generations to come.

FORT SUMTER, CHARLESTON

America's deadliest war exploded into life in Charleston harbor

More than two generations of bitter sectional controversy exploded into armed conflict on April 12, 1861, when Confederate guns fired on Fort Sumter in Charleston Harbor. Ironically, no one was killed during the bombardment. Only after the guns fell silent were two Union soldiers injured firing a salute, making them the first casualties of America's bloodiest war. A few hours later, the Stars and Bars flag of the Confederate states was unfurled over Fort Sumter. Today, Fort Sumter little resembles the three-tiered brick and masonry structure that once dominated Charleston Harbor. The North and the South expended lives and resources liberally in often desperate attempts to hold or capture the fort, which was a symbol for both sides. By the end of the war, the fort's walls had been leveled by a sustained Union siege. Where the Confederate flag once flew, only the ruins of the first-tier gun rooms remain.

The initial bombardment that unleashed the four-year Civil War did little damage to the masonry walls of Fort Sumter. However, heated projectiles fired by the Confederates—known as "hot shot"—set wooden structures within the fort ablaze. In the 1861 image of the fort, the Stars and Bars of the South fly over one of the gutted structures inside the fort.

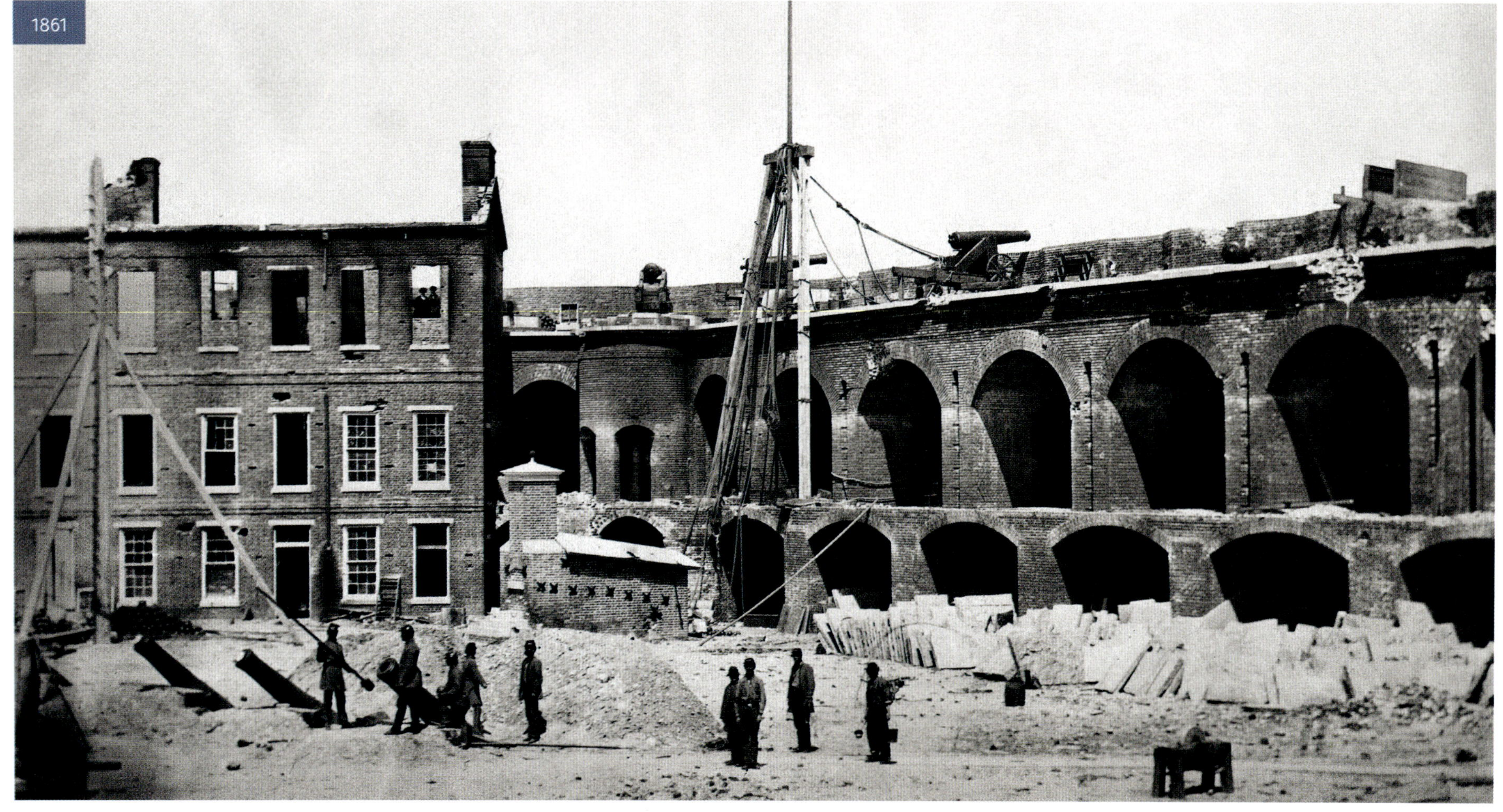

1861

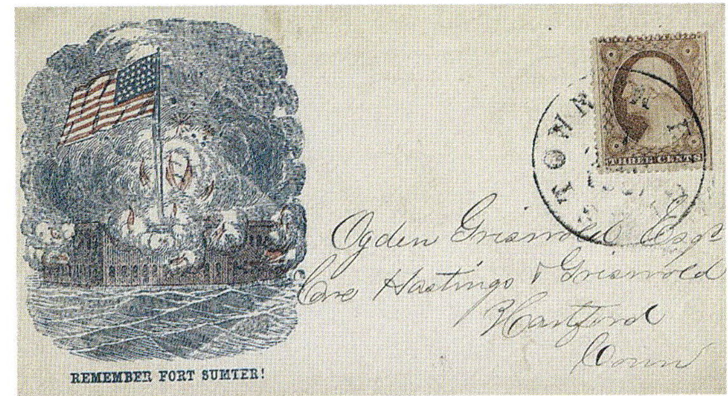

The surrender of Fort Sumter galvanized the North. Prior to the bombardment, there existed strong sentiment in the Northern states to allow the "erring sisters to go in peace," following the Southern states' momentous decision made at the renamed Secession Hall in Charleston. However, the unprovoked attack on Fort Sumter dramatically changed the situation. The response to President Abraham Lincoln's call for 75,000 men to put down the rebellion was overwhelming. Untrained but enthusiastic volunteers flocked to recruiting stations, and the small Union army became a force to be reckoned with practically overnight.

LEFT: Envelope covers like this, inscribed with "Remember Fort Sumter" helped stir sentiment in the North.

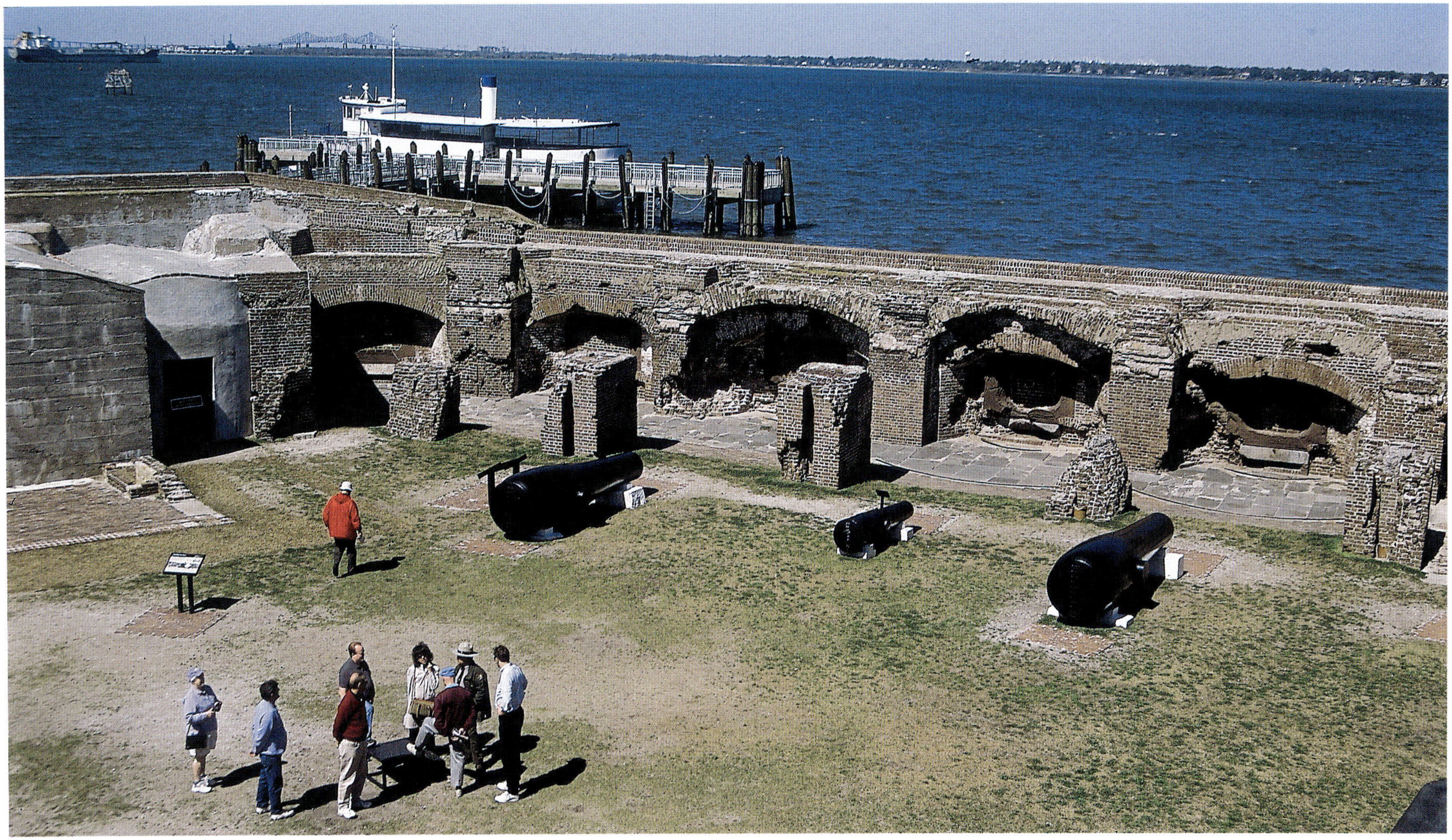

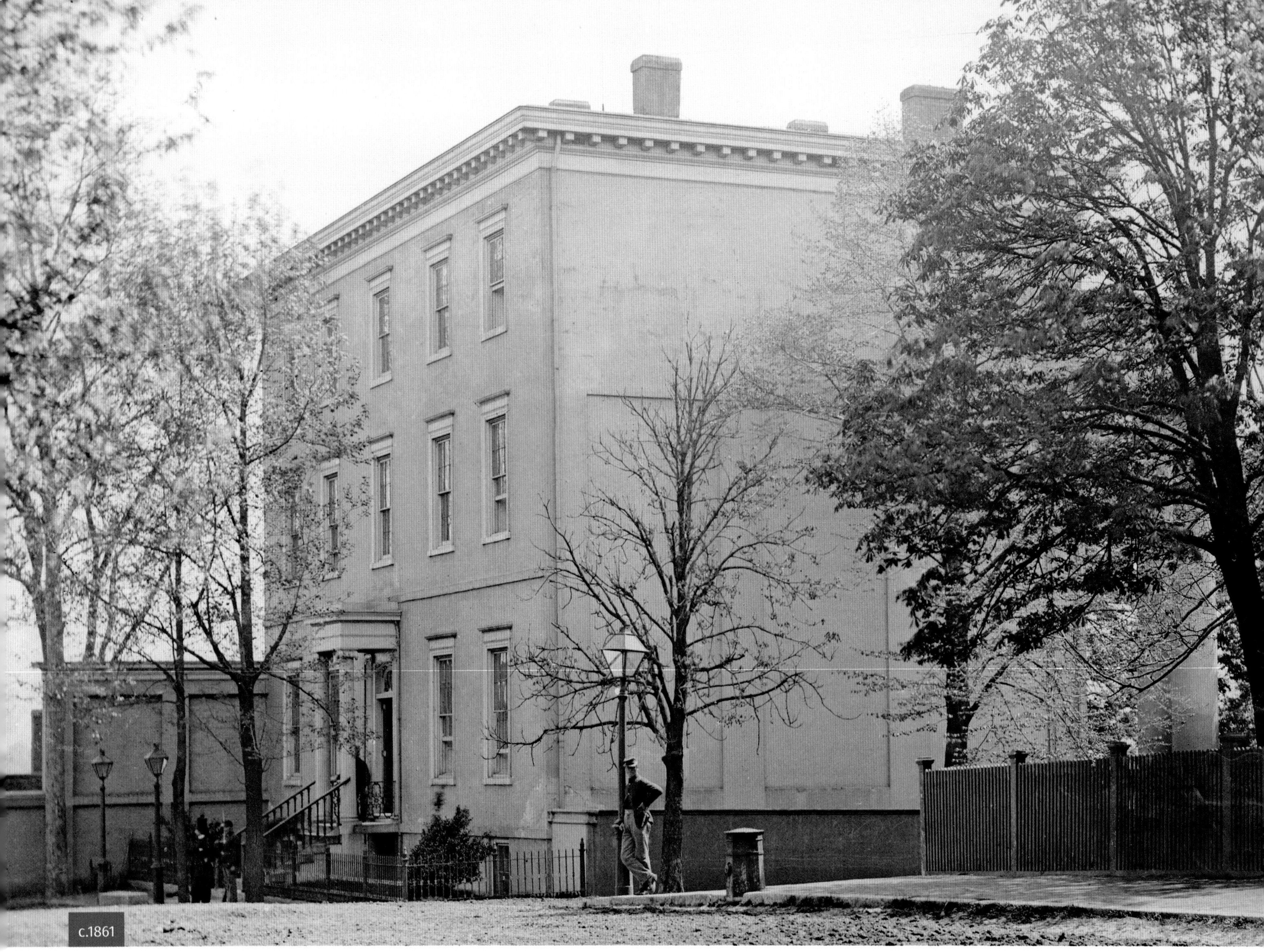

CONFEDERATE "WHITE HOUSE," RICHMOND

Jefferson Davis moved the capital from Montgomery, Alabama, to Richmond, Virginia

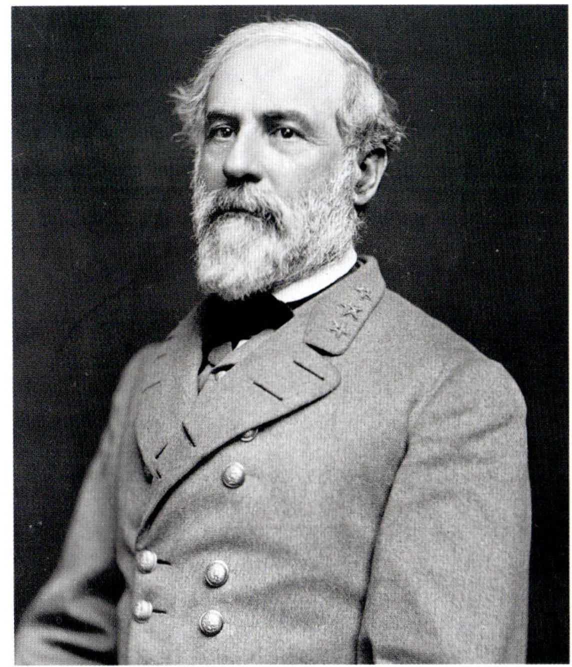

ABOVE: A portrait of Confederate general Robert E. Lee, photographed by Julian Vannerson in 1864.

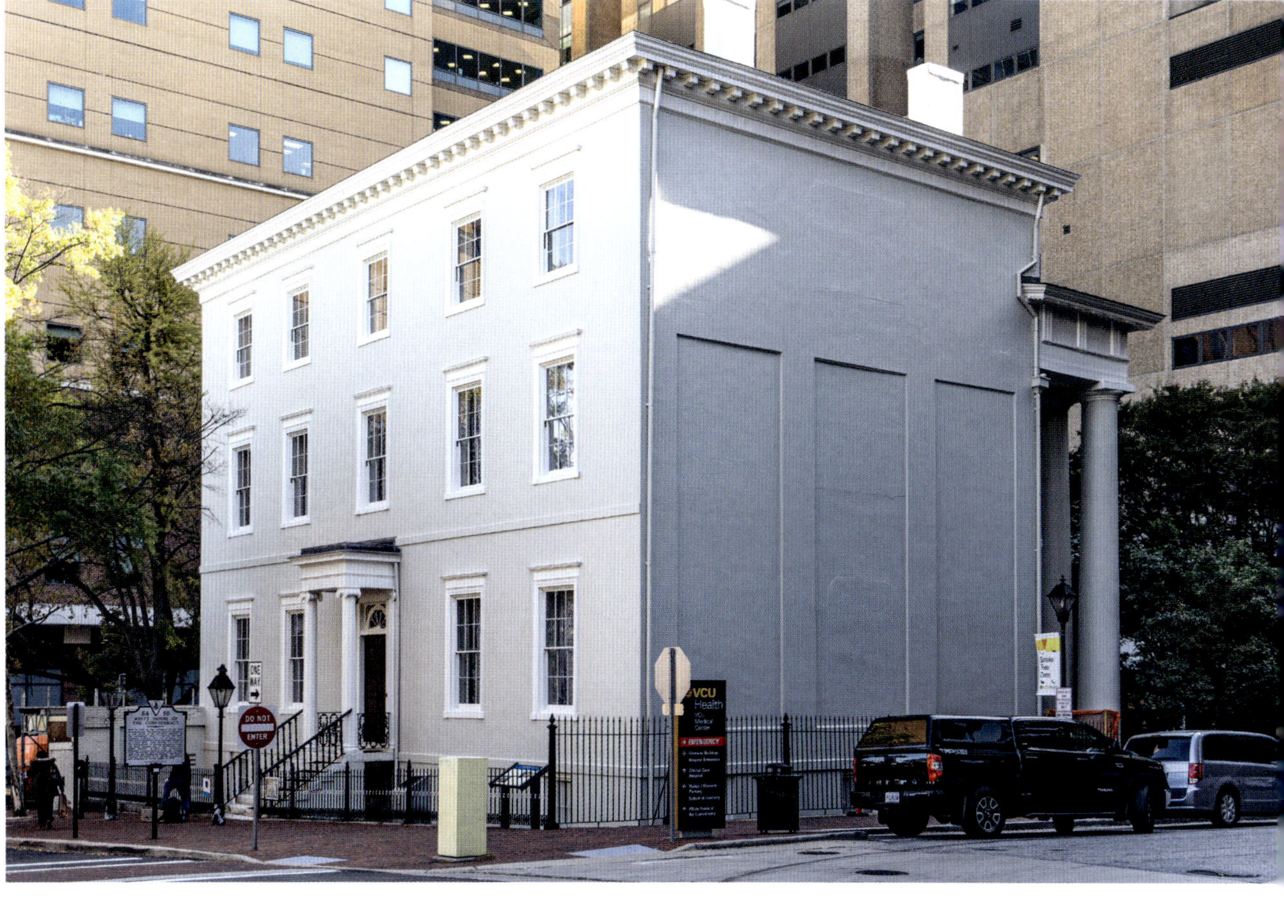

Ninety miles south of Washington, the new Confederate government was establishing itself in the manufacturing center of Richmond, Virginia. Representatives from thirteen Southern states gathered in the stately Virginia Capitol, designed by one of their own, Thomas Jefferson, in 1788. As the war dragged on, the Capitol was the scene of rancorous debates over the handling of the war, the first conscription in America, and the enlistment of slaves in the war's waning days. Throughout the war Richmond became the symbol of Southern resistance. During the early days of the conflict, Northern newspaper editors declared that the city must be captured before the Confederate Congress was able to congregate in Richmond. Throughout the war, "On to Richmond" would be a rallying cry for the Union army in the East.

Jefferson Davis had resigned from the US Senate on January 21, 1861. The Southern statesman had advised his colleagues against secession, but felt it was his duty to follow his native Mississippi out of the Union. A West Point graduate and Mexican War veteran, Davis had hoped for a high rank in the fledgling Confederate army. But the representatives meeting in Montgomery, Alabama, to create a new Southern government selected Davis as the first president of the Confederate States of America in February 1861. Three months later, Davis moved the Confederate capital from Montgomery to Richmond, Virginia.

The Confederate executive mansion at the corner of Twelfth and Clay Streets in the Court End neighborhood of Richmond was built in 1818. Davis often met with his cabinet and generals in this three-story building. It was here that Davis consulted his most successful commander, Robert E. Lee, to plan the ill-fated Gettysburg campaign.

As the war dragged on, the building became something of a refuge for President Davis from the bitter denunciations of his many critics. It survived the bombardment and fire of 1865, when the retreating rebels set fire to their own stores and the conflagration spread. The house then served as the Union army's headquarters, and President Abraham Lincoln briefly sat at Davis's desk.

While the house itself has been restored to its wartime appearance, the one-time executive mansion is now overshadowed by the medical college campus of Virginia Commonwealth University.

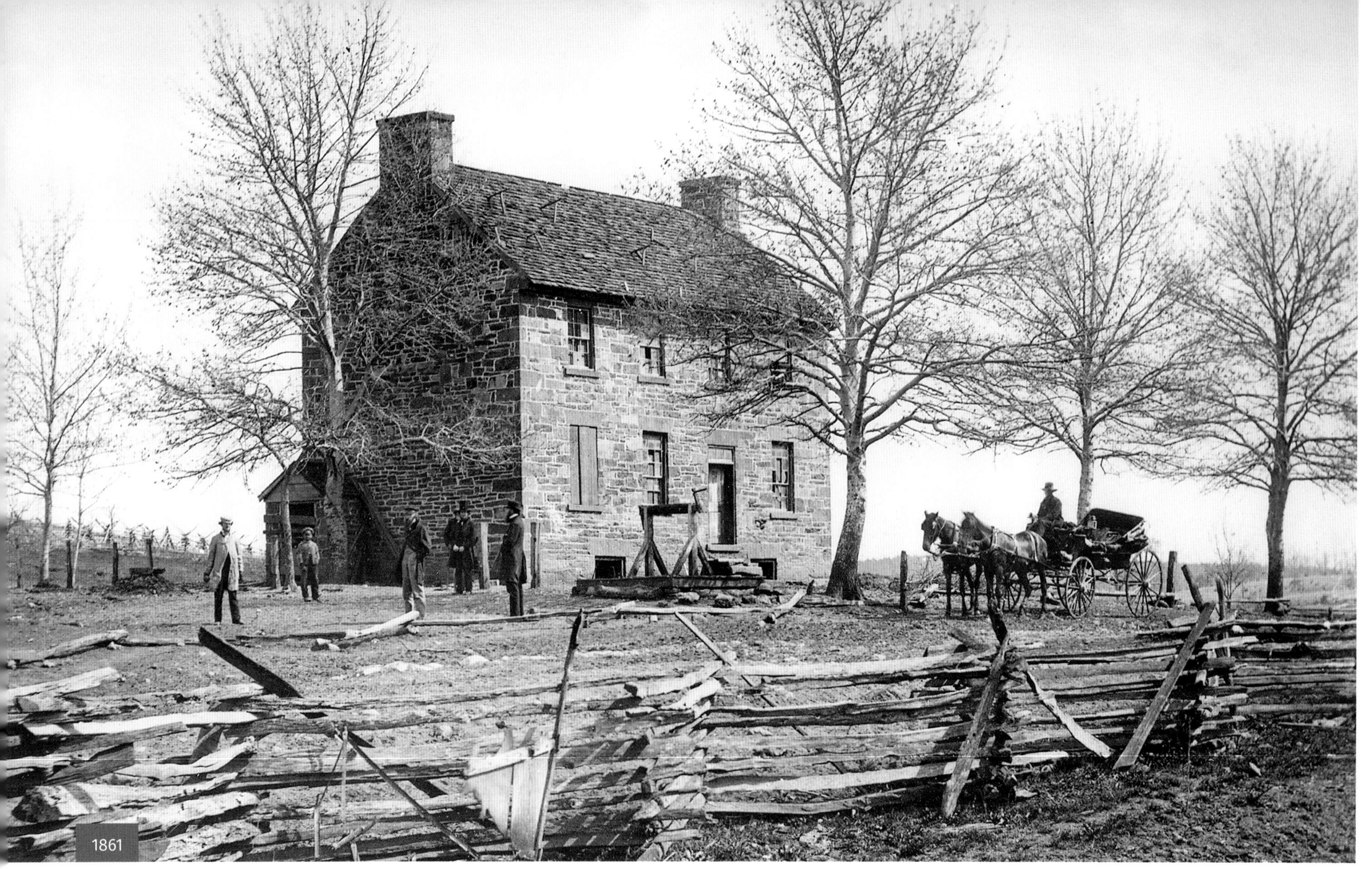
1861

BATTLE OF FIRST BULL RUN/MANASSAS, VIRGINIA

The battle where Stonewall Jackson made his name

The first major land battle of the Civil War is remembered by two distinct names: Northerners referred to the battle as First Bull Run; Southerners called it First Manassas. The difference in names reflects the penchant Northerners exhibited throughout the war to identify battles with rivers and creeks. Their Confederate counterparts tended to name battles after nearby localities. Regardless of the name, the battle was a morale-boosting victory for the Confederates.

One of the most prominent landmarks on the Manassas battlefield is the Stone House, a country tavern located on the Warrenton Turnpike near its junction with Sudley Road. The seemingly victorious Union army surged past the house on July 21, 1861, as it attempted to finish off the remnants of the Confederate army on nearby Henry House Hill. As with most battlefield structures, the tavern was soon filled with the wounded. It was not long before the Union troops were marching past the Stone House again, this time in defeat.

The turning point of the Battle of First Manassas occurred on Henry House Hill, so designated because of a house on the height owned by Judith Henry. Henry was 85 and bedridden at the time of the battle, unable to seek shelter with the rest of her

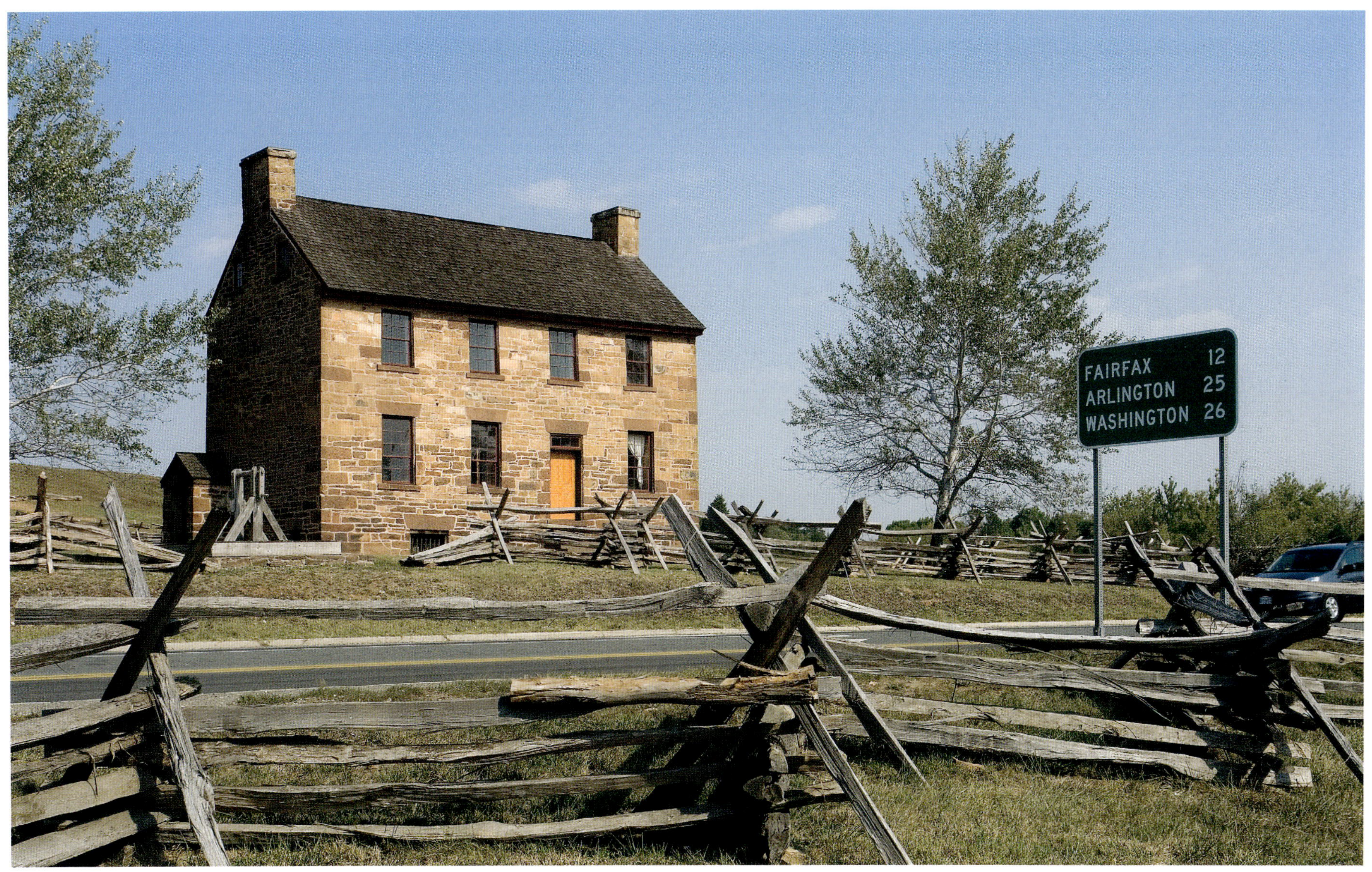

family. As the armies struggled for control of the hill, Confederate sharpshooters firing from the house made it an inviting target. Henry became a casualty of Union counterfire, and is now buried in the family cemetery nearby. The famous stand of General Thomas J. Jackson and his Virginia brigade on Henry House Hill turned the tide of the battle and earned both the general and the brigade the celebrated sobriquet "Stonewall."

The Stone House was soon captured by Virginian troops with fixed bayonets. One year later, the house witnessed another battle—and another Northern defeat. Following the Battle of Second Manassas, the tavern was used by the Confederates to parole Union prisoners. Even today, the house still bears the scars of the two battles and is preserved as part of Manassas National Battlefield Park.

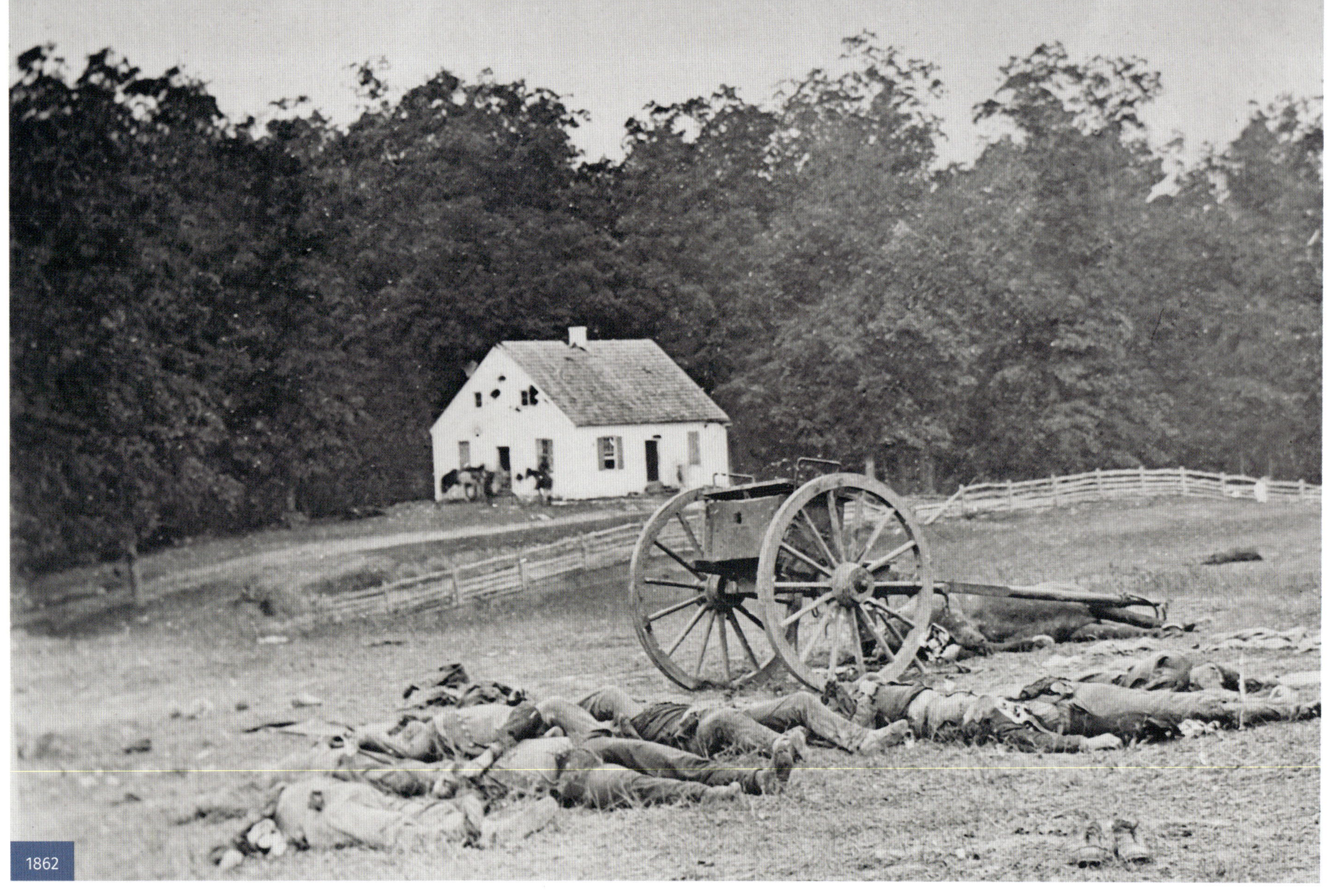

BATTLE OF ANTIETAM, MARYLAND

The bloodiest day in American history

The Battle of Antietam, fought on September 17, 1862, would be the bloodiest day in American history. The two sides inflicted 22,000 casualties on each other over the course of the day, including as many as 4,700 dead or mortally wounded (double the figure of American troops killed on D-Day in World War II). Antietam was also the first battle in history in which the dead of the battlefield were substantially photographed. Some of the first photographs were taken beside the old Hagerstown Pike, where fighting raged in the early morning hours that day. In this vicinity, Stonewall Jackson's command struggled against repeated attacks by three separate Union army corps.

One of the most prominent features on the Antietam battlefield was the church of a German Baptist sect that baptized its members by total immersion—hence the nickname "Dunker Church." In an effort to extricate bluecoats caught in the early fighting on September 17, 1862, Union general John Sedgwick's Second Corps Division launched an attack toward the Dunker Church. The assault turned into a deadly trap as Confederate troops launched almost simultaneous assaults against both of Sedgwick's flanks. Despite the fierceness of the attacks against Sedgwick, the division retired in good order. The Second Corps historian would later note that "not a color is

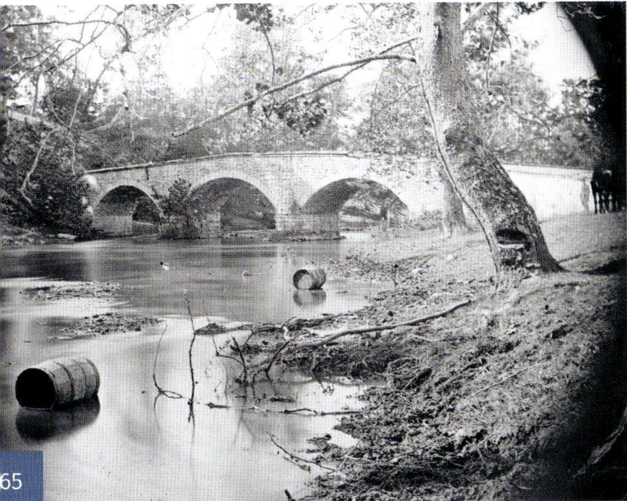

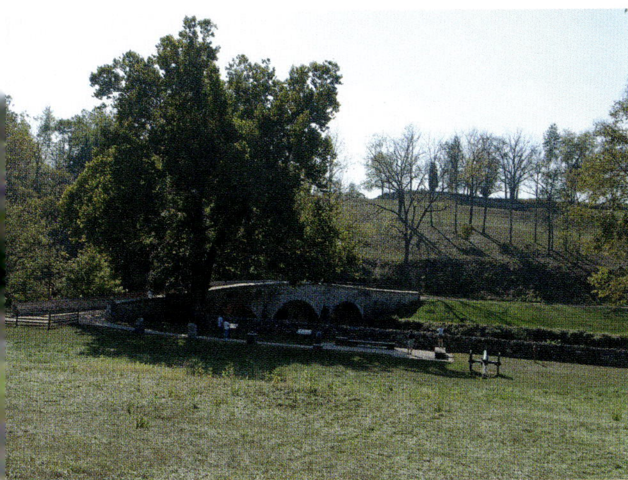

left to become a trophy of that bloody fight." The bullet-scarred Dunker Church also survived the battle, but was later rebuilt.

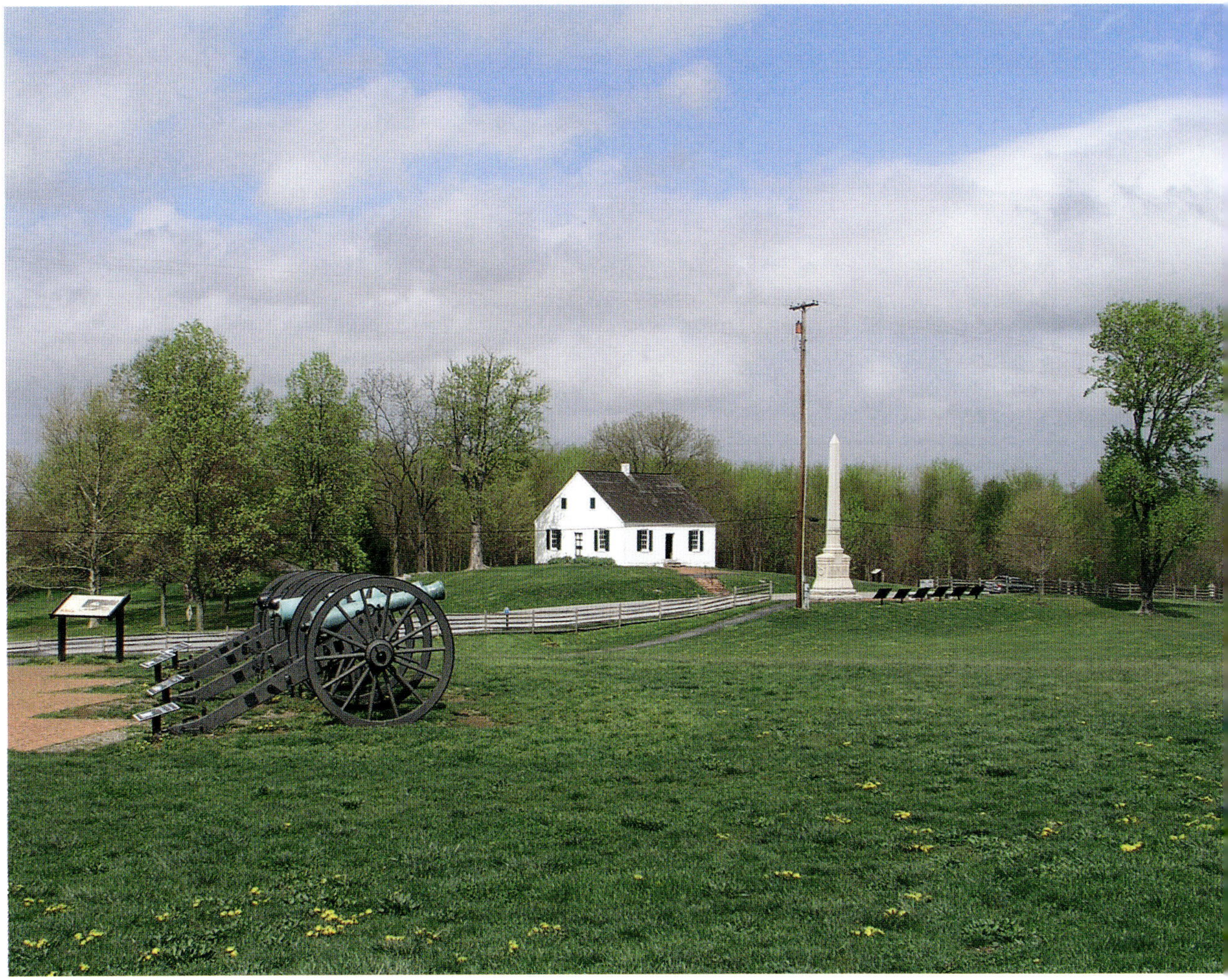

The Battle of Antietam was fought in phases that reflected the piecemeal attacks ordered by General McClellan. The focus of the second phase of the battle, fought by elements of the Second Corps, was a sunken country road that Confederates under General Daniel Harvey Hill were using as a makeshift entrenchment. The repeated assaults against the road would forever earn it the moniker "Bloody Lane."

For four hours, Southern troops staved off their counterparts in blue. The repeated charges gradually thinned the Confederate ranks, and the sunken road became filled with the dead and wounded. Eventually, the Union assault broke the rebel line, opening a path to Lee's rear. However, the exhausted Northerners failed to grasp the opportunity. Today the once blood-soaked lane is dotted with markers and monuments that tell the tale of the struggle waged there.

The final phase of the battle was fought over a triple-arched stone bridge across Antietam Creek. Here, Union general Ambrose Burnside's command was confronted by a handful of Georgian troops positioned on a bluff overlooking the bridge. Despite the enormous numerical superiority of the Federal forces, it took Burnside nearly four hours to capture the bridge today known as "Burnside Bridge." After the capture of the bridge that bears his name, Burnside dawdled for two hours, giving Lee time to bring up badly needed reinforcements. The repulse of Burnside's belated attack brought the Battle of Antietam to an end. Two days later, Lee withdrew his battered but intact army across the Potomac, ending his first invasion of the North.

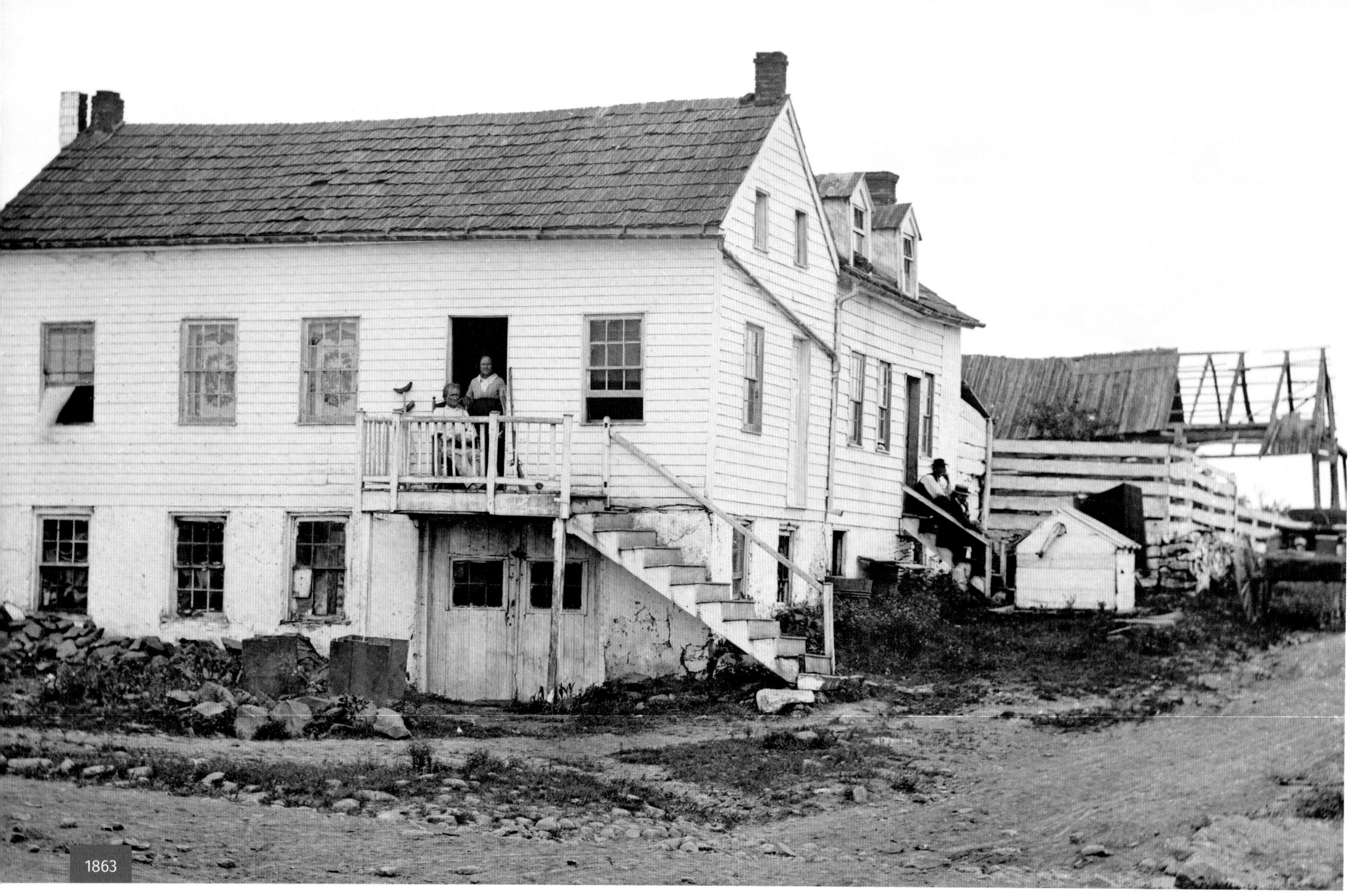

JOHN BURNS' HOUSE, BATTLE OF GETTYSBURG, PENNSYLVANIA

John L. Burns was the oldest combatant fighting at Gettysburg

The twelve roads that enter Gettysburg attracted the two armies like magnets. On the morning of July 1, 1863, thousands of soldiers in blue and gray were converging on the town. The Confederate lines advanced upon McPherson Ridge, only to be thrown back by Union reinforcements. The Southern victory at Chancellorsville notwithstanding, the Confederate cause looked bleak in June 1863. Large parts of Tennessee were occupied, and the Confederacy's last bastion on the Mississippi, Vicksburg, had long been under siege.

Stonewall Jackson had been killed by over-zealous Confederate pickets at Chancellorsville. It fell upon Lee's army to revive Confederate fortunes. In early June, he ordered the Army of Northern Virginia toward the Potomac and Pennsylvania. On

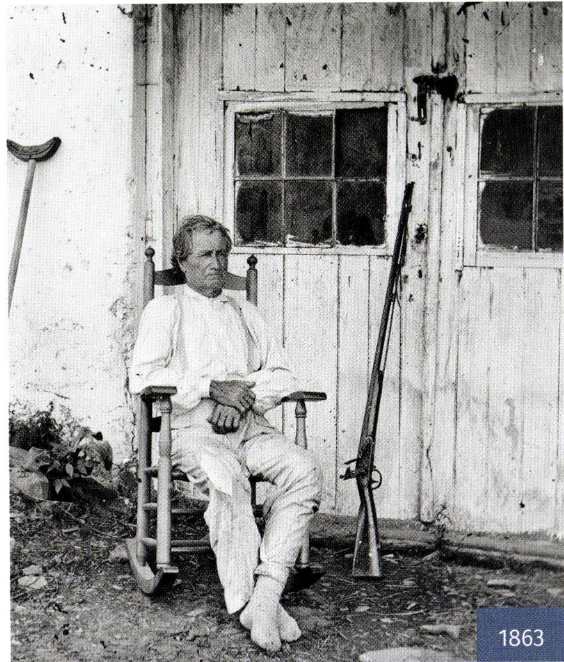
1863

JOHN LAWRENCE BURNS

The "Old Patriot," became one of the most popular subjects for photographers in the days and weeks following the battle. Burns is pictured here, recuperating from his wounds, in an image by Mathew Brady. The flintlock rifle he carried into battle leans against the wall. Born in 1793, Burns was a veteran who had fought in the War of 1812 and the Mexican–American War of 1846–48. At the age of sixty-seven, he volunteered to fight in the Civil War but was rejected as being too old. He was sent to Gettysburg to act as a constable, and was jailed during the town's brief occupation by Confederate forces in June 1863 for the resistance he displayed to Major General Jubal A. Early. He died in 1872 but is immortalized in a statue, rifle in hand, on Stone Avenue, south of Chambersburg Road.

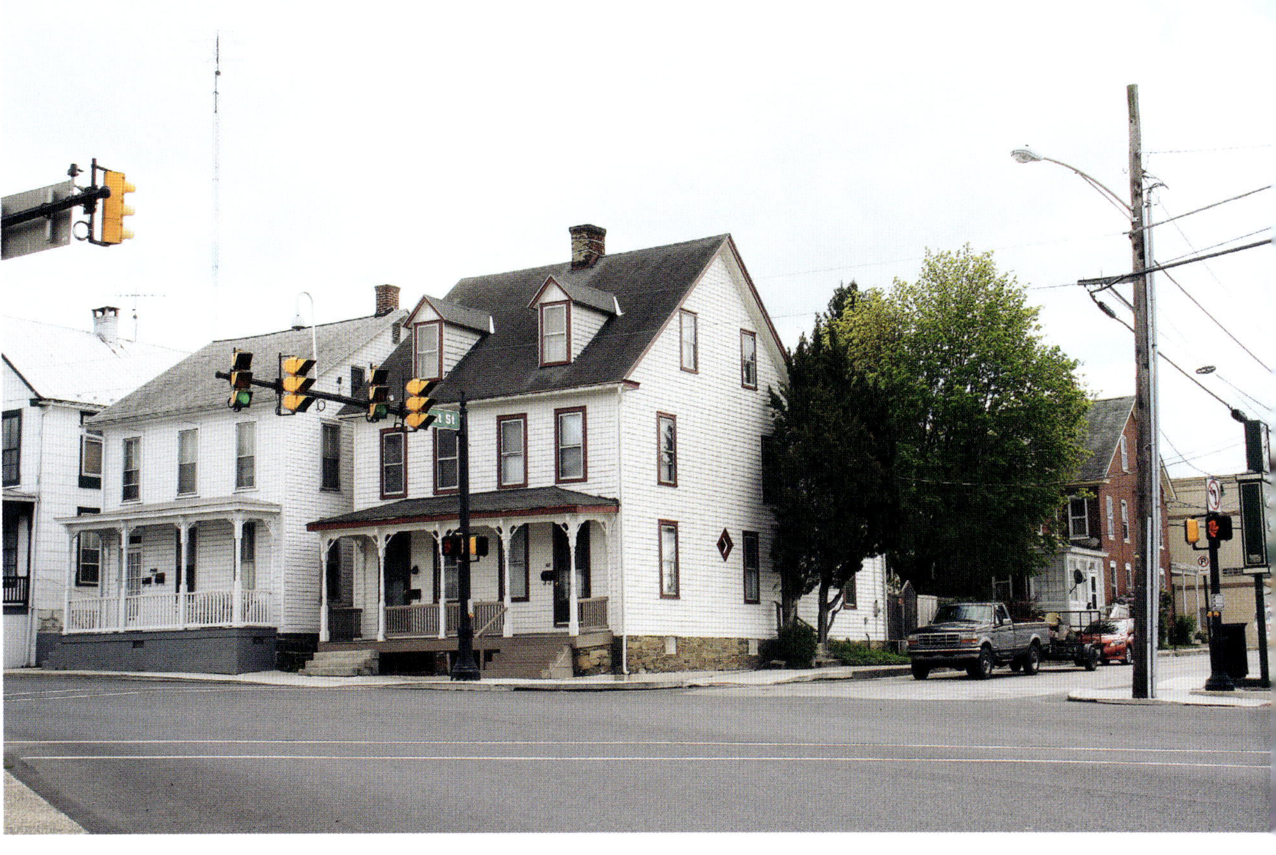

July 1, elements of his army clashed with Union cavalry on the rolling hills outside Gettysburg.

Among the Union defenders on the first day of battle was a 69-year-old former constable, John L. Burns. A veteran of the War of 1812, Burns took up his obsolete flintlock rifle and joined the Federal forces defending McPherson Ridge. On the first day of the battle, Burns had walked to the scene of the fighting with his old flintlock rifle and requisitioned a more modern gun from a wounded Union soldier. He went on to fight with a number of different units before his wounds forced him off the field, and he sought treatment from Confederate medics after convincing them he was a noncombatant.

After the Confederate repulse on McPherson Ridge, a lull descended on the field as the opposing forces brought up reinforcements. In the afternoon, Confederate general Richard Ewell's Second Corps launched an assault north of Gettysburg that overwhelmed the thinly held Union line. The defending Eleventh Corps collapsed, which unhinged the entire Union line. Men in blue were soon fleeing into town, closely pursued by their Southern counterparts, flushed with victory.

BATTLE OF GETTYSBURG, LITTLE ROUND TOP, PENNSYLVANIA

General Lee fails to back up his initial success

The initial Confederate success on the first day of battle convinced Lee of the soundness of continuing the struggle. However, by July 2, 1863, most of the Union army was concentrated in a far stronger position than the previous day. Despite the odds, Lee decided to launch a flank attack against the Union left, similar to Jackson's assault at Chancellorsville, but without Jackson at the helm, it took hours to organize the attack and Lee was unable to build on his initial gains.

Desperate fighting swirled around boulder-strewn Devil's Den and Little Round Top, a key elevation on the Union flank. Just when the rebels appeared poised to take the summit, Federal reinforcements under Colonel Strong Vincent arrived at Little Round Top to save the strategic location.

Today, monument-crowned Little Round Top is one of the most popular tourist stops on battlefield tours.

1863

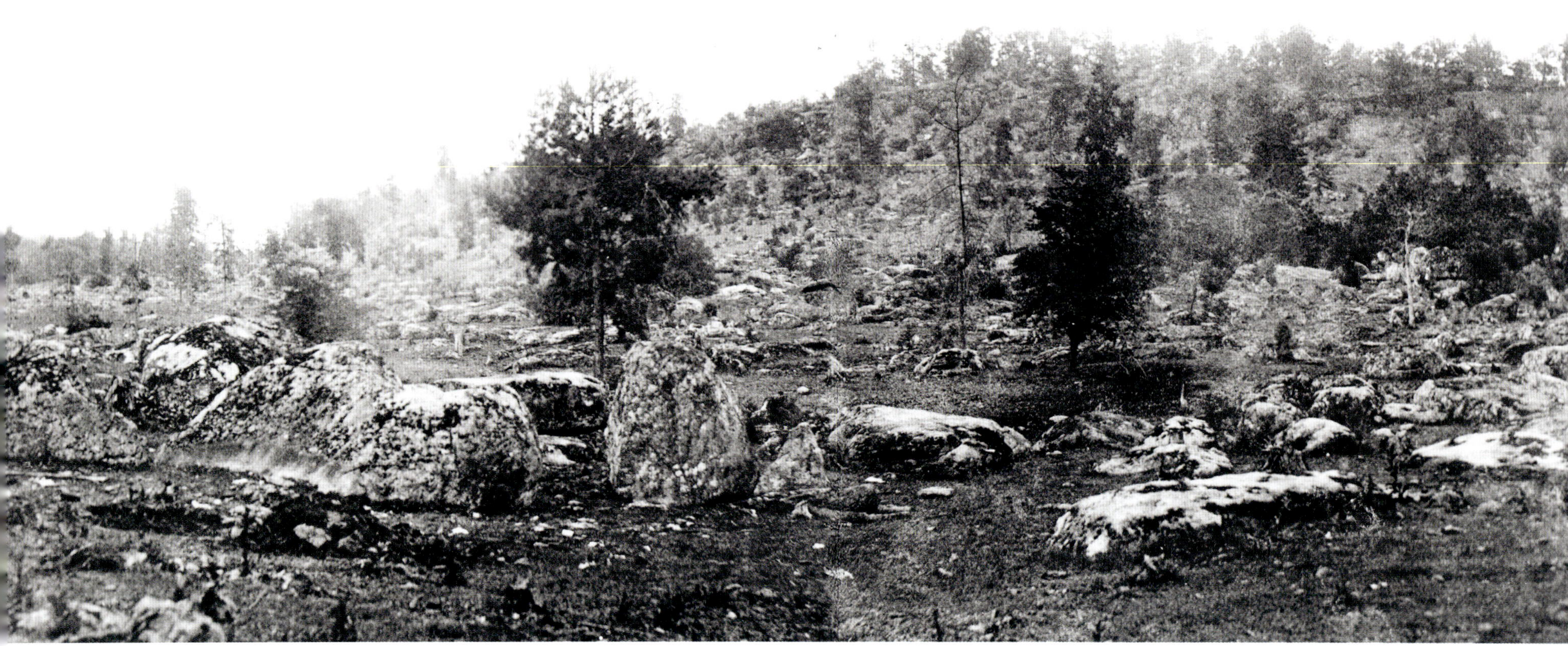

Unable to crush the Union flanks on July 2, Lee opted to storm the Union center on July 3. The attack, known as "Pickett's Charge," was a spectacular failure that only added to the death toll. The charge is named after Major General George Pickett, one of three Confederate generals who led the charge under its commander, Lieutenant General James Longstreet.

In an attempt to weaken the Union defenses, the infantry assault was preceded by a heavy artillery bombardment, but this had little effect. Nine infantry brigades of around 12,500 Confederate soldiers then advanced toward the Union lines under heavy fire. Protected by a low stone wall, the Union men forced back their attackers with over 50 percent casualties. At the end of the three-day contest, the Gettysburg battlefield was strewn with the dead and dying. More than 50,000 men fell at Gettysburg—nearly one out of every three soldiers who participated in the epic battle.

DEVIL'S DEN

Devil's Den, a jumbled cluster of immense boulders at the base of Little Round Top, became a citadel of stone for the remainder of the battle. One of the Southerners killed in the initial battle to take Devil's Den was a young man shot in a nearby field. After the battle, the unburied soldier became the subject of a series of images taken by veteran photographer Alexander Gardner. Dissatisfied with the body's original location, Gardner's crew moved the corpse to an alcove within Devil's Den, which was later claimed by Gardner to be a sharpshooter's den.

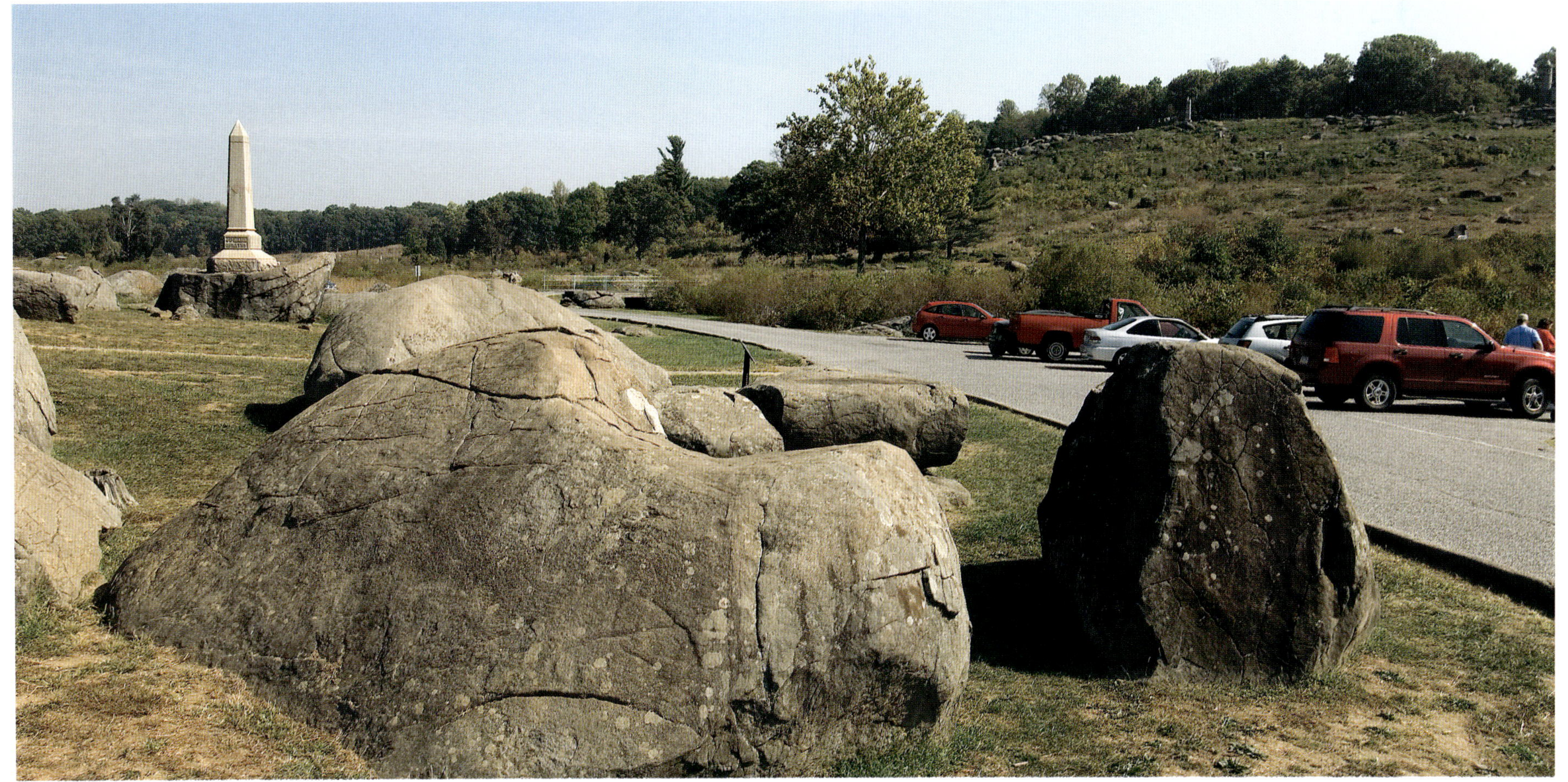

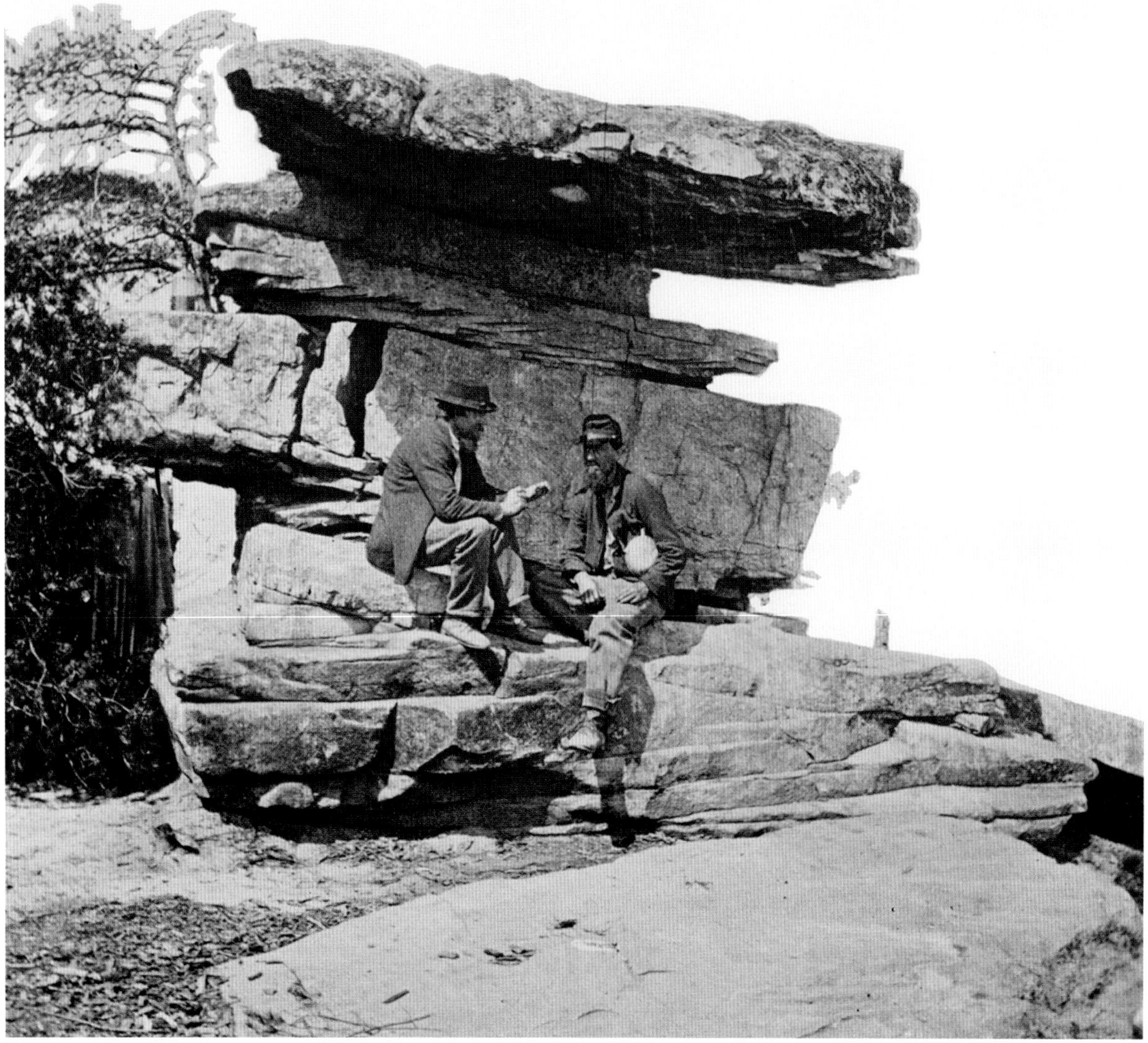

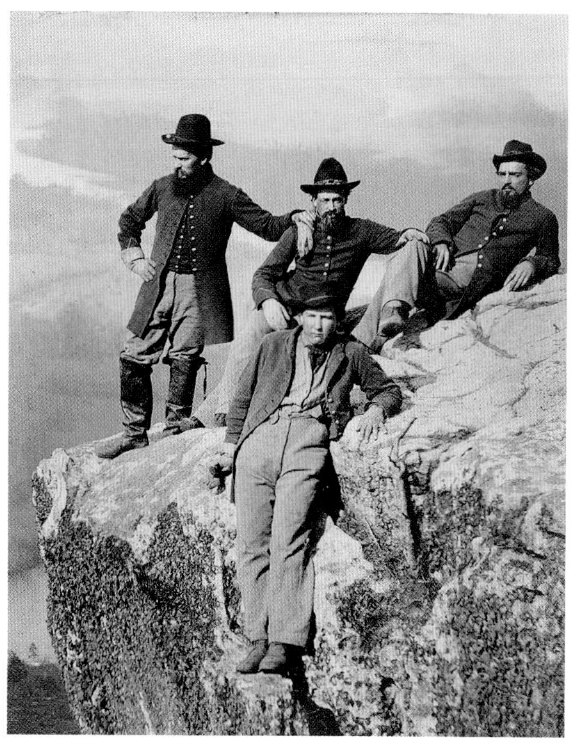

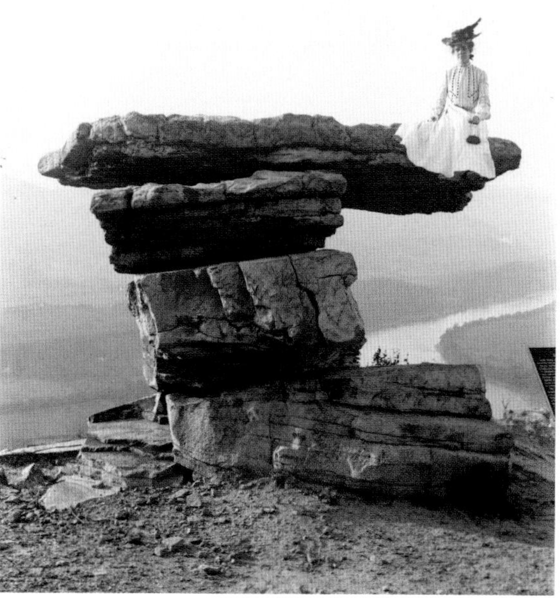

LOOKOUT MOUNTAIN, TENNESSEE

Site of the "Battle Above the Clouds" and the Umbrella Rock viewpoint

The Battle for Lookout Mountain, famously dubbed the "Battle Above the Clouds," was a pivotal engagement during the American Civil War, fought on November 24, 1863, near Chattanooga, Tennessee. Chattanooga was a strategic railway hub vital for control of the South.

Union forces under Major General Joseph "Fighting Joe" Hooker launched an assault on Confederate positions held on the slopes of Lookout Mountain, a towering promontory overlooking the Tennessee River. The Confederate defenders, part of General Braxton Bragg's Army of Tennessee, had fortified the heights to monitor and repel any Union approach.

Hooker's men advanced from the west in thick morning fog that clung to the mountain's slopes, creating the appearance that the fighting was taking place in the sky. As a result, observers from below could only see flashes of gunfire and faint outlines of soldiers above the clouds, giving rise to the "Battle Above the Clouds." After several hours of combat, Union forces succeeded in driving a surprisingly sparse Confederate force from their defensive positions. The next day, Lookout Mountain was firmly under Union control, contributing to the lifting of the Confederate siege of Chattanooga and setting the stage for a decisive Union victory at Missionary Ridge.

After the war, Lookout Mountain and its panoramic vistas became a site of pilgrimage for veterans, tourists, and photographers. One of the most iconic landmarks on the mountain is Umbrella Rock, a large, flat rock formation near the summit. Shaped like an umbrella with a narrow stem, the formation provided stunning views and a sense of thrilling danger due to its steep drop.

In late 1863, brothers Royan and James Linn set up a photographic shed near Lookout Point and photographed soldiers on the rock or near one of the vertiginous drops on the 1,100-foot mountain. This rustic wooden studio operated until 1937, offering souvenir portraits of tourists perched daringly on the rock's edge. The photographers often enhanced the drama of the scene by having subjects pose in period costumes or military uniforms, evoking the Civil War legacy. After its closure, George Thomas Linn demolished the shed in August of that same year.

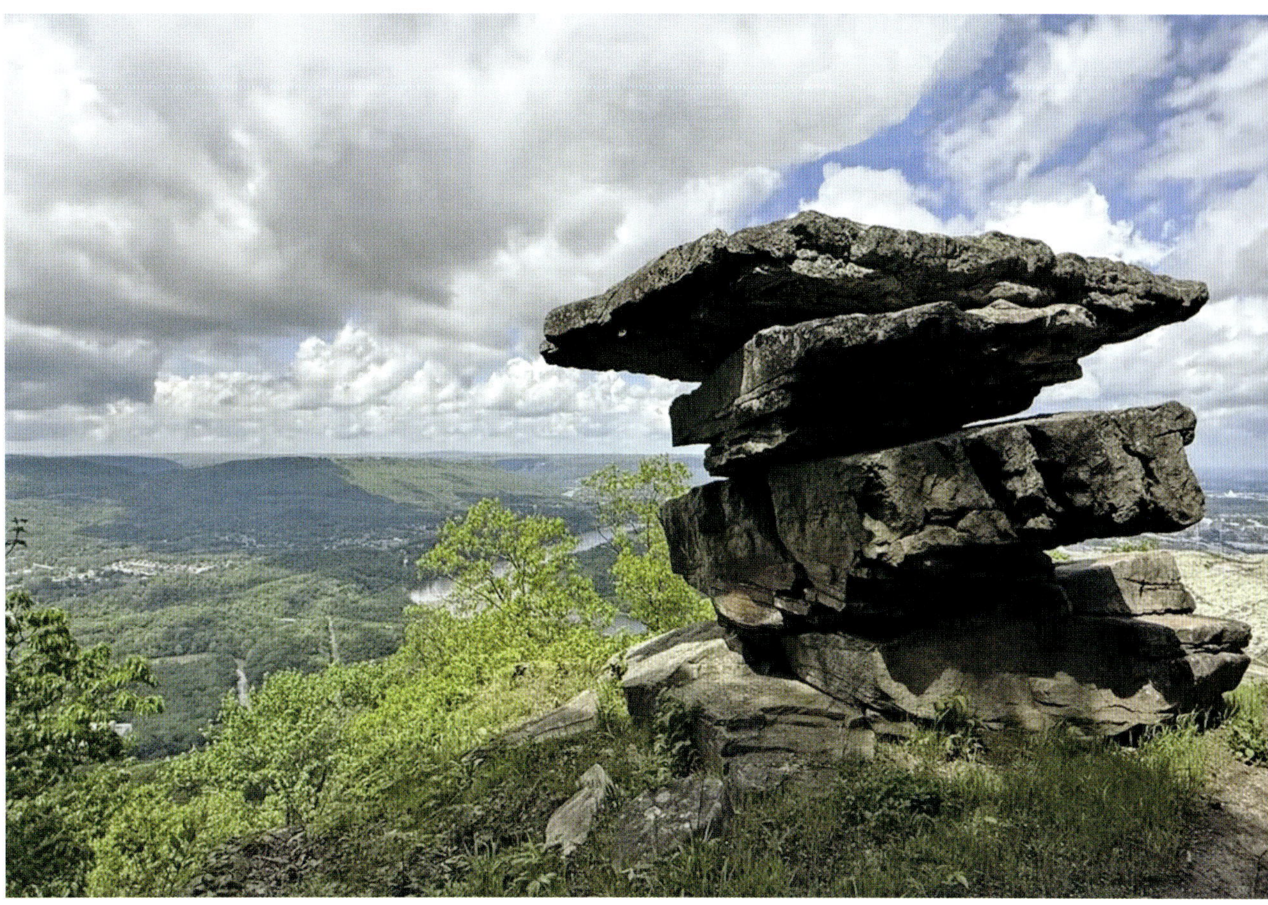

Today, the site is preserved as part of the Chickamauga and Chattanooga National Military Park, where visitors can still trace the footsteps of Union soldiers, though posing on Umbrella Rock or recreating the many Civil War photos posed nearby is not advised.

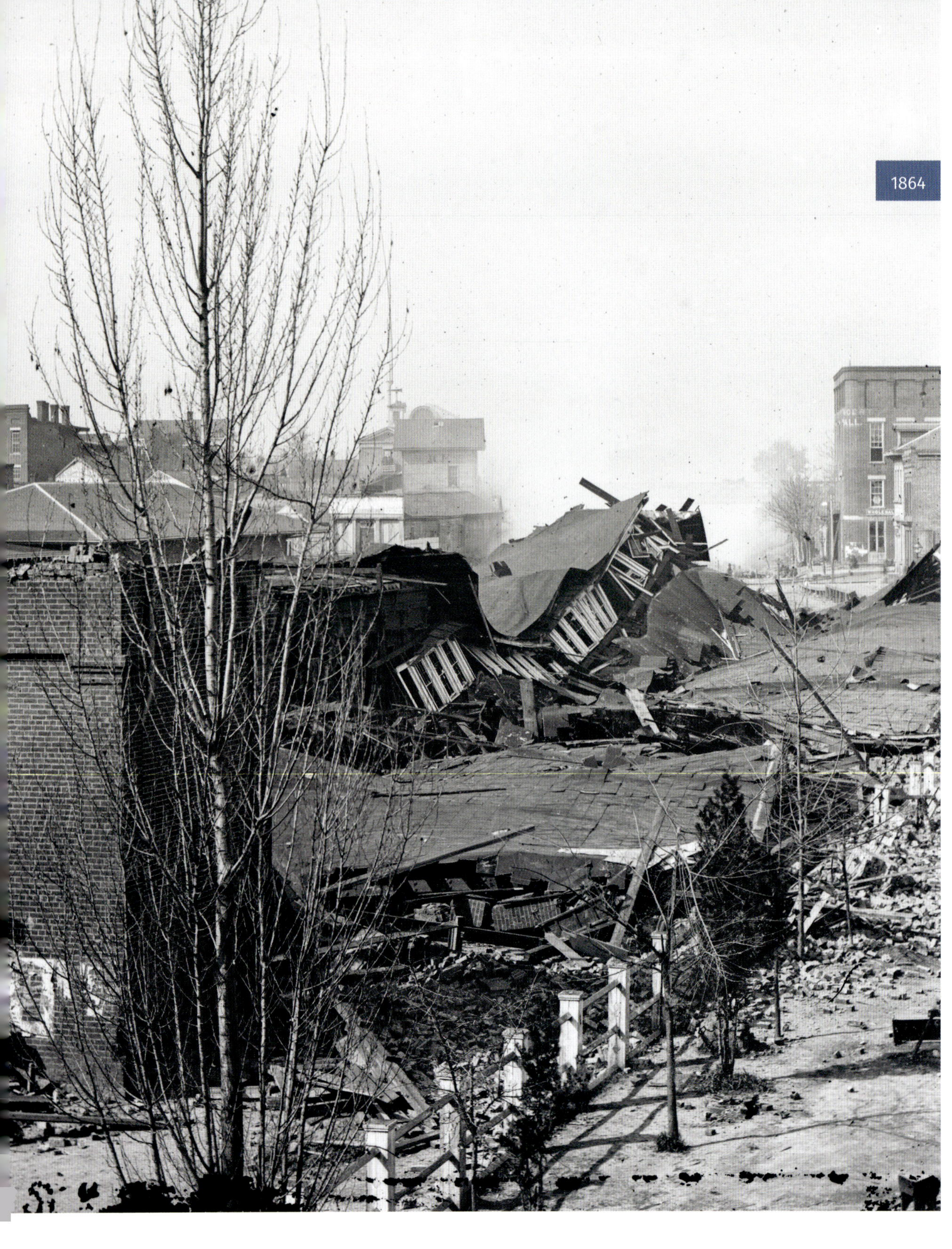

1864

FALL OF ATLANTA, GEORGIA

William Sherman tore down engine sheds, ripped up the railroad tracks, and left Atlanta burning

From the middle of July through the end of August 1864, Atlanta joined the long list of Southern cities besieged by invaders from the North. William Tecumseh Sherman was pushing the Confederates back. General Johnston had dug in, constructing a series of earthen forts around Atlanta. But on July 17, 1864, Confederate President Jefferson Davis replaced the cautious Johnston with General John B. Hood, a soldier more disposed to the offensive than the defensive. Hood's valiant but ill-fated attempts to reverse the Union tide only accelerated the inevitable. The fighting at Atlanta, Ezra Church, and Utoy Creek merely tightened Sherman's stranglehold on the city.

One of the casualties of these early battles was Union general James McPherson, who was killed when he accidentally rode into Confederate lines. A Union photographer later captured the scene of McPherson's death. Fighting raged around Atlanta as Union forces advanced, but a brave and popular general was lost.

By the end of August 1864 an impasse had been reached. Hood's aggressive tactics had cost him more than 11,000 men, leaving his Army of Tennessee demoralized and dispirited. On August 25, Sherman struck southwest of Atlanta, severing the Macon and Western Railroad, Hood's last remaining supply line. After a final, foiled attempt to regain the railroad at Jonesboro, Hood was forced to give up Atlanta. On the night of September 1, 1864, his battered army evacuated and with Hood's men in retreat, Sherman's troops were free to march into a devastated city.

Sherman's triumphant armies entered Atlanta the next day. He telegraphed Washington: "Atlanta is ours,

LEFT: The main railroad shed in Atlanta after Sherman's troops had demolished the sidewalls to collapse the structure.

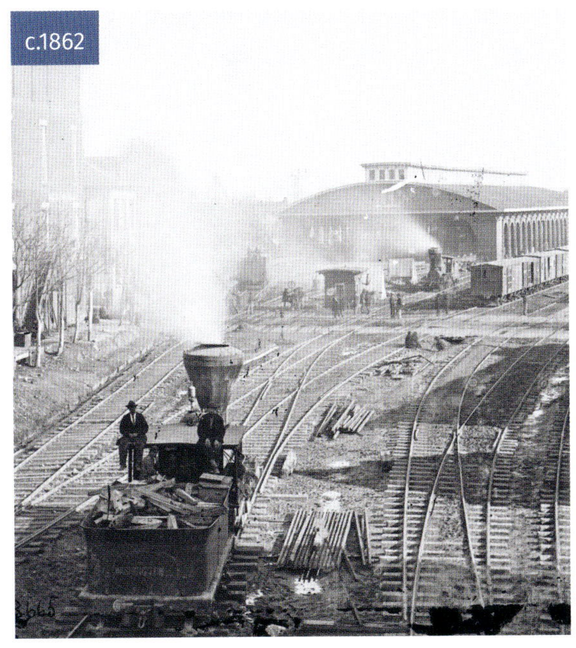

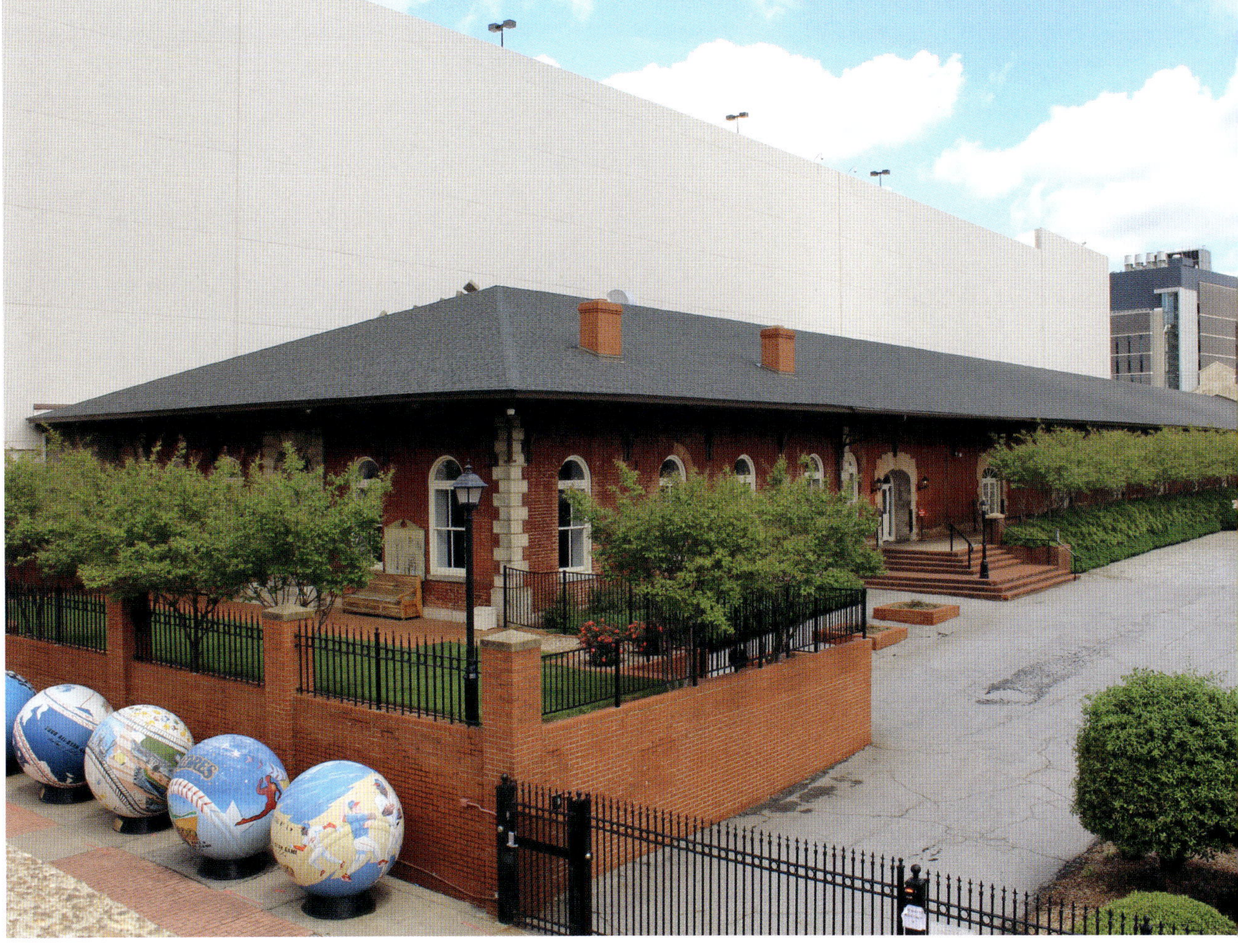

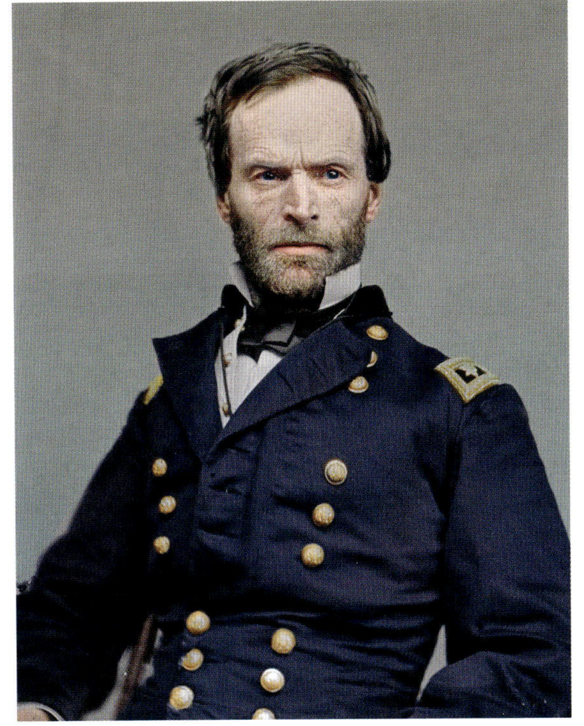

and fairly won." Prior to Atlanta, Northerners—numbed by the endless casualty lists of the past summer—despaired for victory. Lincoln, unable to demonstrate success, was convinced he would lose the November presidential election. The fall of Atlanta transformed Northern opinion toward the war. The end was finally within sight.

ABOVE: The site of the old railroad depot as it looks today.

ABOVE LEFT: Multiple railroad tracks into Atlanta's rail depot are ample evidence of the city's strategic importance to the Federal cause.

LEFT: A colorized portrait of William T. Sherman.

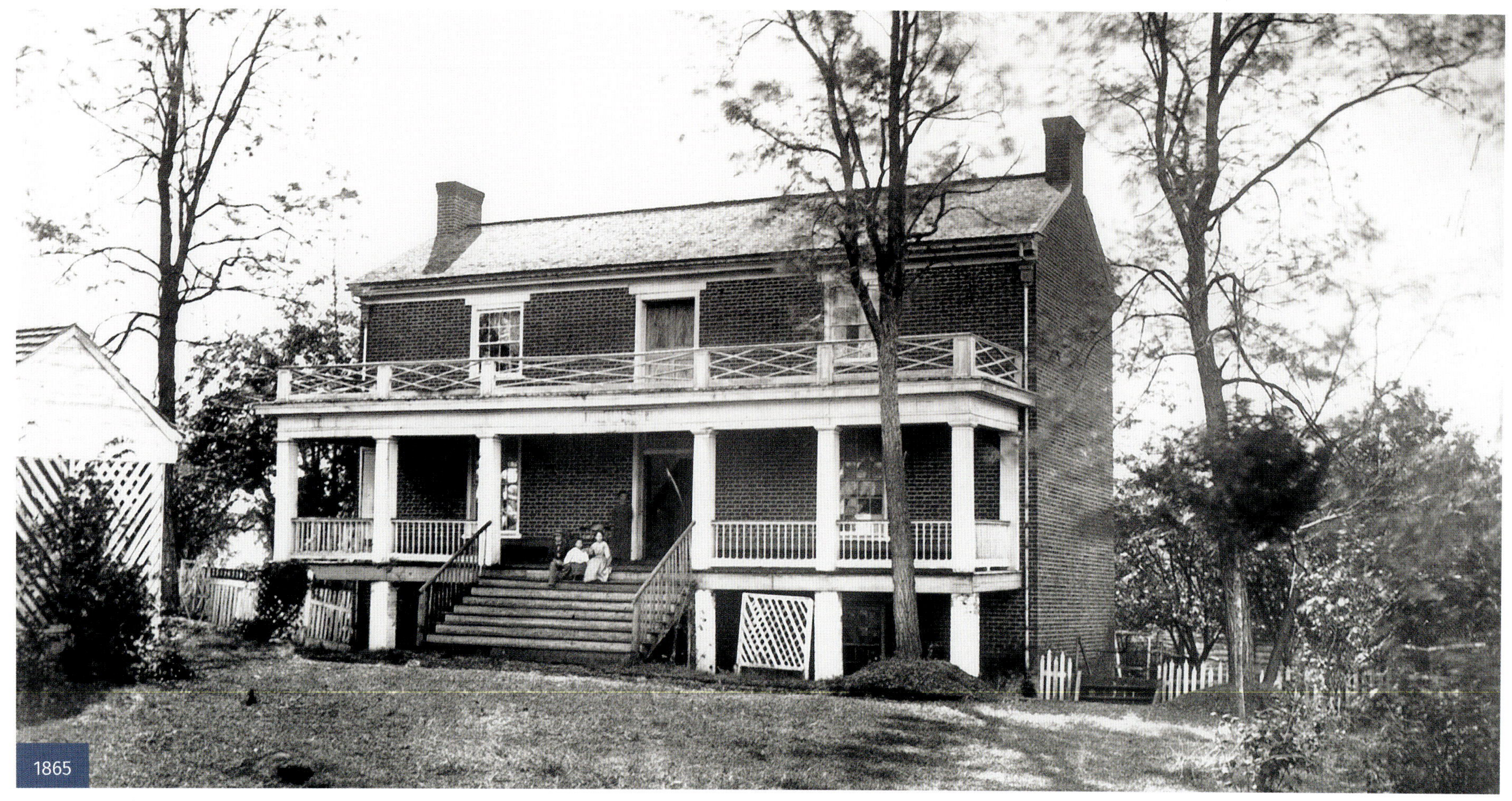

1865

APPOMATTOX COURT HOUSE, VIRGINIA

The Wilmer McLean house was the scene of the surrender of General Lee

At the outset of the Civil War, Wilmer McLean lived on Yorkshire Farm near the banks of Bull Run. His home came under fire on July 18, 1861, in the days leading up to the Battle of First Manassas. Determined to escape the conflict, he moved his family south to rural Appomattox Court House, where the war found him again in April 1865.

Sherman had marched to the sea and taken Savannah at Christmas 1864. He was now heading north through the Carolinas. On April 1, 1865, Grant crushed Lee's right flank at the Battle of Five Forks. The next day, Grant moved in for the kill. His attacks on Petersburg broke Lee's line and forced him to evacuate the town, ending the longest siege in American history. Without the vital rail junction of Petersburg, the Confederate capital of Richmond could no longer be held. The government hastily abandoned the city on the evening of April 2. Before leaving, they set fire to anything of potential value to the approaching Union army. The fire grew out of control, destroying more than 700 buildings as it swept through the city. Within days of Richmond's fall, Northern photographers arrived in the desolate and still-smoldering town. They recorded haunting images, including photos of the nondescript warehouse that had become the infamous Libby Prison.

Freed from having to defend Richmond, General Lee hoped that his smaller, more agile army might still escape Grant's clutches to continue the war elsewhere. However,

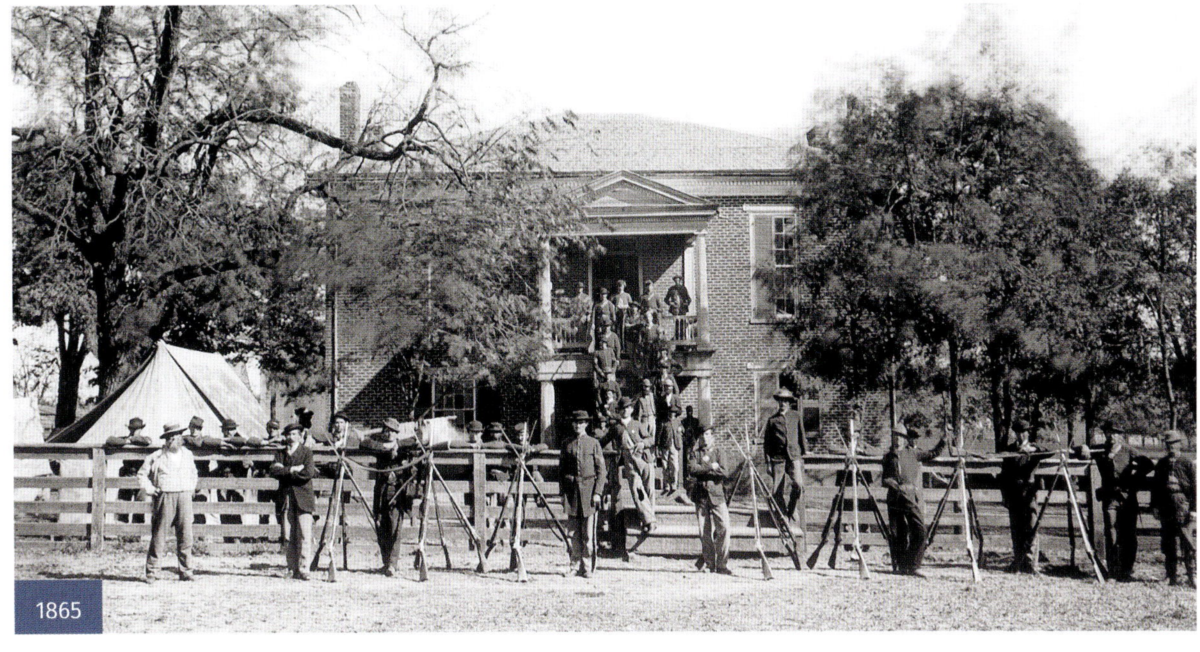

1865

LEFT: A photograph from Timothy O'Sullivan's 1865 series taken at Appomattox. Federal soldiers pose in front of the Court House. Alternative versions of this view feature children standing on the fence among the soldiers

Lee's ill-fed, ill-clad men were no longer capable of the speedy marches that they once were. On April 9, Lee was finally cornered at Appomattox Court House. That morning, dressed in his finest uniform, he surrendered to Grant in the home of Wilmer McLean. The surrender was signed in the front parlor of his house.

After Lee's surrender at Appomattox, the remaining Confederate armies began to topple. Within a week, General Joseph Johnston, again in command of the army facing Sherman, approached his erstwhile adversary about terms for surrender. By the end of May, nearly all the remaining Southern armies had capitulated. The final Confederate general to surrender was Cherokee Indian chief Stand Watie, who surrendered his command on June 23.

Today the building is a visitor center for the Appomattox Court House National Historical Park.

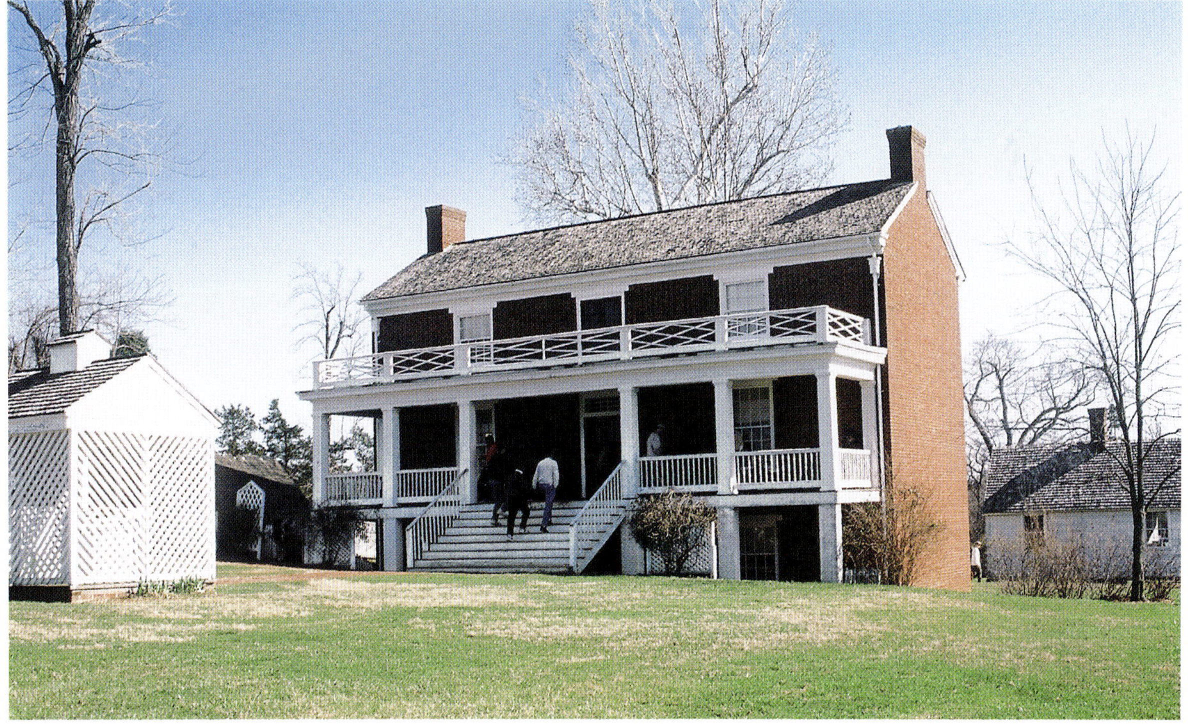

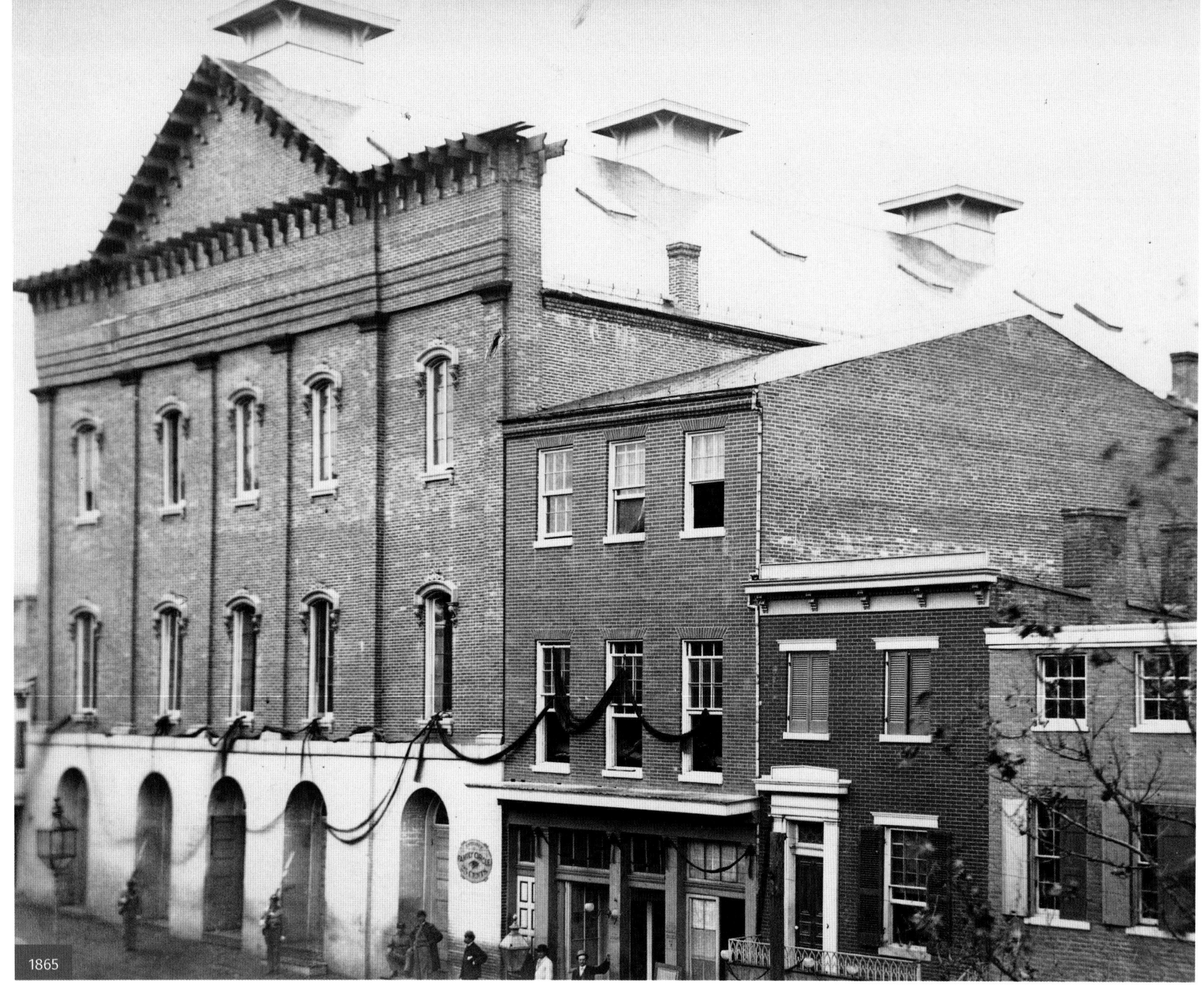

FORD'S THEATRE, WASHINGTON, DC

The euphoria of victory was checked after Lincoln's assassination

Although the defeated South lay in ruins, the first two weeks of April 1865 were a sustained celebration throughout the North. The fall of Petersburg and Richmond, followed by Lee's surrender, meant that the national catastrophe was finally at an end. On the evening of April 14, President Abraham Lincoln, just beginning his second term in office, joined in the revelry by attending a play at Ford's Theatre featuring one of his favorite actresses, Laura Keene.

Lincoln's fatal wounding at Ford's Theatre was the final tragedy of the most tragic war in American history. Shot while sitting in the presidential box by actor John Wilkes Booth, the president succumbed to his wound in a small bedroom across the street from the theater. Upon his death, Secretary of War Edwin M. Stanton was moved to remark, "Now he belongs to the ages."

In the final months of the war, Lincoln's thoughts were focused on the challenges of reuniting the war-torn nation. In his second inaugural address, Lincoln famously asked his countrymen, North and South, to put aside malice, and urged them to "do all which may achieve and cherish a just and lasting peace." He had similar words for his generals, advising them to go easy on the Confederate armies. Unfortunately, with Lincoln's death, all thoughts of a magnanimous peace evaporated. His successors sought retribution against the rebels as well as Booth's accomplices.

Assassin John Wilkes Booth was on the run for twelve days before he was tracked down in northern Virginia. He refused to give himself up and was shot by a Union soldier. Within weeks of the assassination, the Lincoln conspirators were tried by the military and sentenced to death or imprisonment. Four, including Mary Surratt, were hanged in July 1865. Former Confederate President Jefferson Davis was captured on May 10, near Irwinville, Georgia, and thrown into prison for two years; his predicament generated sympathy for him in both the North and South.

Ford's Theatre, after a substantial rebuilding program, is now maintained as a museum by the National Park Service.

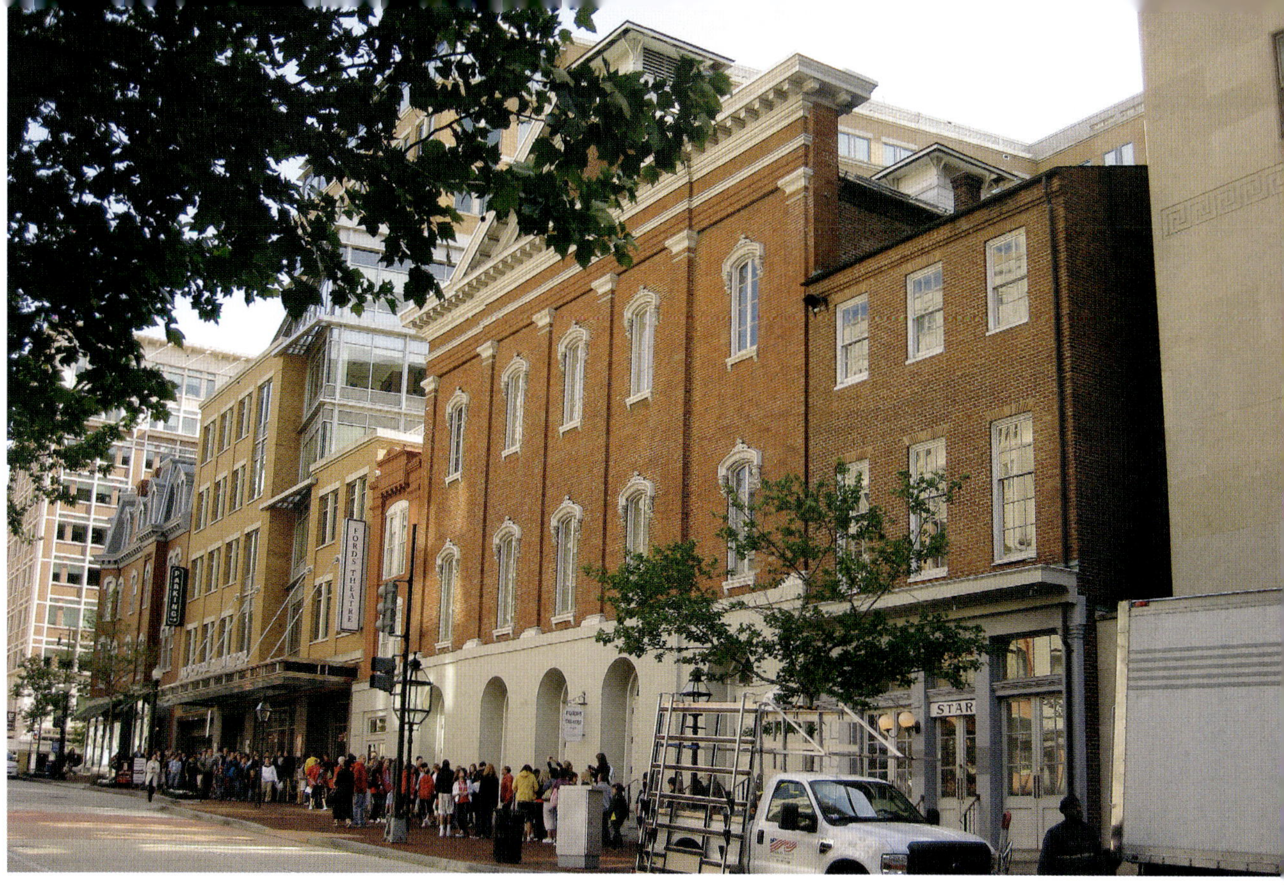

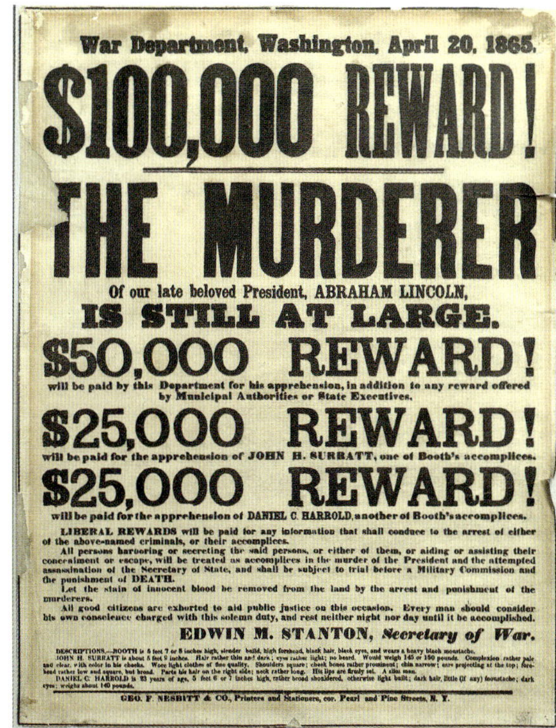

War Department, Washington, April 20, 1865.

$100,000 REWARD!

THE MURDERER

Of our late beloved President, ABRAHAM LINCOLN,

IS STILL AT LARGE.

$50,000 REWARD!

will be paid by this Department for his apprehension, in addition to any reward offered by Municipal Authorities or State Executives.

$25,000 REWARD!

will be paid for the apprehension of JOHN H. SURRATT, one of Booth's accomplices.

$25,000 REWARD!

will be paid for the apprehension of DANIEL C. HARROLD, another of Booth's accomplices.

LIBERAL REWARDS will be paid for any information that shall conduce to the arrest of either of the above-named criminals, or their accomplices.

All persons harboring or secreting the said persons, or either of them, or aiding or assisting their concealment or escape, will be treated as accomplices in the murder of the President and the attempted assassination of the Secretary of State, and shall be subject to trial before a Military Commission and the punishment of DEATH.

Let the stain of innocent blood be removed from the land by the arrest and punishment of the murderers.

All good citizens are exhorted to aid public justice on this occasion. Every man should consider his own conscience charged with this solemn duty, and rest neither night nor day until it be accomplished.

EDWIN M. STANTON, *Secretary of War.*

DESCRIPTIONS.—BOOTH is 5 feet 7 or 8 inches high, slender build, high forehead, black hair, black eyes, and wears a heavy black moustache.

JOHN H. SURRATT is about 5 feet 9 inches. Hair rather thin and dark; eyes rather light; no beard. Would weigh 145 or 150 pounds. Complexion rather pale and clear, with color in his cheeks. Wore light clothes of fine quality. Shoulders square; cheek bones rather prominent; chin narrow; ears projecting at the top; forehead rather low and square, but broad. Parts his hair on the right side; neck rather long. His lips are firmly set. A slim man.

DANIEL C. HARROLD is 23 years of age, 5 feet 6 or 7 inches high, rather broad shouldered, otherwise light built; dark hair, little (if any) moustache; dark eyes; weighs about 140 pounds.

GEO. F. NESBITT & CO., Printers and Stationers, cor. Pearl and Pine Streets, N. Y.

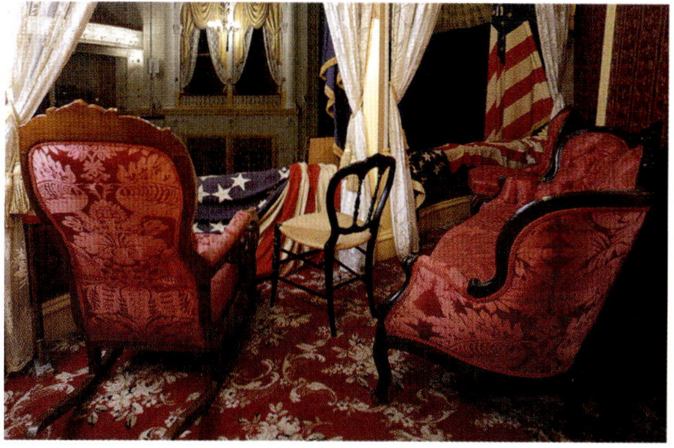

ABOVE: The presidential box where Abraham Lincoln was assassinated. Today Ford's Theatre provides a comprehensive perspective of Lincoln's life and legacy through exhibits and programs at its theater, museum, and education center.

LEFT: A contemporary Reward poster. Four Lincoln conspirators (Lewis Paine, David Herold, George Atzerodt, and Mary Surratt) were hanged in the courtyard of the Washington Arsenal on July 7, 1865. Dr. Samuel Mudd, a physician who treated John Wilkes Booth's broken leg as he evaded capture, narrowly avoided the death sentence and was given a lengthy prison sentence.

PENNSYLVANIA AVENUE, WASHINGTON, DC

The "Grand Review" brought days of parades as the new president and the crowds honored Union forces

Mourning gave way to celebration again in late May 1865 when the grizzled veterans of the Union armies marched into Washington for what would be named the "Grand Review." On May 24 the victor of Gettysburg, General George Meade, led 80,000 men of the Army of the Potomac down Pennsylvania Avenue to the cheers of spectators. The next day, it was Sherman's Army of the Tennessee and Army of Georgia that marched along Pennsylvania Avenue. The new president, Andrew Johnson, sat in a reviewing stand near the White House. Sherman would later describe the review as "a fitting conclusion to the campaign and the war." Today, a statue of Sherman towers over the site where the reviewing stand was once located.

Following the Grand Review, veterans of the fighting at Bull Run decided to return

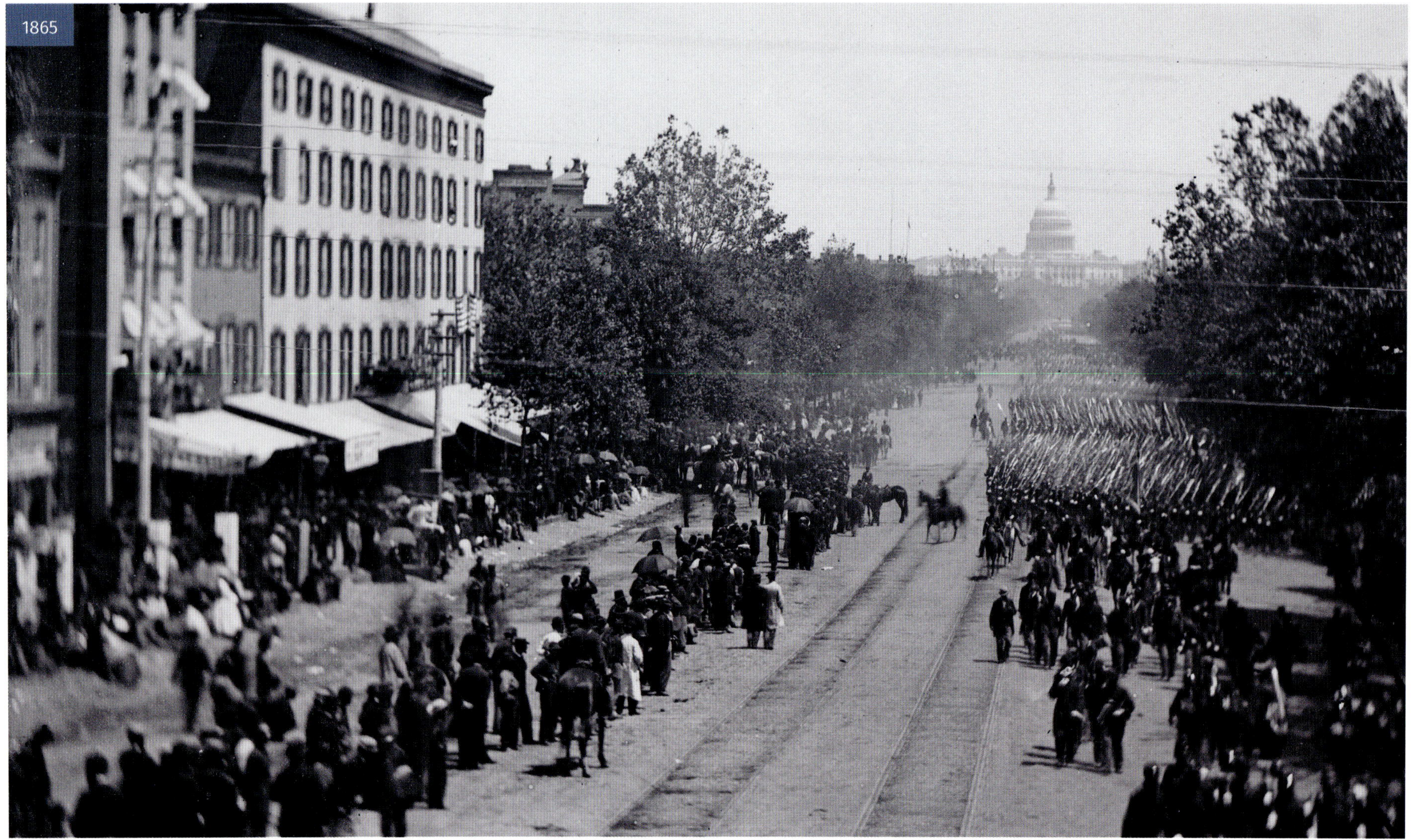
1865

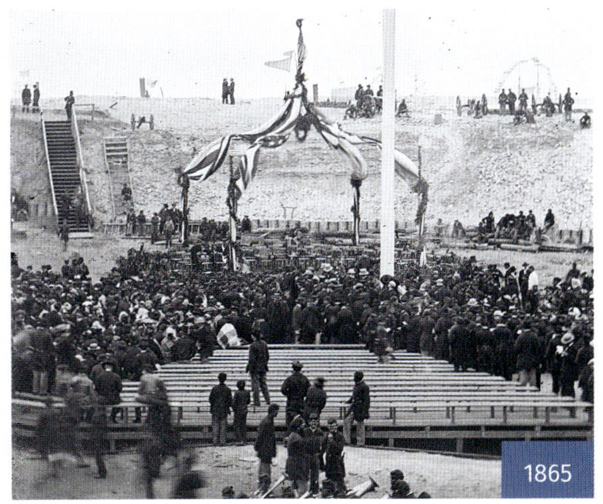
1865

to the battlefield to remember their comrades who had died there. Many of them were appalled by the poor condition of the graves. Bleached bones were visible poking out from the ground where they had been buried in shallow graves. Eventually, the Bull Run/Manassas dead were reinterred in a vault at Arlington National Cemetery. On June 10, 1865, two stone monuments were dedicated on the battlefield, commemorating the two battles fought in 1861 and 1862. One monument was placed on Henry House Hill, not far from the family cemetery were Judith Henry was buried. The second monument was placed near the "Deep Cut" at Groveton, the scene of heavy fighting in August 1862. Today both monuments are protected by the National Park Service.

FORT SUMTER

Fort Sumter, like Charleston, was ultimately evacuated without a fight. On April 14, 1865, four years to the day after he had surrendered the fort, Robert Anderson, now a major general, participated in a special ceremony on the blasted parade ground of the all but ruined citadel (pictured left). Joined by some of the men who served under him during those early days of the war, Anderson raised over Sumter the same battered flag he had lowered in the spring of 1861.

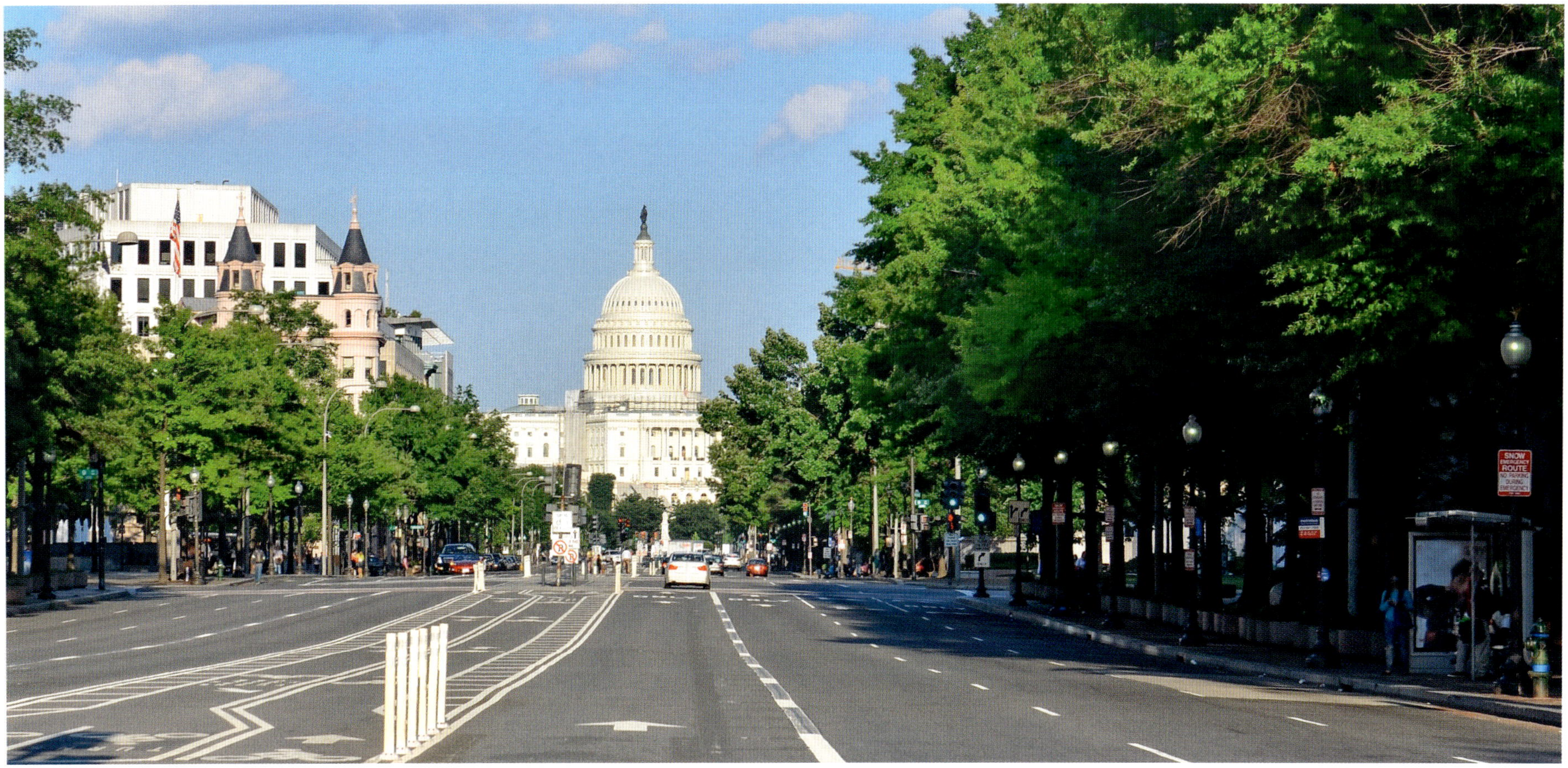

WALT WHITMAN JR HOME, NEW JERSEY

The American poet and essayist, was one of the most influential literary figures in America

Walt Whitman is regarded as one of America's finest poets. Whitman was born on May 31, 1819, in Long Island, New York, and grew up in Brooklyn. The bustling, fast-growing city exposed him to working-class life and politics, all of which became central themes in his poetry. Largely self-educated, Whitman began working as a printer and later became a teacher and journalist.

In 1855, he self-published the first edition of *Leaves of Grass*, a collection of twelve poems that introduced his free-verse style. The book was both praised and criticized for its candid exploration of the human body and spirit, but it quickly positioned Whitman as a new kind of American poet. Over the next four decades, he tinkered and revised *Leaves of Grass* in what would become a lifelong project.

The Civil War deeply affected Whitman. He served as a volunteer nurse in military hospitals in Washington, DC, and witnessed the horrors of war and the resilience of the human spirit. They were experiences that profoundly shaped poems like "The Wound-Dresser" for which he had searing first-hand knowledge.

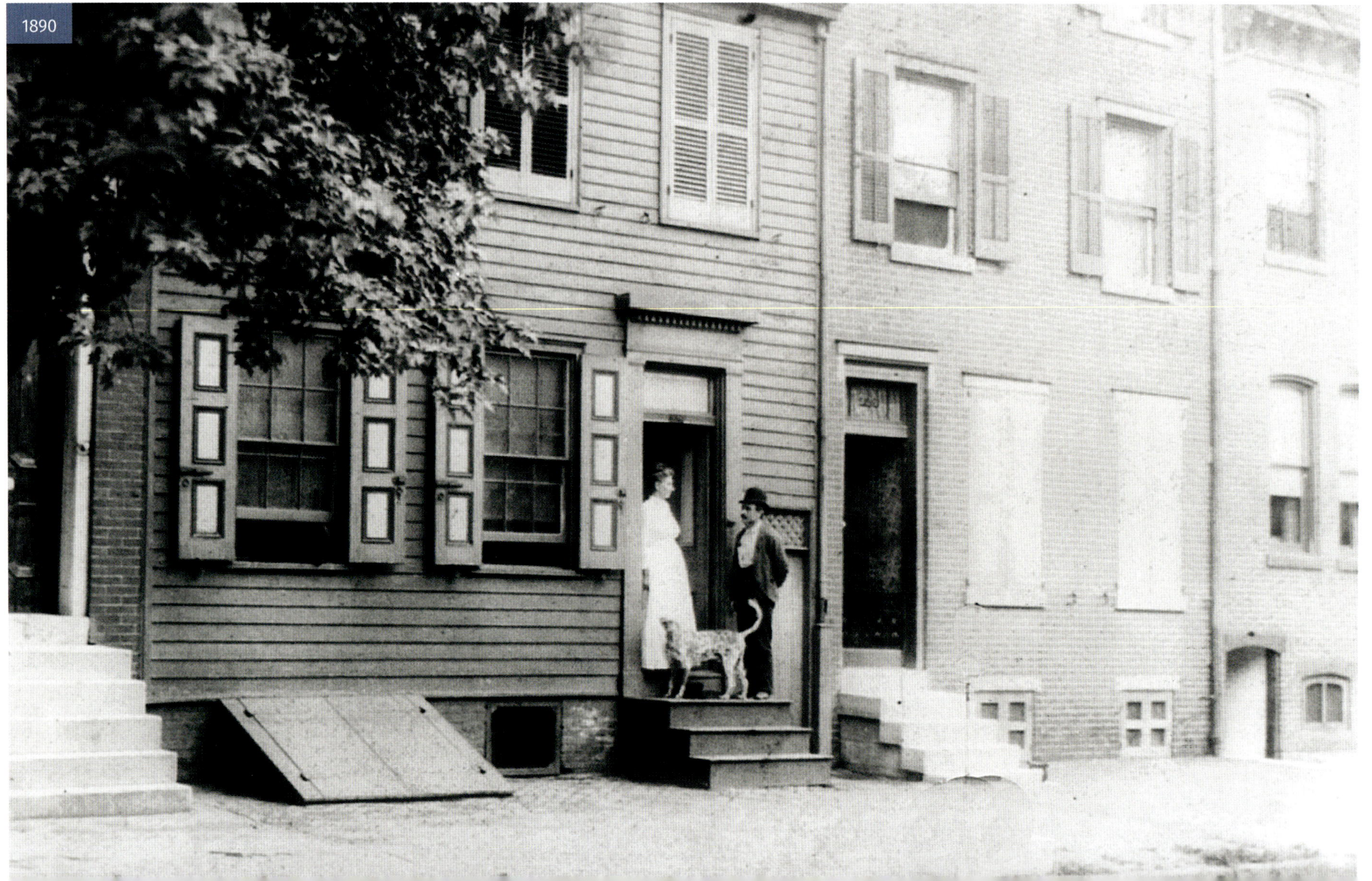
1890

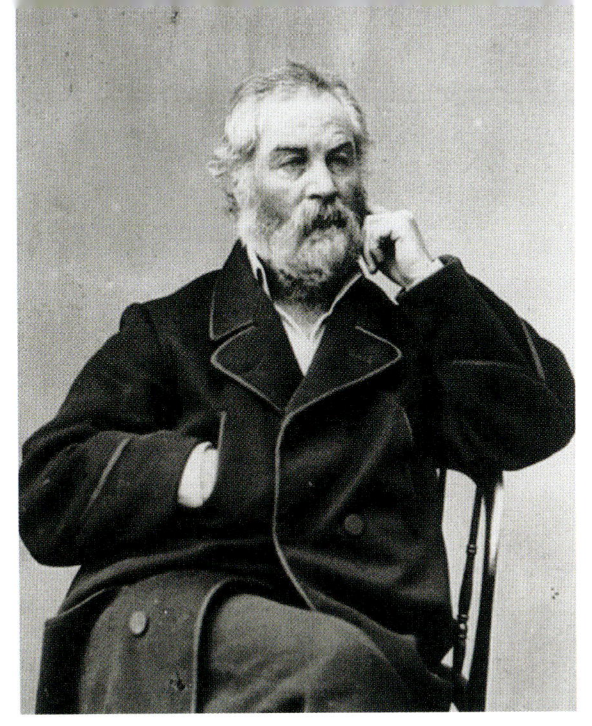

In 1873, after suffering a stroke and the death of his mother, Whitman moved to Camden, New Jersey, to live with his brother George. In 1884, he purchased a small, two-story house at 328 Mickle Street. Despite its modest appearance, the Camden home became a center of literary activity. Visitors from across the country and Europe came to see Whitman in his final years, with his free-flowing white beard giving him the appearance of "Old Father Time."

He oversaw the "Deathbed Edition" of *Leaves of Grass*, and wrote *Specimen Days*, a mix of memoir and observation. Whitman died in the house on March 26, 1892. He was buried in a granite tomb he designed himself in Camden's Harleigh Cemetery. After his death, the house changed hands several times but was eventually preserved by admirers. As Camden's industries dwindled through the twentieth century, the surrounding neighborhood, declined. Mickle Street became Dr. Martin Luther King Jr. Boulevard. Despite the area's challenges, the house remained standing and was declared a National Historic Landmark in 1962.

Today, the interior has been carefully restored to reflect the way it looked in Whitman's time, and it now operates as a museum open to the public. Visitors can walk the same narrow halls, see Whitman's bedroom, and view artifacts such as his original writing desk and personal belongings. The museum also serves as an educational and cultural site.

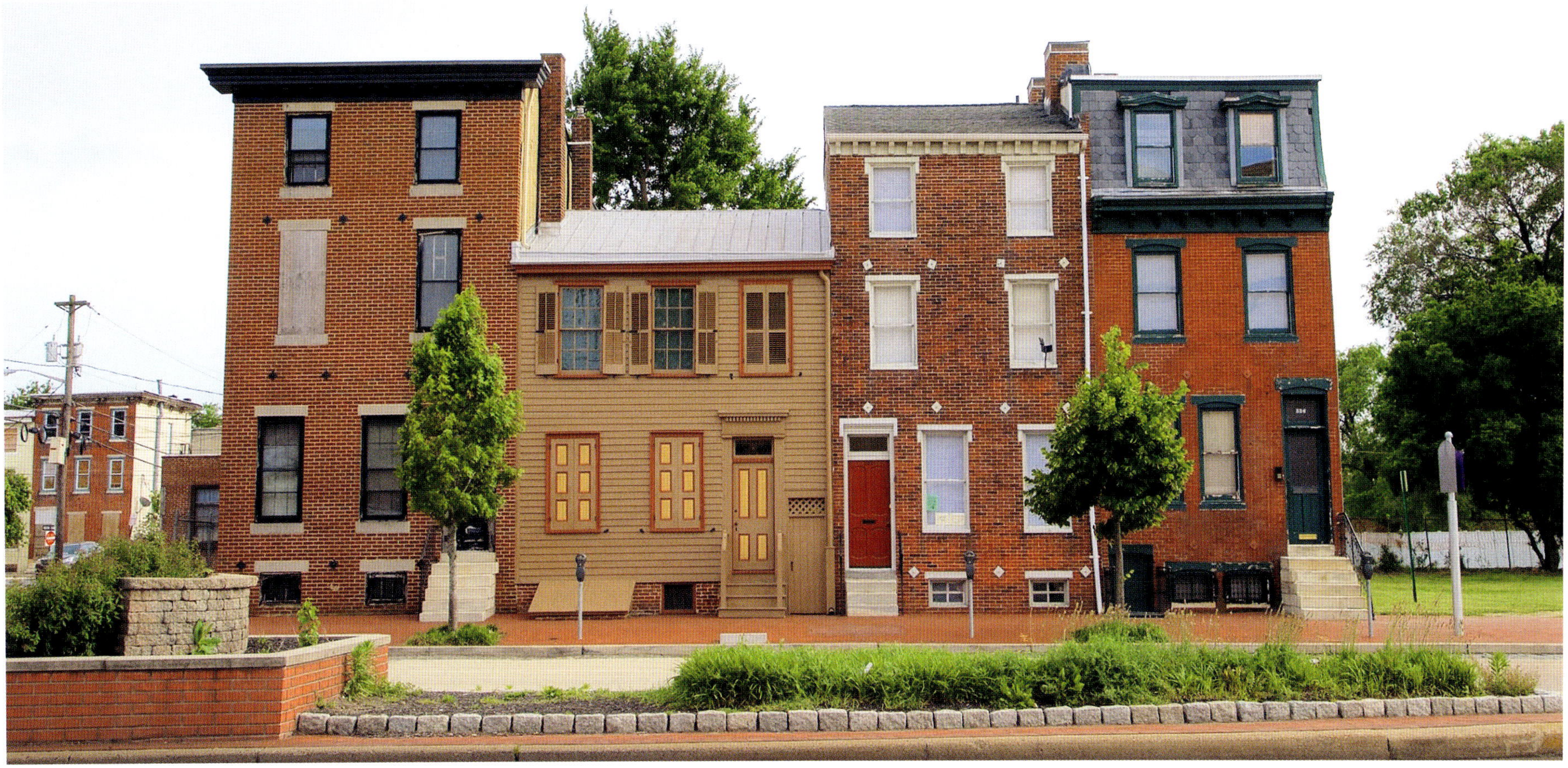

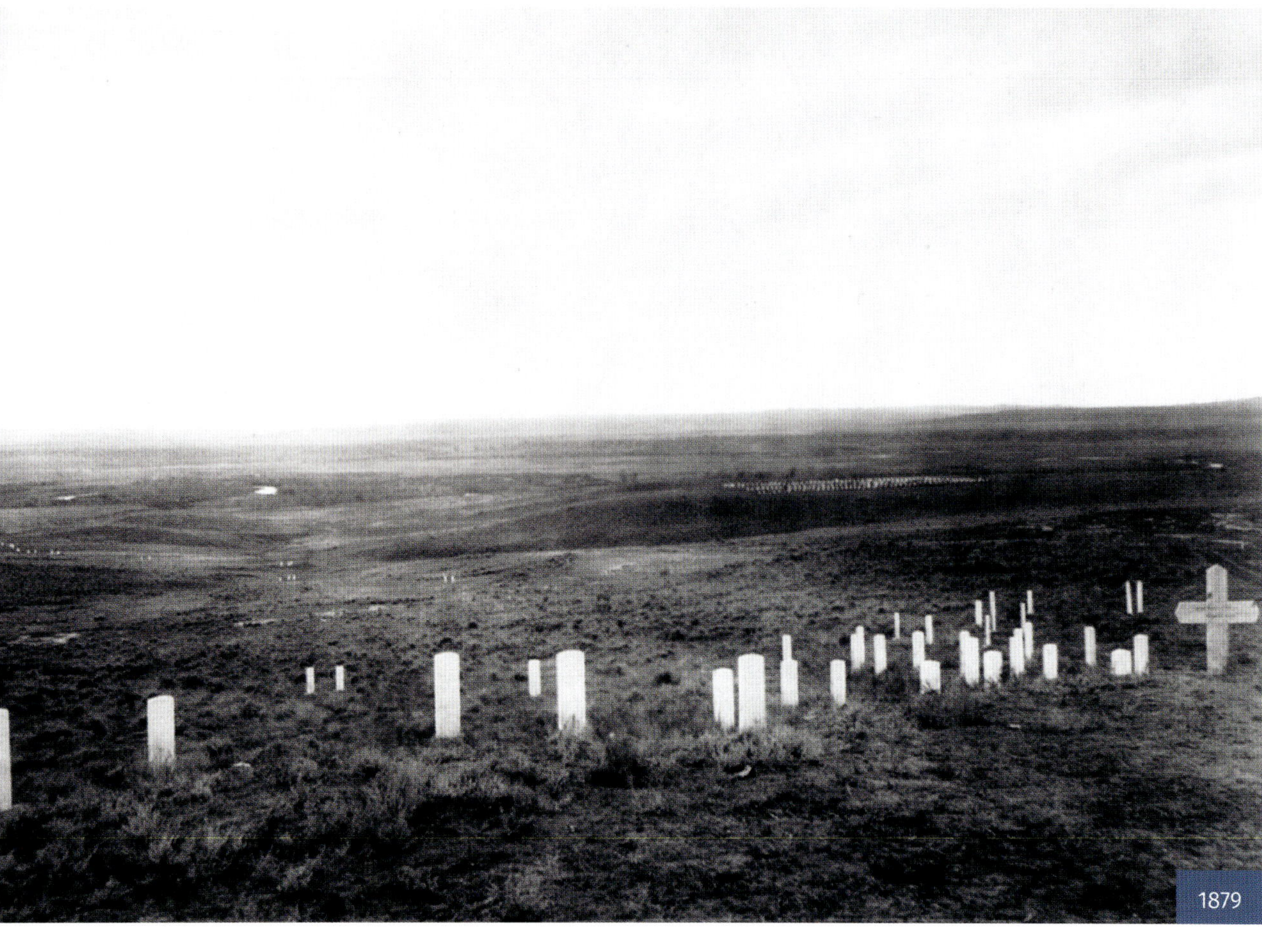

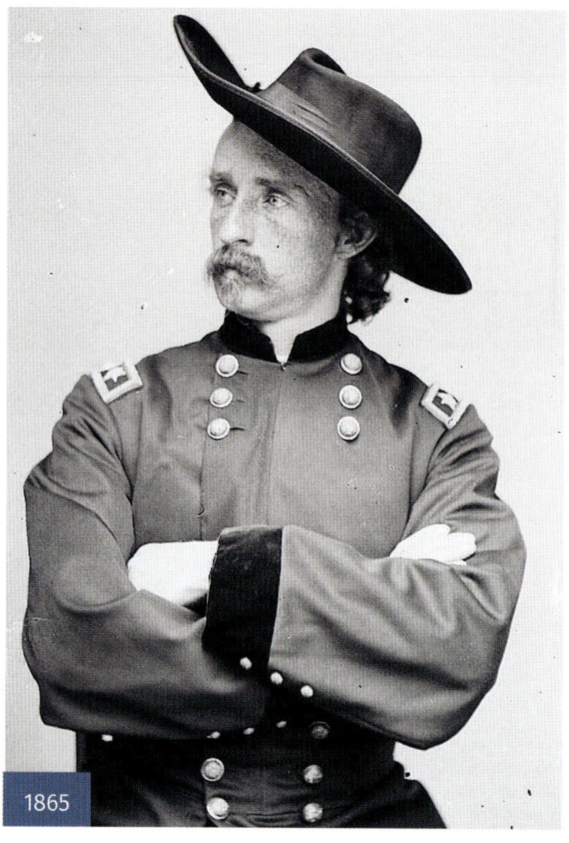

THE BATTLE OF THE LITTLE BIGHORN, SOUTH DAKOTA

Trouble flared when gold was found in the Black Hills of the Lakota Sioux

The Battle of the Little Bighorn, fought on June 25–26, 1876, was the climax of growing tensions between the United States government and several Plains Indian tribes—most notably the Lakota Sioux, Northern Cheyenne, and Arapaho. The roots of the conflict trace back to decades of westward expansion, broken treaties, and increasing encroachment on Native lands.

Following the Fort Laramie Treaty of 1868, the US government guaranteed the Great Sioux Reservation, including the sacred Black Hills, to the Lakota people. However, in 1874 an expedition led by Lieutenant Colonel George Armstrong Custer confirmed the presence of gold in the Black Hills, triggering a rush of gold miners. Rather than stop the trespassing, the government attempted to renegotiate the treaty and purchase the Black Hills. The Lakota, especially leaders like Sitting Bull and Crazy Horse, refused. A treaty was a treaty.

In 1875, the US issued an ultimatum demanding all "non-reservation" Indians report to agencies by January 31, 1876, or be considered hostile. This was unrealistic, especially during winter. Many bands, including those under Sitting Bull and Crazy Horse, chose to resist rather than comply.

By spring 1876, the US launched a three-pronged military campaign to force the "hostiles" back onto reservations. Custer's 7th Cavalry formed one column, and when his scouts located a large Indian encampment near the Little Bighorn River in

ABOVE LEFT: Captain George Kaiser Sanderson created the first Custer battlefield memorial on the site of the Battle of the Little Bighorn in Montana in 1879.

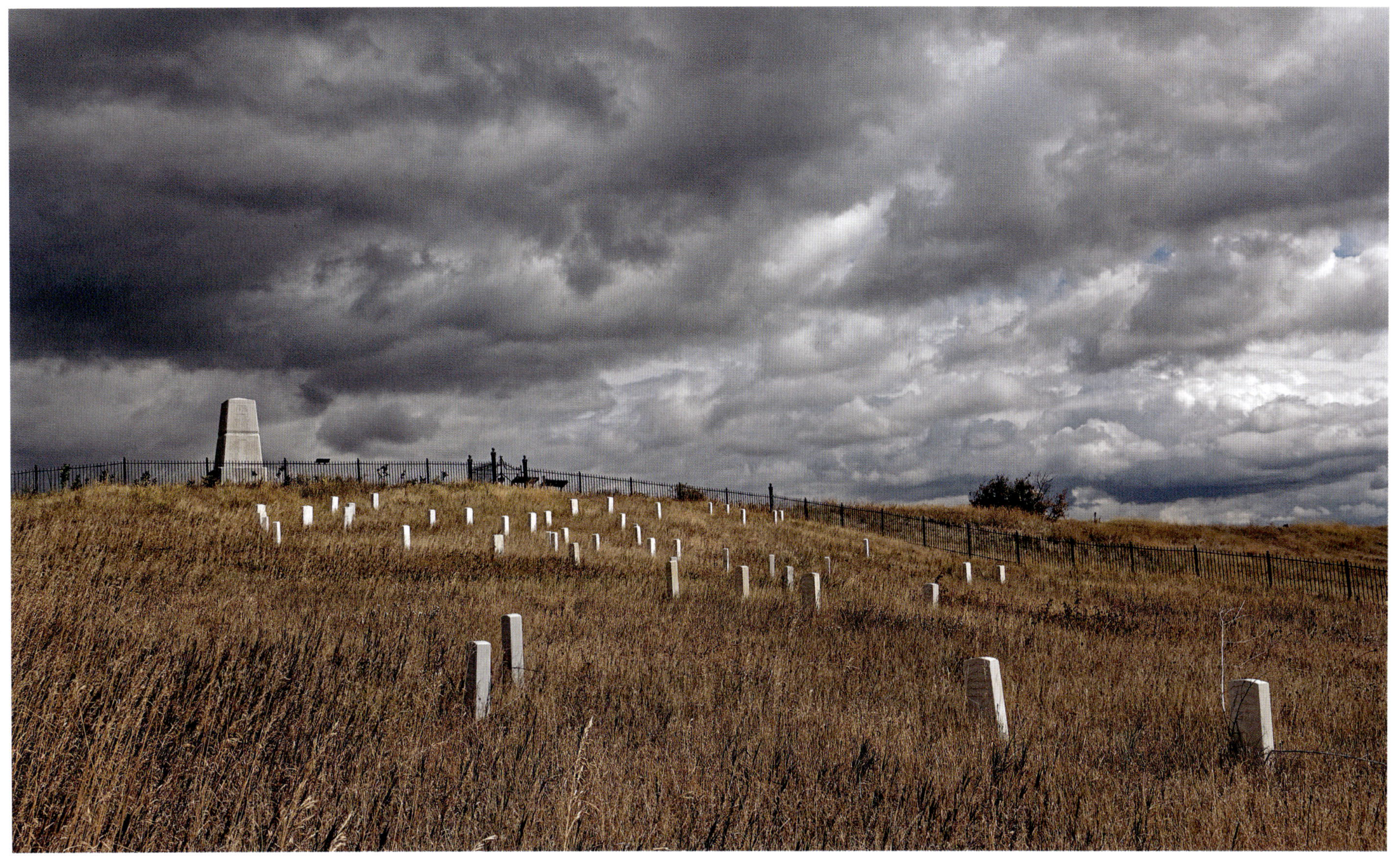

present-day Montana, Custer chose to attack rather than wait for reinforcements. Underestimating the Native forces, he divided his regiment and engaged what turned out to be a massive village of 1,500–2,000. Custer and over 260 of his men were killed in what Native participants viewed as a defensive victory.

Although the battle was a short-term triumph for the Lakota and their allies, the aftermath proved devastating. The American public, shocked and enraged by what was labeled "Custer's Last Stand," demanded a swift and punitive response. The government redoubled its military efforts, sending thousands more troops into the region. Within a year, most of the major Native leaders had surrendered. Crazy Horse was captured and later killed in 1877. Sitting Bull fled to Canada but eventually surrendered in 1881.

Congress then revoked treaty guarantees to the Black Hills and forced the Lakota to cede the territory without consent.

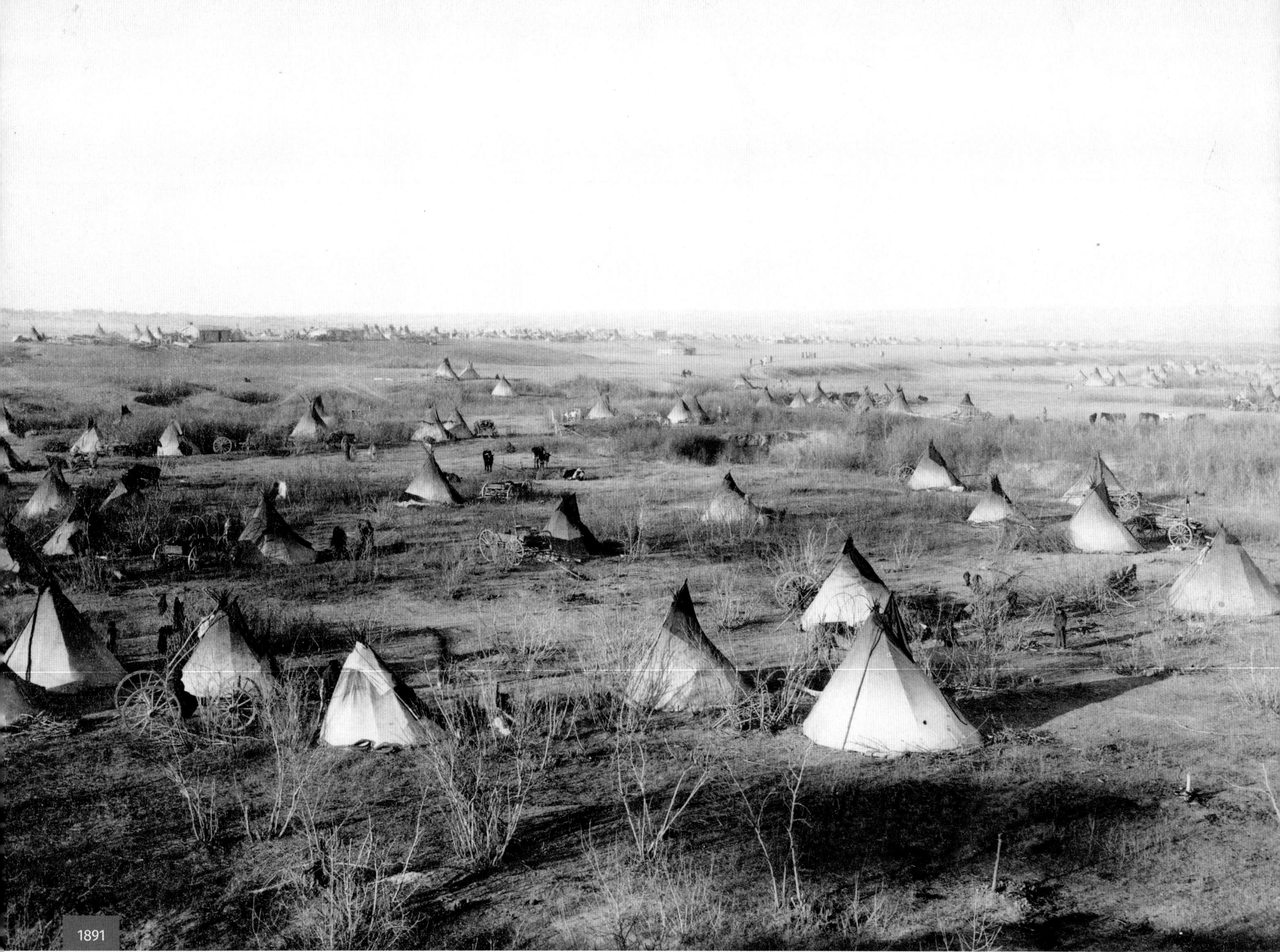
1891

WOUNDED KNEE MASSACRE, SOUTH DAKOTA

The US government were fearful of the Ghost Dance movement

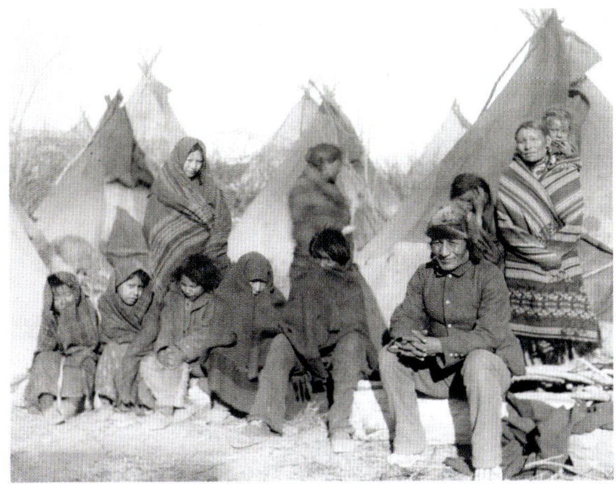

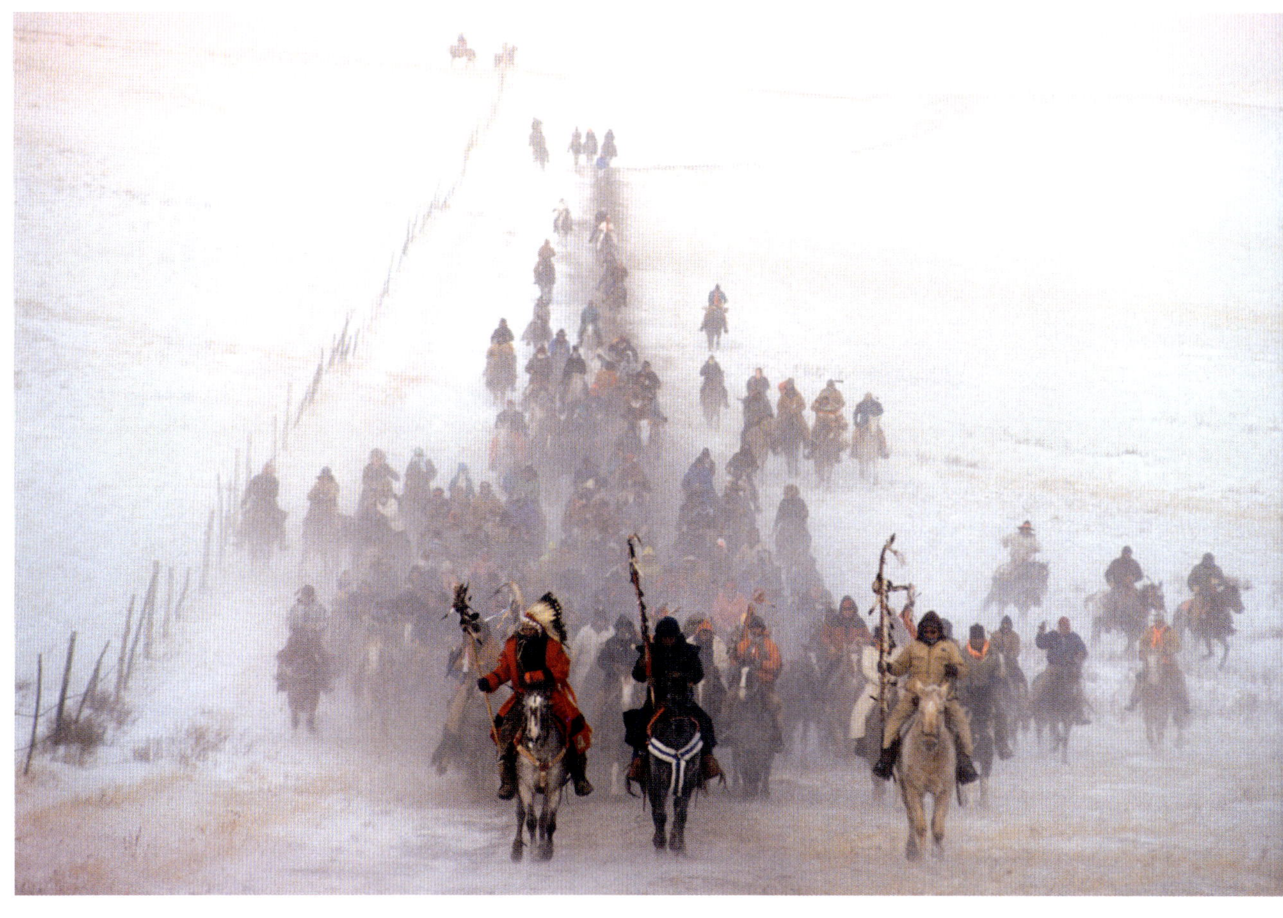

The Lakota, like many Plains tribes, faced starvation due to the decimation of buffalo and inadequate rations from the government. In the late 1880s, a religious revival called the Ghost Dance swept through Native communities. Founded by the Paiute prophet Wovoka, the movement promised a return of Native lands, the disappearance of white settlers, and the resurrection of dead ancestors if followers performed the Ghost Dance rituals.

The government, misunderstanding the spiritual nature of the movement, feared it would incite rebellion. This anxiety peaked with the growing popularity of the Ghost Dance among the Lakota Sioux, particularly those under Chief Sitting Bull. Following the defeat of Custer's 7th Cavalry, he had escaped to Canada in 1877, but returned to surrender in 1881. After working as a performer with Buffalo Bill's Wild West Show, Sitting Bull returned to the Standing Rock Agency in South Dakota. Authorities feared he would use his influence to support the Ghost Dance movement, but on December 15, 1890, he was killed during a hamfisted arrest attempt by the Indian agency police.

In response, many Lakota fled to seek protection under Chief Spotted Elk (Big Foot), who led his band toward Pine Ridge Reservation. The US Army intercepted them and escorted them to a camp near Wounded Knee Creek. On the morning of December 29, the Army attempted to disarm the group. A shot was fired—by whom is still unclear—and soldiers opened fire using Hotchkiss guns, a rapid-fire gun, killing an estimated 250–300 Lakota, most of them unarmed women and children. Chief Spotted Elk was not spared.

The massacre marked a symbolic end to Native armed resistance in the US. Though 20 soldiers received Medals of Honor, the massacre has been widely condemned as an atrocity. It signaled the effective end of the Indian Wars. Young Man Afraid of His Horses, was a respected Oglala Lakota chief and the son of Old Man Afraid of His Horses. He was a moderate and diplomatic leader who consistently sought peaceful solutions with the government. Though not directly involved in the Ghost Dance or Wounded Knee itself, he played a significant role in trying to calm tensions at Pine Ridge in the days leading up to and following the massacre. He helped mediate between Lakota bands and US authorities, working to avoid further bloodshed. His efforts likely helped prevent more violence at Pine Ridge during that volatile time.

OPPOSITE: A Lakota camp near Pine Ridge Reservation in 1891.

ABOVE: Survivors of Wounded Knee huddle against the cold in 1890.

ABOVE RIGHT: In 1990, the Lakota reenacted Chief Big Foot's flight from the 7th Calvary for the 100th anniversary of the Wounded Knee Massacre. They rode in freezing temperatures to the site of the massacre on the Pine Ridge Reservation.

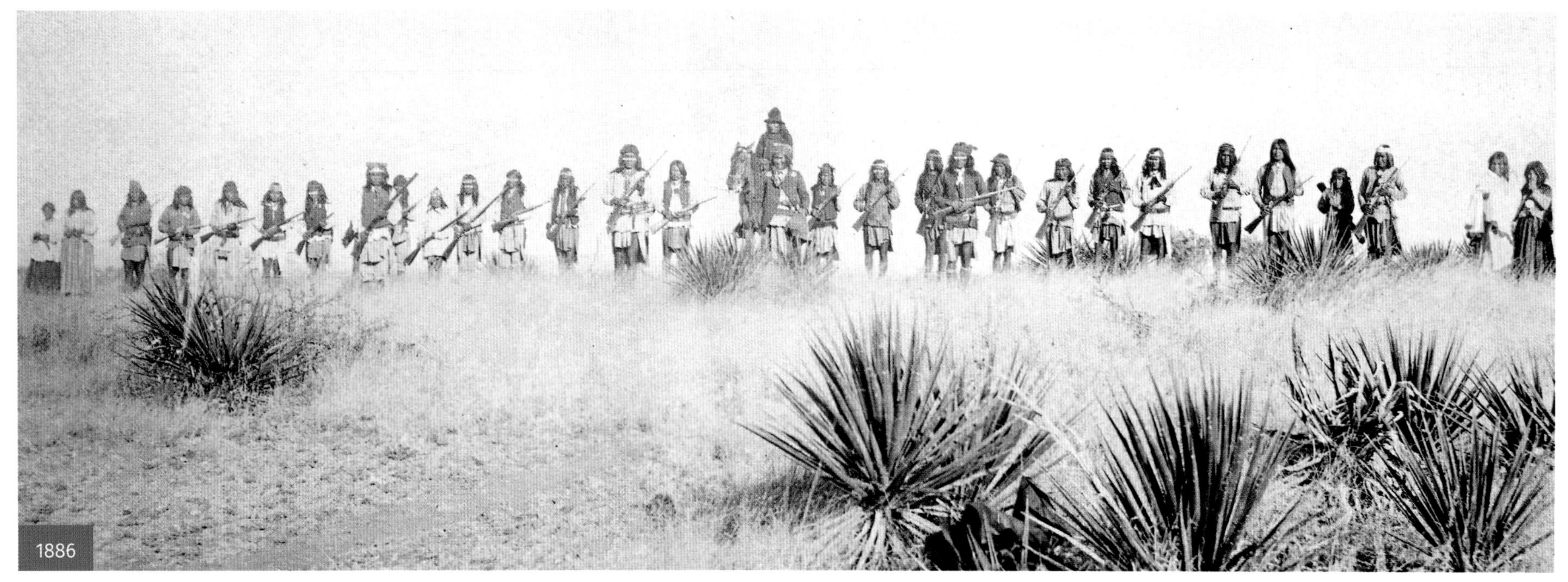
1886

GERONIMO, FORT SILL, OKLAHOMA

The trail of the most fearsome Apache finally ended in 1886

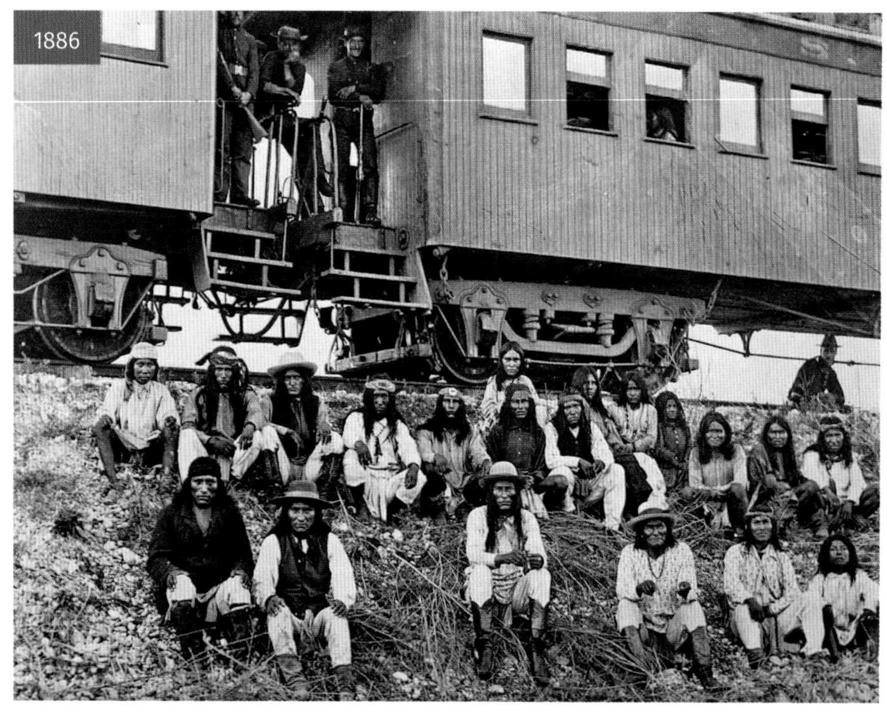
1886

Geronimo (whose tribal name means "One Who Yawns") was born in 1829 in what is now Arizona, and was then a part of Mexico. He was a prominent Bedonkohe Apache and his fierce resistance to Mexican and later American encroachment on Apache lands gained him a fearsome reputation. His animosity intensified after a Mexican raid in 1851 killed his mother, wife, and three children.

Over decades, he led breakouts from reservations, evaded capture, and fought US and Mexican forces. His final campaign ended in 1886. First Lieutenant Charles B. Gatewood, known to the Apache as "Long Nose," led the expedition which brought Geronimo and his followers back to the reservation system for a final time.

Geronimo credited Gatewood for his decision to surrender, as Gatewood was well known to Geronimo, spoke some Apache, and was familiar with and honored their traditions. He acknowledged his pursuers' tenacity for wearing the Apaches down with constant pursuit. He and his followers had little or no time to rest or stay in one place. Completely worn out, the small band of Apaches returned to the US with a full guard and officially surrendered to General Miles on September 4, 1886, at Skeleton Canyon, Arizona.

After his surrender in 1886, Geronimo and about 400 Apache men, women, and children were forcibly removed to Florida, where many died from disease and harsh

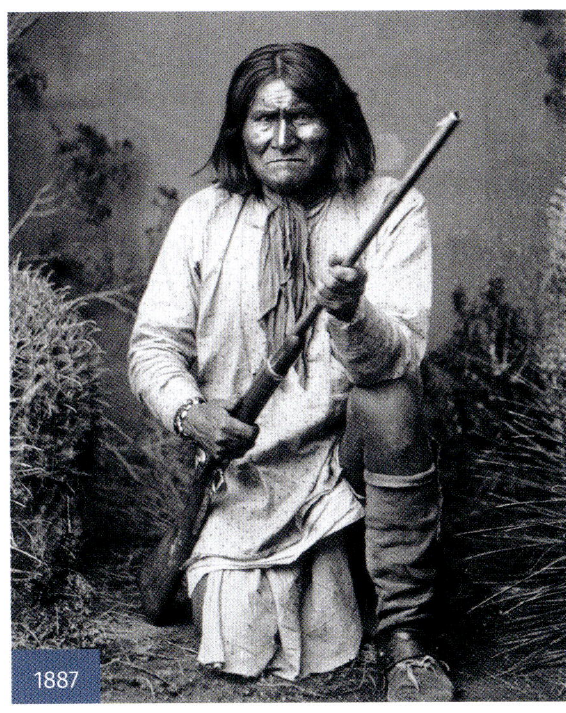

conditions. "In that alien climate," The *Washington Post* reported, "the Apache died like flies at frost time." On the train ride to Fort Sill, many tourists wanted a memento of Geronimo, so they paid 25 cents for a button that he cut off his shirt or a hat he took off his head. As the train would pull into depots along the way, Geronimo would buy more buttons to sew on and more hats to sell.

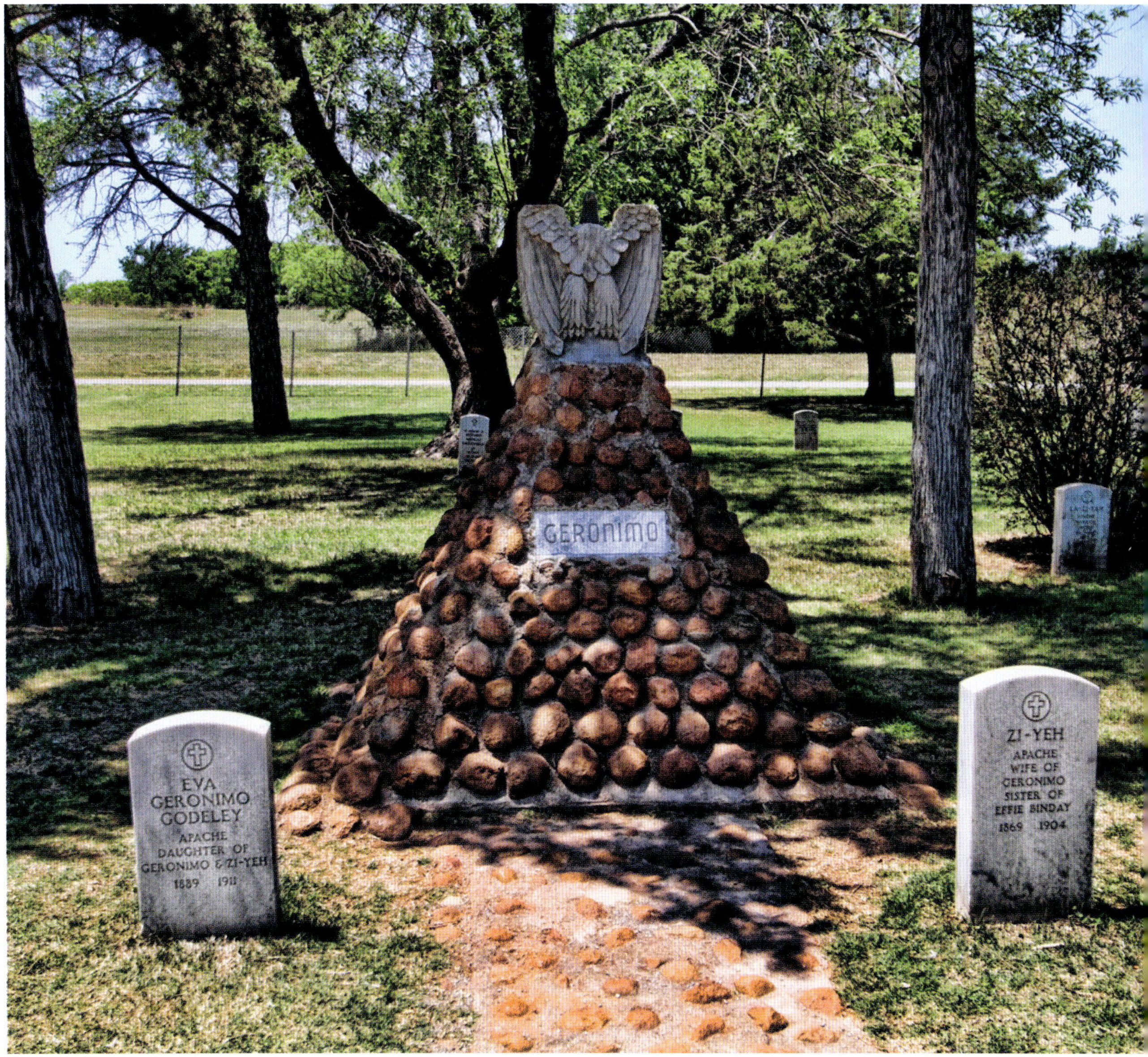

He was a prisoner-of-war for the rest of his days, allowed out on license, but always under armed guard. He made appearances at world's fairs—the Omaha Exposition of 1898 gave Geronimo celebrity status, and for the rest of his life he was in demand as an attraction, including appearances at Pawnee Bill's Wild West shows.

He dictated his autobiography in 1906, *Geronimo: His Own Story*, to S. M. Barrett, which further shaped public perception. Geronimo died on February 17, 1909, after being thrown from his horse and developing pneumonia. He is buried at Fort Sill, Oklahoma, in the tomb pictured above right.

OPPOSITE TOP: Geronimo, at right of the horse at center, stands with his warriors after surrendering in the Sierra Madre Mountains of Mexico.

OPPOSITE BOTTOM: The band of Apache prisoners during a rest stop beside the Southern Pacific Railway, near Nueces River, Texas, on their way into exile. Geronimo and his son are in matching shirts, bottom right.

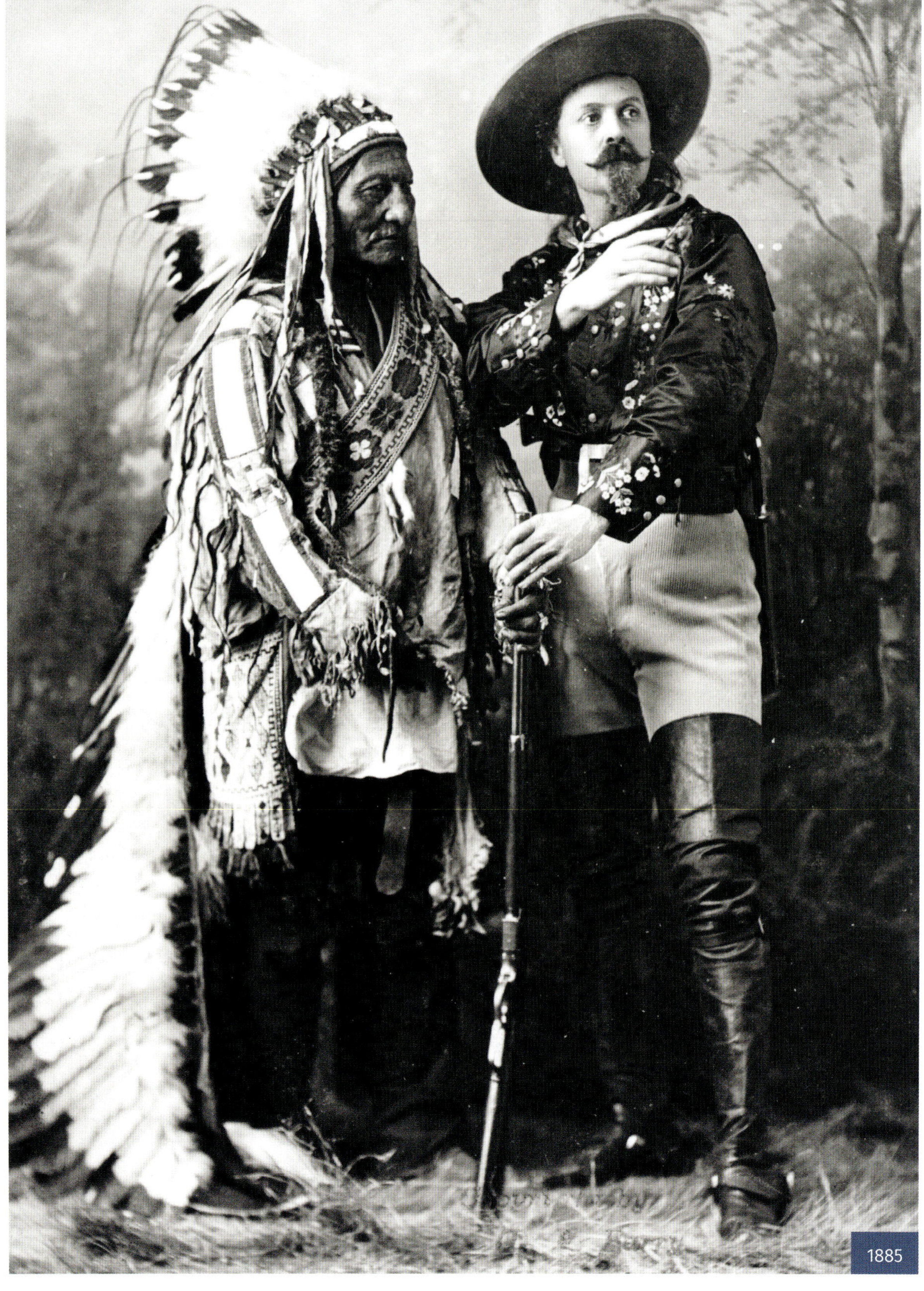
1885

BUFFALO BILL'S WILD WEST SHOW, CODY, WYOMING

The curtain closed on the Old West's greatest showman in 1913

William Frederick "Buffalo Bill" Cody was born in Le Claire, Iowa Territory, in 1846. Cody grew up in Kansas during a time of violent border conflicts and westward expansion. He began working at a young age—first as a messenger, then as a Pony Express rider at just 14. During the Civil War, he served as a Union scout and later became a civilian scout—along with Wild Bill Hickok—for the US Army during the Indian Wars. In 1872, he received the Medal of Honor (later rescinded and posthumously restored) for his services.

Cody earned the nickname "Buffalo Bill" for his work supplying meat to railroad workers. According to his own account, he killed over 4,000 buffalo in 18 months, a feat that contributed to his legend and also symbolized the destructive element of western expansion.

Around the same time, his life began to cross into the realm of entertainment. He starred in a stage play titled *Scouts of the Prairie*, one of the first times a real frontiersman played himself on stage. His natural charisma and storytelling ability captivated audiences.

In 1883, Cody created *Buffalo Bill's Wild West*, a traveling show that would define his career. The show, mounted in a big top, had a variety of elements: sharpshooting with trick shots from Annie Oakley, Frank Butler (Oakley's husband), and Pawnee Bill; cowboy skills such as lasso throwing, roping, and bareback riding; cowboy vs. outlaw chases; stagecoach hold-ups and rescues; battle reenactments, such as Custer's Last Stand, naturally given a heroic twist; and

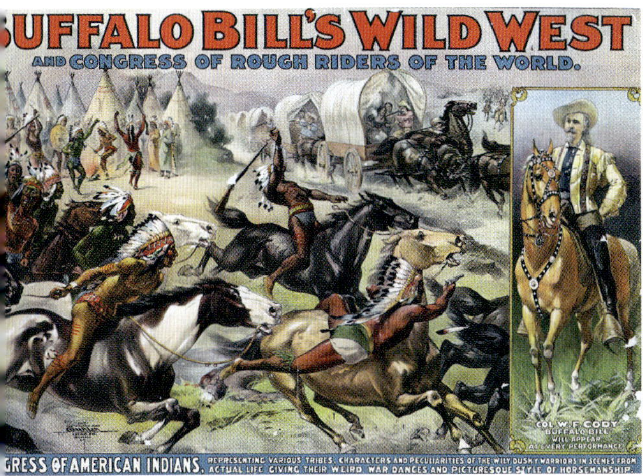

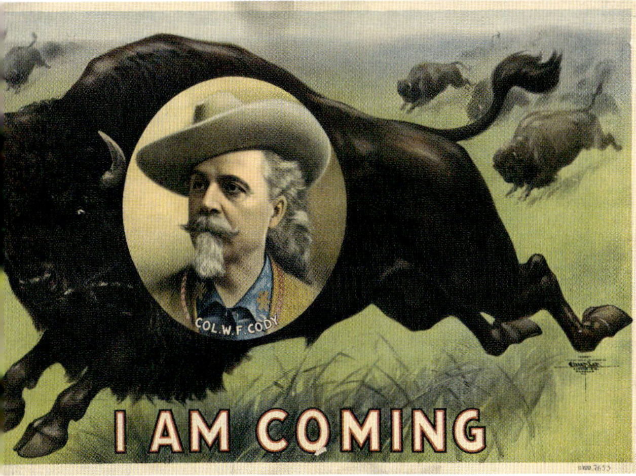

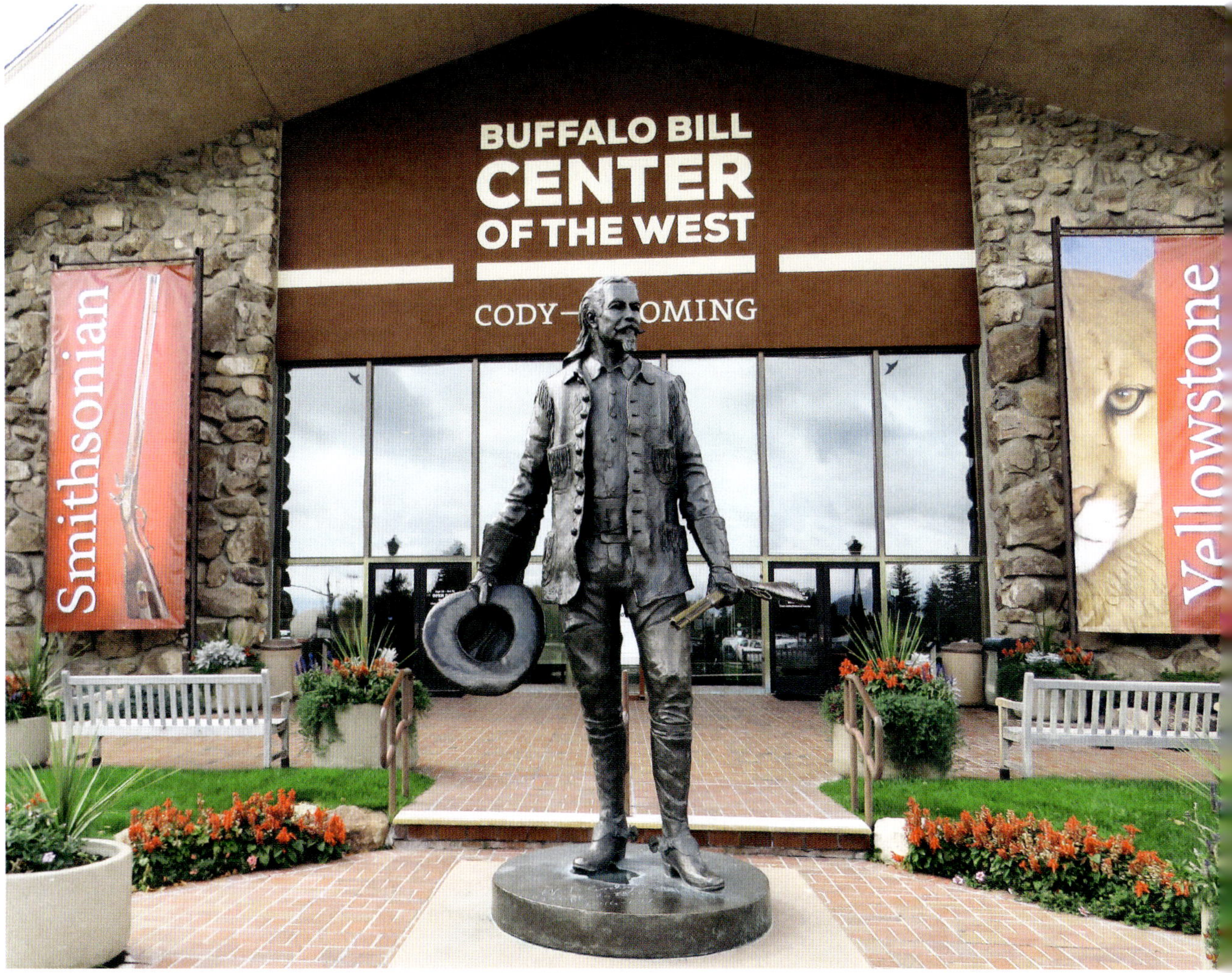

OPPOSITE: Sitting Bull appeared with Buffalo Bill for one season in 1885 and although Cody portrayed them as friends, the great Indian chief was largely motivated by the money.

ABOVE: Two posters advertising the show from around 1899. The top poster depicts Native Americans attacking a pioneer wagon train, but many different cowboy skills were often on show.

ABOVE RIGHT: Buffalo Bill's statue appears out front of the Center of the West museum in Cody, Wyoming.

Native American portrayals of Lakota, Cheyenne and other tribes that included war dances, buffalo hunts, and Indian attacks. Sitting Bull appeared in the show in 1885. The show obscured the brutal realities of Native displacement and frontier violence, but despite profiting from frontier mythmaking, Cody eventually advocated for fair treatment of Native Americans and spoke out against mistreatment by the US government.

The Wild West Show remained popular for decades, touring across Europe and even performing before royalty. However, by the early twentieth century tastes were changing, and Cody faced financial struggles. He went bankrupt in 1913 and his once great show was absorbed by others. Buffalo Bill died in 1917 in Denver, Colorado. He was buried on Lookout Mountain overlooking the Great Plains—a symbolic resting place for a man who embellished Old West history.

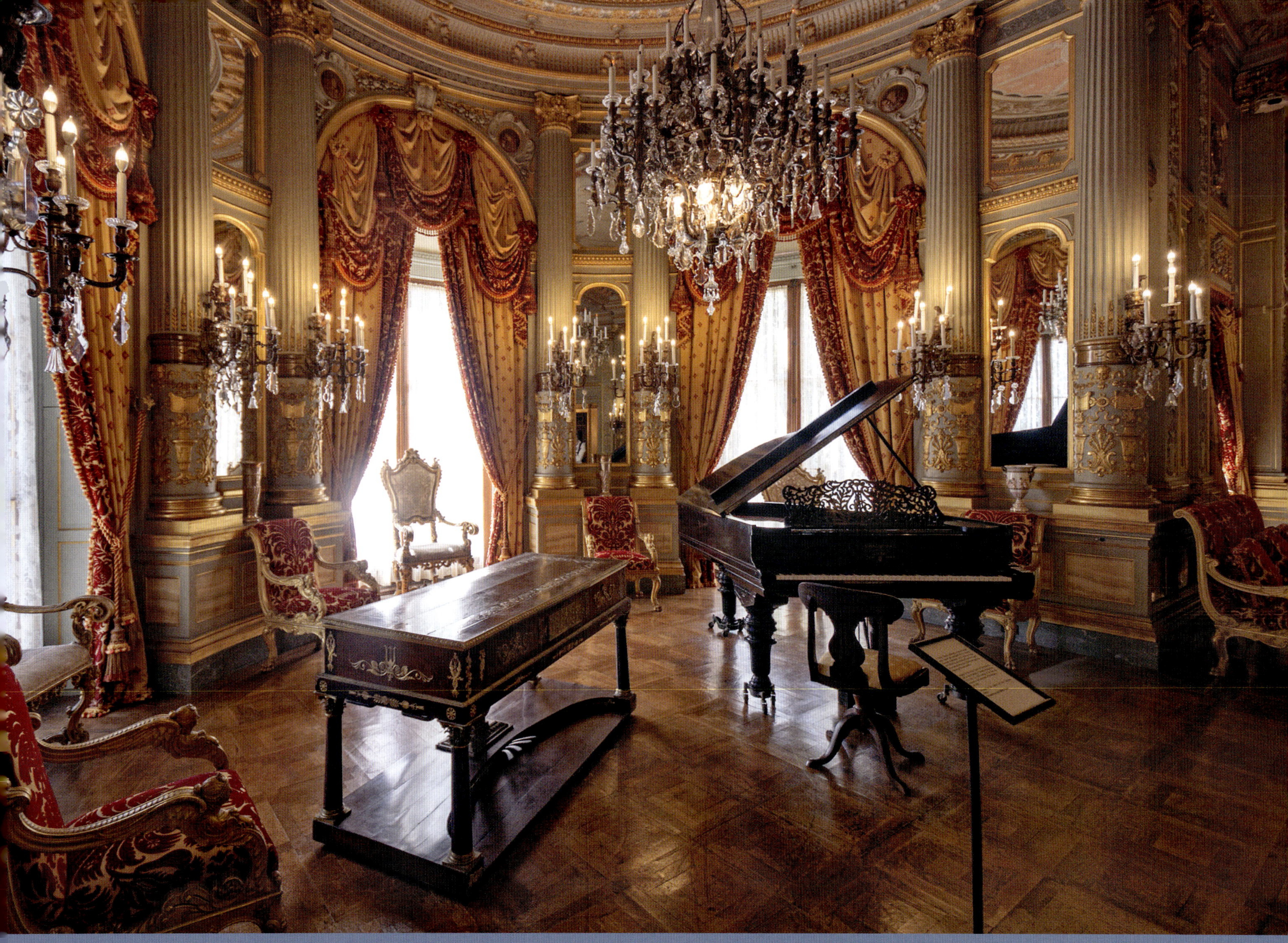

THE GILDED AGE

The Gilded Age—roughly from the 1870s to the turn of the century—was a period of extraordinary change in the United States. It was an age of railroads and robber barons, tycoons and tenements, and some extraordinary architectural and engineering feats. Travel in the newly opened-up territories boomed and luxury hotels boomed alongside. The phrase Gilded Age was coined by Mark Twain and Charles Dudley Warner in their 1873 satirical novel *The Gilded Age: A Tale of Today.* The book mocked a society that glittered with wealth and innovation on the surface, but was riddled with inequality and unrest beneath.

Twain, born Samuel Langhorne Clemens in Hannibal, Missouri, in 1835, emerged as the literary voice of his time. His ascent from Mississippi riverboat pilot to New York salons paralleled the transformation of America from a patchwork of rural states into an industrial superpower.

POST-CIVIL WAR TRANSFORMATION

Following the Civil War, the United States rapidly modernized. The North's industrial engine accelerated, powered by steel, oil, coal, and railroads. The Transcontinental Railroad, completed in 1869, knitted the nation together and opened the floodgates for migration and commerce.

Cities exploded with growth. Chicago rose from the ashes of its 1871 fire into a steel metropolis with a new architectural template, the skyscraper, that allowed architects to build higher and higher. New York, Boston, and Philadelphia became hubs of finance and culture, teeming with new immigrants from Europe who supplied the labor for burgeoning factories.

Carnegie, Rockefeller, J. P. Morgan, Jay Gould and Cornelius Vanderbilt became synonymous with wealth. But *they* had reached the top of the pyramid.

TWAIN: THE MISSOURIAN OBSERVER

As Mark Twain's fame grew, he became a favorite on the East Coast lecture circuit. Though he often mocked the self-absorbed seriousness of elite society, he was also drawn into it. By the 1880s, Twain was mingling with Harvard-educated intellectuals and dining at Newport mansions. He became great friends with Henry Huttleston Rogers, a prominent figure in Standard Oil, who ultimately helped him out of bankruptcy after one too many rash investments.

URBANIZATION AND IMMIGRATION

The Gilded Age also witnessed mass immigration. Between 1870 and 1900 nearly twelve million immigrants arrived, mostly from Southern and Eastern Europe. Italians, Poles, and Slavs settled in ethnic enclaves in cities, seeking opportunity but often finding poverty and discrimination.

At Ellis Island, the primary entry point in New York, families passed through medical exams and interviews. Despite the hardship, most were allowed in, feeding America's demand for labor. They flooded into cities, forming dense ethnic neighborhoods and supplying labor for factories, mills, slaughterhouses, and railroads. Immigrants built America's skyscrapers and dug its subway tunnels. They endured long hours, dangerous conditions, and exploitation—but they also brought culture and dreams of a better life.

Urban landscapes changed. Streetcars moved from horse-drawn, to cable-drawn, to electrically propelled. Some cities took their urban transports above street level, before deciding that below ground was better.

PULLMAN AND FORD

George M. Pullman, an engineer and entrepreneur, revolutionized long-distance rail travel in the 1860s with his luxurious Pullman sleeping cars. In 1880, he established Pullman, Illinois, a planned community on the outskirts of Chicago. It was a model village with neatly arranged brick homes, schools, shops, and parks—all owned and managed by the company. Pullman believed this would ensure worker loyalty and reduce labor unrest. When the Panic of 1890 struck, though, the enforced layoffs created significant unrest.

As Pullman faded, another industrial titan rose. Henry Ford, born in 1863 on a Michigan farm, would transform not only American manufacturing but society itself. In 1908, Ford introduced the Model T, a simple, affordable automobile aimed at ordinary Americans. To mass-produce it efficiently, he pioneered the moving assembly line in 1913, dramatically reducing production time and cost. A Model T, once assembled in over twelve hours, could now be completed in 90 minutes.

Ford's innovations revolutionized labor. He famously introduced the $5 workday, doubling the average wage, and reducing work hours to eight per day. This not only stabilized his workforce but enabled them to afford the very cars they built—a radical shift in industrial economics.

WORLD'S FAIRS: A CELEBRATION OF PROGRESS

The numerous world's fairs of this era were monuments to industrial progress. The 1893 Columbian Exposition in Chicago, commemorating the 400th anniversary of Columbus's voyage, was a defining moment.

With grand neoclassical buildings, electric lights, moving sidewalks, and a massive Ferris wheel, the fair embodied the optimism of the age. Visitors marveled at the inventions on display, including early automobiles, refrigeration, and even a precursor to the zipper. It was a showcase of American ingenuity and its place on the global stage.

The fairs were also deeply symbolic—presenting a sanitized, triumphant version of industrial America alongside its global competitors. By the end of World War I, America had become the world's largest industrial economy. The great industrial boom of the late nineteenth and early twentieth centuries was a time of dazzling possibility.

Mark Twain, who died in 1910, had become both a beloved humorist and a sharp critic of his era. His rise from Missouri to national prominence mirrored the arc of the Gilded Age: rustic origins, meteoric rise, moral conflict, and eventual acceptance. He had this to say about being a patriot: "Patriotism is supporting your country all the time, and your government when it deserves it."

OPPOSITE: **One of the many ornate rooms from The Breakers mansion in Newport.**

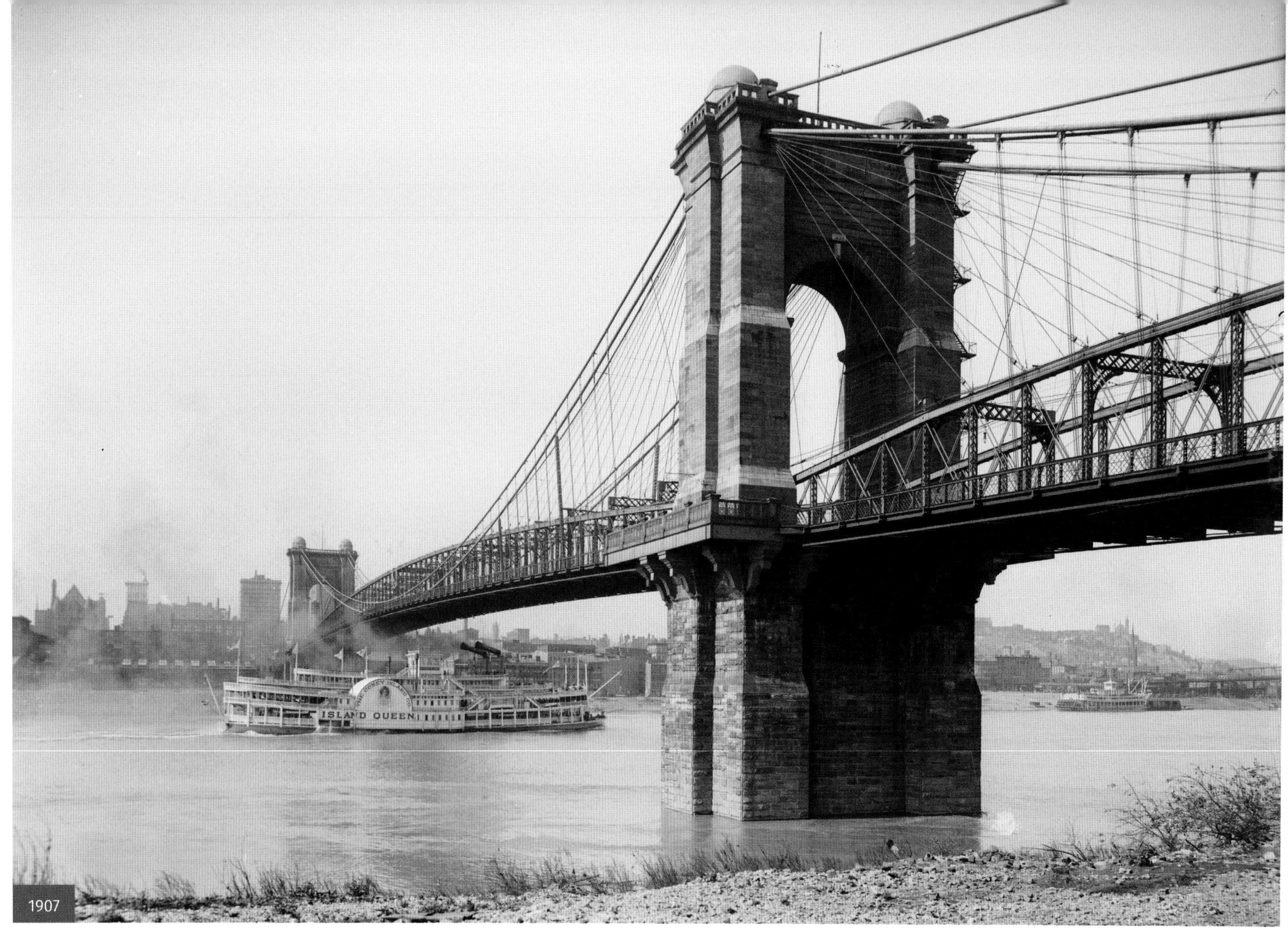

1907

ROEBLING BRIDGE, CINCINNATI

John A. Roebling learned techniques in Cincinnati he would use on a far grander scale

The legacy of the John A. Roebling Suspension Bridge extends beyond Cincinnati. It was the first bridge to cross the Ohio River and the longest suspension bridge in the world at the time. German bridge builder John A. Roebling (born Johann Röbling) was a bridge pioneer and this was the forerunner of his most famous work, the Brooklyn Bridge.

In 1854, a smaller suspension bridge over the Licking River at Newport, Kentucky, had collapsed, an event which deterred investors in the Covington-Cincinnati Bridge Company. Local businessman Amos Shinkle was elected to the board of trustees in 1856 and immediately managed to find new private investors and to garner support from both the Kentucky and Ohio governments.

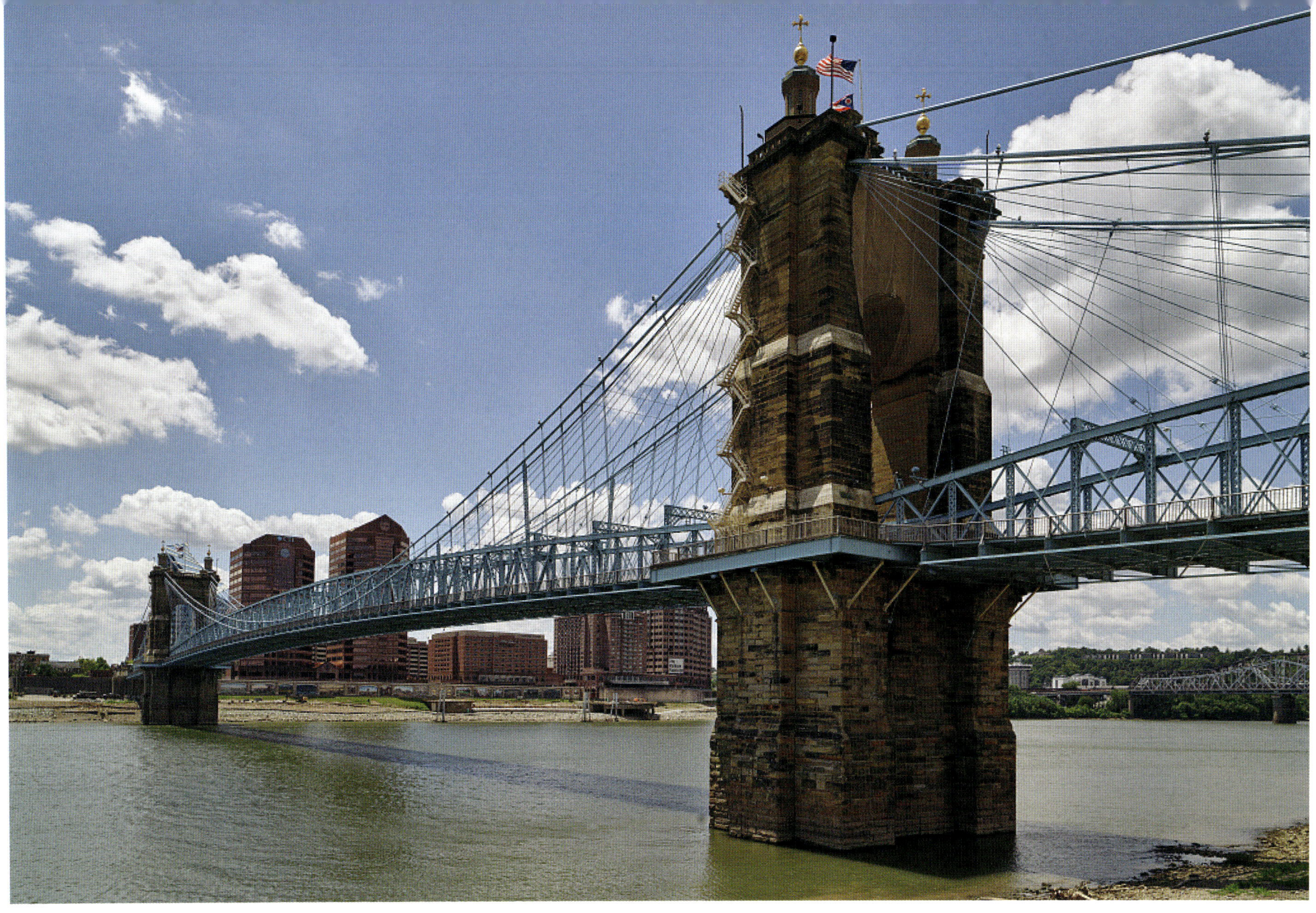

Work on Roebling's pioneering bridge began in 1856, but was halted by the Civil War. In September 1862 Confederate forces moved to invade Cincinnati. The citizens fashioned a pontoon bridge out of coal barges to cross into Kentucky, where they built battlements that dissuaded the rebels. The incident demonstrated the need for Roebling's bridge.

Cincinnati's suspension bridge officially opened on January 1, 1867. Over 166,000 people walked across it in the first two days, charged one cent for the privilege. Drivers of a horse and buggy were charged a toll of 15 cents to cross, while the toll for three horses and a carriage was set at 25 cents.

Inflation of building materials in the post-Civil War construction boom had meant the original deck was made from wood. The bridge piers and hawsers had been engineered to carry the weight of a steel deck, which it duly received in the next century. In 1953, the Commonwealth of Kentucky bought the bridge for $4.2 million and collected tolls until 1963, when it became free to cross.

In the vintage 1907 photo the *Island Queen* steamboat passes underneath, ferrying patrons to and from Coney Island. Coney Island was a seasonal amusement park, opened in 1870, on the banks of the Ohio River approximately ten miles east of the downtown area.

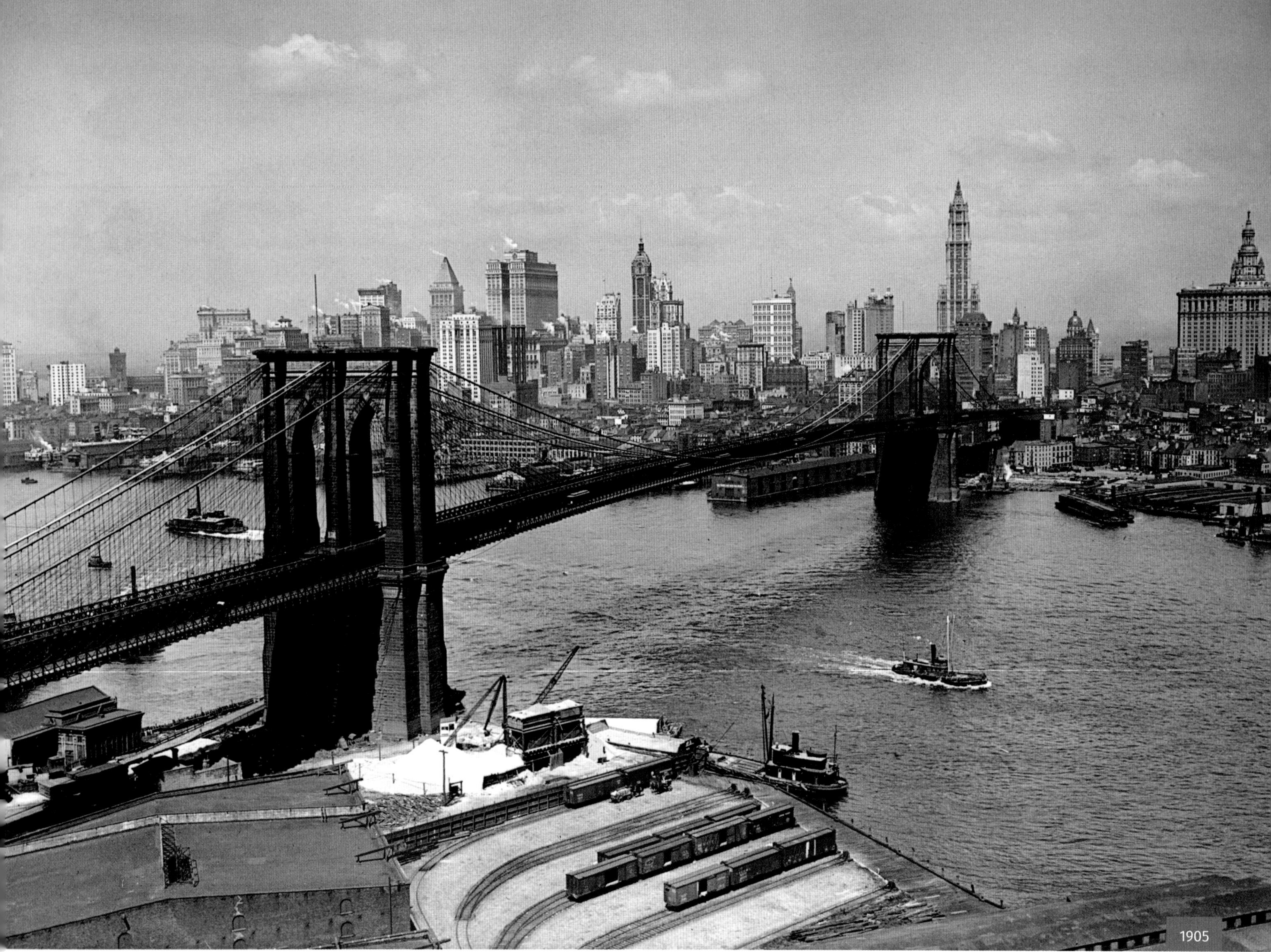
1905

BROOKLYN BRIDGE, BROOKLYN/MANHATTAN

Some early pedestrians were convinced the bridge would fail and plunge into the East River

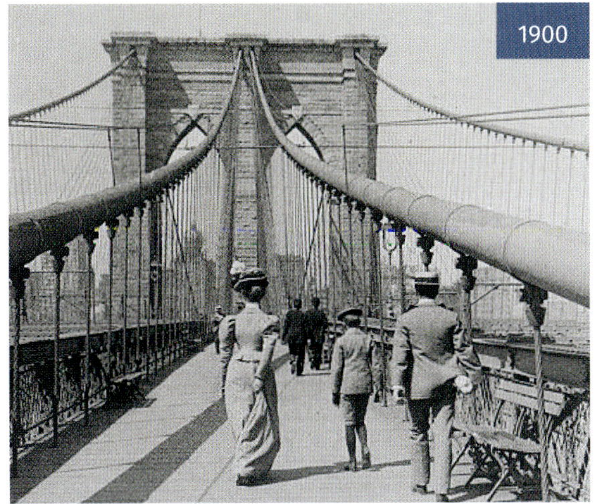

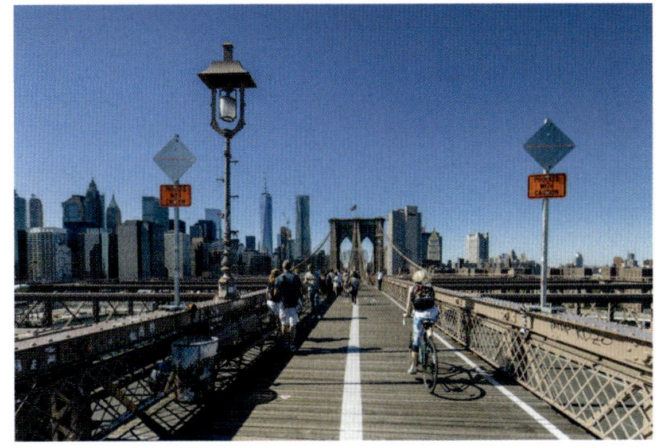

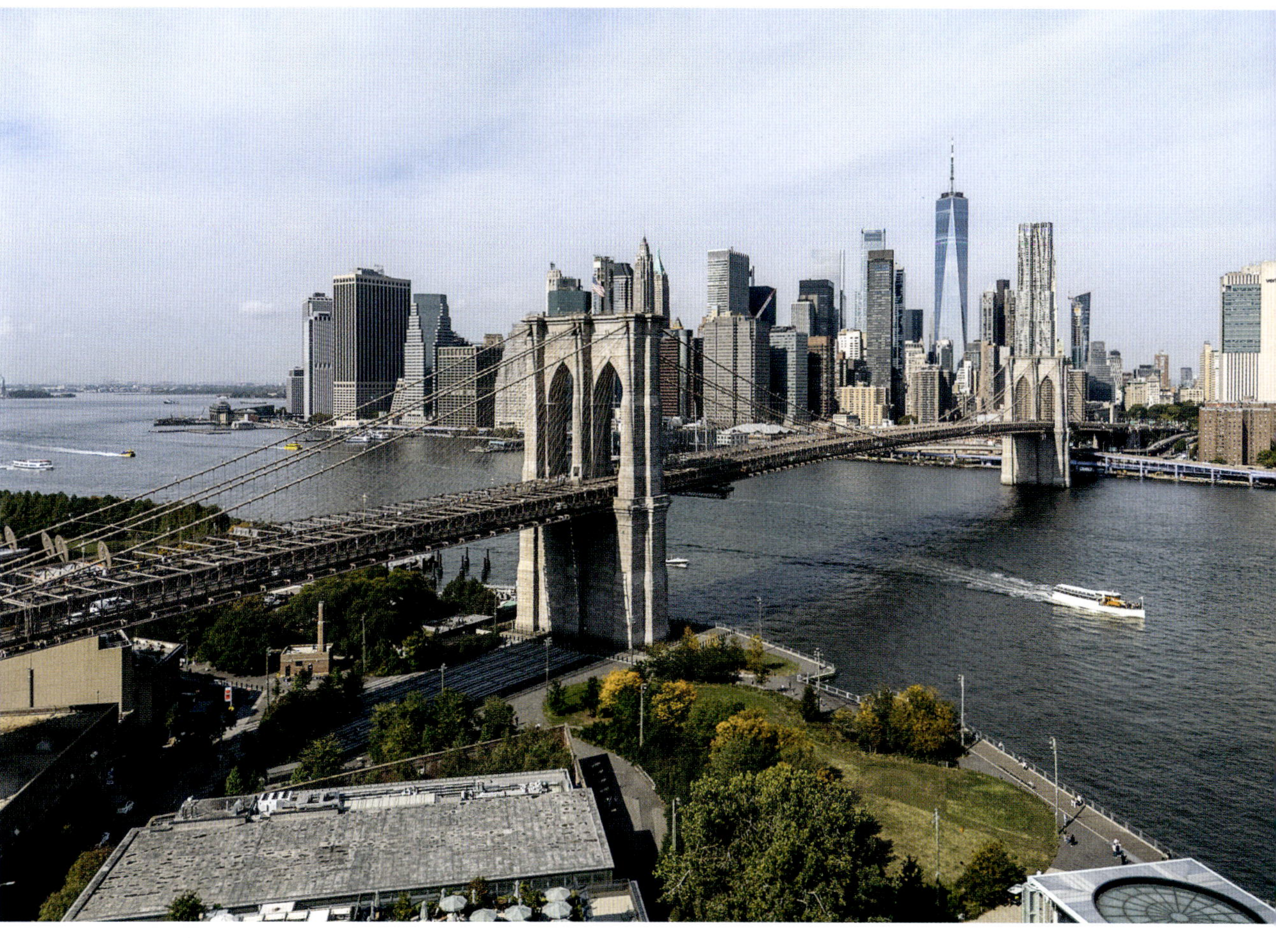

This vintage photo was taken more than two decades after the bridge opened in 1883, the first to span the East River. Proposed in 1857 by German-born engineer John Augustus Roebling, construction of the bridge finally got underway in 1869. John was killed in an accident shortly afterward, and his son, Washington Roebling, took over the demanding work. Injured in one of the caissons, the younger Roebling became an invalid, but with his wife's help, he supervised the project from his bedside window across the river in Brooklyn. It took fourteen years and $16 million to complete, three times the original estimate and more than any other single endeavor of the day. From the day it opened, the Brooklyn Bridge attracted a steady flow of pedestrians eager to experience the new phenomenon. But a tragic accident occurred on Memorial Day 1883, just a week after the opening. In the crush of an uncontrollably large crowd on the stairway leading to the bridge, panic broke out and twelve people were trampled to death. The number of police officers on the bridge was increased, and pedestrians continued to use it, including thousands who walked to work to save the price of the trains. Many others simply came to enjoy a stroll over the city's highest structure and the skyline view of Lower Manhattan.

As cars and trucks supplanted ships and boats, the Brooklyn Bridge proved to be a lasting structure in the modern world with relatively few changes. Nineteenth-century New Yorkers, crossing on cable cars, horse-drawn trolleys, and electric trains, could not have imagined how the bridge would prove adaptable to motorized vehicles. The bridge was built so well that for the first seventy years of its life, well into the age of the automobile, it required only routine maintenance. In 1953, the deck was strengthened to bear the weight of increased motor traffic. No longer the largest or most innovative, the bridge still captures the imagination for its grace and beauty. The benches and walkway along the newly completed East River Esplanade provide a perfect place to enjoy the view.

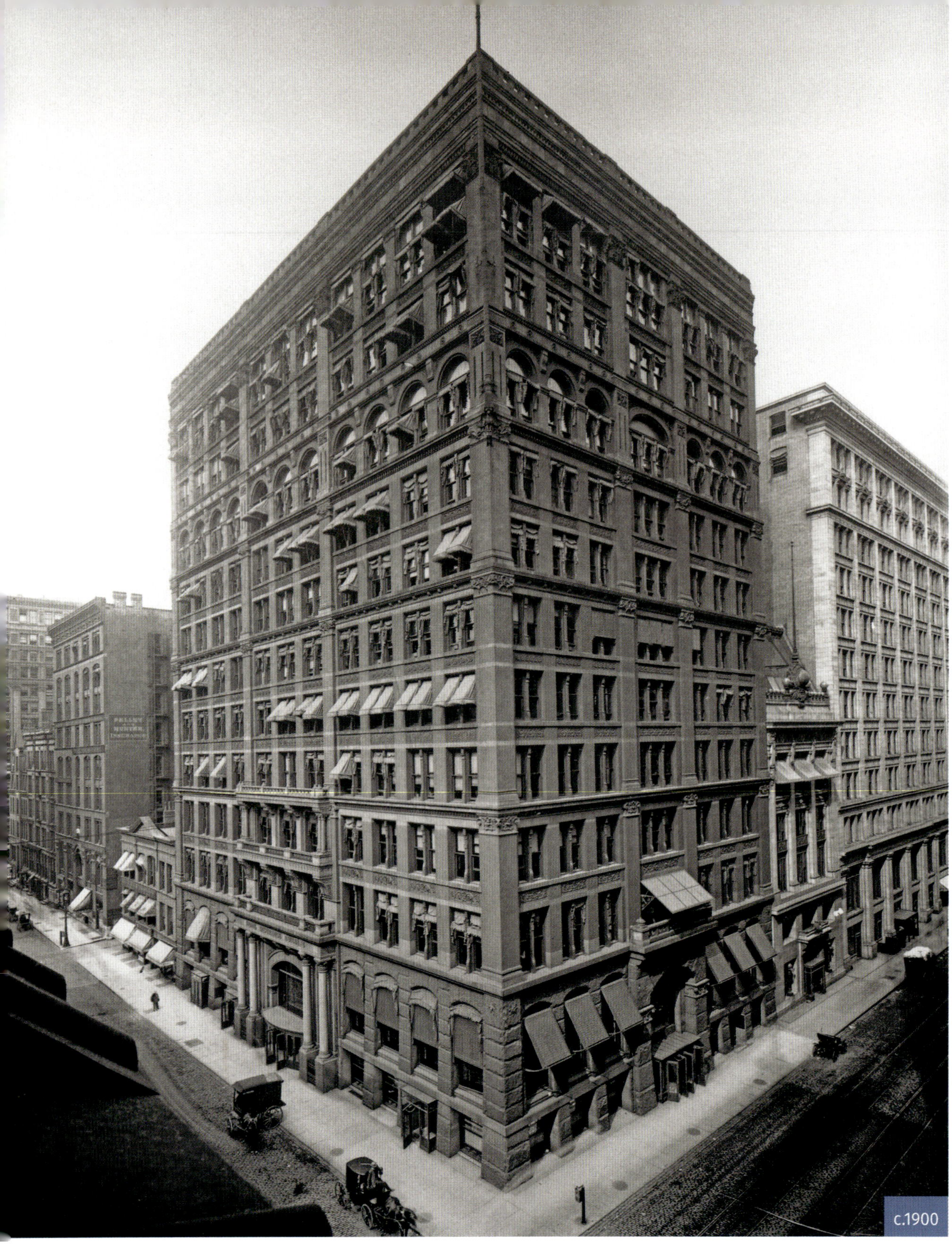

c.1900

HOME INSURANCE BUILDING, CHICAGO

The first real skyscraper to shed its stone exoskeleton

Ditherington Flax Mill (1797) in Shrewsbury, England, has something in common with the Chicago School of architecture. It has been described as "the grandfather of skyscrapers" because of its pioneering use of an iron frame to support its structure, rather than relying solely on heavy masonry walls.

Architect and engineer William Le Baron Jenney took the concept and employed it on a far greater scale when he designed the Home Insurance Building in Chicago. Jenney's design utilized an internal skeleton of iron columns and beams which not only reduced the building's weight but also enhanced its structural

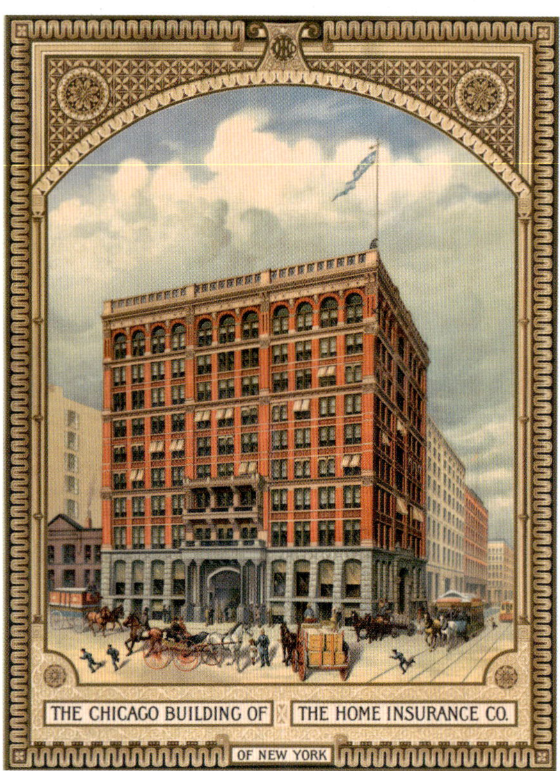

integrity. It was a third of the weight of traditional, stone-built towers, thus demanding less monumental foundations, it was quicker to construct, and it had the potential to go much higher than the ten stories (138 feet) that Jenney had planned. The age of the skyscraper had arrived.

All through its construction Chicago authorities checked the structural integrity of the innovative steel-frame building, anxious that a failure would impact on the city's reputation. It was completed in 1885 to their satisfaction. To prove he could have gone higher from the outset another two floors were added in 1891, bringing its height to 180 feet.

The Home Insurance Building's innovative approach influenced the development of the Chicago School of architecture, which emphasized function, structural expression, and the use of new materials and technologies. Jenney's work inspired contemporaries like Daniel Burnham, Louis Sullivan, and John Wellborn Root, who further advanced skyscraper design. Although earlier structures had employed iron framing, the Home Insurance Building's combination of height, fireproofing, and skeletal construction set a new standard for urban architecture.

Like many of the early skyscrapers, the Home Insurance Building was on too valuable a site for just twelve stories. It was demolished in 1931 to make way for the Field Building (now known as the LaSalle National Bank Building). A plaque in the bank's lobby commemorates the site as the birthplace of the skyscraper. Jenney's pioneering work laid the foundation for the vertical expansion of cities.

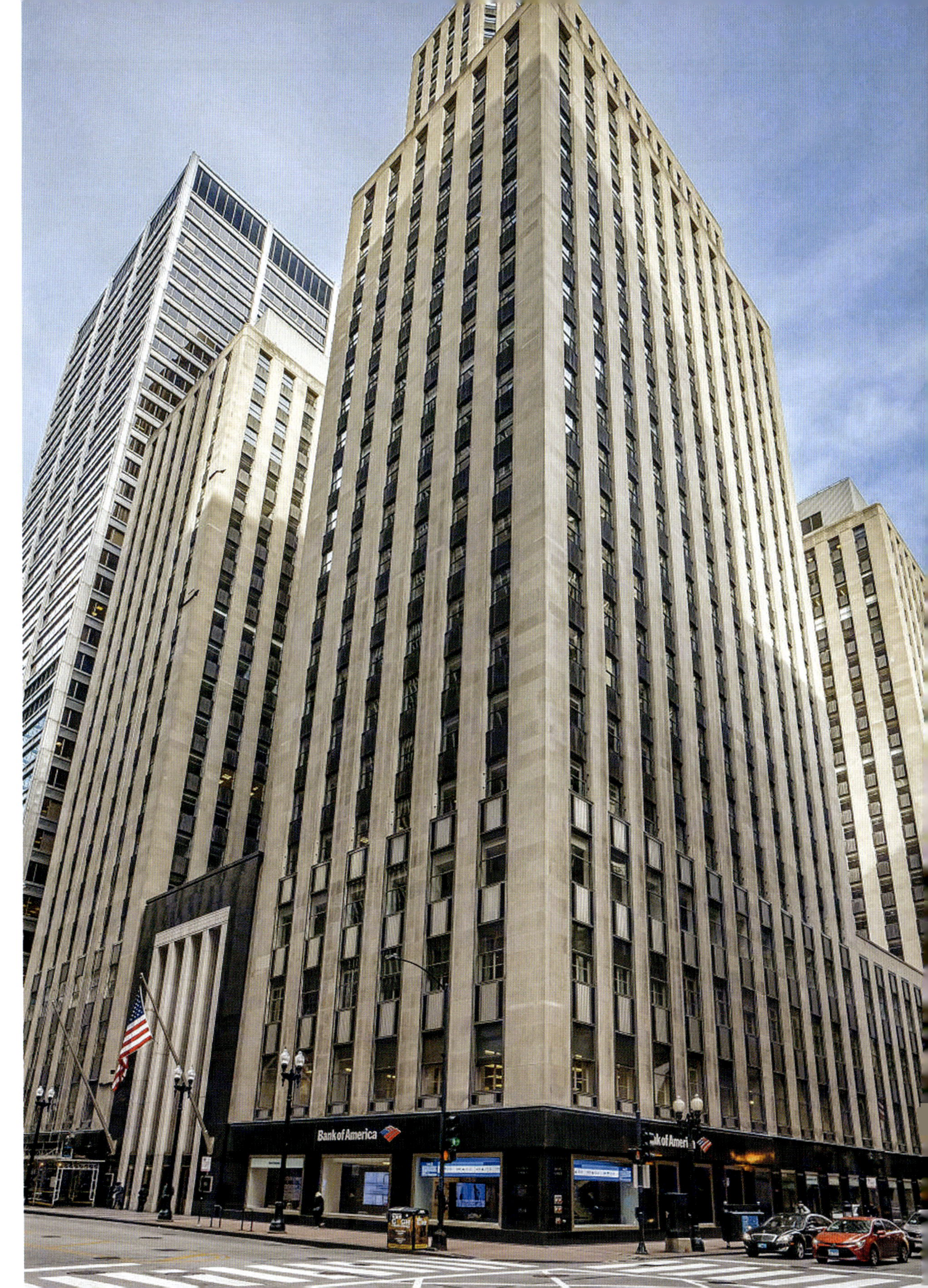

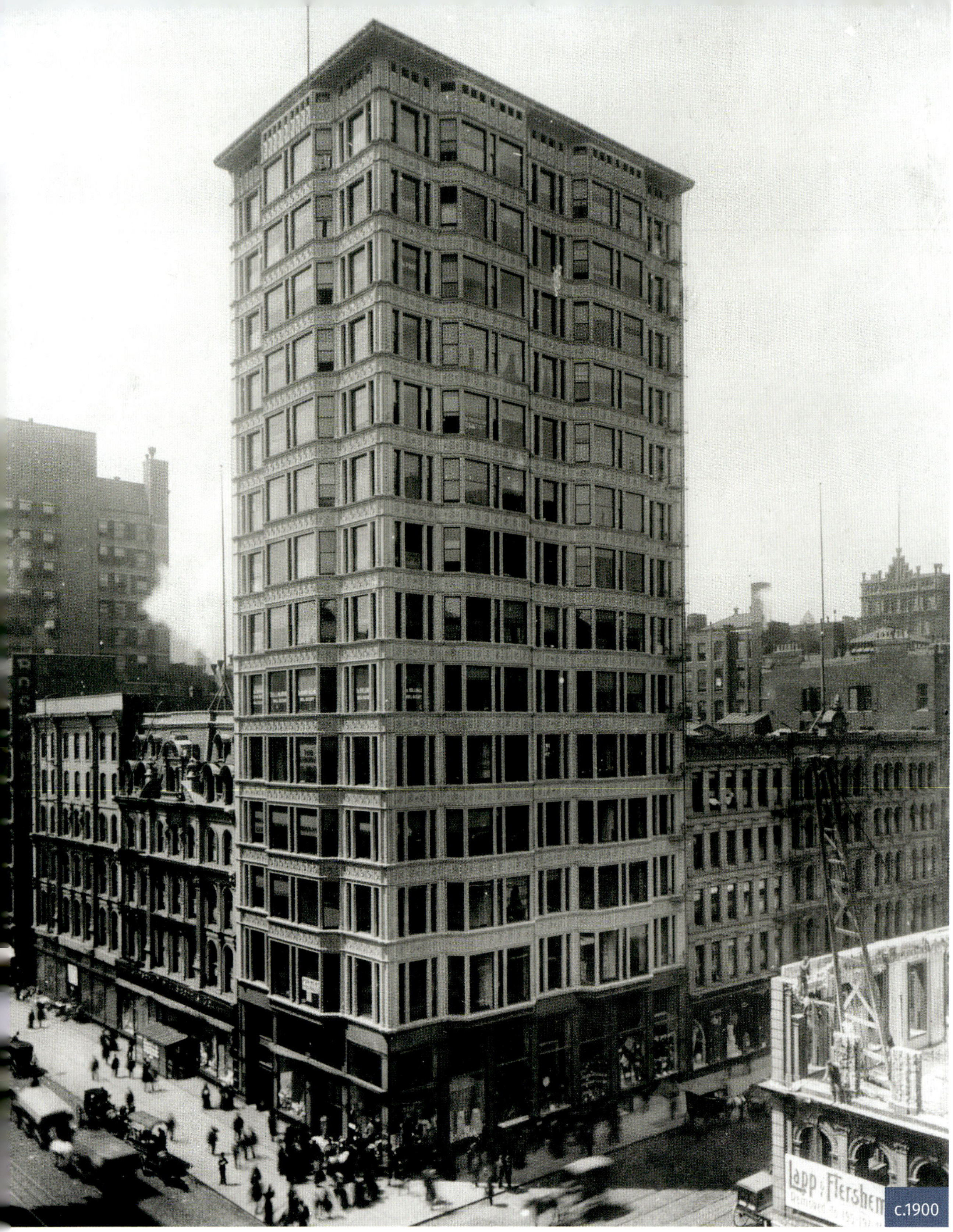

c.1900

RELIANCE BUILDING & OLD CHICAGO STOCK EXCHANGE, CHICAGO

Two buildings that helped establish the Chicago School

The mother of all glass-and-steel skyscrapers—the Reliance Building by Daniel Burnham and John Wellborn Root—changed the course of architecture when it was built in 1890. Located on the southwest corner of State and Washington Streets, the remarkable use of large glass panes gave the world the classic "Chicago window," and the interior steel-frame construction introduced Chicagoans to modern design. Narrow piers, mullions, and spandrels are clad in cream-colored, glazed terra-cotta, enhanced by a Gothic tracery. Thanks to Elisha Otis and his elevator, there seemed no limits to the heights to which buildings could rise. Burnham,

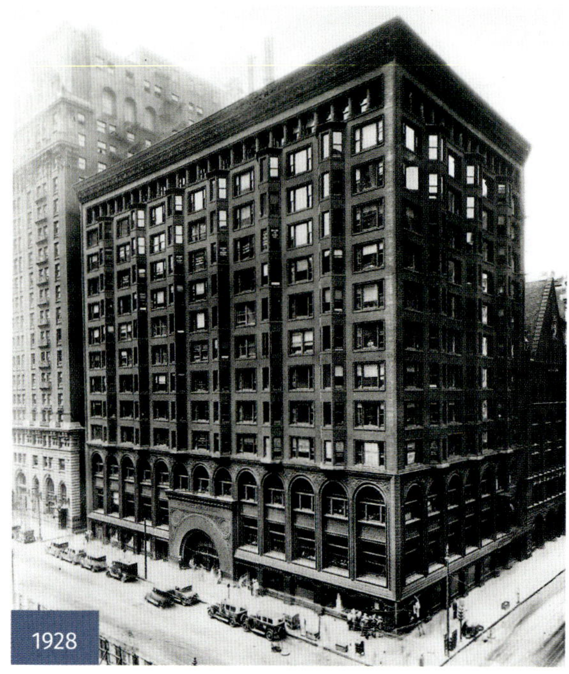

1928

though, was devastated when his long-time partner Root died before the building was finished.

Despite decades of misuse and underappreciation, alongside State Street's decline, the Reliance Building has been refurbished with painstaking skill and is now the Hotel Burnham. After a $27.5 million restoration in 1999, this architectural masterpiece once again shimmers with fresh elegance. Inside, ornamental cast-iron framed elevators and stairways continue to showcase the genius of the building's great architects, justifying its place in a list of the world's 100 most historically significant skyscrapers.

OLD CHICAGO STOCK EXCHANGE

Perhaps no single piece of Chicago architecture is more sadly missed than the 1894 Chicago Stock Exchange (below left), designed by Louis Sullivan and Dankmar Adler. Built at the corner of LaSalle and Washington Streets, the exchange was second in significance among US financial markets only to the New York Stock Exchange. Utilizing the technology of a caisson foundation to adapt to Chicago's marshy soil, Adler and Sullivan created an extraordinary design rich in detail.

No other building in Chicago history was more of a cause célèbre when it was announced that it would fall to the wrecking ball in 1972. Its loss signifies a less intelligent era of Chicago architectural protection. No one worked more diligently to save the building than architectural photographer Richard Nickel, who, when the demolition began, managed to get inside to photograph the tragedy of its destruction. Sadly, Nickel himself became a casualty of the demolition—he was killed while inside the building. Artifacts from the structure became treasured relics of the Prairie style. The interior trading room, with Sullivan's impressive stenciling and stained glass, is preserved at the Art Institute of Chicago, as is the graceful entrance arch, called by one critic the "Wailing Wall of Chicago's preservation movement."

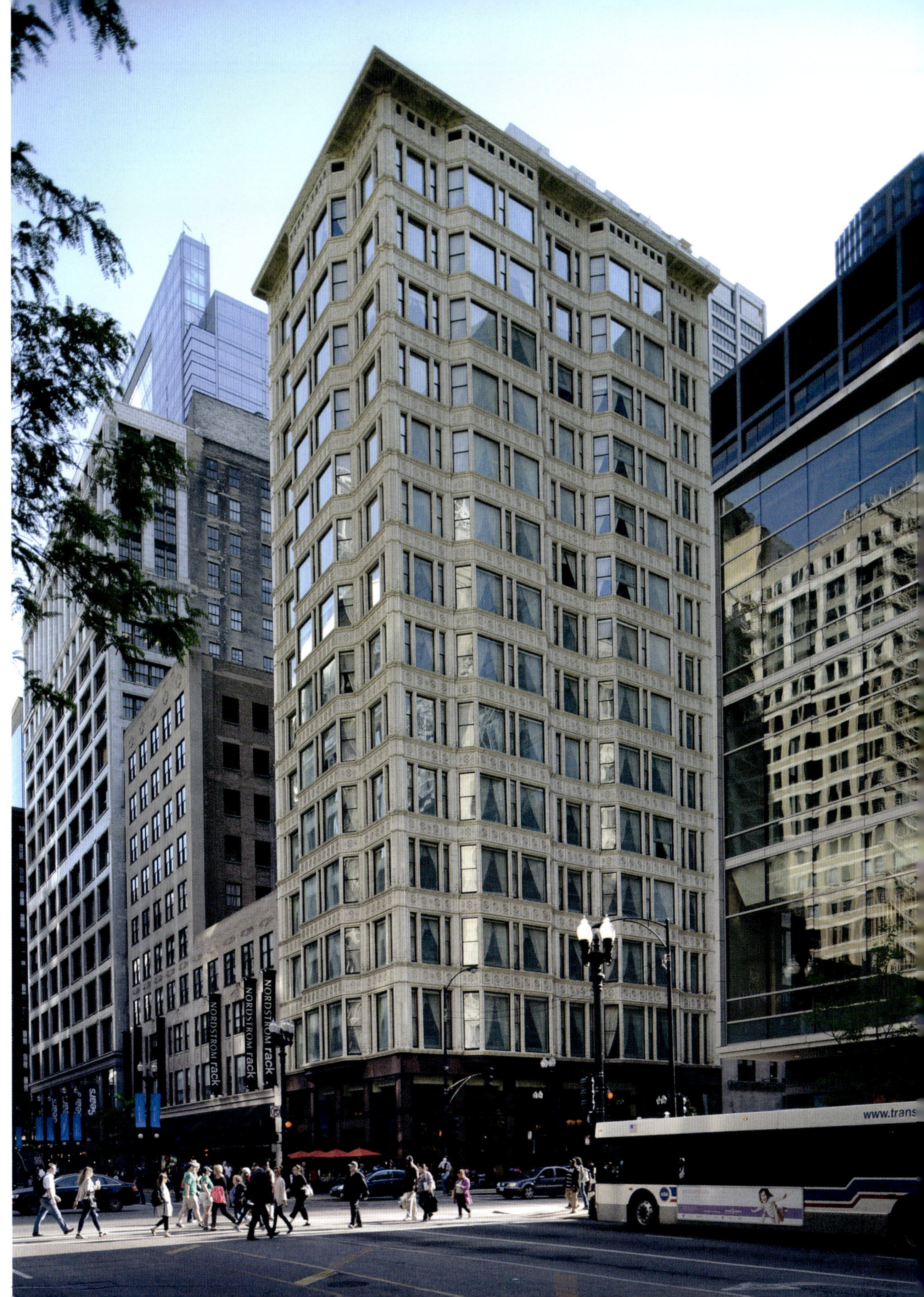

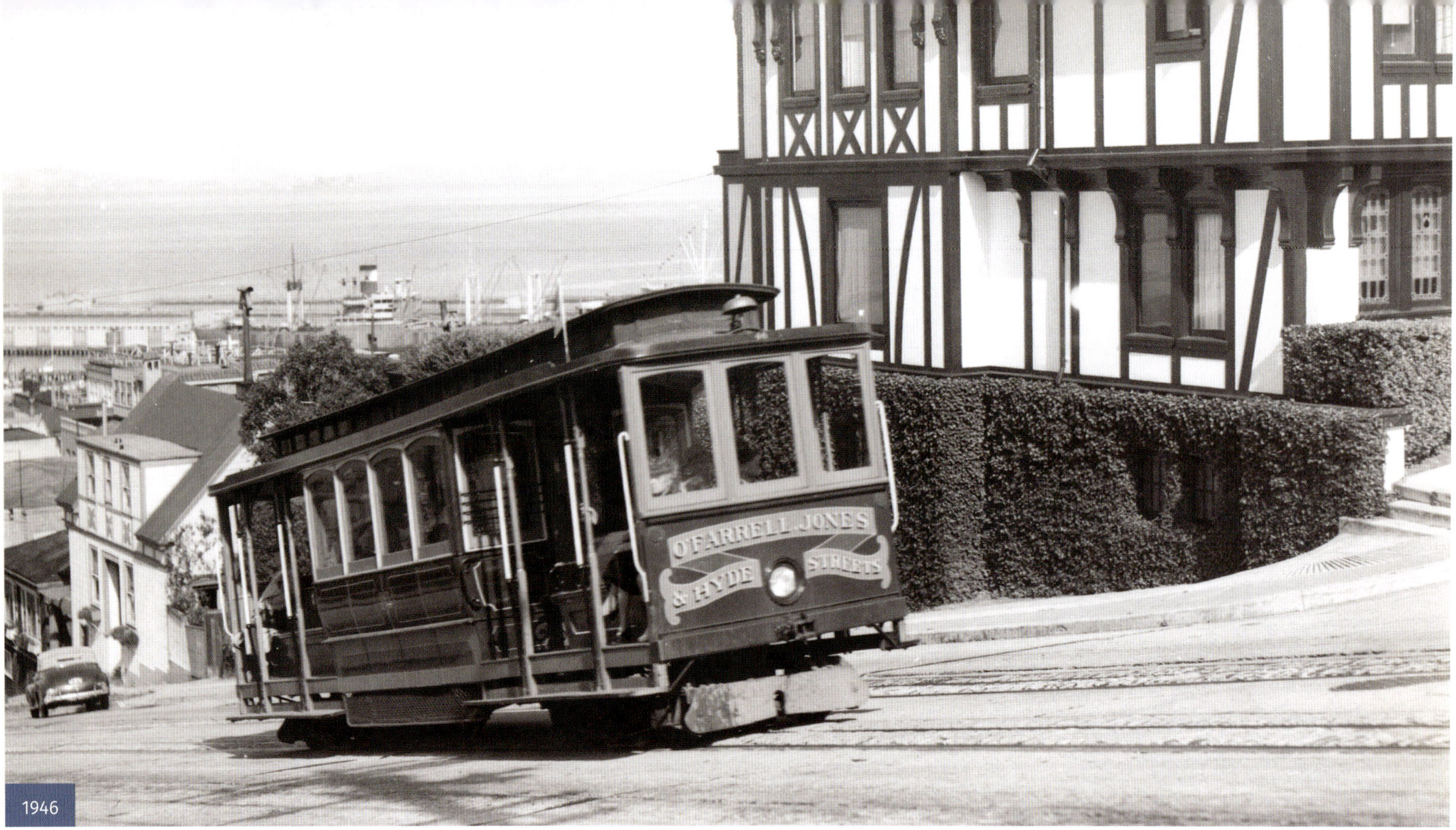

STREETCARS OF SAN FRANCISCO, CALIFORNIA

The west coast city has seen the evolution of streetcars, their demise, and glorious return

Streetcars have played an important role in the development of American cities, creating suburbs along their routes and allowing people to live at far greater distances from their place of work. San Francisco is famous for its streetcars, but horse-drawn rail cars, or “horsecars” were first launched in 1832 in New York City by the New York and Harlem Railroad. It featured small rail vehicles pulled by horses on iron or steel rails embedded in the street. This innovation reduced friction and made for smoother, faster rides than omnibuses on regular roads.

Horsecar systems spread rapidly across the country. Cities like Boston, New Orleans, Baltimore, and Chicago developed major networks. However, horsecars had major

ABOVE: A cable car on Russian Hill, San Francisco.

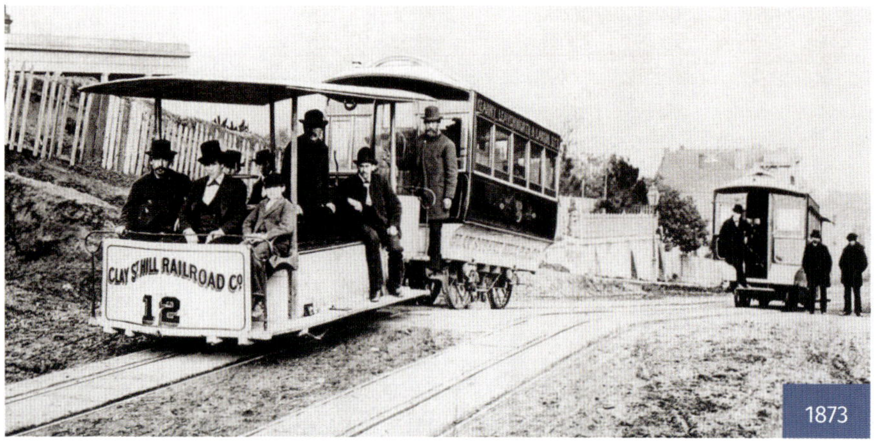

RIGHT: Andrew Hallidie’s Clay Street Line on its debut in 1873. Each train consisted of a grip car and a trailer. The line operated until 1891 when streetcars on Sacramento Street started running.

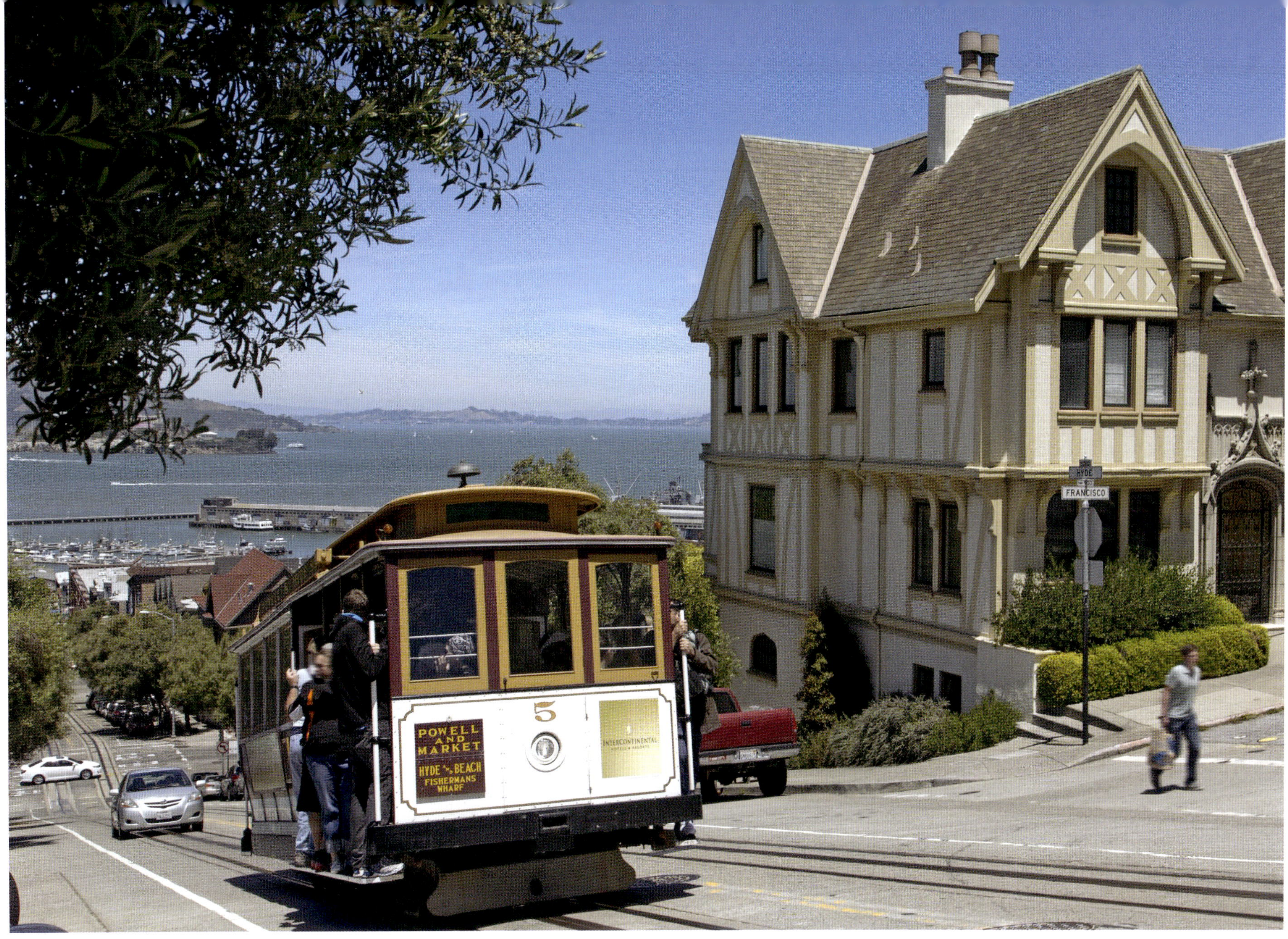

drawbacks: horses tired easily, needed food and stabling, and created substantial "waste." Most routes required a large workforce—both human and equine.

To address the inefficiency of horse-drawn systems—especially in hilly cities—cable cars were introduced. San Francisco pioneered this technology in 1873 with Andrew Hallidie's Clay Street Hill Railroad. Cables powered by a central steam engine ran in underground channels; streetcars latched onto the cable to move, releasing the grip to stop.

Cable cars made for cleaner streets, they were faster, and better suited to steep terrain. They flourished in cities like San Francisco, Seattle, and Chicago. But they were expensive to build and maintain, and as electrical technology matured, a more practical alternative emerged.

The electric streetcar revolution began in 1888 in Richmond, Virginia, under inventor Frank J. Sprague. His design used electric motors powered via overhead wires, offering superior efficiency, and cost-effectiveness. They demanded a greater and more visible infrastructure, but were far less intrusive than the overhead rail lines of New York or Chicago. Sprague's success triggered an explosion of streetcar systems nationwide. By the early 1900s, electric streetcars or "trolleys" were operating in nearly every American city with a population over 10,000. Cleveland, Los Angeles, and Detroit built

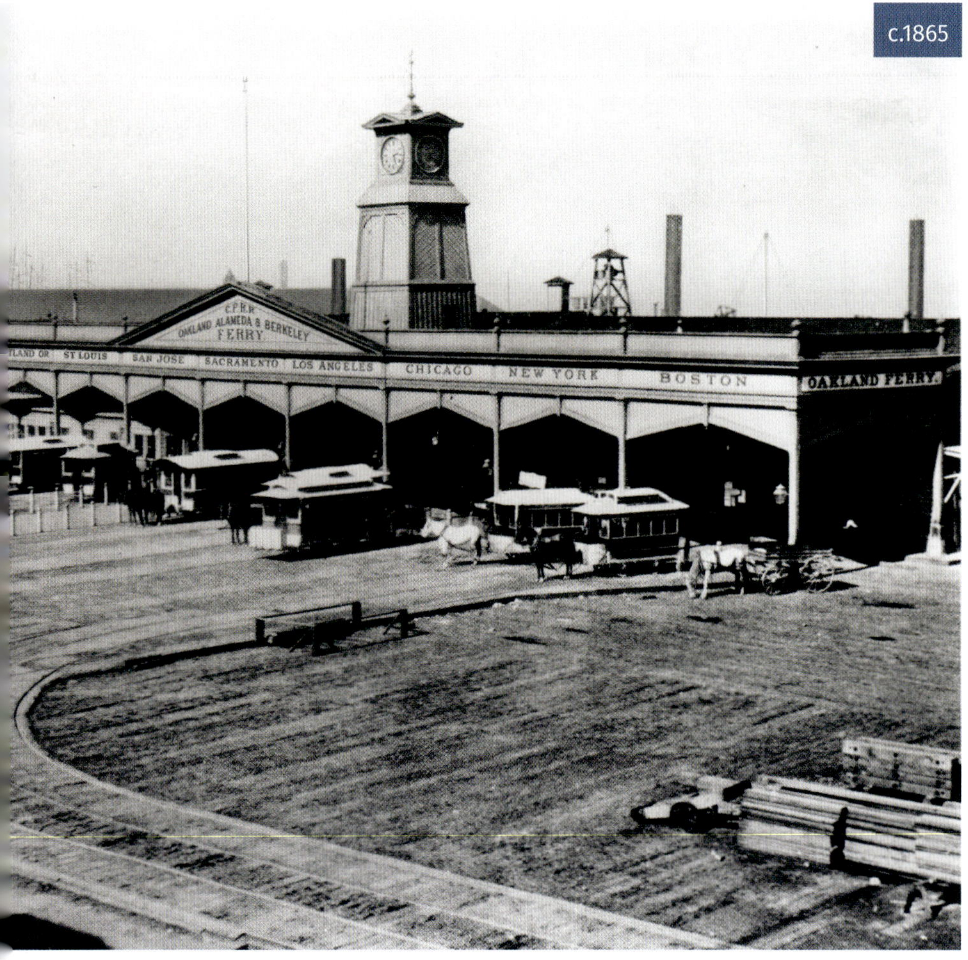

c.1865

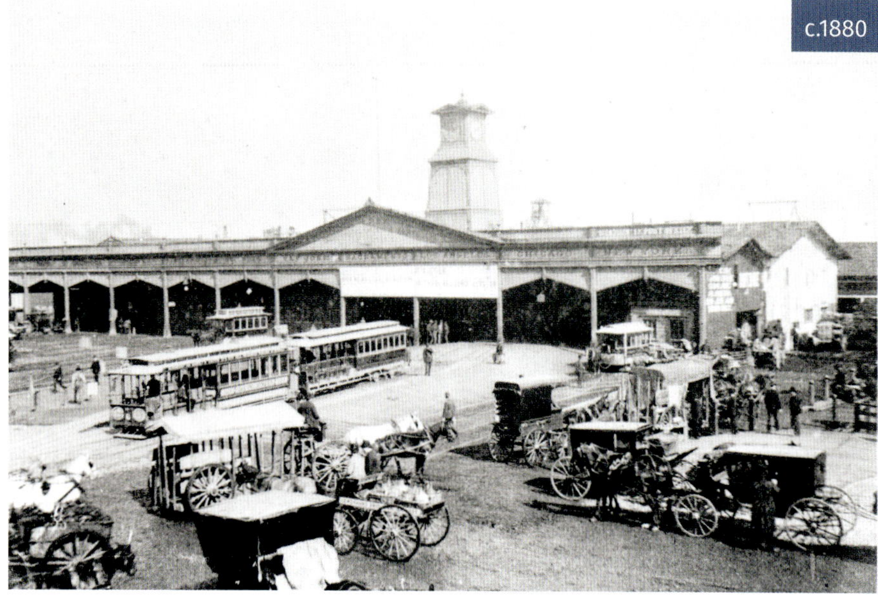
c.1880

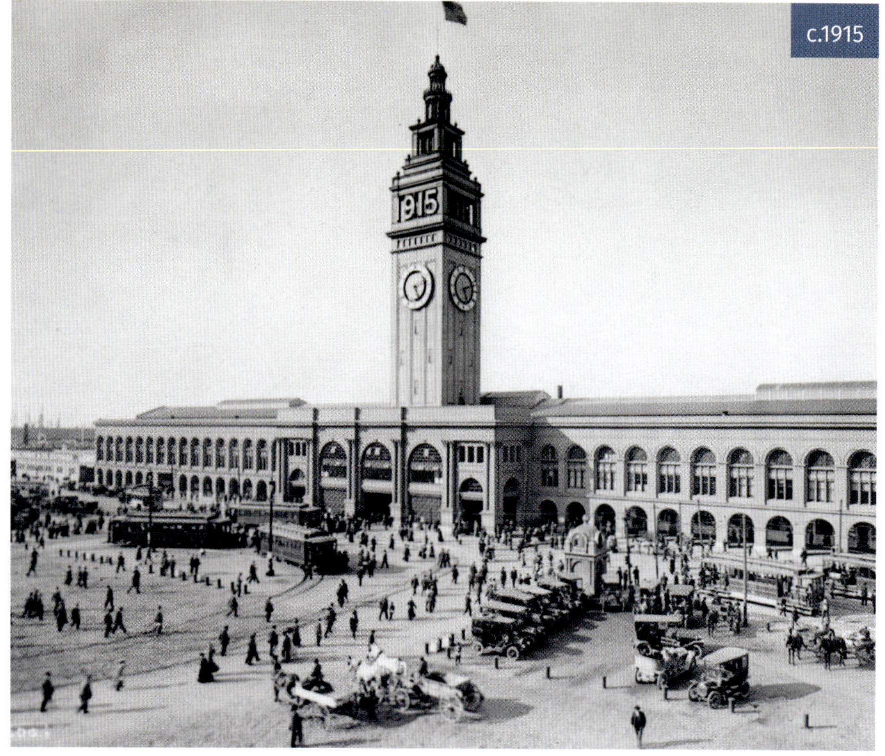

c.1915

extensive systems. In larger urban areas, companies ran hundreds of miles of track, connecting neighborhoods, parks, and factories with downtown and giving rise to "streetcar suburbs." Developers often partnered with transit companies to build lines that would increase land values and attract new residents. In some cities, companies ran both streetcars and electric utilities, as the two businesses were intertwined. Fare policies, ridership rules, and competition were often contentious, leading to regulation and sometimes municipal ownership, as in San Francisco and, later, New Orleans.

Streetcars faced growing pressure in the 1920s and 30s. The rise of the automobile was one pressure point, the other was the cost of maintaining the network of overhead power cables when motor buses were cheaper and far more flexible—traveling farther and adopting any route. They could also tackle inclines only a cable car could previously have taken on.

The most controversial chapter in streetcar decline was the involvement of National City Lines—a company backed by General Motors, Firestone Tire, and Standard Oil. From the 1930s to 1950s, National City Lines acquired and dismantled dozens of streetcar systems, replacing them with bus networks. This campaign sparked accusations of conspiracy and monopolization but, regardless, by the 1960s, most American streetcar systems were gone. Cities like Los Angeles, once home to the world's largest interurban network, had torn up nearly every rail.

San Francisco famously retained some of its cable cars, designating them as historic landmarks in 1964. In 1983, the city also launched the Historic Trolley Festival, which evolved into the permanent F-Market & Wharves line, running vintage electric streetcars. New Orleans kept its St. Charles Avenue streetcar in continuous operation since 1835, making it the oldest continuously running streetcar line in the world. In the late twentieth and early twenty-first centuries, a wave of new light rail and streetcar systems emerged in cities such as Portland, Seattle, Charlotte, and Kansas City, while the streetcars of New Orleans and San Francisco continue to be used by commuters and tourists alike.

OPPOSITE: Three generations of streetcars outside the Ferry Building in San Francisco. The city's cable and streetcar infrastructure was heavily affected by the devastating earthquake and fire of 1906. The 1915 date on the Ferry Building relates to the 1915 Panama–Pacific International Exposition.

RIGHT: The vintage streetcars running in San Francisco today were sourced from places as far afield as Italy, Australia, Switzerland, Canada, Japan, and Germany.

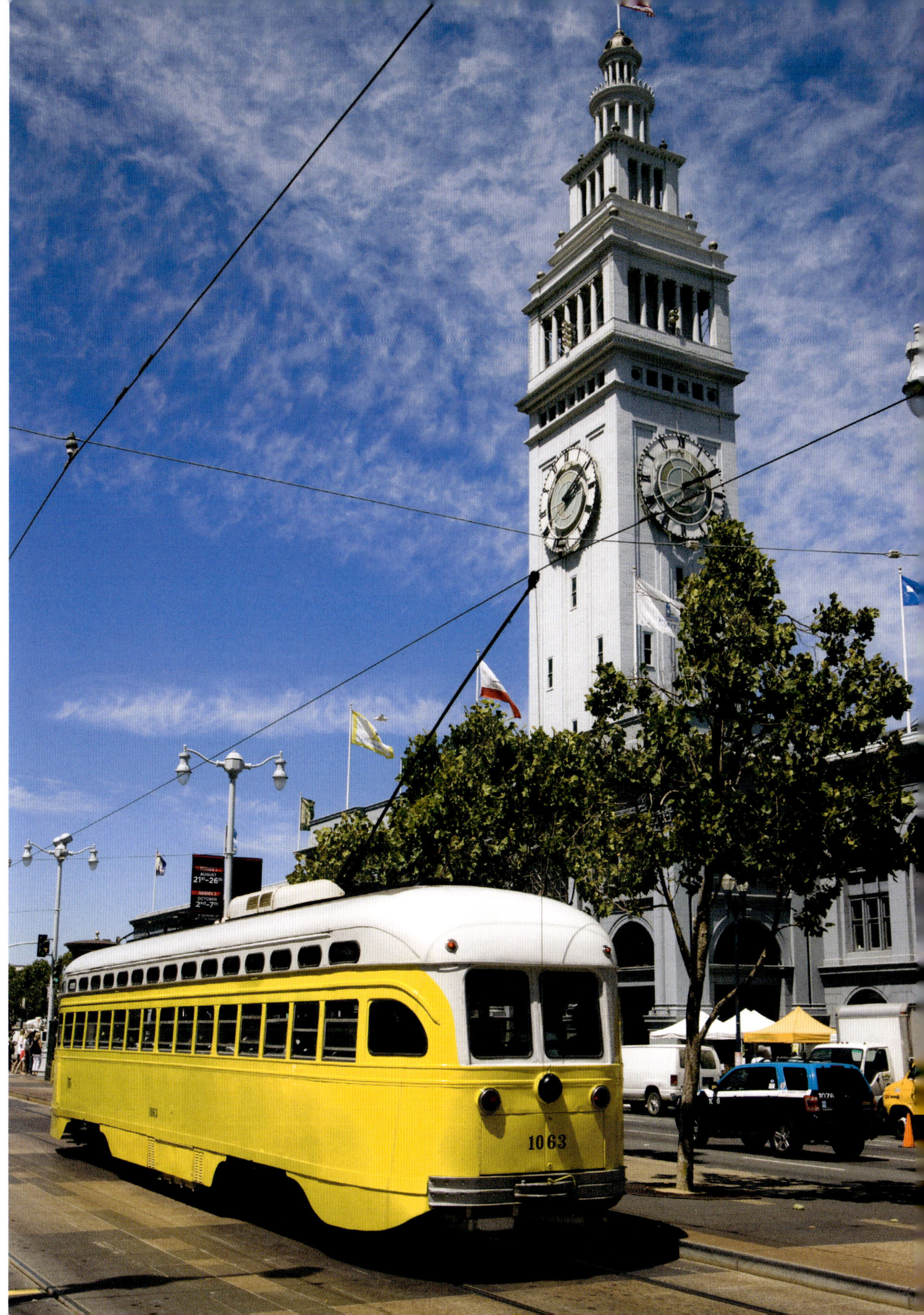

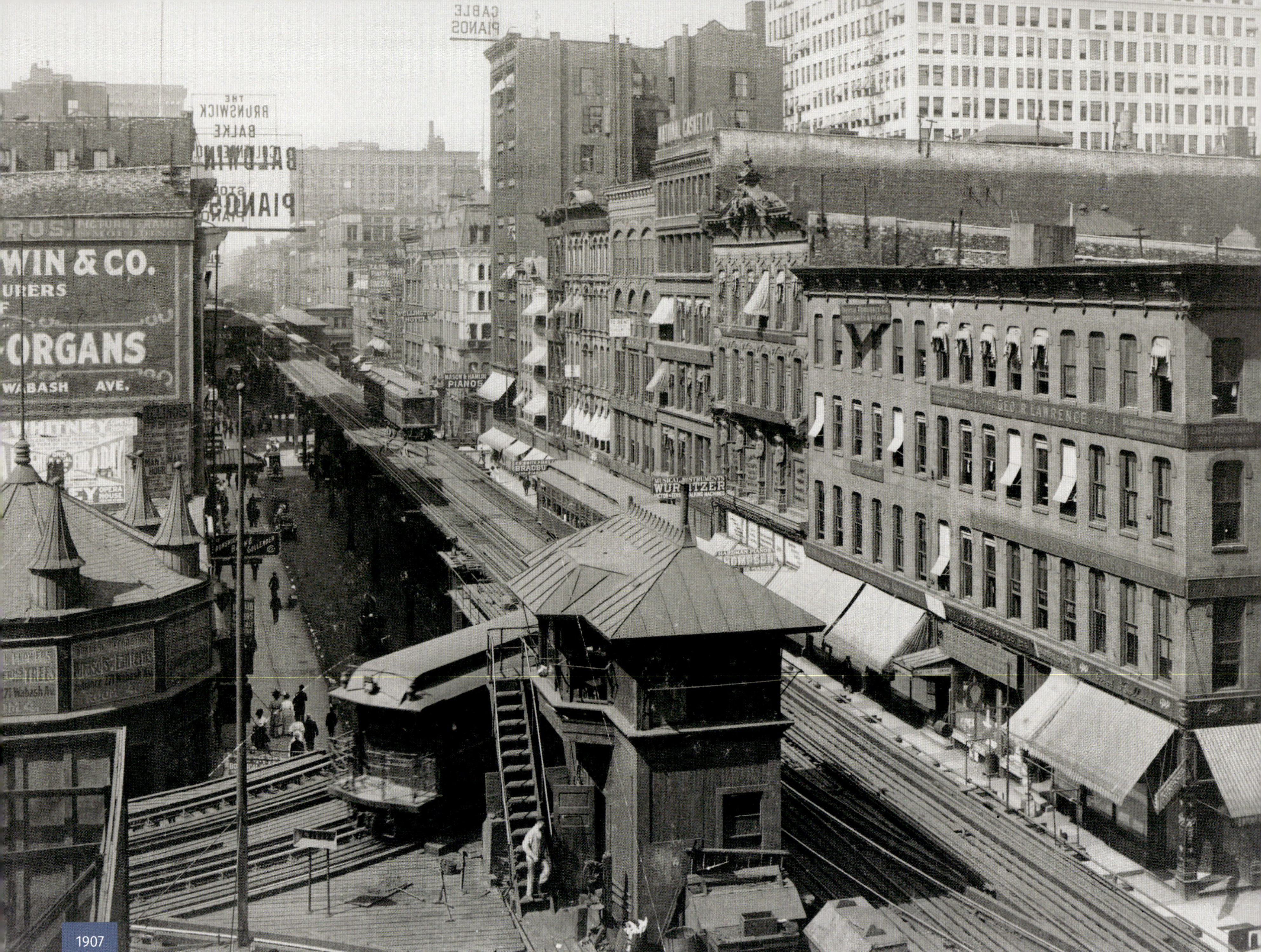

1907

ELEVATED RAILROADS, "THE L," CHICAGO

Chicago still values its "rusty iron heart," while New York's overground rails are long gone

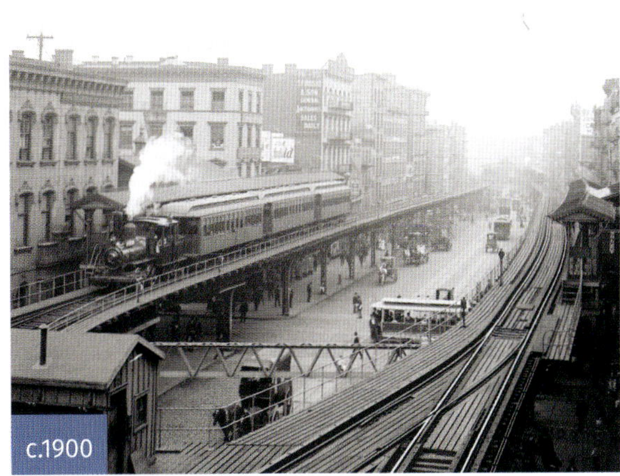

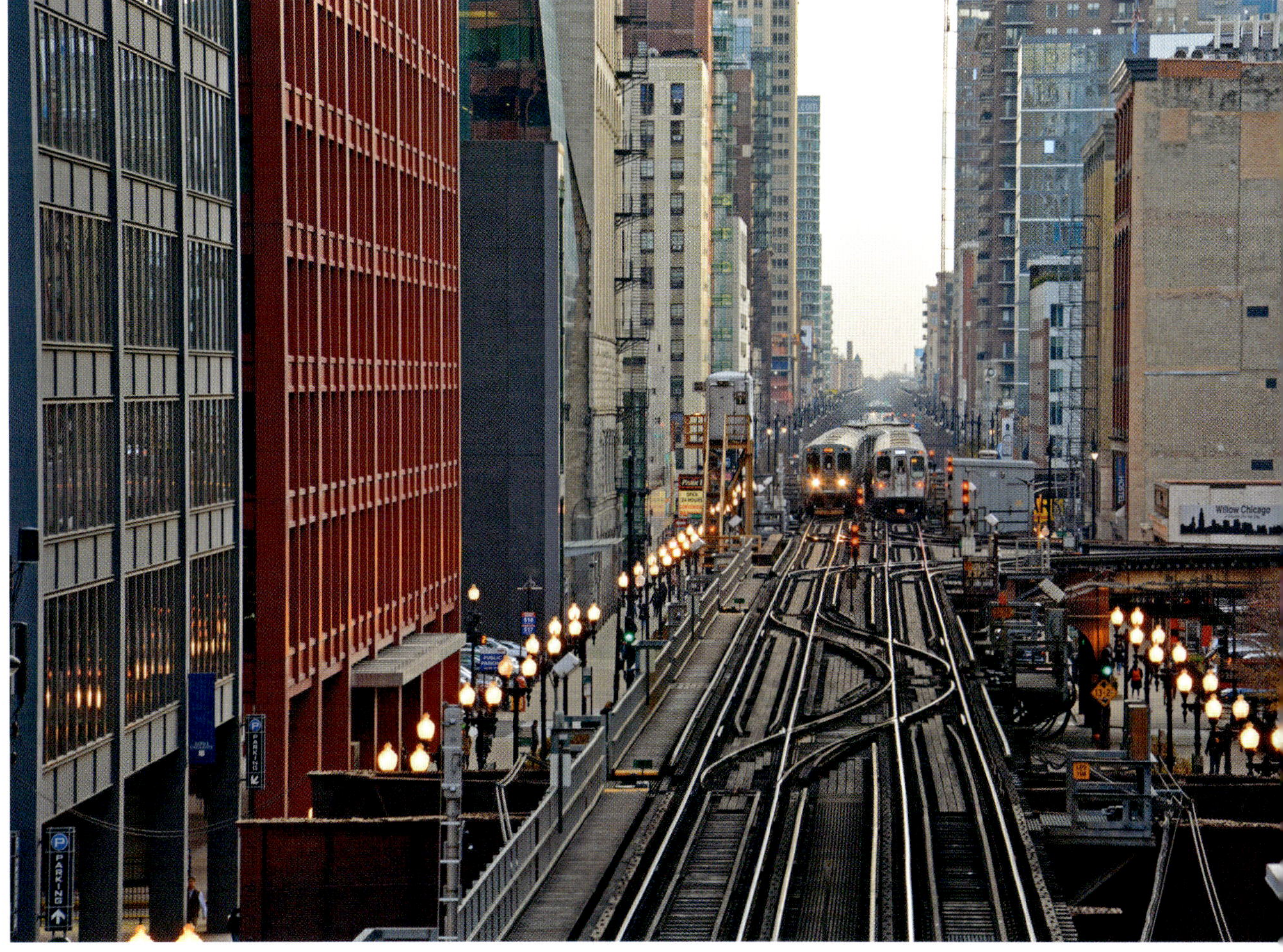

Chicago's elevated railway—commonly known as the "L" (short for "elevated")—is one of the oldest and most iconic urban transit systems in the United States. The "L" officially debuted on June 6, 1892, with the opening of the South Side Rapid Transit line. The first trains were powered by small steam locomotives that ran from Congress Street to 39th Street. By the late 1890s, electrification had replaced steam, and multiple elevated lines were operating across the city. These included the Lake Street Elevated (1893), the Metropolitan West Side Elevated (1895), and the Northwestern Elevated (1900). The construction of the Union Loop—completed in 1897—connected several lines downtown and gave the system its signature identity. Pictured in the vintage photo is the line at Wabash Avenue. Chicago novelist Nelson Algren called the L the city's "rusty iron heart."

It wasn't the first elevated railway in America. The West Side and Yonkers Patent Railway in New York launched in 1868 and was the earliest example of elevated rapid transit, running on steam-powered trains above Greenwich Street in Manhattan. This was followed by more extensive elevated lines operated by the Manhattan Railway Company in the 1870s and 1880s. By the turn of the century, Manhattan had a fully elevated network running north to Harlem and into the Bronx.

Across the East River, Brooklyn had its own set of elevated lines, beginning in 1885 with the BMT (Brooklyn-Manhattan Transit) system. These elevated railroads connected with ferries and streetcars and eventually with the subway system. Brooklyn's elevated lines spread rapidly and, like Manhattan's, were privately operated.

However, beginning in 1904 with the opening of the New York City Subway, emphasis in New York shifted underground. The subways offered smoother rides, less noise, and no visual street blight. Over the next decades, most of Manhattan's and Brooklyn's elevated lines were dismantled.

Unlike other American cities, Chicago never followed suit in dismantling its elevated system in favor of subways or buses during the mid-twentieth century. The L survived, and today the Chicago Transit Authority operates eight color-coded lines over more than 100 miles of track, serving the city and its surrounding areas.

ABOVE LEFT: New York's elevated railroad running through the Bowery at Grand Street.

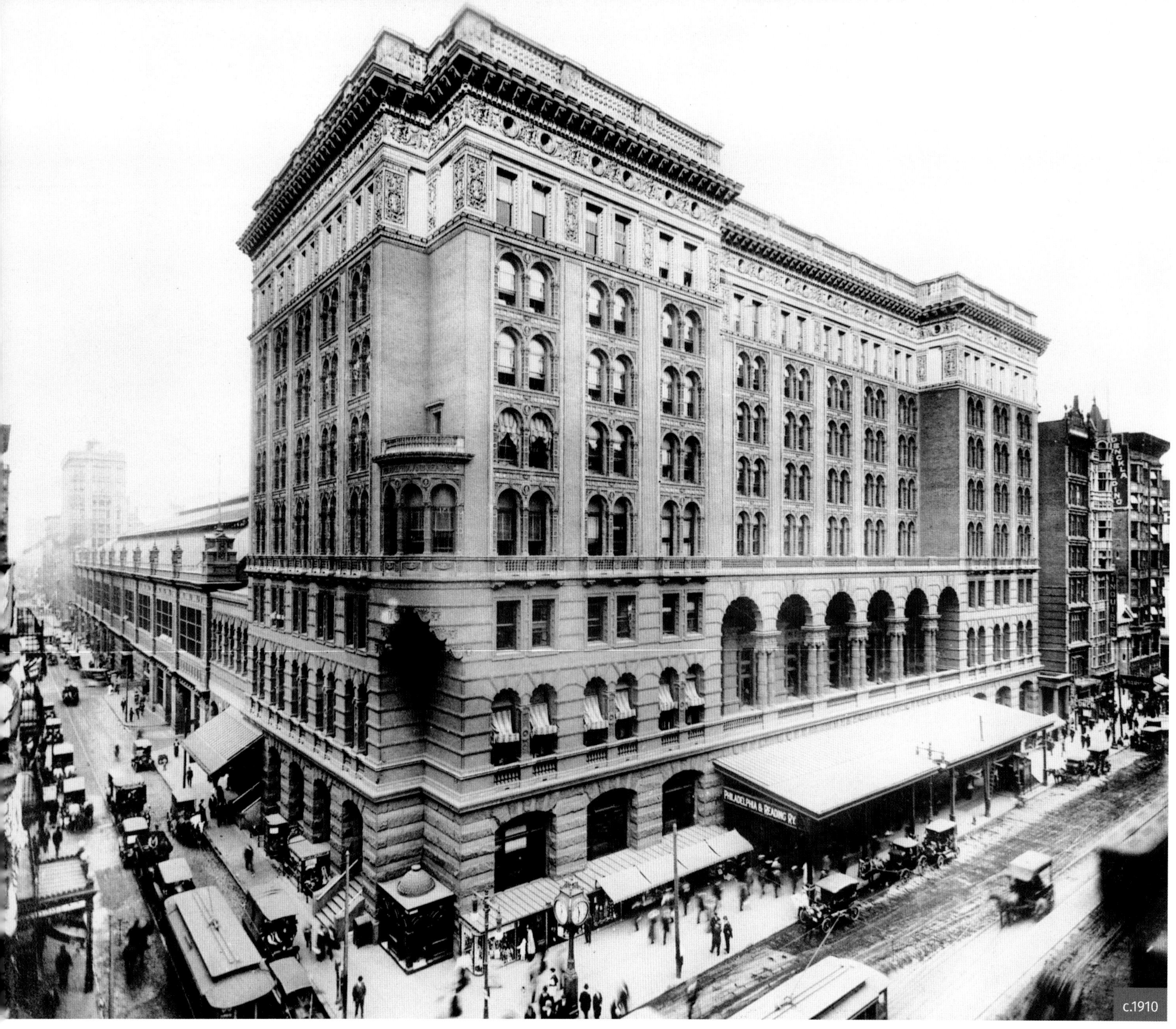

c.1910

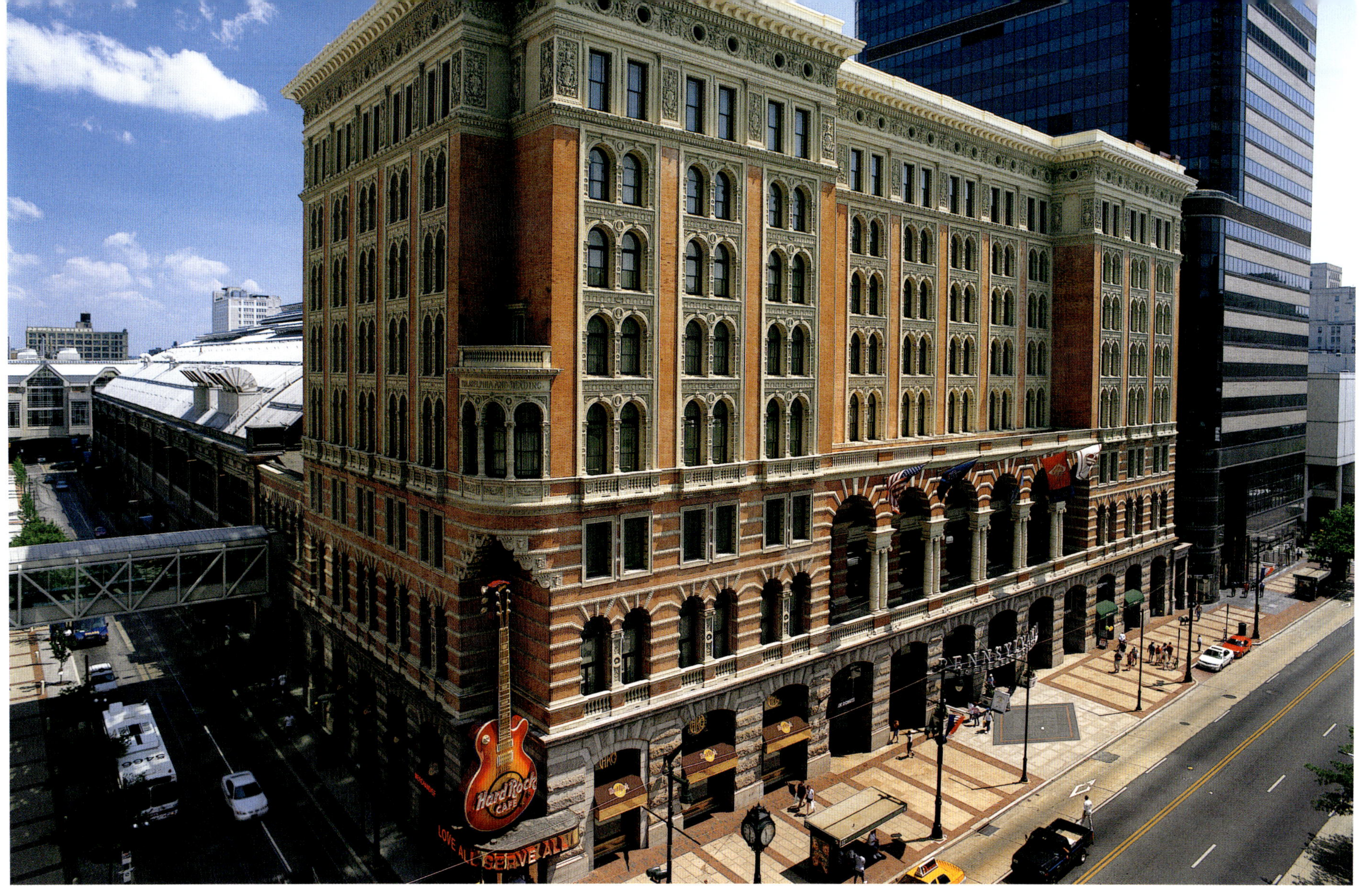

READING RAILROAD TERMINAL, PHILADELPHIA

A grand architectural statement about the power of railroads in the Gilded Age

When the Reading Railroad Terminal was opened in 1893, it brought train passengers right into the heart of downtown Philadelphia. Previously, travelers disembarked at one of the terminals that dotted the city's periphery and took a horse-drawn trolley to their final destination. When the building was completed, it replaced the farmers' and butchers' markets with the indoor Reading Terminal Market. These two previous buildings themselves had been replacements for the original colonial market. That market was an open-air pavilion that extended up the street from the Delaware River past Washington's executive mansion at Sixth Street. Moving the market indoors improved sanitation and opened up the street for trolley tracks.

The headhouse of the Reading Terminal at Twelfth and Market Streets was designed by Francis H. Kimball. The graceful Italian Renaissance Revival building, with brick-bearing walls and cast-iron columns, housed offices and a passenger station until 1984, when the use of electric-powered commuter trains decreased ridership. The building complex was incorporated into the design of the Convention Center in 1993. The train shed, which spreads behind it for two city blocks, features the world's largest steel span arch. After 1997 renovations the landmark train shed has been preserved for a grand entrance and exhibition hall.

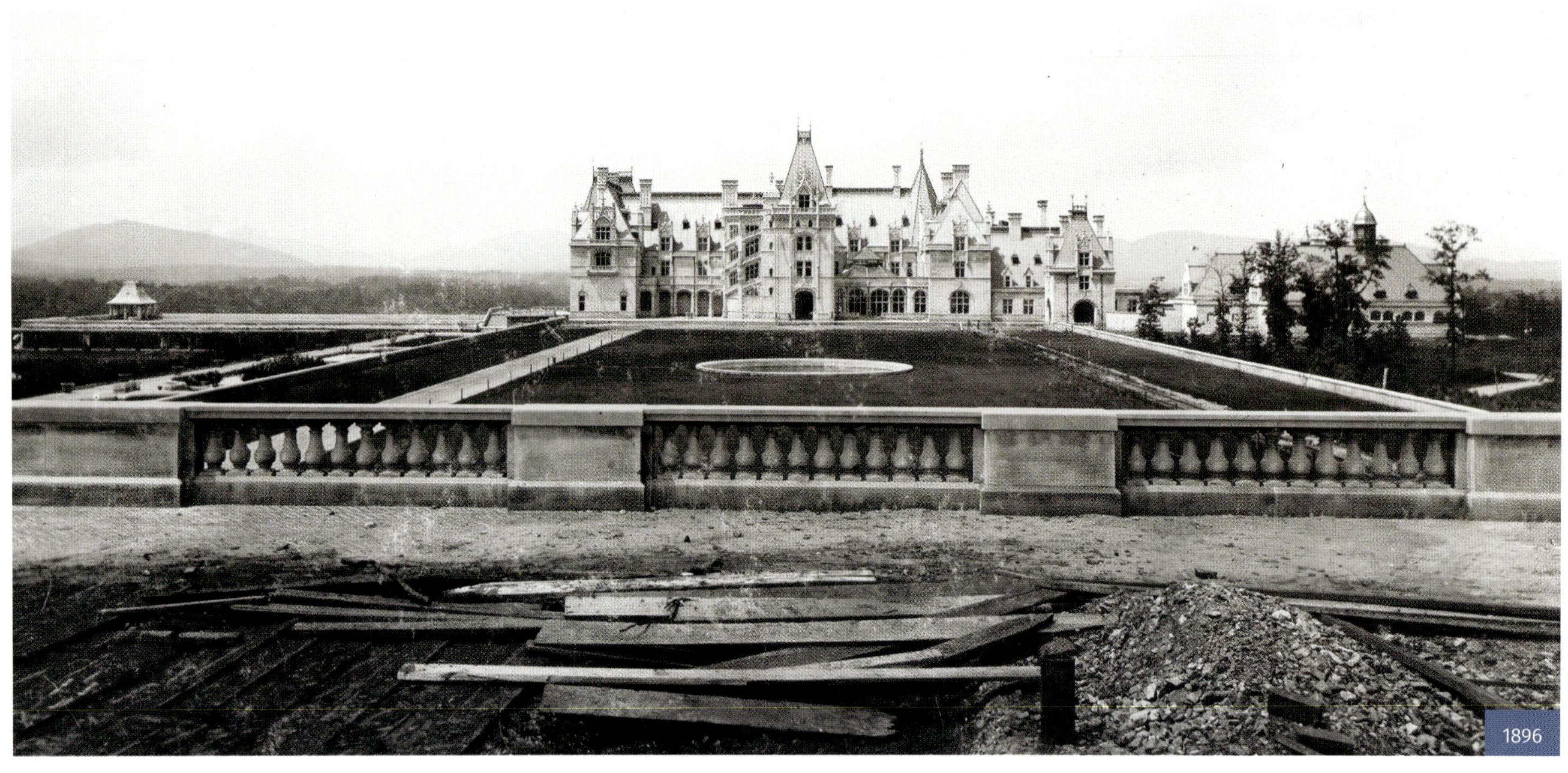
1896

BILTMORE ESTATE, ASHEVILLE, NORTH CAROLINA

Railroad barons didn't spare any expense when building status-symbol mansions

Cornelius Vanderbilt was one of the richest and most powerful industrialists of nineteenth-century America. Known as a "robber baron" by critics and a captain of industry by admirers, Vanderbilt amassed a vast fortune through aggressive business tactics, first in steamships and later in railroads.

Born into a modest Staten Island family, Vanderbilt left school at age eleven and began working with boats. He launched his own ferry service with a $100 loan from his mother, quickly earning the nickname "Commodore," which he carried throughout his life.

During the 1820s and 1830s, Vanderbilt built a successful steamship business, operating routes between New York and surrounding cities. By the 1840s, he dominated coastal shipping, sometimes undercutting competitors with low fares and then buying them out when they collapsed under price wars. In the 1860s, Vanderbilt recognized that railroads were the future of transportation. His first major acquisition was the New York and Harlem Railroad, followed by the Hudson River Railroad, and finally the New York Central Railroad in 1867, which became the core of his transportation empire.

The New York Central and Hudson River Railroad became his model of American railroad consolidation. This allowed Vanderbilt to control a crucial portion of the eastern US transportation network.

His business practices—monopolistic pricing, market manipulation, and strategic takeovers—earned him massive profits and the ire of reformers and competitors alike. By the time of his death in 1877 he had built a considerable business empire, though his personal lifestyle was relatively modest.

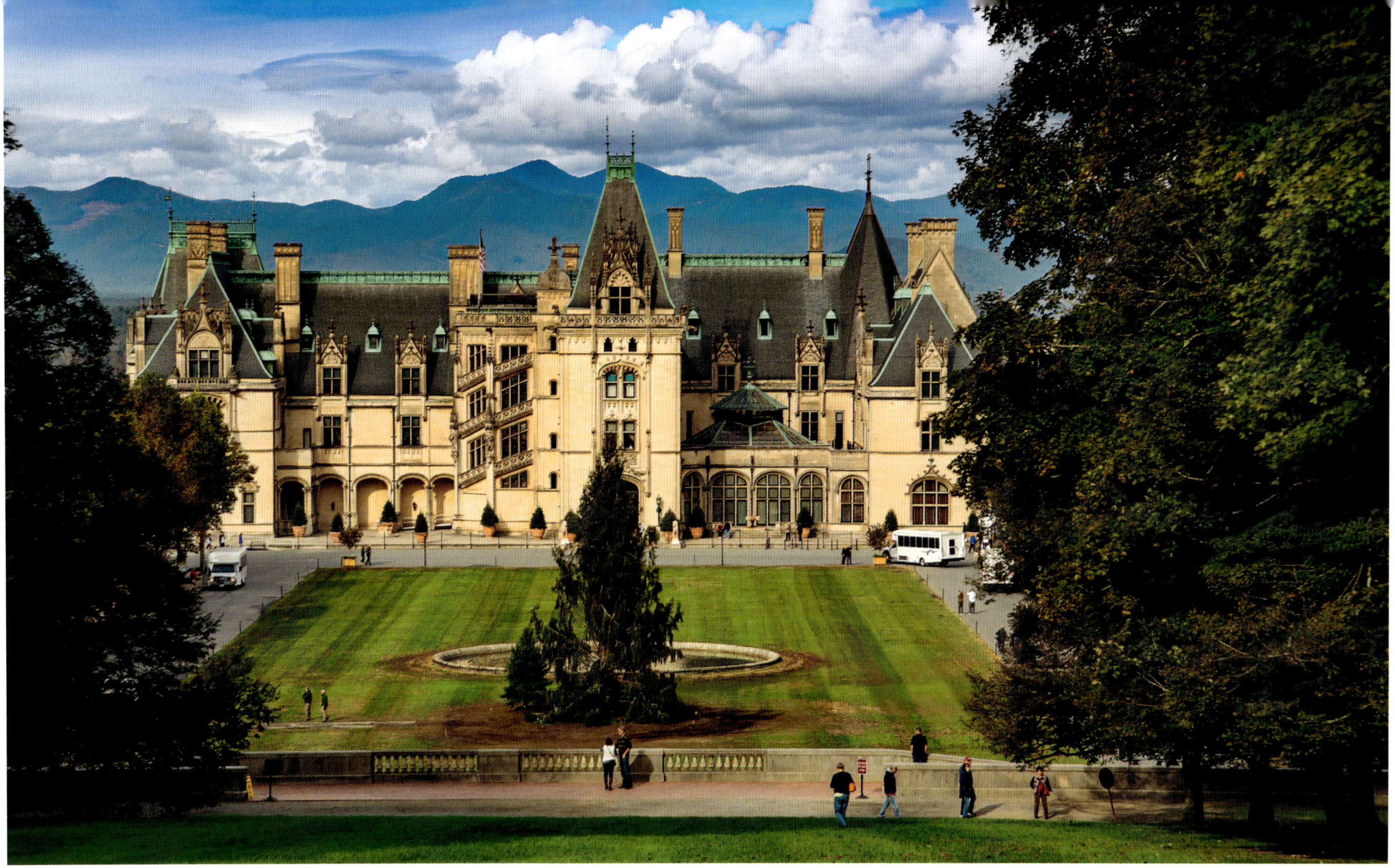

His descendants, on the other hand, lived opulently. His children and grandchildren sought acceptance into American high society and commissioned some of the most extravagant homes of the Gilded Age. The most famous of these is Biltmore Estate in Asheville, North Carolina—built by his grandson George Washington Vanderbilt II. He had fallen in love with the Blue Ridge Mountains during a visit to Asheville in the 1880s. Seeking a country retreat, he began construction of Biltmore (named after Vanderbilt's ancestral home, De Bilt, in the Netherlands and the Anglo-Saxon word for open rolling land, "moor.")

Completed in 1895 (with landscaping by Frederick Law Olmsted) Biltmore remains the largest privately owned home in the United States, with 250 rooms. It was inspired by French Renaissance châteaux and included the latest technologies of its time, such as electricity, elevators, and a refrigeration system. Though many of the New York properties built by railroad tycoons have been demolished, Biltmore and The Breakers, the summer residence of George's brother, Cornelius Vanderbilt II, are mansions that still give a glimpse of the riches created in the Gilded Age.

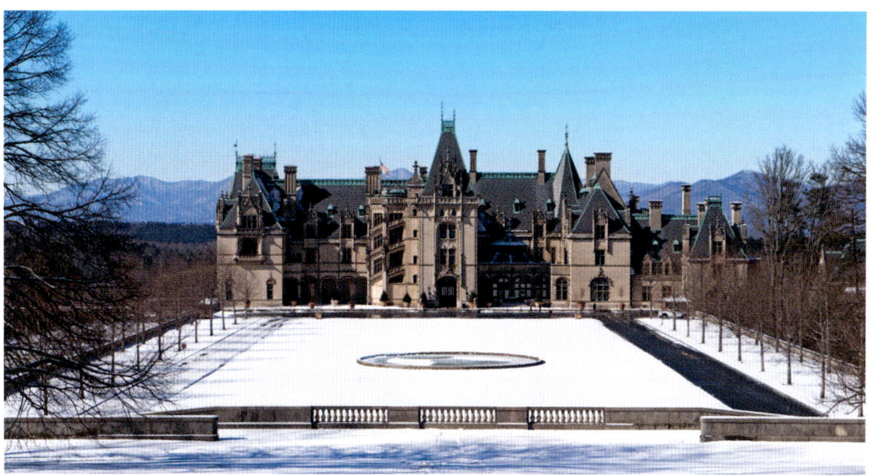

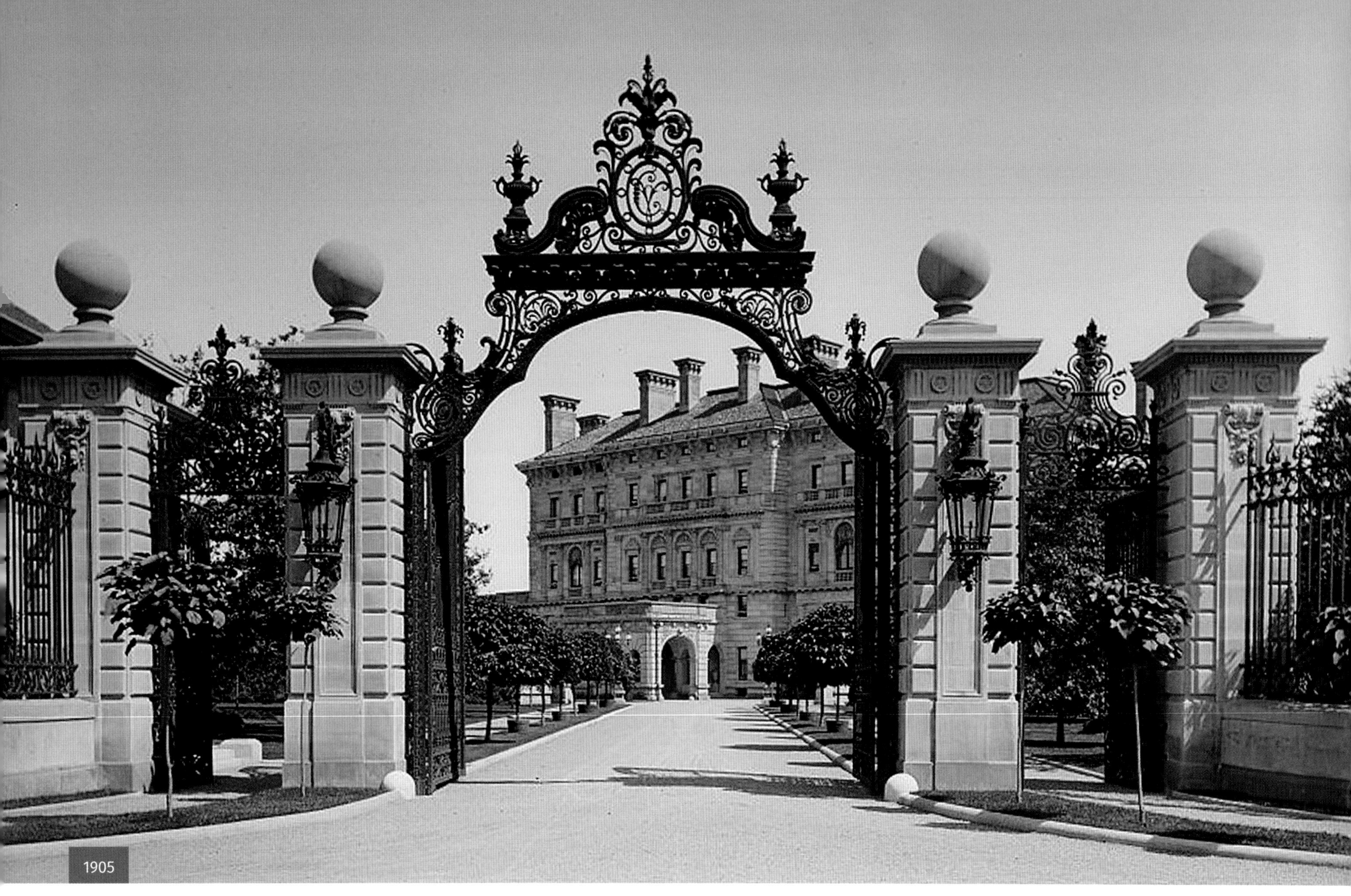
1905

THE BREAKERS, NEWPORT, RHODE ISLAND

A stunning example of ostentatious wealth from a railroad tycoon

No family better epitomized the excesses of the Gilded Age than the Vanderbilts, who built dozens of lavish homes around the world in the late nineteenth and early twentieth centuries. Few of these homes, though, could rival The Breakers, the summer home of Cornelius Vanderbilt II. He was a grandson of family patriarch and railroad tycoon Cornelius Vanderbilt, and had inherited a sizable portion of the family wealth upon his father William's death in 1885. That same year, he purchased a modest house in Newport, the summer playground of New York society. It burned down in 1892, but Vanderbilt set to work on its replacement, hiring architect Richard Morris Hunt to design a 70-room, 125,000-square-foot "cottage" atop the cliffs of Newport. Construction progressed quickly, with the Vanderbilts hiring around 2,000 workers and sparing no expense to have it completed as soon as possible. By the summer of 1895 The Breakers was finished, at a cost of around $7 million, or more than $150 million today.

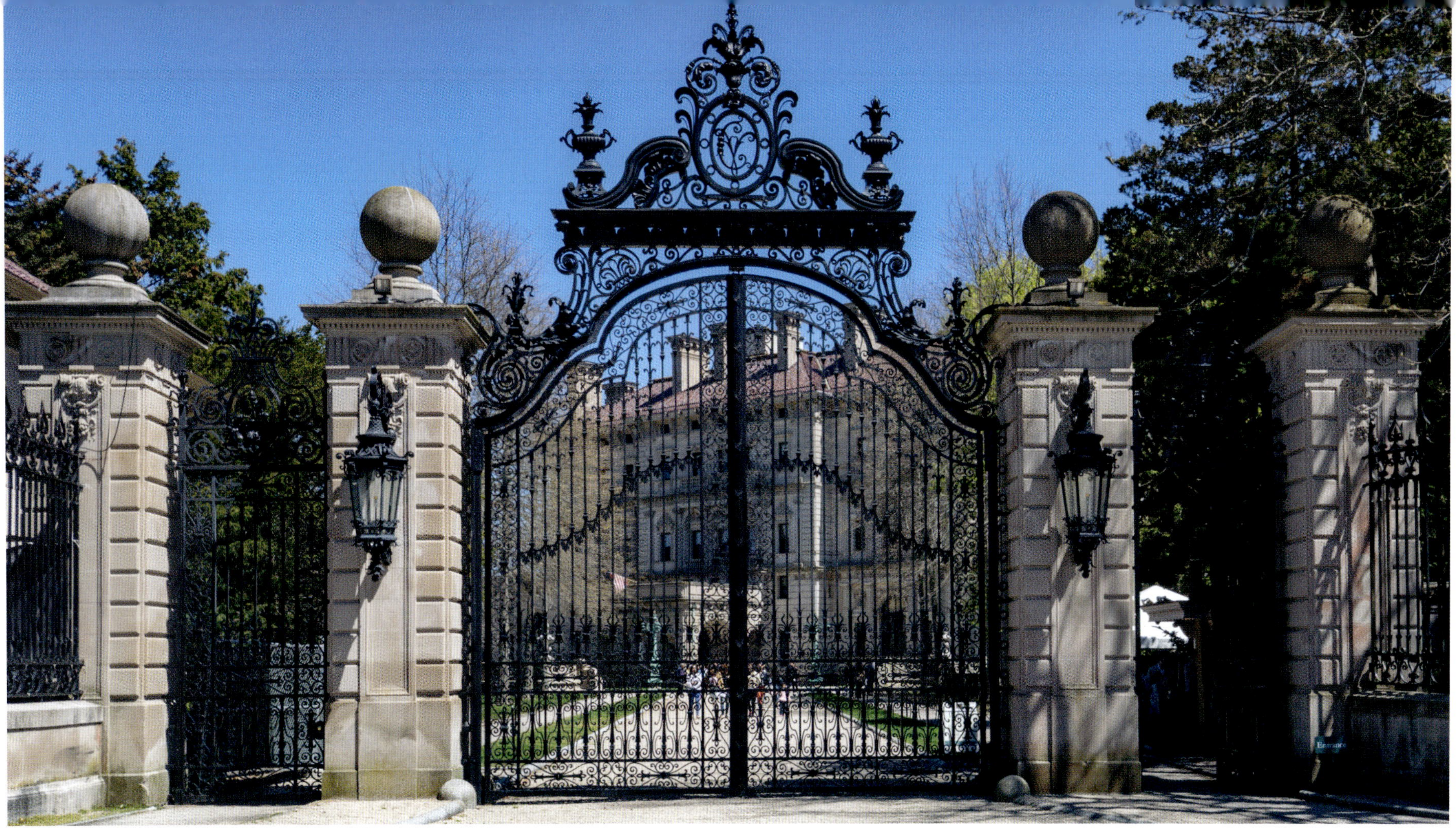

Cornelius Vanderbilt II did not get to enjoy his new home for very long. He suffered a debilitating stroke in 1896 and never fully recovered, dying three years later. His widow Alice survived him by more than three decades and owned The Breakers until her own death in 1934. At this point, the Vanderbilt fortune had largely disappeared, along with so many of the mansions that had been built only a generation or two earlier. The Breakers survived, though, and was inherited by Alice's youngest daughter, Gladys. In 1948, she leased the house to the Preservation Society of Newport County for $1 per year, and her heirs sold the property to them in 1972. Members of the Vanderbilt family continue to maintain a private apartment on the third floor, but the rest of the house is open to the public. It is one of the most popular tourist attractions in Rhode Island, and attracts over 400,000 visitors every year.

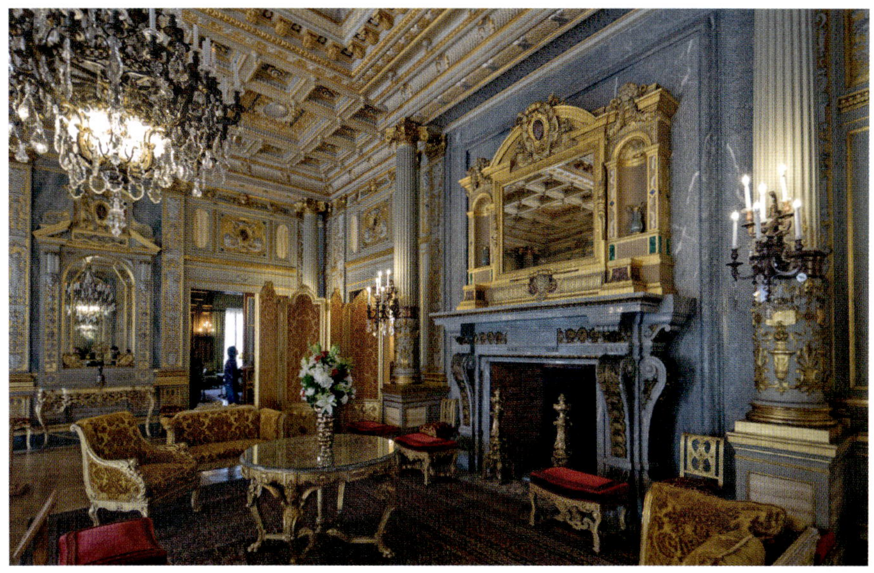

RIGHT: The lavish interior of the Music Room evokes the opulent Parisian interiors of the Second Period. It was used for music recitals for the Vanderbilt family and guests.

HOTEL DEL CORONADO, SAN DIEGO

One of the world's most recognizable and exclusive hotels

The prosperity of the Gilded Age brought new opportunities for travel and leisure, resulting in a boom for luxury hotels across America. Hotel Ponce de León in St. Augustine, Florida, built by Henry Flagler in Spanish Renaissance style, attracted wealthy Northerners escaping the cold.

The same could be said of the Hotel del Coronado, opened that same year of 1888. Elisha Babcock Jr. and Hampton L. Story headed a consortium that bought Coronado, a beach village on the spit of land across the bay from San Diego. Their intention was to create a world-class resort. When the hotel was opened, it had unheard-of modern conveniences, such as a fire alarm system, electricity, elevators, and private bathrooms. Construction began in January of 1887 and by March, one hundred barrels of cement were being used daily. The hotel was planned to have 720 rooms, a 10,800-square-foot ballroom, and its own boathouse. The Queen Anne Victorian architecture, characterized by red-turreted roofs and sprawling wooden facades, was unlike anything else on the West Coast.

John D. Spreckels purchased the holdings of the Coronado Beach Company in 1889 and put in the infrastructure for the entire village of Coronado, including adding

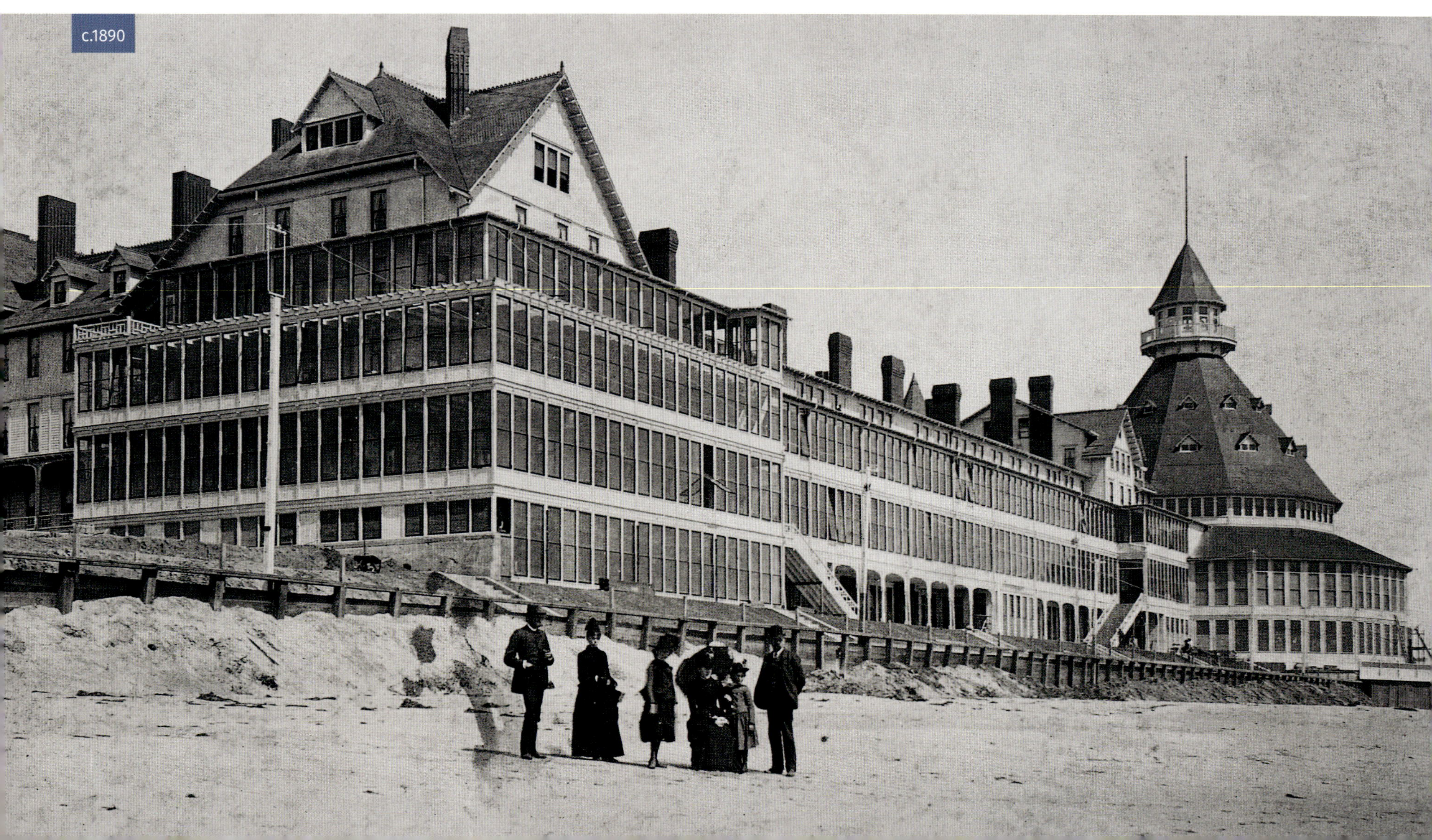
c.1890

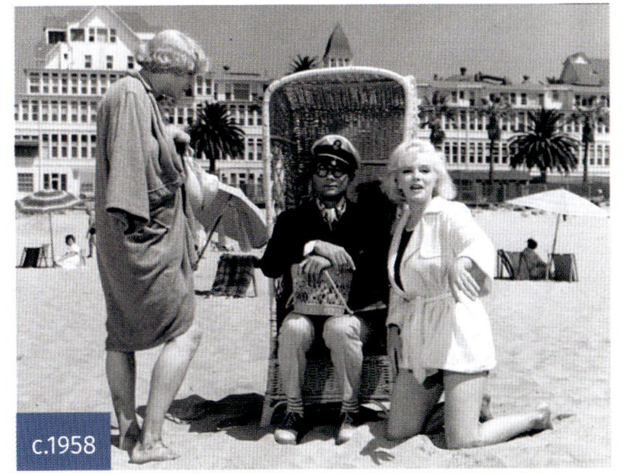
c.1958

streetcar and railway lines, dredging Glorietta Bay, and installing trees along Orange, Palm, and Olive Avenues. By 1913, the hotel even operated its own school for the children of long-term guests.

Though John D. Spreckels' influence on early San Diego was profound, his great love was for Coronado. In 1906 he built himself a mansion nearby in Glorietta Bay (now the Glorietta Bay Inn). For more than one hundred years, the Coronado hotel has been host to the world's famous, including sixteen US presidents. Its royal visitors have included Edward, Prince of Wales, in 1920, who attended the same function as Wallis Simpson—who was then married to a San Diego-based naval commander. It would be fifteen years before they were officially introduced in London.

Wizard of Oz author L. Frank Baum visited Coronado often in the early 1900s, spending months at a time at the Hotel as he wrote several of his Oz books. Some of the nineteenth-century guests are still there—the ghost of Kate Morgan, whose body was found in 1892, is still believed to roam the halls. It most famously featured as a backdrop in the movie *Some Like It Hot* (pictured left) starring Jack Lemmon, Tony Curtis, and Marilyn Monroe.

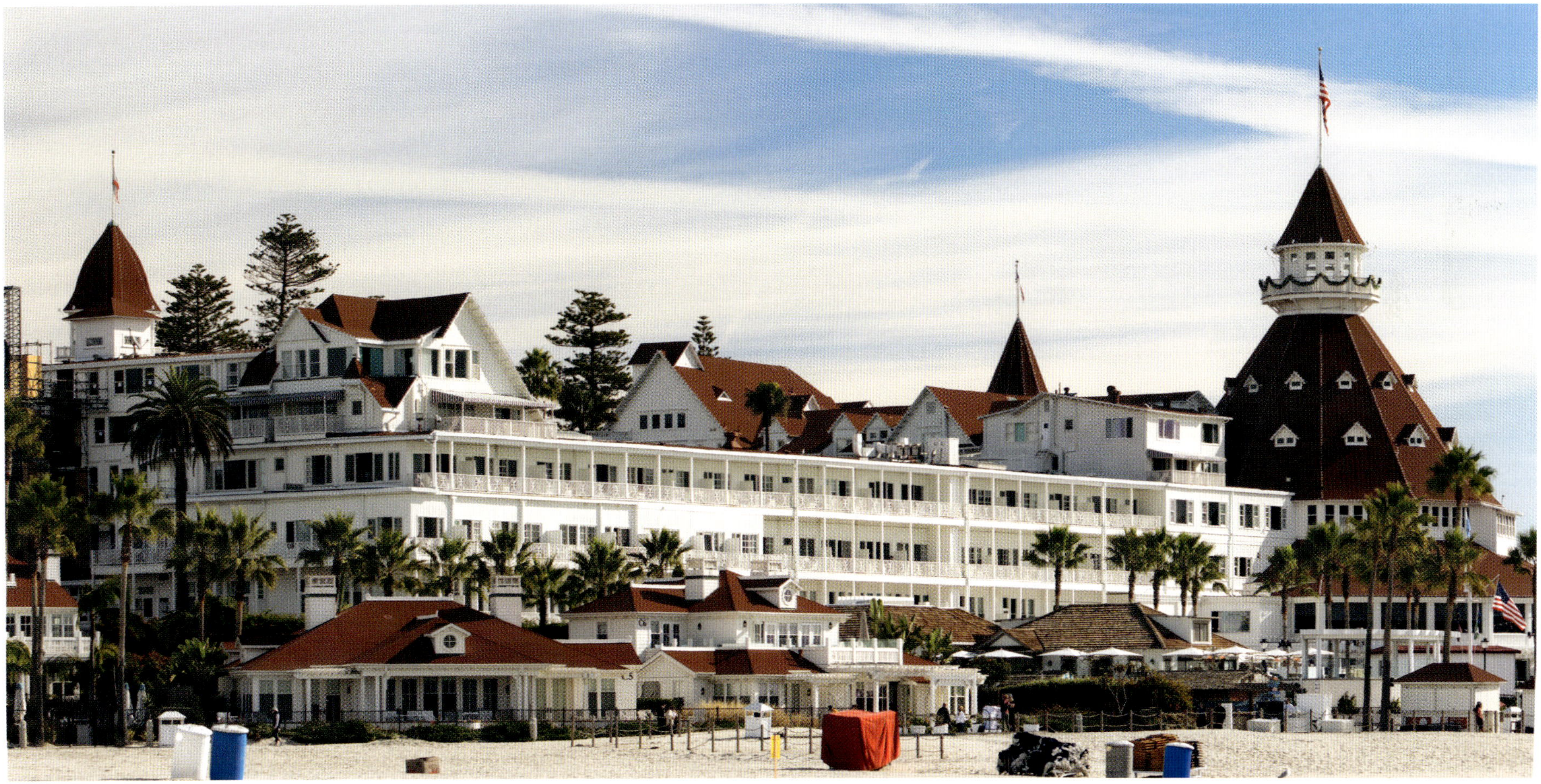

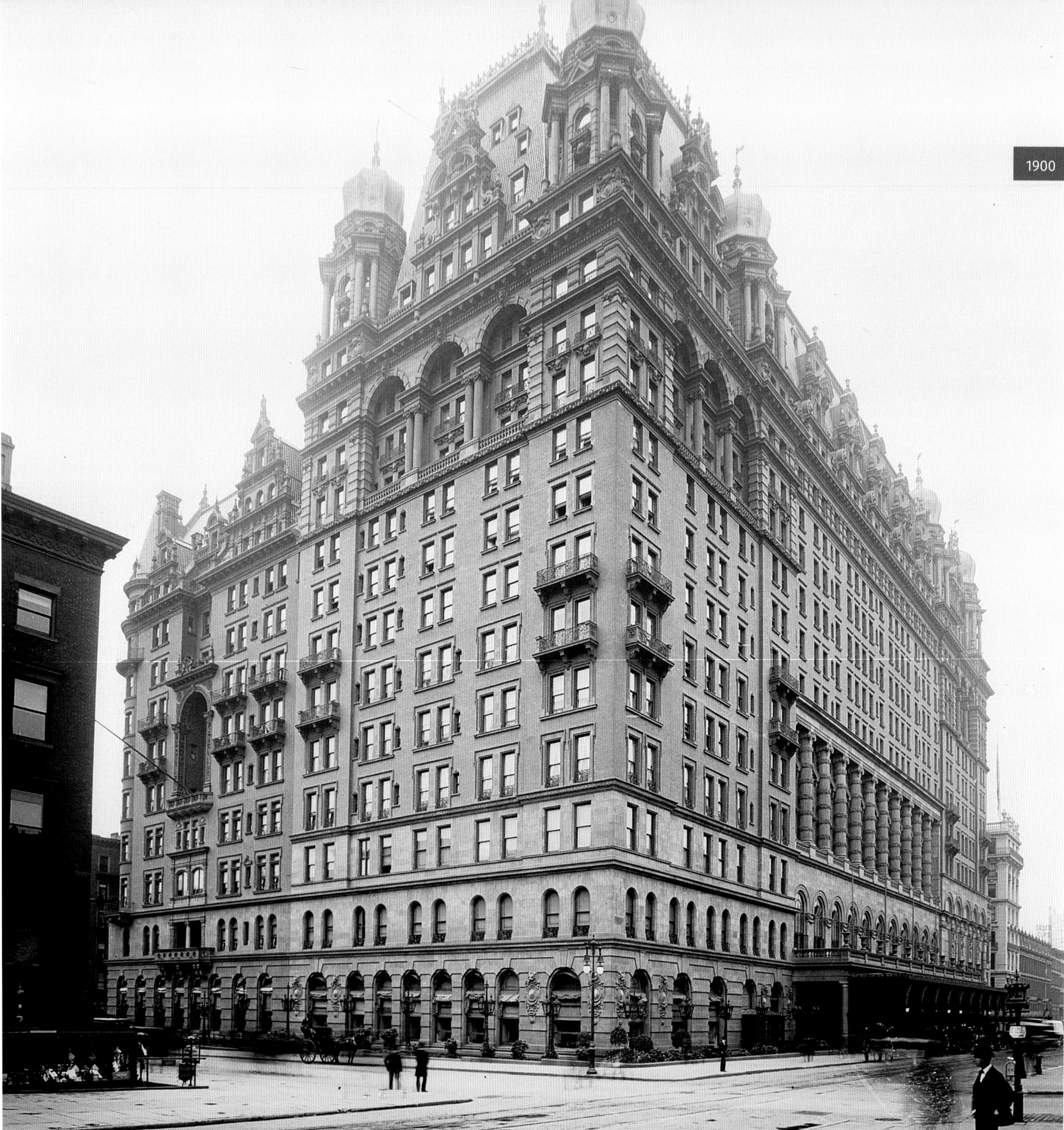

1900

WALDORF-ASTORIA/ EMPIRE STATE BUILDING, NEW YORK

The city's grandest hotel gave way to one of its tallest buildings

The first Waldorf-Astoria was originally two side-by-side hotels built by feuding cousins of the Astor family. William Waldorf Astor built the first one, the Hotel Waldorf, in 1893, overshadowing the neighboring mansion of his despised aunt Caroline. Her son, John Jacob Astor, at first planned to demolish his mother's house and build stables to stink up his cousin's opulent hotel. But since their fortunes were tied together, John Jacob reconsidered and instead built the Astoria in 1897, an even larger, more splendid building. Novelist Henry James called the hotel's amazingly efficient operation "a gorgeous golden blur, a paradise." Hard to imagine, but when the hotels were built between 1893 and 1897 the block was a low-rise residential neighborhood lined with stately brownstones. The architect of both buildings was Henry Hardenbergh who would go on to design New York's Plaza Hotel in 1907.

The two buildings functioned as one hotel, but the cousins agreed that if their alliance fell apart, they could seal off the ground floor connection. Their success was so great that it never happened. Seen here in 1900, the Waldorf-Astoria was the city's grandest hotel and New York society's favorite place to dine, dance, and drink. This view is looking north from Thirty-third Street and Fifth Avenue.

As society moved farther uptown, the original Waldorf-Astoria died of thirst during Prohibition and was demolished in 1929 to make way for the Empire State Building. Both the Empire State and the new Waldorf-Astoria Hotel, a streamlined sophisticate on Park Avenue and Fiftieth Street, were completed in 1931. The Empire State broke all construction records, reaching 102 stories in fifteen months. Opened at the start of the Great Depression, it had no rivals for height but plenty of competition for office space. For years it was called "the Empty State" and survived on entrance fees to its lofty observation deck. It was the city's tallest building until the north tower of the World Trade Center reached 110 stories in 1972. It reluctantly regained the title after the fall of the twin towers, but happily conceded it once again when the steel structure of the new One World Trade Center tower surpassed it on April 30, 2012.

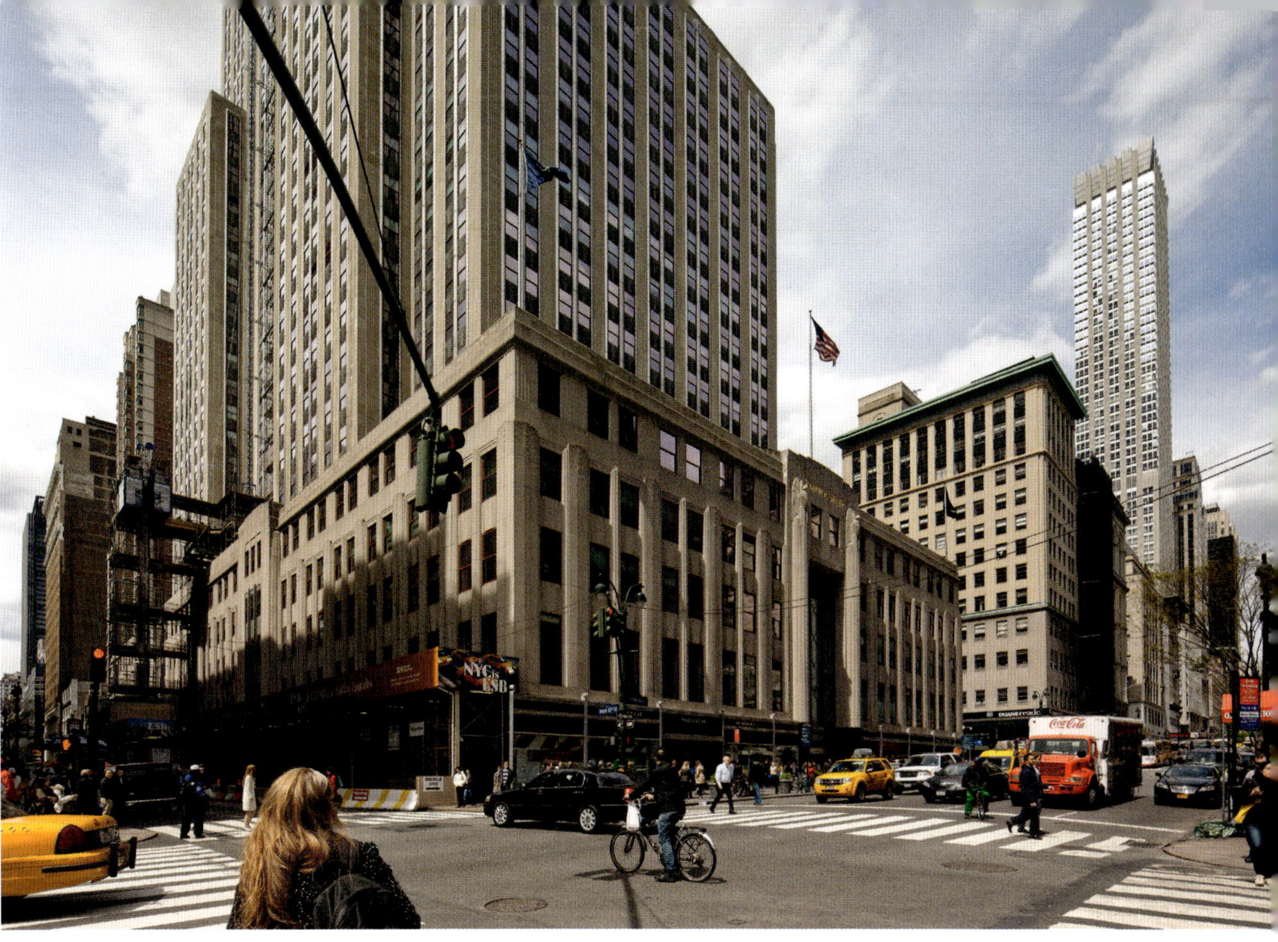

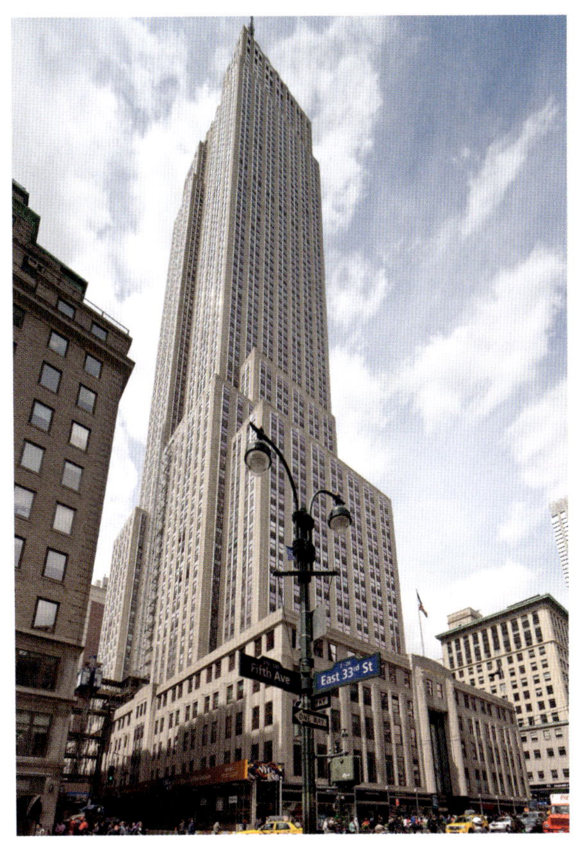

LEFT: With 102 stories, plus a 250-foot antenna, the Empire State Building is 1,454 feet high.

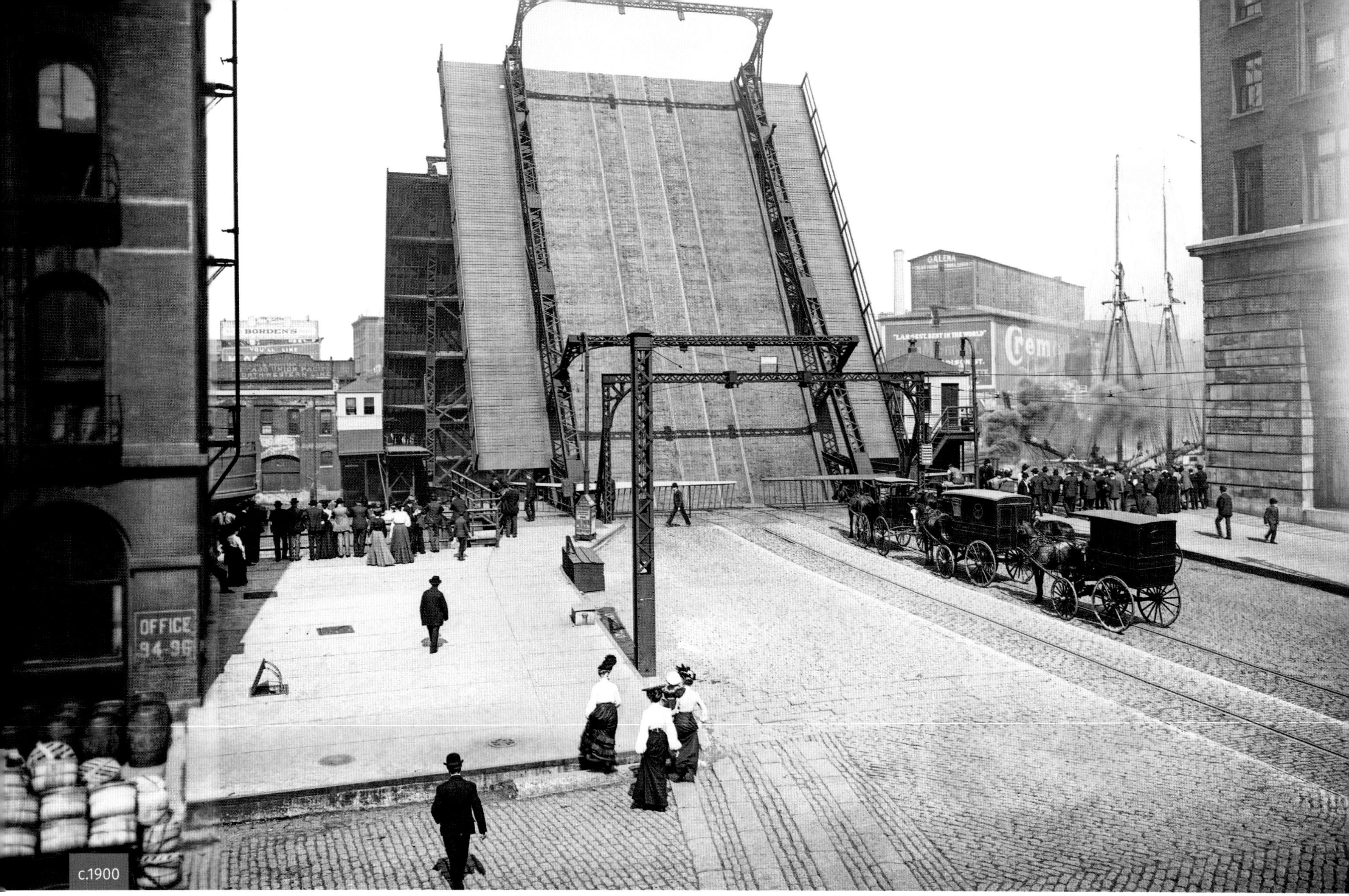

c.1900

STATE STREET BRIDGE, CHICAGO

An important evolution in movable bridge design

As early as 1834, the need for movable bridges across the Chicago River was evident. Major shipping interests relied on the river to accommodate large cargo freights with minimal delays. The first State Street Bridge was of the swing variety, by which the bridge rotated on a large center pier to allow river traffic to pass on either side. Not only were these bridges dangerous for pedestrian traffic stuck on the bridge when it opened, they also created narrow passages that larger ships could not pass through. In 1898 a rolling-lift bridge—an early bascule, or "seesaw", bridge—was installed at State Street, using an improved design that lifted opposite leaves of the bridge on curved runners. The problem with this design was that massive engines were required to lift bridge leaves, which were unstable in their vertical position. It would be more than fifty years before State Street was treated to the design that brought fame to Chicago bridge engineers: the trunnion bascule.

The concept of the trunnion bascule bridge—known worldwide as the "Chicago-style" bridge—is similar to the rolling-lift design, but the major improvement is the use of massive underground weights as precise counterbalances to the weight of the bridge leaves. The 1949 State Street Bridge now accommodates six lanes of vehicle traffic and two pedestrian walkways.

The modern photo also shows a progression of architectural forms, starting with Bertrand Goldberg's Marina City (left), a 1967 mixed-use construction comprising two scallop-edged 65-floor concrete towers plus a ground-level auditorium now occupied by Chicago's House of Blues. Just east of the river rises Mies van der Rohe's IBM Building (center right), completed in 1971 as the architect's final American work. Trump Tower, completed in 2009, is a glimmering 1,131-foot signal of the contemporary age with hints of Chicago's architectural history in its Art Deco setbacks and its steel-and-glass construction.

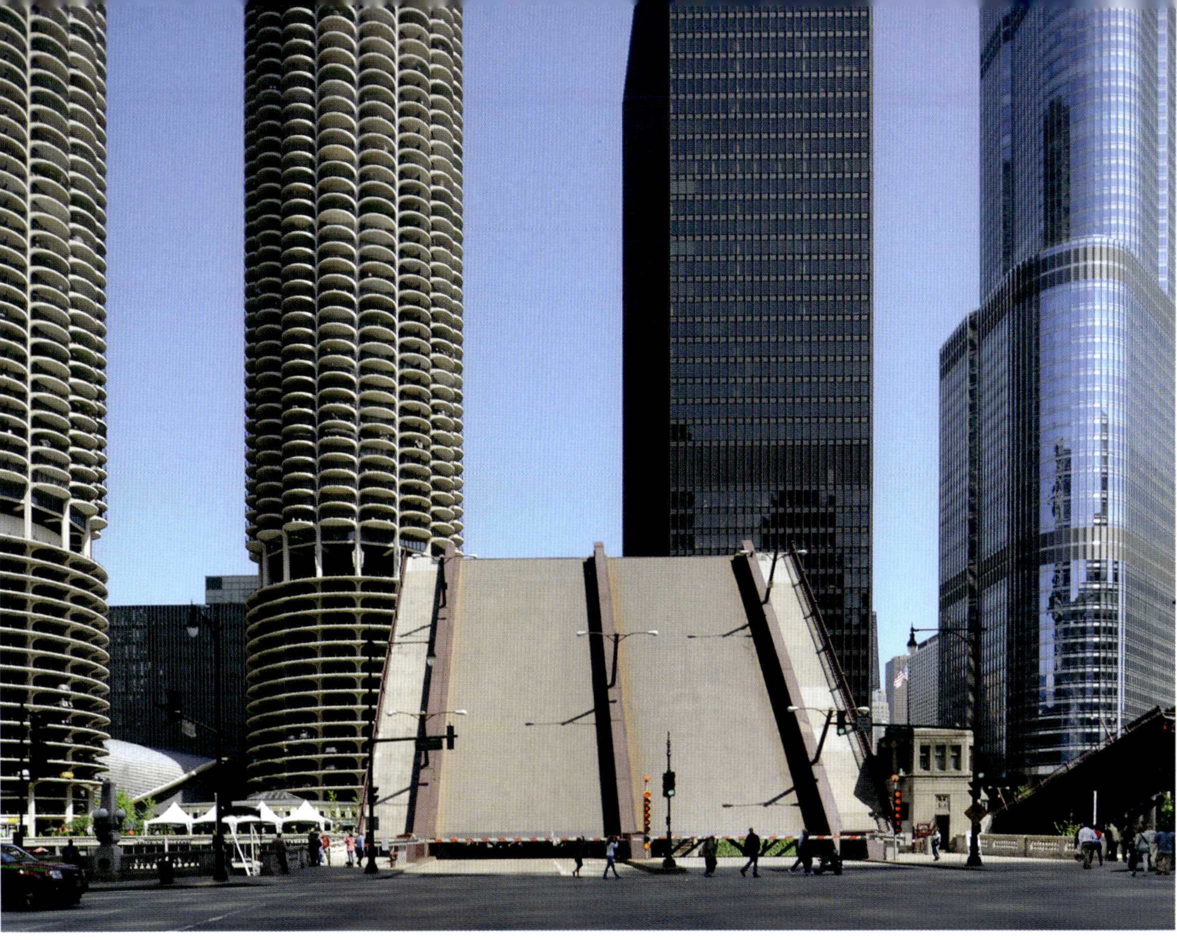

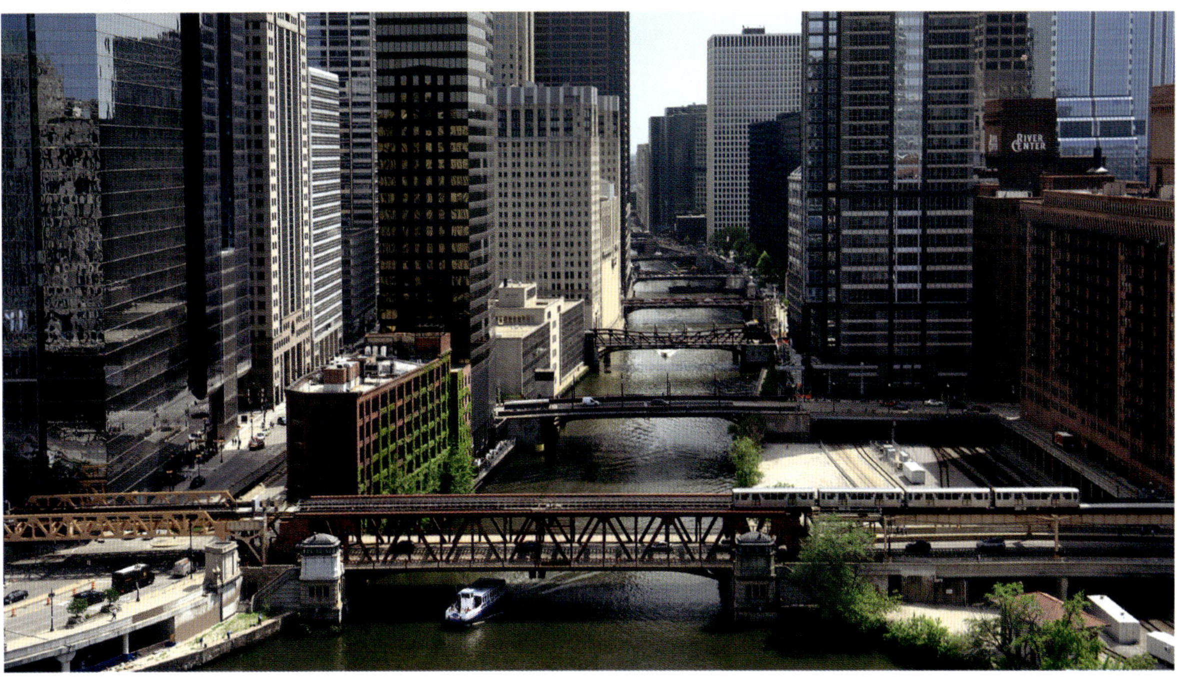

RIGHT: Looking down the Chicago River at the succession of bridges that link north and south. Before the bascule bridges there was a central pillar for each swing bridge, limiting the width of ships to half the size of the river.

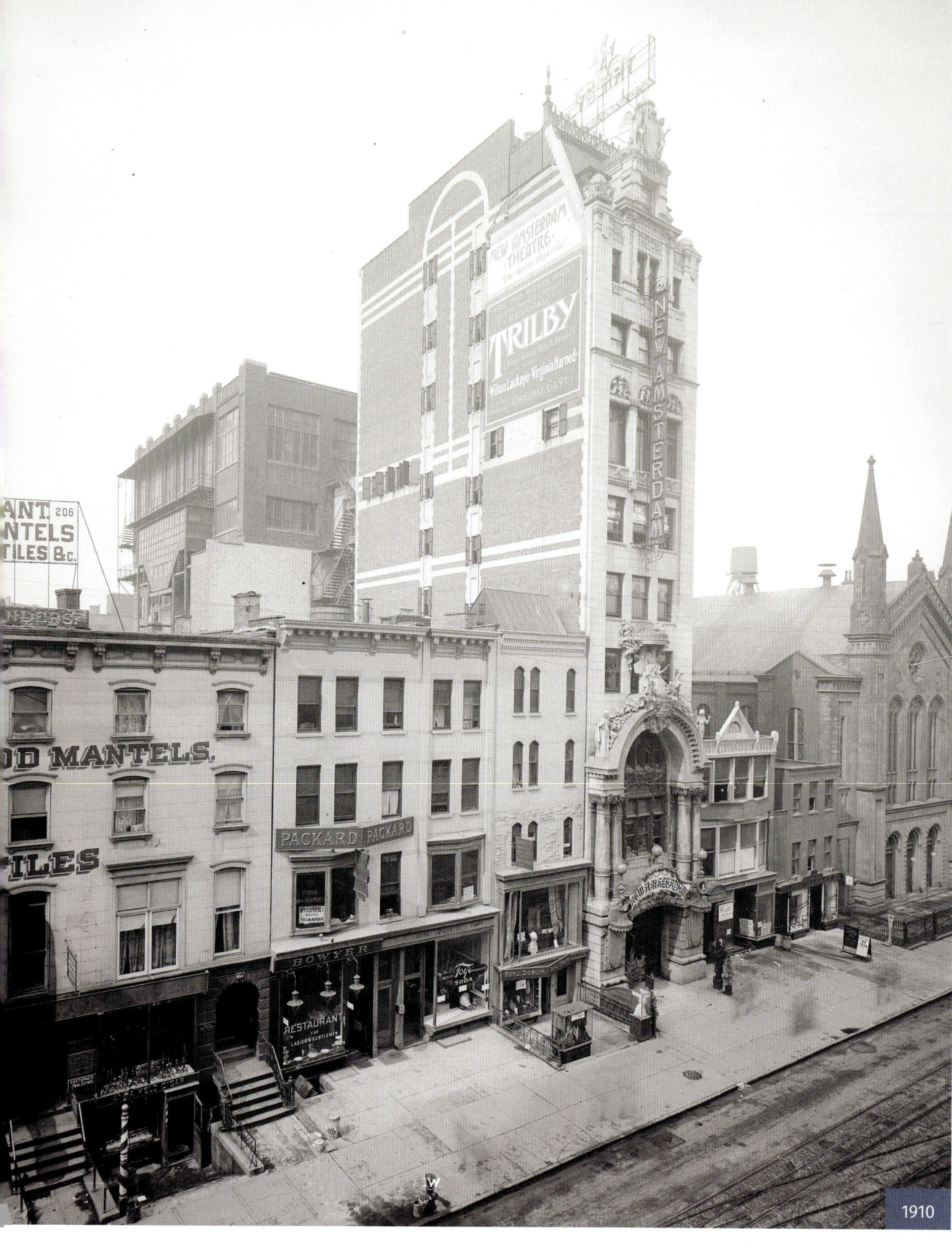

1910

NEW AMSTERDAM THEATRE, NEW YORK

Once the crown jewel of Broadway

Conceived in the late Victorian period and opened in 1903, the New Amsterdam Theatre was the largest theater on Broadway at the time, seating over 1,700 patrons. Located at 214 West 42nd Street by Times Square, impresarios A. L. Erlanger and Marc Klaw opted for a Beaux-Arts-style building. The lavish Art Nouveau interiors were rare in American architecture at the time and its opening marked a turning point in Times Square's transformation into the entertainment capital of the country.

The place quickly became the crown jewel of New York's theater scene, known for its elegance, superior acoustics, and ornate decor. The theater's rooftop also featured the New Amsterdam Roof Garden, a small open-air performance space used during the summer months.

In the 1910s and 1920s, the New Amsterdam Theatre gained national fame as the home of the legendary *Ziegfeld Follies*, produced by Florenz Ziegfeld. These lavish revues blended high art, comedy, dance, and music, and introduced audiences to now legendary performers such as Fanny Brice (portrayed by Barbra Streisand in *Funny Girl* on Broadway and in film), W. C. Fields, and laconic cowboy Will Rogers. The Follies helped solidify the theater's reputation as a venue of glamour and sophistication during the height of the Jazz Age.

However, like much of Times Square, the New Amsterdam Theatre fell on hard times during the mid-twentieth century. The Great Depression hit live performance hard, and by the 1930s, the theater began shifting toward showing movies. By the 1950s its luster had faded significantly, and in 1985, the theater closed due to disrepair and structural concerns. The once glorious building, with its crumbling walls and faded murals, stood vacant for nearly a decade.

A turning point came in the early 1990s with the revitalization of Times Square. In 1993, The Walt Disney Company signed a 99-year lease and committed to restoring the New Amsterdam to its former glory. The renovation cost over $34 million and was painstakingly detailed, with teams of artisans using historic photographs.

The theater reopened in 1997 with Disney's Broadway production of *The Lion King*, followed by *Mary Poppins* and *Aladdin*. It remains both a working theater and a testament to the Gilded Age of American entertainment.

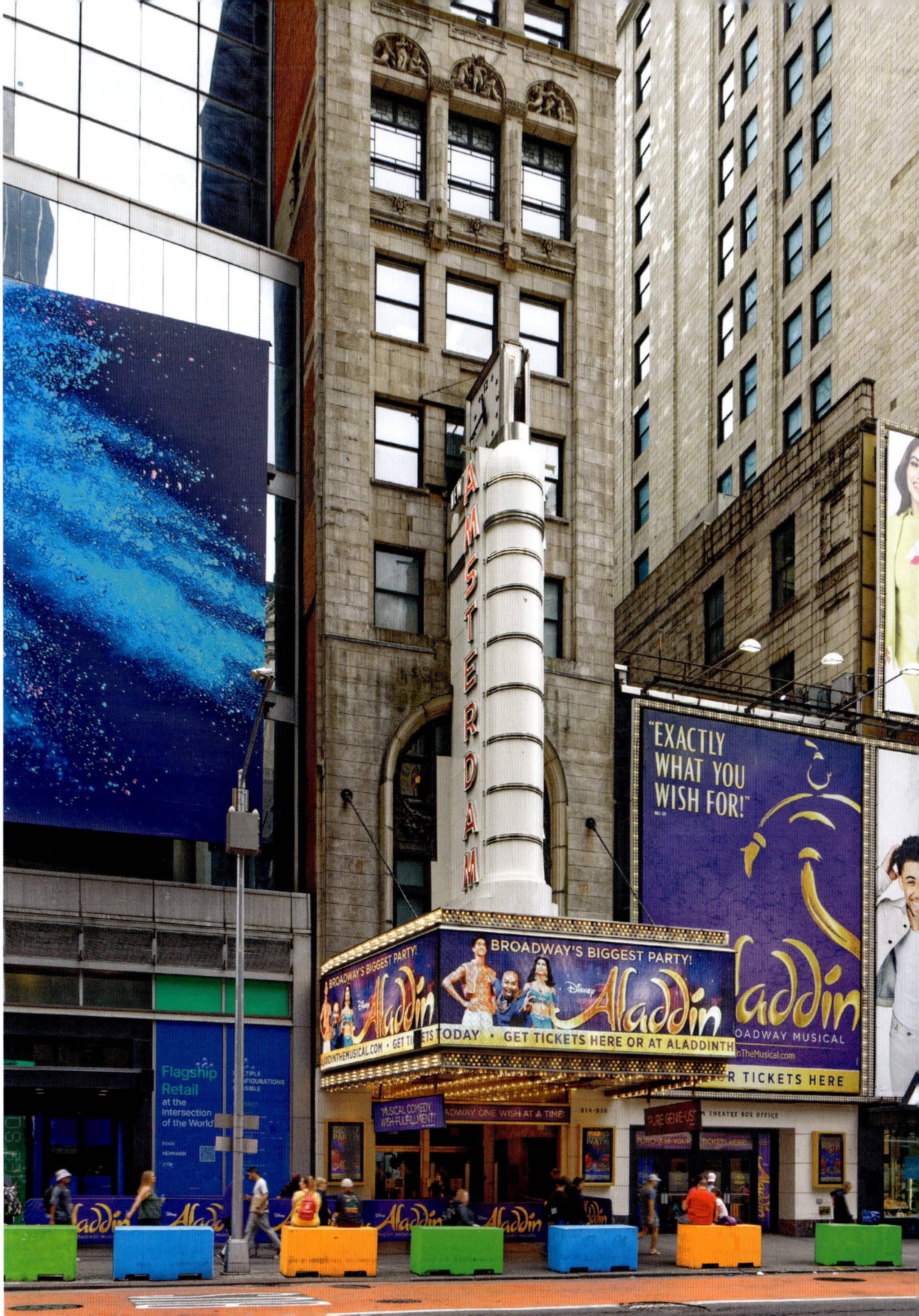

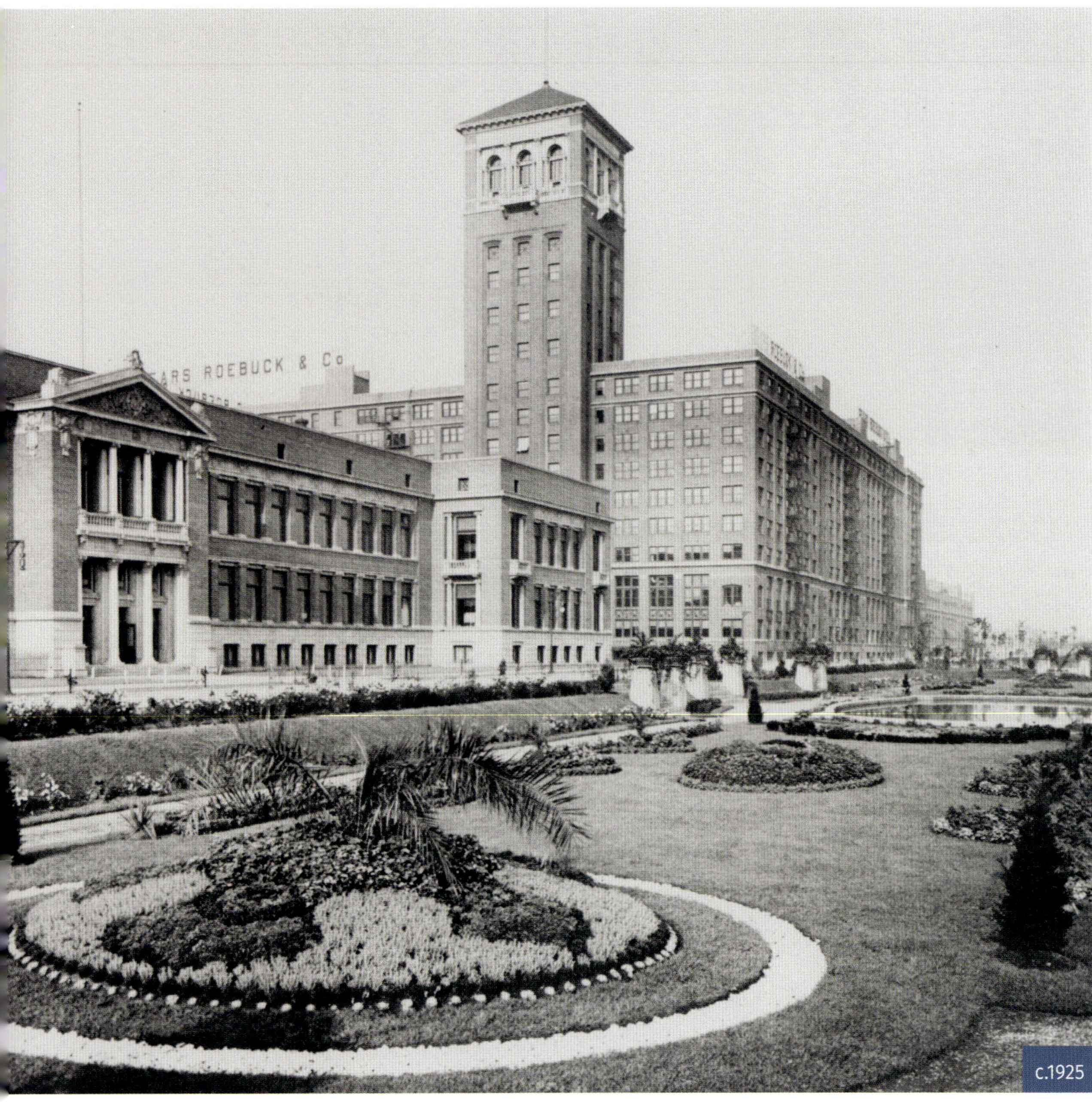

c.1925

SEARS, ROEBUCK AND CO., CHICAGO

For decades the publisher of America's "Consumer Bible"

Sears, Roebuck and Co. was once a giant of American retail. Founded in 1892 by Richard W. Sears and Alvah C. Roebuck, the company began as a mail-order catalog business. With its headquarters in North Lawndale, Chicago, Sears were quick to exploit the expanding railroad network and the needs of rural Americans, offering everything from watches and farm equipment to homes sold in kits.

Its catalogs became known as the "Consumer Bible," reaching millions of households and offering goods at affordable prices. In 1906, Sears opened the first retail store in Chicago. The same year they opened new headquarters in North Lawndale. Connected to downtown via the Burlington Railroad, as well as a direct street route, via Ogden Avenue, North Lawndale was a practical choice. Its new fireproof brick buildings were a lure for Chicago workers still mindful of the Great Fire.

The sprawling Sears complex covered more than 41 acres, and contained three million square feet of office and factory space. It also housed the printing facility for the massive Sears Catalog, and included its own power plant, water system, employee bank, and volunteer fire department. The company held social and athletic events at on-site facilities, which were converted to employee parking lots in 1926. The original fourteen-story Sears Tower offered an observation deck for visitors until the company relocated its headquarters to downtown's new 110-story Sears Tower in 1974.

The post-World War II suburban boom played to Sears' strengths: department stores anchored shopping malls, and the brand became synonymous with American middle-class life. However, by the 1980s and 1990s, cracks began to show. Competition from leaner discount retailers like Walmart and Target, which offered lower prices and more efficient logistics, began eroding Sears' dominance.

Sears sold off the Sears Tower (now the Willis Tower) in 1994 although the company kept the building's naming rights until 2003.

In 2018, Sears filed for Chapter 11 bankruptcy. At the time, it operated fewer than 700 stores, a steep decline from the thousands it once boasted. Today,

Sears exists more as a brand relic than a functioning business, with only a handful of stores remaining. Its story is a cautionary tale of missed opportunities and—like the Kodak company—failing to innovate in a rapidly changing market.

Before its demise, a partnership between Sears, city officials, developers, and community leaders brought about Homan Square, a housing project to revitalize the declining North Lawndale in the early 1990s. Though the other buildings have been razed, the 1906 tower—now Homan Square Tower—has been retained and still overlooks the former home of US mail order.

BELOW: The Willis Tower continues to draw visitors to gaze down from its glass-paneled skydeck.

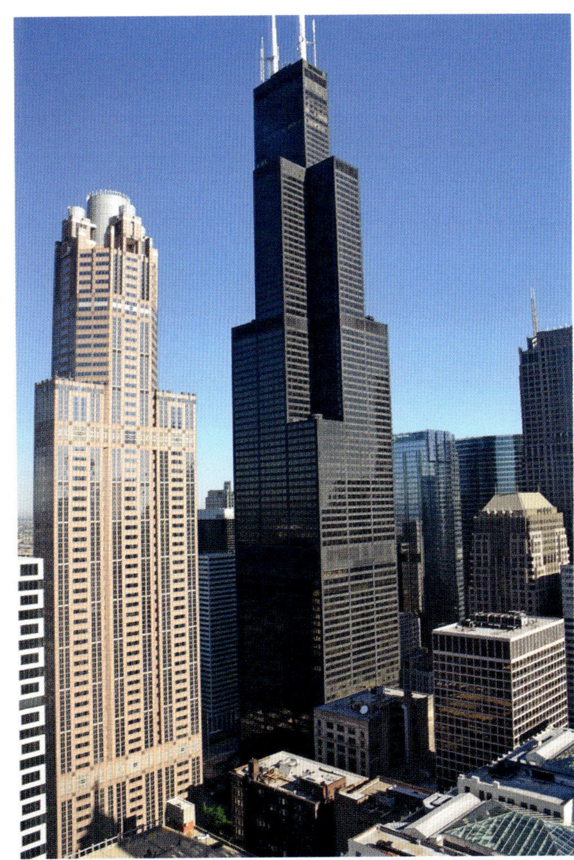

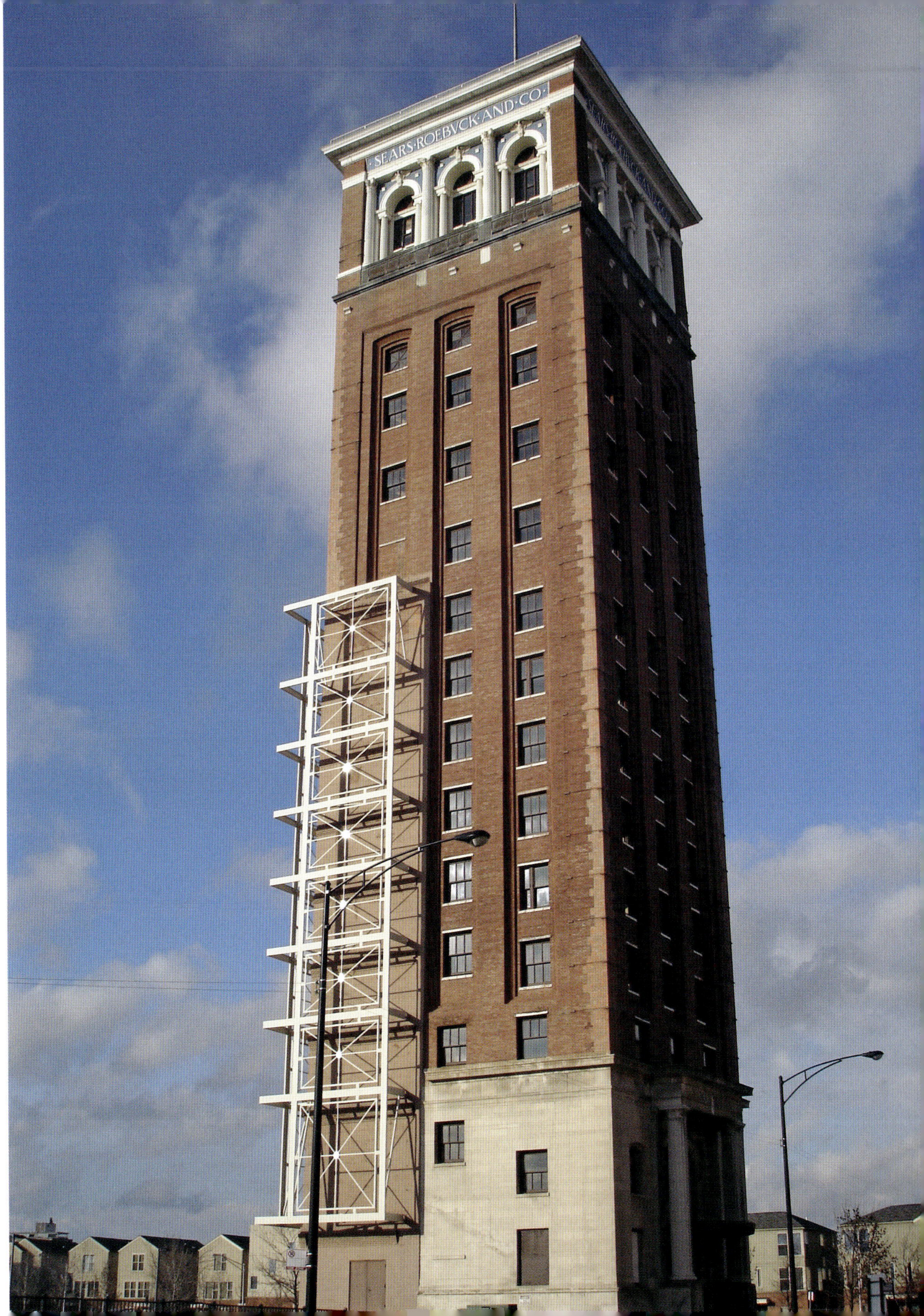

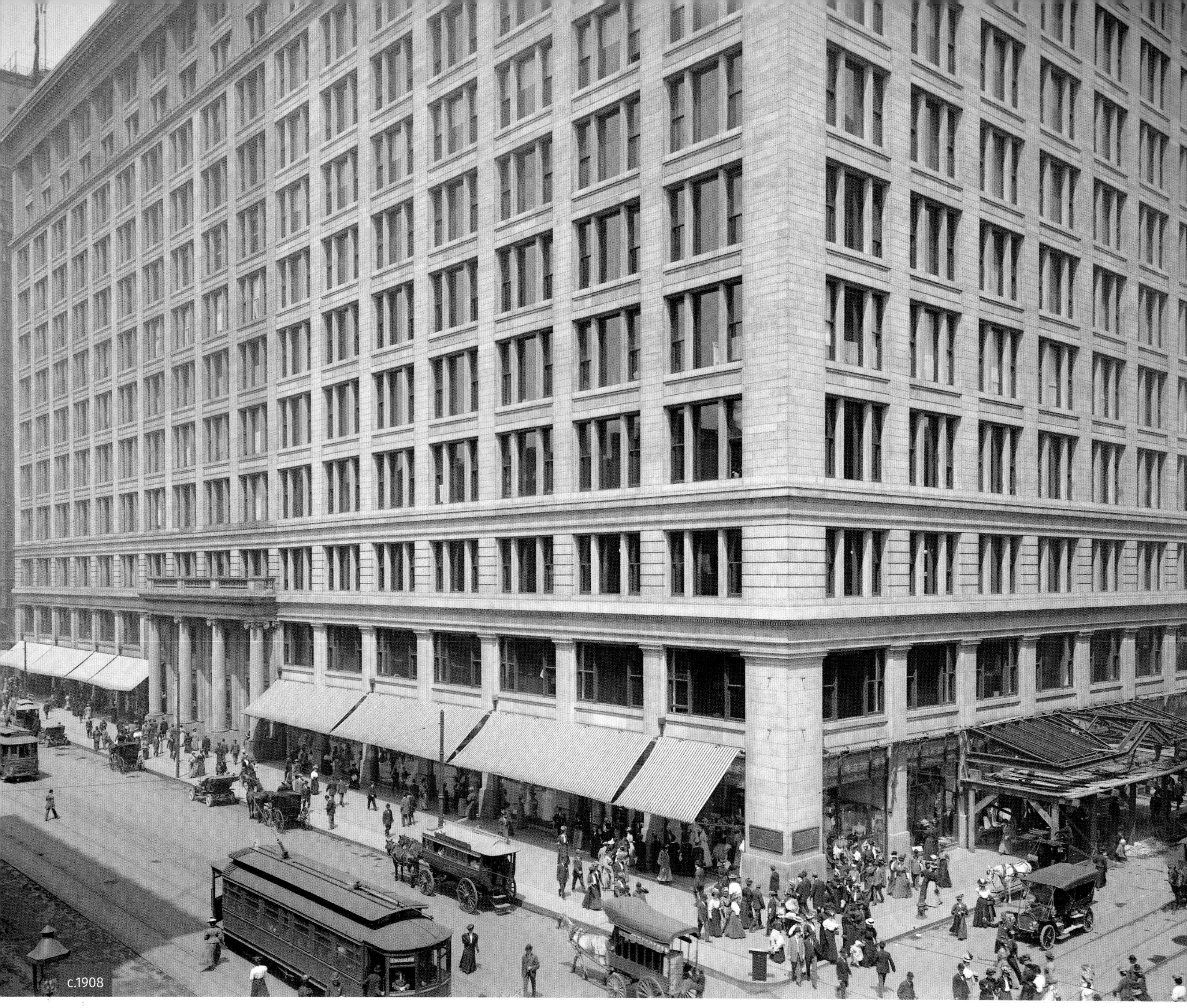
c.1908

MARSHALL FIELD'S/ MACY'S, CHICAGO

The store that gave the lady what she wanted

For more than 150 years, no Chicago business was so closely identified with the character and glamour of Chicago life than Marshall Field and Company. For Chicagoans, Marshall Field invented the department store. He had one goal: "Give the lady what she wants." The enterprising retail magnate moved his business from its original location on Lake Street to State Street in the early 1860s, increasing the street's growth as a shopping hub. Even the Great Fire of 1871 could not keep Chicago's favorite department store down. Marshall Field's would eventually command the streetscape on State Street between Washington and Randolph, occupying all of Wabash Avenue in a series of refined granite structures designed by Daniel Burnham between 1892 and 1907. The store's famous clock became a popular meeting place.

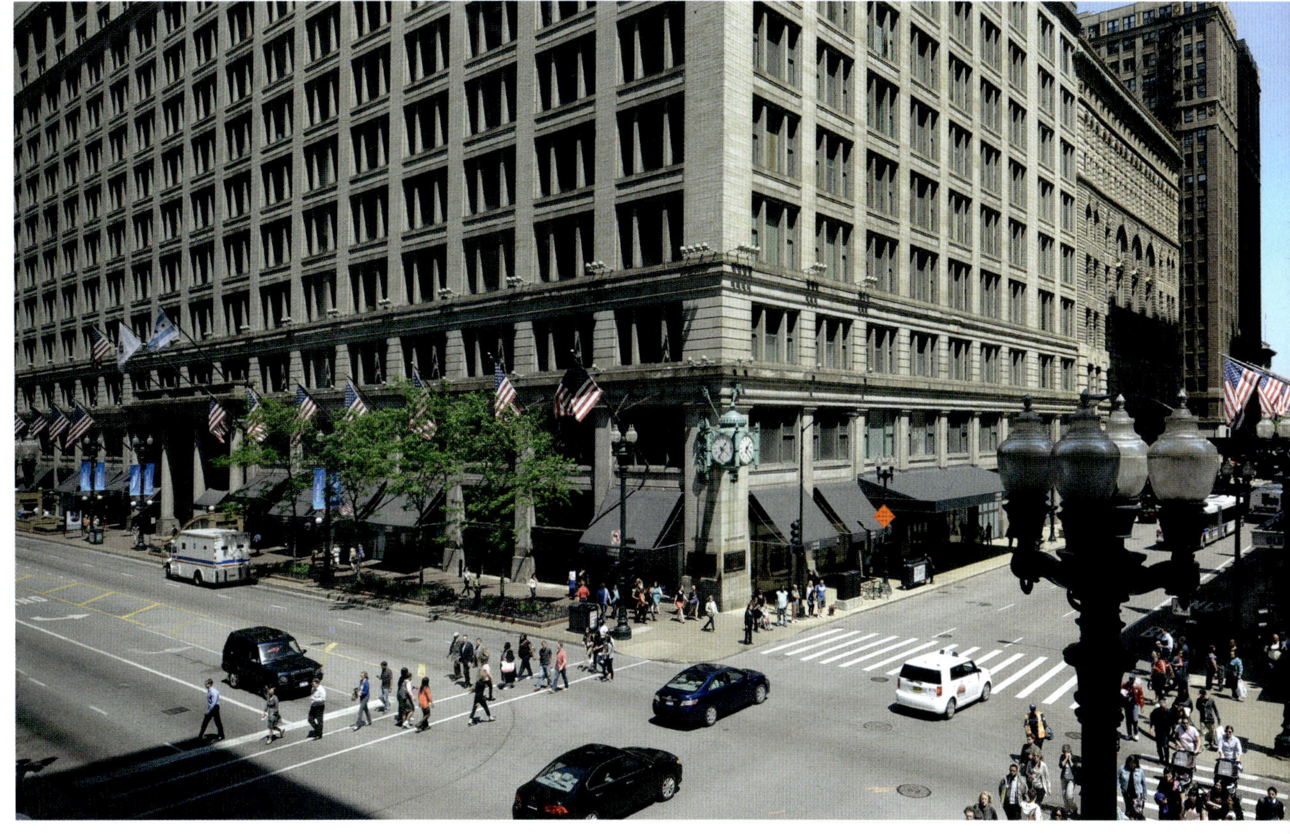

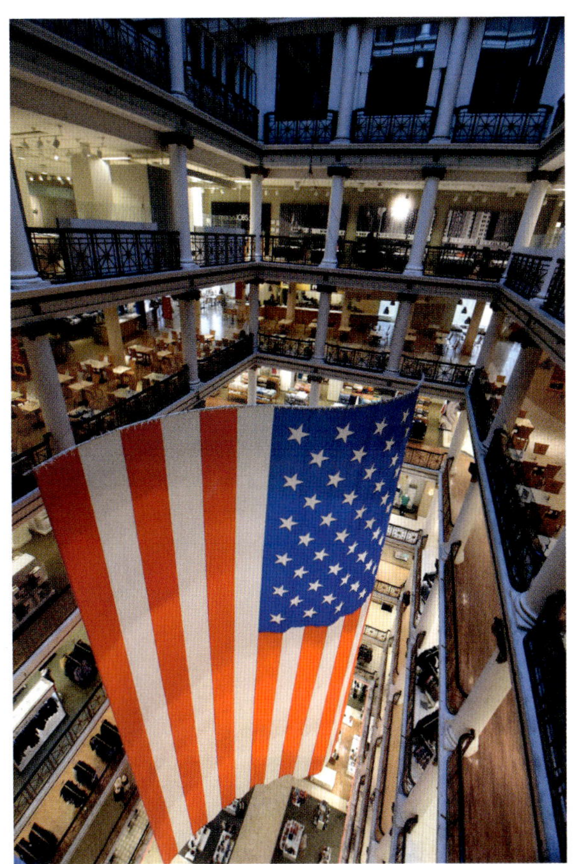

Boasting an interior dome bejeweled with mosaics by artist Louis Comfort Tiffany, the store featured more than 73 acres of merchandise in 450 departments. Sadly, the Loop's grandest enterprise ceased to be in September 2006. Having been purchased by the owners of Macy's, the company made the controversial decision to retire the Marshall Field's name and rebrand all locations under the Macy's banner. The move was met with significant public backlash, especially in Chicago, where Field's held deep emotional and historical significance. Protests and petitions followed, but the name change remained. Though the Marshall Field's name no longer graces its facade, many architectural and cultural elements—such as the Great Clock, the Tiffany ceiling, and the Walnut Room—remain preserved.

The black Macy's awnings have replaced the classic Field green, but the large bronze plaques with the store's original name can still be found on the four corners of the building—all that remains of the grand dame of State Street.

LEFT: A modern interior of the store.

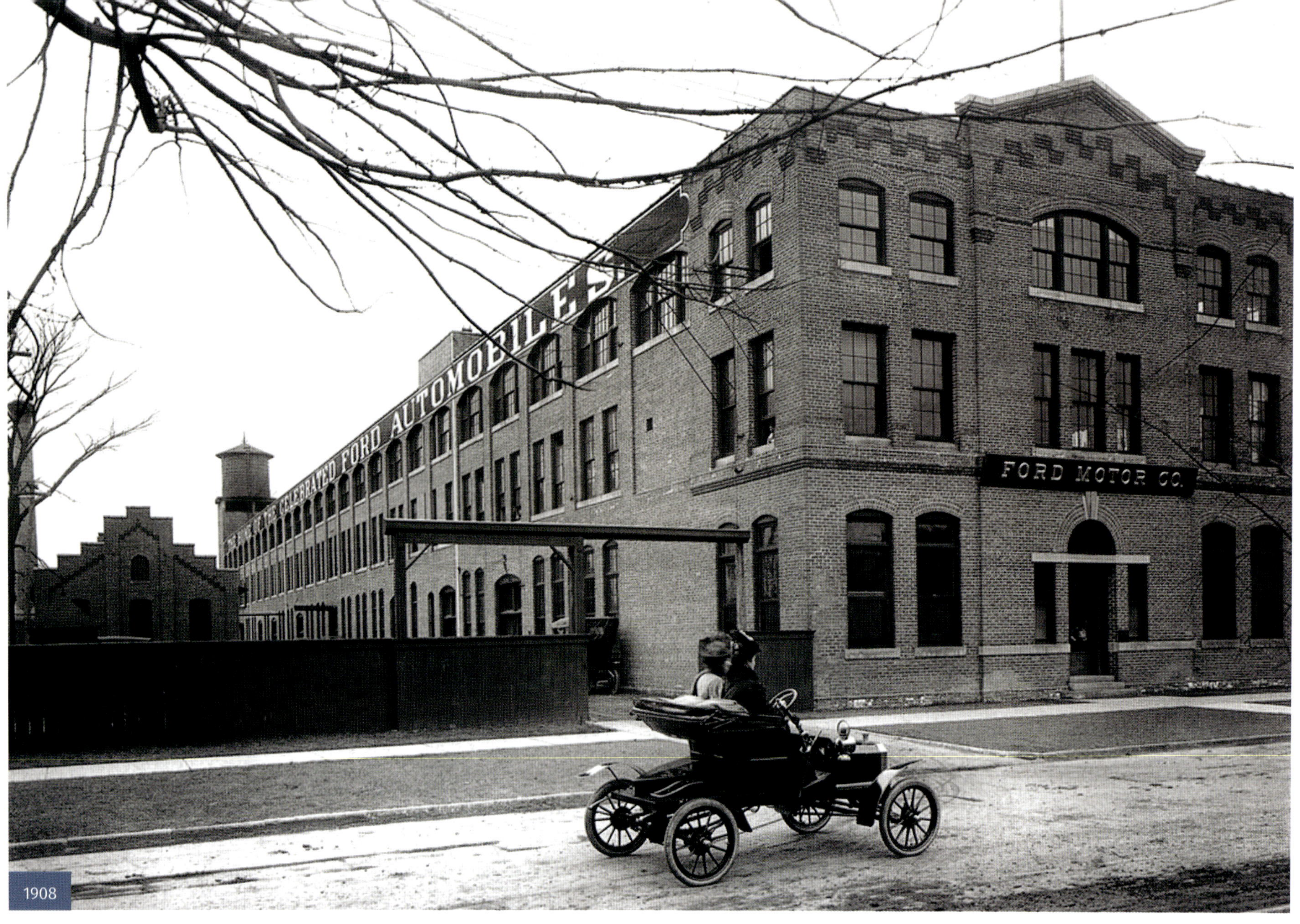

1908

FORD MOTOR COMPANY, DETROIT

Home of the Model T, the world's bestselling car till the Beetle

Henry Ford's first venture into auto production failed. The Detroit Automobile Company, made way for the Ford Motor Company in 1903. Ford's vision was an affordable, reliable auto, simple enough for the average person to operate and maintain. His early models, such as the Model A and Model N, helped establish the company in Detroit, but it was the Model T, introduced in 1908, that transformed the company.

The Model T was initially produced at the Piquette Avenue Plant in Detroit's Milwaukee Junction neighborhood (pictured above). Built in 1904, the Piquette plant was Ford's second production facility and marked a significant step forward in automotive manufacturing. It was at Piquette that Ford and his team, including key engineer C. Harold Wills, developed the Model T, affectionately known as the "Tin Lizzie."

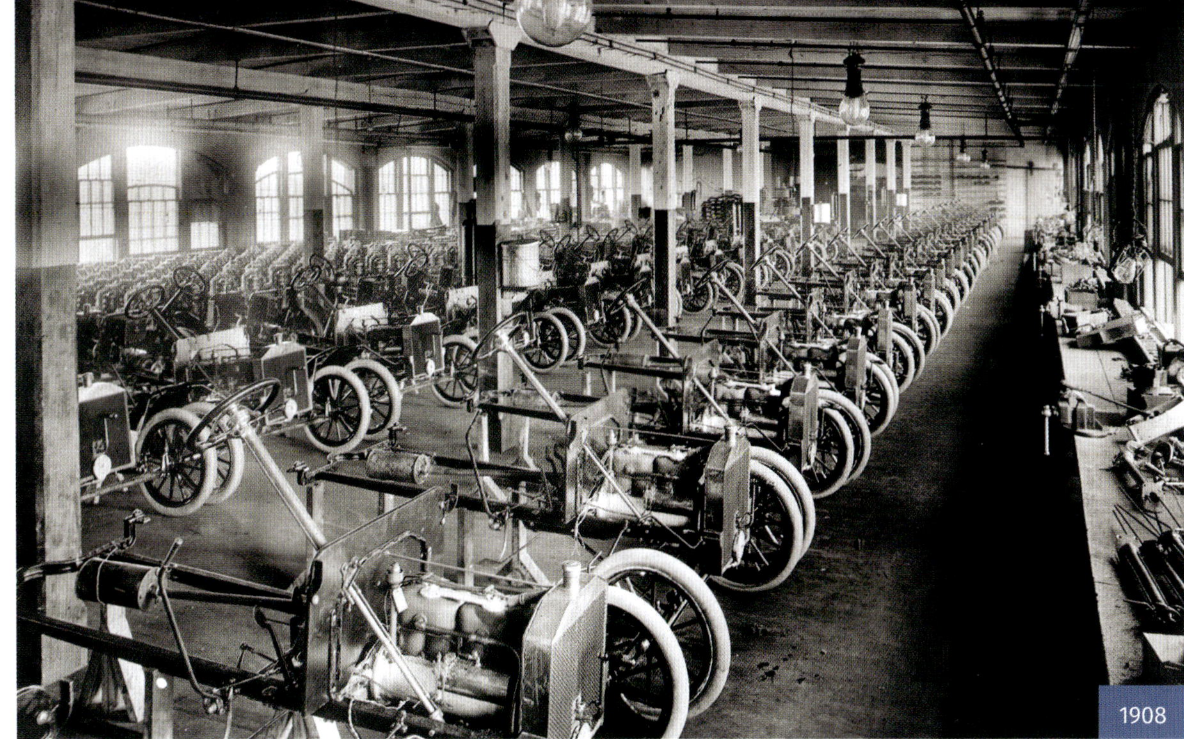

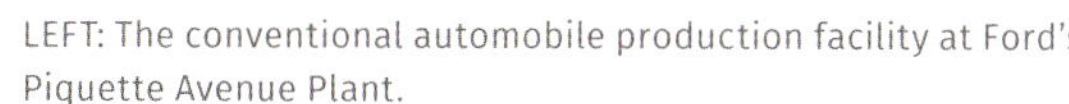
LEFT: The conventional automobile production facility at Ford's Piquette Avenue Plant.

It was inexpensive ($850 at launch and falling to under $300 by the 1920s), sturdy, and easy to drive. It used interchangeable parts and a simple design that allowed mass production at an unprecedented scale. The demand quickly overwhelmed the production capabilities of the Piquette plant, which was still relying on traditional assembly methods with manual labor.

Recognizing the limitations of the Piquette facility, Ford began planning a larger, more modern factory. The result was the Highland Park Ford Plant, opened in 1910 just north of Detroit. Nicknamed the "Crystal Palace," the plant at Highland Park was a model for factories in the twentieth century. The complex consisted of a four-story, 865-foot-long factory, a four-story office, and the power plant topped by five enormous smokestacks. The building was begun in 1909 and, though not fully completed until 1914, was producing cars by 1910.

Automobile production quickly outgrew this facility and was moved to the Ford Rouge factory in the late 1920s, although Ford tractors were produced at Highland Park into the 1970s.

Today, some of the original buildings remain, while the Crystal Palace has been demolished. The facility at Piquette Avenue is now an automotive heritage museum dedicated to the birth of the Model T in what is now a designated US National Historic Landmark.

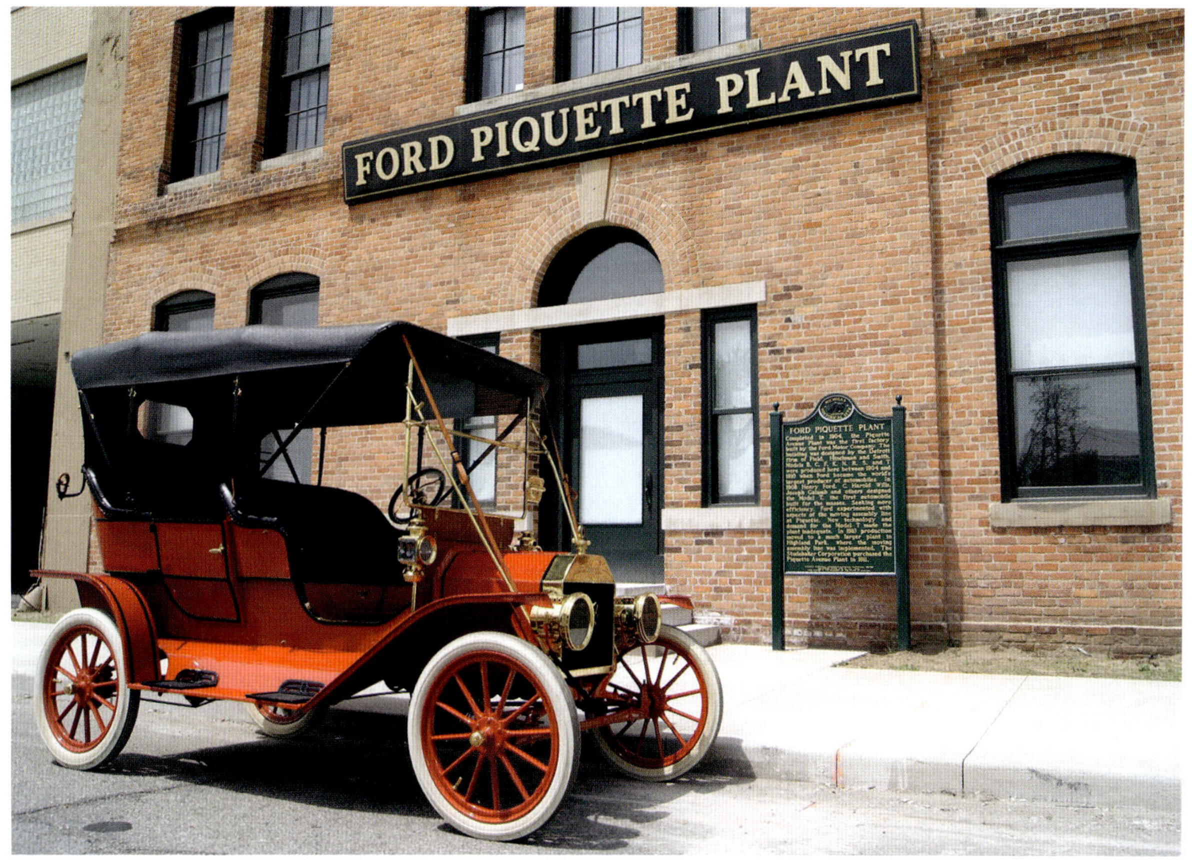

PULLMAN VILLAGE, ILLINOIS

A model industrial village ... until the economy faltered

Railroad magnate George M. Pullman first established the Pullman Palace Car Company in 1867. In need of property for a new factory, Pullman purchased 4,000 acres of land on Chicago's far South Side. Rather than building a factory amid workers in the city, Pullman decided to build a town around his factory. He had been inspired by earlier industrial model towns in Europe, particularly Saltaire in England (founded by Sir Titus Salt), but whereas Salt banned a pub in his industrial village, the Florence Hotel in Pullman served alcohol. Beyond philanthropic motives, Pullman sought to create a controlled environment that would foster productivity and reduce labor unrest.

Designed by prominent Chicago architect Solon Beman—who would go on to design a monument for Pullman's grave—Pullman employees and their families had everything they might need in the town of Pullman There were schools, a library, a theater, church, bank, and post office. All 20,000 of Pullman's workers were required to live in the community. This was an attractive option for Chicago's working-class families, who enjoyed tidy brick row houses with expensive modern conveniences such as gas heating and indoor plumbing. These amenities were provided for reasonable rents and generated an annual six percent profit for Pullman.

Business plummeted during the financial "Panic of 1893," so Pullman laid off thousands of workers and sliced wages twenty-five percent for those who remained. However, he refused to lower rents, resulting in near-starvation conditions. The workers went on strike, and in the spring of 1894 the American Railway Union, led by Eugene V. Debs, voted to support the Pullman strike. After a few episodes of violence, President Grover Cleveland sent in Federal troops to break up the strike. Pullman died in 1897, and the town was sold to its residents in 1907.

The company closed its factory in the Pullman neighborhood of Chicago in 1955. The entire district was declared a National Historic Landmark in 1971, but its isolated position ten miles from downtown Chicago has made a complete renaissance difficult.

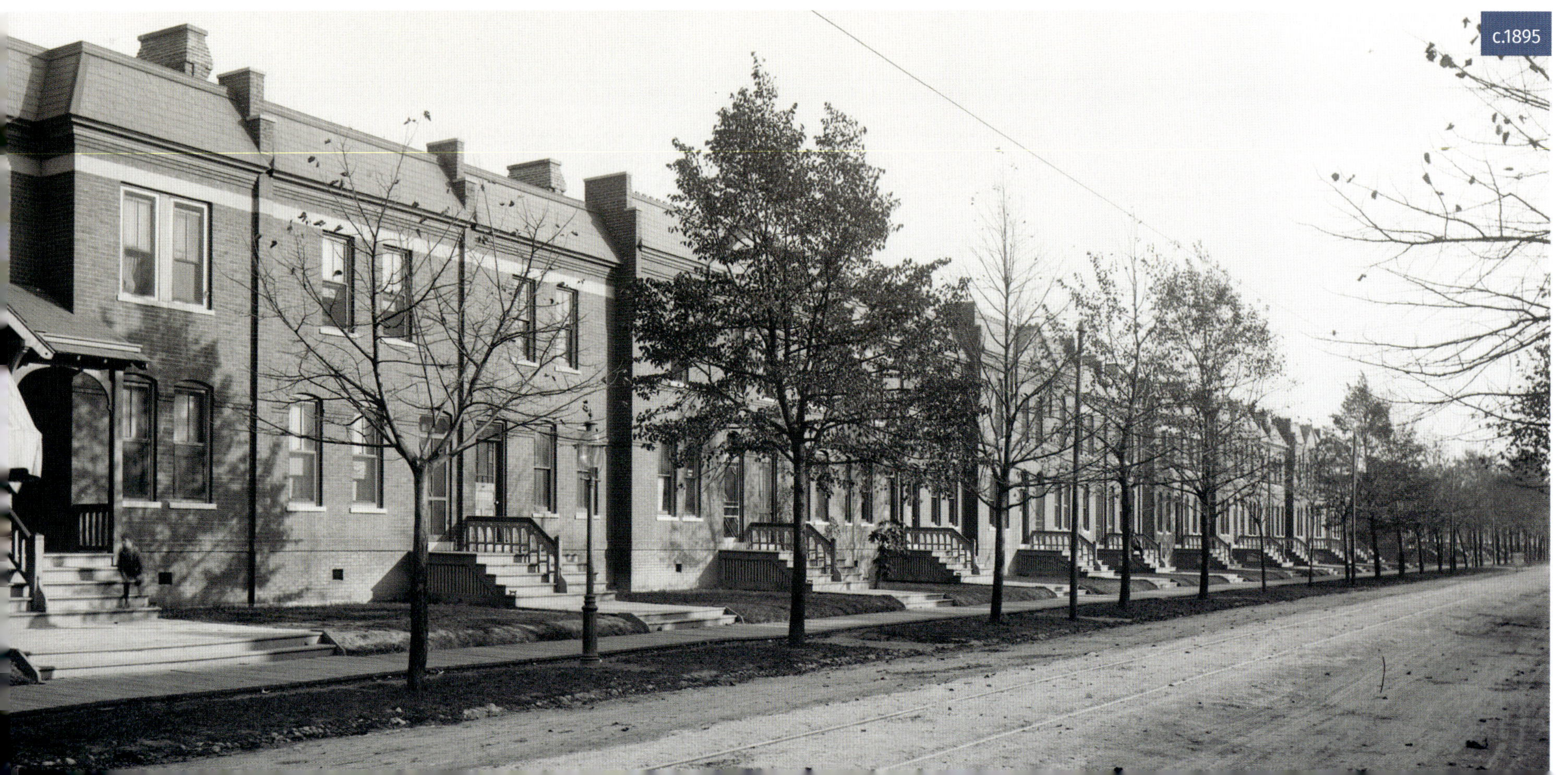

c.1895

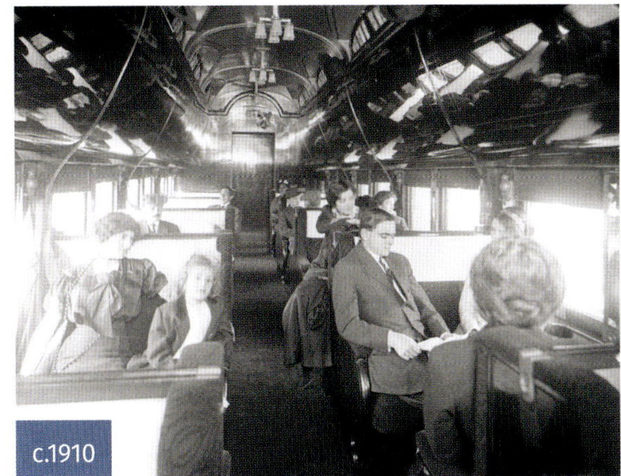

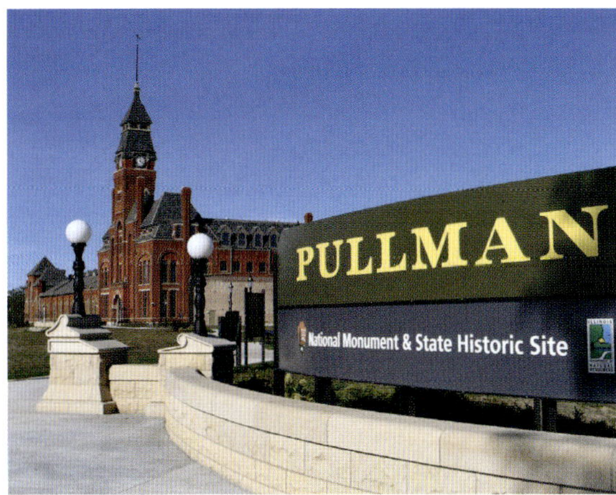

FAR LEFT: A Standard Pullman car on a deluxe Overland Limited train.

LEFT: Today, many of the industrial buildings form part of the Pullman National Monument.

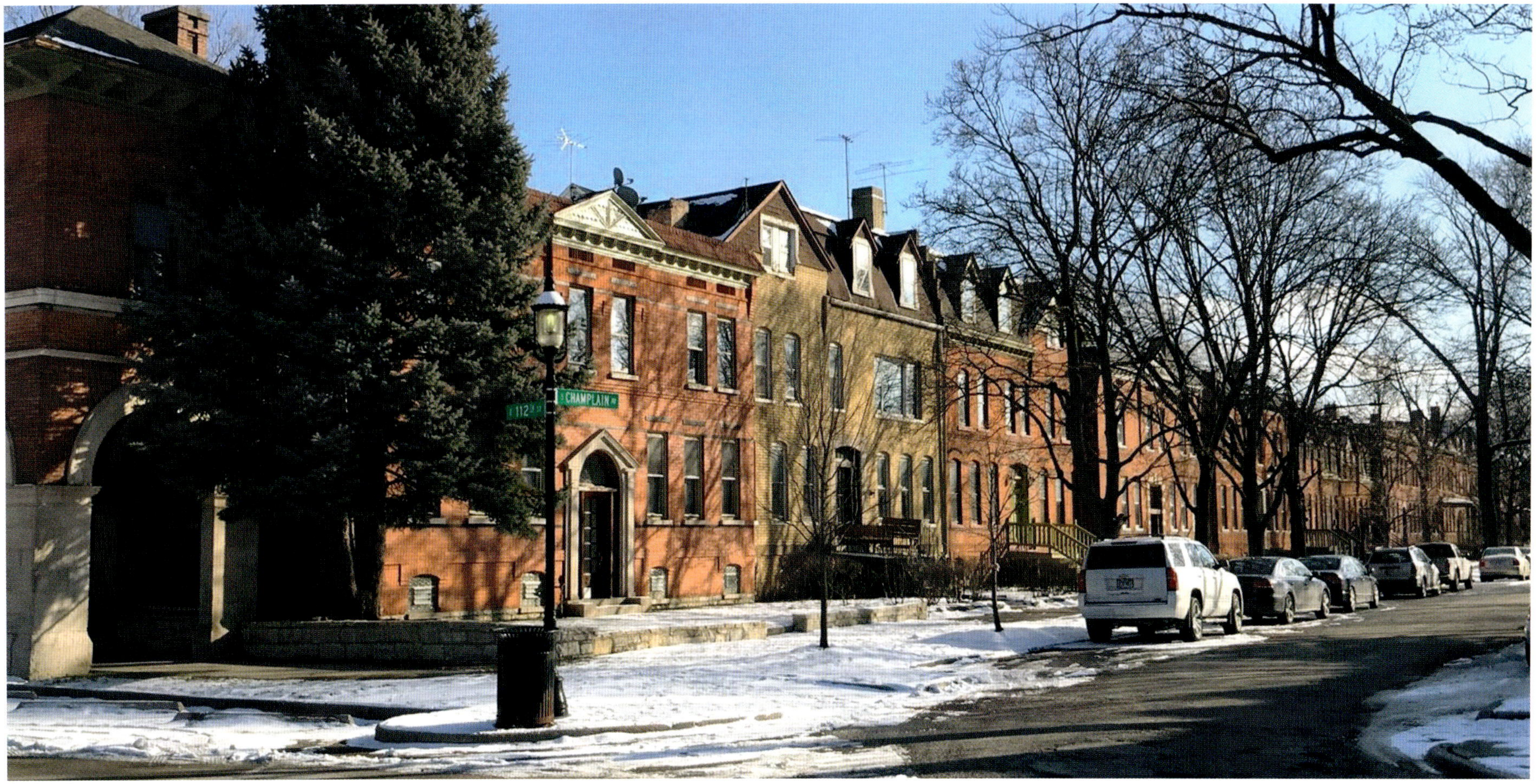

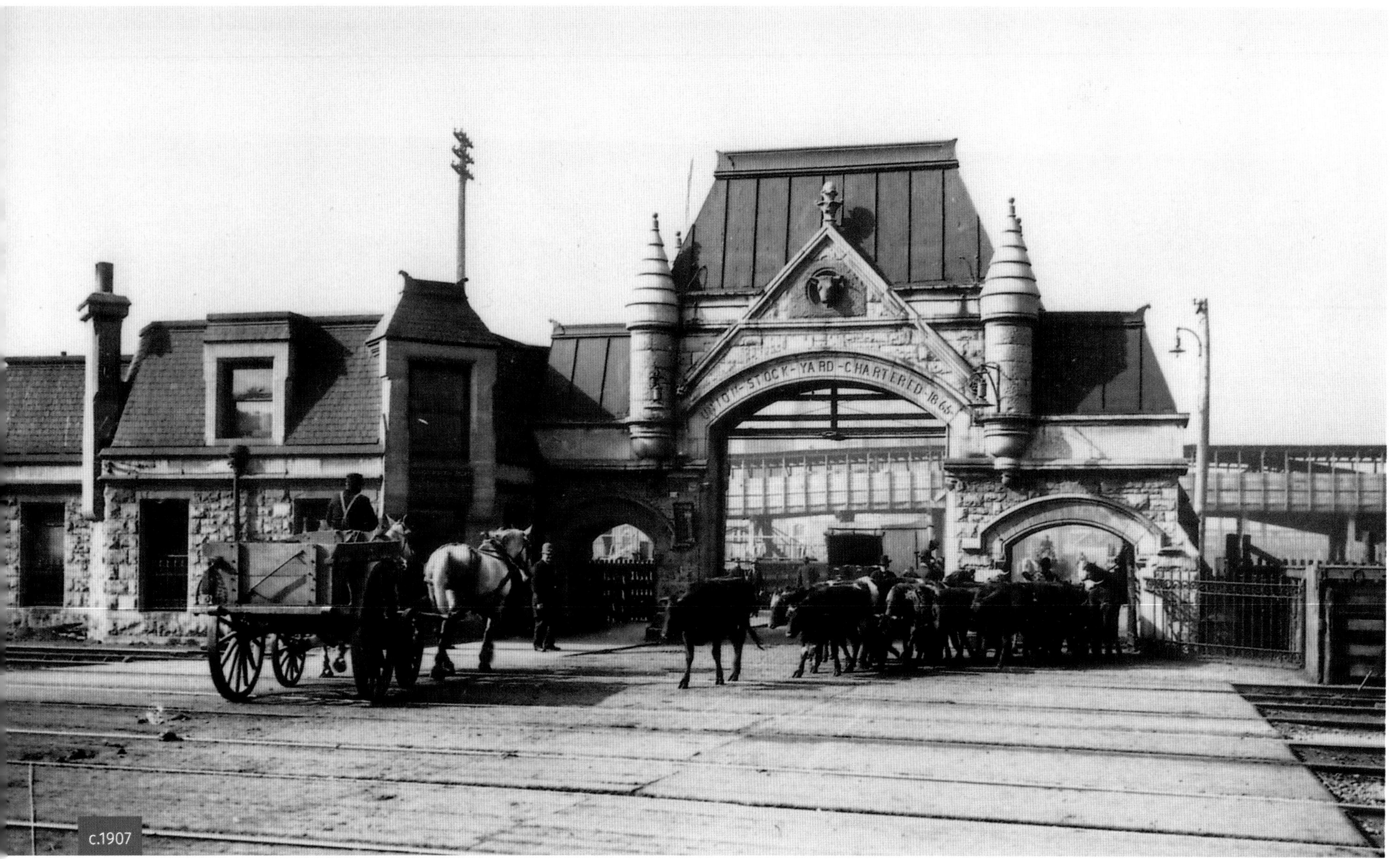

c.1907

UNION STOCK YARDS, CHICAGO

The facility that made Chicago the meatpacking capital of the world

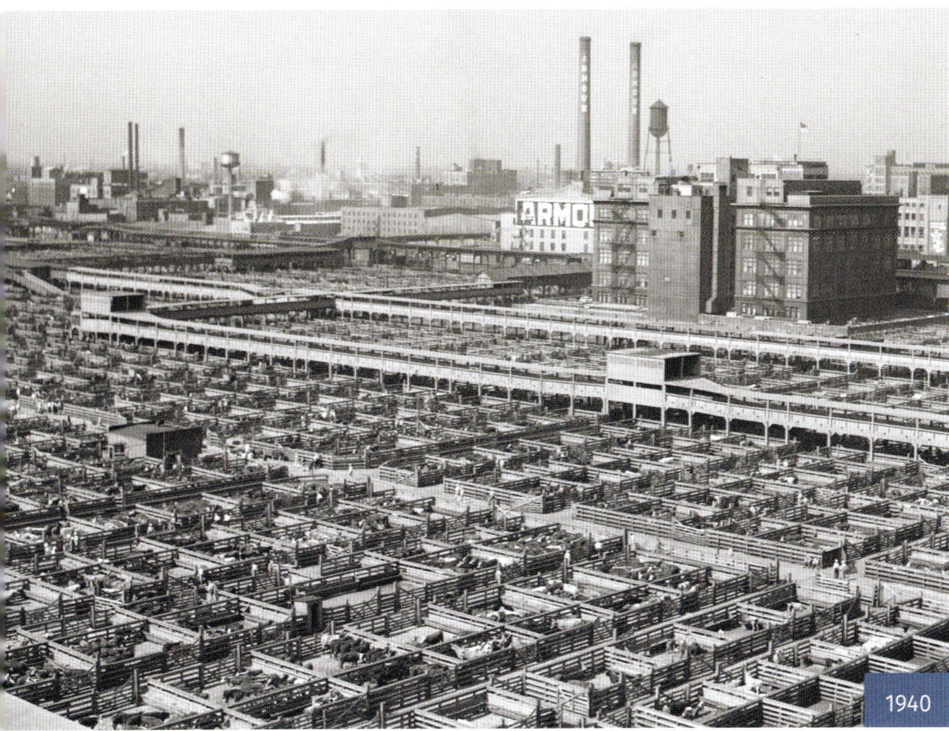

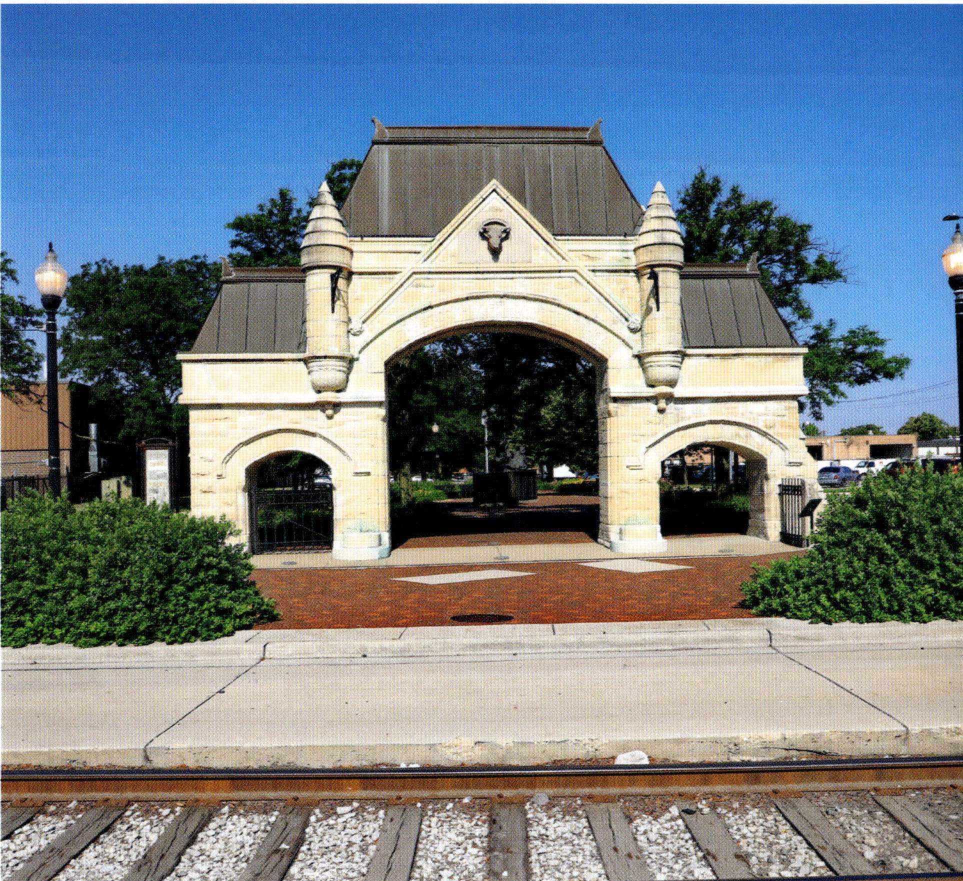

Chicago's Union Stock Yards were established in 1865 on the city's South Side and became a symbol of the city's dominance in the meatpacking industry. Strategically located near rail lines and the Illinois & Michigan Canal, the Stock Yards centralized what had previously been a scattered network of slaughterhouses, drawing animals from across the Midwest and Great Plains.

The city quickly earned the nickname "hog butcher for the world," thanks to its mechanized slaughtering and meatpacking operations. Companies like Armour and Swift pioneered innovations in refrigerated railcars, assembly-line processing, and meat preservation.

Located at 850 West Exchange Avenue at Peoria and designed by preeminent city architects Burnham and Root in 1879, the front gate gave a majestic face to the sprawling Union Stock Yards. The facility covered more than 475 acres. Tourist guidebooks of the nineteenth century marveled at the scale and efficiency of the operation. Almost a city in itself, the yards included pen space for up to 25,000 cattle, 80,000 hogs, and 25,000 sheep.

The yards not only transformed the meat industry but also reshaped labor, immigration, and urbanization patterns. Thousands of immigrants, particularly from Eastern and Southern Europe, found work in its dangerous and grueling conditions, as famously depicted in Upton Sinclair's novel *The Jungle*. The sensational publication of the book in 1906 led to reforms in sanitation and labor conditions for the yards. Gradually the business of meatpacking moved closer to where the animals were farmed, and the yards declined.

After providing employment for the Bridgeport and Back of the Yards communities for over a century, the Union Stock Yards closed in 1971. The gate was designated a Chicago Landmark in 1972. The "bust" over the central limestone arch is thought to be that of "Sherman," a prize-winning steer named after the yards' cofounder, John B. Sherman. Today, industrial parks have filled in some of the vacant space where slaughterhouses once stood.

ABOVE: Despite the rise of other meatpacking centers, the Stock Yards were still going strong in the 1940s, even before World War II intervened.

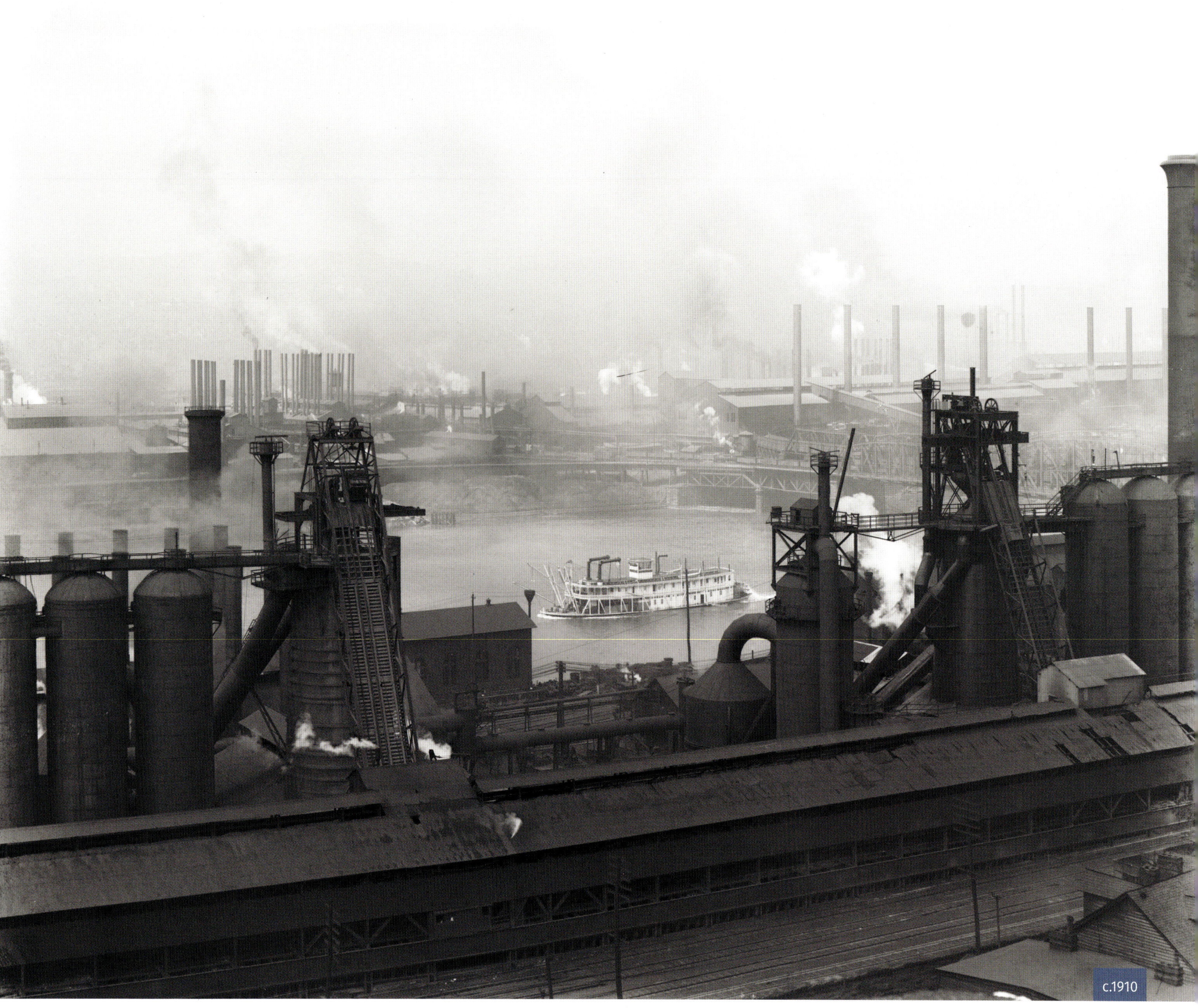
c.1910

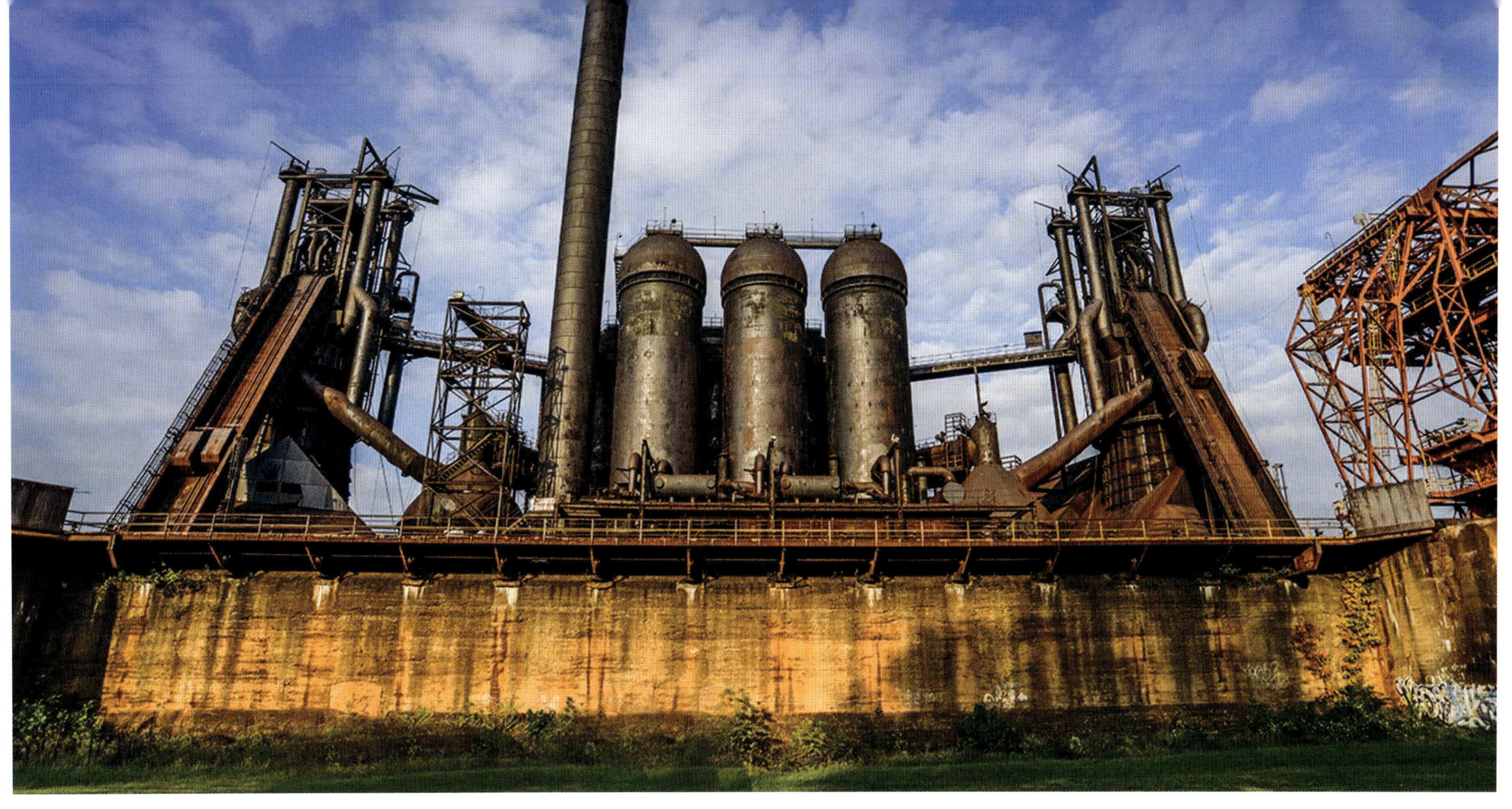

JONES & LAUGHLIN STEEL WORKS, PITTSBURGH

The heavily polluting industry has gone, but some of the silent dinosaurs remain

Pittsburgh, Pennsylvania, was the nation's iron and steel foundry from the late eighteenth and early nineteenth centuries. The city's location at the confluence of the Allegheny, Monongahela, and Ohio rivers, along with nearby coal and iron ore deposits, made it an ideal location for heavy industry.

Scottish immigrant Andrew Carnegie, who became one of the wealthiest industrialists, opened the Edgar Thomson Works in Braddock in 1875. It was the first American plant to successfully use the Bessemer process for mass-producing steel. Named after a Pennsylvania Railroad executive, the Thomson plant was the centerpiece of Carnegie Steel and still operates today under US Steel.

Other major facilities included the Jones & Laughlin steel mills, and the Homestead Steel Works, built in the 1880s just outside Pittsburgh along the Monongahela River. Homestead quickly became one of the most productive steel mills in the world, employing thousands of workers and churning out rails, structural steel, and armor plate.

Despite its industrial achievements, Homestead was the site of one of the most infamous labor conflicts in US history—the Homestead Strike. In 1892, after management, led by Henry Clay Frick, sought to break the power of the skilled union workers, the Amalgamated Association of Iron and Steel Workers was locked out. When Frick brought in Pinkerton agents to protect strikebreakers, violence erupted. A deadly battle ensued, resulting in deaths on both sides and eventually intervention by the Pennsylvania National Guard. The strike ended in defeat for the workers and marked a turning point in American labor history.

At its height during World War II, Pittsburgh produced more steel than any other city in the world, supplying the US military and building materials for infrastructure across the country. By the 1970s and 1980s, global competition and technological changes led to the collapse of Pittsburgh's steel industry. Mills shuttered, jobs disappeared, and the city entered a deep economic downturn. Homestead Works closed in 1986, and much of the former industrial land was repurposed for retail or left abandoned.

Yet the legacy of steel lives on in Pittsburgh's identity. Former mill towns still bear the cultural imprint of their industrial past, and some sites, like the Rivers of Steel National Heritage Area, preserve the memory of the steel era.

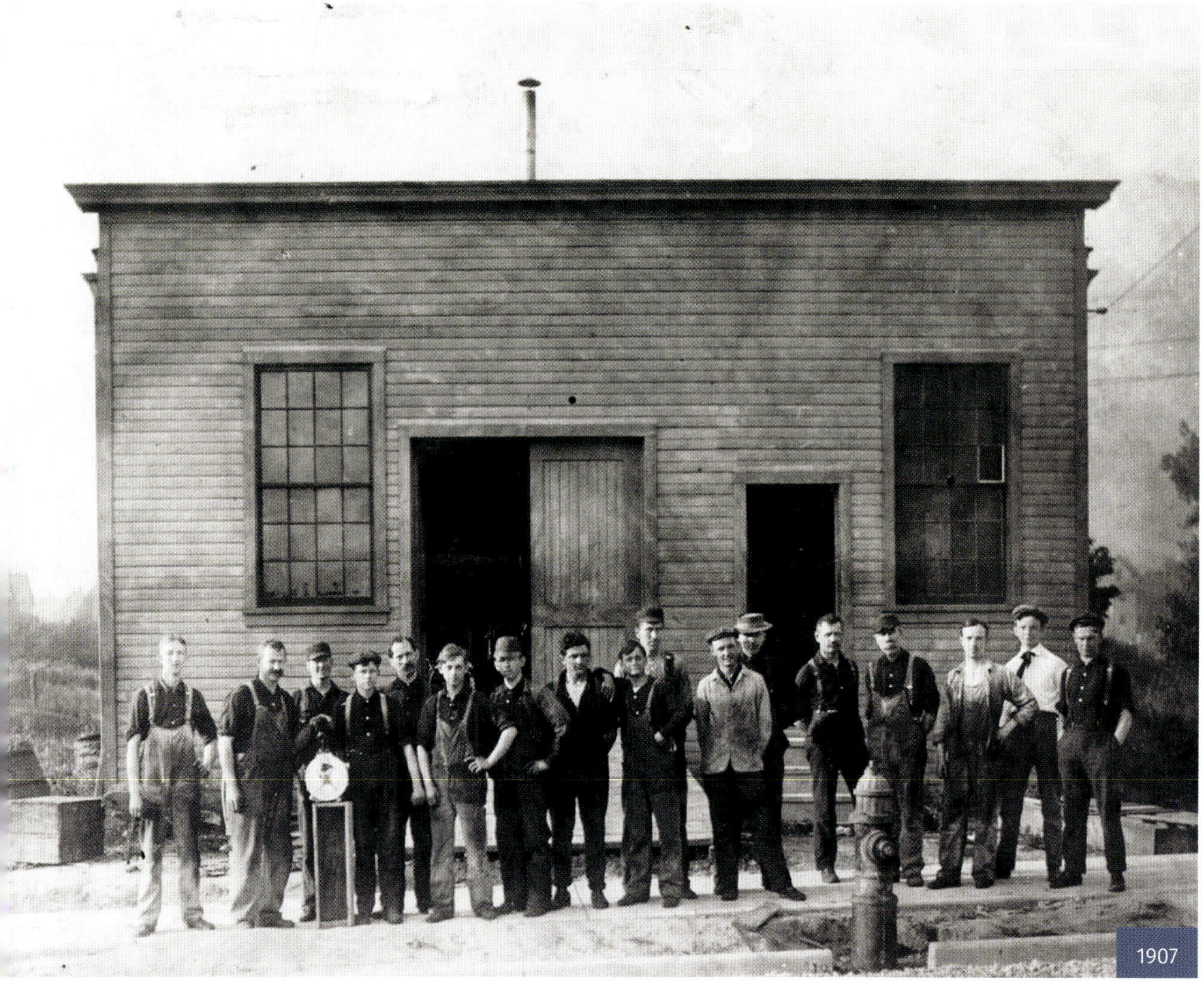

HARLEY-DAVIDSON, MILWAUKEE

Success on the race track helped build spectacular growth for the brand

William Harley met Arthur Davidson when they were both working for a metal fabrication company in Milwaukee. William was a draftsman and Arthur was a pattern maker, and in 1901 they set about making a motorcycle after their plans to build an outboard motor for fishing trips fell through. From a humble, ten-by-fifteen shed emerged what would become the world's most charismatic motorcycle marque. With the help of Arthur's two brothers, William and Walter, three machines were produced in 1903 and again in 1904, until in 1906 they bought their first factory on Chestnut Street, later renamed Juneau Avenue. Our vintage photo shows the four founders of Harley-Davidson Motor Company—William A. Harley, and Walter, Arthur, and William Davidson—posing with their entire staff in front of the Harley-Davidson factory building in 1907.

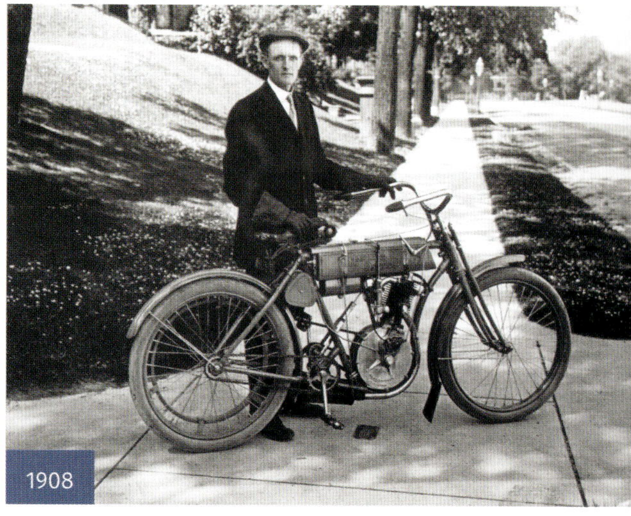

That same year, Harley-Davidson had expanded operations and began selling motorcycles to police departments—a relationship that would prove long lasting. Sales tripled between 1910 and 1912 and the factory on Juneau Avenue was constantly being enlarged, as the *Harley-Davidson Dealer* noted in January 1913: "As soon as one building was finished another was started. While the contractors were finishing the upper floors the lower floors were being used for manufacturing."

Both World Wars supercharged production of the machines, making it at one time the world's largest motorcycle manufacturer, but the brand has survived recurring challenges over the years, each of its own specific nature—the Great Depression, the postwar 1950s image of the bike as portrayed in the 1953 film *The Wild One*, competition from Japan, and a disastrous merger with AMF that led to quality-control issues and declining brand loyalty. Through all, the power of the brand has endured.

ABOVE: Walter Davidson with one of the race-winning machines that helped boost sales of the fledgling company.

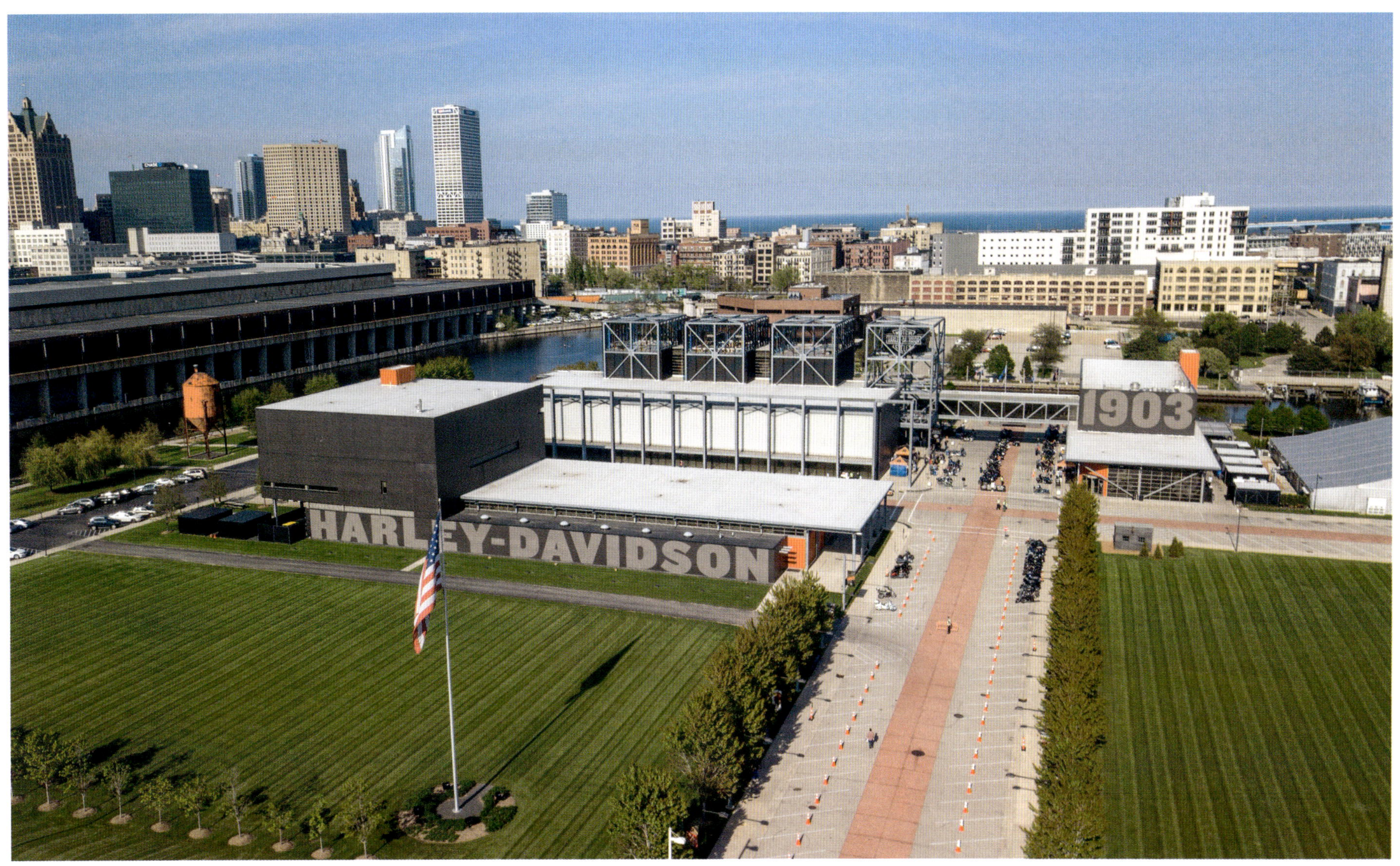

Motorcycle production at Juneau Avenue ceased in 1973. The assembly of machines and the production of engines and transmissions has been spread farther afield throughout the United States, while the former factory is now used as the company's corporate headquarters. It also houses the Harley-Davidson Museum, Harley-Davidson University, a conference center, archives, employee amenities, and other support functions.

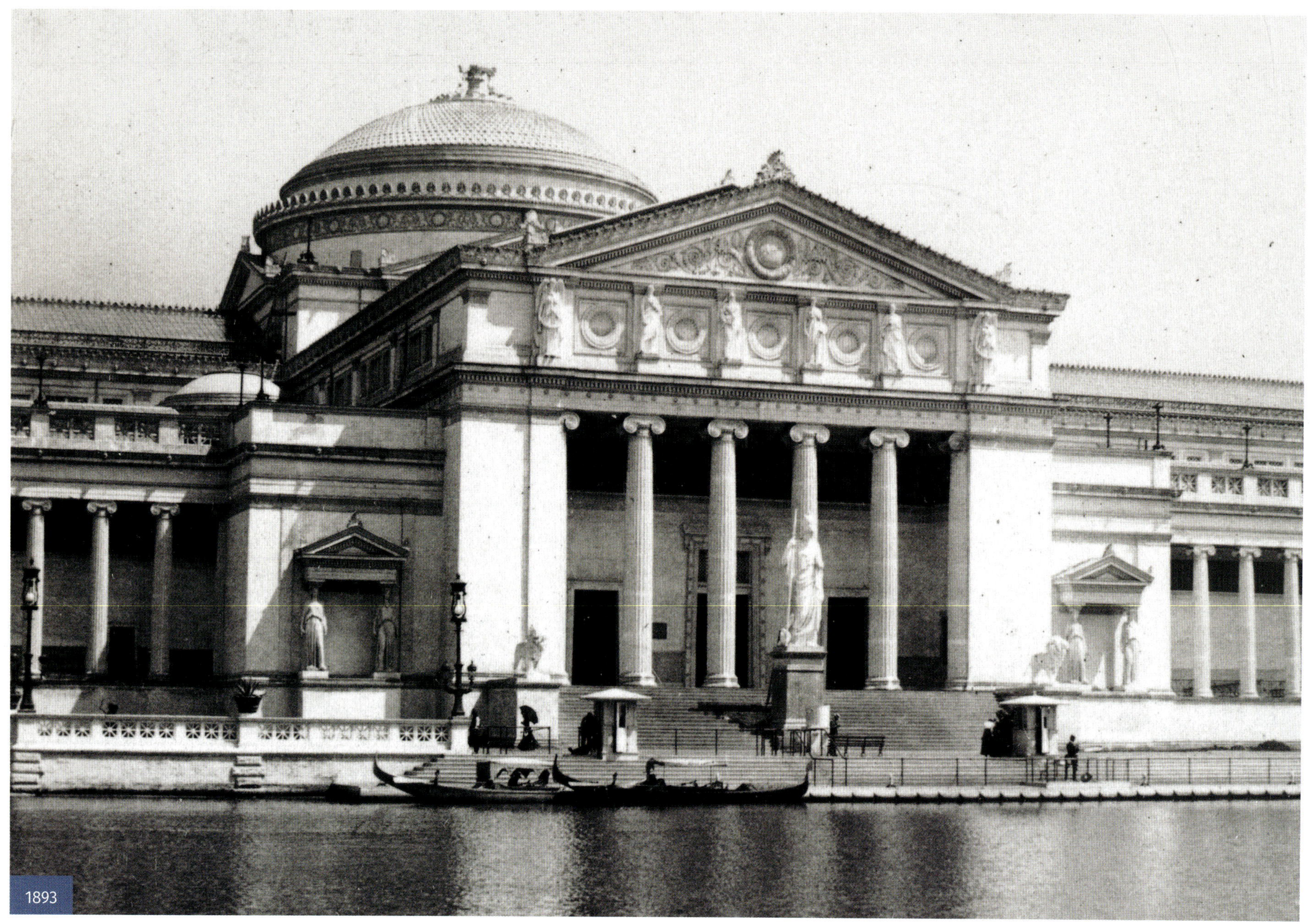

1893

COLUMBIAN EXPOSITION, CHICAGO

The epic exposition in Jackson Park captivated the nation

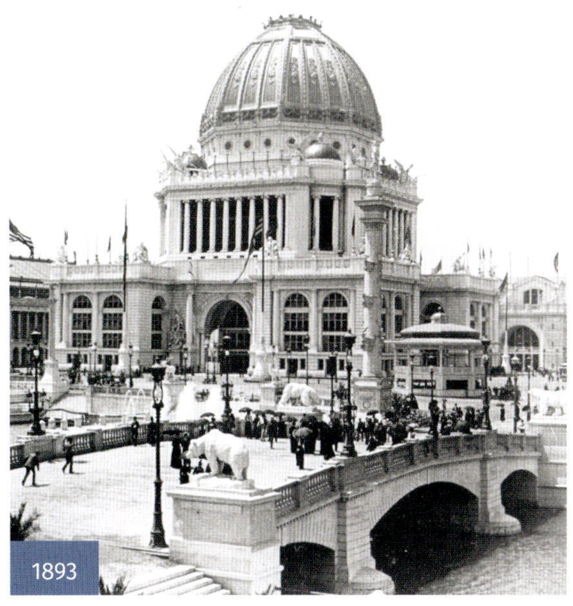

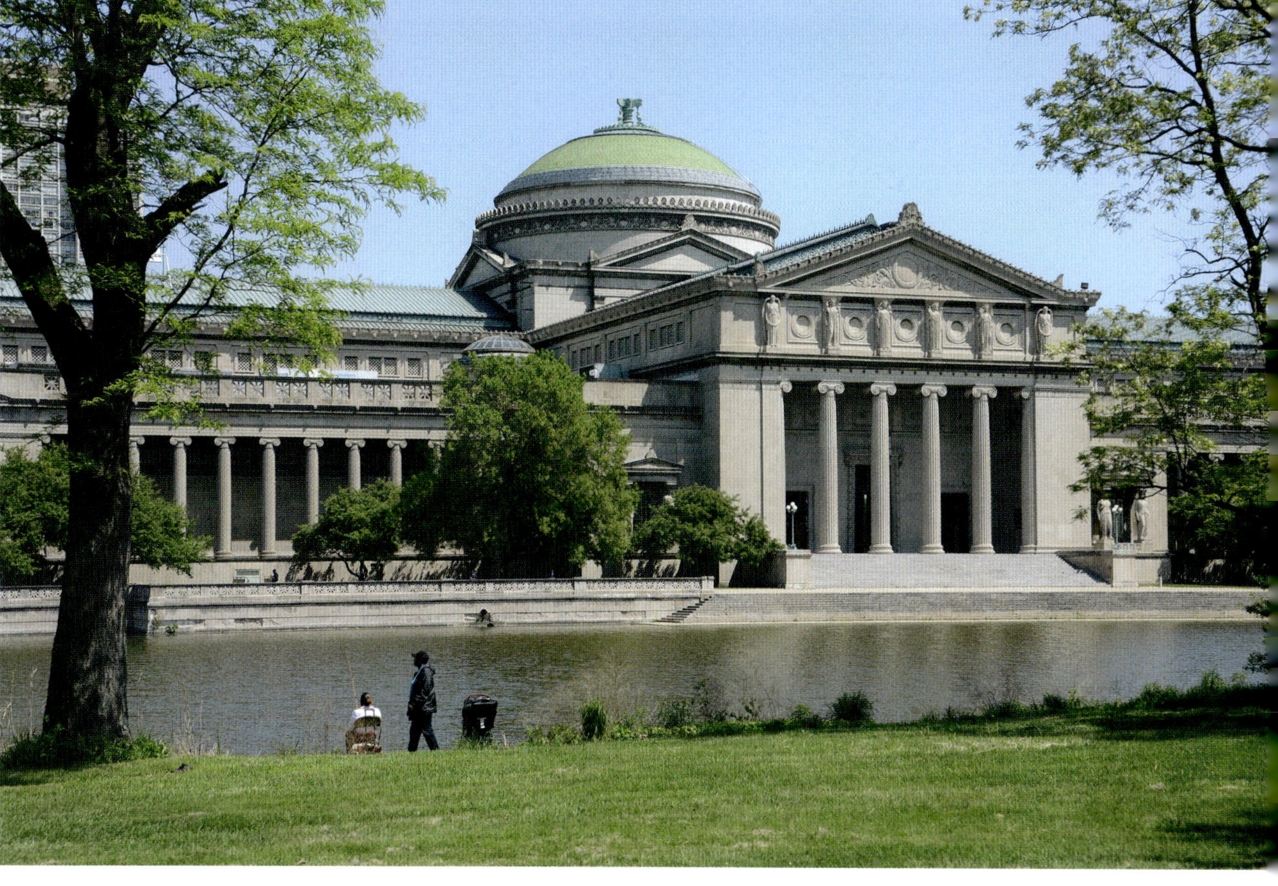

World's fairs showcased industrial and cultural progress from around the world—but in particular that of the host nation. One of the greatest, the 1893 Columbian Exposition, celebrated 400 years of the Americas after Christopher Columbus's discovery voyage in 1492. It was both a celebration of progress and a bold statement of American innovation and ambition at the close of the nineteenth century.

Chicago was selected as the host, marking a symbolic emergence of the Midwest and a statement about the city's recovery after the ruinous 1871 fire. Over 200 buildings went up on reclaimed land at the edge of the lakefront's Jackson Park. Nearly all were designed in a neoclassical style—and made of a mixture of hemp and white plaster—earning it the nickname "The White City." This architectural unity was orchestrated by Daniel Burnham, the fair's chief architect, and Frederick Law Olmsted, who designed the grounds and landscapes.

It introduced millions of visitors to groundbreaking innovations such as the Ferris Wheel—engineer George Ferris's American answer to the Eiffel Tower—and widespread electric lighting powered by Nikola Tesla's alternating current, installed by Westinghouse. The fair become a launchpad for new consumer products and the Midway Plaisance, a mile-long strip of entertainment and ethnographic displays, featured everything from belly dancers to reenactments of African villages.

The exposition drew a record-breaking 27 million visitors during its six-month run—more than a third of the US population at the time. After the fair's conclusion a fire destroyed most of the remaining buildings, but the former Palace of Fine Arts Building survived. The imposing building was reconstructed—albeit in the late 1920s—with Bedford limestone and became the first home of the Field Museum.

In 1928 the name officially changed to the Museum of Science and Industry. Opening in 1933, it was ready for the second great Chicago World's Fair, the Century of Progress, celebrating the city's centennial. Today one of the star exhibits is the U-Boat *U-505*, the German submarine captured on the high seas during the war by Captain (later Admiral) Daniel Gallery, a Chicago native.

1893

ABOVE LEFT: The grand Administration Building of 1893.

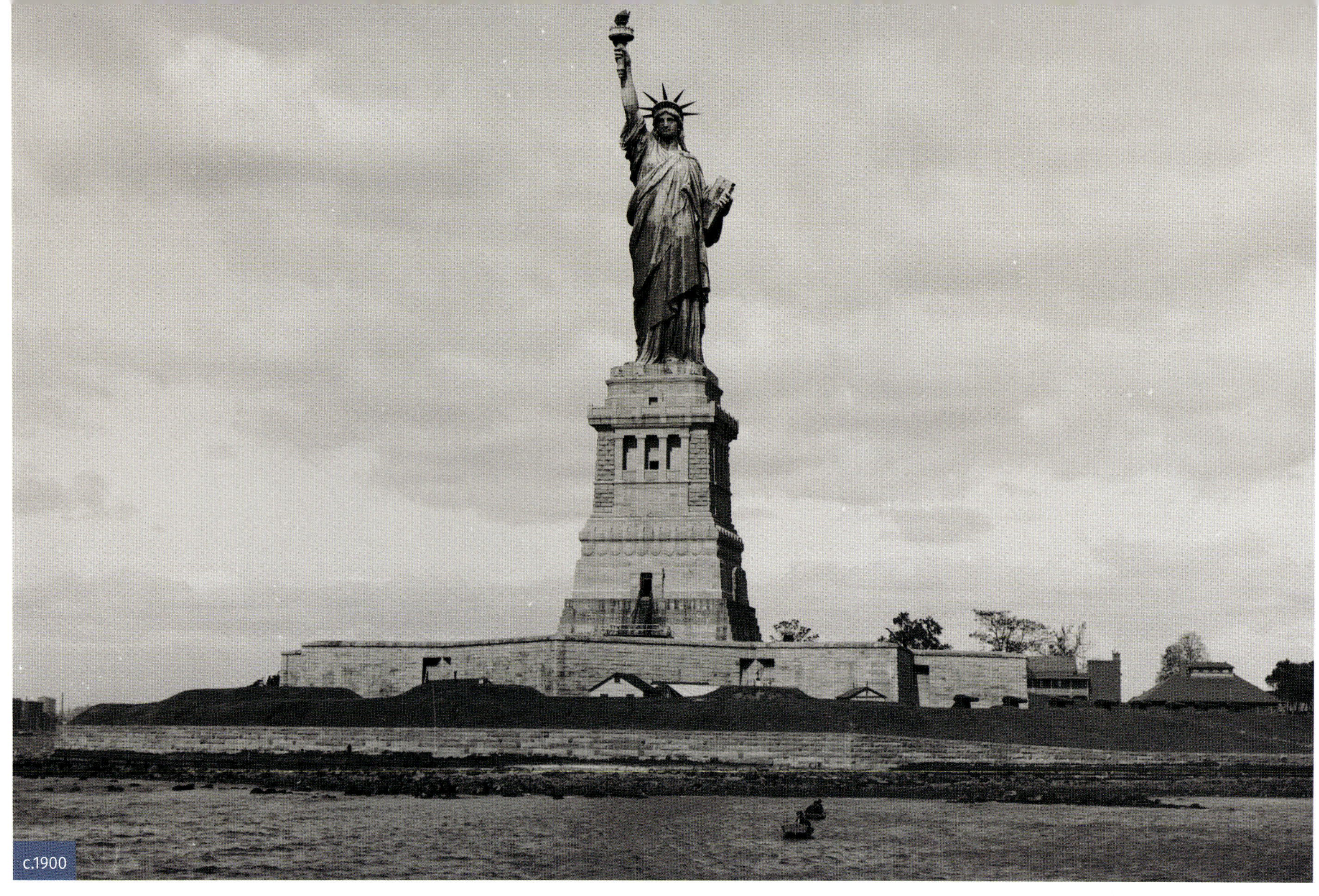
c.1900

STATUE OF LIBERTY, NEW YORK

An American icon, created and gifted by France

The United States' industrial progress relied on a steady stream of labor from the Old World. The colossal figure of the Statue of Liberty became a stirring symbol of welcome to millions of immigrants arriving on steamships to New York in the late nineteenth century. Titled *Liberty Enlightening the World*, the Statue of Liberty had been proposed in France in 1865 during the reign of Napoleon III's repressive monarchy. The man behind the idea, Édouard de Laboulaye, a fervent abolitionist, wanted to celebrate both democratic freedom and the Union victory in the Civil War. The broken shackle and chain at the statue's feet symbolized the emancipation of slaves. Sculptor Frédéric Auguste Bartholdi designed the statue and Alexandre Gustave Eiffel, creator of the Eiffel Tower in 1889, engineered its steel skeleton. In 1903, a plaque was installed inside the pedestal, bearing the now famous lines by Emma Lazarus: "Give me your tired, your poor, your huddled masses yearning to breathe free." In 1916, German saboteurs exploded a cache of dynamite on a nearby wharf, popping some bolts in the statue's arm.

The statue got a total makeover for its centennial on July 4, 1986. French artisans came to New York to work on the statue, as their countrymen had done

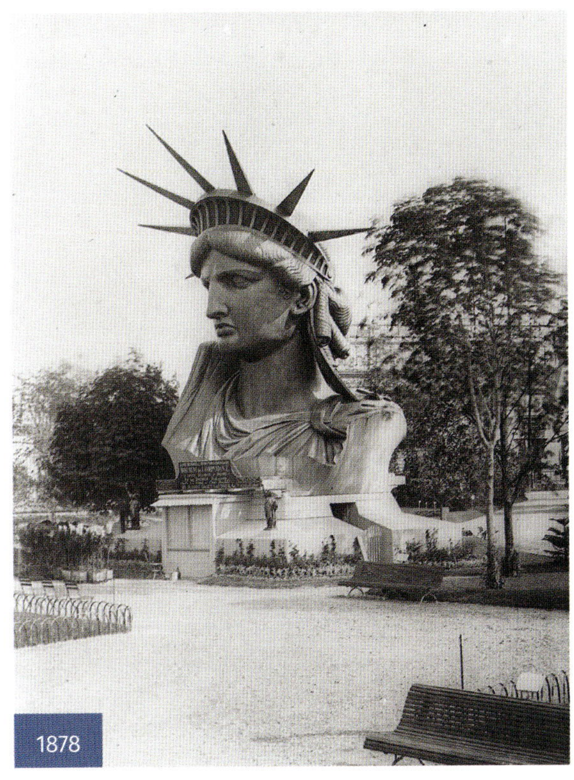

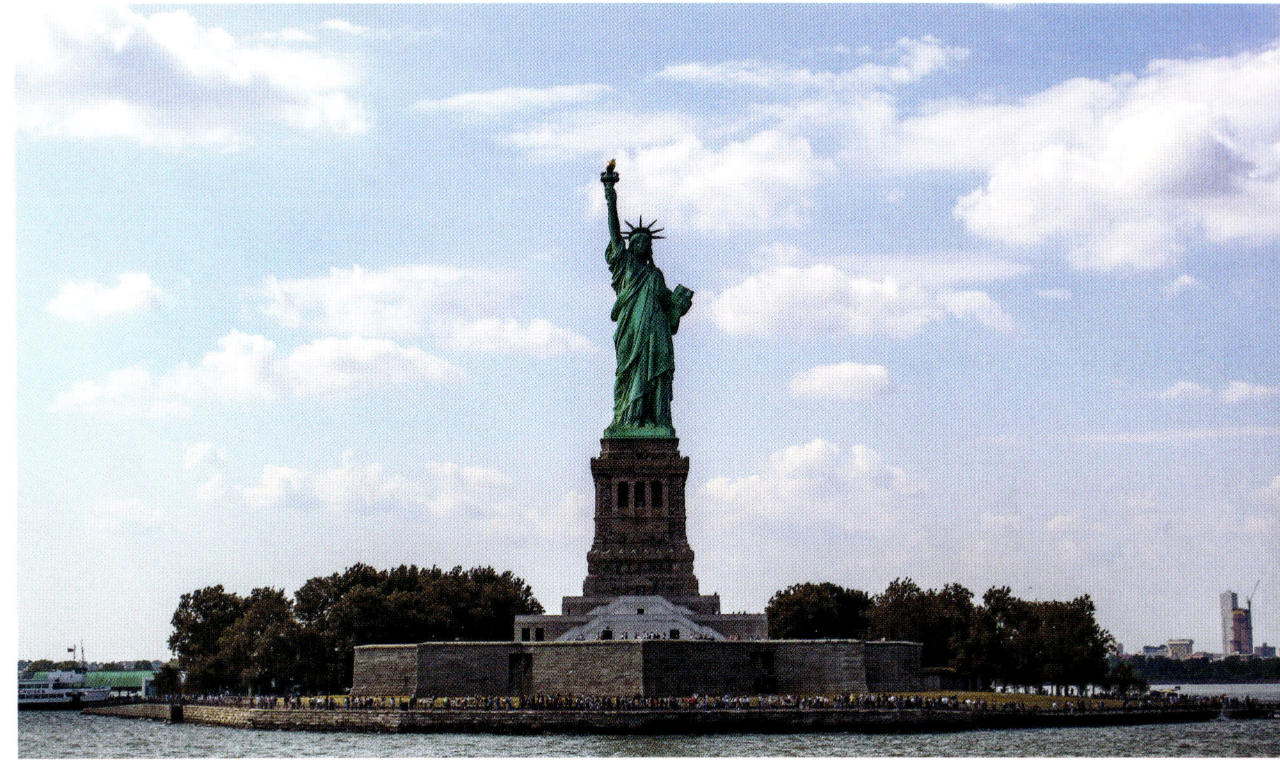

a century before. Although it commemorates the French–American alliance first forged during the Revolutionary War, the statue is clearly an American icon, and the French connection is only a subtext today. Closed after the World Trade Center attacks on September 11, 2001, the Statue of Liberty did not reopen until August 2004. The monumental pedestal, as tall as the statue, has a glass ceiling that affords views into the figure. Visitors who can climb up the 354 steps inside the statue are able to see amazing views from inside her spiked crown.

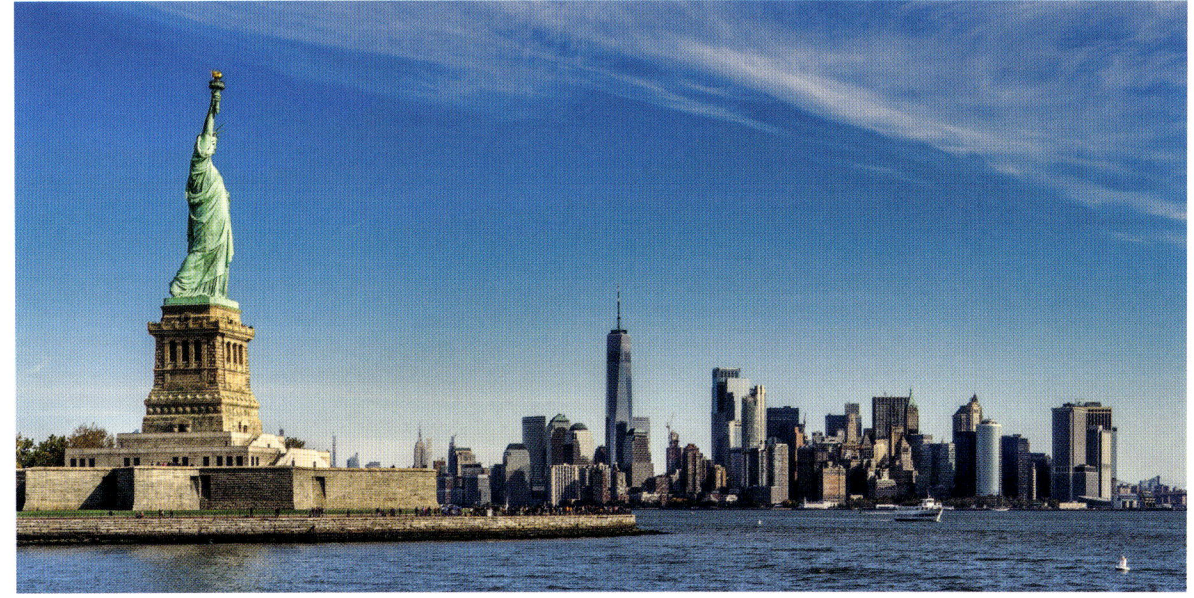

ABOVE: The head of *Liberty Enlightening the World* on display at the Champ-de-Mars, Exposition Universelle, Paris.

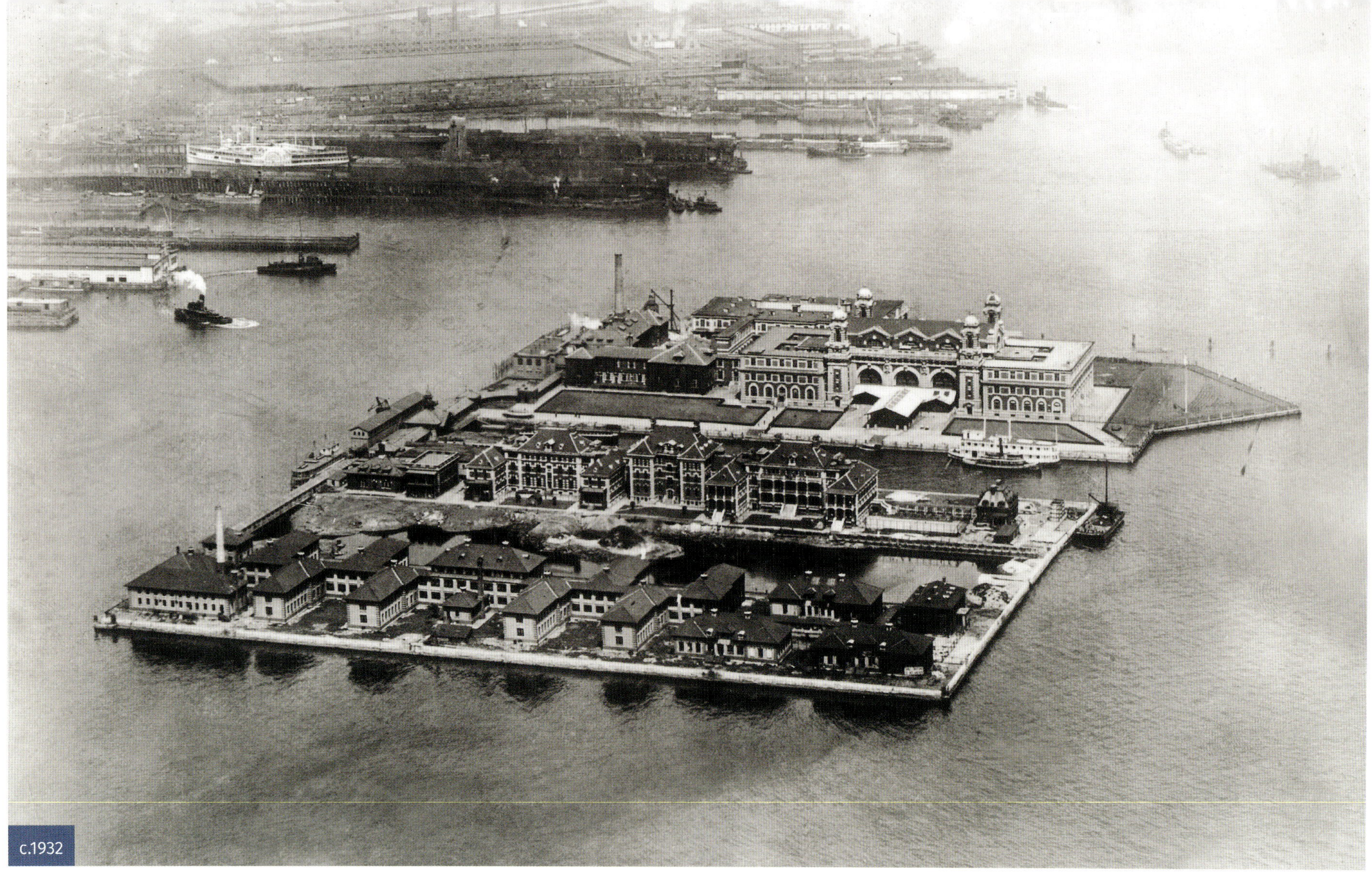

c.1932

ELLIS ISLAND, NEW YORK

The first step of immigrants arriving from the Old World

By the time of this 1930s-era photo, the Ellis Island immigration center was long past its peak. From 1892 to 1924, twelve million people were processed through these buildings. Henry James visited the center at the height of its operation in 1907, the single year in which more than a million people had entered. As he described in *The American Scene*, the arrivals had to undergo a long and tedious process of officially entering the United States: "They stand appealing and waiting, marshaled, herded, divided, subdivided, sorted, sifted, searched, fumigated."

The immigration center, which moved from Castle Clinton to Ellis Island in 1892, at first occupied a series of wooden buildings. The entry process became a bit more humane when those were replaced by the Great Hall in 1900 and supporting facilities by 1906. The island itself was ultimately enlarged through landfill from three to twenty-seven acres. But strict quotas established in 1921 and 1924 severely limited the number of people who could enter the country. From 1925 to the facility's closing in 1954, only 2.3 million immigrants passed through Ellis Island—still more than half of all those entering the United States.

After the immigration center closed, the buildings fell into ruins. Since Congress did not appropriate restoration funds, the deterioration continued even after the island was declared a national monument in 1965. The Ellis Island Foundation, established in 1982, raised millions in corporate and private dollars and reopened the Great Hall as a museum in 1990. Many of the other buildings in the complex still await restoration.

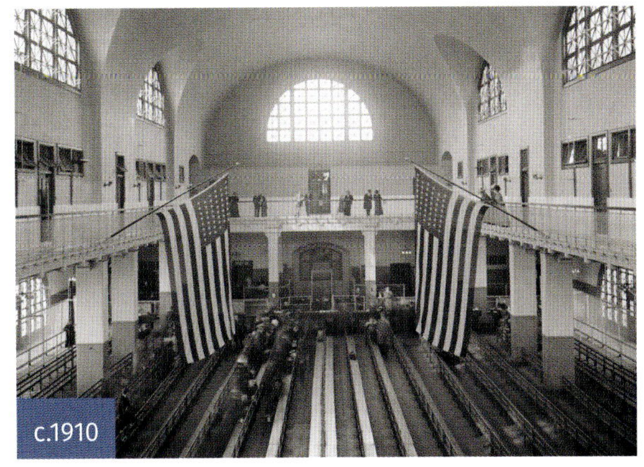

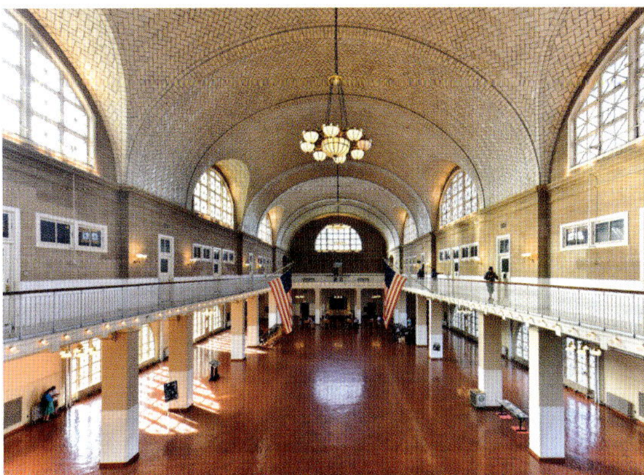

Today, more than forty percent of American citizens can trace their ancestors to arrivals at Ellis Island. Since 1990, more than thirty million have visited the island to trace their heritage. Extensive damage caused by Hurricane Sandy shut down the island from 2012 to 2015.

FAR LEFT: The Great Hall, or Register Room, was often filled to capacity. Prior to the long benches, the hall was divided up into small pens.

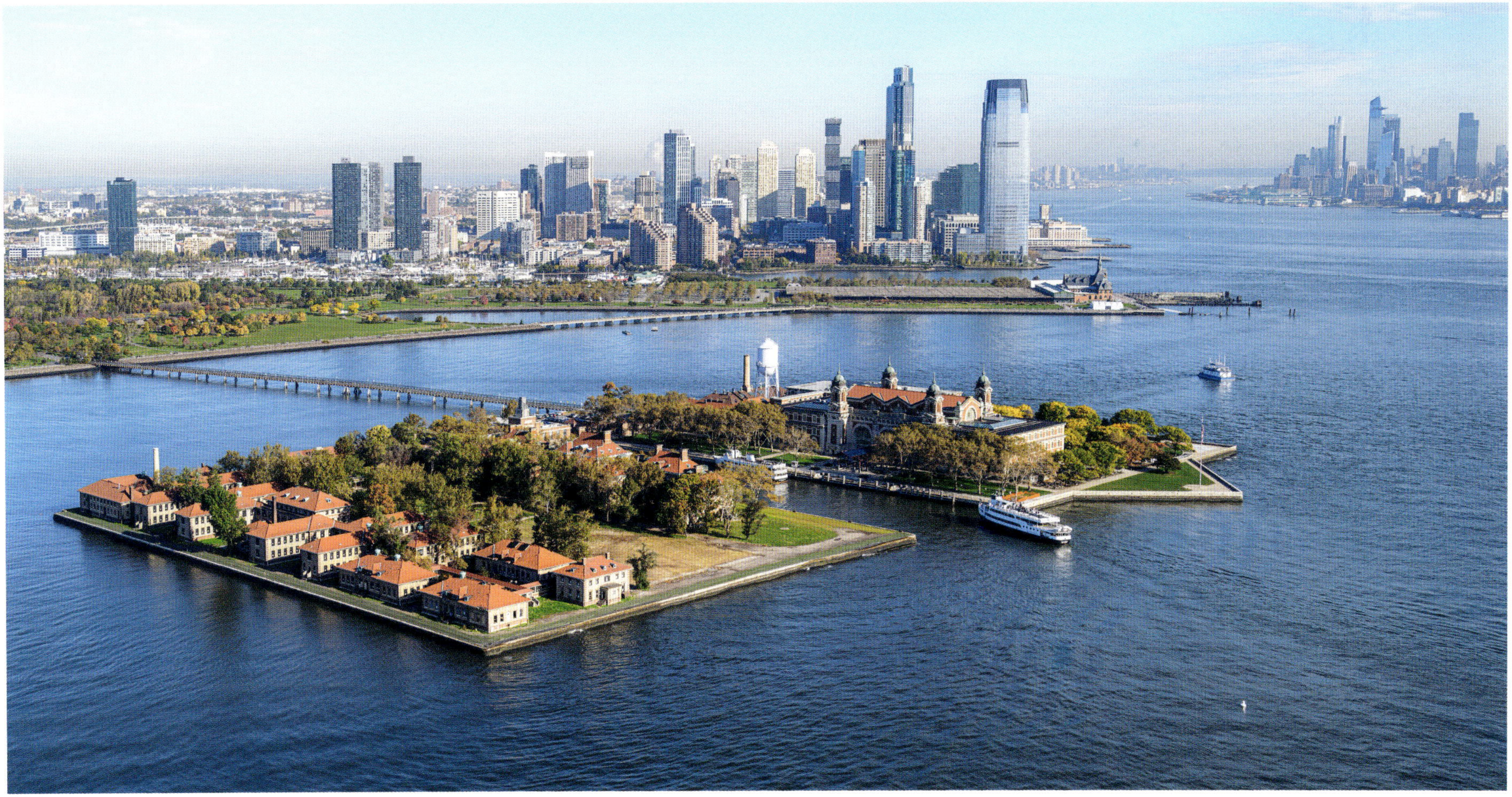

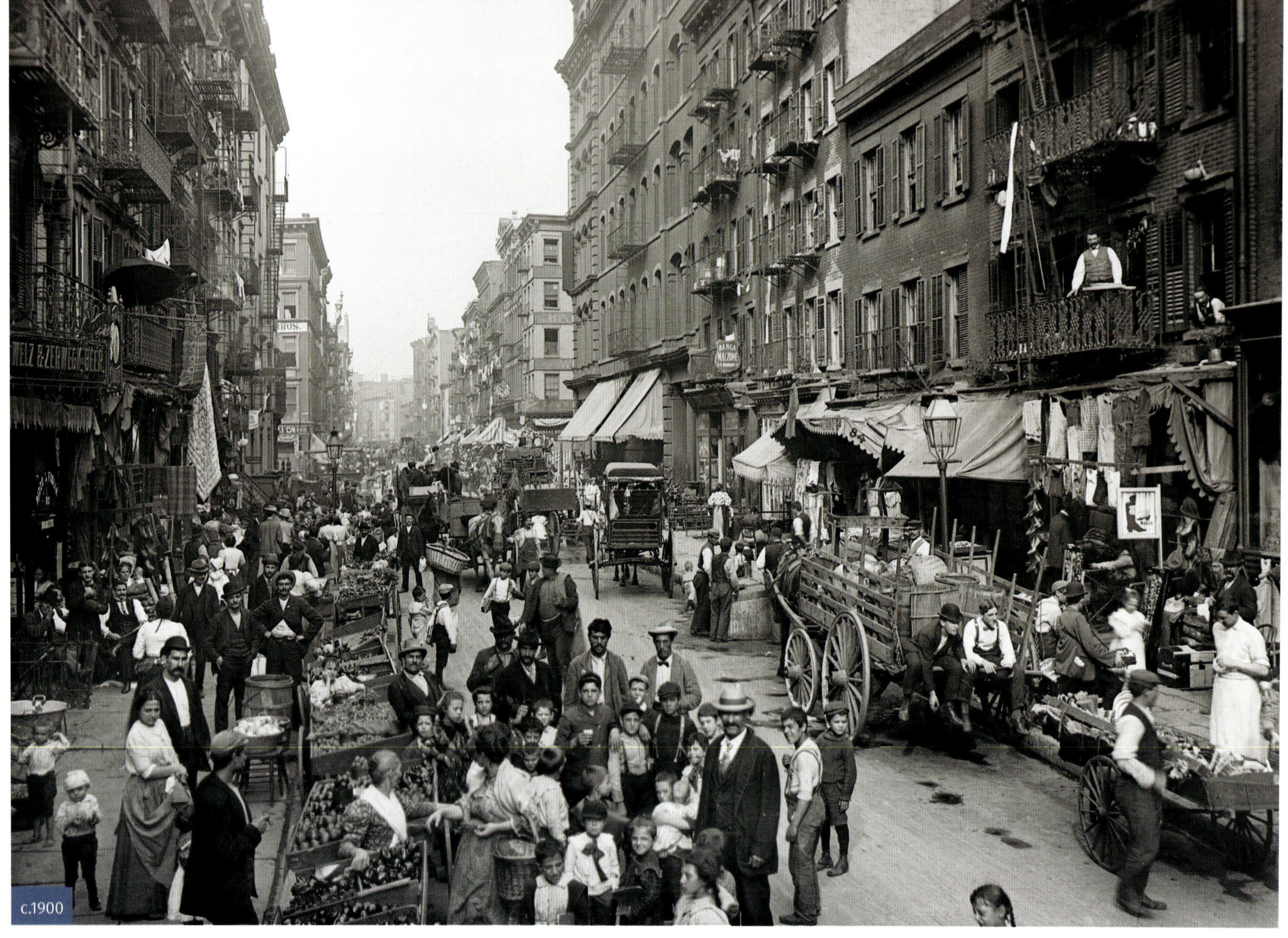
c.1900

MULBERRY STREET, LITTLE ITALY, MANHATTAN

Half a million Italians had made New York home by 1910

Mulberry Street was the heart of Little Italy, the Italian American enclave that rapidly expanded on Manhattan's Lower East Side in the wake of huge waves of immigration from 1899 to 1910. Fewer than 20,000 Italians lived in the city in 1880. By 1910, there were over half a million, more than in any other American city. Like other immigrant groups, they lived in desperately overcrowded tenements, relieved somewhat by daily outdoor handcart markets where they shared the language, food, and customs of their homeland. "When the sun shines, the entire population seeks the street," Jacob Riis wrote in his 1890 book, *How the Other Half Lives*. The vibrant, at times violent, atmosphere of this densely packed area was brought to life in the film *Godfather II* in a murder scene that takes place during a parade on Mulberry Street.

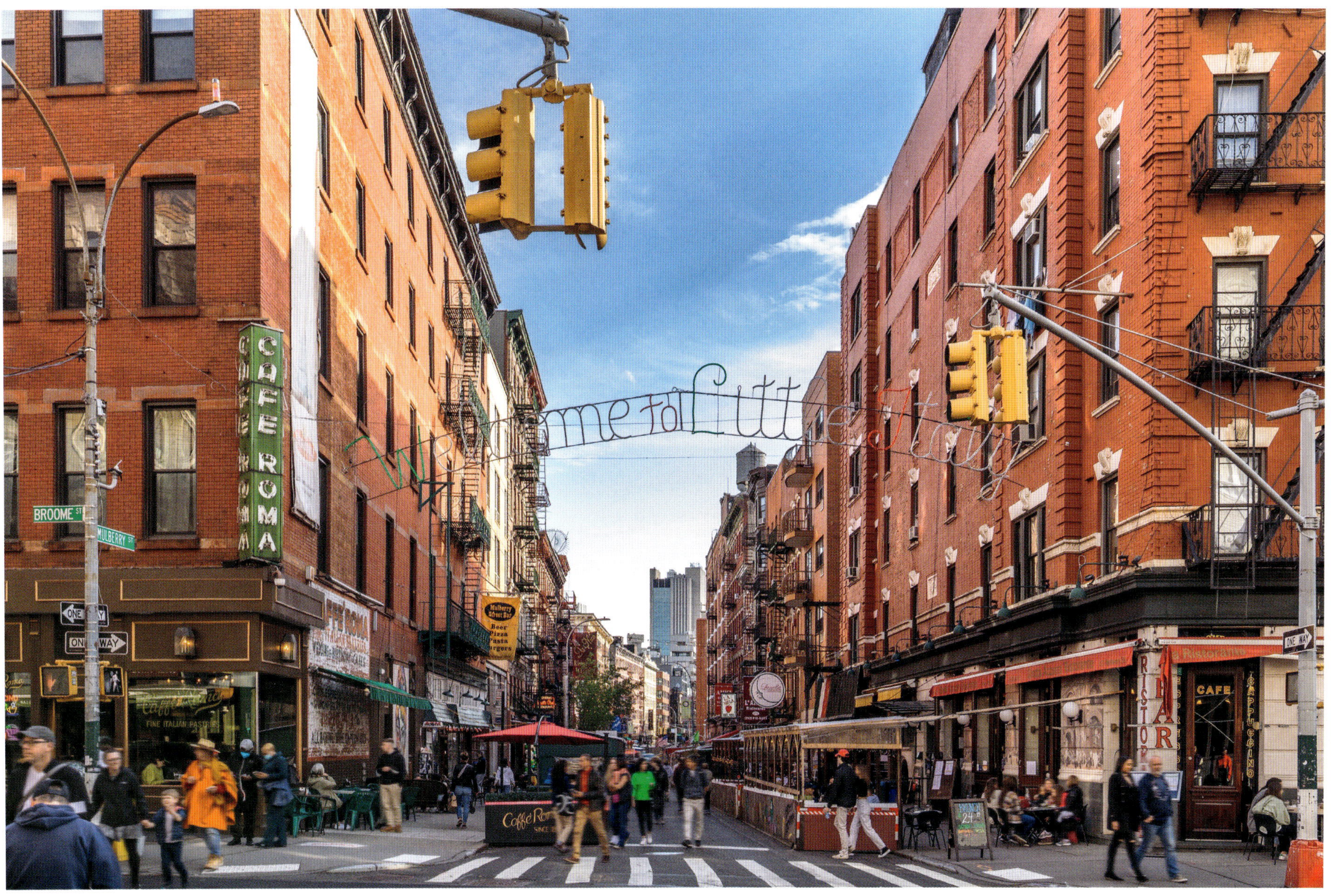

Historically, Little Italy extended for dozens of blocks all around Mulberry Street. Over the years, as Italians moved to other areas and Chinese immigrants moved in, the Italian section shrank to just a few blocks on Mulberry Street alone. Lined with Italian restaurants and shops, it draws locals and tourists seeking the flavors of the old neighborhood. This condensed core of Italian culture temporarily expands every September for the Feast of San Gennaro, an outdoor festival all along Mulberry Street. For the rest of the year, most of the area returns to Chinatown.

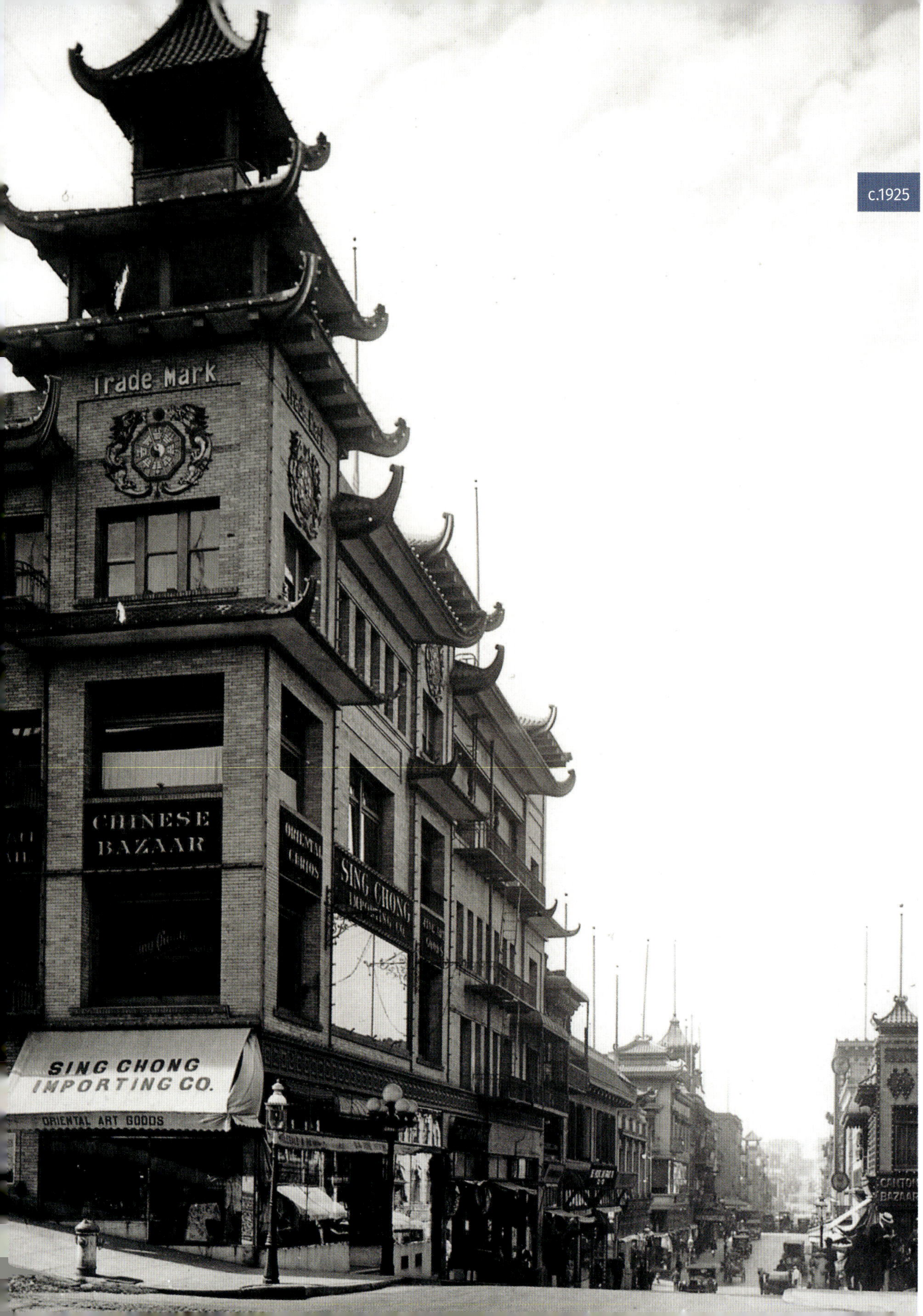

c.1925

CHINATOWN, SAN FRANCISCO

Despite being ravaged by the 1906 fire, Chinatown arose from the ashes

The Trade Mark Building at the intersection of Grant Avenue and California Street lies at the heart of San Francisco's famous Chinatown. The enclave can trace its roots back to the 1850s with the arrival of Chinese immigrants seeking their fortune during the California Gold Rush or to work on the Transcontinental Railroad. These immigrants, mostly from Guangdong Province, faced intense racism and exclusion from mainstream society. To survive and support one another, they

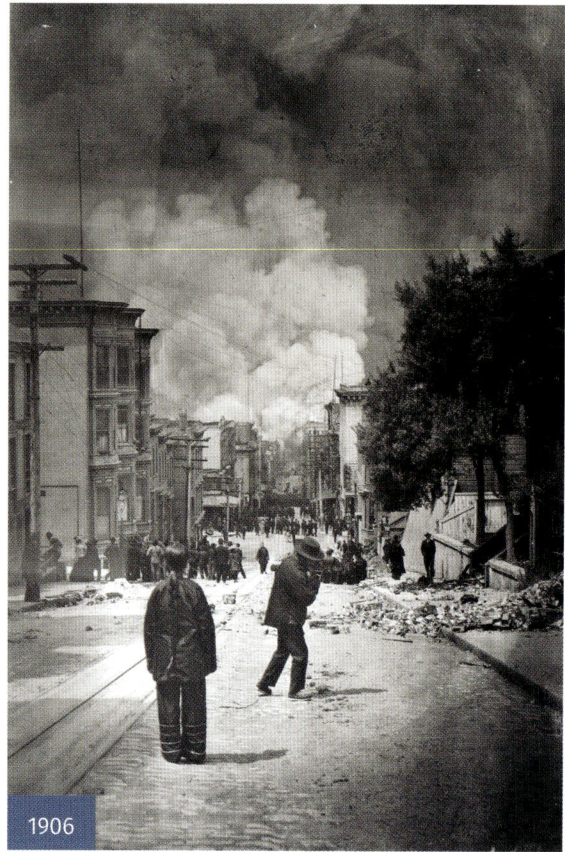
1906

formed a tight-knit community along Grant Avenue (formerly Dupont Street) in what became Chinatown. The area quickly developed into a cultural and economic hub, offering Chinese-operated businesses, herbal medicine shops, theaters, temples, and Chinese newspapers posted on walls.

Despite their contributions to the economy, Chinese residents were subject to regular discrimination. The Chinese Exclusion Act of 1882 was the first significant federal law to ban immigration based on nationality, targeting Chinese laborers and severely restricting their ability to gain citizenship. These laws, combined with local anti-Chinese sentiment, confined many Chinese immigrants to the Chinatown district.

In 1906, much of Chinatown was destroyed by the San Francisco earthquake and fire, but Chinese leaders fought off efforts to relocate the community and instead rebuilt it with Orientalist architecture—pagodas, dragon motifs, and colorful facades—designed to attract tourism and promote cultural pride. This post-reconstruction era helped reshape Chinatown's image from a feared enclave of vice and opium dens to a tourist destination.

Today, Grant Avenue and San Francisco's Chinatown remains a vibrant living and working neighborhood, while also a must-visit tourist destination along with the Ferry Building and Fisherman's Wharf. While it continues to face challenges—such as gentrification and rising costs—it also serves as a powerful symbol of resilience and cultural preservation.

OPPOSITE: A woman stands transfixed in the street as the fire, which has taken hold downtown, is about to sweep up the hill.

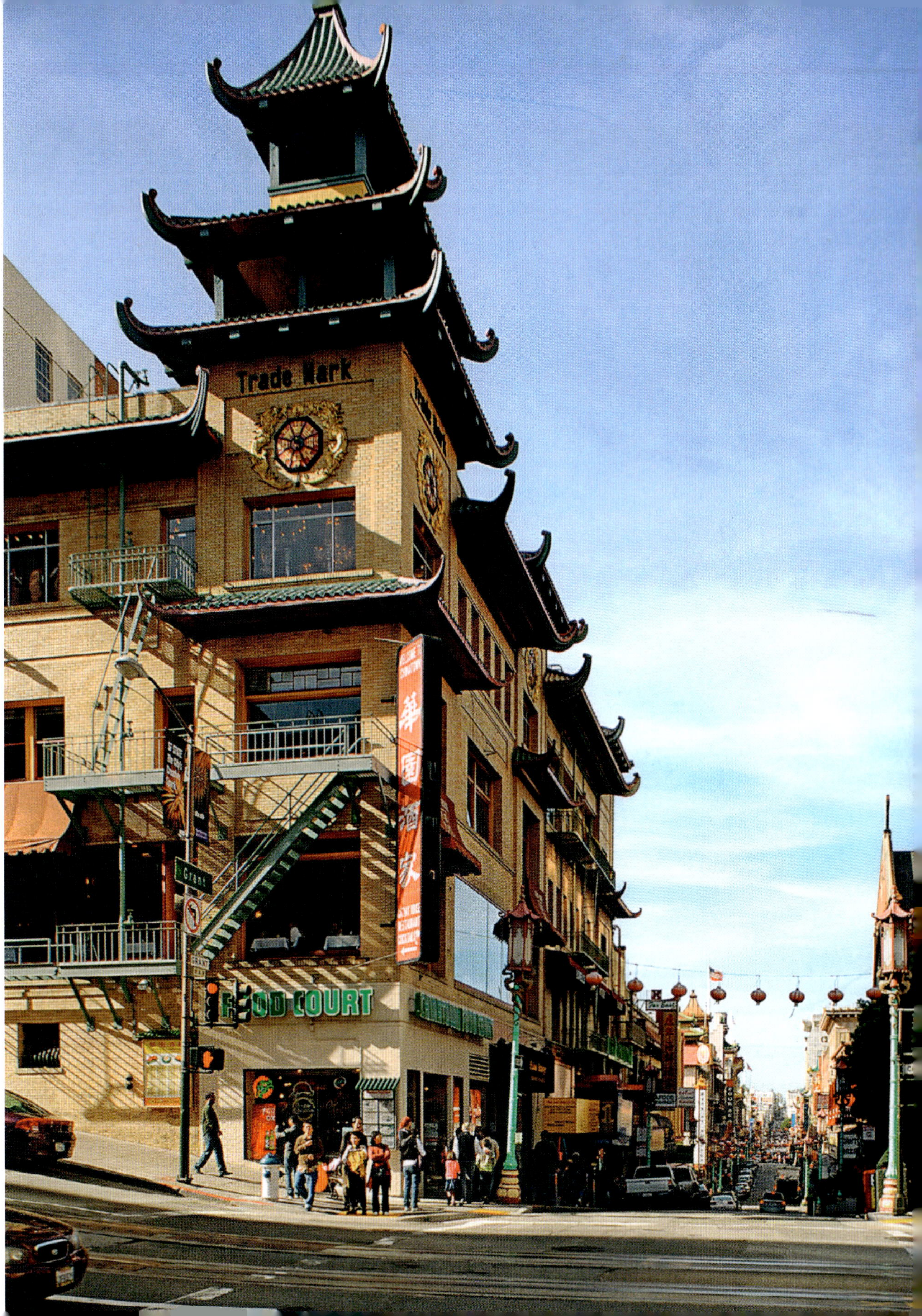

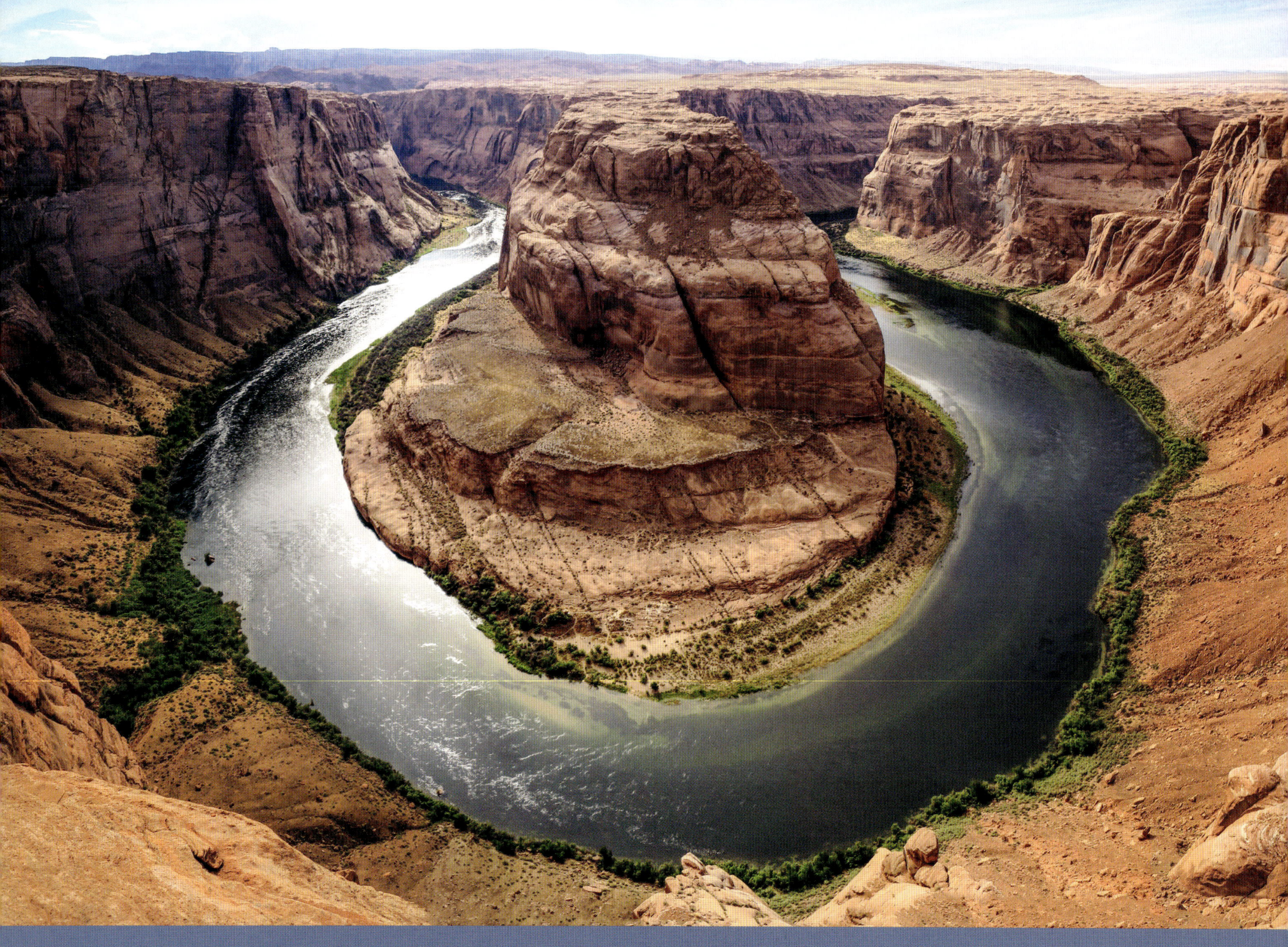

PRESERVING THE PAST, PROTECTING THE FUTURE

Once it could afford to, the United States demonstrated an unparalleled commitment to preserving both its natural wonders and its rich cultural legacy. This dual effort has resulted in the creation of the national park system and the establishment of major cultural institutions. From the sweeping landscapes of Yellowstone and Yosemite to the vast collections of the Smithsonian Institution and the Metropolitan Museum of Art, America's approach to preservation reflects a belief that its heritage is of crucial value to future generations.

BIRTH OF THE NATIONAL PARK

The American national park system was born out of a nineteenth-century drive to protect the country's most awe-inspiring natural landscapes from agricultural exploitation. The idea of preserving land for the public good was revolutionary, especially at a time when workers had few leisure hours and limited vacation time. In 1872, Yellowstone National Park was established as the world's first national park. Spanning parts of Wyoming and Montana, and a scrape of Idaho, Yellowstone became a model for conservation. Center stage were dramatic geysers, such as Old Faithful, which rarely strayed from its show-stopping schedule. There was wildlife—sometimes on the verge of extinction following decades of hunting—such as bison and bears, and a largely untouched ecosystem, all of which inspired national pride.

Yosemite in California became the focus of further preservation efforts. In 1864, President Abraham Lincoln had signed a bill granting Yosemite Valley and the Mariposa Grove to the state of California for public use and preservation—this was the first time the federal government acted to protect natural scenery. Yosemite became a national park in 1890, and it played a central role in the formation of environmental ethics in the US, thanks in large part to naturalist John Muir. Muir's advocacy influenced public opinion and policymakers, eventually helping to establish the National Park Service in 1916.

Crater Lake, located in Oregon, joined the national park system in 1902. Formed by the collapse of a volcano thousands of years ago, its pristine, deep-blue waters and unique geological history captivated early explorers and scientists.

When the National Park Service was created in 1916, it was originally focused on protecting landscapes and wilderness. Over time, its mission expanded to include historic and cultural sites. Today, many of the 400-plus sites managed by the NPS are historic battlefields, presidential homes, Native American heritage sites, and architectural landmarks.

CULTURAL PRESERVATION

By the early twentieth century the movement to protect America's natural heritage was echoed by efforts to safeguard cultural achievements. At the heart of this effort was the Smithsonian Institution, established in 1846 through a bequest from British scientist James Smithson. It has grown into the world's largest museum and research complex, with 21 museums and the National Zoo. The Smithsonian serves as a steward of America's cultural and scientific artifacts, housing everything from the Wright brothers' airplane to African American history, indigenous art, and space exploration memorabilia.

Another cornerstone of cultural preservation is the Library of Congress. Founded in 1800 it was intended to serve the government but has since expanded to become the largest library in the world. It holds millions of books, manuscripts, photographs, maps, and recordings, and it functions not just as a national archive but as a symbol of the nation's intellectual heritage.

Andrew Carnegie, a Scottish-born American industrialist and philanthropist, played a pivotal role in expanding public access to knowledge through the creation of libraries across the United States. Believing that self-education was key to personal advancement, Carnegie donated over $60 million to build more than 1,600 public libraries in the US between 1883 and 1929. These "Carnegie libraries" were typically built in small towns and cities, often under the condition that local governments provided the land and agreed to fund ongoing maintenance. Carnegie viewed libraries as "instruments for the elevation of the masses" and his vision transformed the American public library system, establishing a nationwide network of learning institutions that remain central to communities today.

AMERICAN ART AND URBAN MUSEUMS

Beyond Washington, DC, the nation's major cities also developed institutions dedicated to the visual arts and sciences. These museums have played vital roles in democratizing access to culture and advancing scholarship.

The Art Institute of Chicago, founded in 1879, is one of the oldest and most respected art museums in the country. It houses an exceptional collection of French Impressionist and Post-Impressionist paintings, including works by Monet, Van Gogh, and Seurat. The museum reflects Chicago's emergence as a cultural hub during the Gilded Age and the concerted efforts of Bertha Palmer, who donated twenty-nine Monets and eleven Renoirs and bolstered the collections ahead of the 1893 World's Fair.

In New York City, two institutions exemplify the city's cultural vibrancy. The Metropolitan Museum of Art (The Met) opened in 1870 and has one of the most comprehensive art collections in the world. From Egyptian antiquities to European masters and American decorative arts, The Met embodies the ambition of a young nation eager to match the artistic grandeur of Europe.

Just a few miles away, the American Museum of Natural History, established in 1869, is a monument to scientific curiosity. Its dioramas, dinosaur fossils, and planetary exhibits are designed not just to educate, but to inspire wonder. Like the national parks, the museum promotes an appreciation for the natural world and the deep history of life on Earth.

YELLOWSTONE NATIONAL PARK, WYOMING/MONTANA

The geothermal wonders of Yellowstone have captivated explorers for years

On March 1, 1872, President Ulysses S. Grant signed the Yellowstone National Park Protection Act. Yellowstone became the first national park in the United States, widely considered to be the first of its kind in the world.

The region that would become Yellowstone had been inhabited by Native American tribes for thousands of years. Tribes such as the Shoshone, Crow, and Blackfeet lived in and traversed the area, holding deep cultural and spiritual connections to the land. European-American exploration of the Yellowstone region began in earnest in the early nineteenth century. The Lewis and Clark Expedition (1804–1806) skirted the northern edge of the Yellowstone area, but it wasn't until later that more detailed exploration occurred. Fur trappers and mountain men, such as John Colter, a member of the Lewis and Clark Expedition, entered the region and returned with tales of "fire and brimstone," geysers, and steaming rivers. Colter's stories were often met with skepticism and dubbed "Colter's Hell."

Many expeditions in the late 1860s confirmed Colter's findings, but it was the 1871

1902

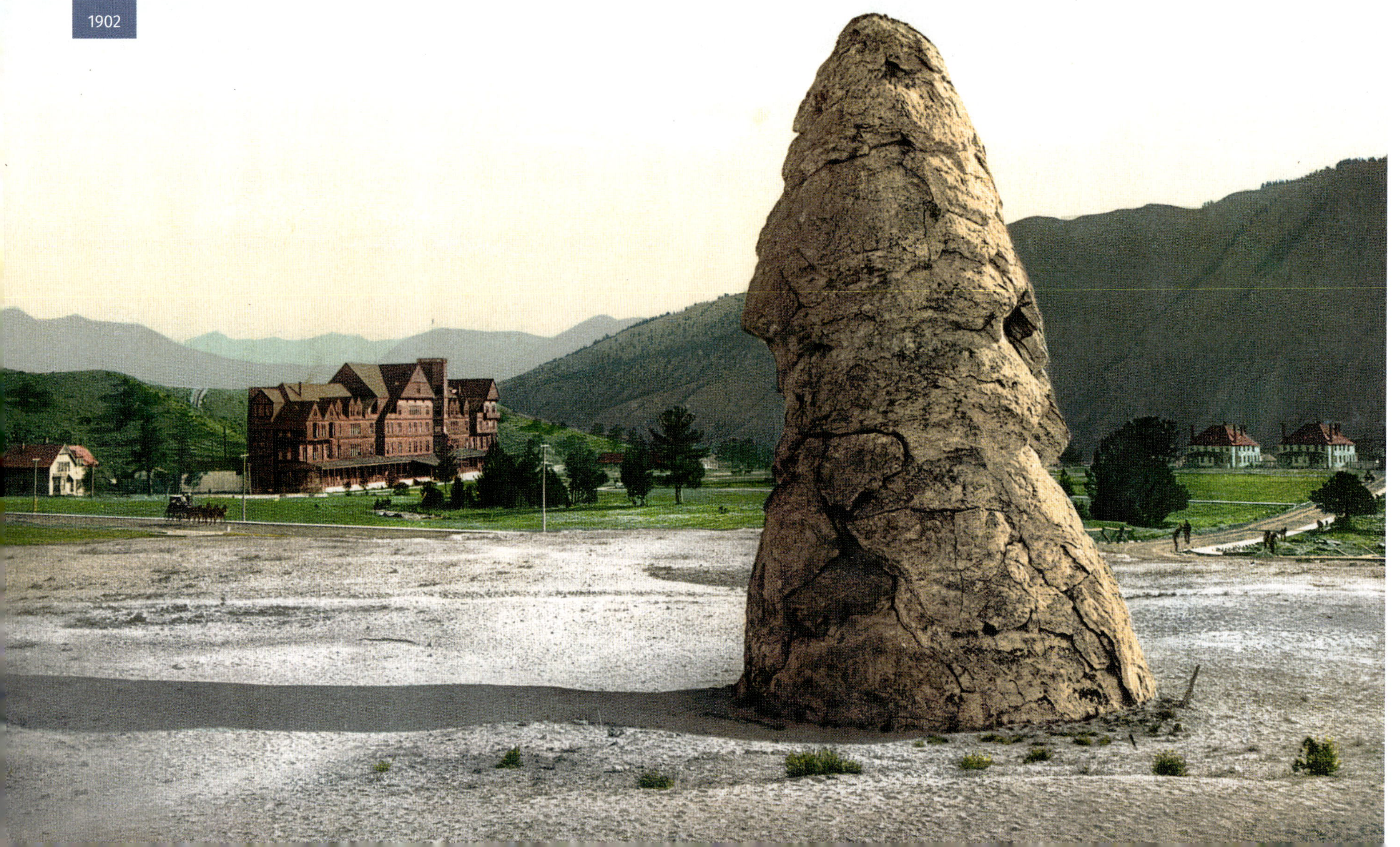

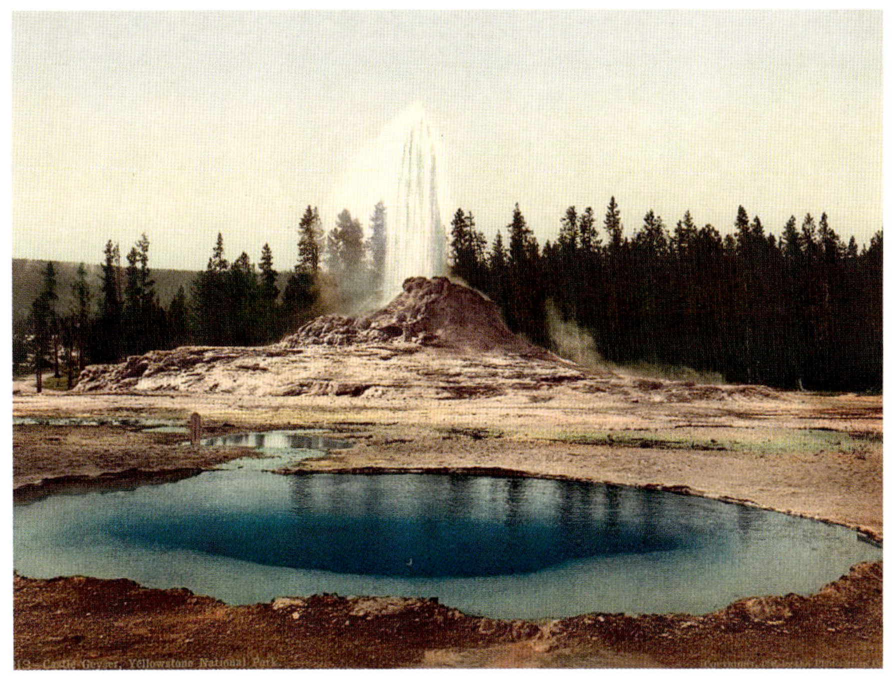

Hayden Geological Survey, led by geologist Ferdinand V. Hayden, that proved crucial in persuading Congress to act. Accompanied by photographer William Henry Jackson and artist Thomas Moran, the survey brought back stunning images and paintings that visually captured the park's unique landscape. These visuals were instrumental in convincing Congress and the public that Yellowstone was worth preserving.

At the time, there was increasing awareness of the need to protect wild spaces from commercial exploitation. Unlike national monuments or forest reserves that came later, Yellowstone was not set aside for its mineral resources but rather for its unparalleled natural beauty and geothermal features. The Yellowstone Act created a 3,472-square-mile park, "dedicated and set apart as a public park or pleasuring-ground for the benefit and enjoyment of the people."

Tourism followed, with Americans anxious to see the spectacular geothermal features. The Mammoth Hotel (pictured opposite), built between 1882 and 1883, was the first grand hotel to be constructed in Yellowstone National Park. Its name referenced both its size and the fact that nearby was the largest concentration of mineral-depositing hot springs in the world. The current Mammoth Hot Springs Hotel and Cabins dates to 1937–38.

LEFT: A hand-tinted photo of the Castle Geyser from 1898.

BELOW: The Liberty Cap rock.

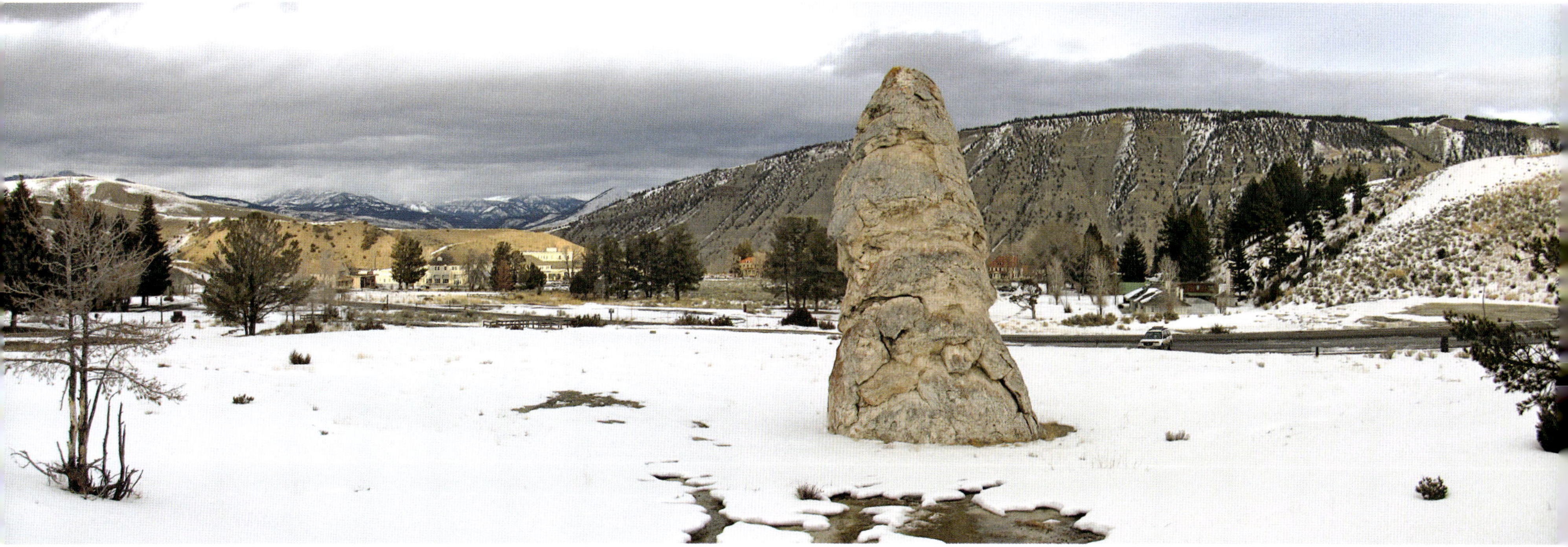

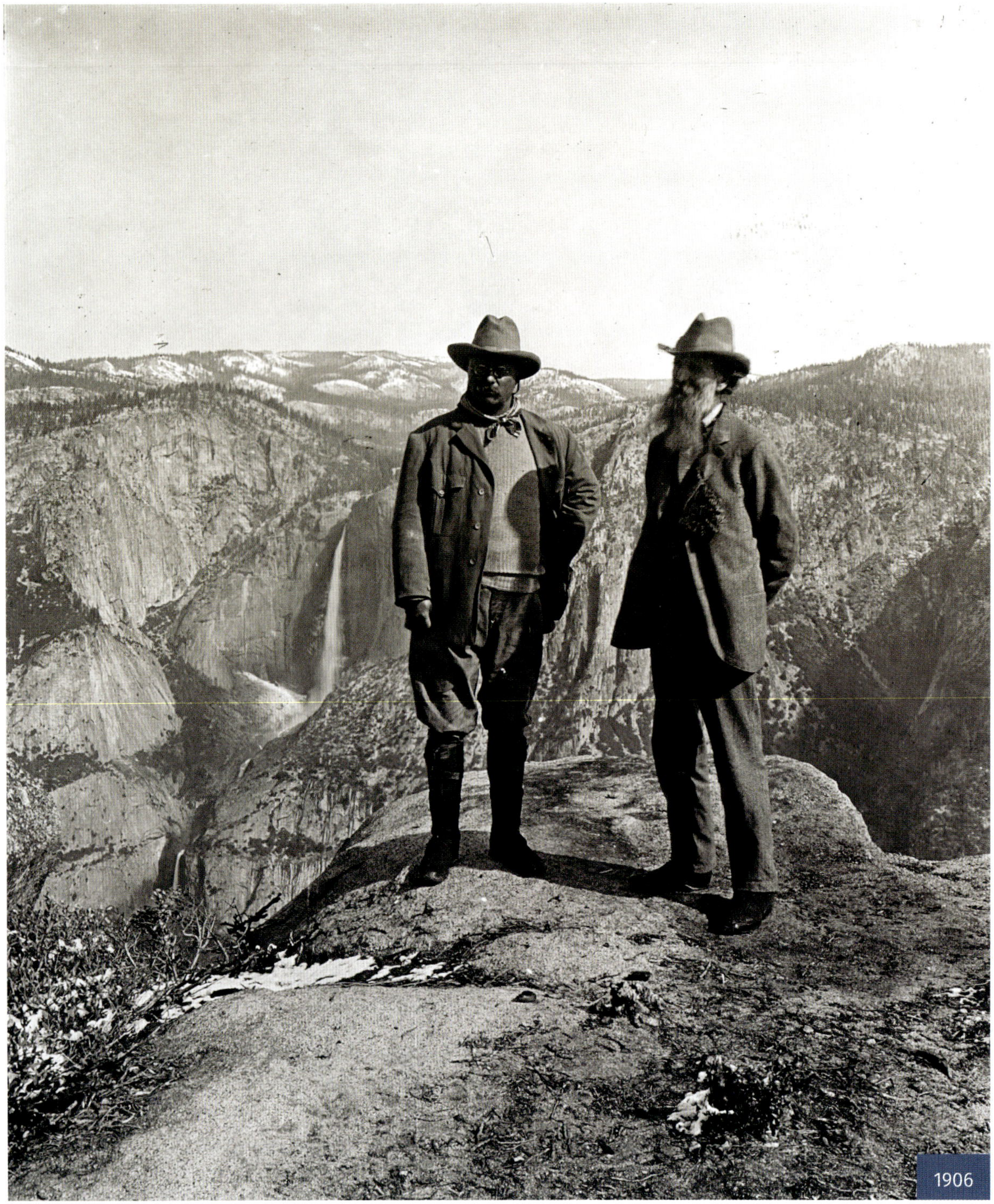

1906

YOSEMITE NATIONAL PARK, CALIFORNIA

Naturalist John Muir was a key figure in stopping development of Yosemite

Yosemite National Park is famous for its towering granite cliffs, majestic waterfalls, and ancient giant sequoias. Yosemite's path to becoming a national park is a rich story of exploration, advocacy, and the early conservation movement in America.

The first significant contact between European Americans and the Yosemite Valley occurred during the Mariposa War of 1850–51. A state militia group called the Mariposa Battalion entered the valley in pursuit of Native American groups accused of attacking mining settlements during the California Gold Rush. One of the battalion's leaders, Major James D. Savage, and his men were reportedly the first non-indigenous people to view the Yosemite Valley. While the purpose of the expedition was to remove Native people from their homelands, the soldiers were stunned by the valley's natural beauty and began sharing accounts that would draw the interest of explorers and settlers.

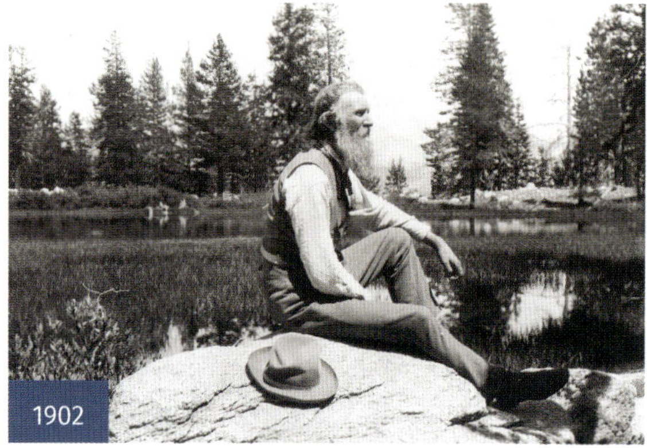

ABOVE: Naturalist John Muir was an expatriate Scot.

LEFT: Muir with President Teddy Roosevelt against the backdrop of the 2.400-foot Yosemite Falls.

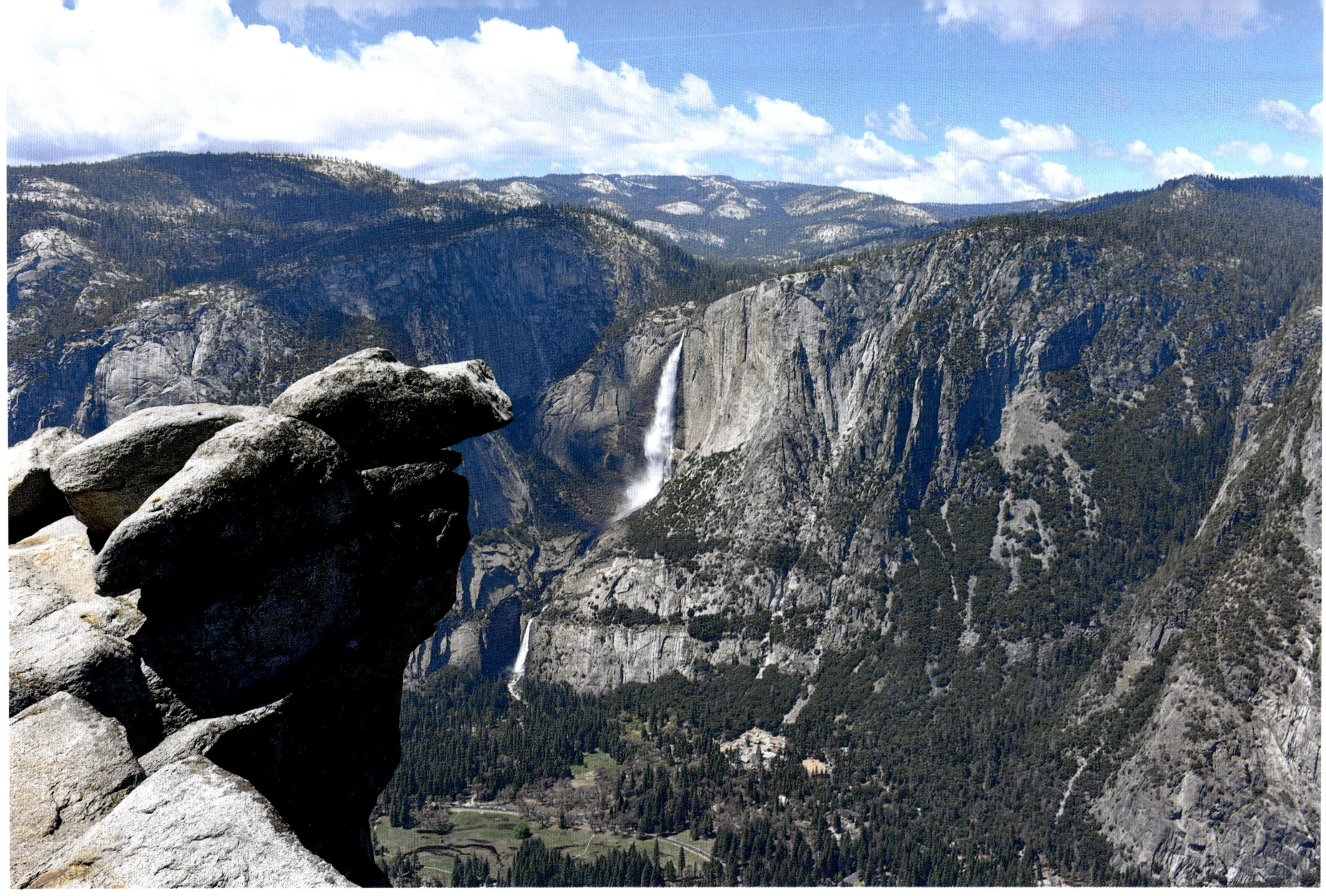

Interest in Yosemite grew throughout the 1850s and 1860s. Artists, writers, and photographers traveled to the area. Among the most influential was photographer Carleton Watkins, whose large-format photographs of Yosemite were displayed in Washington, DC, and played a significant role in swaying public opinion.

In 1864, during the height of the Civil War, President Abraham Lincoln signed the Yosemite Grant Act, which set aside the Yosemite Valley and the Mariposa Grove of Giant Sequoias as protected public lands. This was a historic moment—the first time the US government had acted to preserve land for public enjoyment and protection. The Yosemite Grant was managed by the state of California, and it predated the creation of Yellowstone National Park by eight years.

Management of the Yosemite Grant was initially inconsistent. Over time, growing threats from overgrazing, commercial logging, and tourism prompted calls for stronger federal protection. One of the most passionate advocates for Yosemite's preservation was John Muir, a Scottish-American naturalist and writer who spent years exploring the Sierra Nevada and writing about its beauty. Muir described cattle grazers who cleared forest land as "hoofed locusts" and his essays and activism were crucial in shaping public opinion.

Thanks largely to Muir's efforts, Congress passed legislation to create Yosemite National Park in 1890. The National Park Service, established in 1916, took over management of the park, balancing the need for preservation with increasing public use. Today, Yosemite National Park spans over 750,000 acres, encompassing alpine meadows, rivers, waterfalls like Yosemite Falls and Bridalveil Fall, and the granite monoliths El Capitan and Half Dome.

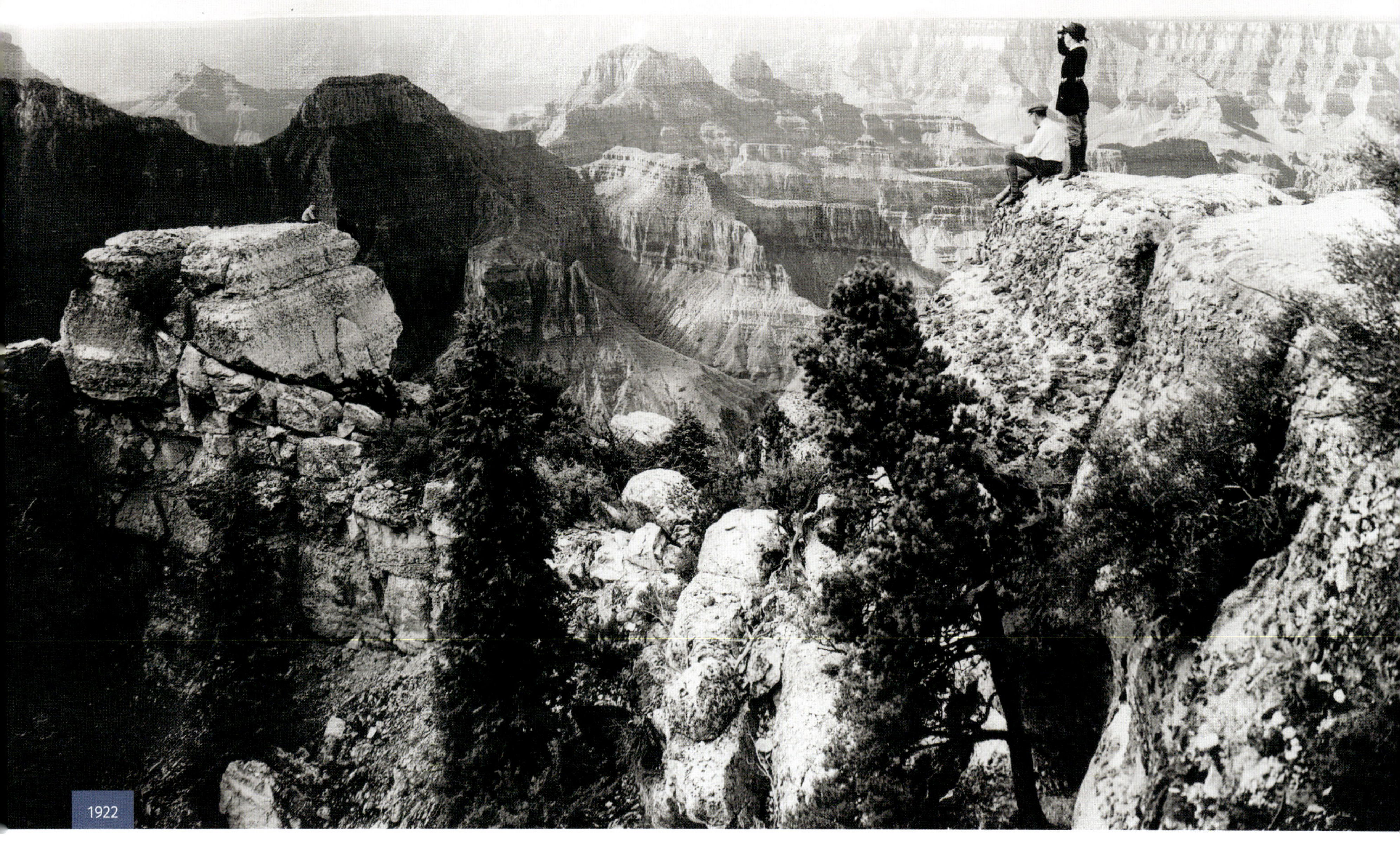
1922

THE GRAND CANYON, SOUTH RIM, ARIZONA

The view of the Colorado River's massive gorge never fails to impress

The recorded history of the Grand Canyon began with Spanish explorers in the sixteenth century. In 1540, members of the Spanish expedition led by Francisco Vásquez de Coronado became the first Europeans to lay eyes on the Grand Canyon. Led by Hopi natives, the Spanish were searching for the fabled Seven Cities of Gold and were struck with awe when they reached the South Rim. It wasn't until the nineteenth century that American explorers began to map and document the canyon in earnest. One of the most significant early expeditions was led by John Wesley Powell in 1869. A one-armed Civil War veteran, Powell and his team navigated the

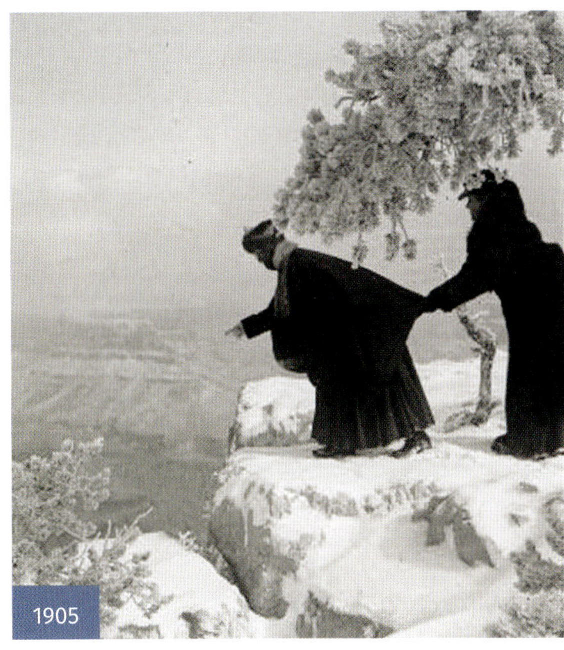

1905

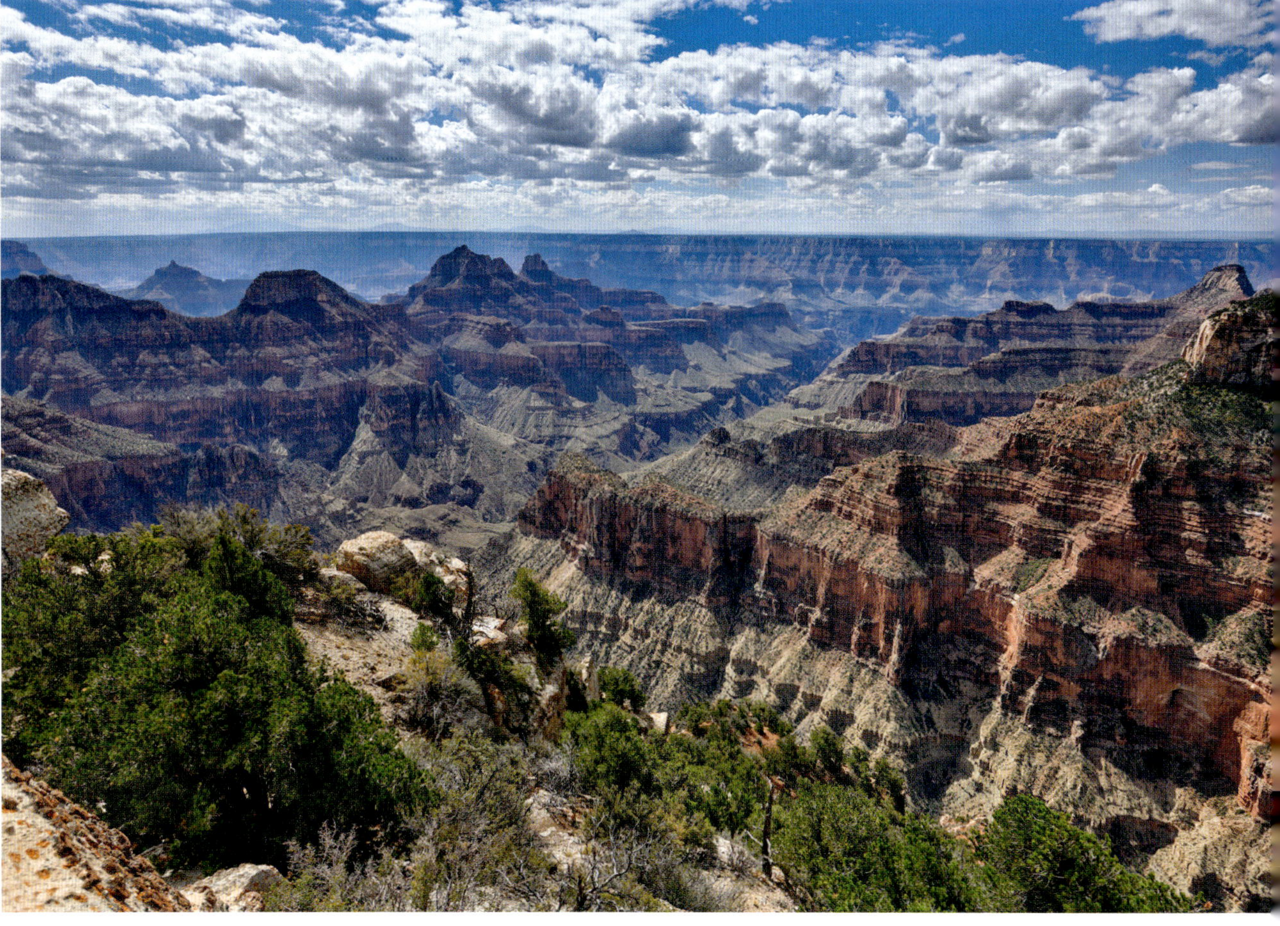

Colorado River through the canyon in wooden boats, enduring harsh conditions and significant danger. His scientific surveys and vivid accounts captivated the American public and drew attention to the canyon's geological significance.

The late nineteenth century marked a turning point for the Grand Canyon as it transitioned from a remote geological marvel to a burgeoning tourist destination. The construction of the railroad to nearby Williams, Arizona, in 1882—and later the spur to the South Rim in 1901—made the canyon far more accessible. The Santa Fe Railway, along with entrepreneur Fred Harvey, played a crucial role in promoting tourism. Harvey Houses offered upscale lodging and dining to travelers, and the (carefully chaperoned) Harvey Girls provided an early example of hospitality tourism in the American West.

By the early twentieth century, the Grand Canyon had become a fashionable destination for adventurous and affluent travelers. In 1905, the El Tovar Hotel opened on the very edge of the South Rim, offering luxurious accommodations with a rustic charm. Other early draws included mule rides down the precipitous Bright Angel Trail, first offered in the 1890s and a necessity for those burdened with Victorian skirts.

With other precious wilderness areas gaining national park status, conservationists began lobbying for federal protection of the Grand Canyon and its over-exploitation. President Theodore Roosevelt declared the Grand Canyon a National Monument in 1908. After decades of advocacy, it was officially designated a national park in 1919, with the National Park Service taking over its management.

Today, the Grand Canyon National Park is one of the most visited national parks in the country. Annual visitor numbers routinely exceed 4.5 million, with travelers from all over the world coming to experience its dramatic vistas, layered rock formations, and sweeping river-carved chasms. The South Rim remains the most accessible and popular area, offering panoramic viewpoints like Mather Point, Desert View, and Yavapai Observation Station. The North Rim, more remote and less developed, appeals to those seeking solitude and cooler summer temperatures

OPPOSITE: A view of the Grand Canyon from Bright Angel Point on the South Rim.

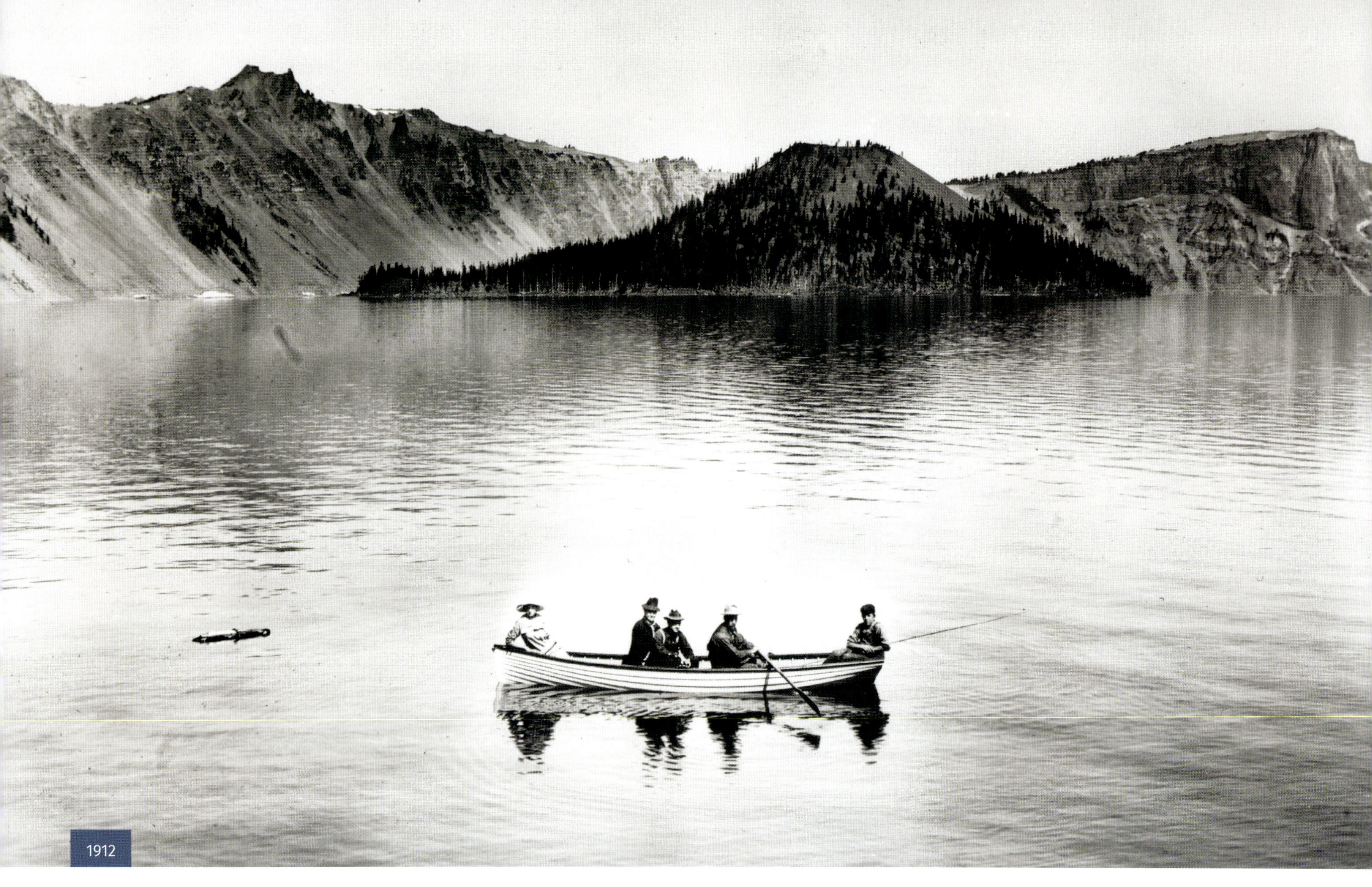

CRATER LAKE NATIONAL PARK, OREGON

A unique national park with a lake fed by rainwater

Crater Lake National Park, in southern Oregon, is home to one of the most striking natural wonders in the United States. Its defining feature, Crater Lake, at 1,943 feet, is the deepest lake in the country, with water as clear as Lake Tahoe.

Formed nearly 8,000 years ago by an enormous volcanic eruption, the lake and its surrounding landscapes have long captured the imagination of scientists, explorers, and conservationists.

The lake lies within the caldera of Mount Mazama, a once towering volcano that erupted violently around 5,700 BCE. The eruption, one of the most powerful in North America in the past 10,000 years, caused the mountain to collapse inward, forming a massive bowl-shaped depression. Over time, rain and snow filled the caldera, creating the deep, brilliantly blue lake we see today. Crater Lake has no rivers flowing in or out—its water level is maintained solely by precipitation and evaporation.

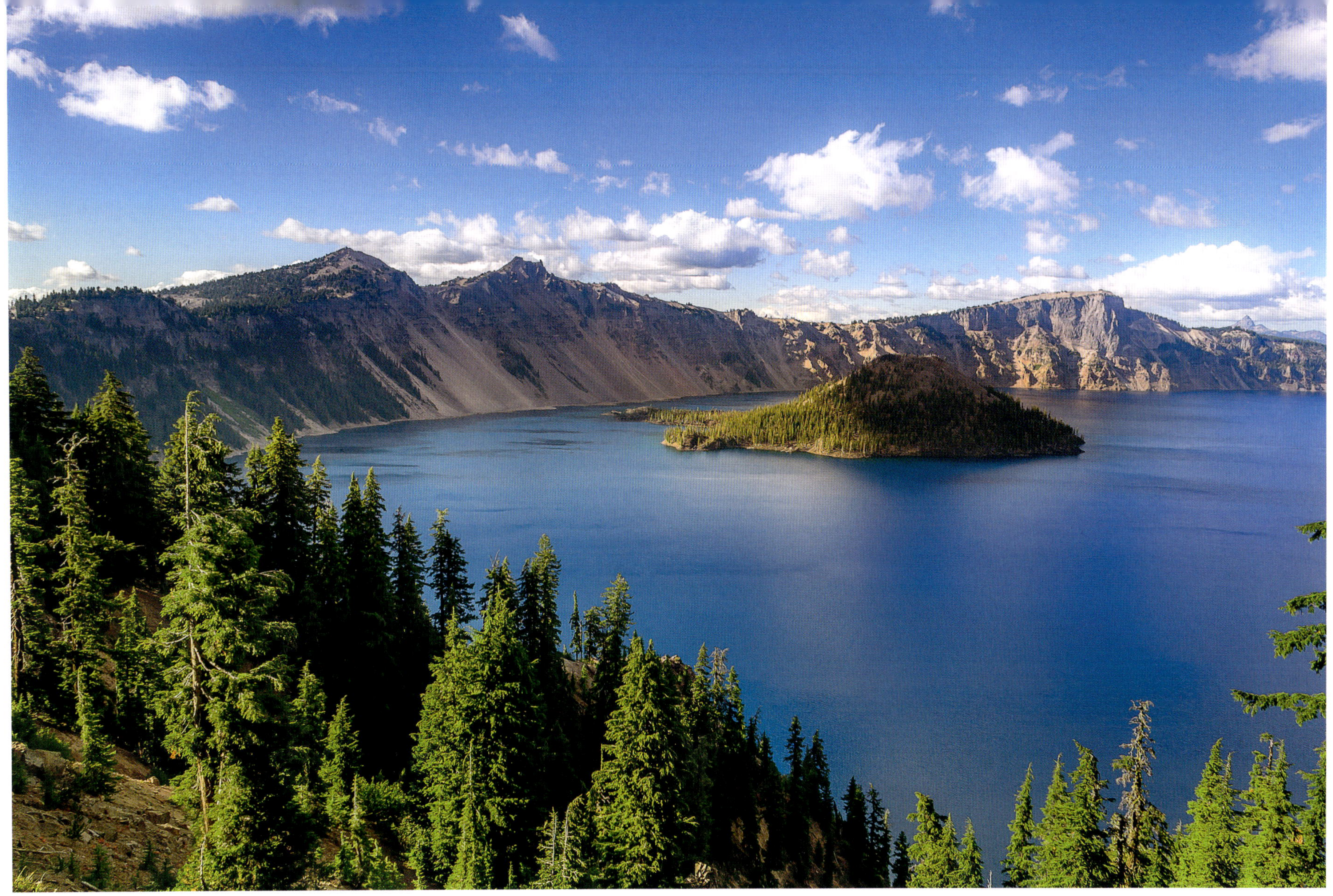

According to the oral traditions of Native American tribe the Klamath, the eruption of Mount Mazama was a result of a battle between the spirit of the sky (Skell) and the spirit of the underworld (Llao), a myth reflecting the real geological violence that shaped the land. The Klamath considered the lake sacred and often avoided its rim out of reverence and caution.

The first documented European American sighting of Crater Lake occurred in 1853 during a gold prospecting expedition. A group led by John Wesley Hillman stumbled upon the lake and were astonished by its vivid blue color and immense depth. They named it "Deep Blue Lake."

William Gladstone Steel, after reading about the lake as a young boy, first visited Crater Lake in 1885 and began a decades-long campaign to have it designated a national park. The journalist from Ohio wrote extensively, gave public lectures, and lobbied politicians, arguing that the lake's unique geological features and stunning natural beauty warranted federal protection. Steel's efforts finally bore fruit when, on May 22, 1902, President Theodore Roosevelt signed legislation creating Crater Lake National Park. This made it the first national park in the Pacific Northwest. The park protected over 150,000 acres of wilderness, including the lake, surrounding forests, and volcanic features like Wizard Island, a cinder cone that rises above the lake's surface.

Over the years, the park developed facilities for tourism and scientific study. In 1915, the construction of the Rim Drive, a scenic road encircling the caldera, allowed visitors to take in panoramic views of the lake. The Crater Lake Lodge, completed in 1915 and later renovated, has become a central hub for park visitors.

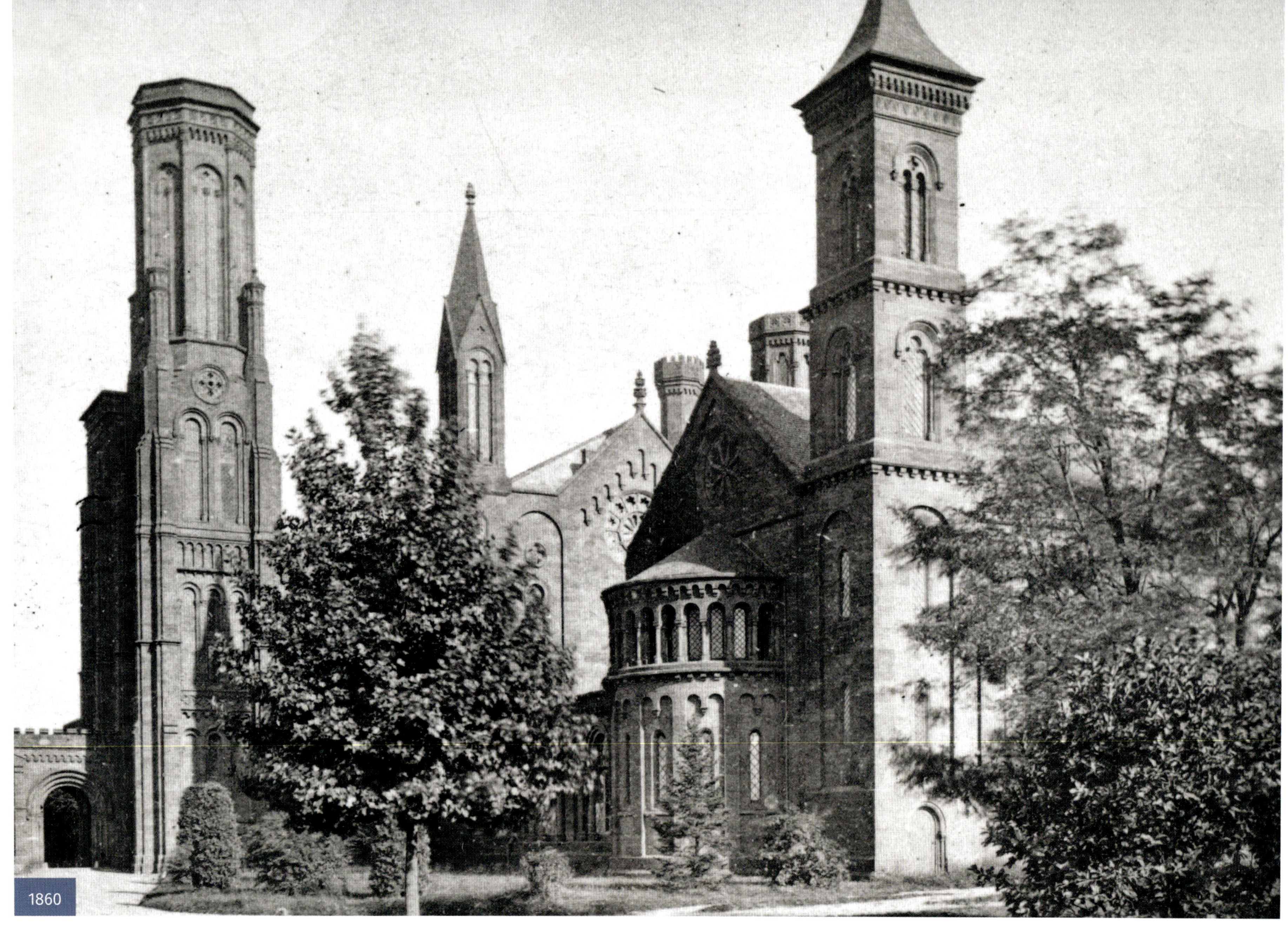
1860

SMITHSONIAN CASTLE, WASHINGTON, DC

The starting point for America's largest museum system

When English scientist James Smithson passed away, he left a bequest of $550,000 to the United States for the creation of "an establishment for the increase and diffusion of knowledge." The United States, although excited at the prospect of creating such an institution, was unsure of the best way to achieve Smithson's wish. Upon receiving the bequest in 1835 the United States welcomed a decade of debate on what "the diffusion of knowledge" meant, and how it could best be achieved. A university in Smithson's honor was suggested, as was a scientific research institution, a national publishing house, and a museum—all establishments connected with knowledge and education. With everyone from scientists to congressmen and the public weighing in with their suggestions, it became clear that just one of these institutions wasn't going

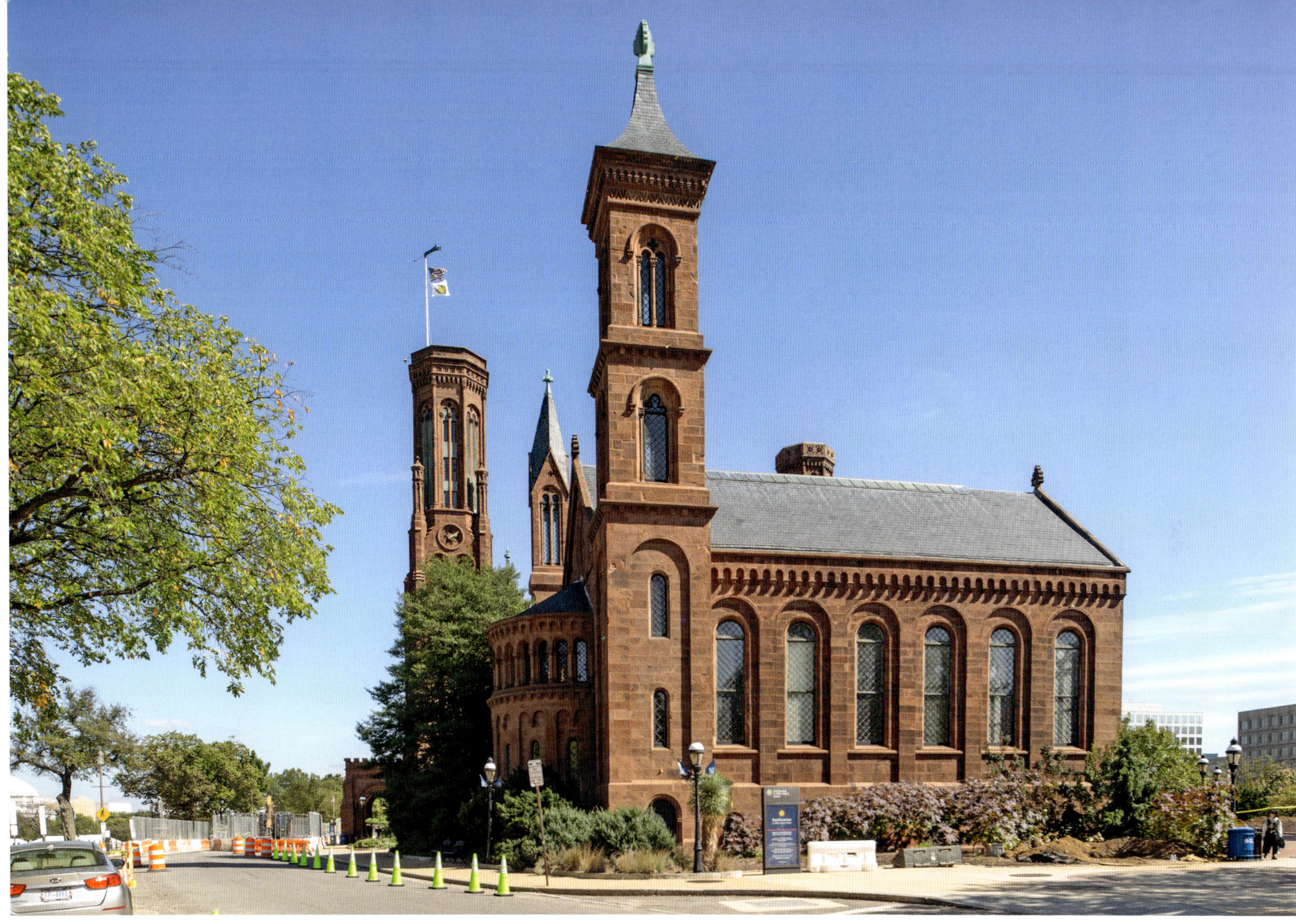

to be satisfactory. On August 10, 1846, Congress passed legislation that was immediately signed into law by President James Polk. This was the creation of the Smithsonian Institution, founded as a combination of the many different ideas suggested, including the scientific research center, an educational publication source, and a museum.

Designed by James Renwick, Jr. and completed in 1855, the Smithsonian Institution Building, now known as the Smithsonian Castle, was created to house the United States' collection of scientific research and historical artifacts. Made of red sandstone from nearby Maryland and in a late Romanesque and Gothic style, this building has been a mainstay of the National Mall since before the Civil War.

The Smithsonian Castle has had many different responsibilities in its lifetime. In its earliest years, the Secretary of the Smithsonian, visiting scientists, specimens, and more all resided under its roof. In the 1880s, the yard around the building was used for the National Zoo, and in 1901 the first children's museum was installed in the Castle. Since its beginnings as a debated idea and a multipurpose educational facility, the Smithsonian Institution has expanded greatly.

The institution now includes many different avenues of education including 20 museums (with more on the way), a national zoo, more than 150 million objects varying from scientific specimens to artistic masterpieces, and an astrophysical laboratory. Now used for administrative support, the Smithsonian Castle continues to represent the United States' successful attempt to fulfill Smithson's last wish.

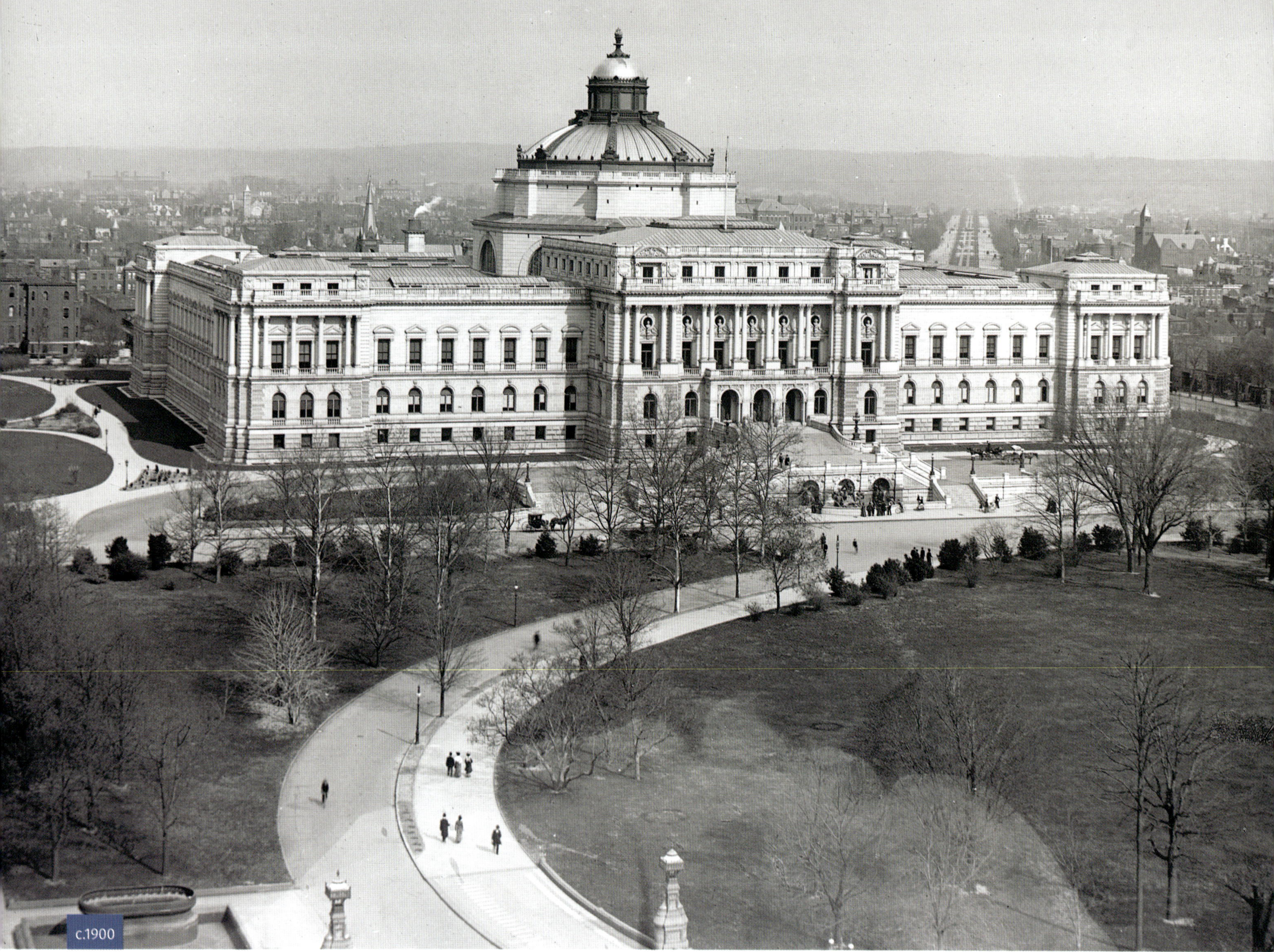

LIBRARY OF CONGRESS, WASHINGTON, DC

America's national library, housed in one of the capital's most elegant buildings

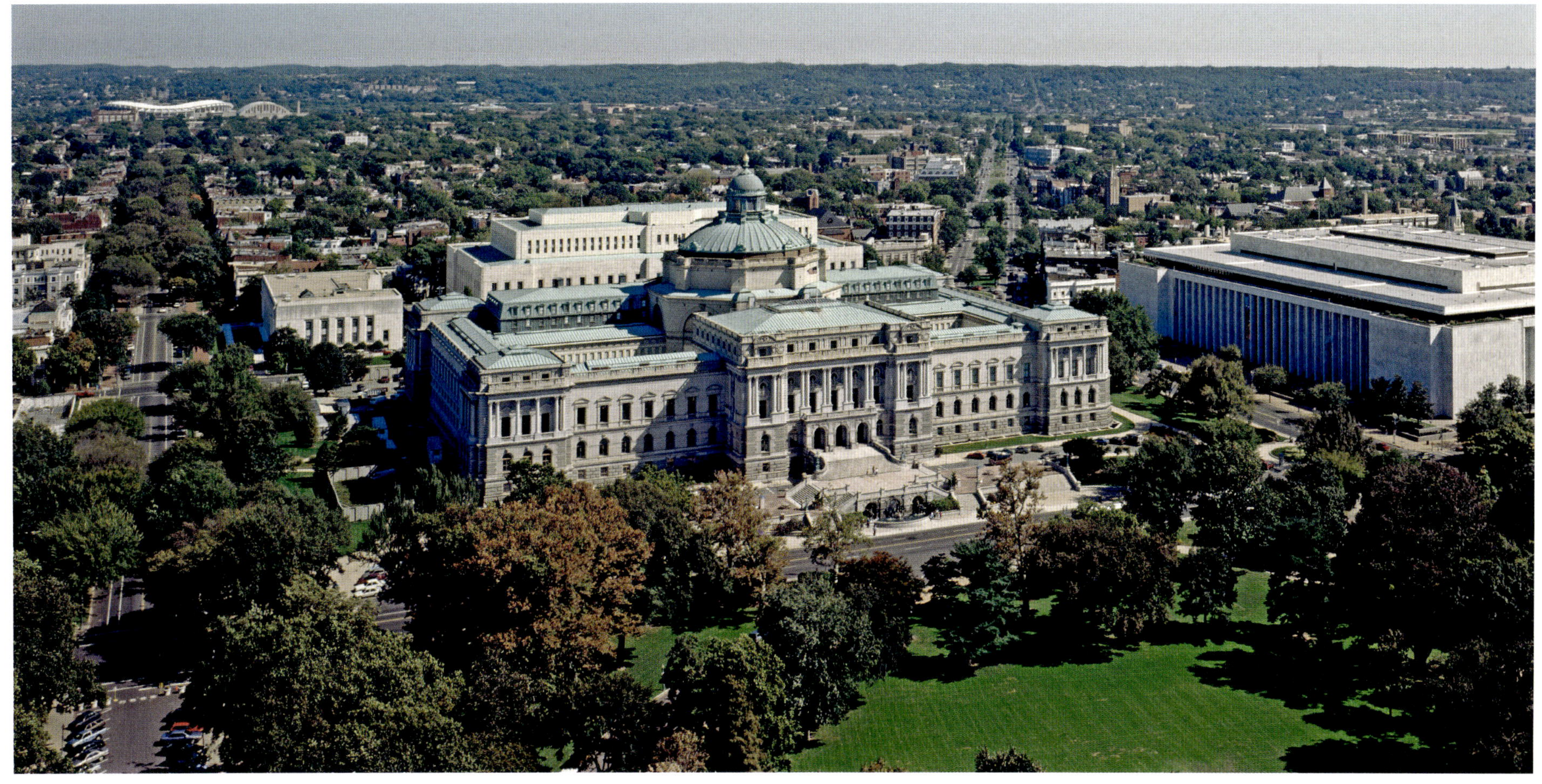

In the year 1800, Washington received its official title as the capital city of the United States. As they established themselves in the federal city, Congress requested $5,000 in funds to be used for Congressional books. This was the start of the Library of Congress, a library primarily for legislative purposes in its earliest years, housed in the US Capitol building for easy congressional access. Unfortunately, the collection of 3,000 books met an early demise in 1814, when British soldiers invaded Washington and set the new capital ablaze, taking the library's contents with it.

Instead of rebuilding their collection book by book, 72-year-old former President Thomas Jefferson offered to donate his personal collection of over 6,000 books to the library ... but required the sum of $23,950 ($650,000 in today's money) for his troubles. Congress agreed the purchase to restore their reference materials.

The Librarian of Congress from 1864–1897, Ainsworth Rand Spofford, enlarged the scope of the library's collections. Spofford's term also saw the construction of the Library of Congress Building as the new home for the rapidly growing collection. Built in 1897 in a Beaux-Arts style the Library's new home was close to Congress for legislative needs, and also served as the American public's national library.

As the library's collection grew, so did its physical space in Washington; the building now known as the John Adams Building opened to the public in 1939. One of the library's largest periods of expansion, both nationally and internationally, was throughout the 1950s to the 1970s as global networks increased.

The library now boasts over 164 million items in its collection, spanning multiple centuries, formats of expression, languages and various subjects. Recognized as the largest library in the world, the Library of Congress still serves its original purpose of supporting the United States Congress but has also developed a new role throughout its expansive history—as the national library for the United States. Today visitors can tour its museum and gallery spaces, and those doing research can procure a free library card and grab a chair in their Main Reading Room.

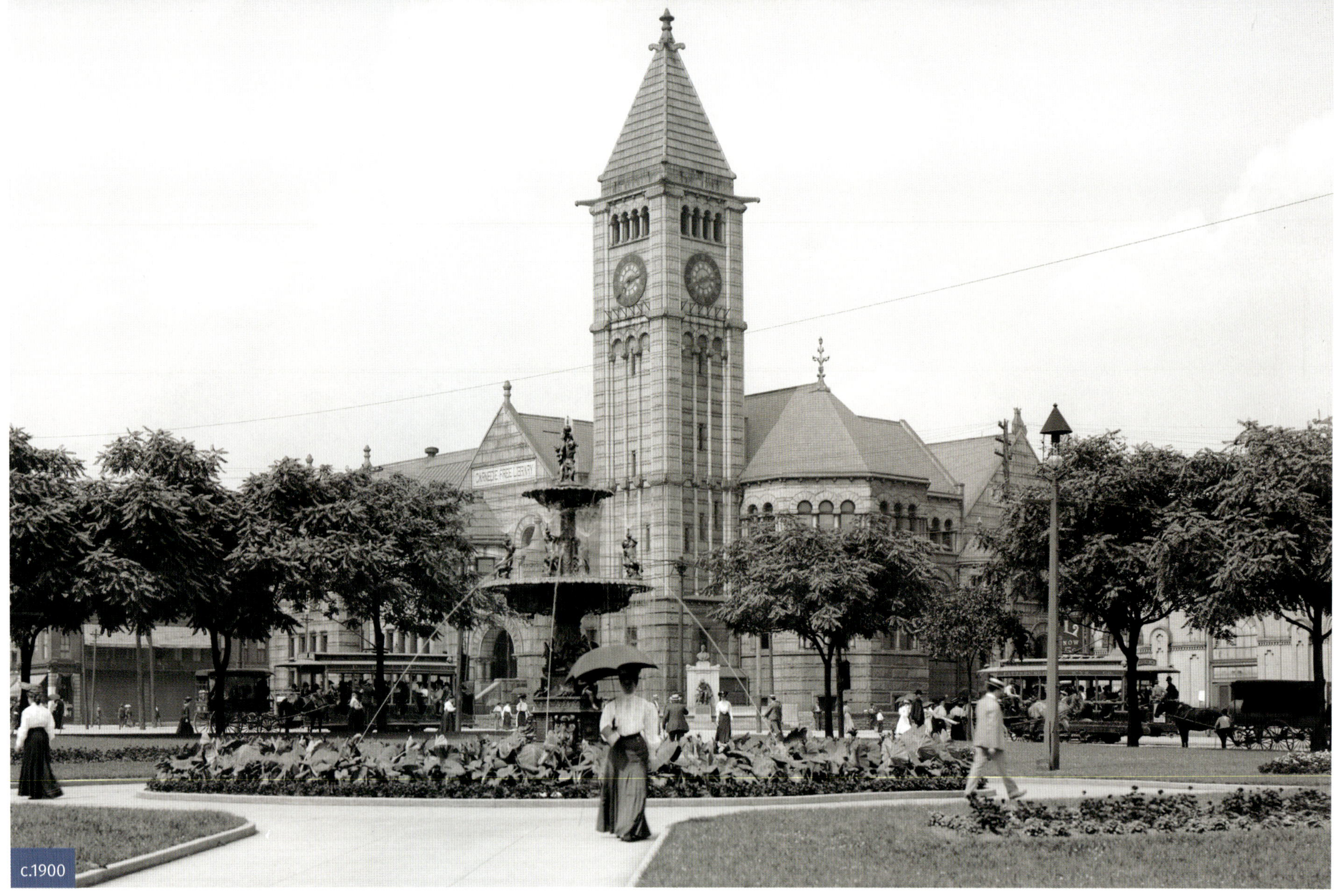

c.1900

CARNEGIE LIBRARY, NORTH PITTSBURGH

Andrew Carnegie held the belief that the wealthy had a strong moral obligation to help the poor

The Carnegie libraries represent one of the most significant philanthropic efforts in American history. Financed by industrialist Andrew Carnegie, these libraries reshaped public access to knowledge in the late nineteenth and early twentieth centuries. Andrew Carnegie was born in Scotland in 1835 and immigrated to the United States as a child. As a young man working in a Pittsburgh telegraph office, he was allowed to borrow books from a local private library—an opportunity that shaped his view on the importance of free access to information and learning.

After amassing a fortune in the steel industry during the Gilded Age, Carnegie turned to philanthropy. Influenced by his belief in the *Gospel of Wealth*—his 1889 essay—he that argued the rich had a moral obligation to use their wealth for the public good: "The man who dies thus rich dies disgraced."

Carnegie's first library grant in the US was given to Allegheny, Pennsylvania (now part of Pittsburgh) in 1881, though the first library to open with his funding was in Braddock, Pennsylvania, in 1889. Braddock's library set a high standard—it included not only books, but a music hall, gymnasium, and billiards room. However, Carnegie quickly realized that to make the greatest impact, he needed a more scalable approach.

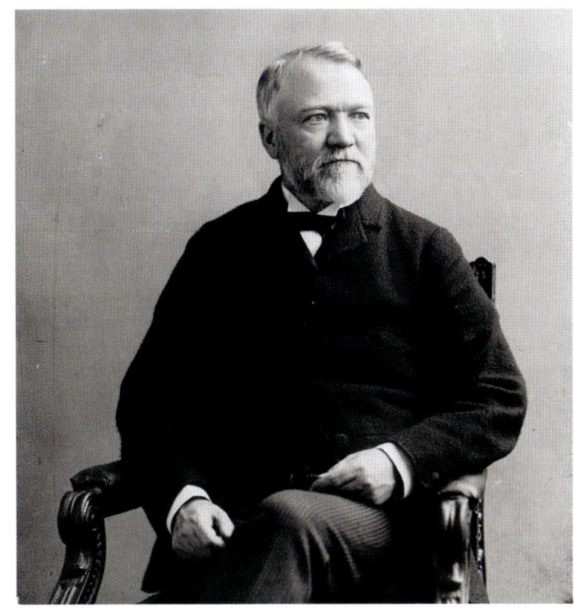

From the 1890s to the 1920s, Carnegie developed a system for awarding library grants to cities and towns across the United States. Communities had to apply for a grant and meet specific conditions: they had to demonstrate a need for a library, provide the land, and commit to annually funding the library's operation—typically at a rate of 10% of the initial grant amount. This model ensured that local governments were invested in the success of their libraries and that the facilities would remain open and maintained.

The results were extraordinary. Between 1883 and 1929, Carnegie funded 1,679 public libraries across the United States and 2,509 libraries worldwide.

These libraries were typically modest in size, but architecturally distinctive—often designed in Classical Revival or Beaux-Arts styles, with high ceilings, open reading rooms, and large windows to maximize natural light. Many became civic landmarks in their communities.

OPPOSITE: The Carnegie Library on Pittsburgh's North Side, emphasizing its free access.

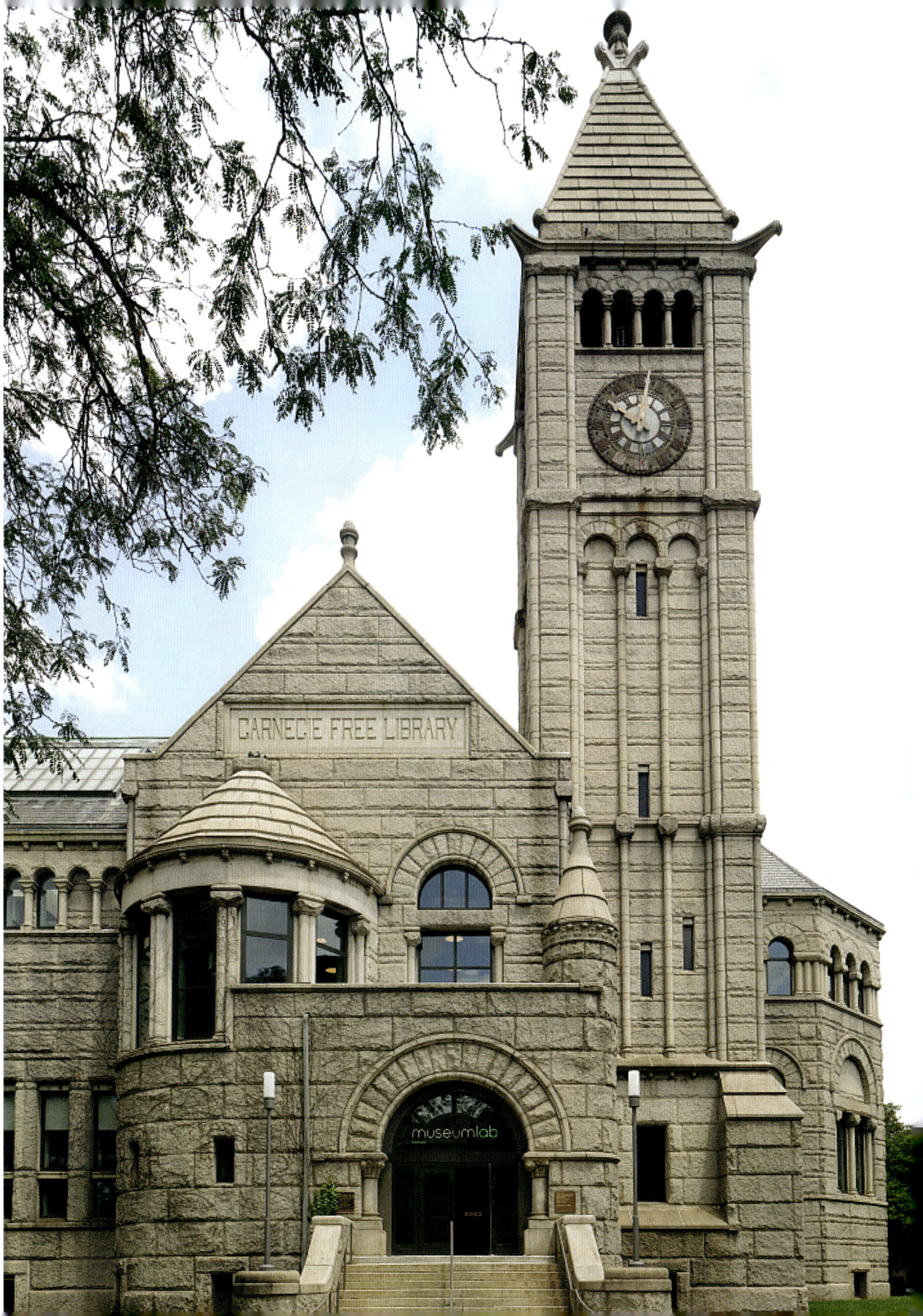

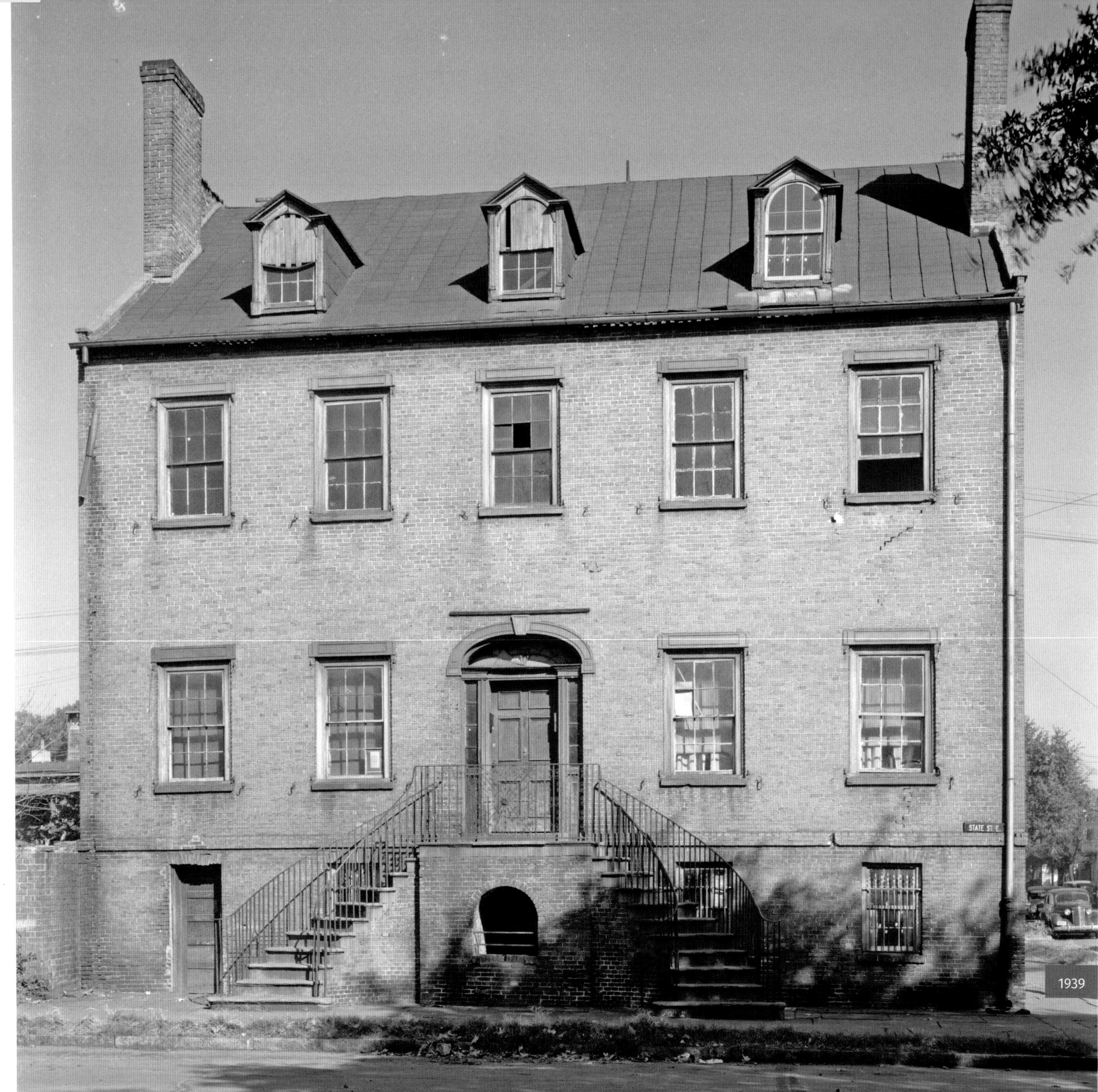

1939

ISAIAH DAVENPORT HOUSE, SAVANNAH, GEORGIA

The birth of the architectural preservation movement in Savannah was generated by the threat to this house

Isaiah Davenport moved from Rhode Island to Savannah in 1799, only three years after Savannah's devastating fire of 1796. He was a master builder and constructed his own home on Columbia Square to showcase his skills. He designed and built it between 1815 and 1820 in the Federal style, with which he was familiar. Symmetry and balance were maintained inside and out, with a center hallway on both floors.

Exacerbated by the Great Depression, the local economy slumped with the loss of the cotton industry when the boll weevil decimated the South's cotton crop. Davenport House became a tenement, as did so many other beautiful old homes in Savannah. By 1954 it was destined for demolition. The menacing machine with the wrecking ball was idling on Habersham Street, waiting for the signal.

Alarming destruction was taking place throughout the Savannah Historic District. Priceless old homes were being knocked down for their handmade Savannah gray bricks to build new houses in the southern part of the city. Wooden structures deemed not up to code were flattened overnight. Having lost the colorful City Market on Ellis Square for a parking garage just one year earlier, seven courageous Savannah women turned the tide of demolition in favor of preservation. After purchasing the Davenport House, they formed the Historic Savannah Foundation, which today is a model to the world for creative restoration and renovation. The 2.5 square miles of tenderly restored buildings and preserved landmarks can be credited to Katherine Judkins Clark, Elinor Adler Dillard, Anna Colquitt Hunter, Lucy Barrow McIntire, Dorothy Ripley Roebling, Nola McEvoy Roos, and Jane Adair Wright.

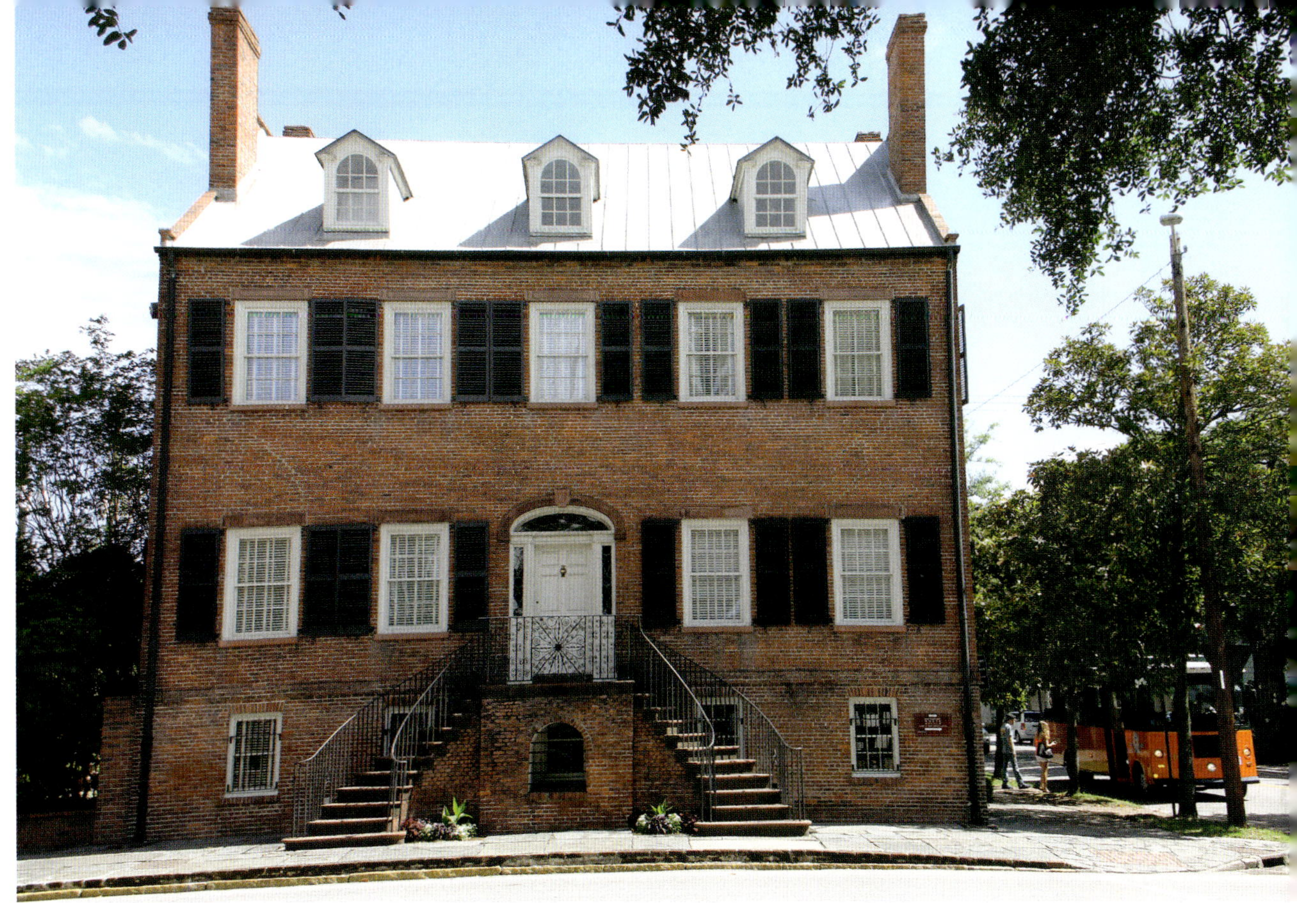

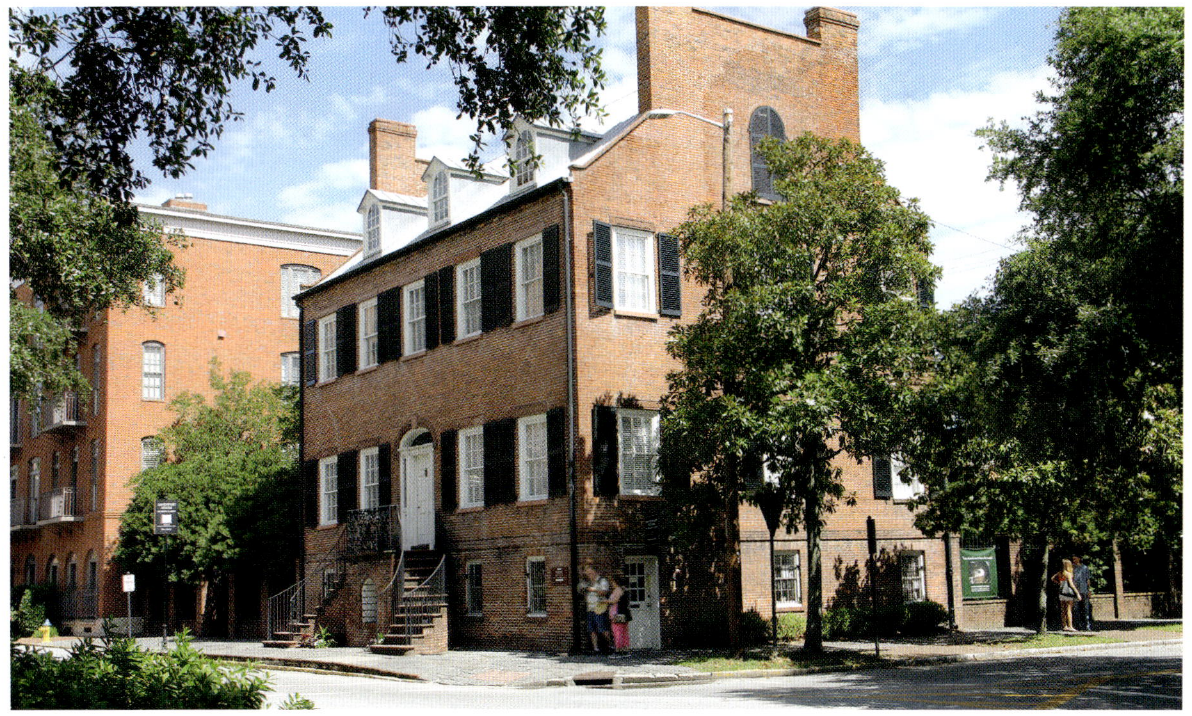

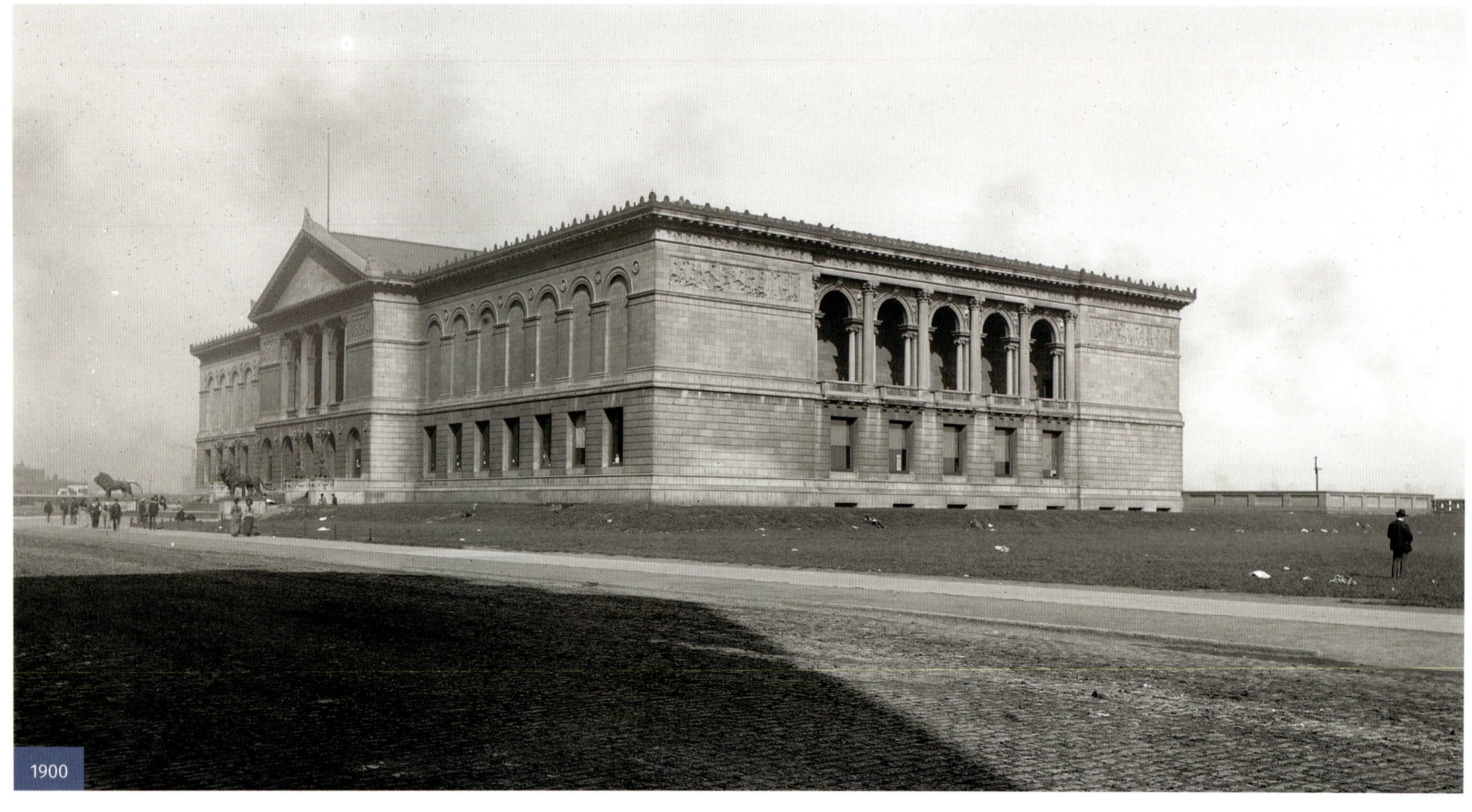

1900

ART INSTITUTE OF CHICAGO, GRANT PARK, CHICAGO

A legacy building of one of the greatest world's fairs

Though it was some distance from the main 1893 World's Fair site, architects Shepley, Rutan and Coolidge designed the grand building at Michigan and Adams as the location for the exposition's Parliament of Religions. The Columbian Exposition celebrated the 400-year anniversary of Columbus's arrival in the New World and, unlike the majority of the buildings at the "White City" in Jackson Park, the future home of the Art Institute of Chicago was a truly permanent structure.

The solid horizontal lines and tall arches evoked the Richardsonian Romanesque style, still a force in 1890s Chicago. There are Beaux-Arts influences too, with the embellished rooflines, sculpted ornamentation, and classical elements like the second-floor Corinthian columns. The site gained historical significance even before any paintings were installed—Indian delegate Swami Vivekananda delivered a much-reported speech at the Parliament of Religions calling for religious tolerance and an end to disruptive fanaticism. American artist Edward Kemeys exhibited his massive plaster sculptures of wild animals—including two majestic lions—at the World's Fair. The lions were subsequently cast in bronze and installed at the entrance of the Art Institute.

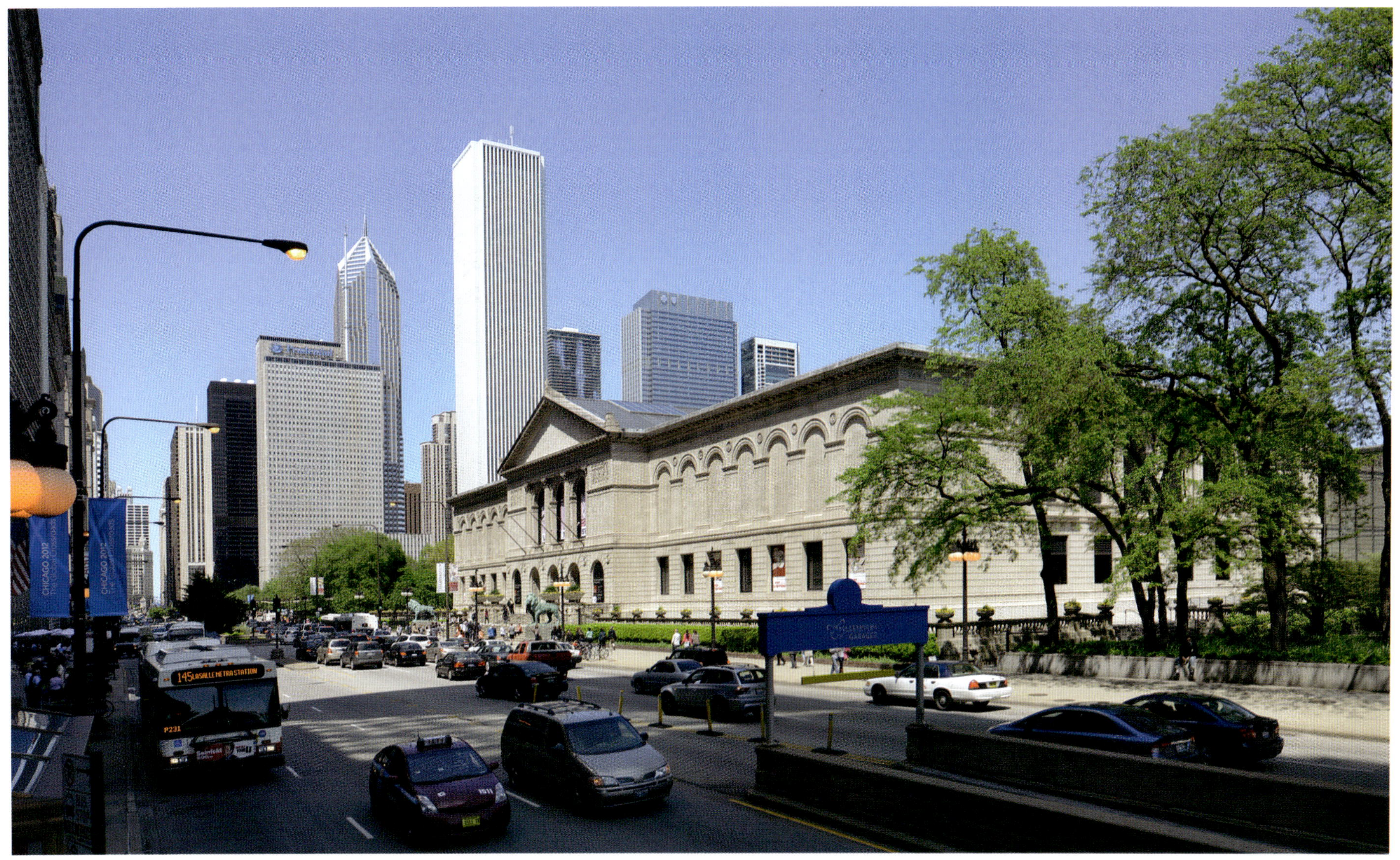

The museum's collection was aided by the gift of Bertha Honore Palmer's art collection in 1922. Bertha and her husband Potter Palmer—developer of the Palmer House Hotel—began collecting Impressionist art in the 1890s.

The institute received works by Claude Monet, Pierre-Auguste Renoir, Edgar Degas, Camille Pissarro, and Mary Cassatt. A few years later, the Helen Birch Bartlett Memorial Collection was donated, including Georges Seurat's *A Sunday Afternoon on the Island of La Grande Jatte*, now one of the most visited works in the museum.

Today the museum is responsible for one of the world's most comprehensive collections of modern art. The new Modern Wing, designed by architect Renzo Piano and completed in 2009, now houses this vast collection, including many works that were in storage for years. This expansion, the largest in the museum's history, connects the Art Institute to Millennium park via the Nichols Bridgeway, creating an unbroken artistic flow along Michigan Avenue. Kemeys' lions remain on guard at the entrance and are adorned with Chicago Bears merchandise whenever the Bears win big—something that fans fear is unlikely to happen any time soon.

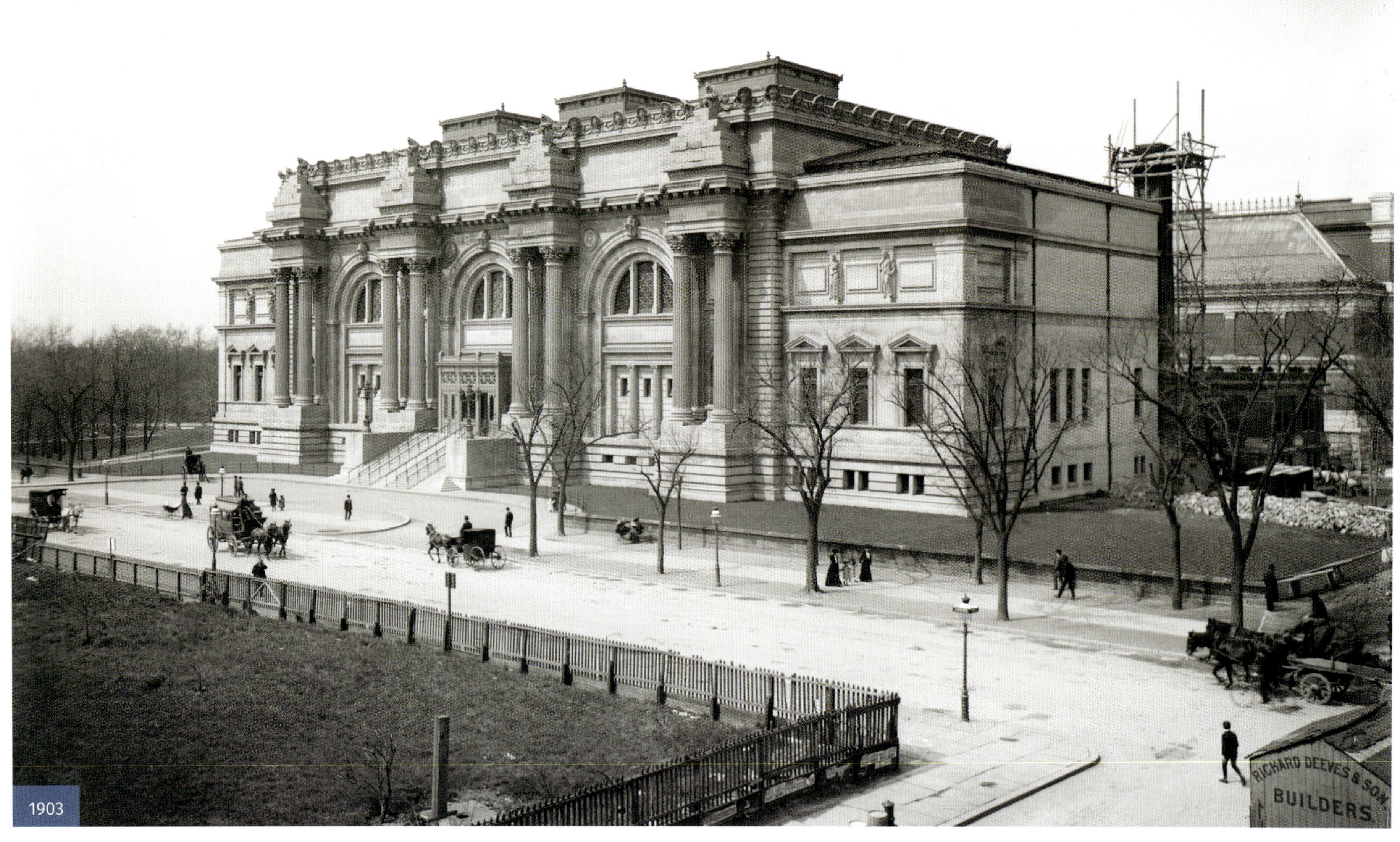

THE METROPOLITAN MUSEUM OF ART, NEW YORK

America needed a museum to rival the great institutions of Europe

The idea for "The Met" was born in 1866, when a group of Americans in Paris discussed the need for an art museum in the United States that could rival the great institutions of Europe. They believed that such a museum would serve to educate and inspire the American public. Upon returning to New York, these men, along with civic leaders, businessmen, artists, and philanthropists, began planning what would turn out to be The Met.

The Metropolitan Museum of Art was officially founded on April 13, 1870, by lawyer John Jay, publisher George Palmer Putnam, and railroad executive William T. Blodgett. The museum first opened its doors in February 1872 in a modest building at 681 Fifth Avenue, New York. At the time, its collection consisted of just a few dozen European paintings and a small quantity of decorative arts. Eight years later, in 1880, The Met moved to its current location in Central Park on Fifth Avenue and 82nd Street. The original red-brick structure, designed by architects Calvert Vaux and Jacob Wrey Mould, has since been vastly expanded into the monumental building we know today. Over the decades from 1880, The Met grew rapidly, thanks to strategic acquisitions, donations, and major benefactors such as J. P. Morgan, who served as board president in the early twentieth century and played a vital role in expanding the museum's holdings and international reputation.

The museum's vast and diverse collection is organized across numerous departments. Highlights include the Egyptian Art collection, with the iconic Temple

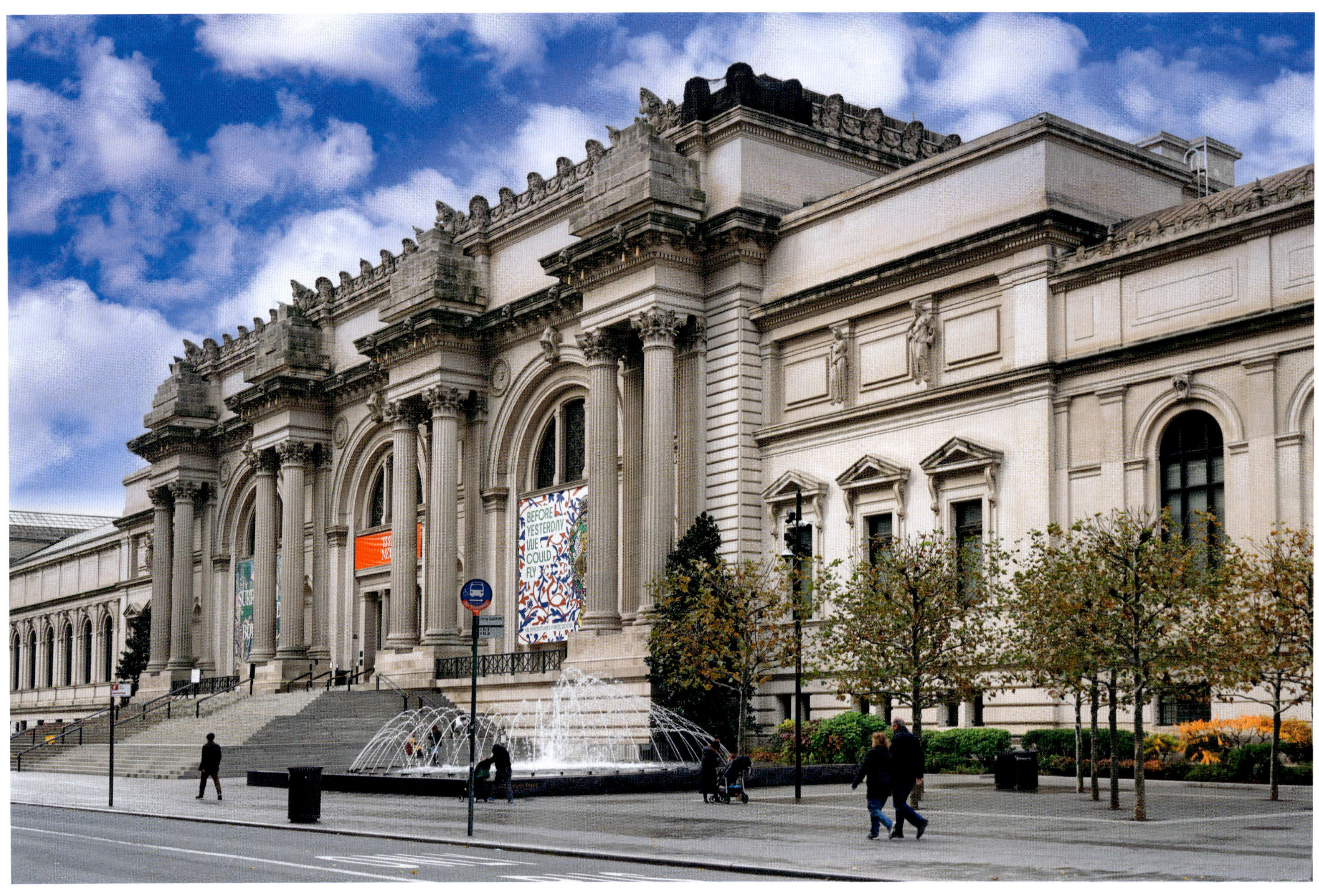

of Dendur (a gift from Egypt to the United States in 1965); the European Paintings wing, which features masterpieces by Rembrandt, Vermeer, Velázquez, Monet, and Van Gogh; and the American Wing, celebrating centuries of American art and design.

Today, The Met houses over two million works of art spanning 5,000 years of history, from ancient civilizations to contemporary art. Like all museums it only has a fraction of its collections on display. Highlight of the social calendar is the fundraising Met Gala, pioneered by Eleanor Lambert in 1948, where individual tickets cost $75,000 (2025)—and many of the stars attending pay even more for the carefully designed/assembled/curated outfits they arrive in.

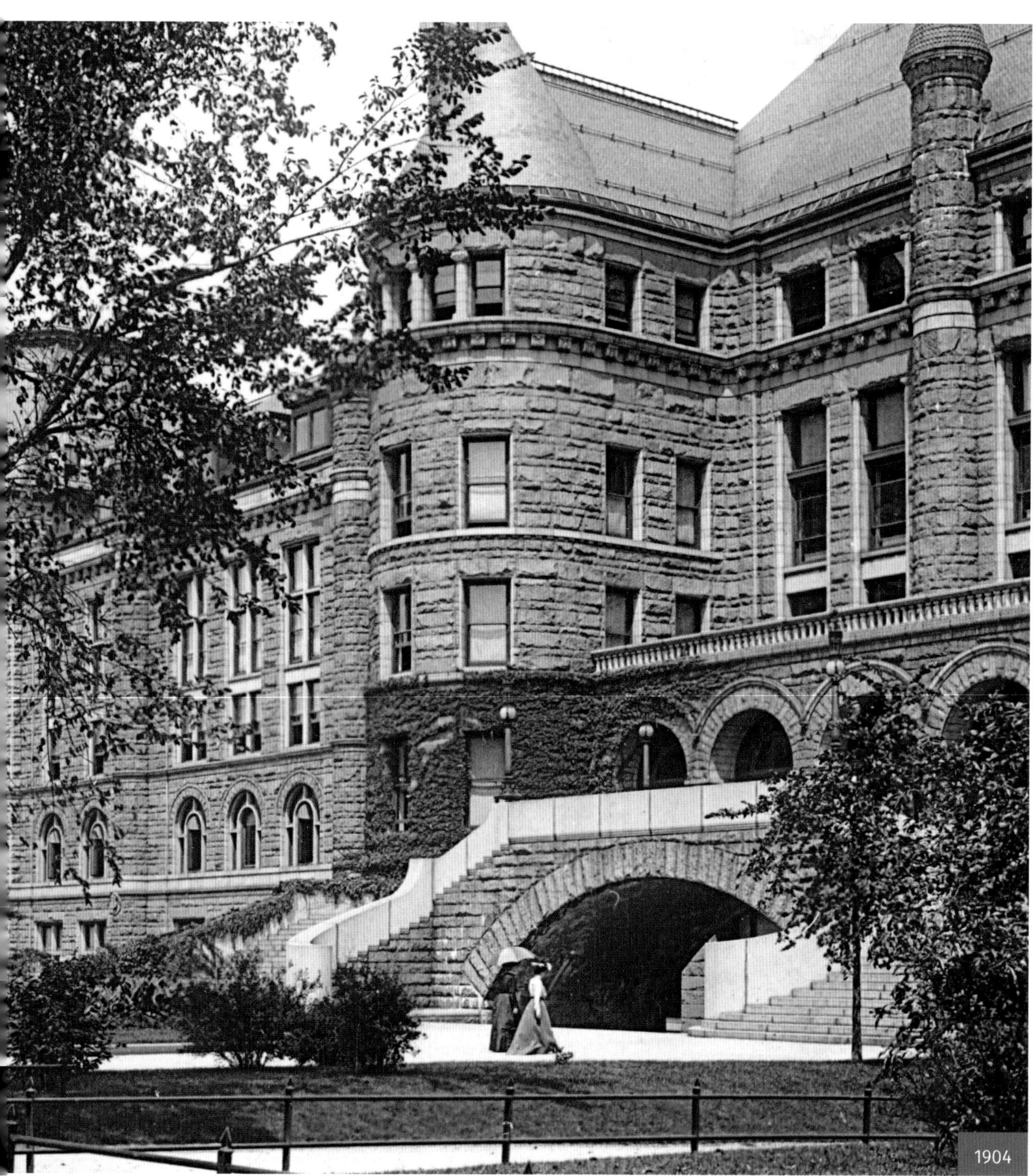
1904

NATURAL HISTORY MUSEUM, NEW YORK

The vision of naturalist and ardent beachcomber Albert Bickmore

The American Museum of Natural History (AMNH), located in New York City, is one of the most comprehensive museums of its kind in the world. It was the brainchild of naturalist Albert S. Bickmore who reportedly "grew up on the beach in Maine" collecting shells and sea urchins and noting the local flora and fauna. He devised the idea for the American Museum of Natural History in 1861 and spent almost a decade in advocacy for the project. The museum was officially founded in April 1869 with the support of prominent figures such as Theodore Roosevelt Sr., financier J. P. Morgan, and industrialist Morris K. Jesup.

The AMNH first opened in 1871, occupying a modest space in the Arsenal building in Central Park. However, its founders had grander aspirations, and in 1877, the museum moved to its present site across from Central Park on Manhattan's Upper West Side. The museum's first purpose-built structure in Theodore Roosevelt Park was designed by Calvert Vaux and Jacob Wrey Mould and opened on December 22, 1877. Numerous wings have been added over the years, including the main entrance pavilion in 1936 and the Rose Center for Earth and Space in 2000.

From its early days, the museum has sponsored significant scientific expeditions. One of the most famous was led by Roy Chapman Andrews to the Gobi Desert in the 1920s, which uncovered the first fossilized dinosaur eggs. A hallmark of the museum is its world-class fossil halls, featuring towering dinosaur skeletons like the *Tyrannosaurus rex* and *Barosaurus*, as well as an extensive collection of prehistoric life. The Rose Center for Earth and Space modernized the museum's reach into astronomy and planetary science, with its striking glass cube housing the Hayden Planetarium and extensive exhibits on cosmology.

Today, the AMNH welcomes over five million visitors per year, who wander in awe through its two million square feet of exhibition space.

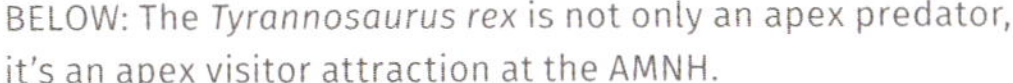

BELOW: The *Tyrannosaurus rex* is not only an apex predator, it's an apex visitor attraction at the AMNH.

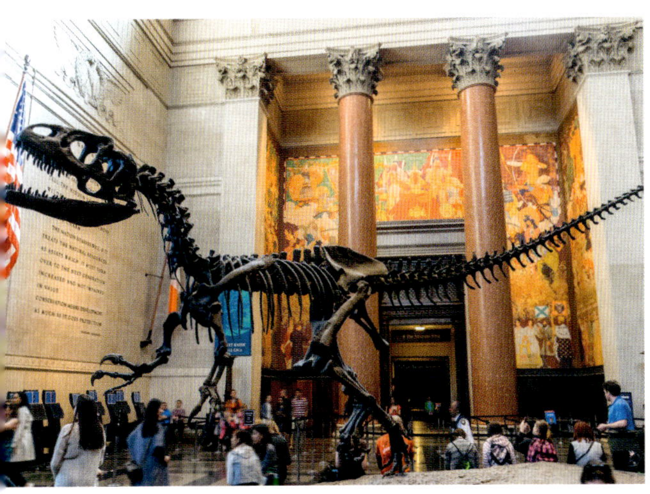

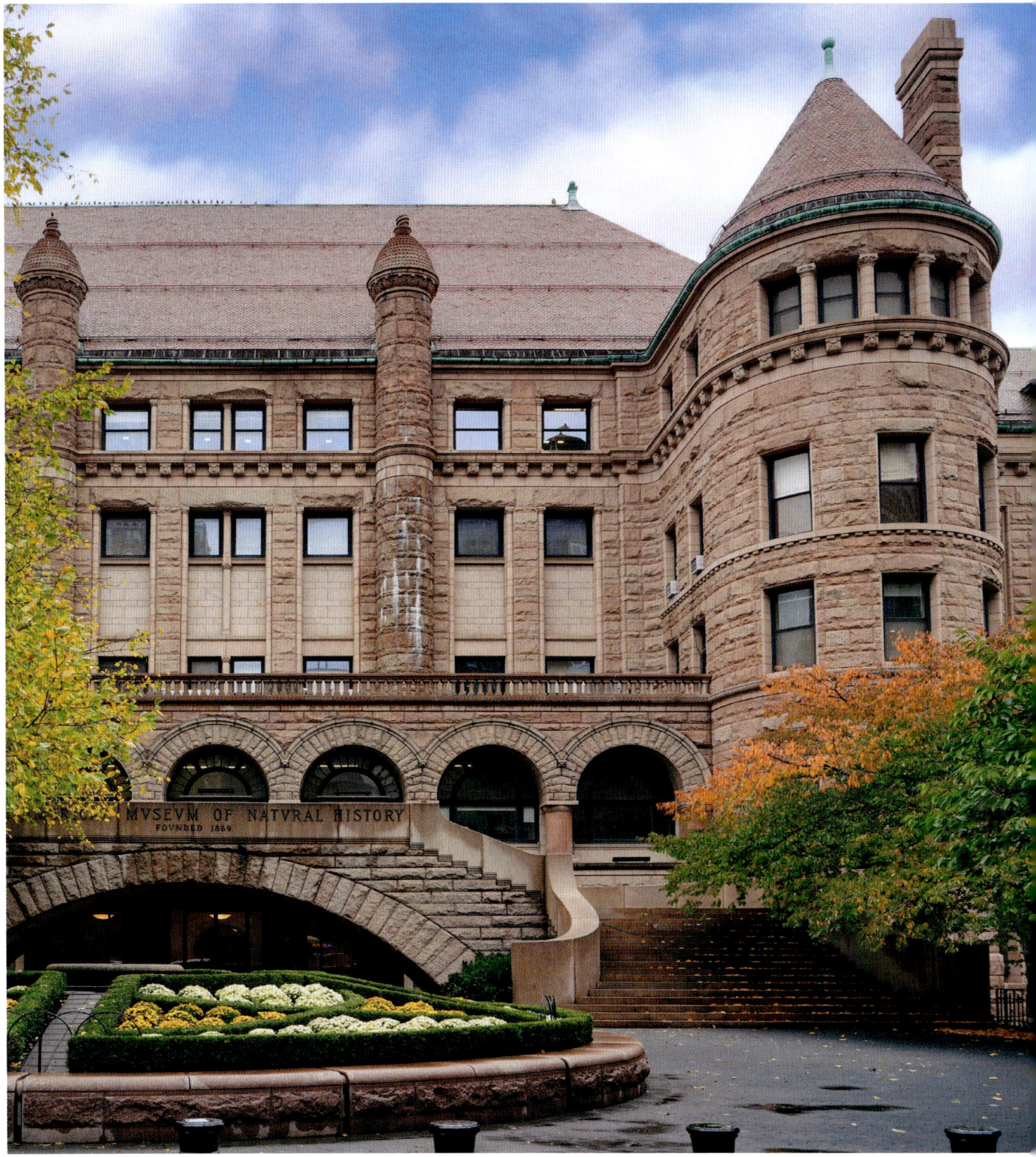

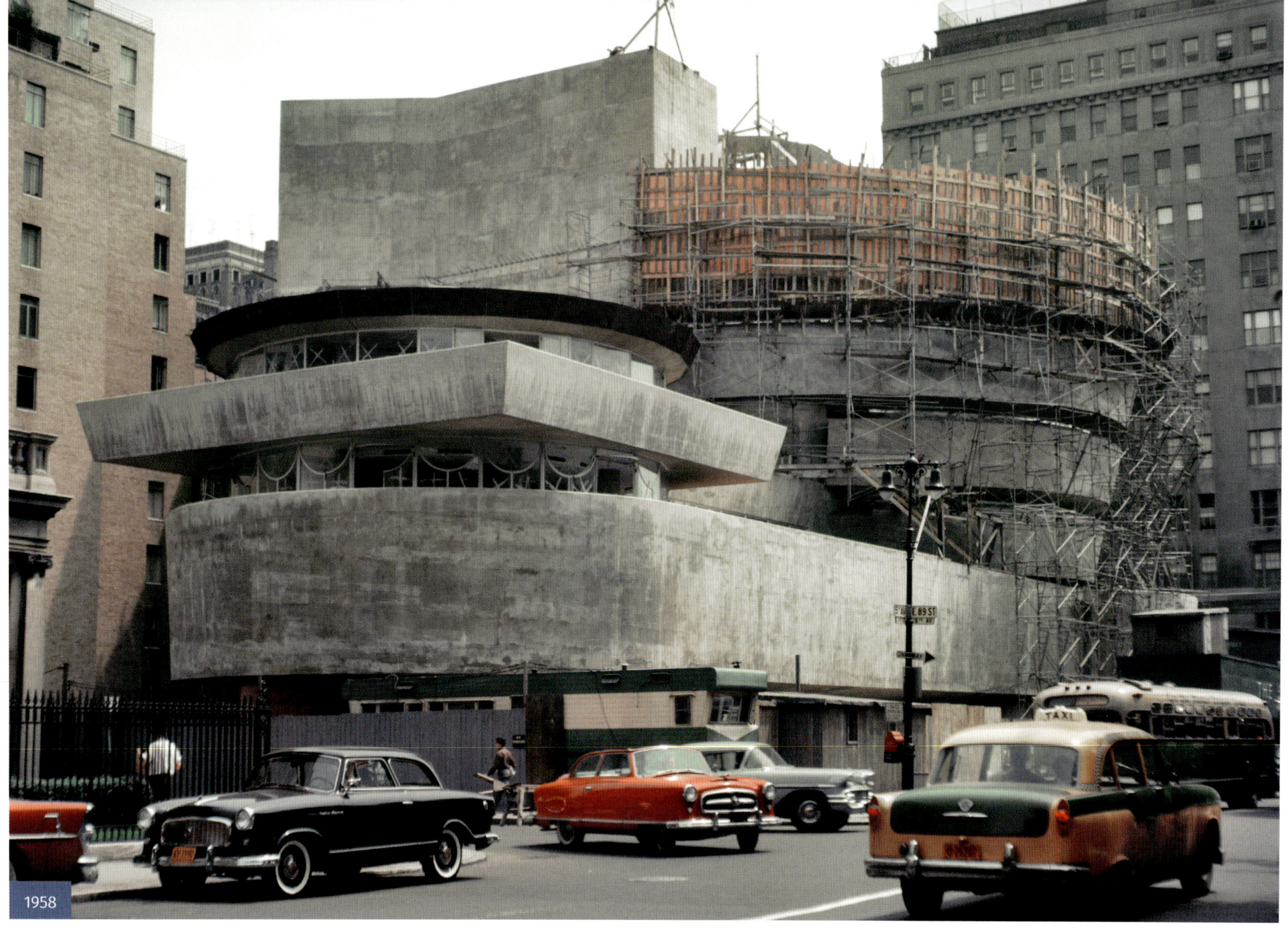

1958

SOLOMON R. GUGGENHEIM MUSEUM, NEW YORK

Frank Lloyd Wright's design posed some tricky questions for the curating staff

Solomon R. Guggenheim's wealth came from the gold-mining industry, which allowed him to start collecting art in the 1890s, and to concentrate on his passion full-time after World War I. Under the guidance of artist Baroness Hilla von Rebay he amassed a major collection of modernist paintings which at first were displayed at the Museum of Non-Objective Painting on East Fifty-fourth Street. By the 1940s the collection of avant-garde paintings was so large that in 1943 Guggenheim commissioned Frank Lloyd Wright to design a suitably modernist museum for the ever-expanding collection. Located at 1071 Fifth Avenue, on the corner of East Eighty-ninth Street, the landmark building split the opinion of critics from its opening in 1959. The cylindrical core of the museum building was wider at the top than the bottom, with a unique

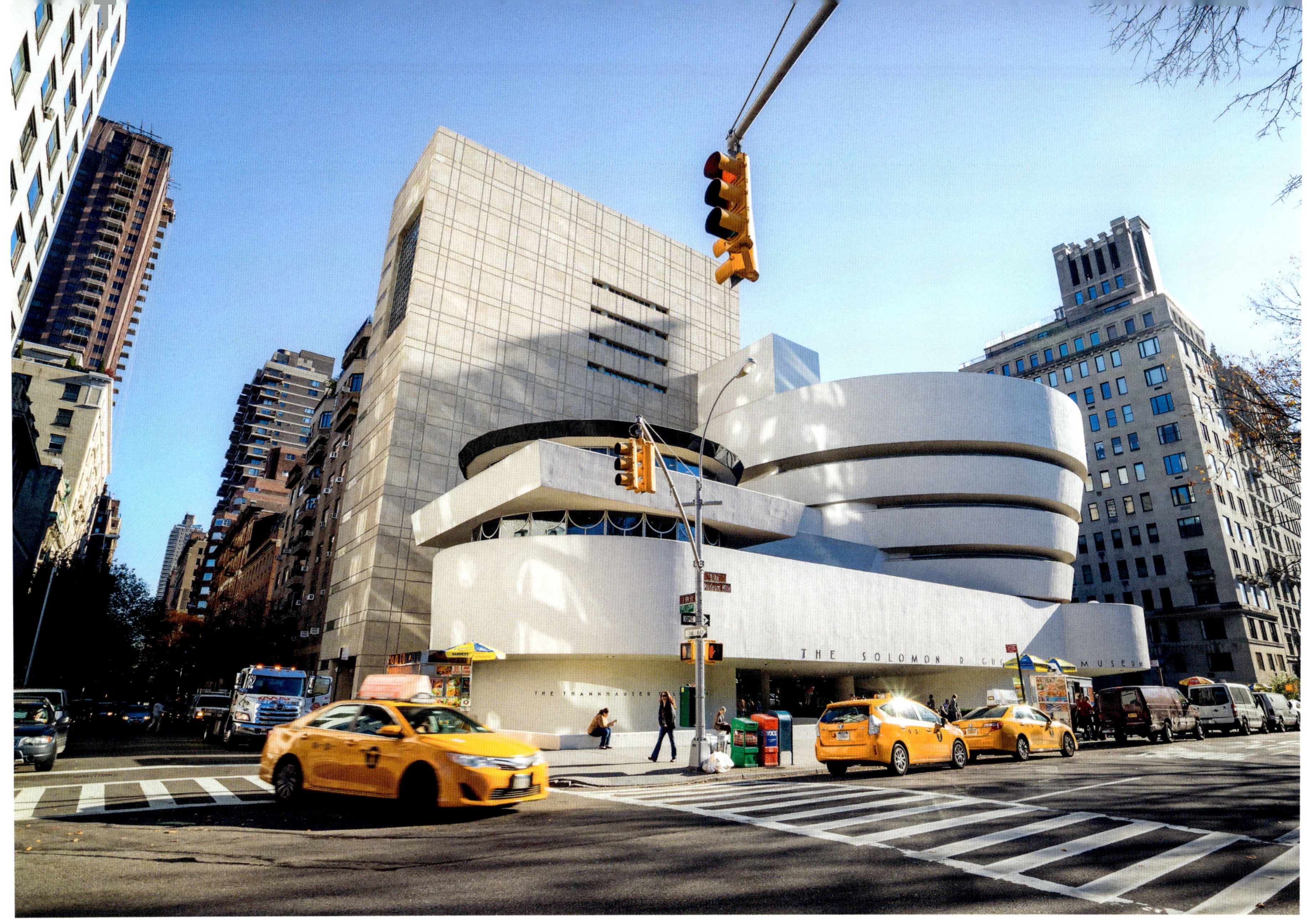

ramp gallery extending in a spiral, from ground level along the outer edges of the building to the widest point at the top. Wright's plan was for visitors to take the elevator to the top floor and descend the spiral at their leisure, viewing the installed pieces as they went.

Guggenheim died in 1949 and never got to see the building to which his name will always be attached. Frank Lloyd Wright died in the April before the museum opened in the October of 1959. Had they both lived, they might have been surprised at the vehement opposition expressed by some artists to the new gallery space. There was a great challenge in presenting art on non-vertical, curved walls with a floor that was tilting. A group of 21 artists signed a letter protesting the display of their work in such a space. However, gallery director Thomas M. Messer devised ways of displaying the art so that it wouldn't appear as though it were leaning backward, as though resting on an easel. A major expansion to the museum came in 1992 under the guiding hand of Thomas Krens, museum director from 1988 to 2008. The exhibition space was expanded considerably by the addition of an adjoining ten-story, limestone tower designed by Gwathmey Siegel & Associates, who consulted the original Frank Lloyd Wright sketches for the project. At the same time, the main gallery skylight, which had been obscured for years, was uncovered to recreate the natural lighting that Lloyd Wright had intended. The Guggenheim, with over a million visitors annually, continues to be one of New York's most visited attractions.

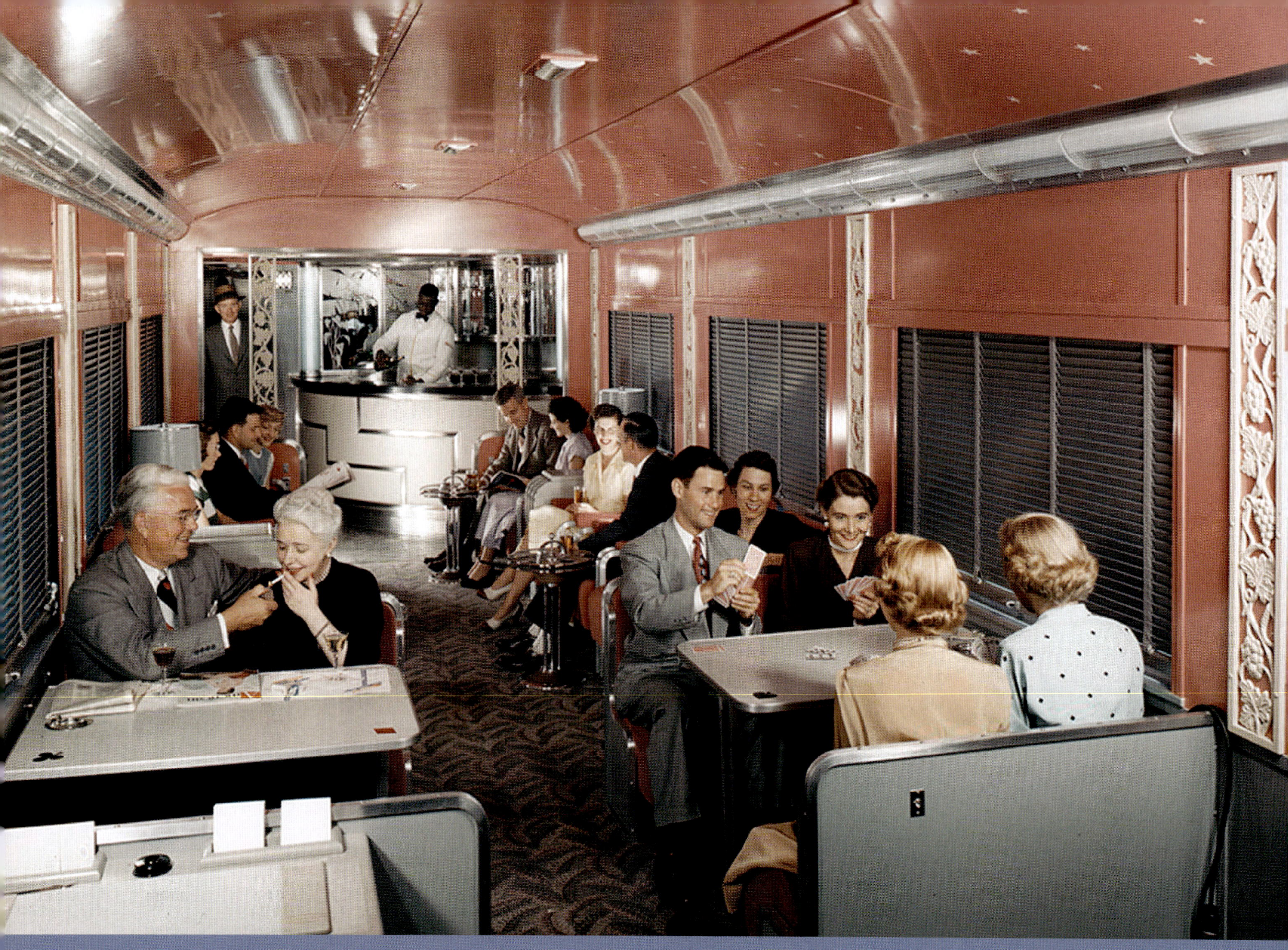

ON THE MOVE: AMERICA'S REVOLUTION IN TRANSPORT

The twentieth century saw the United States transform from a rail-bound continental power into the global leader of aerial and extraterrestrial transportation. In little more than a lifetime, Americans went from boarding steam trains and ocean liners to driving automobiles, flying across the world in hours, and launching astronauts into orbit.

THE GOLDEN AGE OF RAIL AND ITS ECLIPSE

At the dawn of the twentieth century, railroads were the arteries of America. Thousands of miles of track stitched the country together, enabling the movement of goods and people. Major cities owed their growth to rail hubs, and luxurious long-distance trains—like the Twentieth Century Limited, the Super Chief, and the Southern Pacific Railroad's Sunset Limited (pictured left)—offered elegant travel with dining cars and sleepers. Yet, by mid-century, their dominance began to wane.

The reasons were many: automobiles moved beyond the "boneshaker" models into sedans in which long journeys could be accomplished in relative comfort. Motels and Auto Courts sprung up along popular, long-distance routes to cater for "tin can tourists." In the 1950s, the construction of the Interstate Highway System under President Dwight D. Eisenhower fundamentally altered American habits. By the 1970s, private passenger rail was no longer profitable, leading to the creation of Amtrak in 1971, a government-run effort to preserve intercity passenger services. The Sunset Limited, run between New Orleans and Los Angeles is the country's longest-running scheduled service and is one of the last vestiges of the Golden Age.

Freight rail has remained strong, but the age of the train as the primary passenger mover in America had come to an end. The automobile had embedded itself in the American psyche as a vehicle of autonomy, innovation, and identity—and it remains there today.

THE DEATH OF THE OCEAN LINER

For much of the early twentieth century, transatlantic travel meant taking a ship. Ocean liners like the RMS *Lusitania*, RMS *Queen Mary*, and SS *United States* were floating cities—symbols of national pride, technological prowess, and luxury. Immigrants arrived in steerage aboard liners while the wealthy traveled in opulent first-class cabins.

But the jet age killed the liner. After World War II, advancements in aviation and the introduction of long-range passenger planes made it possible to fly from New York to London in a matter of hours. By the 1960s, commercial airlines had displaced ships as the dominant form of transatlantic travel. The once glorious liners were scrapped, turned into museums, or converted into cruise ships. What had been a symbol of luxury faded into nostalgia and Manhattan's shipping piers sought new occupations.

THE AGE OF AVIATION

America's leadership in aviation began in a humble bicycle shop in Dayton, Ohio. In 1903, the Wright brothers made the first powered flight in Kitty Hawk, North Carolina—a brief, airborne flirtation that nonetheless changed history.

By World War I, aircraft had become tools of reconnaissance and combat. Between the wars, daring pilots like Charles Lindbergh and Amelia Earhart crossed the Atlantic solo, with the latter's disappearance most keenly felt. Airlines like Pan American and TWA emerged in the 1930s and 1940s, connecting cities and continents. Any aspiring US city needed to have its own airport and Fiorello LaGuardia made sure New York didn't lose out.

World War II accelerated aviation technology. Postwar, veterans brought skills and expectations that propelled commercial flight into the mainstream. The introduction of jet airliners, beginning with the Boeing 707 in 1958, dramatically reduced travel time and helped boost aircraft production. Soon, American aerospace companies like Boeing, Lockheed, and McDonnell Douglas led the global market. Aviation reshaped business, warfare, and leisure, while shrinking the world in practical terms.

THE RACE TO SPACE

The most dramatic transportation frontier of the twentieth century was outer space. After World War II, the Cold War fueled a new kind of competition: not for land or seas, but for the cosmos.

In 1957, the Soviet Union launched Sputnik, the first artificial satellite. A startled America responded with urgency, founding NASA (National Aeronautics and Space Administration) in 1958. A decade of rapid development followed, culminating in 1969 when Neil Armstrong became the first human to walk on the Moon, during the Apollo 11 mission. His words—"That's one small step for man, one giant leap for mankind"—marked the height of American space dominance.

The Saturn V rocket, one of the most powerful machines ever built, carried humans beyond Earth's orbit. Satellites improved global communication, weather forecasting, and navigation. The Space Shuttle program, beginning in 1981, aimed to make space travel more routine, with reusable vehicles.

Whether on roads, in the skies, or among the stars, American transportation shaped a modern world where distance became less of a barrier to overcome. As the twentieth century closed, America stood as the country that had invented not just new ways to move—but the prime force in space exploration.

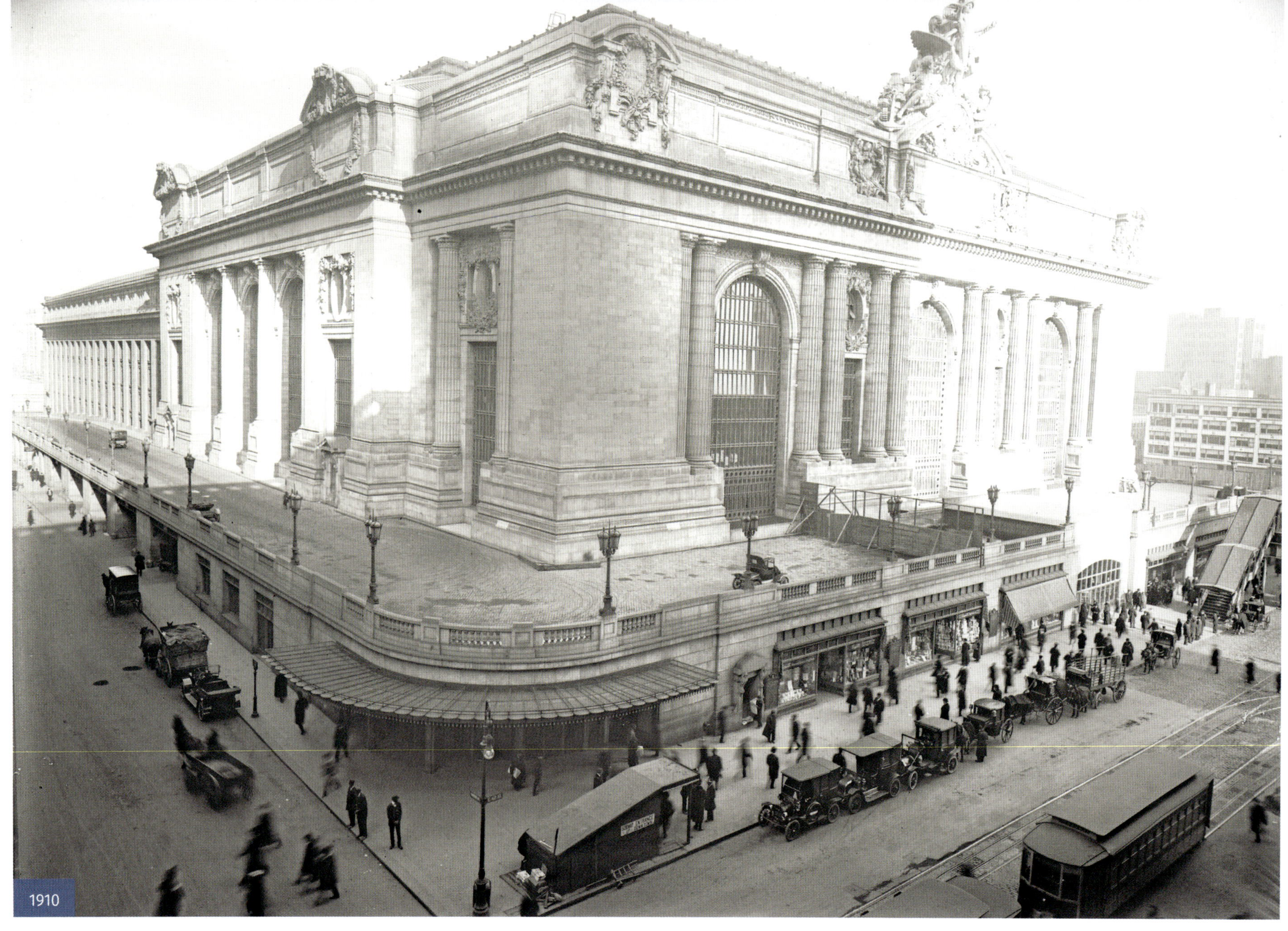

1910

GRAND CENTRAL STATION, NEW YORK

Resisting the fate that befell Penn Station, Grand Central is a top tourist destination

Elevated on a platform above Park Avenue with a triple-arched facade, Grand Central Terminal was built as a gateway to New York City. Completed in 1913, it replaced the first Grand Central Depot of 1871, when that street was at the northern end of the city. The new terminal, the crowning glory of Cornelius Vanderbilt's New York Central Railroad, brought several railroad lines together under one roof and spearheaded the city's expansion beyond Forty-second Street. Next door was the Commodore Hotel, built by Vanderbilt in 1919, who was known as the "Commodore" from his first career in shipping lines. The hotel was part of Terminal City, a complex of hotels and office buildings developed by the railroad and connected by underground passageways to Grand Central.

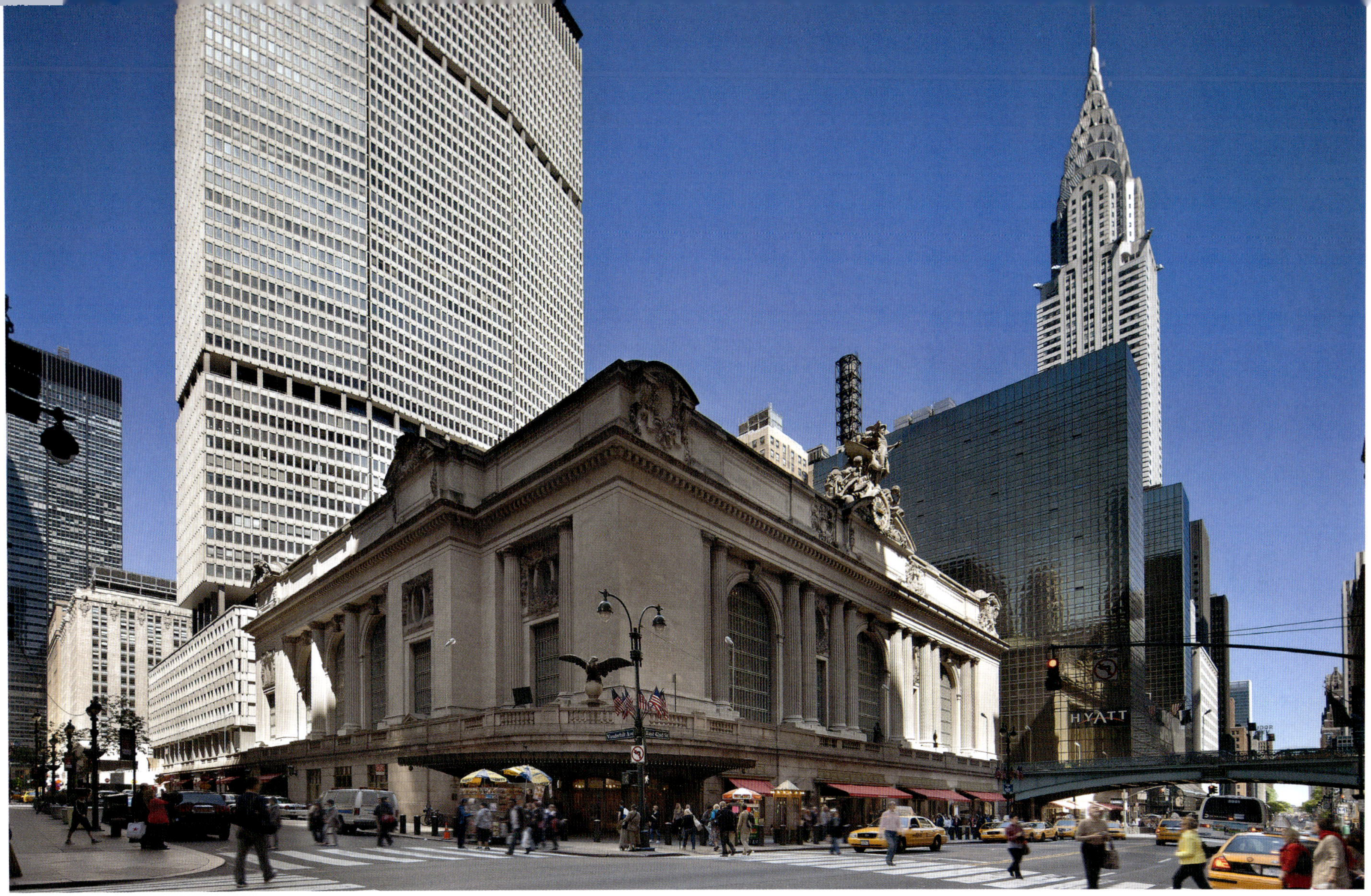

Over the years, Grand Central Terminal was surrounded by much taller buildings. Behind it is a glass slab built in the 1960s, the Pan Am Building, now renamed the Met Life Building. Critics called it "a monstrous bland blanket." In the late 1970s, the railroad and the Commodore Hotel were on the brink of bankruptcy. Donald Trump bought the hotel and reopened it as the glass-sheathed Grand Hyatt in 1980.

The main concourse is a glorious space today, thanks to a decades-long preservation battle that saved the terminal from destruction. With train service declining in the 1950s, the ceiling lights of the zodiac went out, grime stained the stone columns, and a giant screen advertising Kodak film covered the wall of grand windows. At first, the railroad tried to demolish the terminal, and when that failed, tried to build a skyscraper on top of it that would have pierced this room with steel columns. In 1978, after years of lawsuits, the US Supreme Court upheld the terminal's landmark protection. Twenty years later, the Kodak screen finally came down, a marble staircase went up in its place, the cerulean blue ceiling was cleaned and its stars were lit once again. Filled with bustling shops and restaurants, the concourse is now a vibrant place for tens of thousands of commuters and tourists.

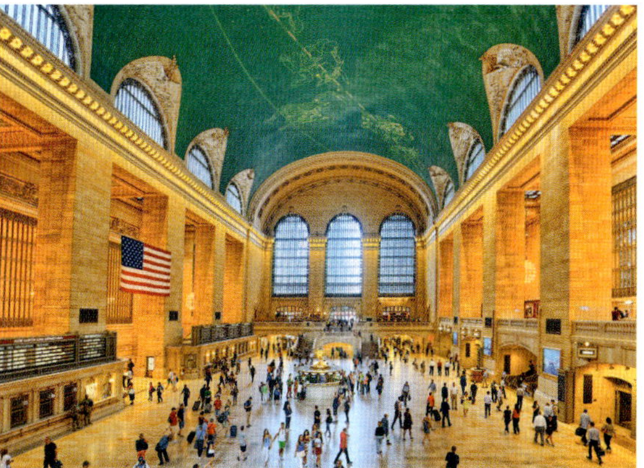

UNION STATION, HOUSTON

Houston's Union Station building survived, but the trains have departed

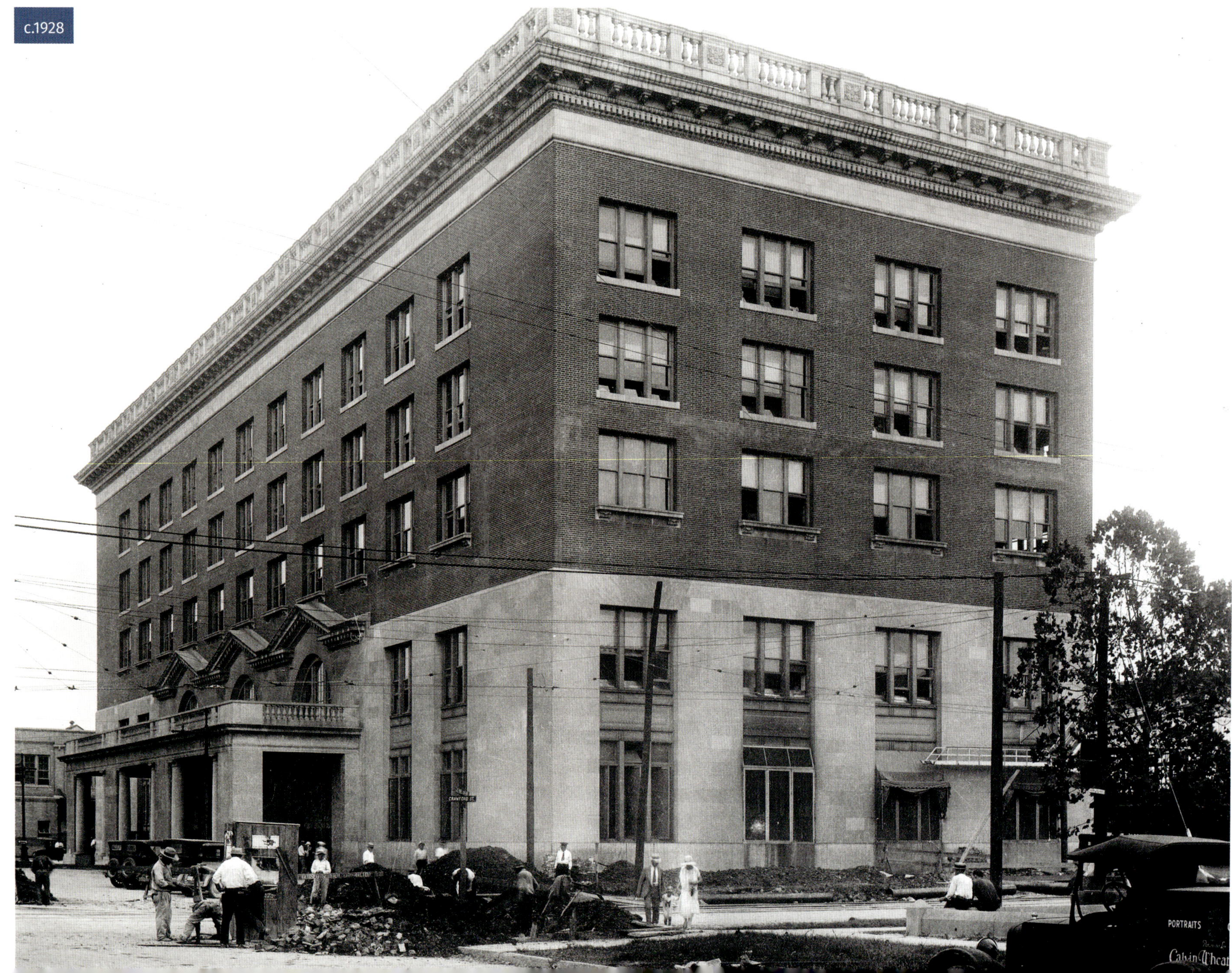

c.1928

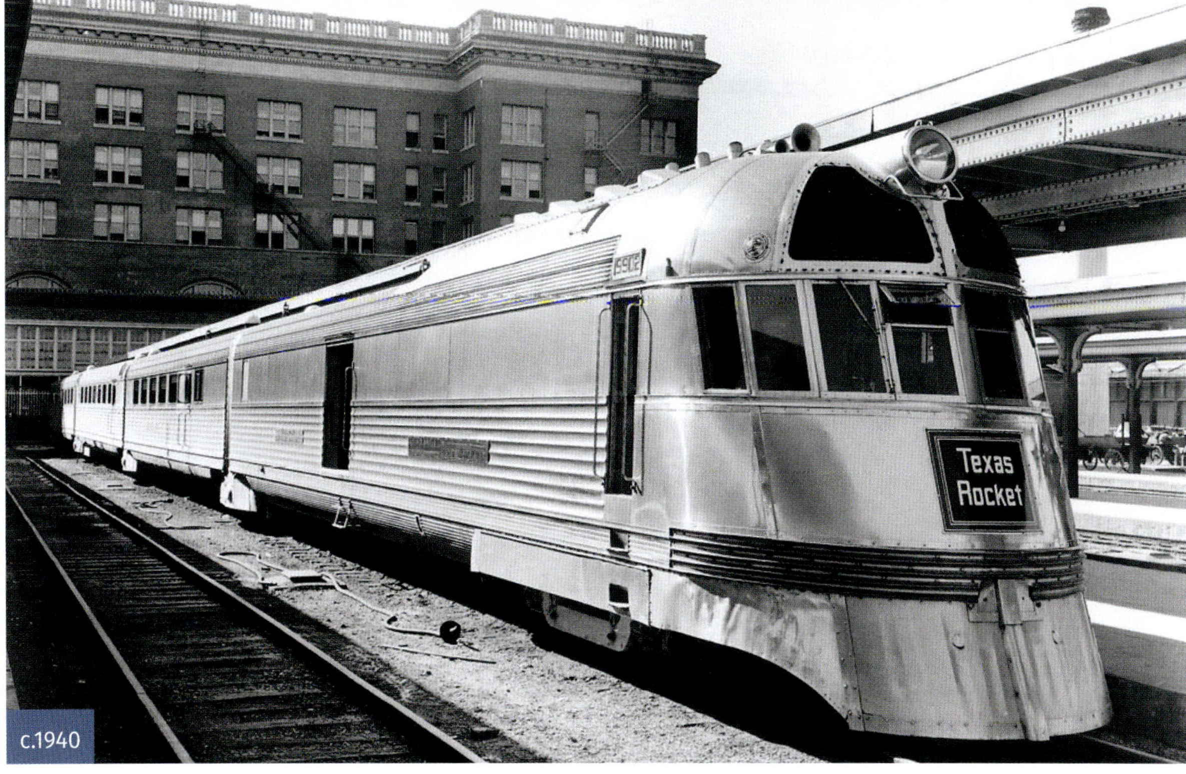

c.1940

LEFT: The *Texas Rocket*, owned by the Burlington-Rock Island Railroad ran between Dallas and Houston from the late 1930s. Its counterpart, the Sam Houston Zephyr, also covered that route.

The heart of Houston transportation for generations, Union Station was built in 1911 at Crawford Street and Texas Avenue. The grand, three-story train station was designed by the architectural firm of Warren & Wetmore (who also designed the Grand Central Terminal and the Ritz-Carlton in New York City). Union Station was part of a $5 million downtown train terminal and warehouse complex that brought together multiple railways via thirteen tracks. The building boasted a main hall with grand columns and arches featuring a lunch counter and the Harvey House dining room—an upscale franchise restaurant throughout the West, where gentlemen were required to wear jacket and tie. Harvey House served the original "blue plate special," served on a blue china plate. As Houston grew, the building saw more traffic, and more floors were added later too.

The shiny futuristic train (inset) was the *Texas Rocket*, which ran from Houston to Fort Worth from 1937 to 1945. The Rockets have departed, but the Astros have since arrived to take their place. Throughout the United States, passenger rail declined in the late 1960s and early 1970s. Union Stations across the country were closed, diminished or repurposed, and Houston couldn't buck the trend: in the mid-1970s, it halted services, and remaining industrial rail service trickled off to other random connections. Abandoned in a now underdeveloped section of east downtown Houston, it seemed doomed. What would save it? Of all things: baseball. The Houston Astros had been shopping for a new venue—and decided it would be a good idea to build on the old Union Station. The result was a beautiful restoration and reconstruction; the Astros made the old train station part of their new ballpark. In 2000 it was christened Enron Field after its primary corporate sponsor. Following the high-profile and scandalous derailment of Enron, the stadium was rededicated as Minute Maid Park.

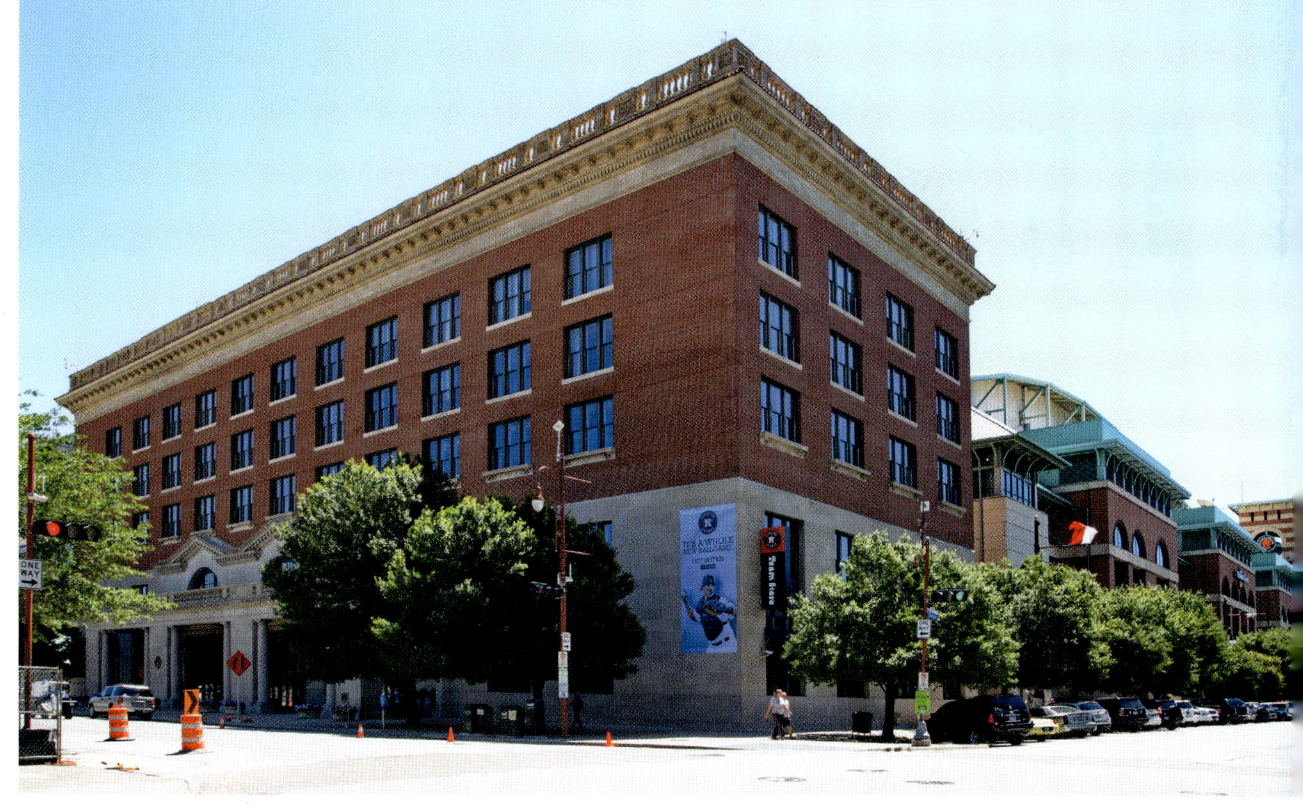

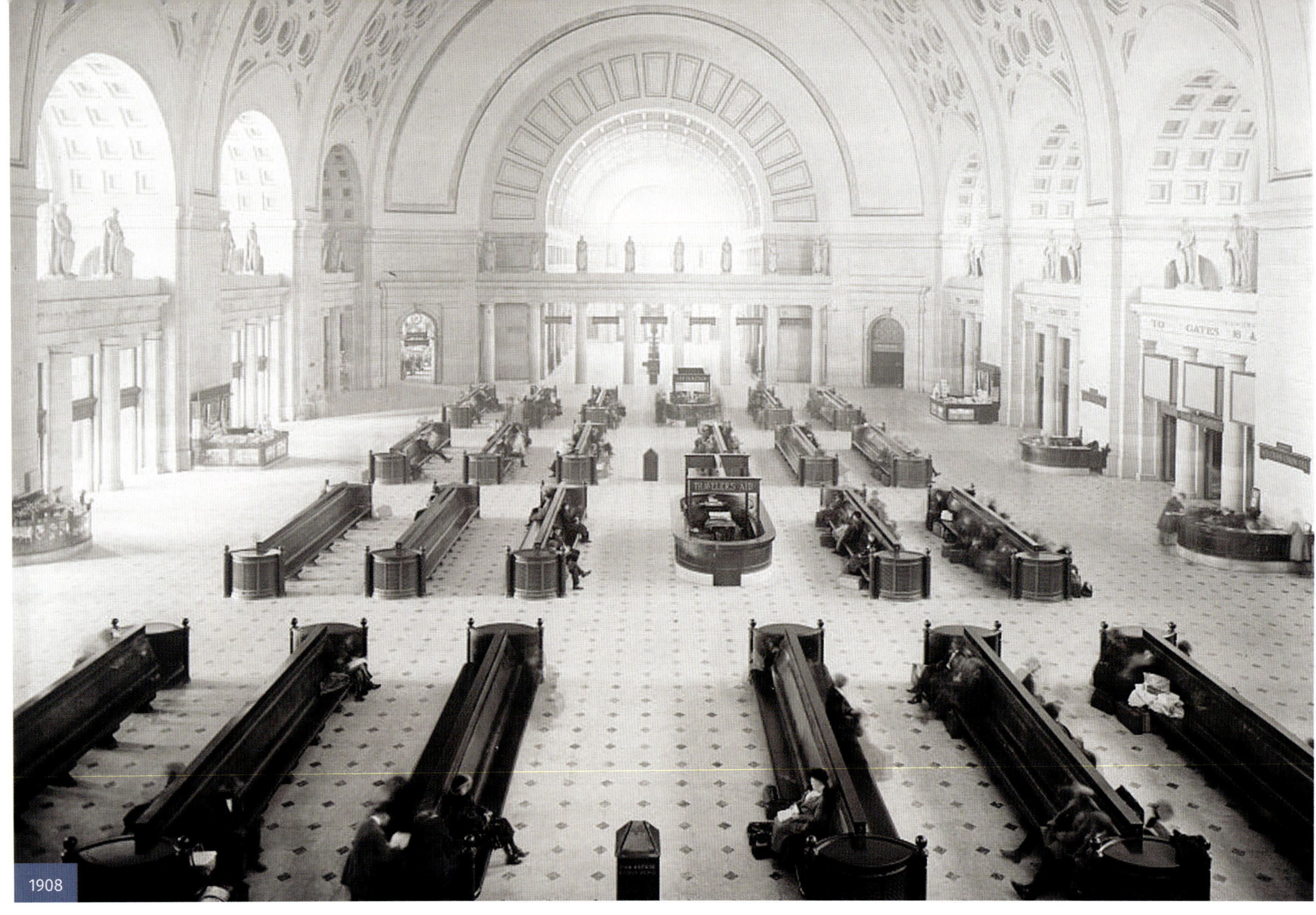

1908

UNION STATION, WASHINGTON, DC

One of the great cathedrals of American transport

Since 1853 different railroad stations had surrounded downtown Washington, servicing multiple railroad companies. In 1903, work began on architect Daniel Burnham's central station. The structure was built on the edge of Swampoodle, a former Washington neighborhood largely populated by Irish and Italian immigrants who were responsible for the building's construction. On October 27, 1907, the last train left the old B&O terminal, and just a few hours later arrived as the first train in Union Station. With its inclusion of different railroad companies, Union Station was the ideal center point for all involved. The station was an immediate success and by 1928 a train arrived or departed from the station every five minutes, with tens of thousands of passengers commuting through it. During World War II the station was the area's primary place of departure.

Designed with the classical architecture of the ancient Greeks and Romans in mind, the building was grand, with a waiting room (pictured above) that the Washington Monument could fit in if laid on its side. The statues were completed in Beaux-arts

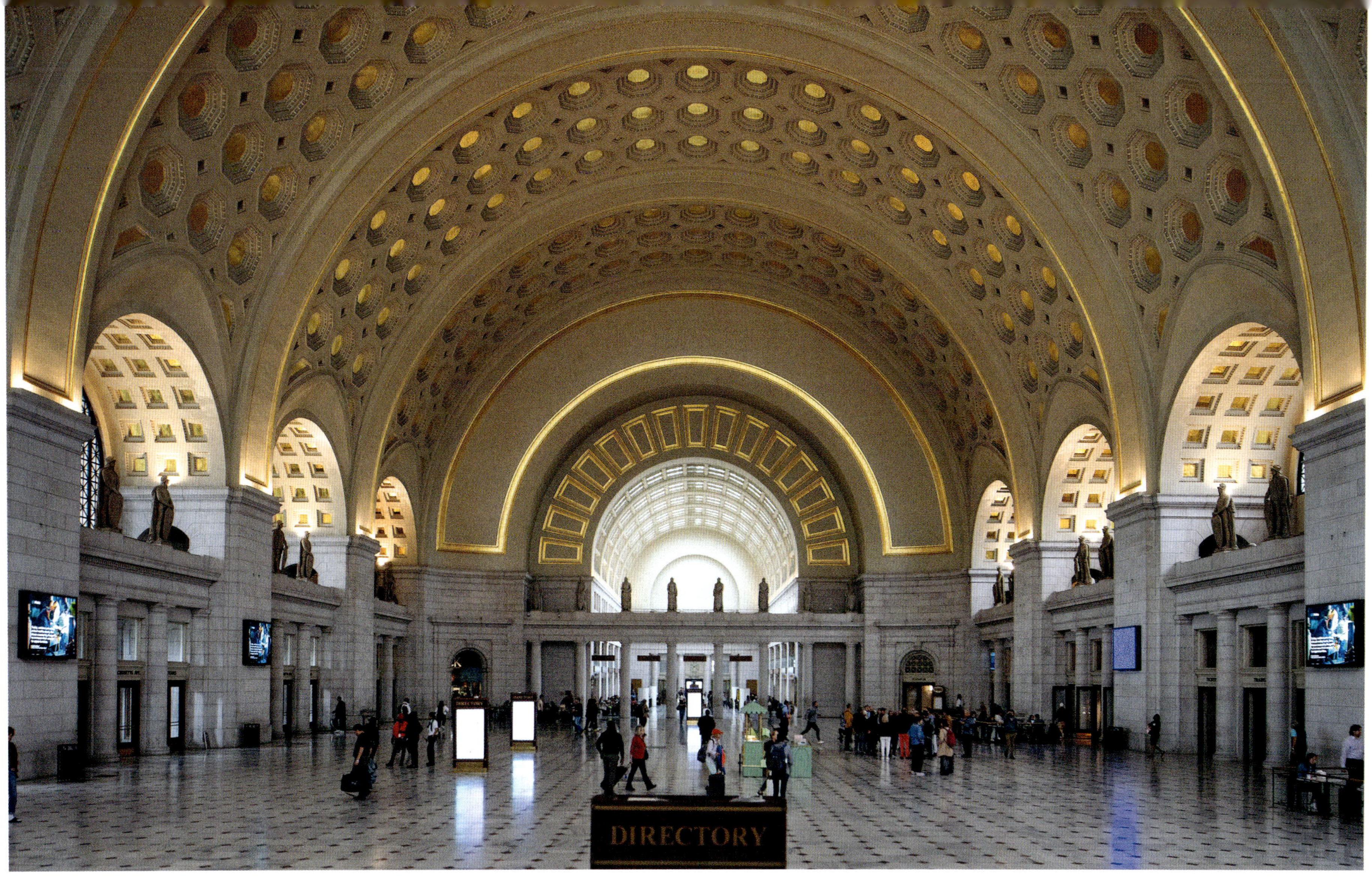

style by artist Louis Saint-Gaudens. The station housed restaurants and stores for those waiting to transfer trains, and for locals coming to cool off during one of DC's brutally hot summers. The train and station employees worked around the clock hauling luggage or managing shops to support the bustling station and patrons from all walks of life. Visitors included foreign political leaders, such as Winston Churchill and Nikita Khrushchev, as well as political actors and domestic tourists.

By the 1960s, owing to a drop in revenue from $80,000 a day to less than $30,000, decreased train arrivals and departures, and a near fatal runaway car that crashed into the station, the station no longer resembled the gateway to Washington it was intended to be. Through the late 1960s and into the 1970s, the station was converted into the National Visitor Center for the Bicentennial of America in 1976, although on completion it was unpopular. The station's need for purpose was not its only struggle: the structure itself faced challenges. In 1977 the building was headed for major structural collapse.

Union Station finally closed, although many believed it still had a future in Washington, DC. Among those who believed in Union Station's future was the United States Congress. In 1981, Congress passed the Union Station Redevelopment Act of 1981, amending the Act that established the National Visitor Center and restored the building back to its original purpose. With the support of Amtrak, the station reopened in 1988 with three levels of retail space, a connected bus terminal, and an Amtrak terminal that was structured behind the original concourse. Restorations of the original statues and other interior design elements were also completed.

Since the station has reopened, the Union Station Plaza has greeted locals and visitors traveling to and from the nation's capital. While Union Station has faced hard times since its reopening, the resilience of Washington's grand railroad station continues to impress.

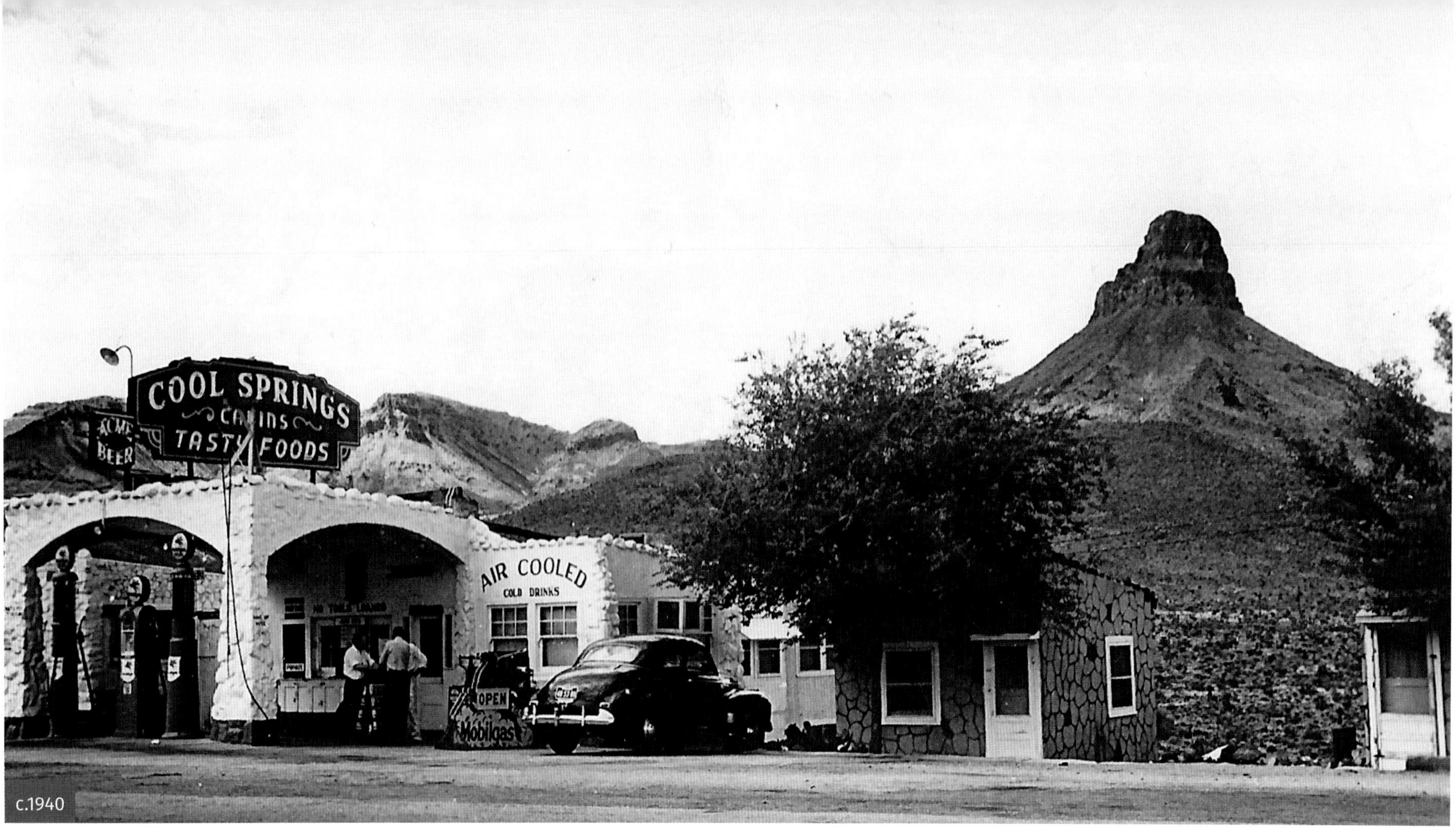

c.1940

ROUTE 66, ARIZONA

Historic Route 66 was brought back to life by an Arizona barber

US Route 66, or the "Mother Road," is the most famous American highway. Established on November 11, 1926, Route 66 originally stretched approximately 2,448 miles from Chicago, Illinois, to Santa Monica, California, passing through eight states: Illinois, Missouri, Kansas, Oklahoma, Texas, New Mexico, Arizona, and California. During the Great Depression in the 1930s, thousands of families, particularly from the Dust Bowl-ravaged Midwest, used Route 66 to head west in search of a better life in California. John Steinbeck famously charted the misery of a migrant family in his novel *The Grapes of Wrath*. Over the decades, Route 66 facilitated tourism, wartime transportation, and postwar road trips.

The development of the Interstate Highway System in the 1950s and 60s, especially the construction of I-40, led to Route 66's gradual decline. Towns that once thrived on the constant flow of travelers saw traffic diverted, leading to economic stagnation, and in some cases near-abandonment (McLean, Texas). By 1985, Route 66 was officially decommissioned by the federal government, erasing it from highway maps.

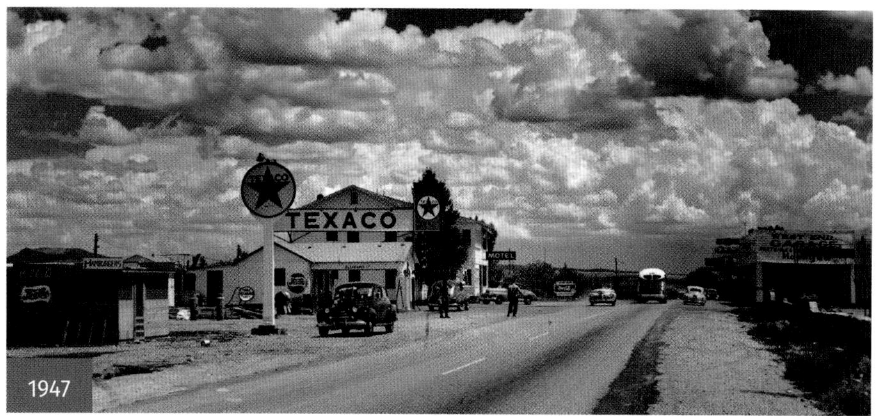

1947

ABOVE: A famous *Life* magazine photo of a hitcher in Seligman. The road was widened to a four-lane highway before it was abandoned to I-40. All the structures in the vintage photo have gone, replaced on the left by Roadkill 66 Cafe, whose motto is: "You Kill It, We'll Grill It."

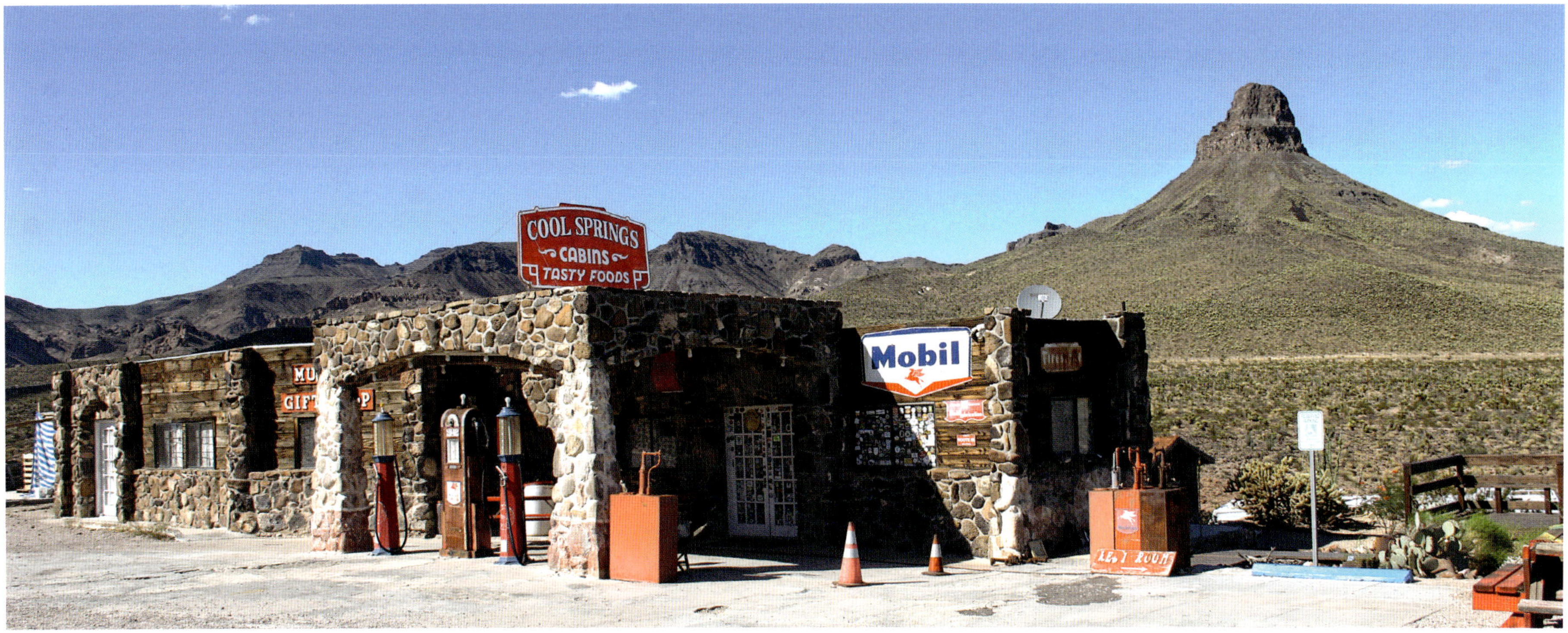

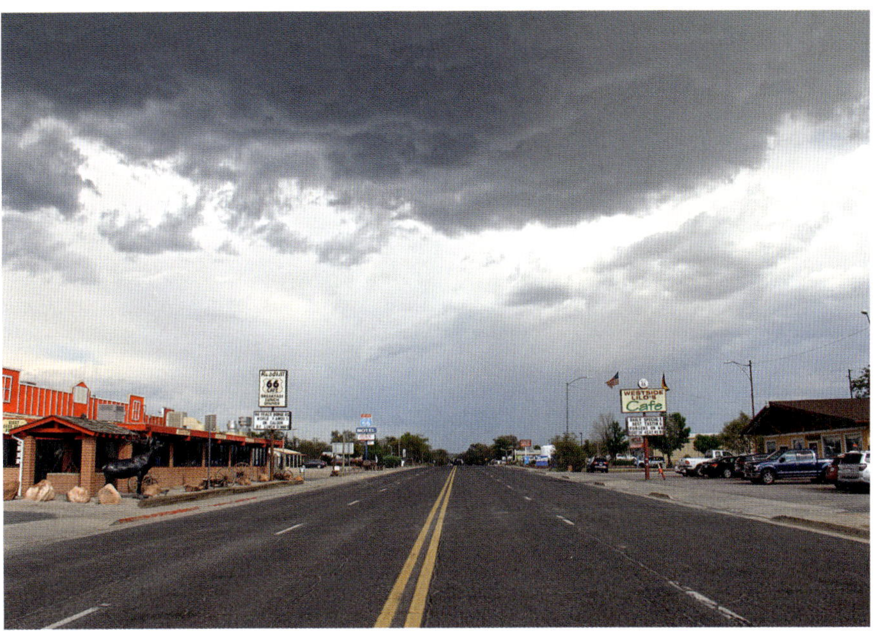

However, one small town in Arizona—Seligman—would become the center of a grassroots movement to preserve the spirit of Route 66, largely thanks to the passion and determination of Angel Delgadillo. Born in Seligman in 1927, Angel Delgadillo was a local barber and business owner who had witnessed the rise and fall of Route 66 at first hand. When Seligman was bypassed in 1978, it suffered tremendously, like many other towns along the route, with all the passing trade vanishing overnight.

Refusing to accept this fate, Angel became a tireless advocate for preserving the legacy of Route 66. In 1987, he founded the Historic Route 66 Association of Arizona, the first organization of its kind dedicated to promoting the cultural significance of the highway. The association successfully lobbied for the state of Arizona to designate Route 66 as a historic highway, setting a precedent that other states would follow.

Angel's barbershop in Seligman transformed into an unofficial visitor center, museum and gathering place for Route 66 enthusiasts from around the world. Thanks to Delgadillo's efforts, Seligman became a must-stop destination for Historic Route 66 road trippers. Delgadillo's legacy even inspired elements of the animated film *Cars* (2006), in which the fictional town of Radiator Springs parallels the real-life story of Seligman. Today, Route 66 lives on as a symbol of Americana, a small slice of twentieth-century history celebrated in road trips from the Chicago lakefront to Santa Monica Pier, with some beautifully preserved gas stations (such as Cool Springs above) along the route.

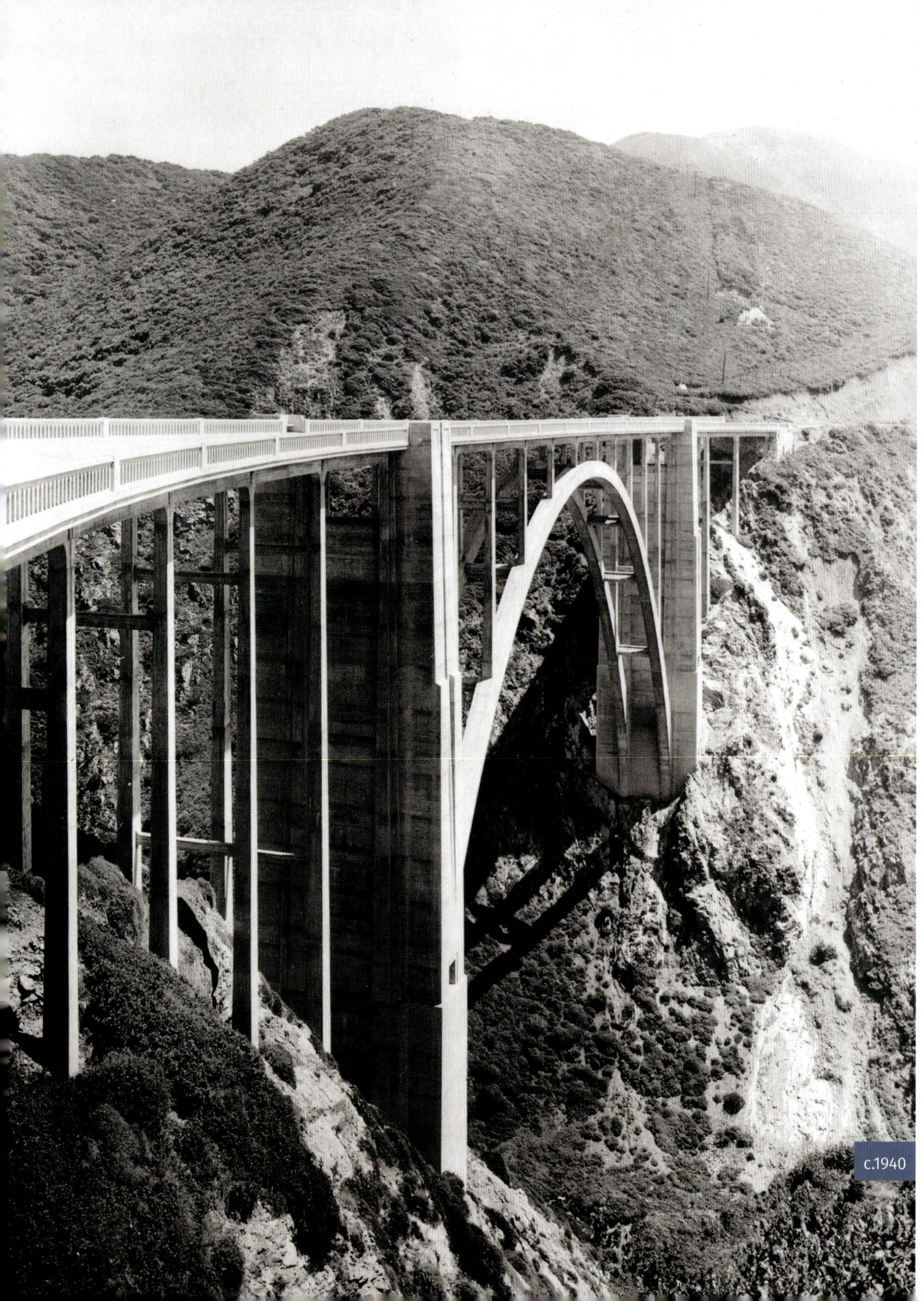

c.1940

PACIFIC COAST HIGHWAY, CALIFORNIA

One of America's most celebrated scenic roads—that demands a convertible

The Pacific Coast Highway (PCH), officially designated as California State Route 1 (SR 1), is a north–south highway that runs along most of the Pacific coastline of California. It spans approximately 656 miles from Dana Point in Orange County to Leggett in Mendocino County, where it terminates at US Route 101. The highway was established in 1934, but construction began in earnest in the early twentieth century, with funding and labor coming later from New Deal programs such as the Works Progress Administration (WPA). One of the most significant and challenging segments is the route through Big Sur, completed in 1937. This section required extensive engineering work due to the rugged terrain.

The Bixby Creek Bridge, completed in 1932, is one of the most famous structures on the PCH. Located in Monterey County, it spans 714 feet across Bixby Creek. Built with reinforced concrete, the bridge allowed uninterrupted travel along the Big Sur coast and remains one of the most photographed bridges in California due to its dramatic coastal backdrop.

The PCH has faced recurring challenges from natural disasters. Landslides, particularly in Big Sur, have repeatedly damaged and closed parts of the highway. The Mud Creek Slide in 2017 buried a quarter mile of the highway under millions of tons of earth, closing the road for over a year and costing more than $54 million to repair.

The 2025 Palisades Fire significantly impacted the PCH in Malibu, causing extensive damage and disruptions. The wildfire, which ignited on January 7, 2025, and was only fully contained on January 31, scorched over 23,700 acres and destroyed more than 6,800 structures across Pacific Palisades, Topanga,

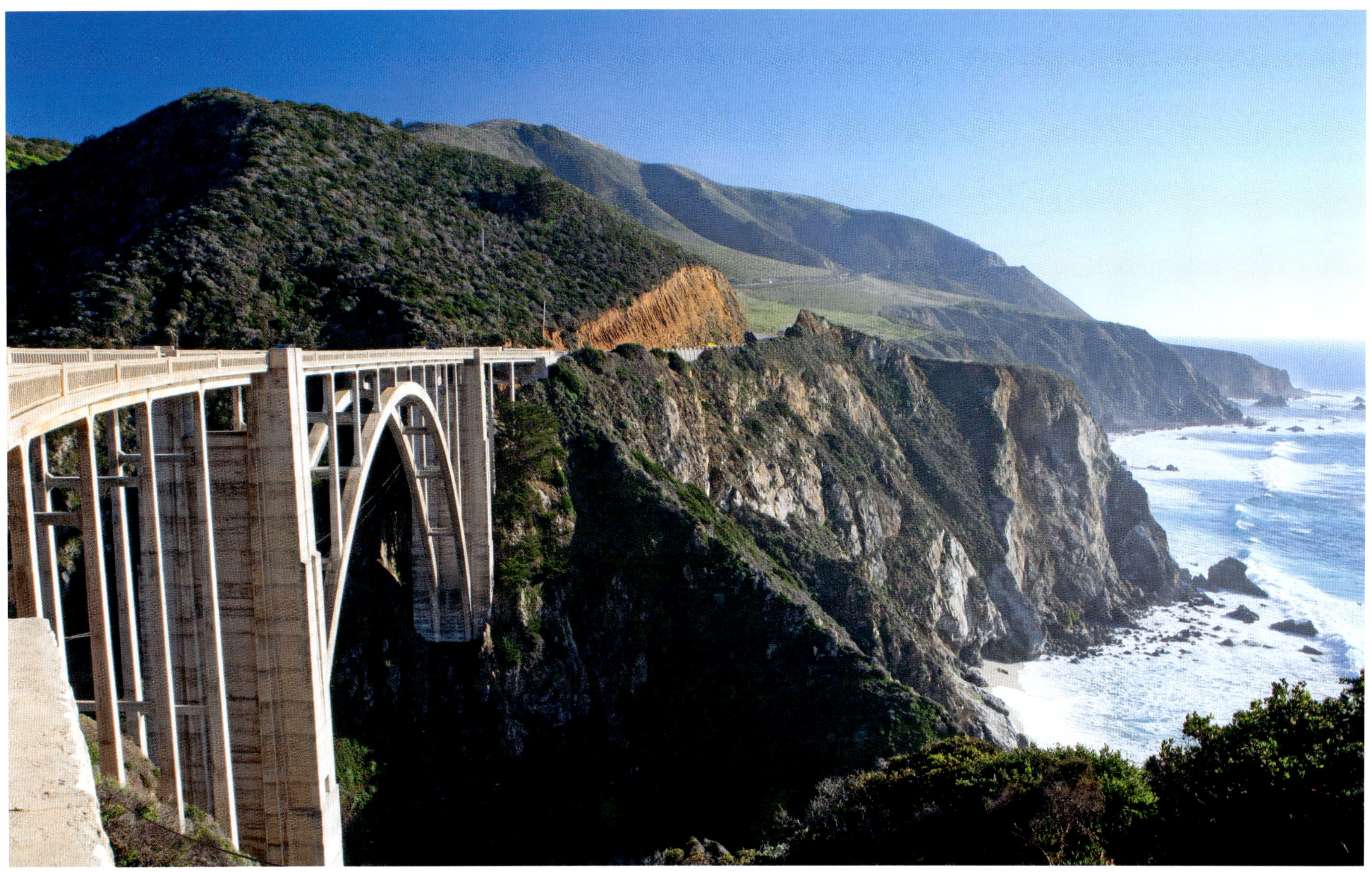

and Malibu. Sections of the highway were closed to the public, with access restricted to residents, essential businesses, and repair crews. Mud slides followed to worsen the problem. The clean-up involved an estimated 90,000 truckloads of debris, with full restoration taking several months.

A report by Pepperdine University's School of Public Policy estimated that the city of Malibu would lose approximately $9.5 million per month in taxable sales due to the PCH closures and the resulting decline in tourism.

THE OVERSEAS HIGHWAY, FLORIDA

An engineering marvel connecting Key West to the mainland

Before the Overseas Highway—or indeed even the railroad—was built, reaching Key West was a serious undertaking. In the nineteenth century, travel to the Keys required a long and often unpredictable sea journey. Steamships from Miami or Tampa were the primary mode of transportation, and rough waters or storms could delay travel for days.

That isolation began to change with the vision of Henry Flagler, a Standard Oil tycoon and railroad magnate who played a pivotal role in developing Miami and Florida's east coast. After building the Florida East Coast Railway from Jacksonville to Miami by 1896, Flagler set his sights on an ambitious goal: extending the railroad all the way to Key West. He believed Key West's deep-water port would make it a hub for trade with Latin America and the newly opened Panama Canal.

Construction of the "Overseas Railroad," officially known as the Key West Extension, began in 1905. The project was a monumental engineering challenge, involving the building of long bridges over open water and enduring numerous hurricanes. After nearly a decade of construction, the first train arrived in Key West on January 22, 1912, with 82-year-old Flagler aboard. Dubbed the "Eighth Wonder of the World," the railroad connected the Keys to the mainland and brought prosperity to the region.

However, the railroad's triumph was short lived. On September 2, 1935, one of the most powerful hurricanes to ever strike the US—the Labor Day Hurricane—devastated the Keys. With winds over 185 mph and a massive storm surge, the hurricane destroyed large portions of the railway and killed more than 400 people. The damage was so extensive that the Florida East Coast Railway abandoned the line.

Rather than rebuild the railroad, the state of Florida saw an opportunity to create a highway using the existing railroad foundations and bridges. Funded in part by the federal government, construction began in the late 1930s. In 1938, the Overseas Highway officially opened, repurposing parts of the railway bridges to accommodate automobile traffic. The road ushered in a new era of tourism and growth.

Since its opening, the Overseas Highway has undergone significant upgrades. In the 1980s, many of the original railroad bridges—converted for car use decades earlier—were replaced with modern spans, including the longest (pictured right), a new Seven Mile Bridge parallel to the old one. The historic Old Seven Mile Bridge still exists and now serves as a pedestrian and cycling path to Pigeon Key, a former workers' camp and now a museum site.

Today, US Route 1 through the Keys is a scenic marvel and also a vital lifeline. It connects over 40 islands, serving both residents and millions of tourists who travel to enjoy the tropical climate, coral reefs, and laid-back, "Ernest Hemingway-esque" culture of the Keys.

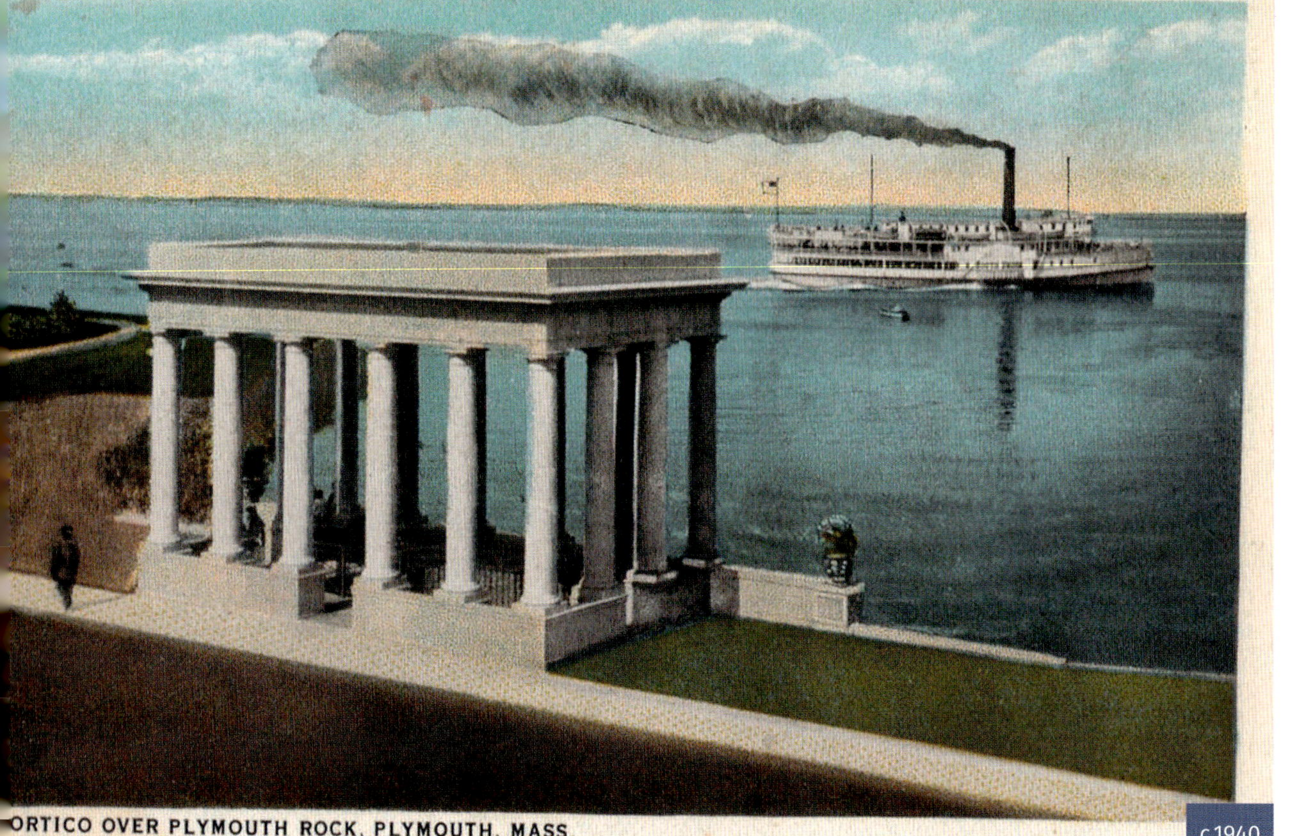

c.1940

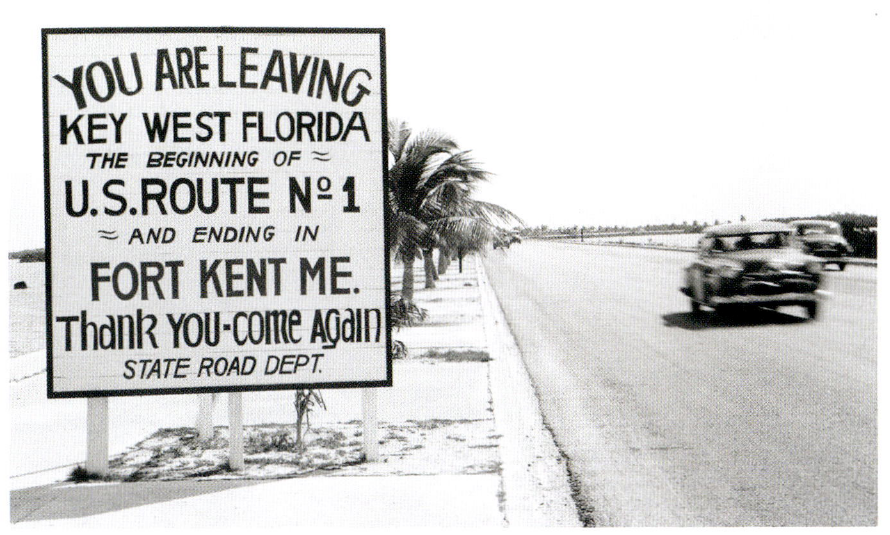

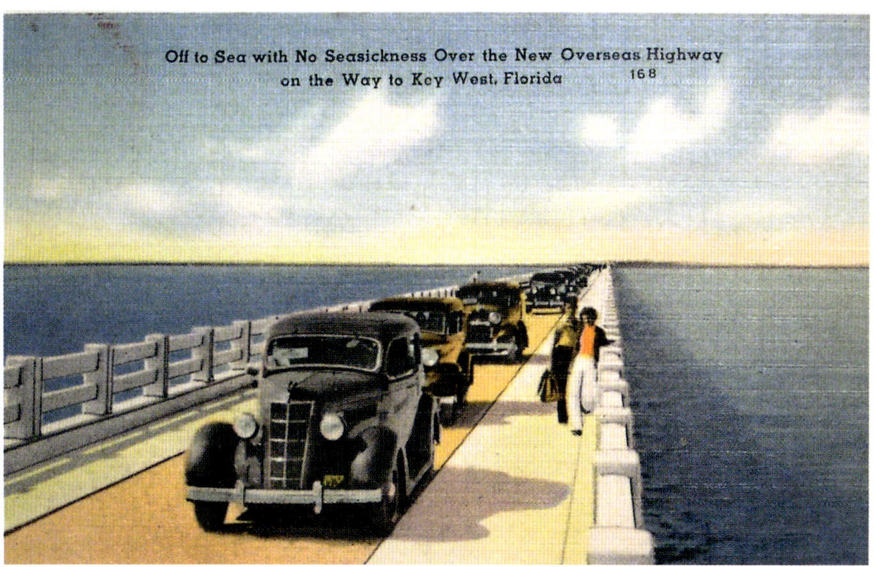

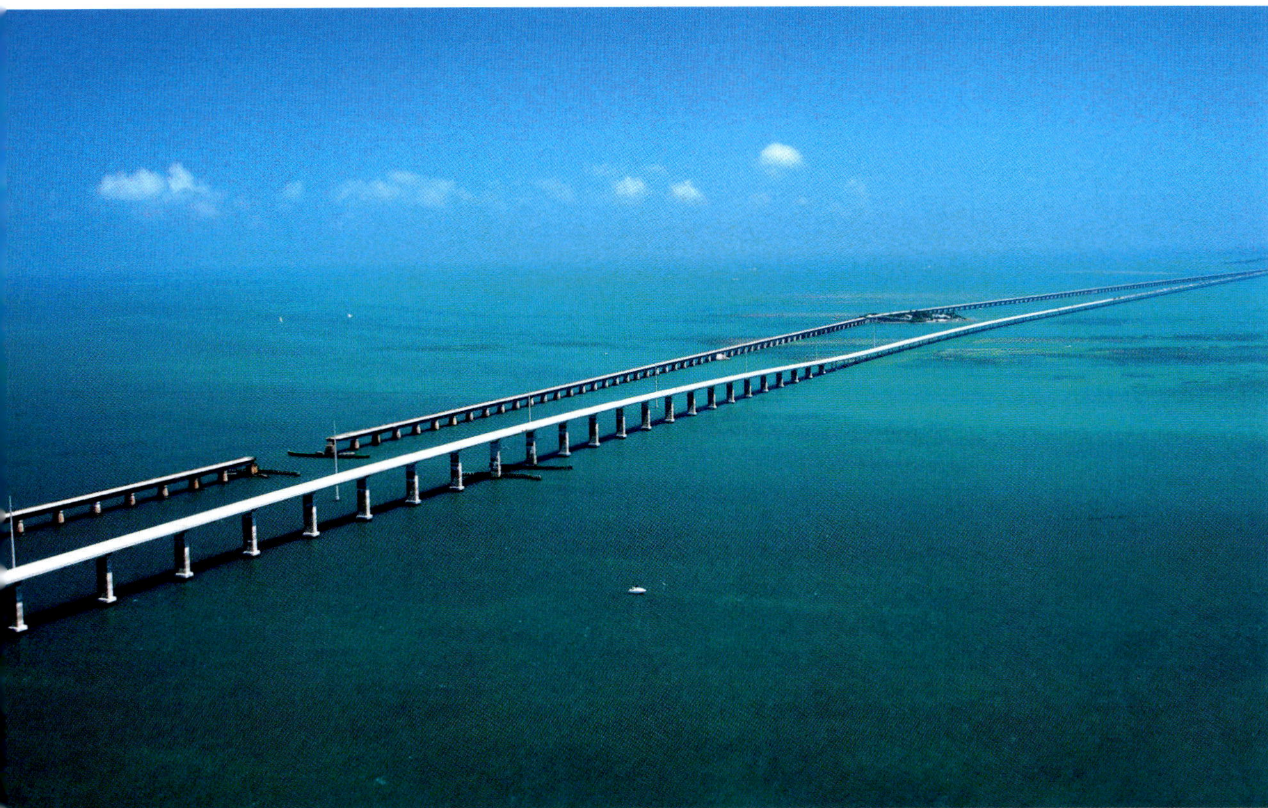

ABOVE: Two postcards from the 1940s celebrating the epic journey over water.

LEFT: The new Seven Mile Bridge alongside the old, with Pigeon Key at top right.

NEW JERSEY TURNPIKE, NEW JERSEY

The highway that transformed road travel in the north of the Garden State

The New Jersey Turnpike—celebrated in song by Paul Simon and featured prominently on the opening titles of HBO's hit series *The Sopranos*—stretches for 117 miles from Pennsville in the south to Ridgefield in the north. The idea for a high-capacity, limited-access highway traversing New Jersey emerged in the early twentieth century as growing automobile use and interstate commerce overwhelmed the state's existing roadways. By the 1940s, traffic congestion was a serious issue, especially around urban centers.

In 1949, the New Jersey Turnpike Authority was created by the state legislature to finance, build, and operate a major toll road. The goal was to construct a highway that could carry large volumes of vehicles quickly and safely, without relying on taxpayer funding. Construction began in 1950, and was carried out at a remarkable pace. Despite the scale of the project—requiring hundreds of bridges, interchanges, service areas, and overpasses—much of the mainline was completed in just over two years.

On November 30, 1951, the full original Turnpike opened to traffic from Deepwater (near the Delaware Memorial Bridge) to Ridgefield Park, connecting with major roads into New York City. At the time of its opening, it was considered an engineering marvel—straight, wide, and built for speed. It featured dual carriageways, designed

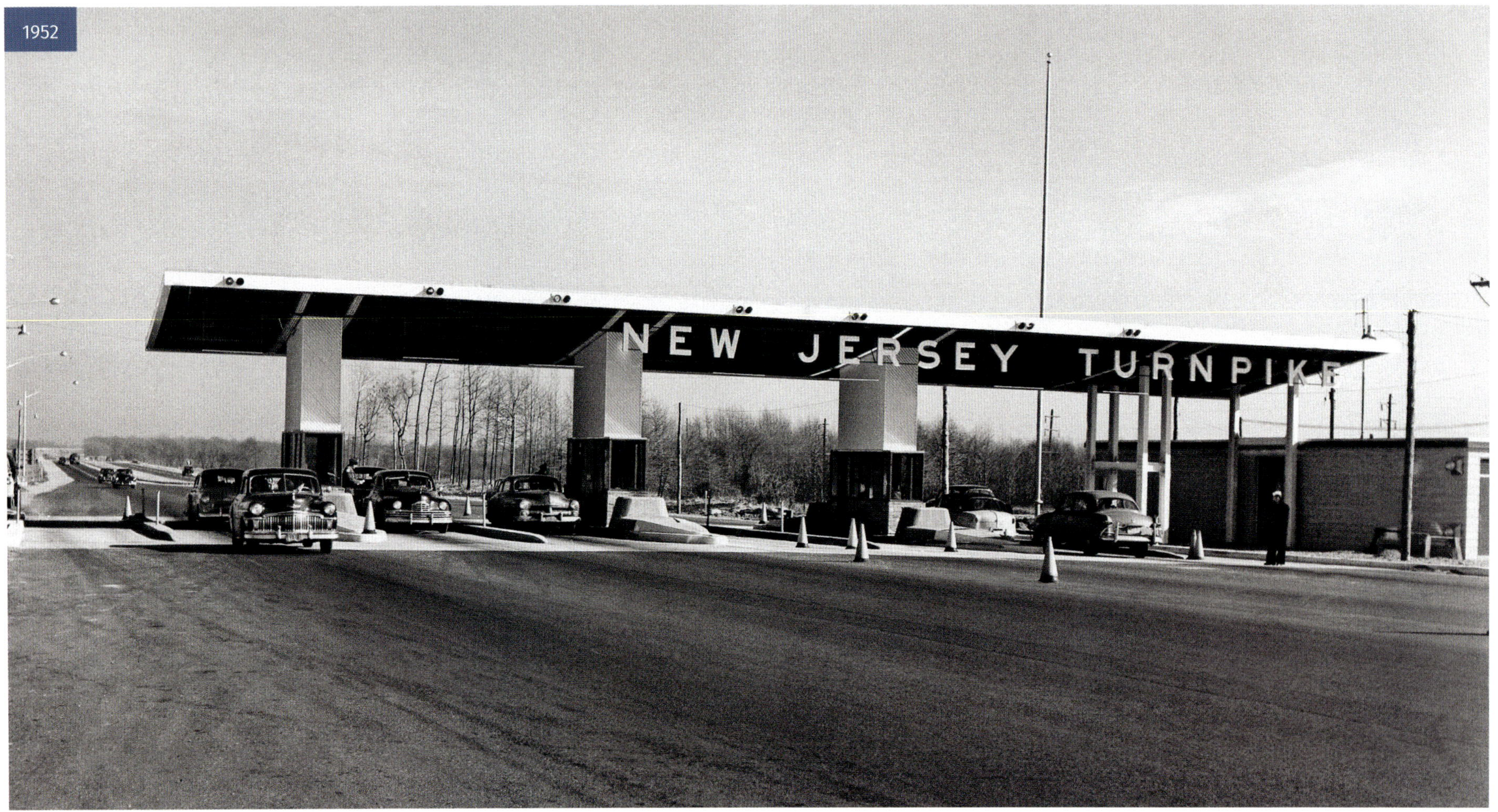

1952

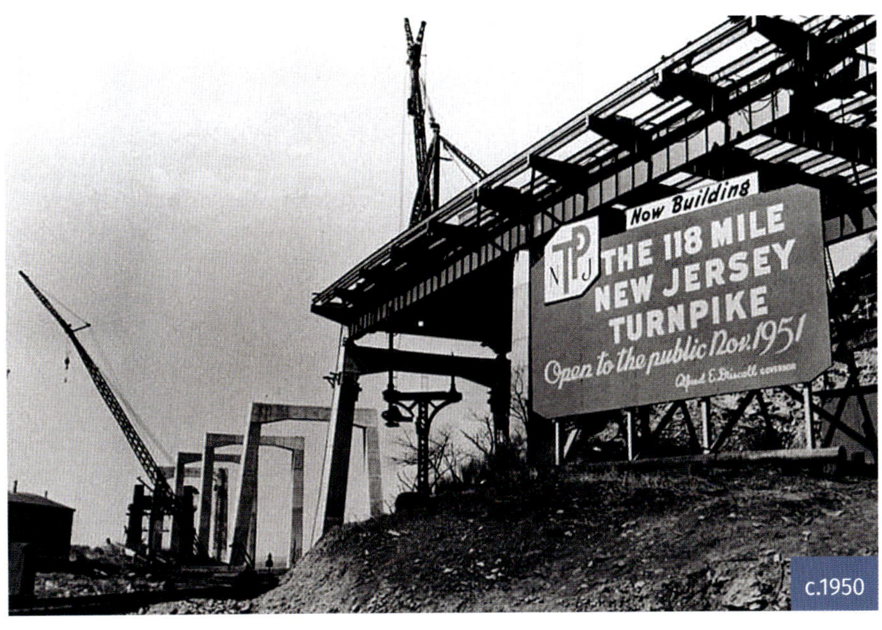

for both cars and trucks. Its location through industrial northern New Jersey, including near Port Newark and Elizabeth, allowed it to serve one of the most important shipping and logistics hubs in the nation. Warehouses, distribution centers, and industrial parks sprung up along the route.

The Turnpike entered popular culture as a symbol of modern travel with its distinctive signage, and with its rest areas named after famous New Jerseyans, such as Thomas Edison, Clara Barton, Walt Whitman and NFL star Vince Lombardi.

Electronic toll collection through E-ZPass, introduced in the late 1990s, has helped streamline travel, and today the New Jersey Turnpike carries over 200 million vehicles annually, making it one of the most heavily used toll roads in the country. Despite competition from I-95 and other corridors, it remains indispensable due to its directness and connections.

OPPOSITE: The toll plaza on the New Jersey Turnpike at Deepwater in 1952, where a connection could be made directly with the Delaware Memorial Bridge

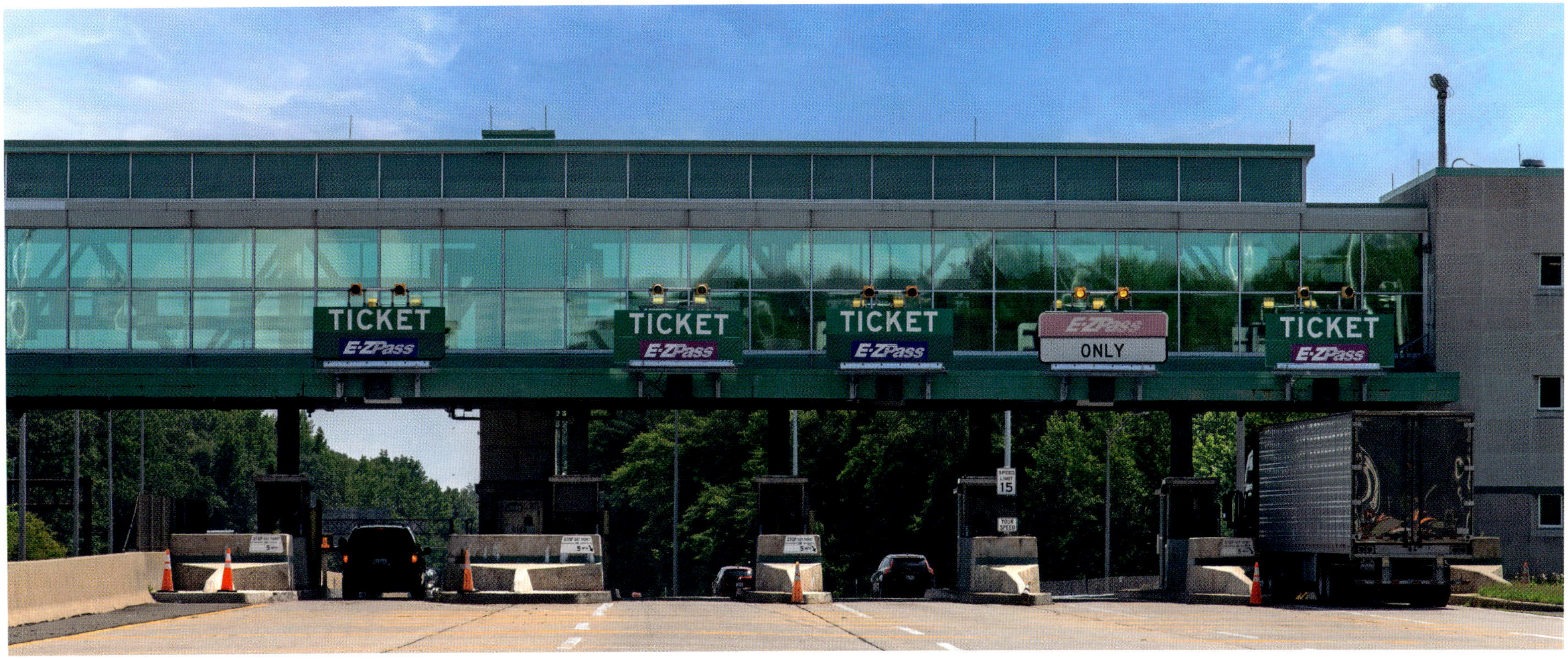

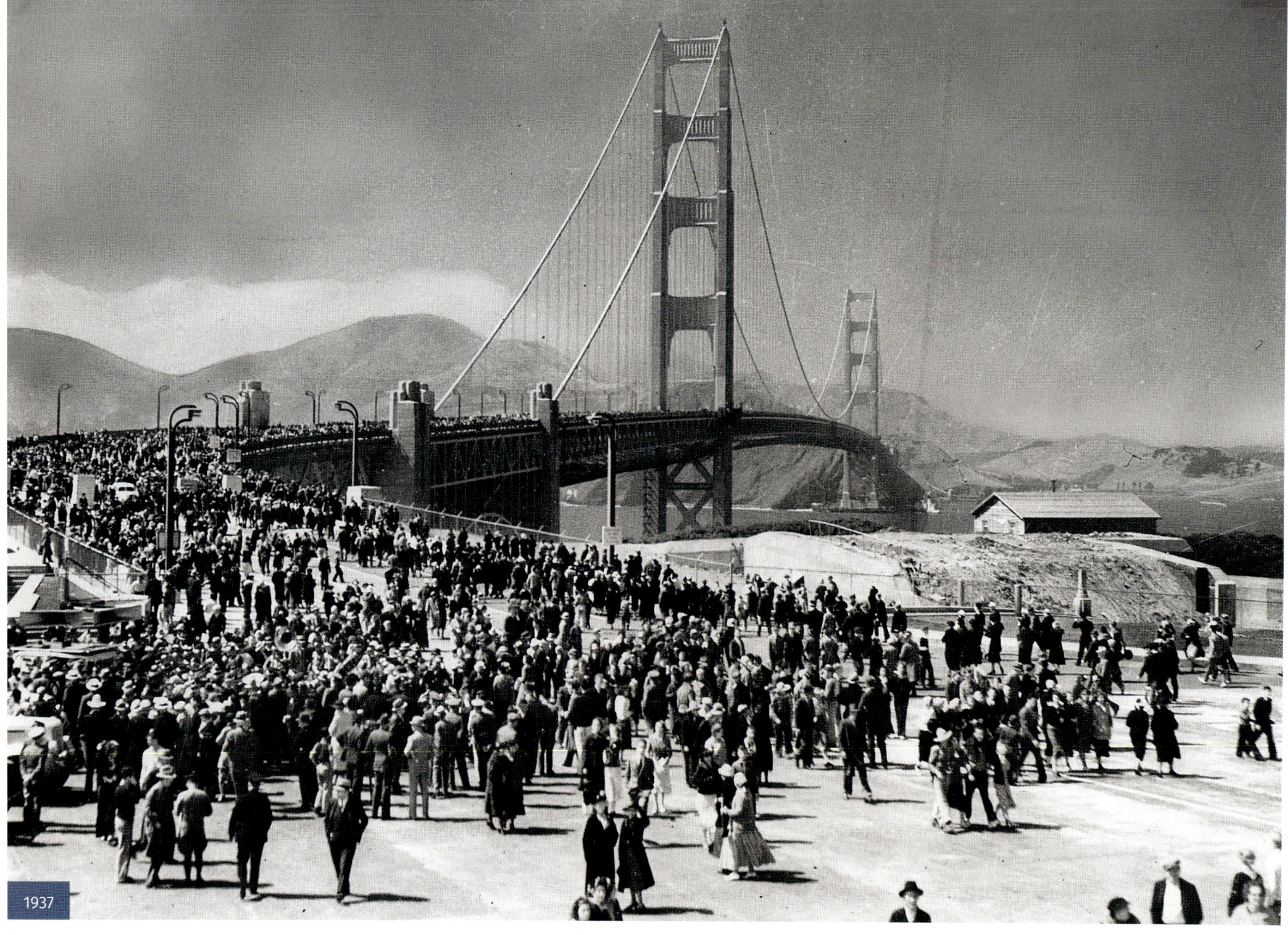
1937

GOLDEN GATE BRIDGE, SAN FRANCISCO

Hailed as a wonder of the Modern World when it opened, its critics said it could never be built

Before the arrival of the Golden Gate Bridge, San Francisco relied on ferries from the Hyde Street Pier to transport motorists to Sausalito and Marin County. The crossing took around 20 minutes depending on weather conditions and cost $1. Critics of the bridge plan believed the cost of construction would make tolls prohibitive and pointed out the strong winds and persistent fogs that beset the 6,700-foot strait.

Original plans for the construction of the bridge, drawn up in the 1920s, called for the bastion at Fort Point (1861) to be demolished. However, bridge builder Joseph Strauss considered Fort Point such an important thread in San Francisco's history that he commissioned a special arch over the fort, allowing the bridge to be built without destroying the fort.

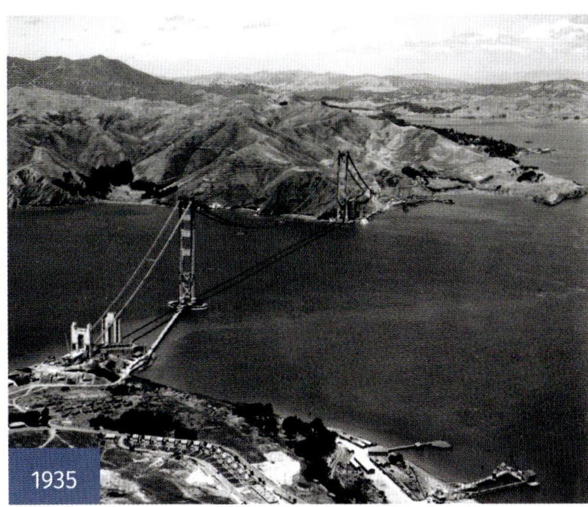
1935

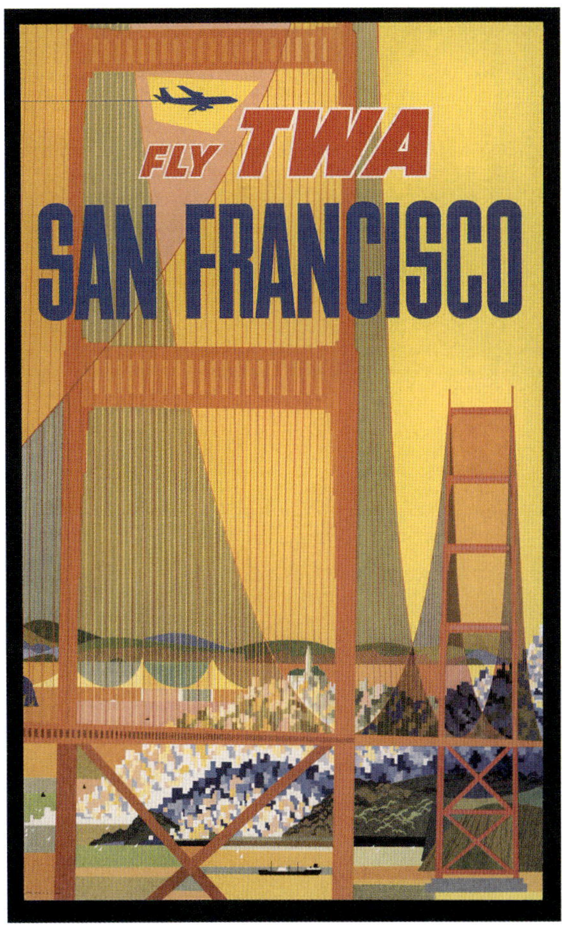

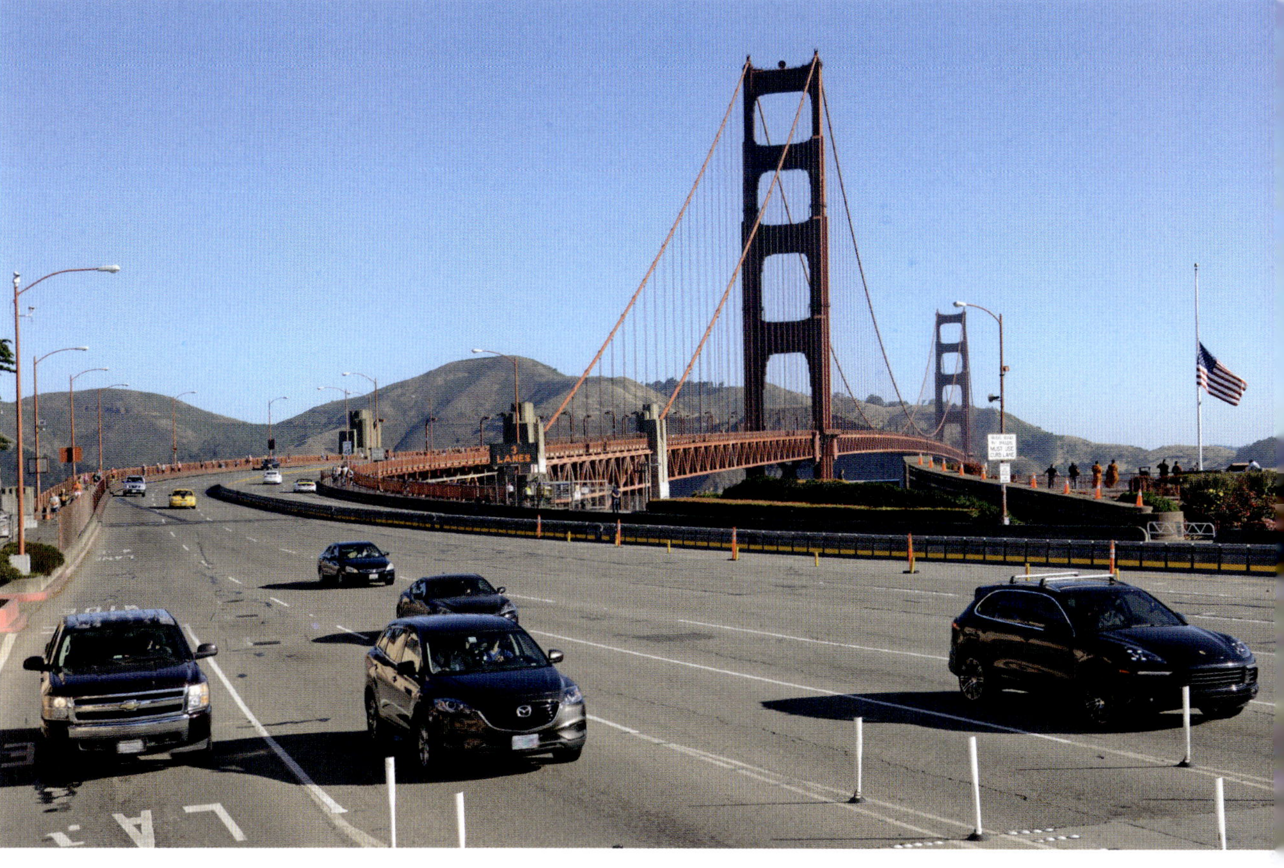

There were countless opponents. The US navy feared that the bridge might collapse and block the entrance to one of its main harbors and if it were to go ahead, wanted it painting with black and yellow stripes for visibility. The Southern Pacific Railways operated the ferries which would lose money and used their commercial muscle to lobby against the bridge—a move that backfired with a ferry boycott.

The final suspension design was conceived by Leon Moisseiff, the engineer of the Manhattan Bridge in New York City. He was aided by Senior engineer Charles Alton Ellis, while Irving Morrow, designed the overall shape of the bridge towers, including the Art Deco elements and the color. The whole project was coordinated by Strauss, who worked hard to claim all the credit when the bridge was pronounced a success and a new "Wonder of the Modern World" after it opened in 1937.

At the time of its opening it was both the longest (the main span is 4,200 feet) and the tallest suspension bridge in the world. Although it has since relinquished both records it remains easily the most photographed bridge in the world. A team of sixteen ironworkers and 28 painters work against the elements to keep the bridge in working order, an occupation that demands strong nerve and a tolerance for fog.

HUDSON RIVER PIERS, MANHATTAN

Where the great transatlantic liners once docked

From the late nineteenth century to the mid-twentieth century, the Hudson River piers in Manhattan was the place where the Old World arrived to inspect the New. By the 1880s, major shipping lines such as Cunard, White Star Line and Hamburg-Amerika Linie, established regular transatlantic service to and from Manhattan's west side, particularly between West 14th and West 59th Streets. These companies built or leased piers along the Hudson River, forming the heart of the Chelsea and Hell's Kitchen waterfronts.

The early twentieth century marked the golden age of ocean liners. Iconic ships like the RMS *Lusitania*, RMS *Mauretania*, *Schnelldampfer Deutschland* and the RMS *Titanic* and *Oceanic* were among the era's marvels. Though *Titanic* was bound for Pier 59,

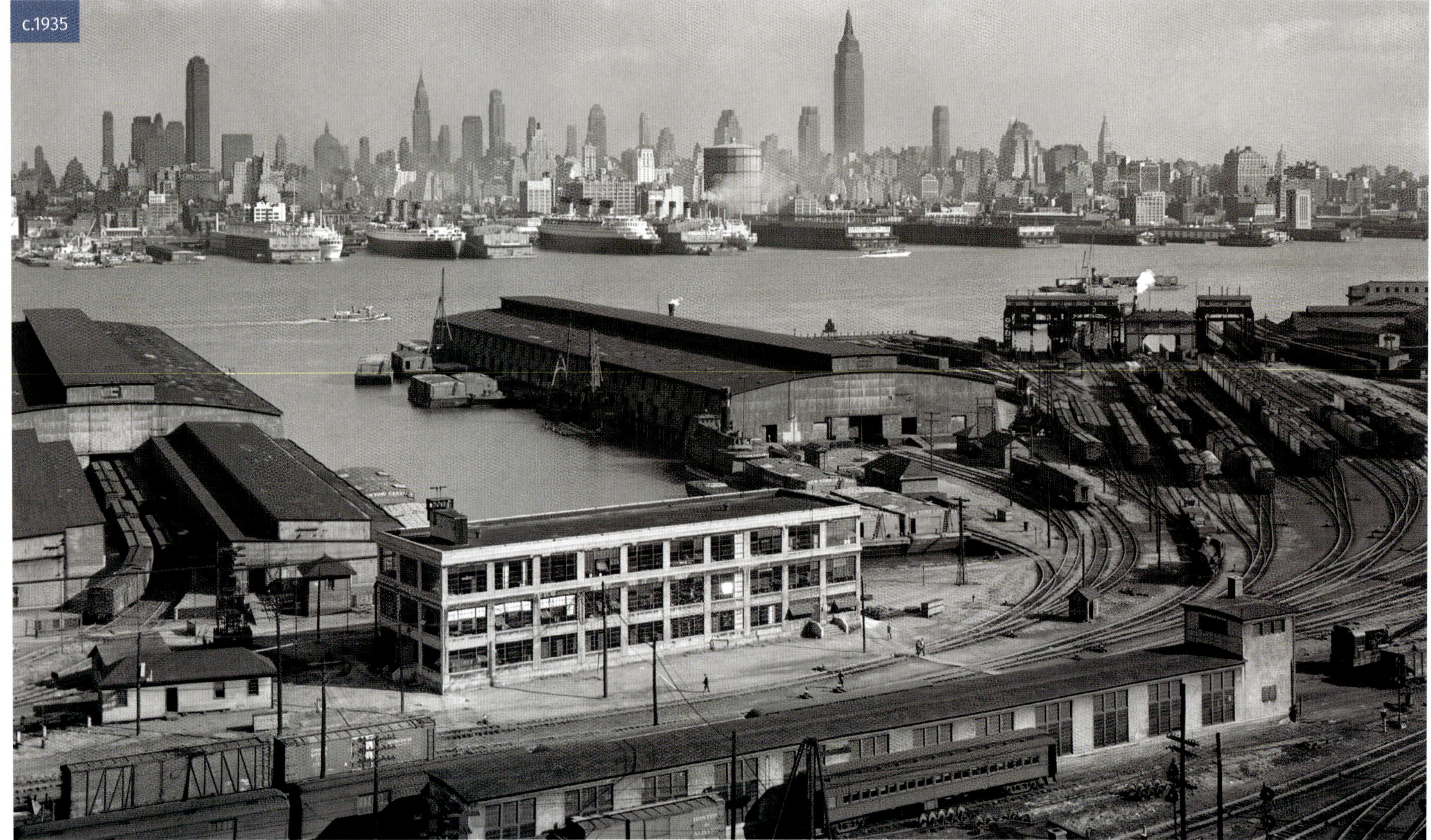

c.1935

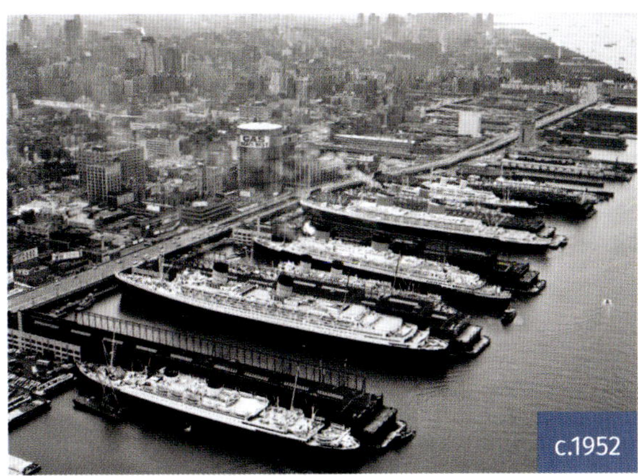

OPPOSITE: A view of the ocean liner piers and Manhattan taken from Weehawken, New Jersey.

she famously never arrived. Her tragic sinking in 1912 shocked the world and had major repercussions for maritime safety regulations.

During World War I, but especially World War II, many ocean liners were requisitioned as troop transports. The piers themselves became military zones—famous liners like the *Empress of Canada* and *Queen Mary* docked at the Cunard piers around West 50th Street and moved hundreds of thousands of Allied troops.

After World War II, the liner business surged again. From the late 1940s into the early 1960s, ships like the SS *United States*, SS *America*, and RMS *Queen Elizabeth* were symbols of national pride and technological prowess. The SS *United States*, which docked at Pier 86, broke transatlantic speed records. However, by the early 1960s, air travel was faster, more convenient, and increasingly affordable. The transatlantic liner trade rapidly declined. Many of the great ships were retired, the *Queen Mary* went to Long Beach and the once glamorous piers grew quiet. Some were filled in and some were repurposed as recreational areas. Hudson River Park, stretching roughly from Chambers Street to 59th Street, occupies land that was partially built on old pier platforms and bulkhead extensions.

In recent decades, New York has worked to revitalize its waterfront. The Manhattan Cruise Terminal, occupying piers 88, 90, and 92, now hosts cruise ships bound for the Caribbean and beyond. The Intrepid Sea, Air & Space Museum at Pier 86 features the decommissioned aircraft carrier USS *Intrepid* and preserves some of the area's maritime heritage.

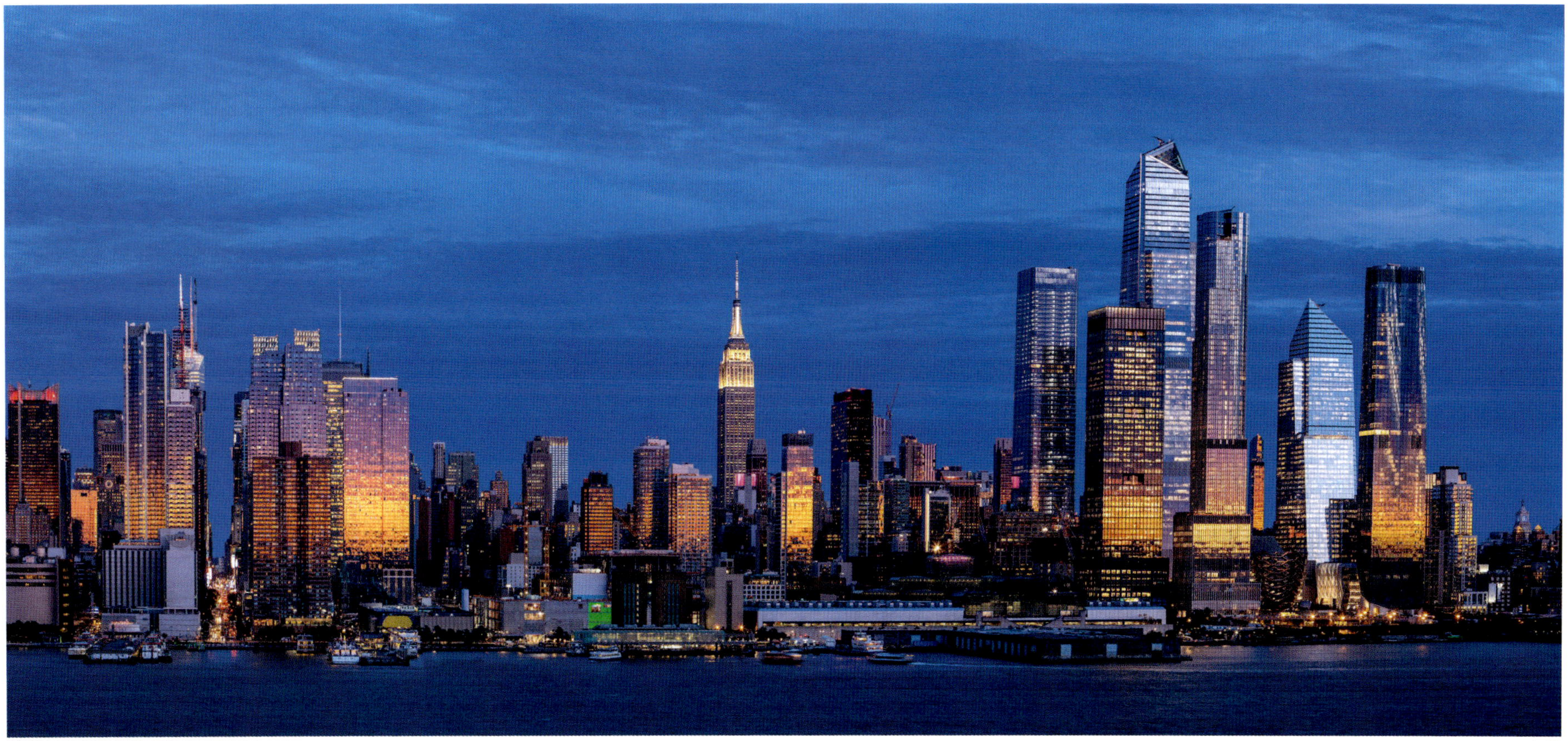

KITTY HAWK, NORTH CAROLINA

The Wright Brothers made a key breakthrough in how to control an airplane

In 1892, brothers Wilbur and Orville Wright opened a cycle shop in Dayton, Ohio. By the mid-1890s they were building their own models, the Van Cleve and the St. Clair, but they had other ambitions. Inspired by aviation pioneer Otto Lilienthal, a German glider enthusiast who died in a crash in 1896, they studied the principles of aerodynamics. By 1899, they began experimenting with kites and small gliders, focusing on the idea of control—an area where many previous inventors had failed. The Wrights believed that solving the problem of how to control an aircraft in flight was more important than building a powerful, lightweight engine.

In 1900, the brothers chose Kitty Hawk, North Carolina, as their testing ground. Its steady winds, soft sand dunes, and relative isolation made it ideal for glider trials. That fall, they brought their first glider to the site. Although its lift was less than expected, it confirmed that their theories about wing design were sound. After failures of lift in 1901, they were prompted to build a homemade wind tunnel back in Dayton where they tested over 200 wing shapes to understand lift and drag more precisely. In 1902, they returned to Kitty Hawk with a new glider that incorporated a movable rudder, working in conjunction with their wing-warping system for roll

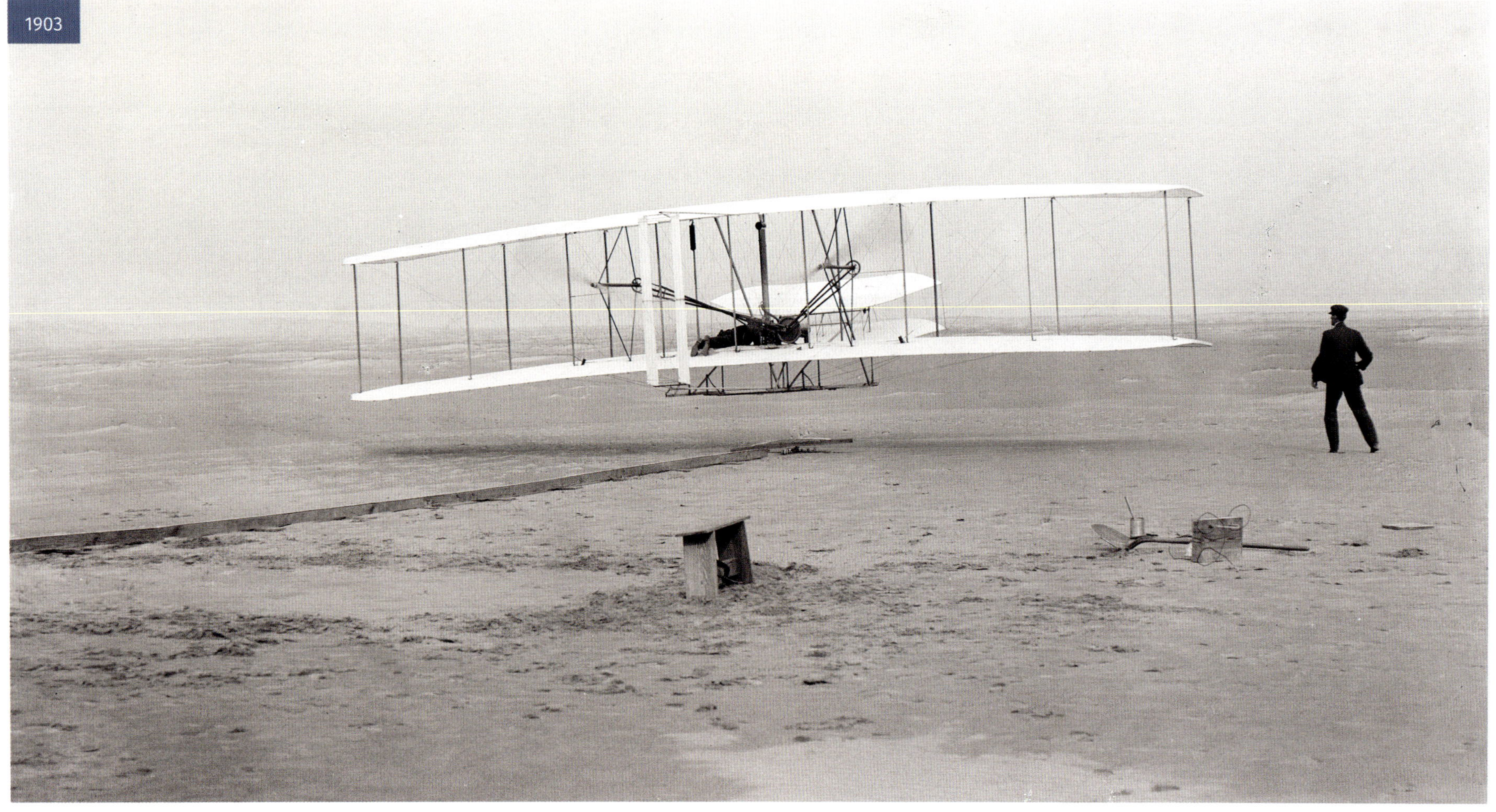
1903

control. This three-axis control—pitch, roll, and yaw—is still the fundamental principle behind airplane maneuvering today. With this 1902 glider, they achieved hundreds of successful flights and had essentially solved the problem of controlled flight.

The next step was adding an engine. Since no suitable lightweight engine existed, the brothers designed and built their own with the help of their mechanic, Charlie Taylor. By late 1903, they had completed the Wright Flyer, a biplane with a 12-horsepower engine. On December 17, 1903, after days of poor weather, they made four flights at Kill Devil Hills near Kitty Hawk. The first flight, piloted by Orville, lasted 12 seconds and covered 120 feet. The fourth flight, with Wilbur at the controls, lasted 59 seconds and covered 852 feet. These were the first powered, controlled, and sustained flights in history. By 1905, they had built the *Flyer III*, capable of flying for over 30 minutes and making controlled turns and circles.

Convincing the skeptical French and even the Smithsonian that they were first took a considerable effort, but history has proven that the brothers made their breakthrough in 1903, a year that saw the debut of Harley-Davidson and the Ford Motor Company. Some year!

BELOW: A monument to the Wright Brothers at Kitty Hawk, North Carolina, giving the state its motto: "First in Flight."

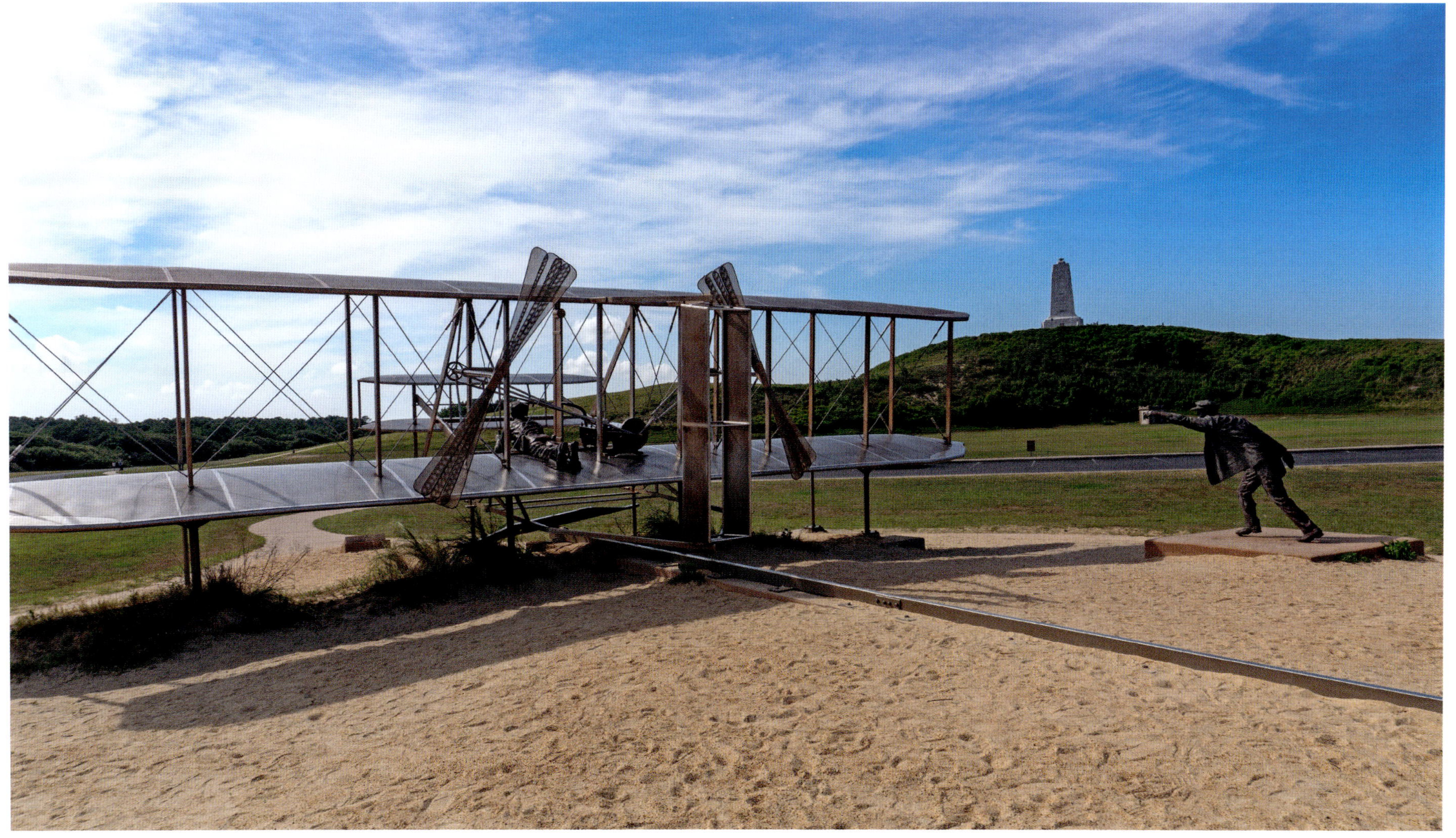

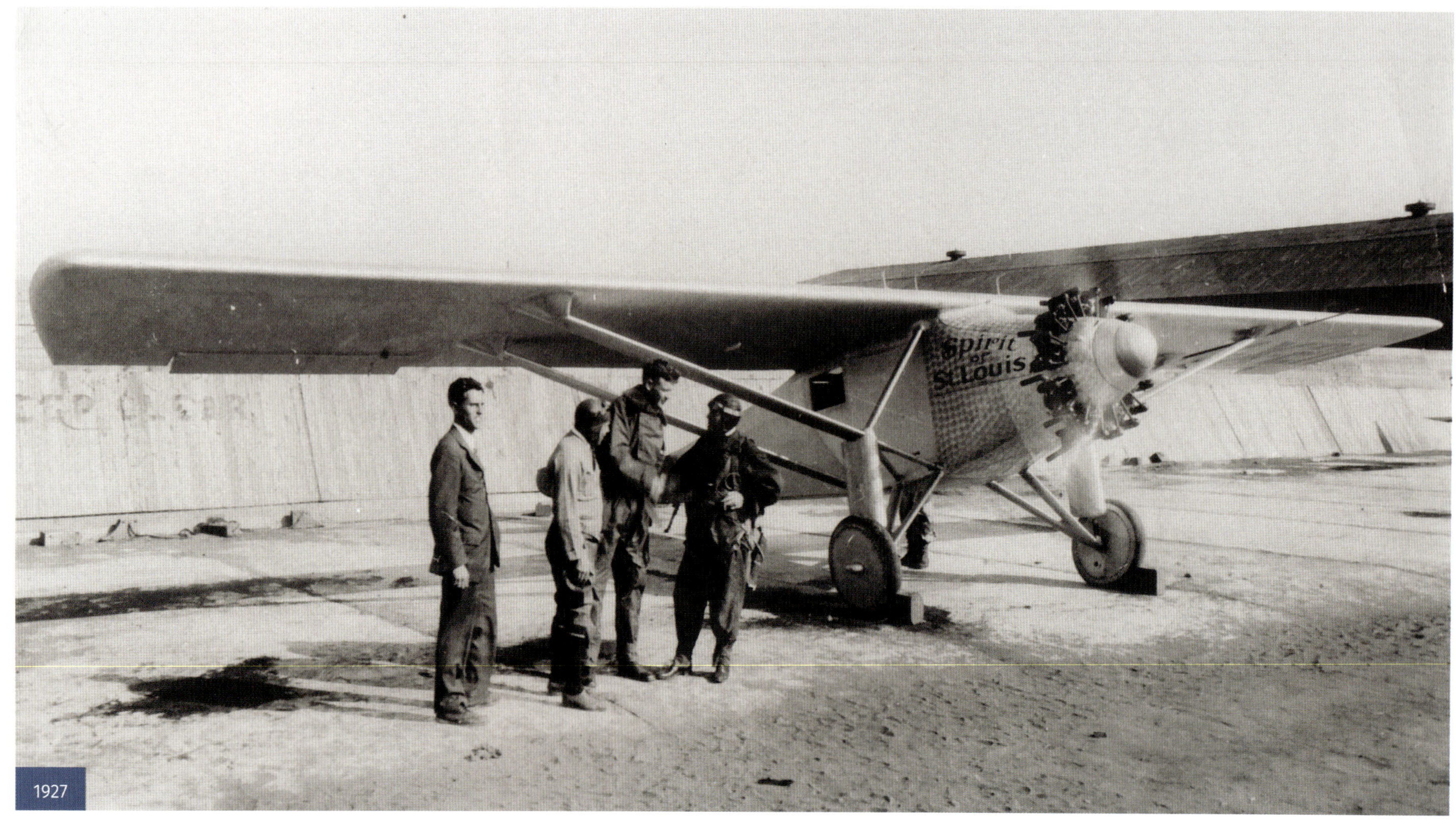

1927

TRANSATLANTIC FLYERS, LINDBERGH AND EARHART

Two of America's finest aviators

Charles Lindbergh began his flying career in the 1920s, initially working as a barnstormer and later as a US Air Mail pilot. The first transatlantic flight had been made by Alcock and Brown in a Vickers Vimy biplane in 1919, but nobody had flown the ocean solo. Lindbergh's fame skyrocketed in 1927, when at just 25 years old, he made the first solo nonstop transatlantic flight in his monoplane, the *Spirit of St. Louis*. Lindbergh flew for 33.5 hours from Roosevelt Field, Long Island, to Le Bourget Field near Paris—a distance of over 3,600 miles. This historic flight earned him a permanent place in the annals of aviation, and he became a global celebrity overnight.

Following the flight, Lindbergh used his fame to promote aviation and played a key role in the development of airlines such as Pan American. However, Lindbergh's public image shifted dramatically in the late 1930s and early 1940s. After visiting Nazi Germany in 1936 on behalf of the US military attaché, Lindbergh praised German aviation and accepted a medal from Nazi Luftwaffe chief, Hermann Göring. He was a strong advocate for US neutrality before and during World War II and

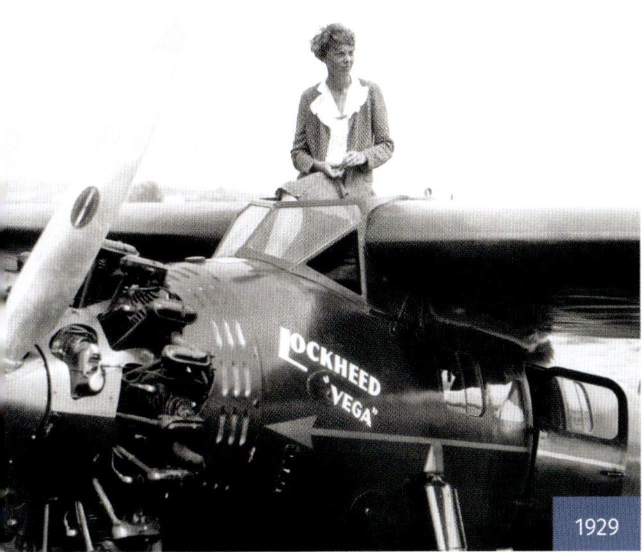

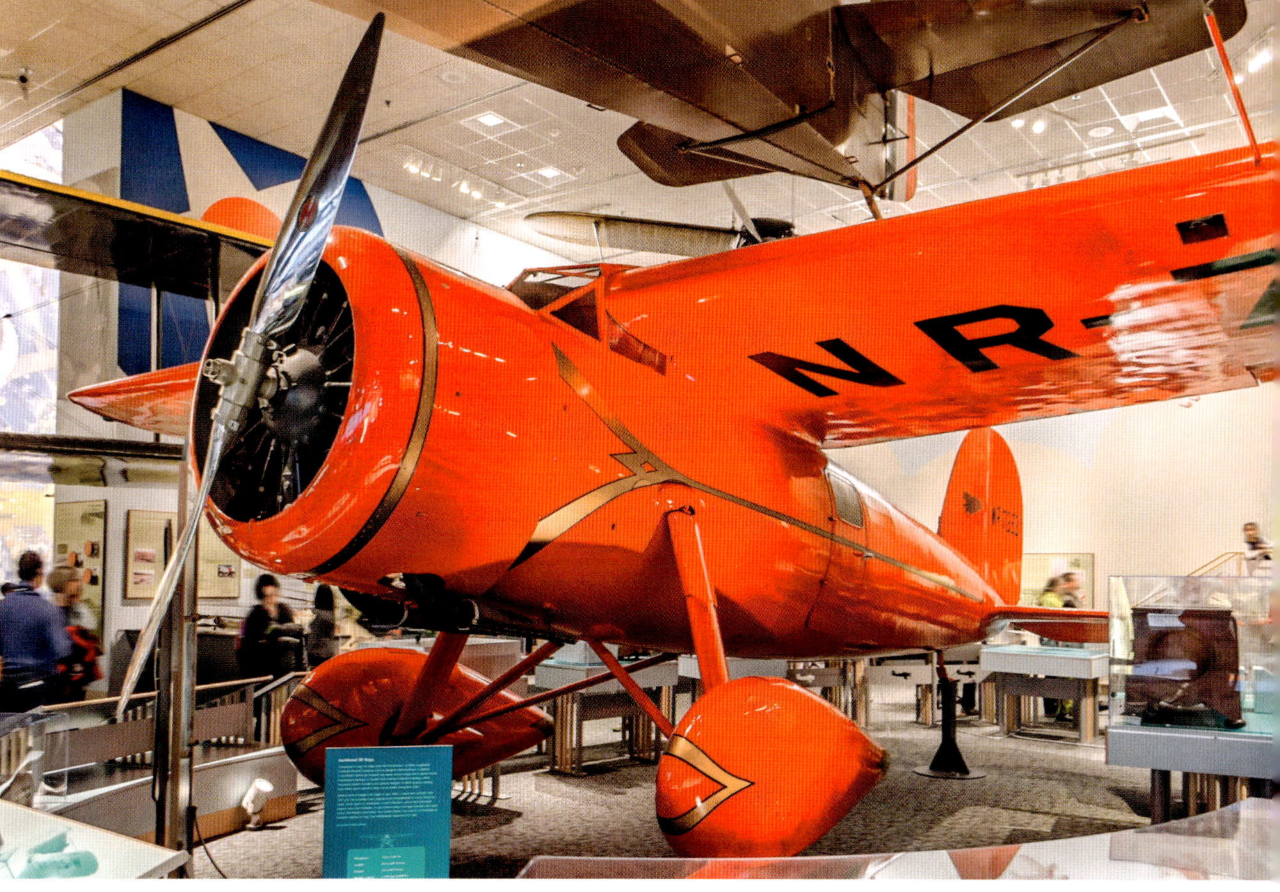

his speeches were widely criticized as isolationist and even anti-Semitic.

After the war, Lindbergh retreated from the public spotlight, but made many trips to Germany. In the early 2000s—after his death in 1974—a new and startling aspect of his personal life emerged. A German woman named Brigitte Hesshaimer revealed that Lindbergh had fathered three secret children with her during the 1950s and 60s. It was subsequently revealed that he had additional children with two other German women as well. These long-term affairs were kept entirely hidden from his American family and the revelation added a new, complex layer to Lindbergh's legacy.

Amelia Earhart, born on July 24, 1897, in Atchison, Kansas, became one of the most influential figures in early aviation. Earhart's fascination with flying began in her early twenties, after a 1920 plane ride in California with World War I pilot Frank Hawks.

ABOVE: Amelia Earhart prepares for the National Women's Air Derby at Long Beach, California, August 1929.

OPPOSITE: The tall figure of Charles Lindbergh and his record-breaking plane, now on display at the Smithsonian National Air and Space Museum in Washington, DC.

The experience was transformative. Soon after, she began taking flying lessons and purchased her first plane—a secondhand Kinner Airster she nicknamed "The Canary." In 1922, she set a women's altitude record, flying to 14,000 feet.

Her big break came in 1928, when she was invited to join a transatlantic flight sponsored by publisher George P. Putnam, whom she later married. Determined to make her own mark as a pilot, Earhart accomplished a historic feat in 1932, when she became the first woman to fly solo nonstop across the Atlantic. On May 20, 1932, exactly five years after Charles Lindbergh's solo flight, she took off from Newfoundland and landed in a pasture near Londonderry, Northern Ireland.

In the years that followed, Earhart continued breaking records: she was the first woman to fly solo nonstop across the US and the first to fly solo from Hawaii to California.

In 1937, Earhart set out on her most ambitious goal yet: to become the first woman to fly around the world. She and her navigator, Fred Noonan, departed from Oakland, California, heading eastward. By June, they had completed 22,000 miles of the journey. On July 2, they took off from New Guinea, en route to Howland Island in the Pacific. They never arrived. Despite an extensive search, no conclusive evidence of their fate has ever been found and theories about her disappearance have persisted ever since.

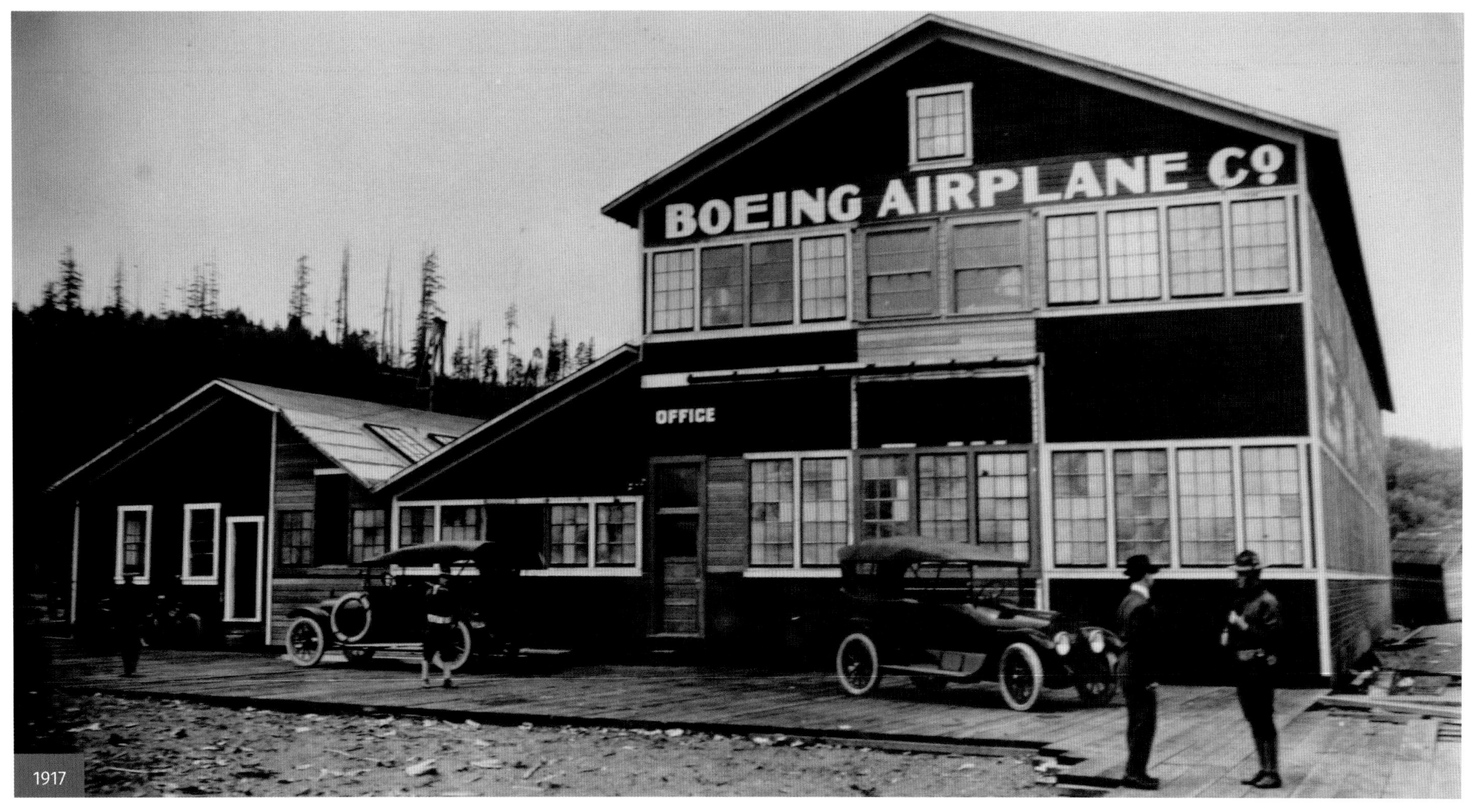

1917

BOEING AIRPLANE COMPANY, SEATTLE

Boeing started off building seaplanes in the Red Barn

William E. Boeing was a wealthy lumberman with a keen interest in aviation. After a flying boat he co-owned was damaged in 1916 and then took months to repair, Boeing believed he could build a better aircraft himself. Along with US Navy engineer George Westervelt, he founded Pacific Aero Products Co. in Seattle. Their first plane, the B&W Seaplane (named after their initials), was built in a small boatyard on the Duwamish River. This facility, an old red-painted wooden building formerly used by the Heath Shipyard, became known as the Red Barn. It served as Boeing's first manufacturing plant.

In 1917, shortly after the United States entered World War I, Boeing renamed the company Boeing Airplane Company. The military's need for aircraft provided the fledgling business with its first significant contracts, particularly for training aircraft like the Model C. After the war ended, military demand plummeted, and Boeing diversified into furniture and boats. But by the 1920s, with the government supporting commercial air mail services, Boeing re-emerged as a key player in aviation.

World War II marked another major turning point. Boeing produced thousands of aircraft, including the iconic B-17 Flying Fortress and the B-29 Superfortress. Postwar,

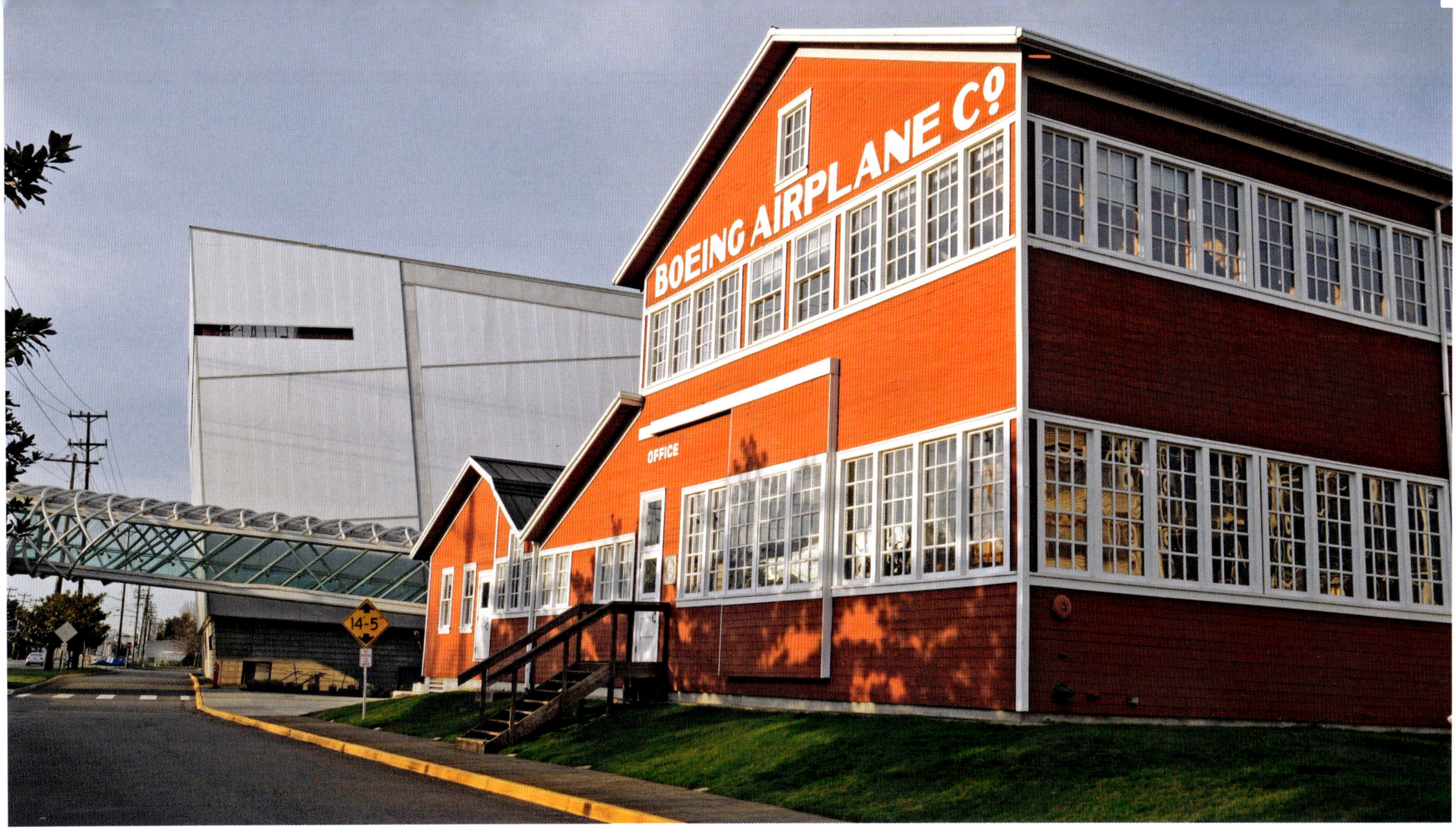

Boeing turned its focus to commercial aviation. The introduction of the Boeing 707 in 1958 helped usher in the Jet Age.

Although preceded by the de Havilland Comet (1952) the 707 was the first successful American commercial jetliner. It revolutionized air travel with faster, longer-distance service, cementing Boeing's status as a leader in global aviation. In 1967, the company launched the market-leading 737, which would become the world's bestselling commercial jetliner, followed by their first wide-body aircraft, the iconic 747 "Jumbo Jet" in 1970.

The company moved its headquarters from Seattle to Chicago in 2001, and later to Arlington, Virginia, in 2022. Production is based in Everett and Renton, Washington, and Charleston in South Carolina. Despite triumphs like the 777 and the fuel-efficient 787 Dreamliner, Boeing has faced recent challenges, notably with the grounding of the 737 MAX after two fatal crashes in 2018–2019.

Today, the original Red Barn is preserved as part of the Museum of Flight in Seattle.

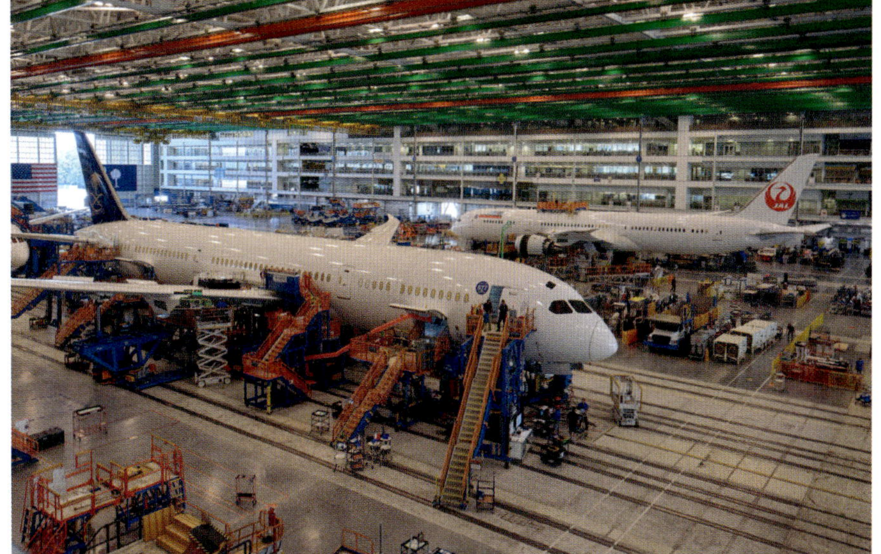

RIGHT: Boeing's modern production facility near Charleston, South Carolina.

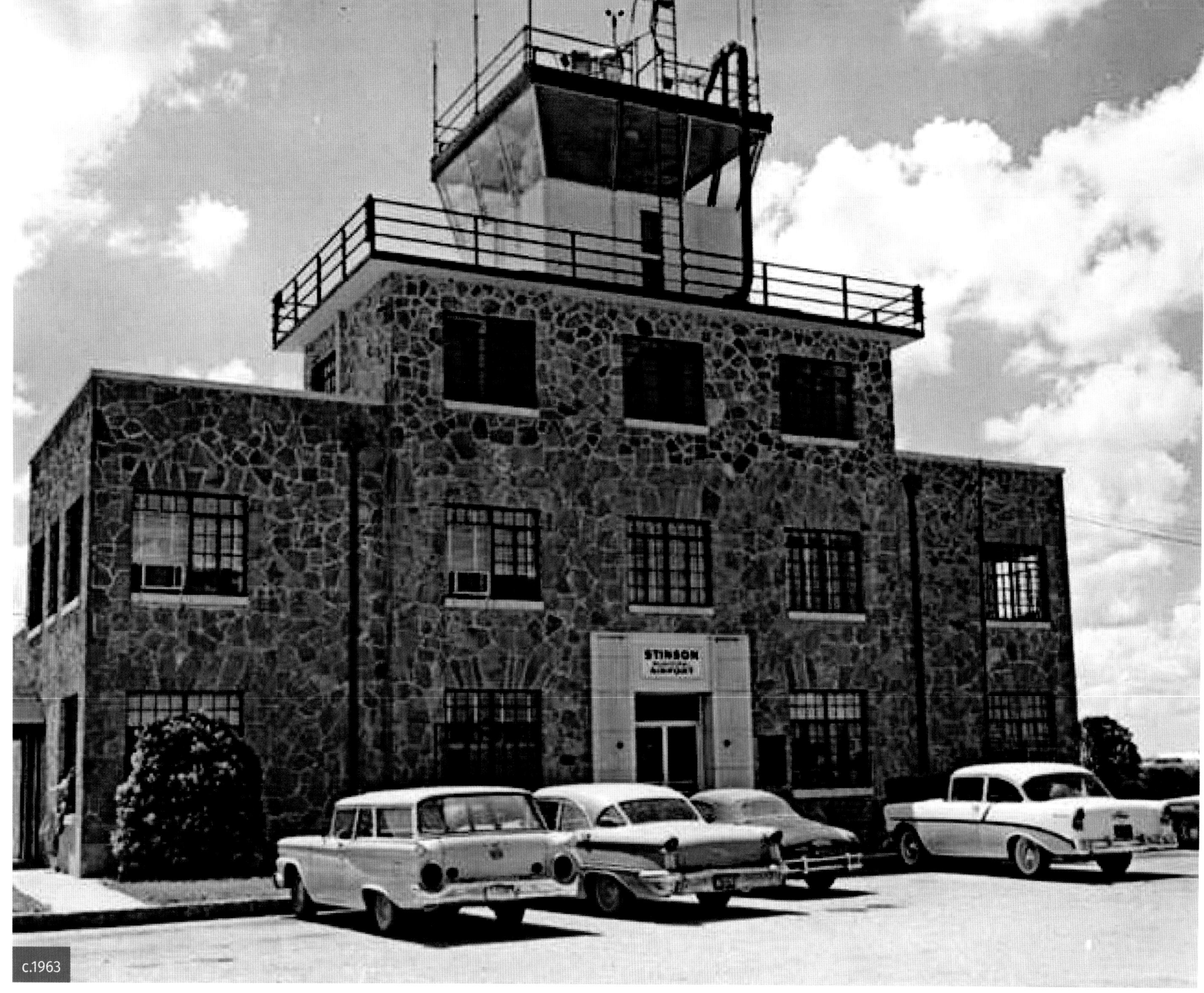

c.1963

STINSON FIELD, SAN ANTONIO, TEXAS

Named after a family of remarkable aviation pioneers

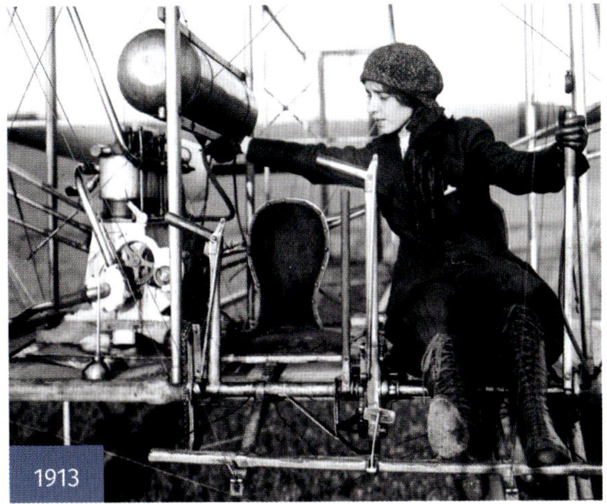
1913

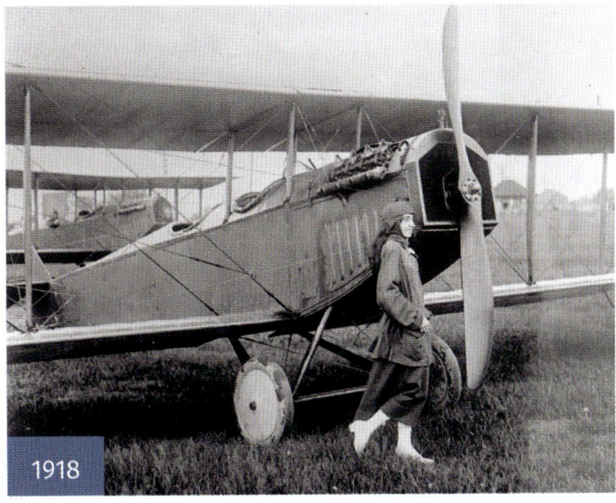
1918

TOP: On the flying exhibition circuit, Katherine Stinson was dubbed "the flying schoolgirl" even though she was twenty-one years old. The Stinson School in San Antonio did not last out World War I, and Katherine then became a Red Cross ambulance driver in Europe before returning home. She died in 1977 at the age of eighty-six.

ABOVE: Katherine Stinson preparing for her flight from Buffalo to Washington, DC, for American Red Cross week: "Miss Stinson donated her services to the American Red Cross paying all expenses incident to the trip." Flying in a Curtiss Military Tractor she picked up the contributions, at Buffalo, Rochester, Syracuse, Albany, New York, Philadelphia and Baltimore.

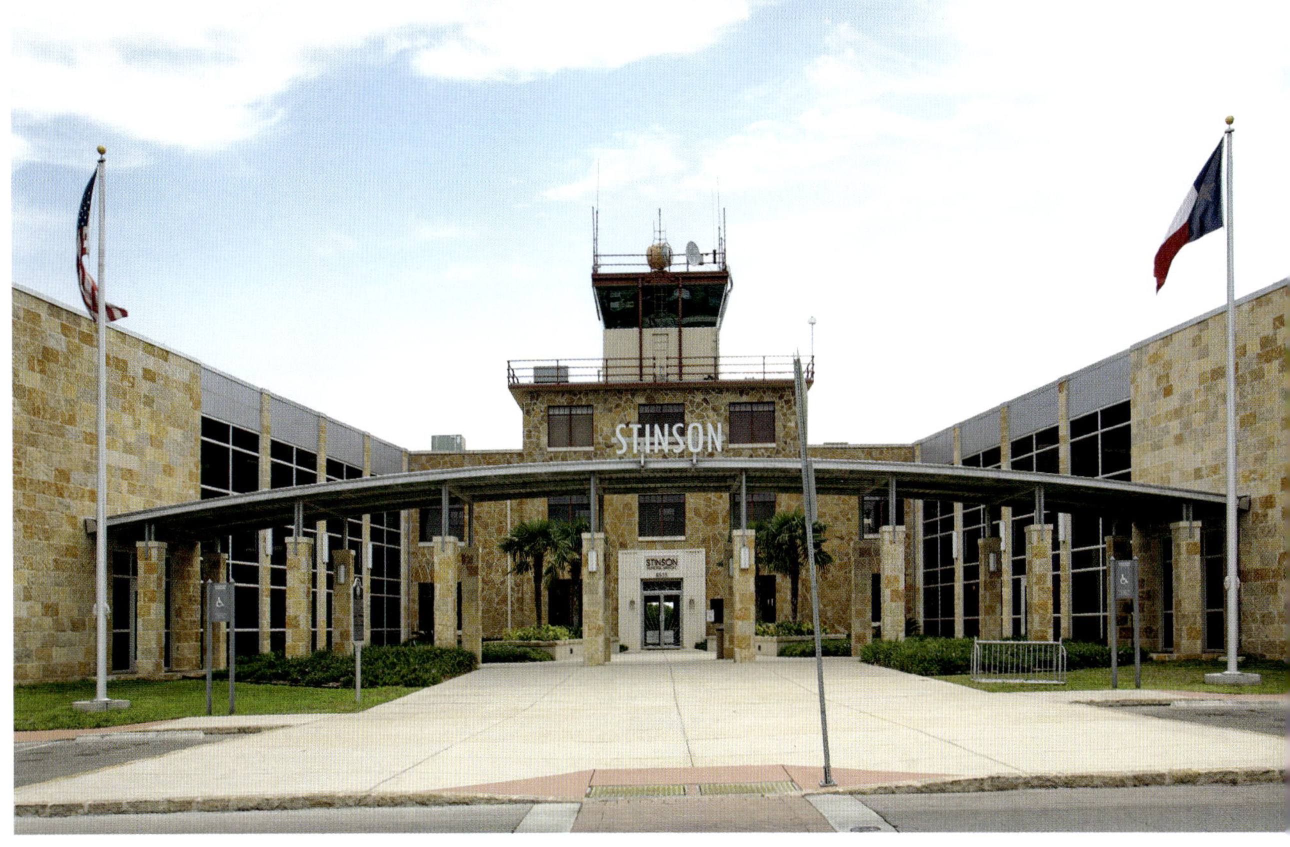

The rise of regional municipal airports in the 1920s and early 1930s is typified by San Antonio's original airfield on Mission Road. Stinson Field was named after the prominent Stinson family of aviators. Stinson Field was earlier than most: it opened in 1915 and has been in continuous operation ever since. The Stinsons were a colorful family and they took up flying when it was still a novel affair. Katherine Stinson was taught to fly by one of the Wright brothers' pilots and flew exhibitions, specializing in a loop-the-loop maneuver. She was America's fourth licensed female pilot (her sister, Marjorie, was the ninth). Her brother Eddie was also a stunt pilot and formed the Stinson Aircraft Company. The family ran a flying school at Fort Sam Houston before leasing land from the city to start the airport.

After World War I the airfield was run by the City of San Antonio. In 1936 a new terminal was completed as part of the Works Progress Administration program, and during World War II the military used the facility as a training base. Today, Stinson is the second-oldest, continually used airport in the United States. The place is still hopping with oilmen flying private jets, recreational pilots taking toys for a spin, regional air carriers shuttling Texans around the country, and three flight schools—as well as a fair amount of helicopter traffic. In 2008 a major terminal expansion was completed, adding 24,000 square feet, though the original terminal was left intact.

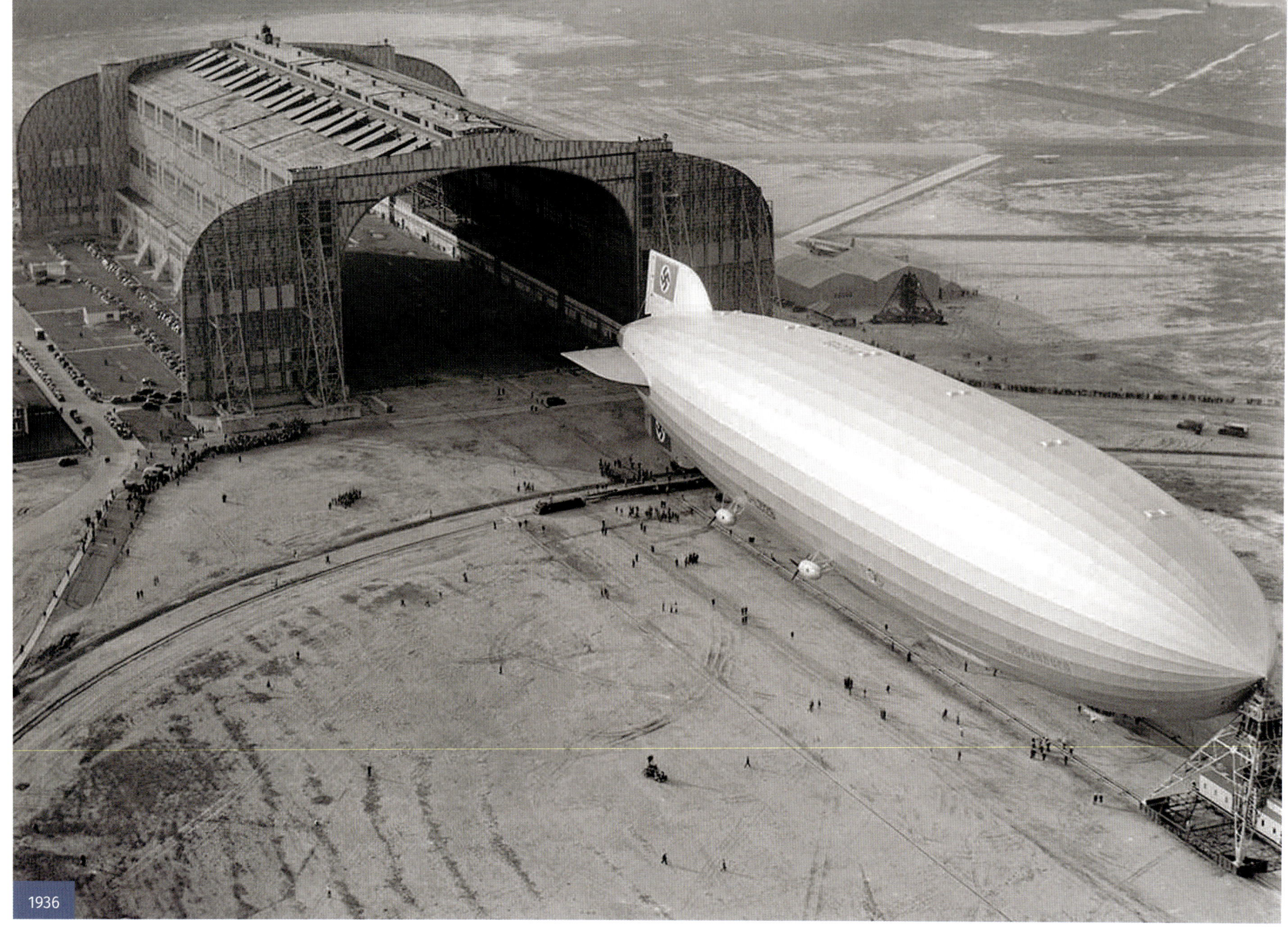
1936

LAKEHURST NAVAL AIR STATION, NEW JERSEY

Forever associated with the tragic Nazi airship

The Lakehurst Naval Air Station was established in the early twentieth century and became a hub for American and international airship activity, especially during the golden age of dirigibles in the 1920s and 1930s. In 1921, Lakehurst was officially commissioned as Naval Air Station (NAS) Lakehurst. One of its key features was Hangar One, completed in 1921. At over 800 feet long and 200 feet tall, it was one of the largest freestanding structures in the world at the time and capable of housing the largest airships ever built.

In the 1920s and 1930s, the Navy based its own fleet of rigid airships there, including the USS *Shenandoah*, *Los Angeles*, *Akron* and *Macon*. These airships were used for reconnaissance, long-range patrols, and experiments in airborne aircraft launching.

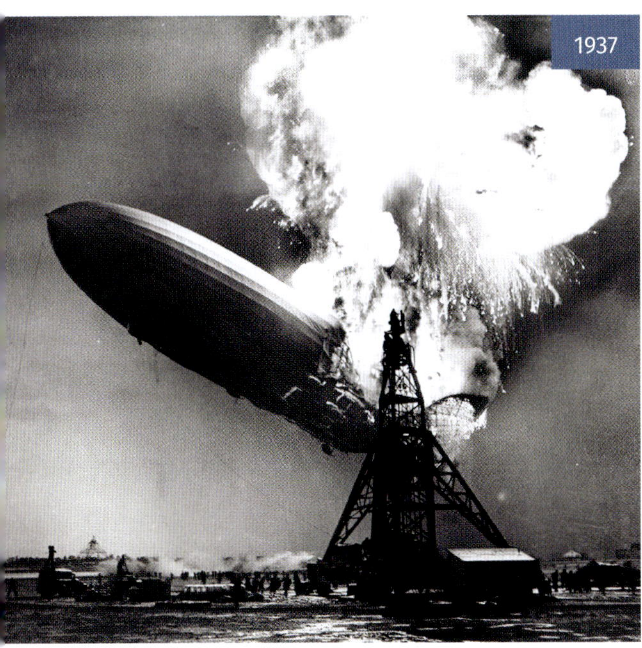
1937

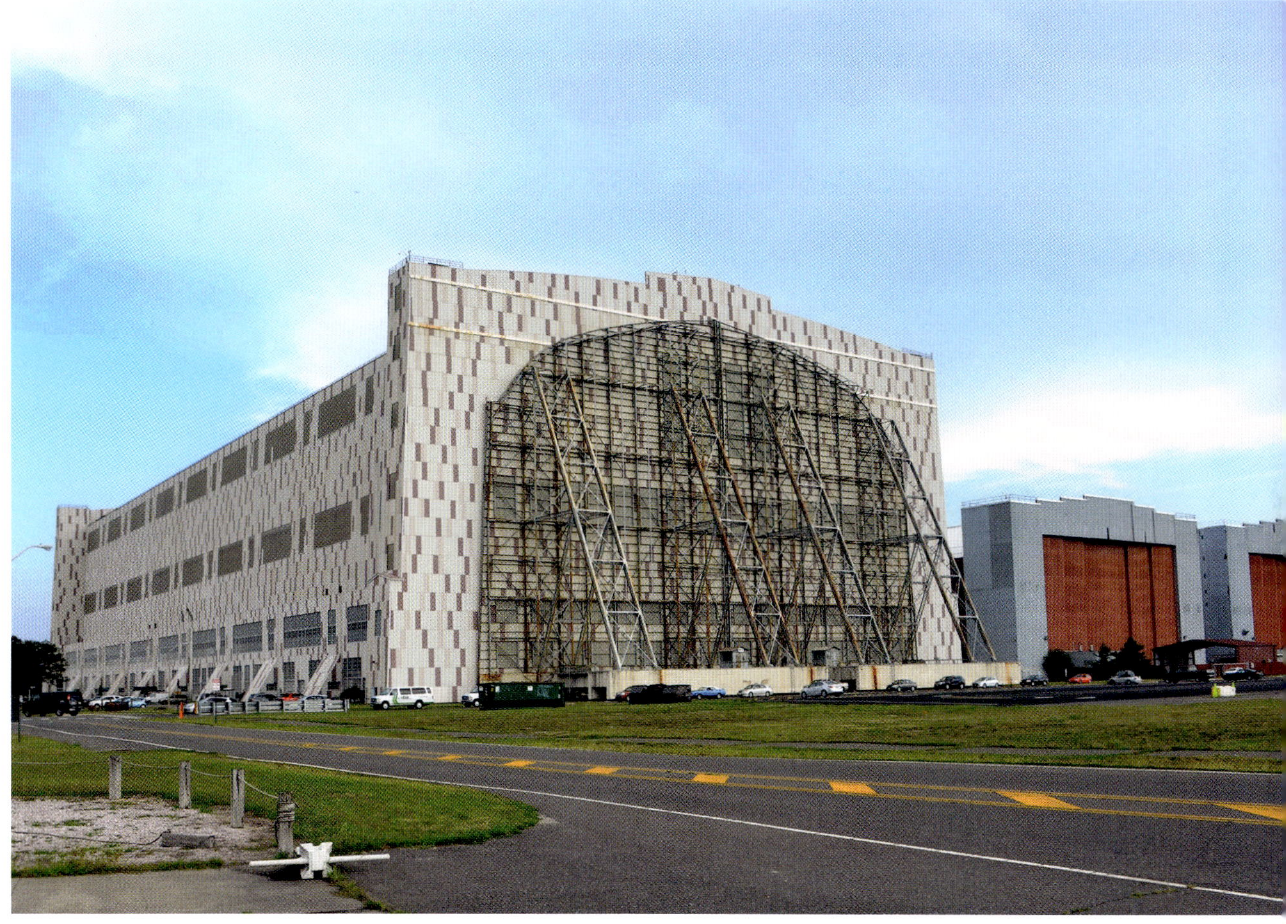

While promising, the technology proved to be risky and several of these vessels crashed in storms or due to structural failure.

The infamous event in Lakehurst's history occurred on May 6, 1937, with the destruction of the German airship LZ 129 *Hindenburg*. At the time, the *Hindenburg* was the pride of German engineering—a massive, luxurious airship operated by Deutsche Zeppelin-Reederei that provided elegant passenger service between Europe and the United States.

On its first North American flight of the 1937 season, the *Hindenburg* departed Frankfurt, Germany, carrying 97 people—36 passengers and 61 crew. As it approached Lakehurst for landing, high winds delayed the docking process. At around 7:25 p.m., while attempting a final mooring, the airship suddenly burst into flames and crashed to the ground in just 34 incendiary seconds.

The disaster killed 35 people on board and one ground crewman, while amazingly, considering the size of the inferno, 62 survived. The horrifying footage, widely captured by newsreels, was accompanied by the famous radio broadcast from Herbert Morrison exclaiming, "Oh, the humanity!" It shocked the world and brought a tragic end to the dream of commercial airship travel.

The exact cause of the fire remains debated. The most widely accepted theory is that a static electricity spark ignited hydrogen gas leaking from one of the airship's cells. Unlike helium, which is nonflammable, hydrogen was highly combustible—but at the time, the US embargoed helium exports, and Germany had no access to it.

Today, Lakehurst remains a functioning military site, part of Joint Base McGuire–Dix–Lakehurst, and still houses Hangar One, which is listed as a National Historic Landmark.

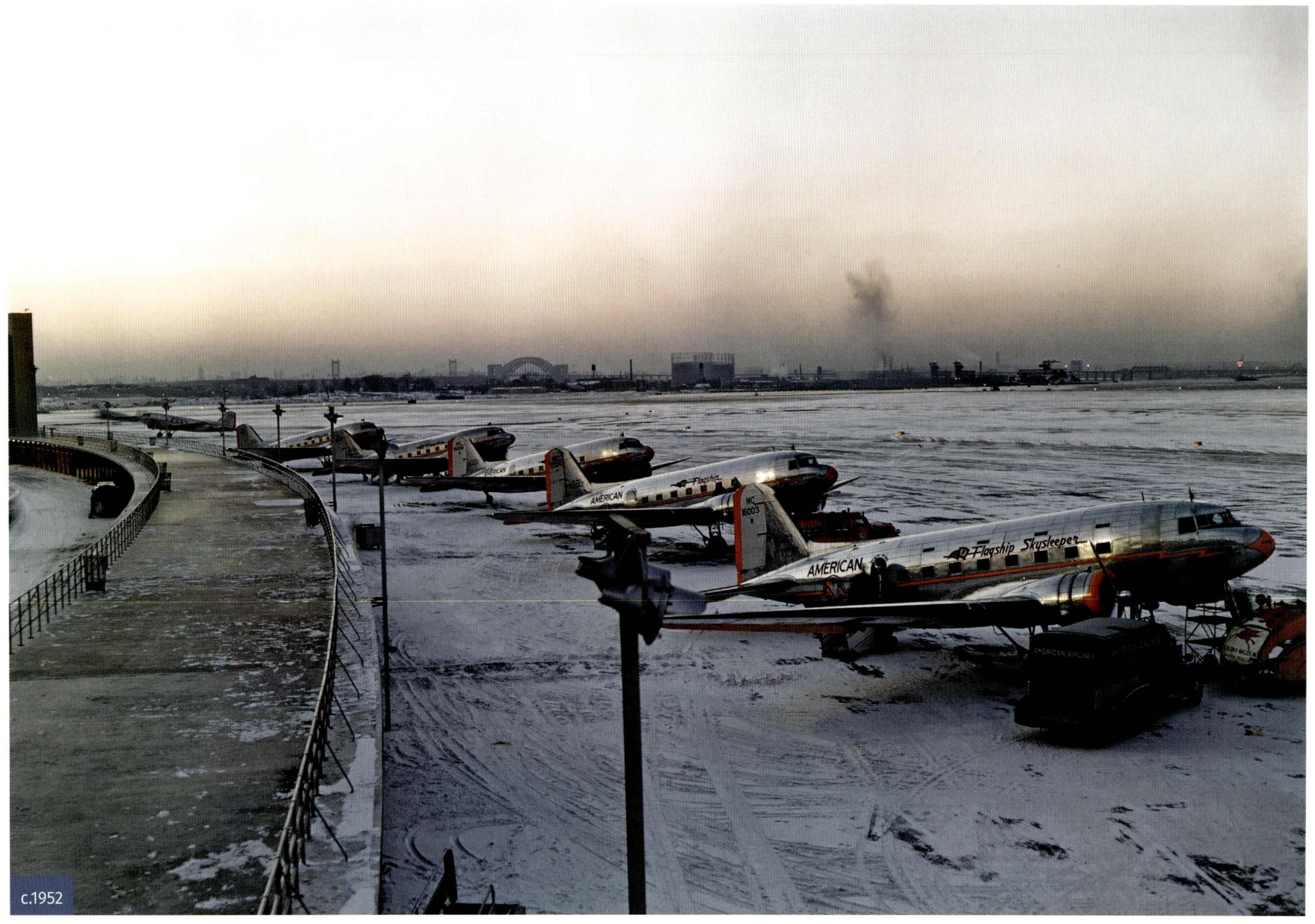

c.1952

LAGUARDIA AIRPORT, NEW YORK

Fiorello LaGuardia was insistent his city should have its own airport

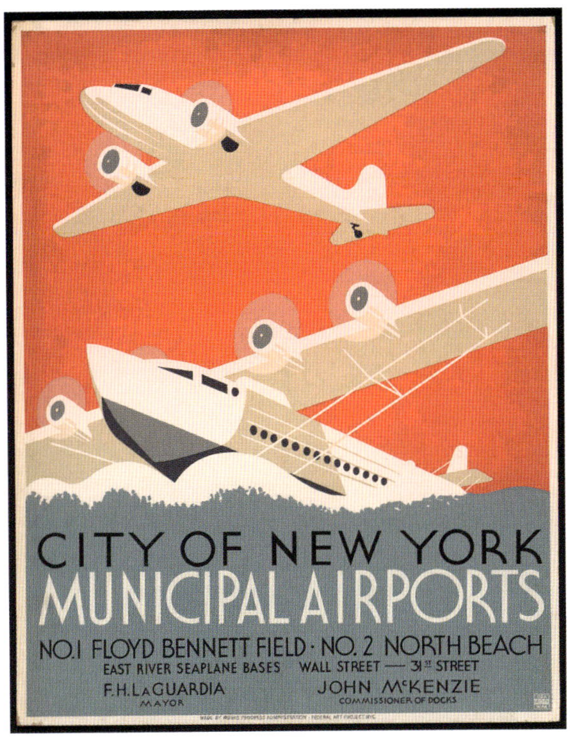

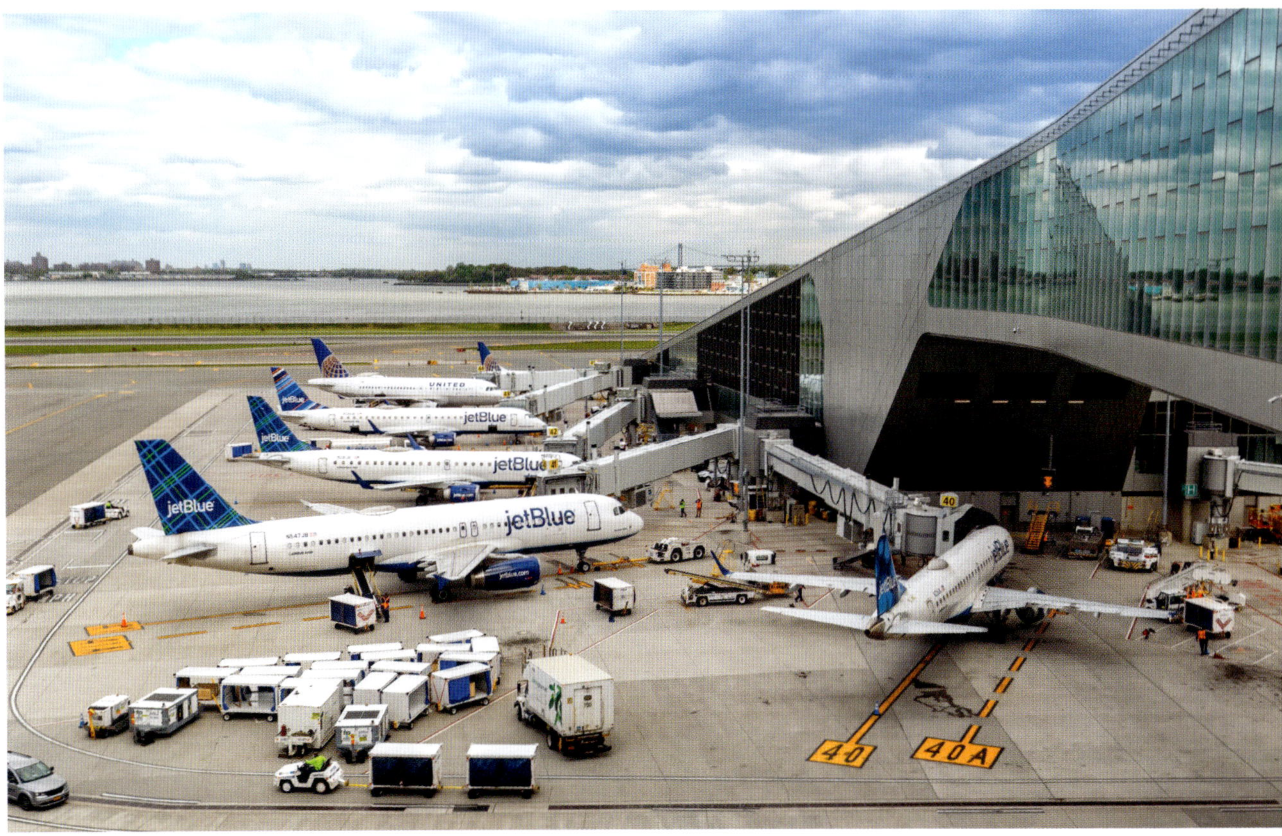

New York City Municipal Airport in Queens once had two terminals. One on the East River for seaplanes and an aerodrome next door. Influential New York mayor Fiorello H. LaGuardia had lobbied for an airport in 1934, a time when most airlines used Newark, New Jersey. The mayor famously refused to disembark from a flight that landed in Newark, insisting that his ticket said "New York" and not New Jersey.

His protest highlighted the need for a New York City-based airport, prompting city officials to develop the site of the old Gala Amusement Park on the East River, which had already been converted into a small airfield known as Glenn H. Curtiss Airport. In 1937, the city began construction of a much larger commercial airport on the site, using landfill to expand the land area into Flushing Bay.

LaGuardia Airport officially opened to commercial flights in December 1939 as New York Municipal Airport–LaGuardia Field. The airport was an immediate success, drawing over 250,000 passengers in its first year—an impressive number for the time. In 1947, the Port Authority of New York and New Jersey took over operations, and the name was shortened to LaGuardia Airport in honor of the former mayor who championed its creation.

The Marine Air Terminal (MAT), located on the western edge of the airport along Bowery Bay was constructed in 1939. It was specifically designed to accommodate Pan American Airways' "Clippers," the luxurious flying boats used to fly passengers to Europe via intermediate stops in places like Newfoundland and the Azores.

The terminal itself was a masterpiece of Art Deco architecture, but its original use was short lived. Advances in land-based aircraft during and after World War II, rendered seaplanes obsolete for most commercial routes. By 1947, Pan Am ended its seaplane operations at LaGuardia, and the Marine Air Terminal's role changed.

Throughout the 1940s and 1950s, LaGuardia was a bustling hub for domestic flights. However, its short runways were not designed to handle jet aircraft or large-scale traffic, and airplanes were only getting bigger. To alleviate congestion, many long-haul and international flights were redirected to the newer (1948) Idlewild/John F. Kennedy International Airport (JFK), while LaGuardia focused primarily on short-haul and domestic routes.

Following criticism from Vice President Joe Biden, who compared the facilities at LaGuardia to "some third-world country," a massive $8 billion redevelopment project began in 2016, led by the Port Authority and LaGuardia Gateway Partners. The investment has transformed the airport's image.

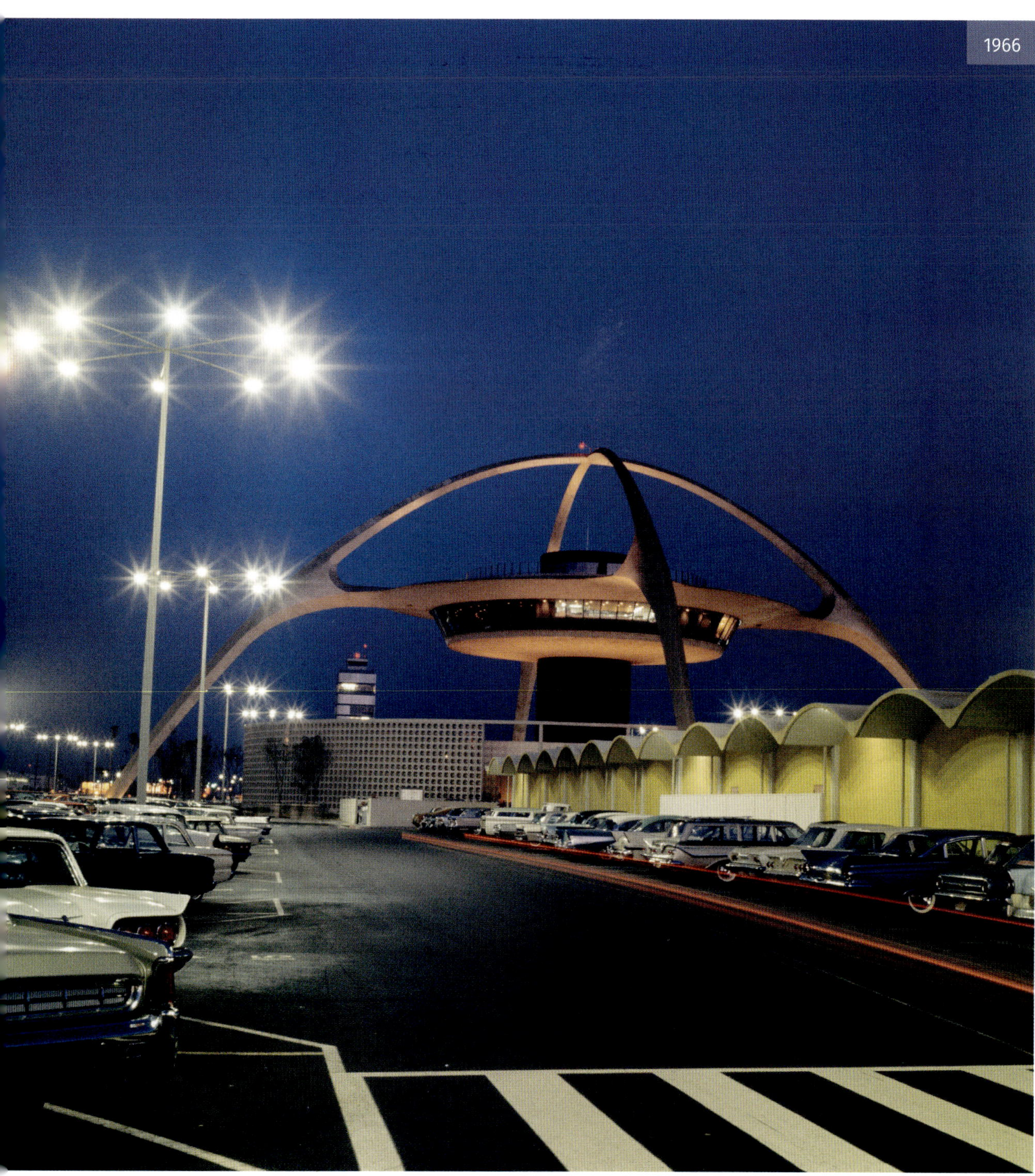

1966

THE THEME BUILDING, LAX, LOS ANGELES

A space-age building towering over the world's fifth-busiest airport

Los Angeles' main airport, LAX, is built on an air strip named Mines Field near Inglewood. Since 1928 it had become the Los Angeles Municipal Airport, serving the army, navy, air force and small commercial planes. By the late 1950s the airport had been developed into the Los Angeles International Airport, known as LAX. In 1961 the iconic space-age Theme Building opened at a cost of $50 million.

It was a classic example of style-over-function, influenced by "Populuxe" architecture, it is an example of the Mid-century-modern design movement, later to become known as "Googie." The flying-saucer-shaped design was created by William Pereira, Charles Luckman, Paul Williams (who designed the classic shell-shaped La Concha Motel in Las Vegas, now used for the Neon Museum), and Welton Becket. In the beginning, the restaurant on the top rotated slowly, providing a unique dining experience, but it was later made stationary. Above the restaurant is the Observation Deck with a 360-degree view of incoming and departing planes.

The structure was designated a Los Angeles Cultural Heritage Monument in 1993, but has rarely, if ever, turned a profit. The Walt Disney Imagineering team then designed a $4 million renovation and the new

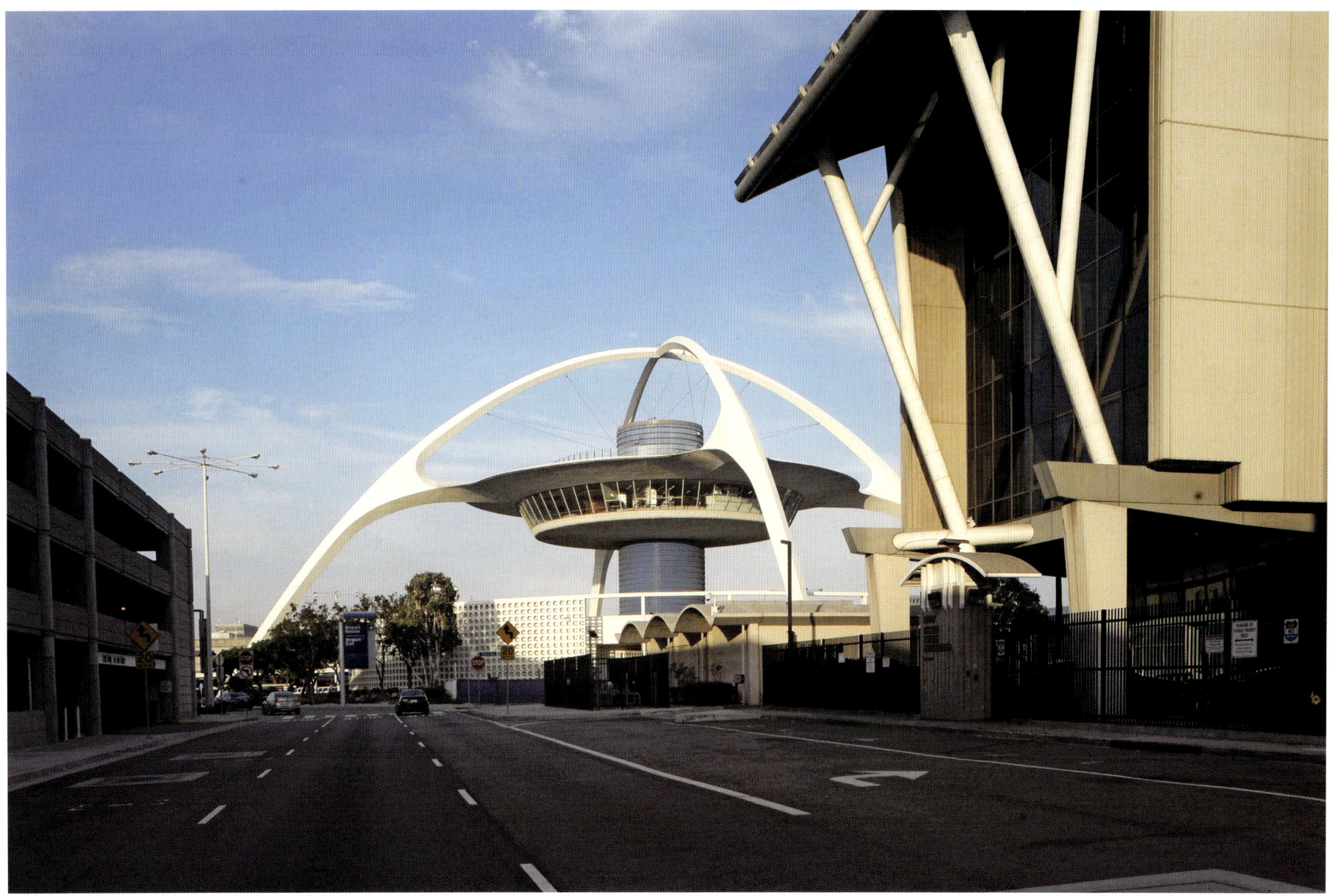

Encounter Restaurant opened in 1997. In 2007 a $14.3 million seismic upgrade and retrofit was started after a half-ton chunk of stucco fell onto the restaurant roof. New engineering was used for the arch system and a unique, steel, 600-ton, tuned mass damper was installed in the roof to absorb any earthquake motion. This upgrade was completed in 2010. The restaurant closed in 2013, with no plans to reopen.

The Observation Deck is now open only on Saturdays and Sundays following the 9/11 tragedy. A $14 billion upgrade of LAX began in 2017 aimed at integrating all the airport terminals and buildings, including the Theme Building, which stands as a classic 1950s view of what the future would be.

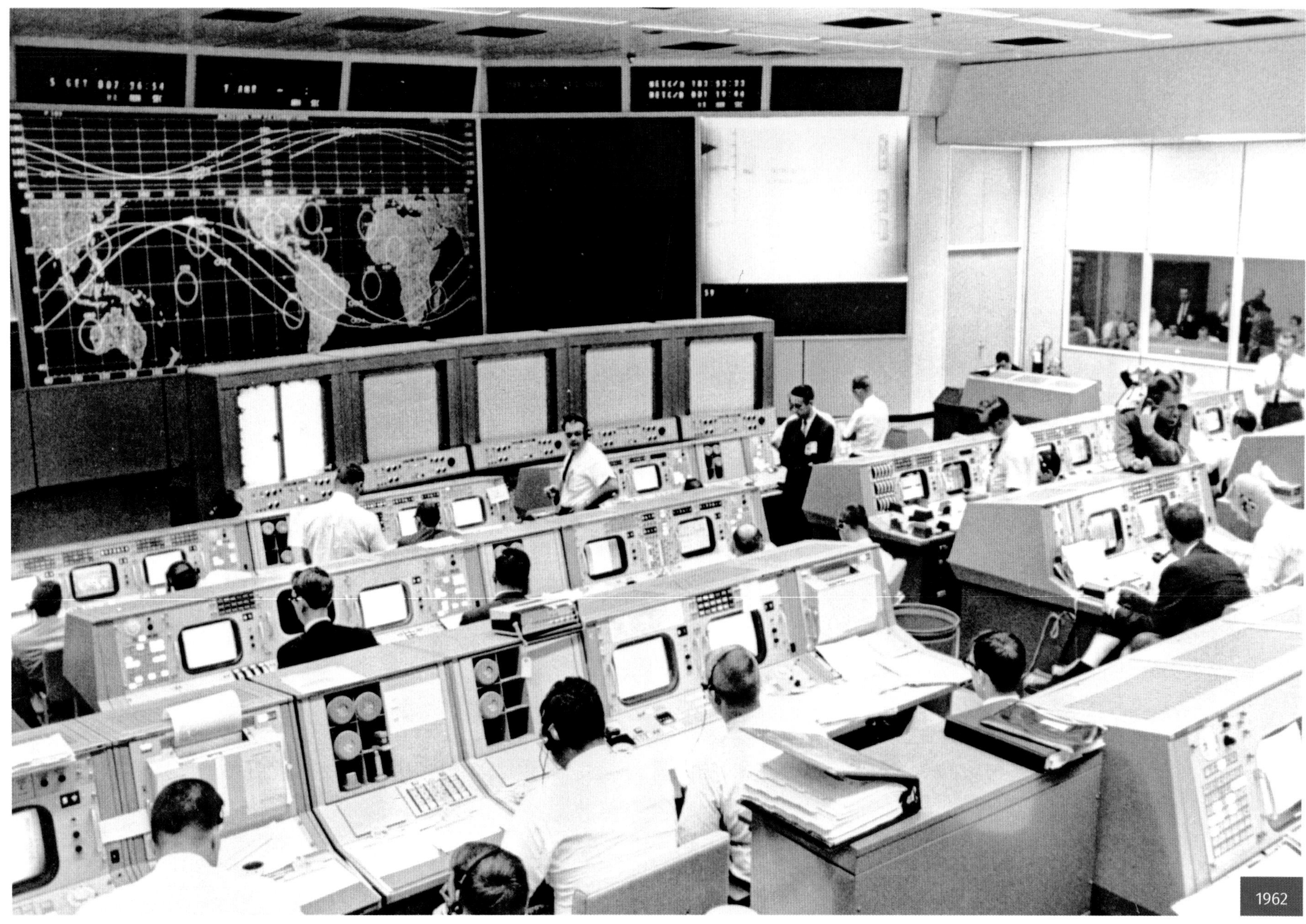

1962

JOHNSON SPACE CENTER, HOUSTON

Mission control for the Gemini and Apollo space programs

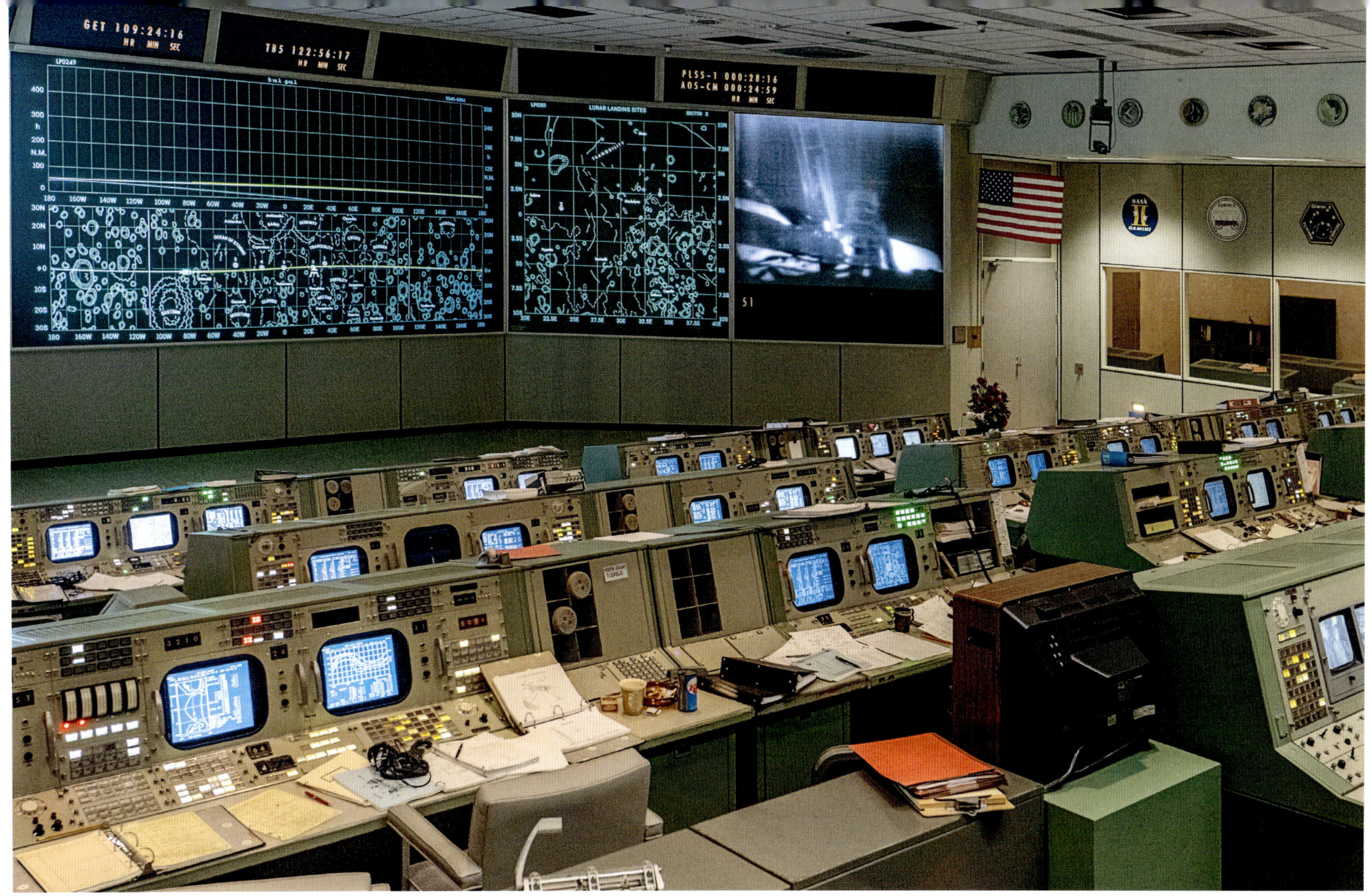

The vintage photo shows the control room at NASA's Johnson Space Center (JSC) in 1962. In 1961 President John F. Kennedy threw down the gauntlet to put a man on the moon by the end of the decade. But for this big goal, they needed a big space in which to work. The initiative's selection team chose Houston for its many technical workers, logistical infrastructure, mild climate, and proximity to both the San Jacinto Ordinance Depot and major academic institutions such as Rice University. Rice owned the land on which the JSC now stands, about 25 miles southeast of Houston. The university donated the undeveloped cattle-grazing land to NASA for the facility, which was originally called the Manned Spacecraft Center.

It was renamed the Lyndon B. Johnson Space Center in 1973 to honor the late president. Fittingly, it was Texan Charles Duke who uttered the famous words from Mission Control in Houston after Apollo 11's lunar module took longer than expected to reach the moon's surface: "Tranquility, we copy you on the ground. You got a bunch of guys about to turn blue. We're breathing again."

Over the years, the JSC was updated and served as primary flight control for NASA, supporting major space programs such as Gemini, Apollo, Skylab, the Space Shuttle, and the International Space Station. The original Apollo control room (above) was retrofitted as a museum exhibit in 2019 to mark the 50th anniversary of the moon landing.

The JSC today is a complex campus of facilities, including what is now called the Christopher C. Kraft Jr. Mission Control Center, which has primary responsibility for coordinating and monitoring all manned American spaceflight. Its multiple rooms, computers, and controls used to handle those responsibilities look as if they come straight out of *Star Trek*. The site also houses extensive and elaborate training facilities, a moon rock lab, and the directors of the White Sands Test Facility in New Mexico. Building 30, the famous Apollo Mission Control Center, is now a National Historic Landmark.

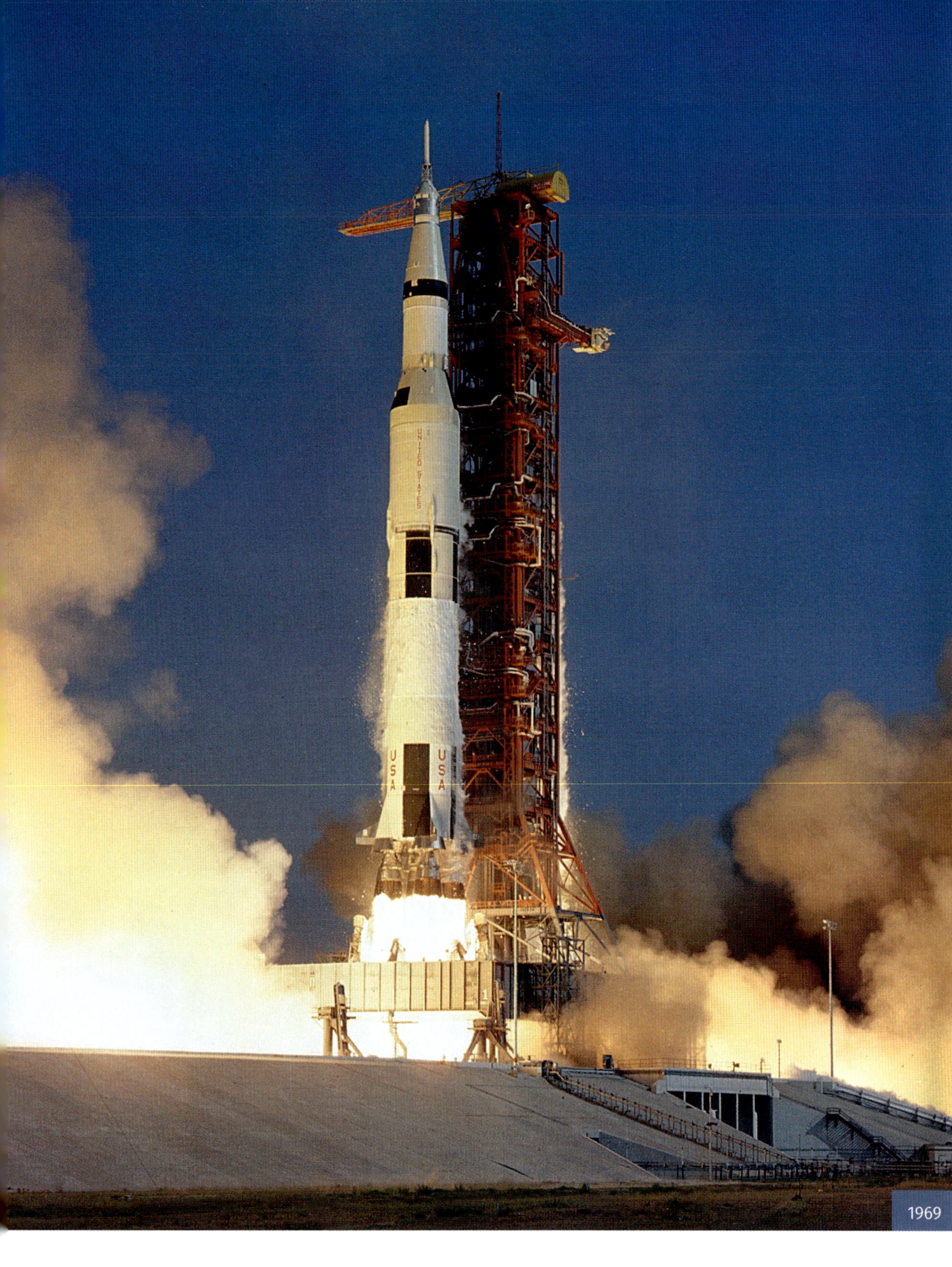

CAPE CANAVERAL SPACE FORCE STATION, FLORIDA

America and the Apollo program made one giant leap for mankind

The Apollo space missions were announced in John F. Kennedy's speech to a joint session of Congress, setting the goal of landing a man on the Moon and returning him safely to Earth before the end of the decade. It was a Cold War space race with the Russians that JFK didn't intend to lose. At the heart of this historic program was Cape Canaveral, Florida, which served as the primary launch site for Mercury, Gemini, and finally Apollo missions.

Cape Canaveral, on Florida's Atlantic coast, had been used for missile and rocket testing since the 1940s. In 1963, part of the Cape was renamed Cape Kennedy in honor of the fallen president, though the name reverted to Cape Canaveral in 1973. Adjacent to the Cape is Merritt Island, which became home to the Kennedy Space Center (KSC)—NASA's primary launch complex for manned spaceflight.

The centerpiece was Launch Complex 39, specially built for Apollo's enormous Saturn V rocket. Two pads, 39A and 39B, were constructed to handle the weight and power of the 363-foot Saturn V. The nearby Vehicle Assembly Building (VAB) housed the massive rocket stages, where they were stacked vertically before being moved to the launch pads.

On July 16, 1969, Apollo 11 launched from Launch Pad 39A with astronauts Neil Armstrong, Buzz Aldrin, and Michael Collins aboard. The world watched as the Saturn V thundered into the sky above Cape Canaveral, beginning a mission that would resonate for millennia.

The country that had only sought independence in 1776 had reached another planet. Four days after liftoff, Armstrong and Aldrin descended in the Lunar Module (Eagle) to the Moon's surface (pictured above), while Collins orbited above them in the Command Module, Columbia.

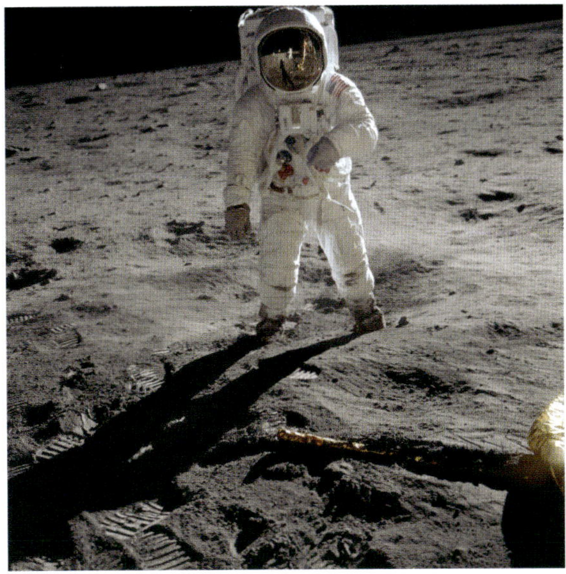

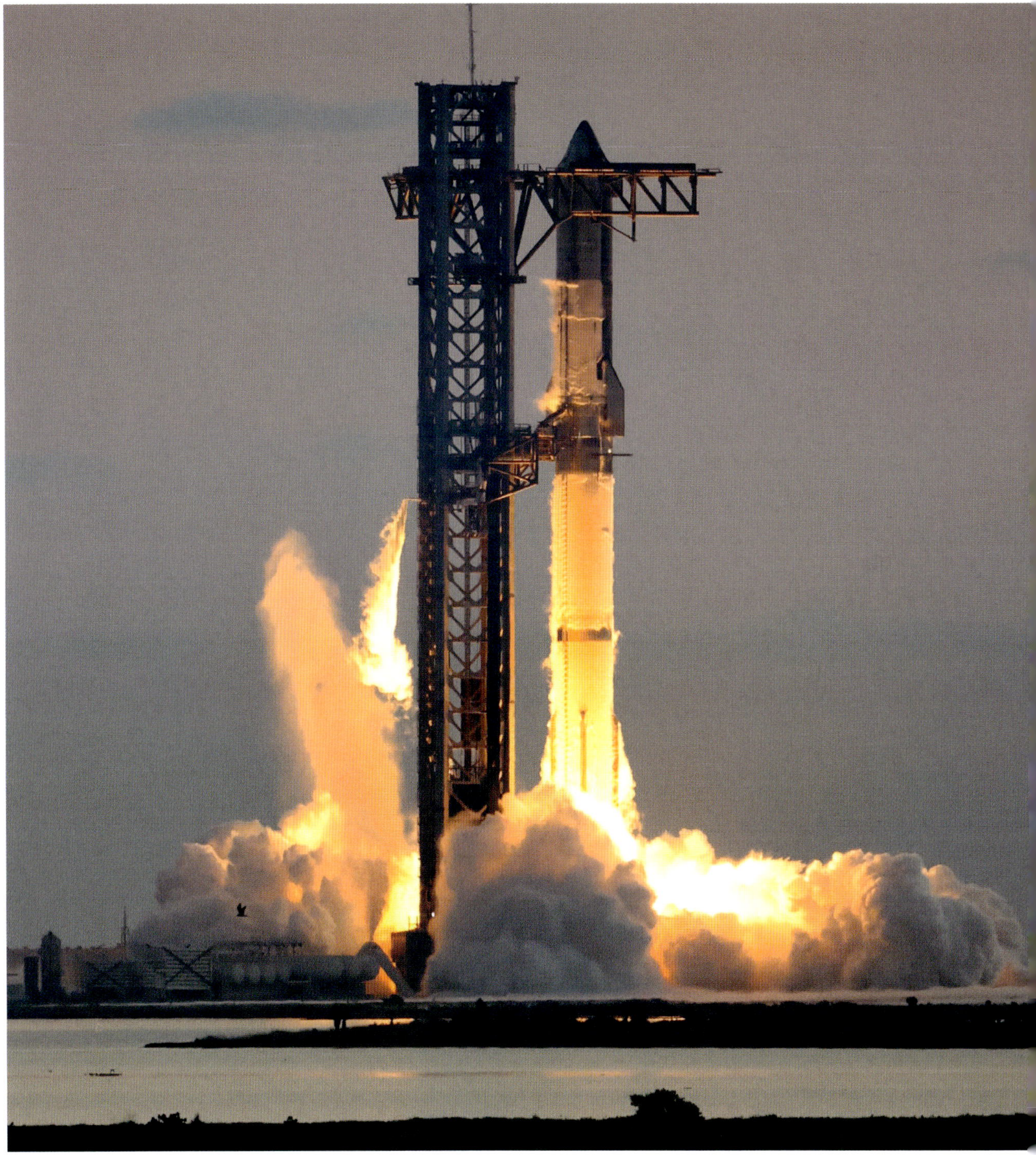

On July 20, Armstrong stepped onto the Moon and delivered the historic words: "That's one small step for man, one giant leap for mankind." Although he had actually said "*a* man," the "a" wasn't picked up on audio.

Following Apollo 11, six more missions attempted lunar landings; five were successful. Apollo 13 famously suffered a near-fatal malfunction en route to the Moon but was safely guided back to Earth in a dramatic rescue effort. The final lunar mission, Apollo 17, launched in December 1972, marking the end of a defining era in space exploration. After Apollo, Cape Canaveral and the Kennedy Space Center continued to serve as launch sites for the Space Shuttle program, satellite launches, and more recently, commercial spaceflight by companies like SpaceX and Blue Origin. Launch Complex 39A, once the starting point for Moon missions, is now leased by SpaceX and used for Falcon 9 and Falcon Heavy launches (as pictured right).

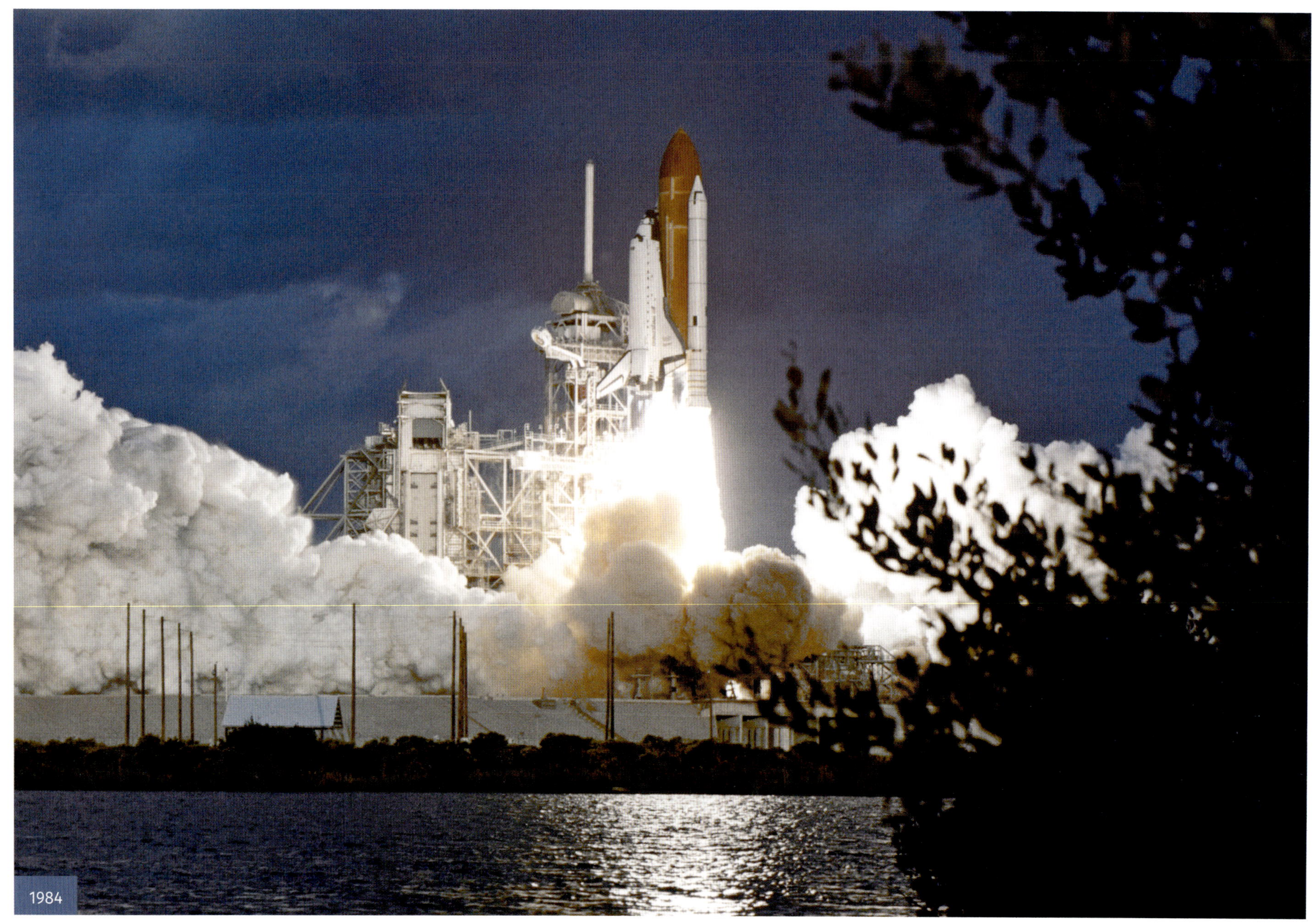
1984

SPACE SHUTTLE, SMITHSONIAN/UDVAR-HAZY AEROSPACE MUSEUM

Apollo's successor had more commercial ambitions

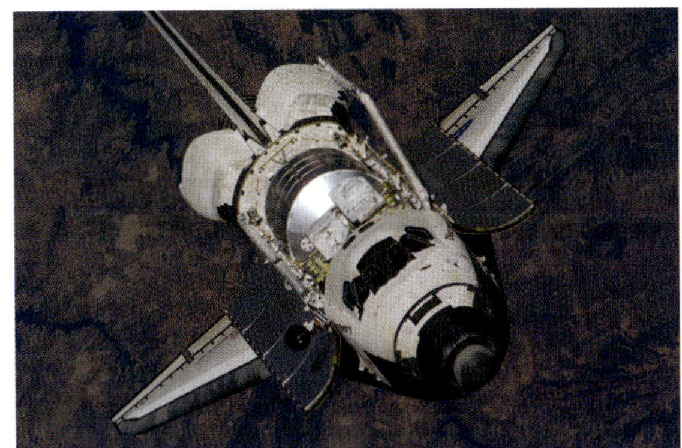

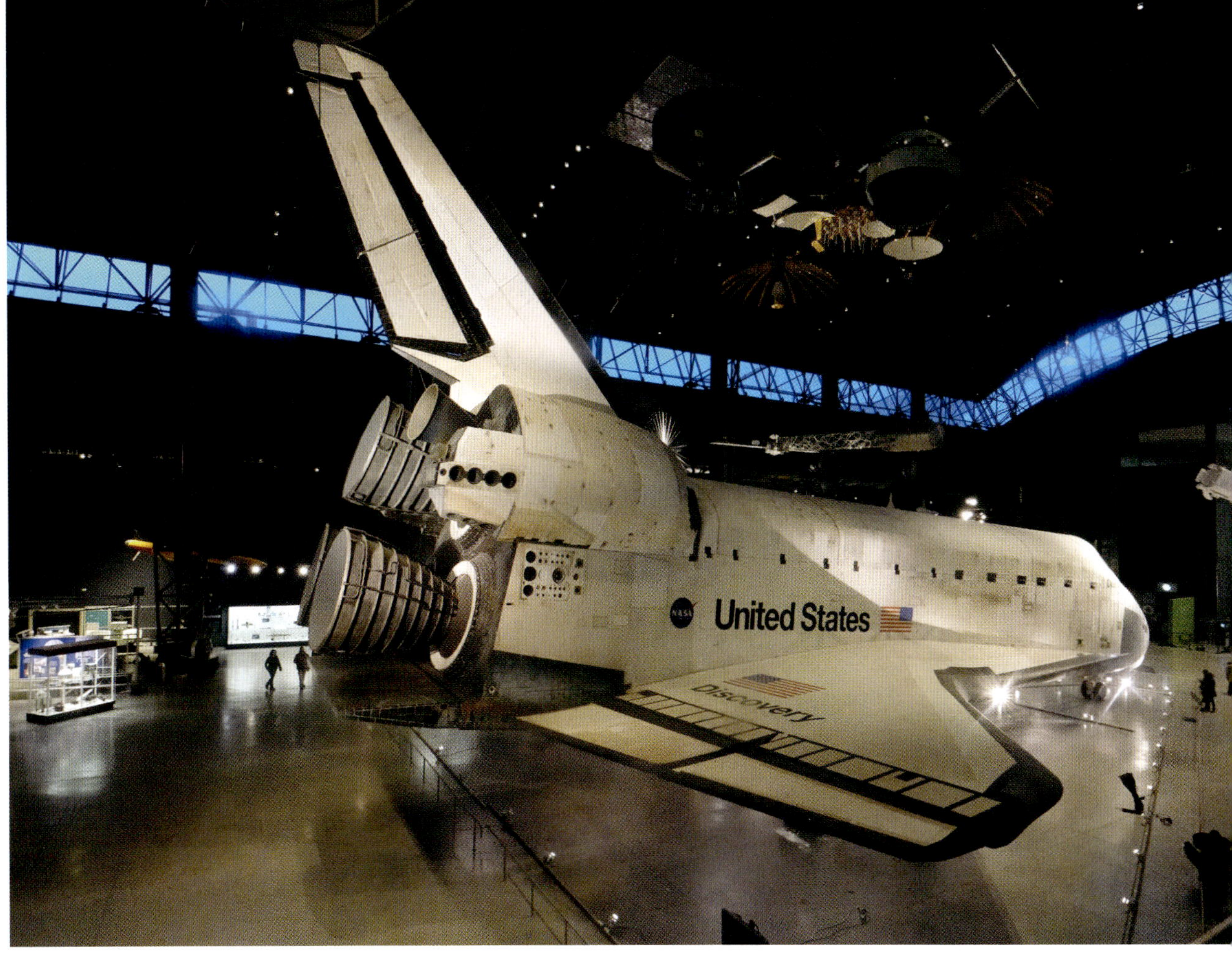

The Space Shuttle program was NASA's ambitious effort to create a reusable spacecraft capable of transporting astronauts and cargo into low Earth orbit. The Apollo lunar missions came at enormous expense and so the space agency began exploring ways to make spaceflight more economical. In 1972, President Richard Nixon approved the development of the Space Shuttle—a partially reusable spacecraft that could launch like a rocket, orbit Earth, and then return to land like a plane. Running from 1981 to 2011, the program marked a new chapter in human spaceflight. Development was complex and expensive, with the first orbiter, Enterprise, built in 1976 for approach and landing tests (but never spaceflight). The first operational shuttle, Columbia, launched on April 12, 1981.

Over 30 years, the shuttle program flew 135 missions and carried more than 350 people into space. Five orbiters were built and flown: Columbia, Challenger, Discovery, Atlantis, and Endeavour. The program's mission was to boldly go and deploy satellites, the Hubble Space Telescope (launched by Discovery in 1990), and later to help construct the International Space Station (ISS), whose assembly was largely carried out using flights from the late 1990s onward.

Despite its achievements, the shuttle program suffered two catastrophic disasters. On January 28, 1986, Challenger broke apart 73 seconds after launch due to a failed O-ring seal in one of the Solid Rocket Boosters. All seven crew members, including teacher Christa McAuliffe, perished. The disaster grounded the fleet for nearly three years as NASA overhauled its safety procedures. Tragedy struck again on February 1, 2003, when Columbia disintegrated during reentry due to damage sustained on launch. A piece of foam from the external tank had struck the wing, compromising its heat shield. Again, seven astronauts were lost.

After Columbia, NASA flew only essential missions, primarily to complete construction of the ISS. The final shuttle flight, STS-135, was undertaken by Atlantis on July 8, 2011. It concluded three decades of US-operated human spaceflight—until the arrival of commercial crew vehicles like SpaceX's Crew Dragon nearly a decade later.

Discovery is now the star exhibit on display at the Smithsonian/Udvar-Hazy Aerospace Museum in Washington, DC, parked right alongside some of the tiny, earliest space capsules, a testament to the United States' incredible achievement in space.

OPPOSITE: The launch of the Space Shuttle Discovery from the Kennedy Space Center, November 8, 1984.

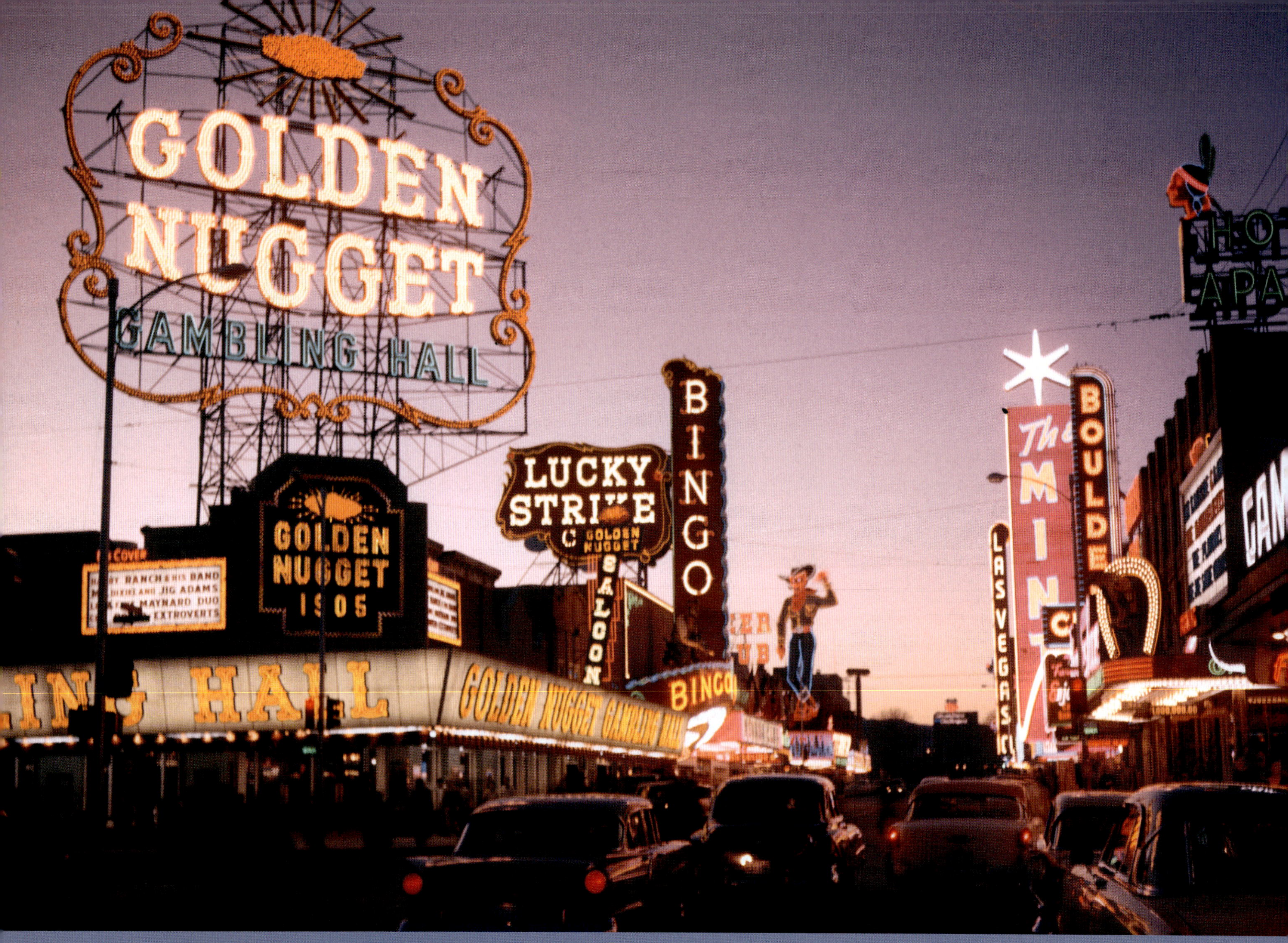

GLOBAL ENTERTAINMENT CAPITAL

From silent films to the pizzazz of the Super Bowl, from the blues legends of Mississippi to the shows of Las Vegas, America has defined and exported entertainment for over a century.

Sports have long been a part of national life, but in the twentieth century, they became entertainment spectacles. Few nations have commercialized and celebrated sports with the same flair and scale as the United States.

The National Football League (NFL), founded in 1920, rose to supremacy in the postwar decades. Its blend of strategy and aggression made it America's favorite sport. The Super Bowl, launched in 1967, evolved into a national institution and a global media event—complete with multimillion-dollar ads and superstar musical performances.

Baseball, known as "America's pastime," was the sport of the early twentieth century. It gave rise to legends like Babe Ruth and Jackie Robinson, the latter breaking the color barrier in 1947 and helping sports lead the charge in civil rights.

Golf (like baseball) imported from the Old World, always had great potential given the land available for epic courses to be set. America's earliest golf legend, Bobby Jones, created a course near his home in Georgia that has become the most recognizable in the game, thanks to its annual hosting of the Masters.

Even auto racing became a uniquely American form of spectacle. The Indianapolis Motor Speedway (IMS), home to the Indianapolis 500, remains one of the world's most prestigious motorsport circuits and the single largest sporting venue in the world, with seated space for 250,000.

THE SOUND OF AMERICA: BLUES, JAZZ, SOUL, AND ROCK

In the early twentieth century, the blues emerged in the Mississippi Delta, its mournful chords capturing the struggle and resilience of Black life in the South. Pioneers like W. C. Handy, Robert Johnson, and Muddy Waters laid the foundation for countless genres.

In the 1920s, jazz born in New Orleans fused African rhythms with European harmony and improvisation. Icons like Louis Armstrong, Duke Ellington, and Ella Fitzgerald gave America its first major cultural export.

By the 1950s, a new fusion emerged: rock 'n' roll, blending blues with country and gospel. Elvis Presley, Chuck Berry, and Little Richard lit up the stage with a sound that shocked older generations and thrilled youth around the world. The rebellious edge of rock made it a voice of teen identity.

The 1960s and 70s brought soul music, a gospel-inflected blend driven by stars like Aretha Franklin, Otis Redding, and Marvin Gaye, while Motown Records turned Detroit into a hit factory of crossover Black artists. Meanwhile, Nashville was carving out its own role as the home of Country Music.

HOLLYWOOD: THE MYTH FACTORY

The rise of Hollywood in the early twentieth century marked the start of West Coast influence. The film industry first took root in New York and New Jersey, but producers soon fled to Southern California for its cheaper land, better weather, and distance from Edison's patent enforcers.

By the 1920s, Hollywood had become synonymous with film. Studios like Paramount, Warner Bros., Universal, and MGM built vast backlots and controlled production and distribution, and held their stars on permanent contract. Stars like Charlie Chaplin, Clara Bow, and later Clark Gable and Marilyn Monroe became global icons. Hollywoodland also had a massive sign attracting real estate investors.

With the advent of "talkies" in 1927 (notably *The Jazz Singer*), the building of luxurious picture palaces only increased from the pioneer days of the "silents." Grauman's Chinese Theatre in Los Angeles was just such an extravagant movie house where no expense was spared, and no promotional opportunity went unexplored.

Traditional theater and vaudeville took a back seat—existing theaters often being forced to convert to movie houses. This trend, since the advent of Blockbuster Video, DVDs and now streaming, has reversed, with conversion back to live performances for those venues that resisted the wrecking ball (including the Radio City Music Hall, which came under threat).

LAS VEGAS: THE CITY OF SPECTACLE

Nowhere is American entertainment more visible than in Las Vegas, a city built in the desert on neon and excess. Originally a railroad stop, Las Vegas boomed after Nevada legalized gambling in 1931. By the 1950s, mob-backed casinos like the Flamingo and Sands turned the city into a playground for adults. Frank Sinatra, Sammy Davis Jr. and Elvis Presley gave Vegas its cool. The formula was simple: gambling, music, and frequently risqué shows.

In the late twentieth century, Vegas rebranded. Massive themed resorts like The Mirage, Luxor, Bellagio, and The Venetian offered not just gaming but family-friendly spectacles, elite dining, and Broadway-style shows. There had always been boxing contests to bring in the high-rollers, but to this heady mix has been added other world-class sports events such as the NFL's Raiders and the Formula 1 Las Vegas Grand Prix.

While other nations have vibrant cultural scenes, America has created a global *lingua franca* of entertainment which has created some of the most iconic venues in the world.

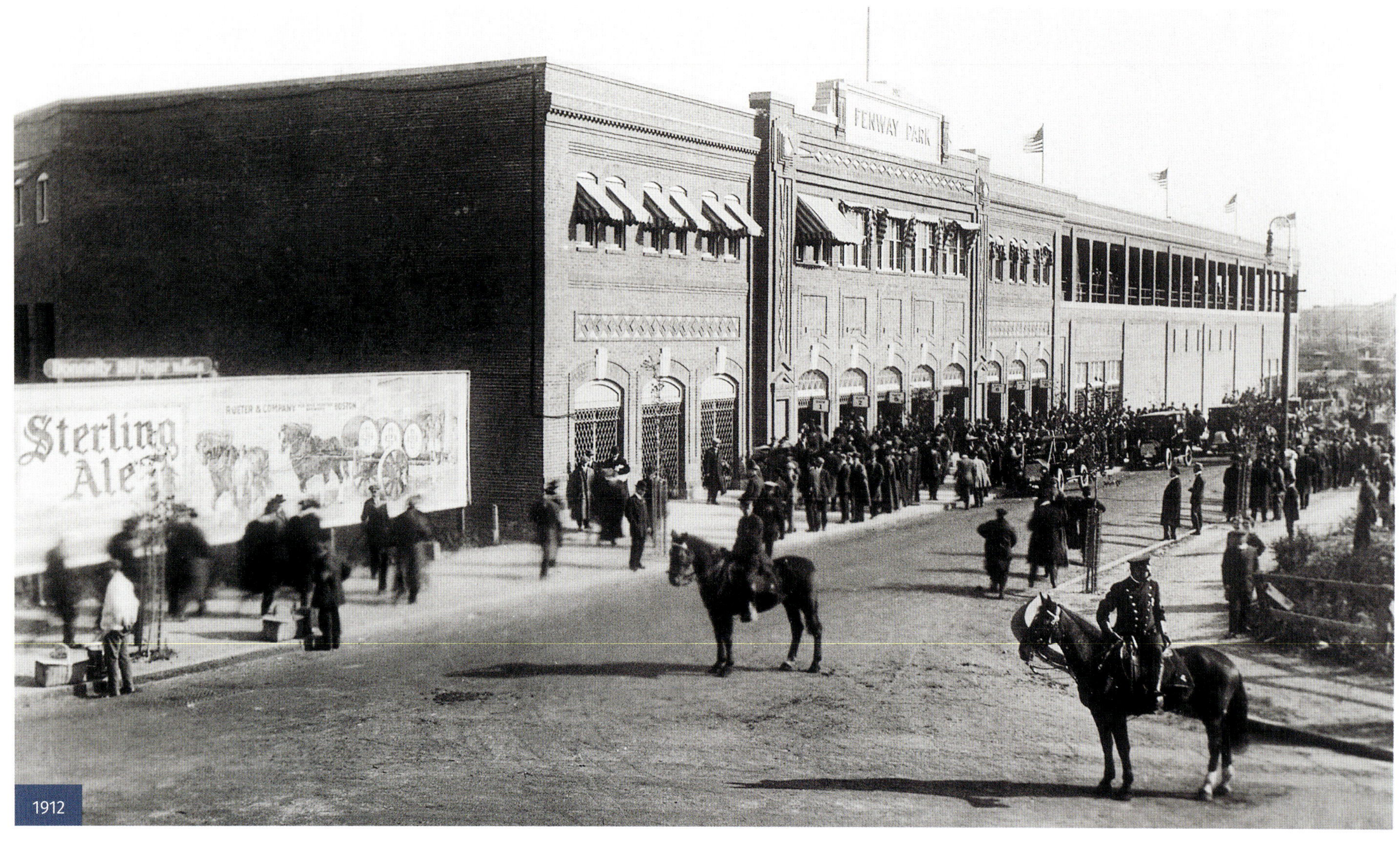

1912

FENWAY PARK, BOSTON

MLB's oldest baseball stadium, home to the Green Monster

The filled-in land around the Back Bay Fens was Boston's new frontier at the turn of the twentieth century. Where once lay a no-man's-land of tidal flats plus the mainland marshes of Roxbury's Gravelly Point, streets were now laid out, and cultural institutions took root. In 1912, Red Sox owner John Taylor—of the family that owned the *Boston Globe*—moved his team to his brand-new ballpark by the Fenway. The 24,000 spectators who filed in through the gates on Jersey Street (later Yawkey Way) on Opening Day watched the Sox beat the New York Highlanders (later Yankees), 7–6.

Fenway Park was renovated after a major fire in 1934, and after several expansions now seats 37,755 (night games). It is difficult to overstate the place that Fenway Park—the

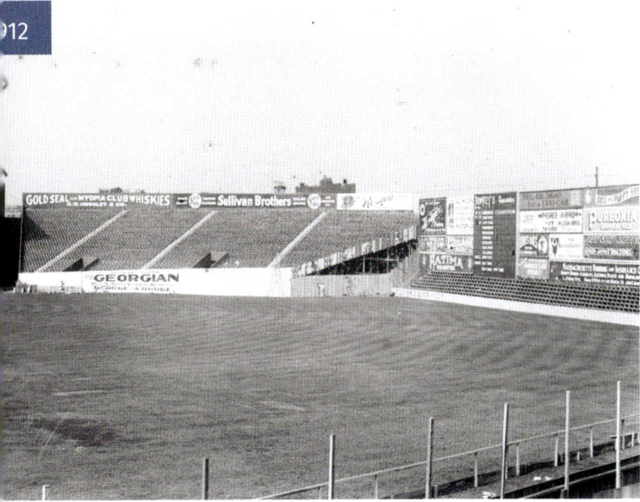

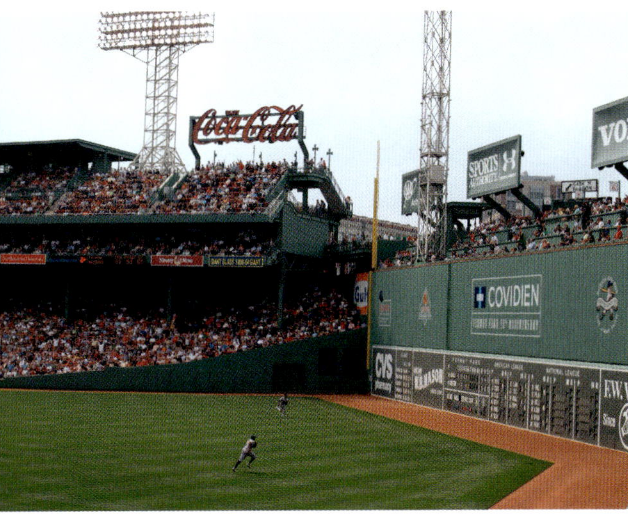

ABOVE: Two photos of the left-field wall: one in its original form from the opening season, and below it the "Green Monster" that it has become.

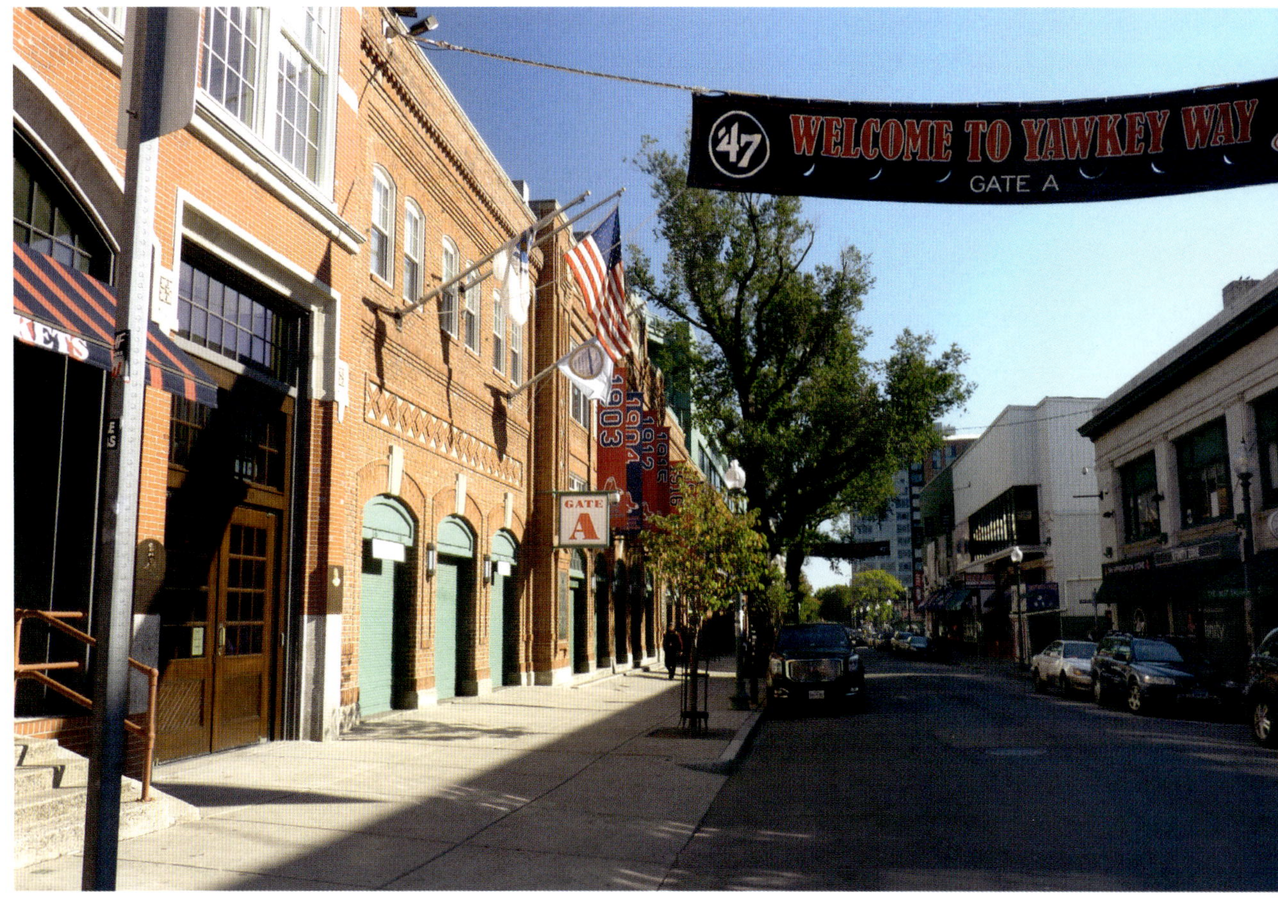

oldest and smallest park in the major leagues—holds in the hearts of New Englanders. The Sox won five World Series before trading power-hitting pitcher Babe Ruth to the New York Yankees, and then entering an 86-year title drought that ended in 2004, literally as a blue moon occurred in the night sky. "The Curse of the Bambino" was a popular sports curse attributed to the sale of Babe Ruth, "the Bambino," to the New York Yankees in 1920. The team's history has been marked by its intense rivalry with the Yankees, arguably the fiercest and most historic in North American professional sports ... and this didn't help. However, to make up, the Red Sox became the first team to win four World Series trophies in the twenty-first century, with championships in 2004, 2007, 2013, and 2018.

Fenway's most famous feature is its 37-foot-high left-field wall the "Green Monster," the popular nickname for the wall, situated 310 feet from home plate at the left-field foul line. Part of the original ballpark construction of 1912, facing Lansdowne Street, it was not painted green until 1947; before that, it was a glorified billboard and for most of its history was simply called "The Wall."

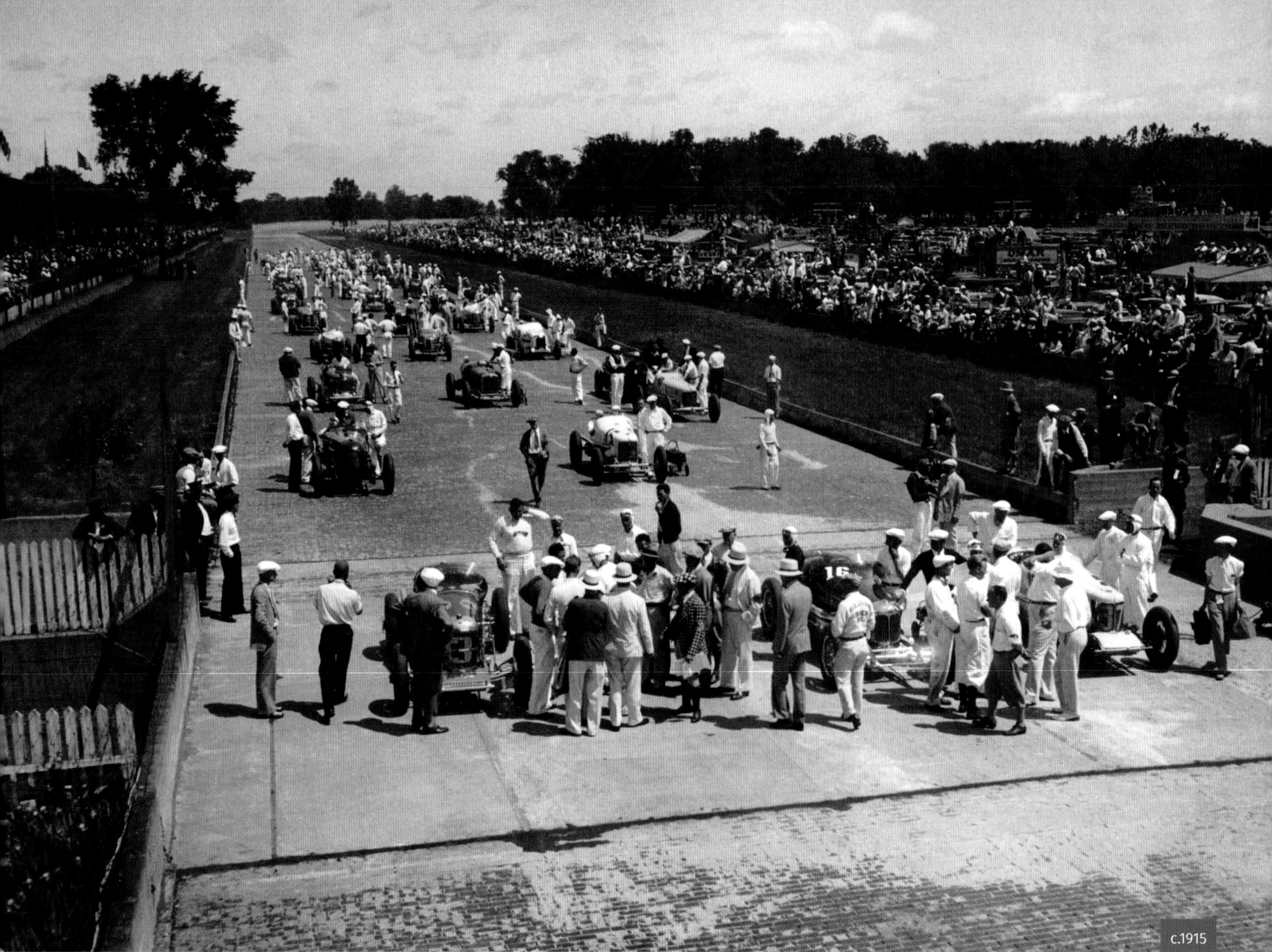

c.1915

INDIANAPOLIS MOTOR SPEEDWAY, INDIANA

The world's largest sporting venue comes alive in May

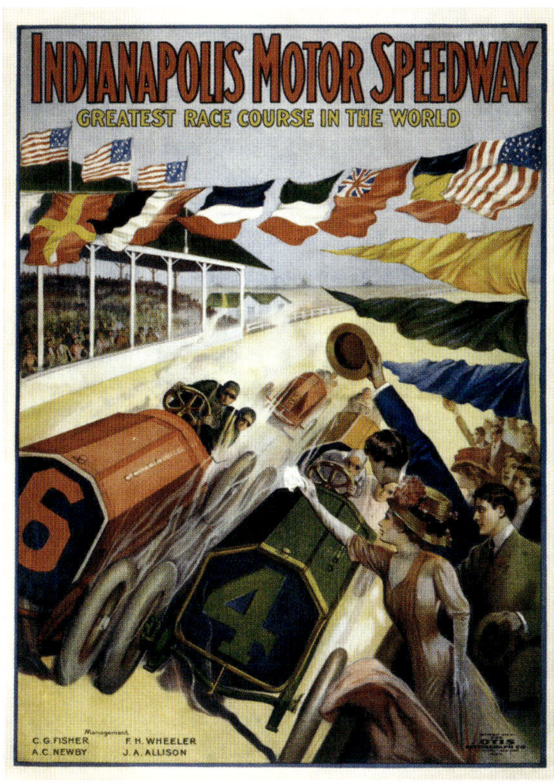

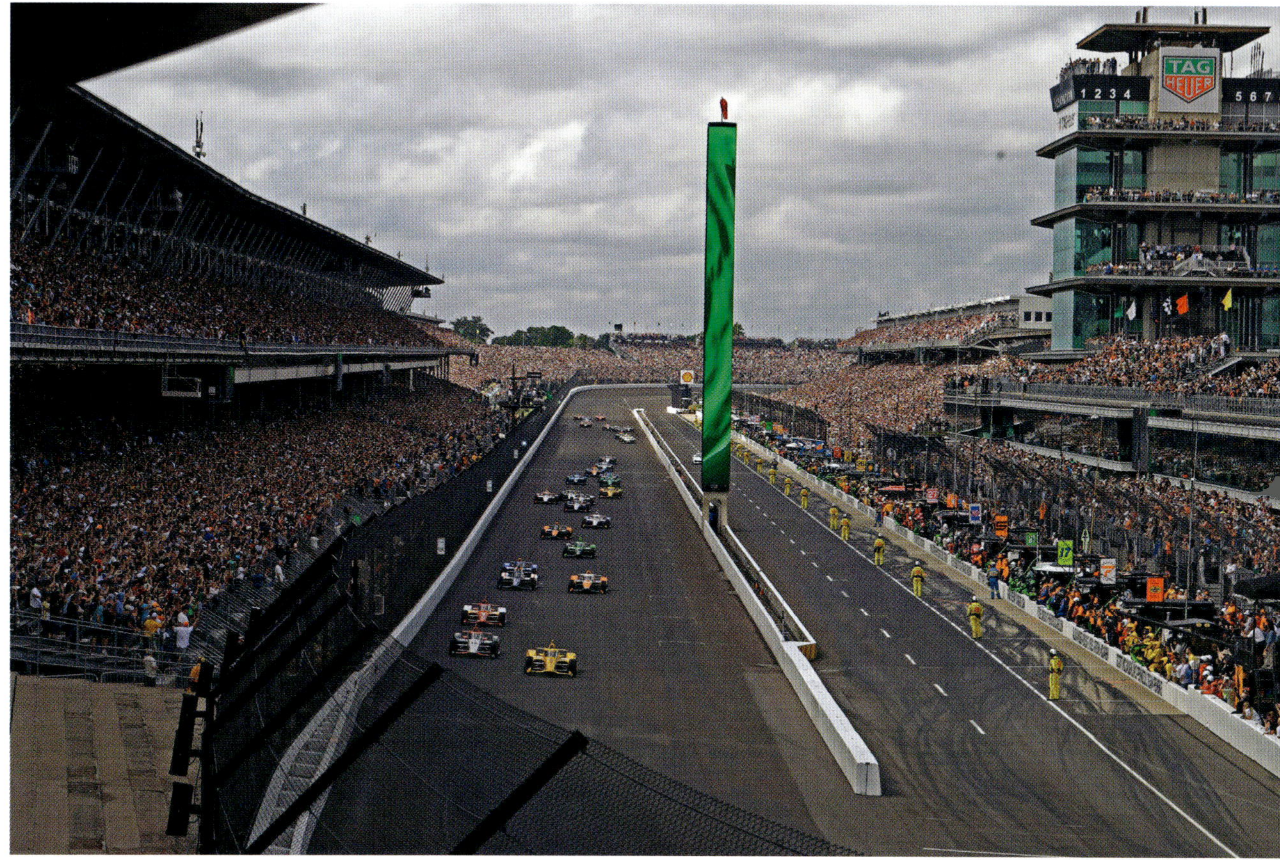

The Indianapolis Motor Speedway (IMS), located in Speedway, Indiana, has played a central role in the development of auto racing and American motorsport culture for well over a century. In 1908, local businessman Carl G. Fisher began planning a track that could host races and test new automotive technologies for Indiana-based auto makers.

Construction began in 1909 on a 2.5-mile oval circuit laid over 328 acres of farmland. The track was originally surfaced with crushed stone and tar, which quickly proved unsafe. After a disastrous first motorcycle race and a chaotic automobile event that resulted in multiple fatalities, the track was resurfaced later that year with 3.2 million bricks, earning it the nickname "The Brickyard."

The track's owners realized that rather than holding frequent smaller races, a single, large event would better capture the public's imagination. This led to the creation of the Indianapolis 500, a 500-mile race first run on May 30, 1911. The inaugural event was won by Ray Harroun, driving a Marmon Wasp. "The Month of May" is a phrase interchangeable with the Indy 500, as for four weeks teams assemble to test and qualify.

The Indy 500 quickly became the premier racing event in the United States (with the highest prize money in world motorsport) and attracted global attention. Over time, the track evolved to meet modern safety and technical standards. The original brick surface was gradually replaced by asphalt, though the symbolic "Yard of Bricks" at the start/finish line remains. In 1927, the facility was sold to Eddie Rickenbacker, a World War I flying ace and former Indy 500 driver, who managed it until World War II. The original Pagoda control tower building has been replaced several times, but always maintaining the Japanese styling.

While the Indianapolis 500 remains the crown jewel, in 1994 the Brickyard 400, a NASCAR race, was introduced and became one of the most popular races on the stock car circuit. The speedway has also hosted Formula 1, with the United States Grand Prix, and MotoGP motorcycle racing. These races used an infield track as well as the start/finish straight.

With a permanent seating capacity of over 250,000—making it the largest sports venue in the world by capacity—it continues to draw hundreds of thousands of fans every Memorial Day weekend for the Indy 500.

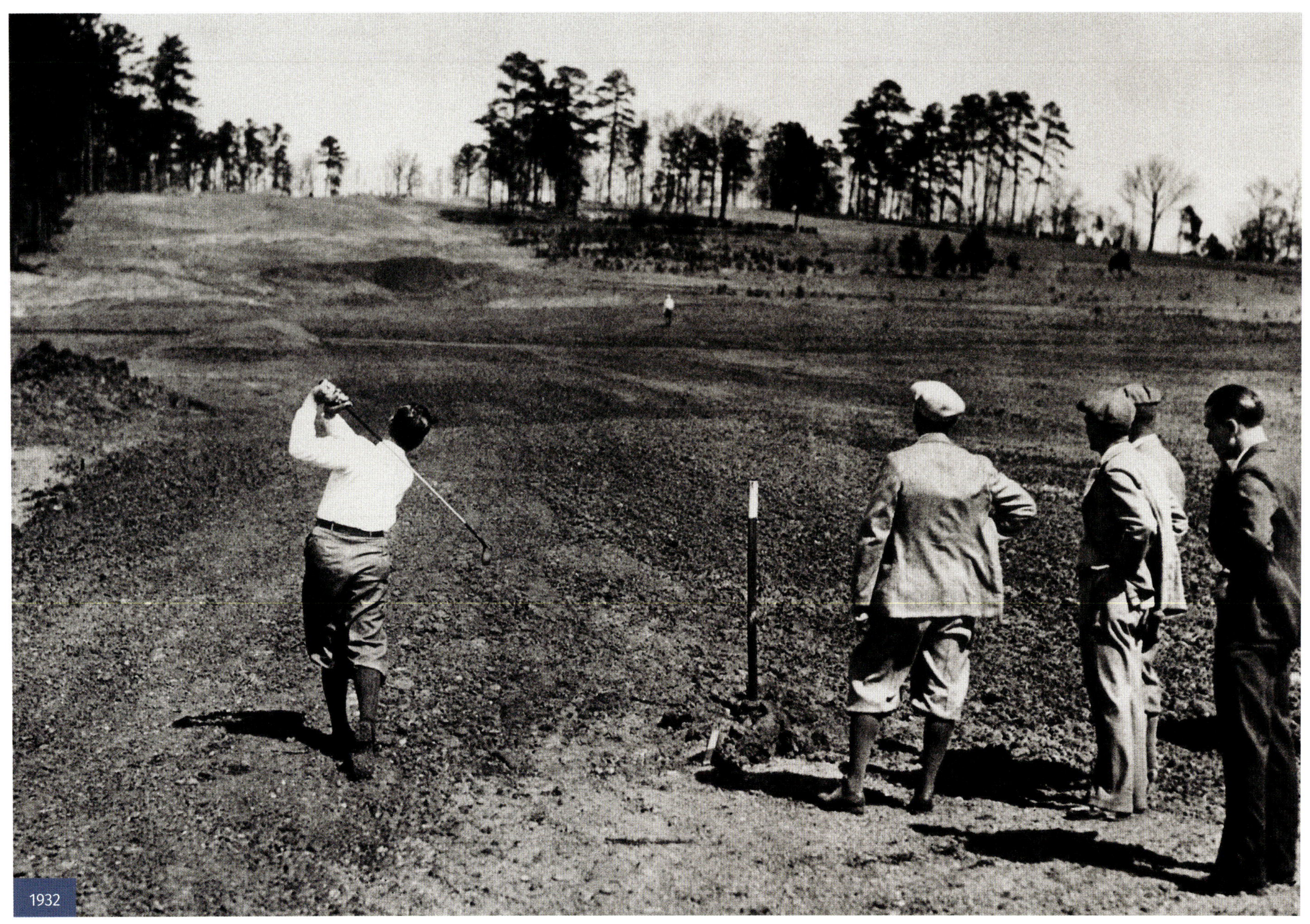

1932

AUGUSTA NATIONAL GOLF CLUB, GEORGIA

Bob Jones helped create an iconic golf course—in equal parts majestic and terrifying

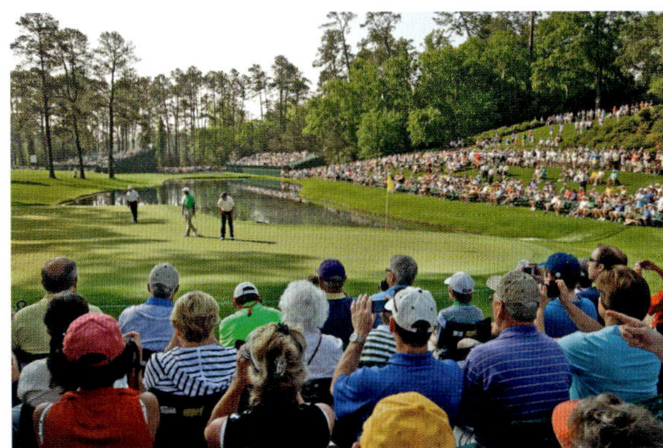

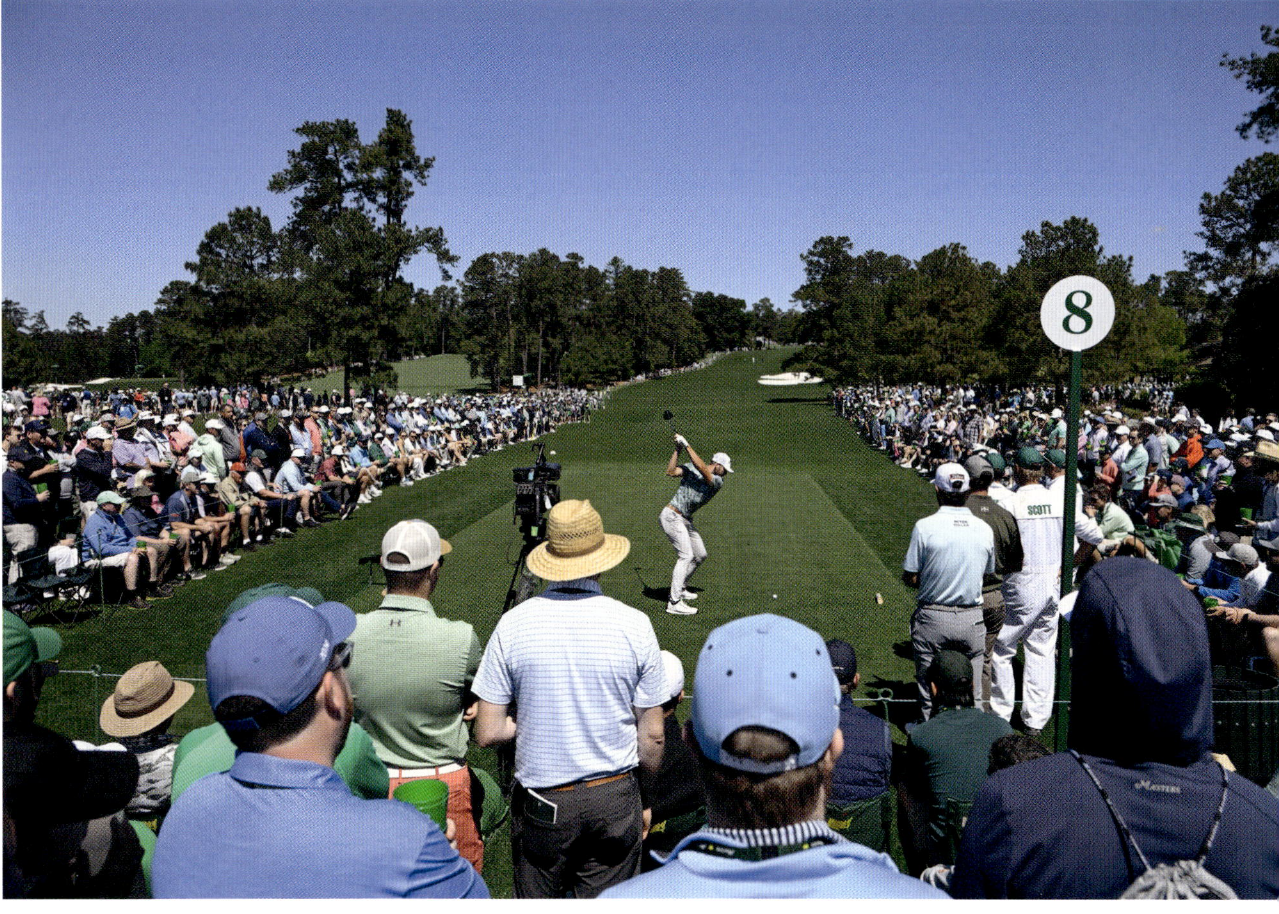

It may be less than a century old, but the Augusta National Golf Club is one of the most revered institutions in golf. Best known as the home of the Masters Tournament, Augusta National combines rich tradition, a pristine course, superfast greens, and a challenging 18 holes.

Augusta National was founded in 1931 by Bobby Jones, a world-class amateur golfer, and Clifford Roberts, a wealthy New York investment banker. Jones had recently retired from competitive golf after winning the Grand Slam in 1930 and wanted to create a golf course that would embody his vision of perfection in the game. They chose the site of a former tree nursery—Fruitland—which offered rolling terrain, flowering plants (all the holes are now named after flowers and trees), and ample space.

Jones enlisted famed British course architect Alister MacKenzie (Pebble Beach, Royal Melbourne, The Worcestershire) to help design the layout. Together, they created an 18-hole course that emphasized strategy over brute strength. MacKenzie died shortly before the course officially opened in 1933, but his architectural principles remain deeply embedded in its design.

In 1934, the first Masters Tournament—then called the Augusta National Invitational—was held. Jones wanted the course to host the US Open, but governing body the PGA of America thought Georgia would be too hot in June. The name "Masters" was adopted in 1939, reportedly at the insistence of Clifford Roberts, though Jones initially resisted the term as too self-important.

The Masters quickly distinguished itself from other golf tournaments. It was invitational, always held at the same course, and has become steeped in traditions: the Green Jacket awarded to the winner, the Champions Dinner and the pre-tournament Par-3 Contest.

Over the decades, Augusta National has undergone numerous changes, but always with an eye toward maintaining its original spirit. While the course has been lengthened to keep up with modern equipment, its key features—elevated greens, Rae's Creek, and fast putting surfaces—continue to test the world's best golfers. In 1997, Tiger Woods' historic Masters victory at age 21 brought global attention and new audiences to Augusta.

Augusta National's influence stretches far beyond Georgia. The Masters is one of golf's four major championships. It is broadcast worldwide and revered for its meticulous presentation—immaculate fairways, blooming azaleas—and, unlike many other golf events, highly respectful spectators.

OPPOSITE: Bobby Jones teeing off at the 8th hole in 1933, while the course is under construction. Alongside him are Clifford Roberts and Alister MacKenzie.

ABOVE RIGHT: A view from behind the modern 8th tee during the 2024 US Masters. The development of golf equipment over the years has necessitated the lengthening of many tee shots.

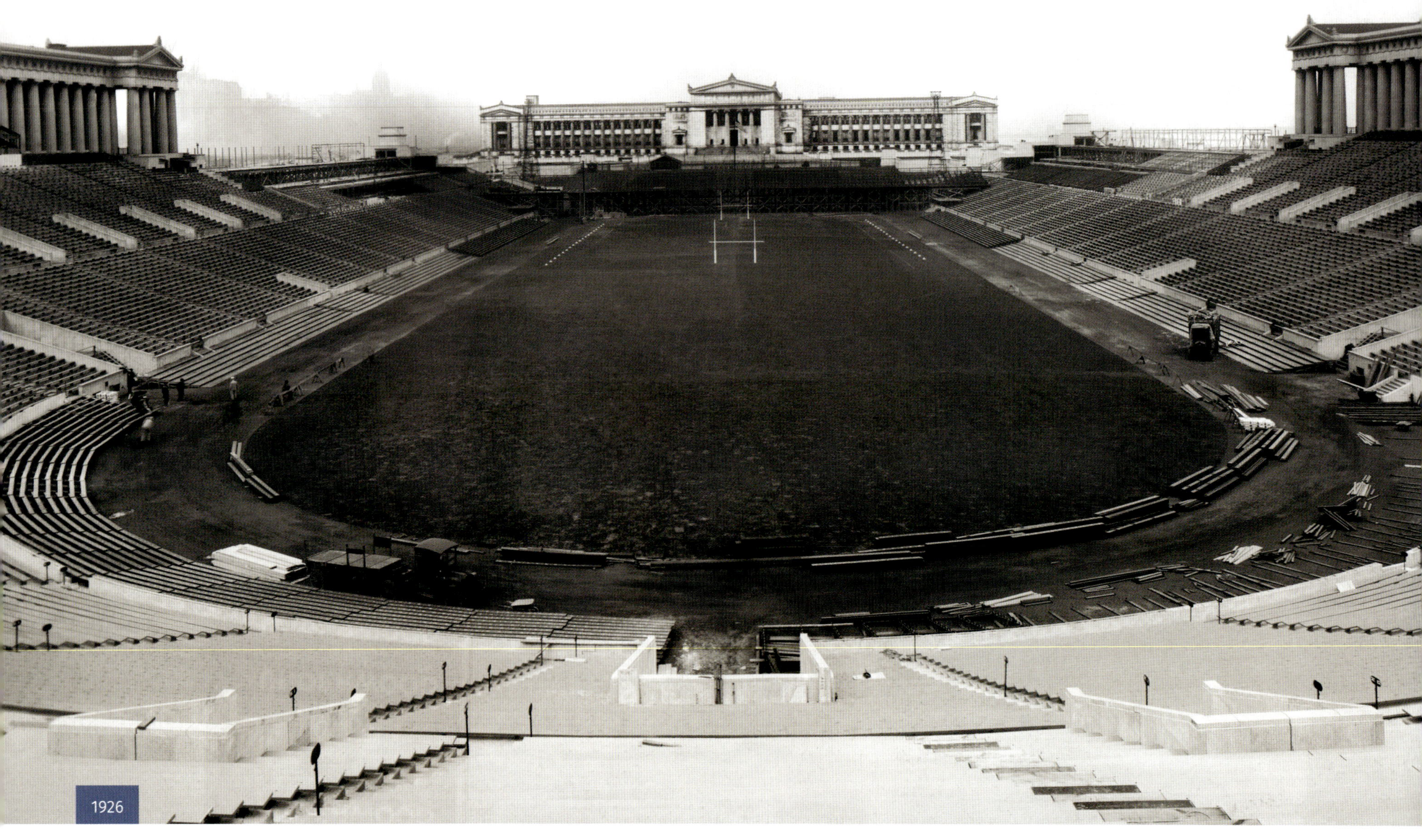
1926

SOLDIER FIELD, CHICAGO

The oldest stadium used in the NFL, but not the longest used...

Though over a century old, Soldier Field's role as the home of the NFL's Chicago Bears is relatively recent (compared to the Green Bay Packers' Lambeau Field). It was originally conceived as a multipurpose municipal stadium, Grant Park Stadium, but was renamed Soldier Field to honor soldiers who fought in World War I. In November 1926, the annual Army vs. Navy college football game was held in Chicago to formally dedicate the field. The stadium had been designed to host large-scale events such as track meets, political rallies, and college football games. It has even hosted midget car racing and military re-enactments. Its original seating capacity was over 74,000, expandable to over 100,000 with temporary seating, making it one of the largest stadiums in the country.

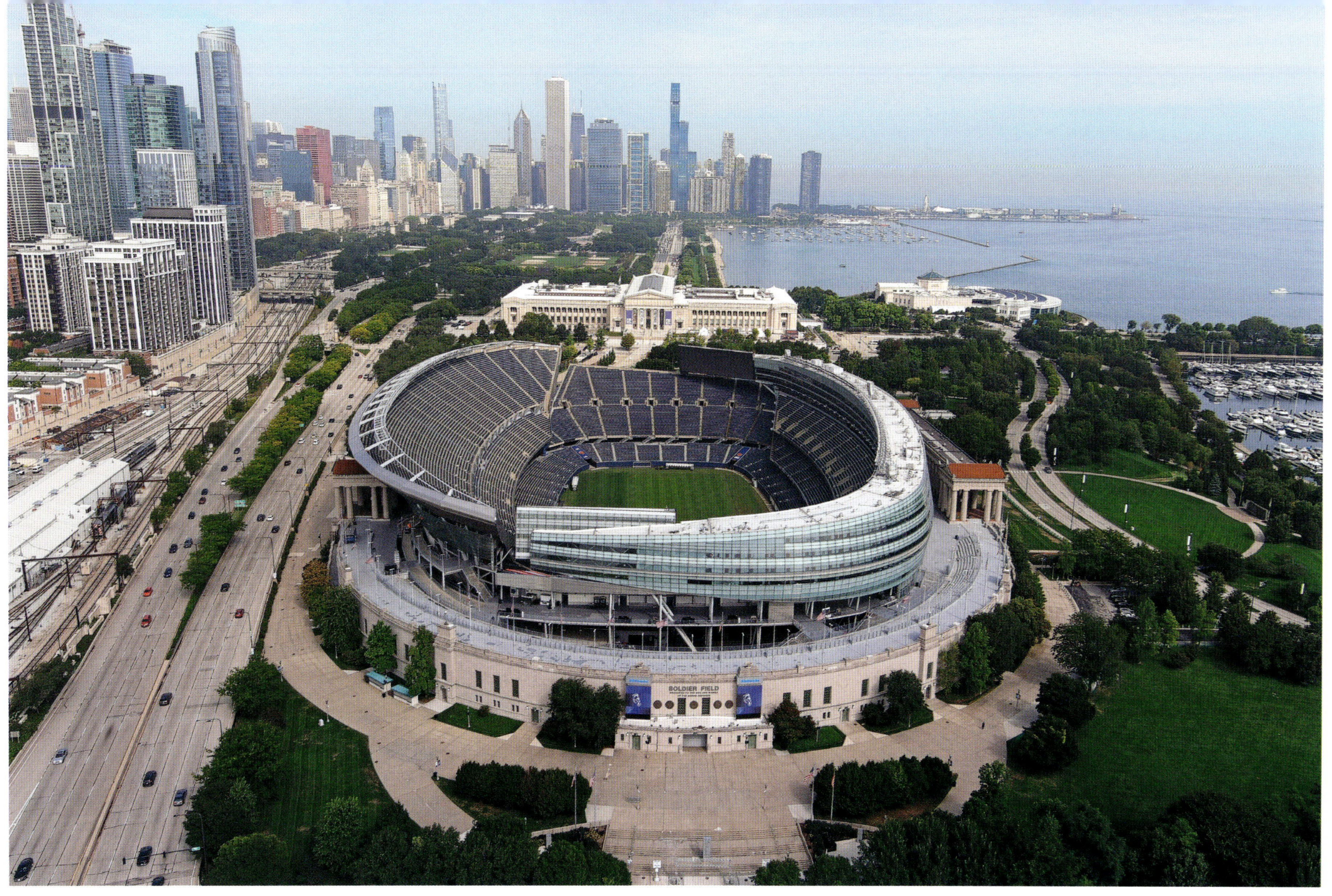

The Chicago Bears were founded in 1919 as the Decatur Staleys and relocated to Chicago in 1921. They originally played at Wrigley Field, sharing it with the Chicago Cubs baseball team. However, by the late 1960s, it became increasingly clear that the cramped Wrigley Field was inadequate for an expanding NFL, especially for a team with a massive and passionate fan base. After years of negotiations, the Bears moved to Soldier Field in 1971.

During the 1985 season, led by head coach Mike Ditka and defensive coordinator Buddy Ryan, the Bears assembled one of the most dominant defenses in NFL history. The Bears finished 15–1 and dominated opponents en route to Super Bowl XX, where they defeated the New England Patriots 46–10.

By the late 1990s, Soldier Field was showing its age. It lacked modern amenities and revenue-generating features such as luxury suites. After much debate, a controversial $690 million renovation was undertaken in 2002–2003. The interior of the stadium was entirely rebuilt while the historic colonnades on the exterior were preserved. The result was a stark contrast between old and new, leading some critics to nickname it the “spaceship inside a coliseum.”

The renovation reduced capacity to around 61,500, making it one of the smaller NFL stadiums. Despite backlash from preservationists—Soldier Field even lost its National Historic Landmark status in 2006—the renovation ensured that the Bears would remain in downtown Chicago. In 2023, the Bears signed a purchase agreement for a site in Arlington Heights, signaling a future relocation. The Bears’ current lease at Soldier Field with the Chicago Park District expires in 2033.

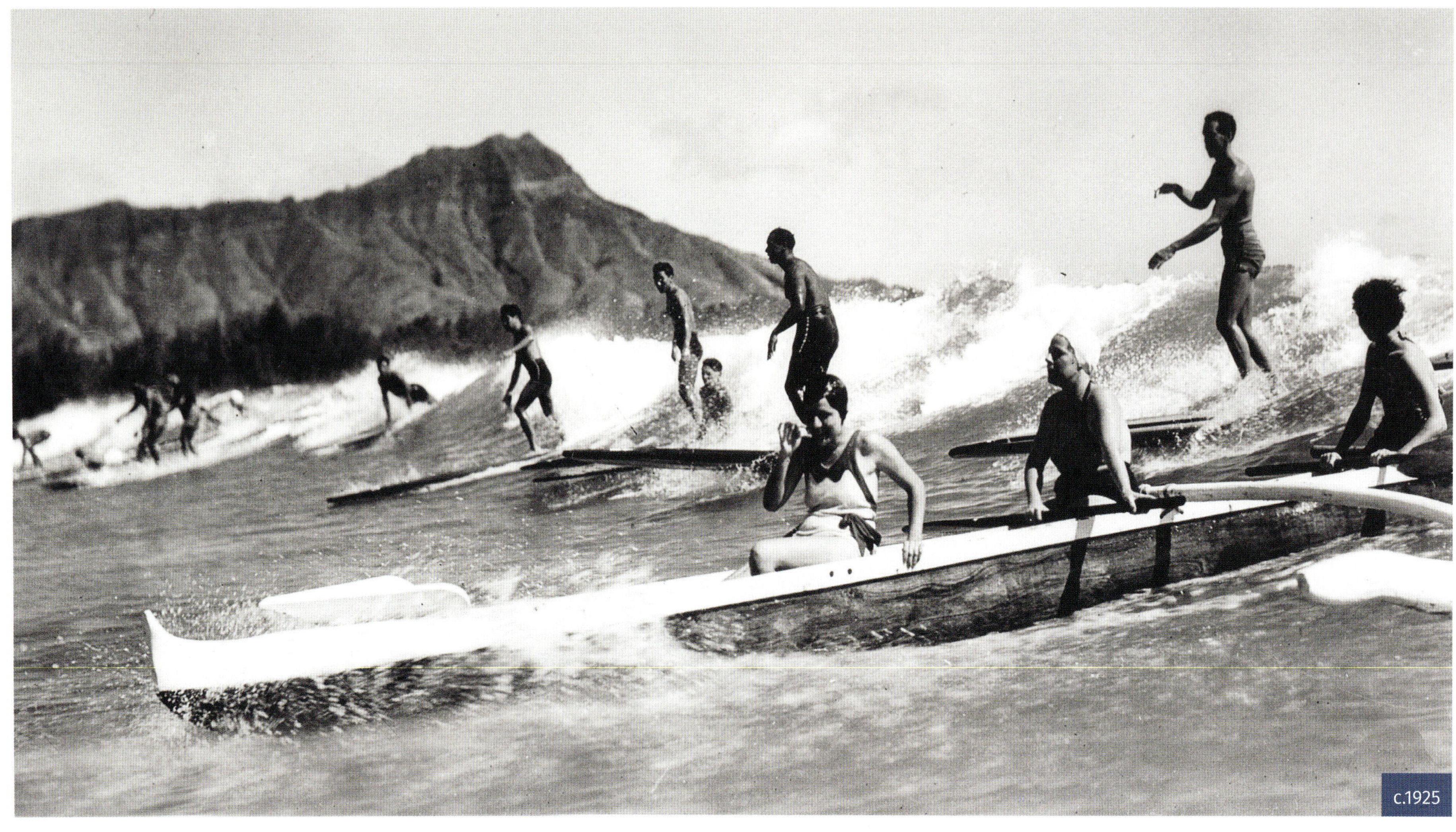
c.1925

SURFING AT WAIKIKI, HONOLULU, HAWAII

Duke Kahanamoku was the ambassador for a sport now embraced across the globe

Surfing, known as *heʻe nalu* in Hawaiian, has deep roots in the islands of Hawaii, particularly the famous beach of Waikiki in Honolulu on the island of Oahu.

Surfing in ancient Hawaii was a central part of the culture, practiced by both men and women, royalty and commoners. By the nineteenth century, however, the influence of Western colonization began to take effect. Christian missionaries, and the islanders' changing lifestyles led to a decline in traditional Hawaiian practices, including surfing.

In the early twentieth century surfing enjoyed a resurgence centered on Honolulu and the gentle rolling waves of Waikiki Beach. This revival coincided with increased interest in Hawaii as a destination for leisure and exotic culture. Local beachboys gave surf and outrigger canoe rides to tourists (as pictured above) which played a major role in keeping the sport alive. Chief among them was Duke Kahanamoku, born in Honolulu in 1890 and an extraordinary waterman. He first gained international fame not through surfing but as an Olympic swimmer. He won his first gold medal in the

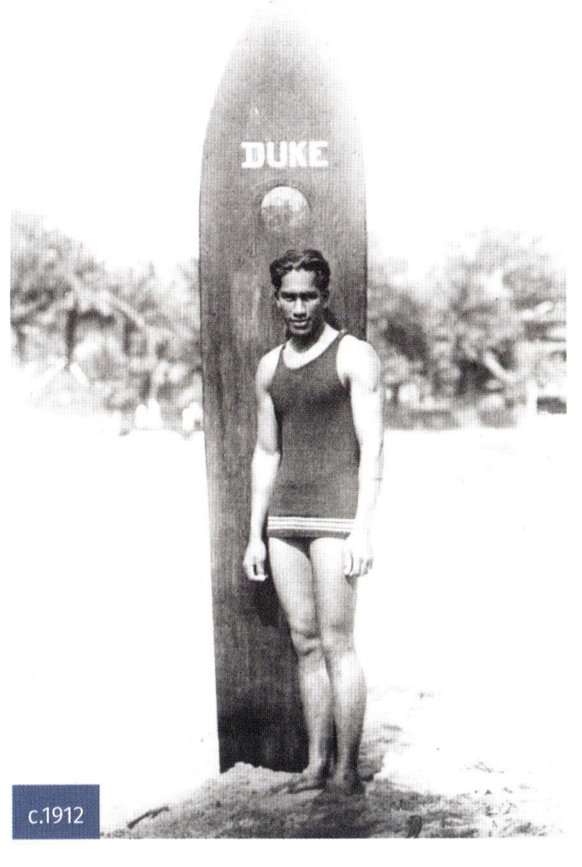

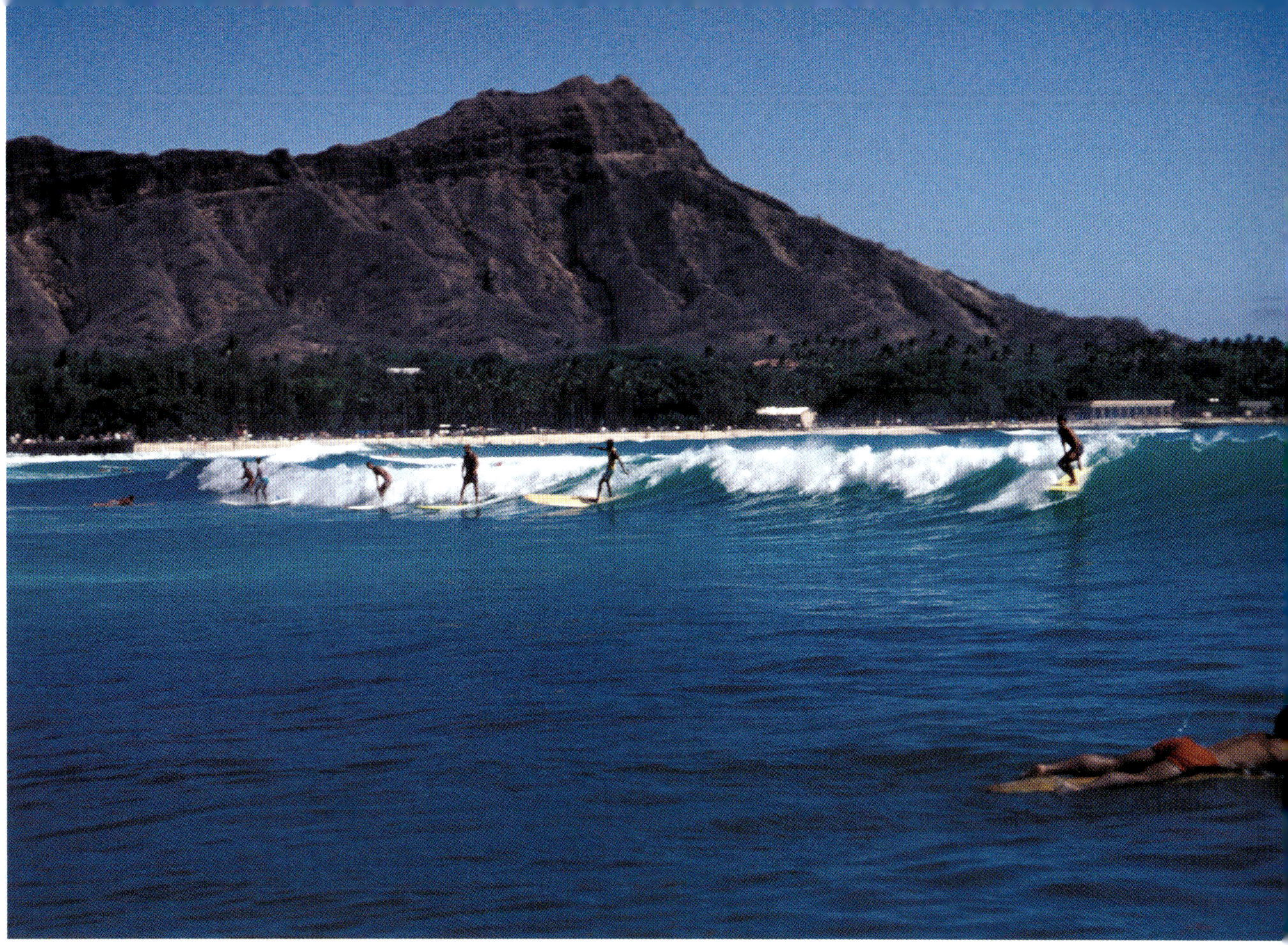

100-meter freestyle at the 1912 Stockholm Olympics and went on to compete in four Olympic Games, earning five medals. Tall, graceful, and charismatic, Duke became a global celebrity—and he used his fame to share his love for surfing with the world.

Between Olympic appearances and exhibitions, Duke traveled to mainland United States, Australia, and even Sweden. On these trips, he would bring his handcrafted surfboards (no mean achievement given their size) and introduced surfing to audiences who had never seen it before.

In 1915, he gave a surfing exhibition at Freshwater Beach in Sydney, Australia, effectively planting the seed for Australian surf culture. In California, he drew crowds at beaches from San Diego to Santa Monica, helping to inspire the first generation of mainland surfers.

Back in Honolulu he was a founding member of the Hui Nalu surf club, one of several groups dedicated to preserving Hawaiian water sports traditions. Along with the Outrigger Canoe Club, these organizations fostered a growing community of surfers and watermen.

After World War II, Hawaii's tourism industry boomed with the rise of jet travel, and surfing became a defining symbol of island life. Waikiki, with its gentle waves and scenic beauty, remained a popular spot for beginners, while more advanced surfers began exploring the challenges of the island's North Shore. Surf culture exploded on the mainland in the 1950s, promoted by movies like *Gidget* (1959) and reinforced by the music of the Beach Boys.

Duke Kahanamoku lived to see surfing go global. He remained a beloved ambassador of *aloha* until his death in 1968. A statue of Duke now stands near the spot where he once surfed on the beach at Waikiki, greeting visitors with outstretched arms and his trademark welcoming smile.

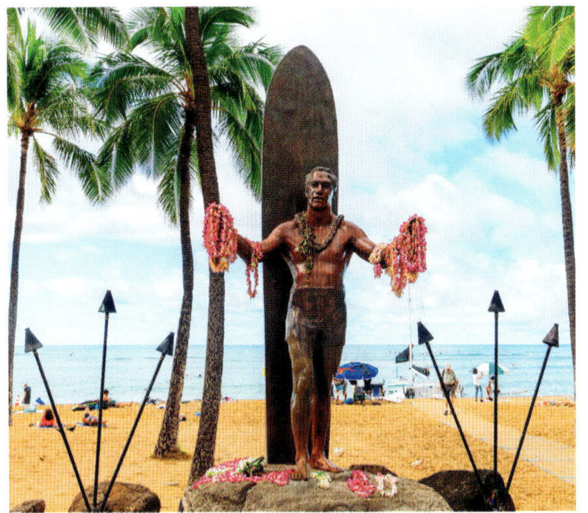

LEFT: Duke Kahanamoku with a relatively short board for the era and, below, his commemorative statue at Waikiki.

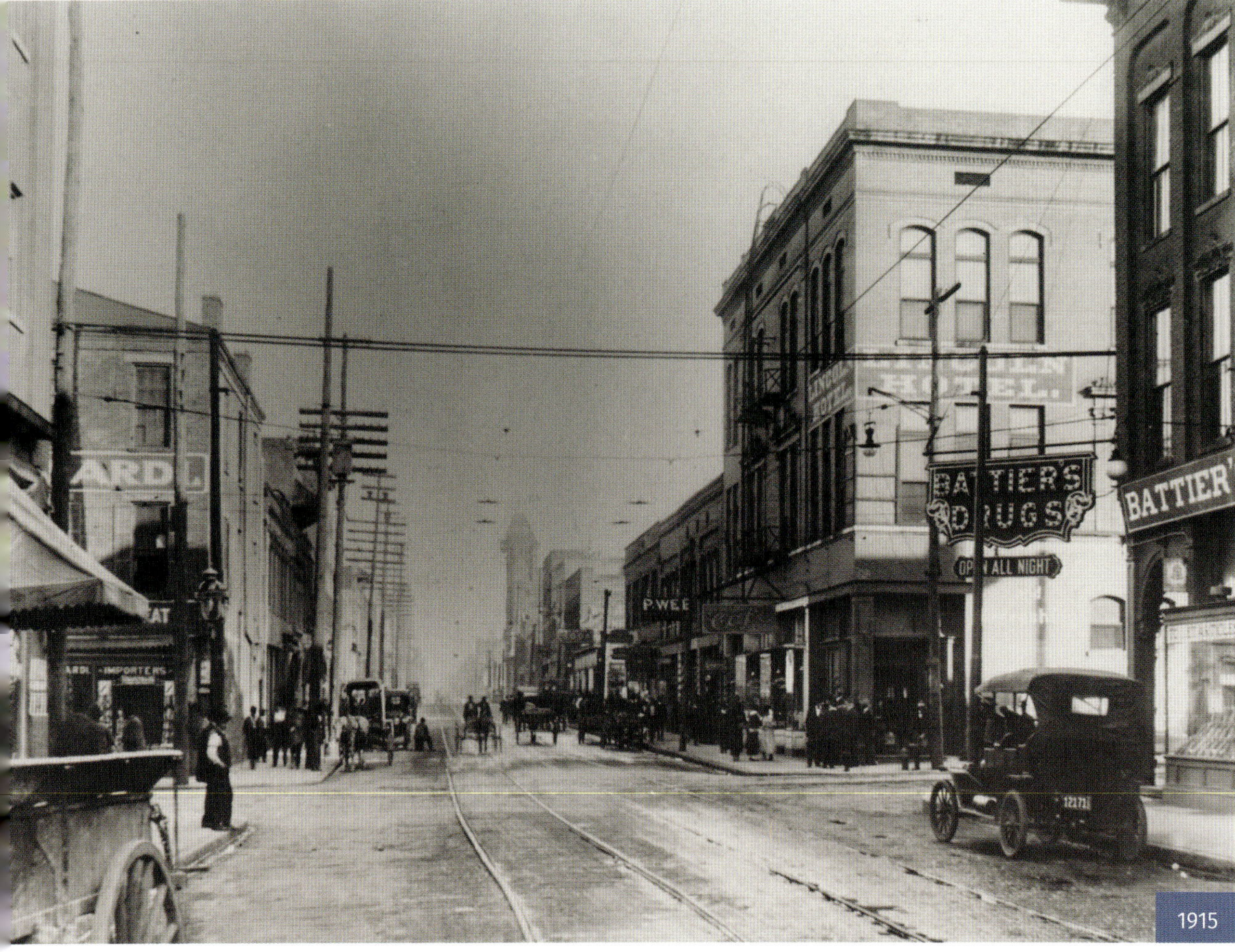

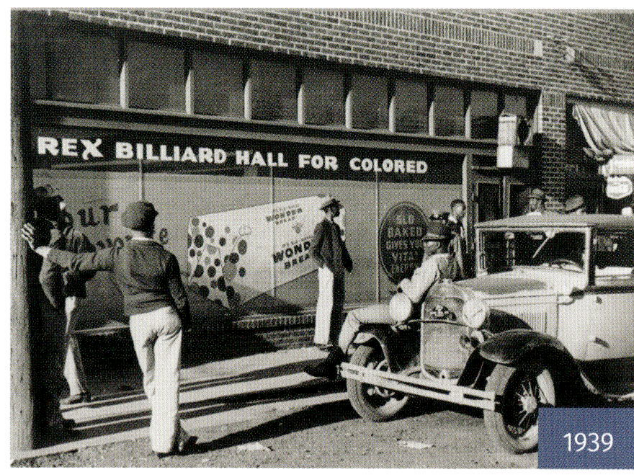

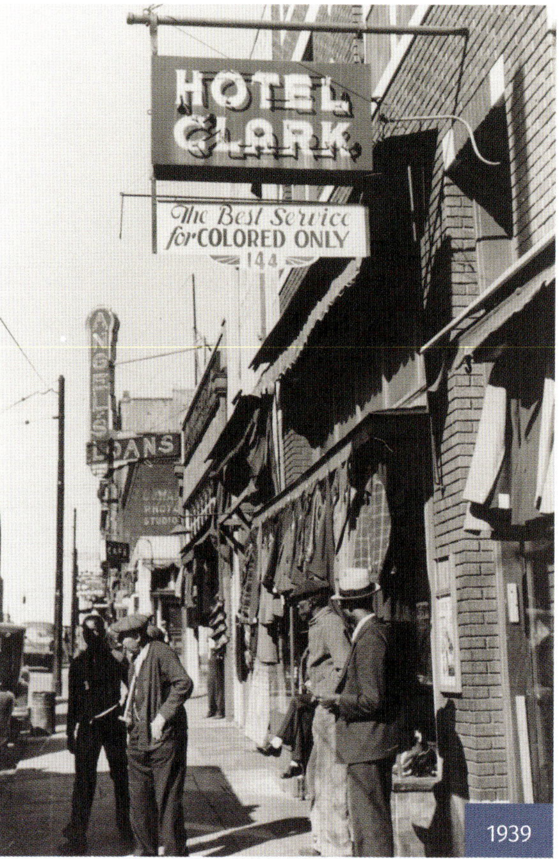

ABOVE: The Scene on Beale Street in the late 1930s, with second-hand clothes stores and loans businesses.

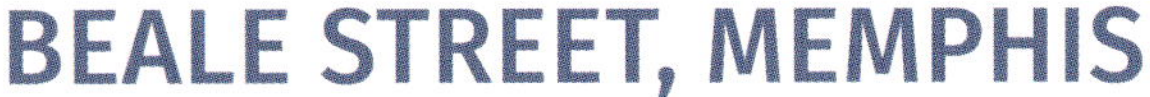

BEALE STREET, MEMPHIS

Where W. C. Handy wrote his blues standards

Memphis, Tennessee, holds a revered place in the history of American music as a cradle of the blues. It was born out of the hardships of Black life in the post-Reconstruction South. By the early 1900s, the Mississippi Delta had become a hotbed for this new sound, and Memphis—sitting at the northern edge of the Delta and serving as a major port on the Mississippi River—became a natural gathering place for musicians. The city's famous Beale Street soon became the heart of the Memphis blues scene.

William Christopher Handy was born in 1873 in Florence, Alabama. Despite his father's view that "musical instruments were tools of the devil," he trained as a classical musician. Handy was deeply drawn to the music of the people—the raw, emotional expressions he heard from Black laborers, street

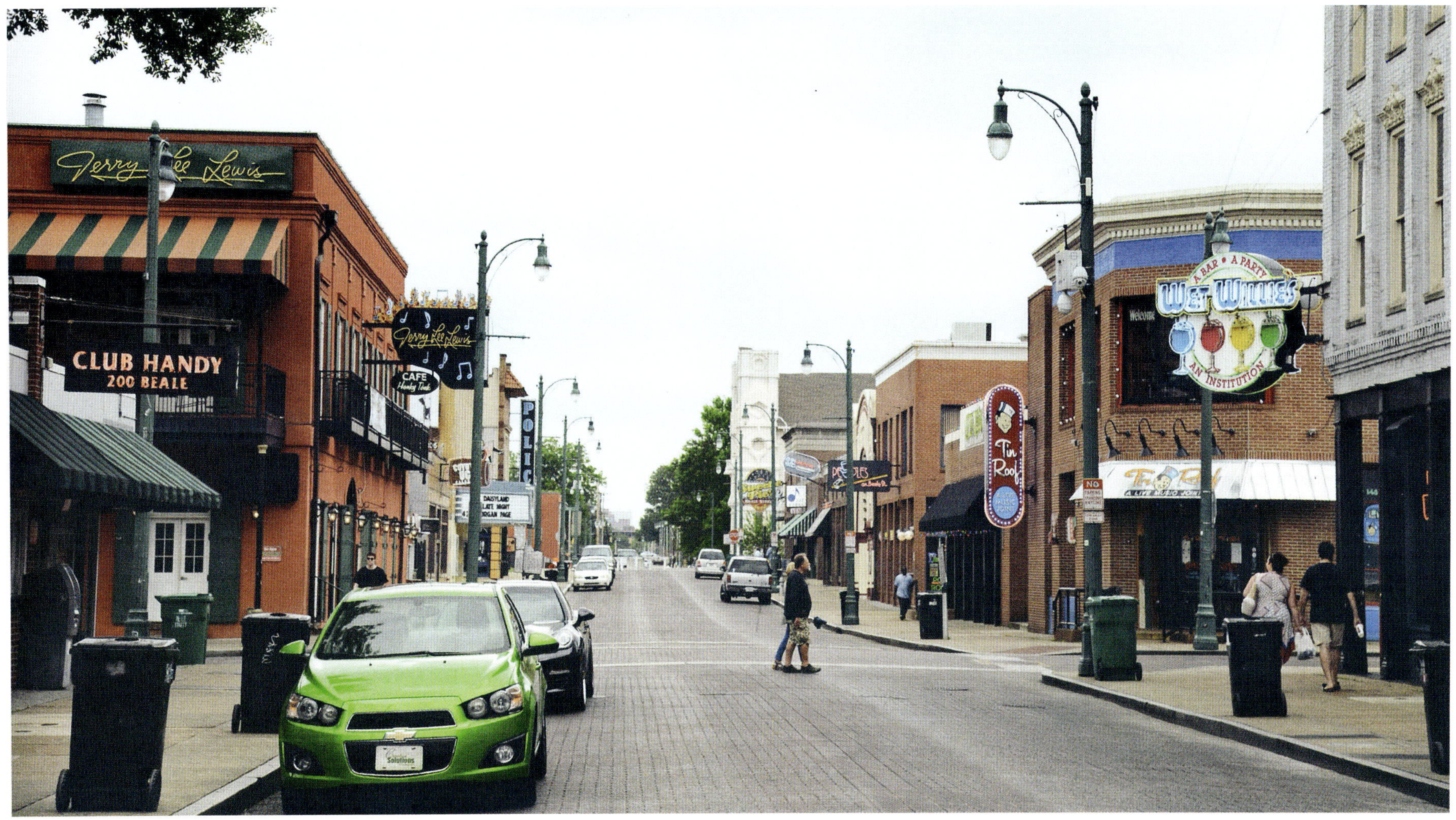

performers, and traveling musicians. Memphis provided Handy with the perfect environment to absorb, and ultimately elevate the blues.

Handy's key contribution was not that he invented the blues, but that he formalized it—writing it down, arranging it for orchestras and bands, and publishing it in sheet music form. In 1912, he published *Memphis Blues*, and while it wasn't a commercial success straight away, it marked the first time the blues had been published in a structured musical format. Then, in 1914, Handy published *St. Louis Blues*, which became a massive hit and brought blues to mainstream audiences, especially when performed and recorded by artists like Bessie Smith and Louis Armstrong.

As blues grew in popularity, Beale Street blossomed as the center of Black culture and music in Memphis. The street featured clubs, theaters, and juke joints that hosted countless musicians. While Handy's blues were orchestrated and polished, many of the street performers offered a raw style, using guitars, harmonicas, and makeshift instruments.

This 1915 view down Beale Street shows many of the buildings that made Beale Street notorious. Just to the right of center is a sign for the Pee Wee saloon. This restaurant and bar is the place where Handy wrote *Memphis Blues*. The nightlife on Beale continued at a slower pace until it became virtually nonexistent in the late 1940s. In the early 1980s a planned Beale Street renaissance began, with the simple realization that people came to the street for the blues—it has thrived ever since, becoming the most popular tourist destination in Tennessee.

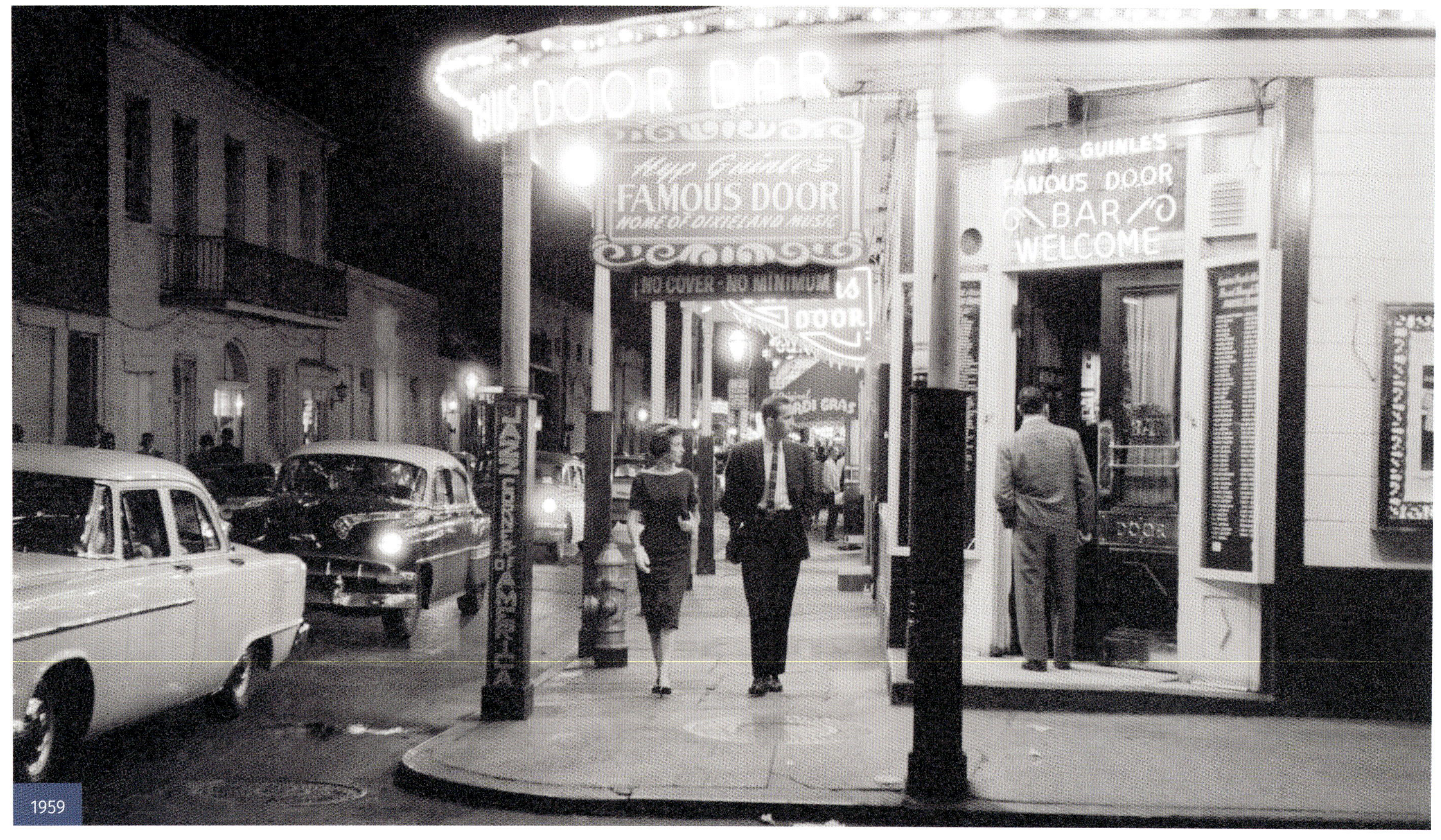

1959

THE FAMOUS DOOR, BOURBON STREET, NEW ORLEANS

New Orleans was the birthplace of jazz and helped introduce both zydeco and Cajun music

The building at 339 Bourbon Street dates from 1826 and was built by Frenchman (Don) Andre Guillory. Prior to 1934 it housed a pharmacy, before Hypolite "Hyp" Guinle leased the building for $50 a month and opened the Famous Door Club as a music venue. The Door wasn't so famous at first but gained its name after Hyp asked visiting celebrities to sign the guest book. He declared the corner of Bourbon and Conti the "Jazz Corner of America" and erected plaques either side of the door with the famous jazz musicians who had played there, including George Girard and Louis Armstrong. The extensive list is visible in the vintage 1959 photo. Hyp ran the club for over 30 years until his death in 1965. His widow, Genevieve, continued his musical legacy for another eight years until 1973 when she sold the property to local club owner Nick Karno.

The Karno family had many businesses along Bourbon Street. Nick Karno had bought the 500 Club across the street from the Prima Bothers in the late 1950s

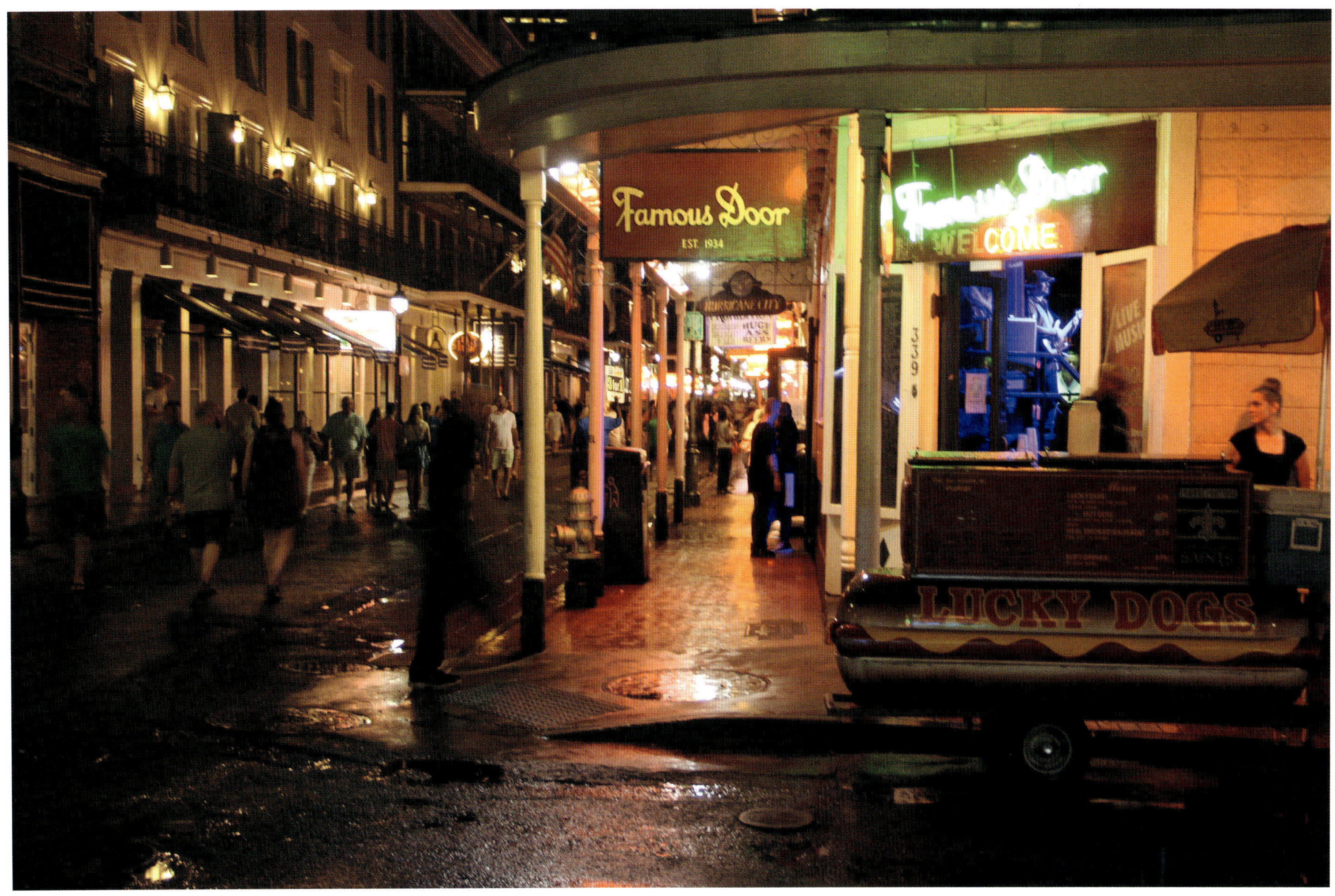

and his son Louis remembers being allowed to carry the $60,000 in cash for the purchase. Both Guinle and the Karnos had to run the gauntlet of the New Orleans mafia during that period, headed by mob boss Carlos Marcello. The Famous Door was eventually sold to the Wehner family in August 1992 and run by John Wehner. They invested money in a new stage and sound system. The list of 261 musicians originally displayed has gone , but over the years jazz musicians have been supplemented by visits from Elvis Presley and Ringo Starr, and a thirteen-year-old piano prodigy. The son of a Louisiana Supreme Court Justice and a New Orleans District Attorney might have got into trouble for appearing in licensed premises at that tender age, but Harry Connick Jr. survived the experience.

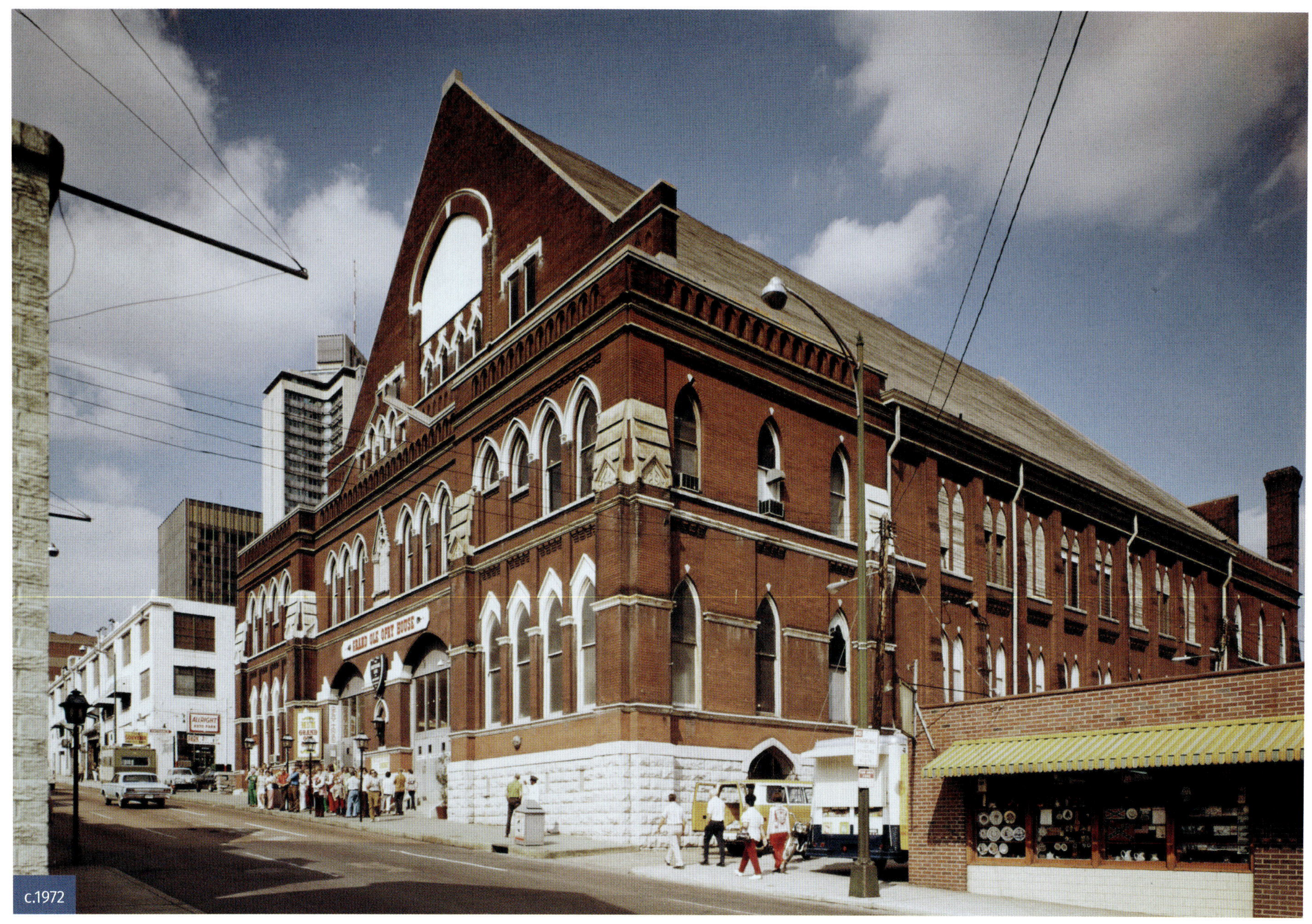

c.1972

RYMAN AUDITORIUM, NASHVILLE

The "mother church" of country music

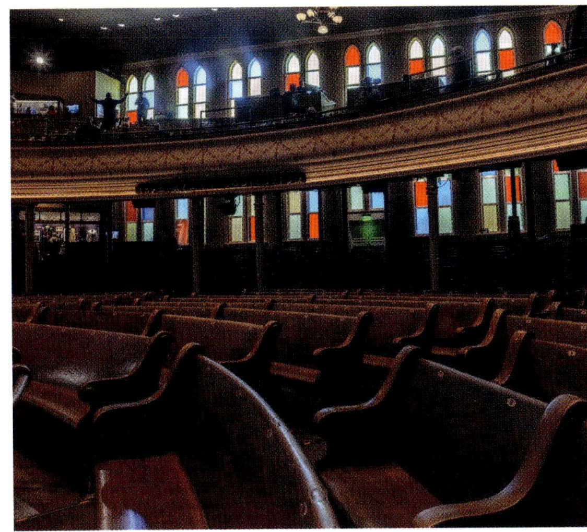

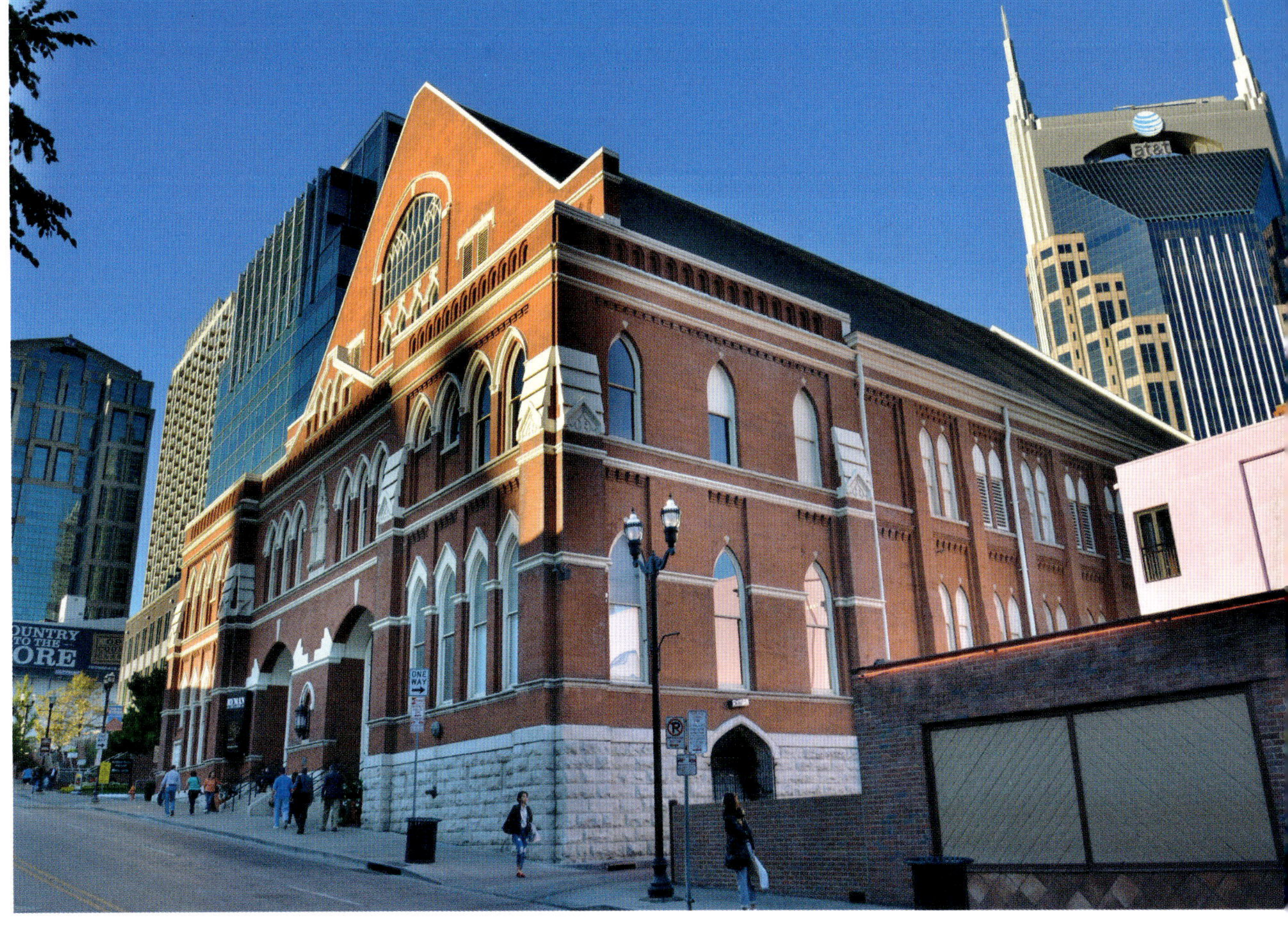

Together, the Grand Ole Opry and the Ryman Auditorium represent the beating heart of country music in Nashville. The Opry began as a simple radio broadcast. On November 28, 1925, George D. Hay, a radio personality known as "The Solemn Old Judge," launched a Saturday night program on Nashville radio station WSM called the WSM Barn Dance. The show featured live performances of old-time music—what would later be called country.

The program grew rapidly in popularity. In 1927, Hay famously remarked that listeners had just heard an hour of classical music, but now they would hear "something decidedly different." He dubbed the show the "Grand Ole Opry," a name that stuck. By the 1930s and 1940s, the Opry became a national institution.

The Ryman Auditorium began life as a church. Built in 1892, it was originally named the Union Gospel Tabernacle. Businessman and riverboat captain Thomas G. Ryman financed its construction after a religious awakening. Following Ryman's death in 1904, the building was renamed in his honor. Over time, it became a prominent performance venue in Nashville, hosting speakers, opera singers, and vaudeville acts. Thanks to its flawless acoustics, it earned a reputation as one of the finest venues in the South.

In 1943, the Grand Ole Opry moved into the Ryman Auditorium and that pairing would last for the next 31 years. The cramped backstage areas and pew-style seating gave the venue a unique intimacy, and the building's church-like atmosphere (pictured above left) added to its mystique. Performers like Hank Williams, Patsy Cline, Johnny Cash, and Loretta Lynn all graced the Ryman stage. The venue wasn't just a concert hall; it was a proving ground where careers were made—or sometimes broken—based on how well artists connected with its passionate audience.

By the early 1970s, the Ryman was showing its age. The Opry had outgrown the small venue. In 1974, the Grand Ole Opry moved to a new, custom-built venue: the Grand Ole Opry House, located in the Opryland complex east of downtown Nashville.

After the Opry left, the Ryman fell into decline and was nearly demolished. Fortunately, preservationists and music lovers rallied to save it. In the 1990s, a major renovation restored the building to its former glory. The Ryman reopened as a world-class performance venue in 1994, and the Opry has since returned to its original home for special broadcasts and anniversary shows.

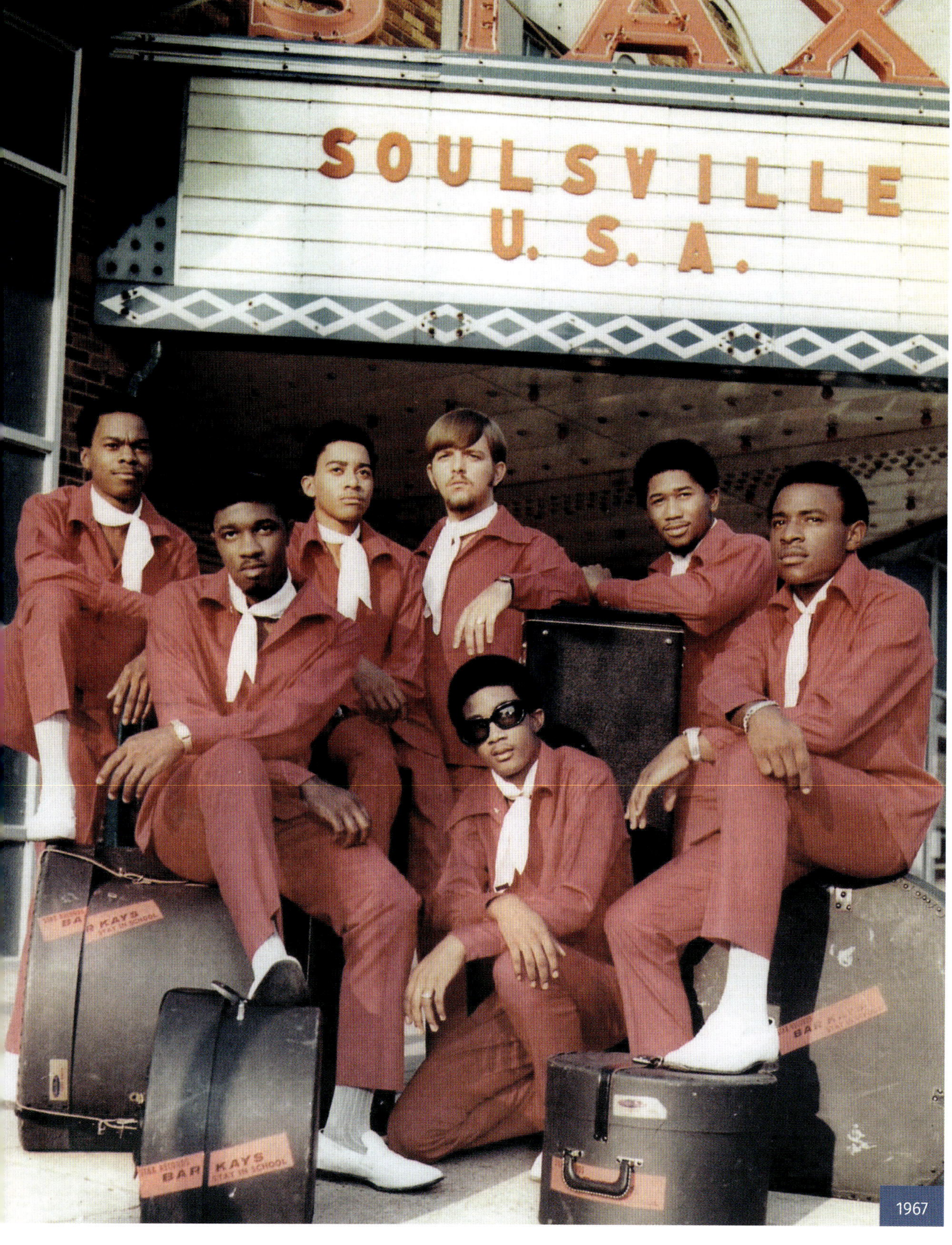

1967

STAX RECORDS, MEMPHIS

The South's answer to Tamla Motown

Founded in 1957 in Memphis, Stax Records became one of the most influential soul music labels in American history. Alongside Motown in Detroit, Stax helped define the sound of 1960s and 1970s soul, with a grittier, more gospel- and blues-infused style that reflected the heart of the South.

Stax began as Satellite Records, established by Jim Stewart, a country fiddler who initially focused on country and rockabilly music. His sister, Estelle Axton, joined him in 1959 and together they moved the label into a former movie theater at 926 East McLemore Avenue in a predominantly Black neighborhood in South Memphis. The theater's sloped floor and high ceiling gave the studio its signature warm sound.

Stax became a creative hub for Black and white musicians working together at a time when racial integration was rare, especially in the South. This multiracial environment helped foster a unique and authentic sound. The label's in-house band, Booker T. & the M.G.'s, backed most of its artists and became legends in their own right. Stax launched the careers of soul icons such as Otis Redding, Isaac Hayes, Sam & Dave, Rufus and Carla Thomas, and The Staple Singers. Otis Redding, in particular, emerged as the label's biggest star until his tragic death in a 1967 plane crash.

After Redding's passing and the loss of a distribution deal with Atlantic Records, Stax faced financial problems. Despite a revival under Al Bell, the label closed in 1975. Today, the original Stax studio site is home to the Stax Museum of American Soul Music, preserving the powerful legacy of a label that gave voice to a generation and changed the sound of American music.

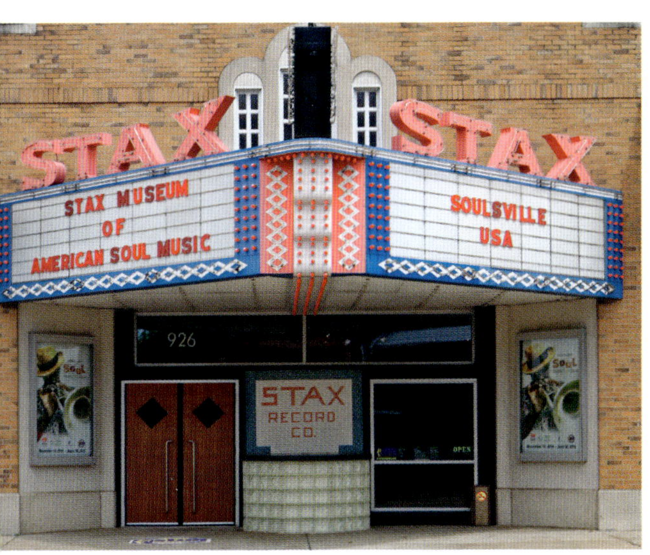

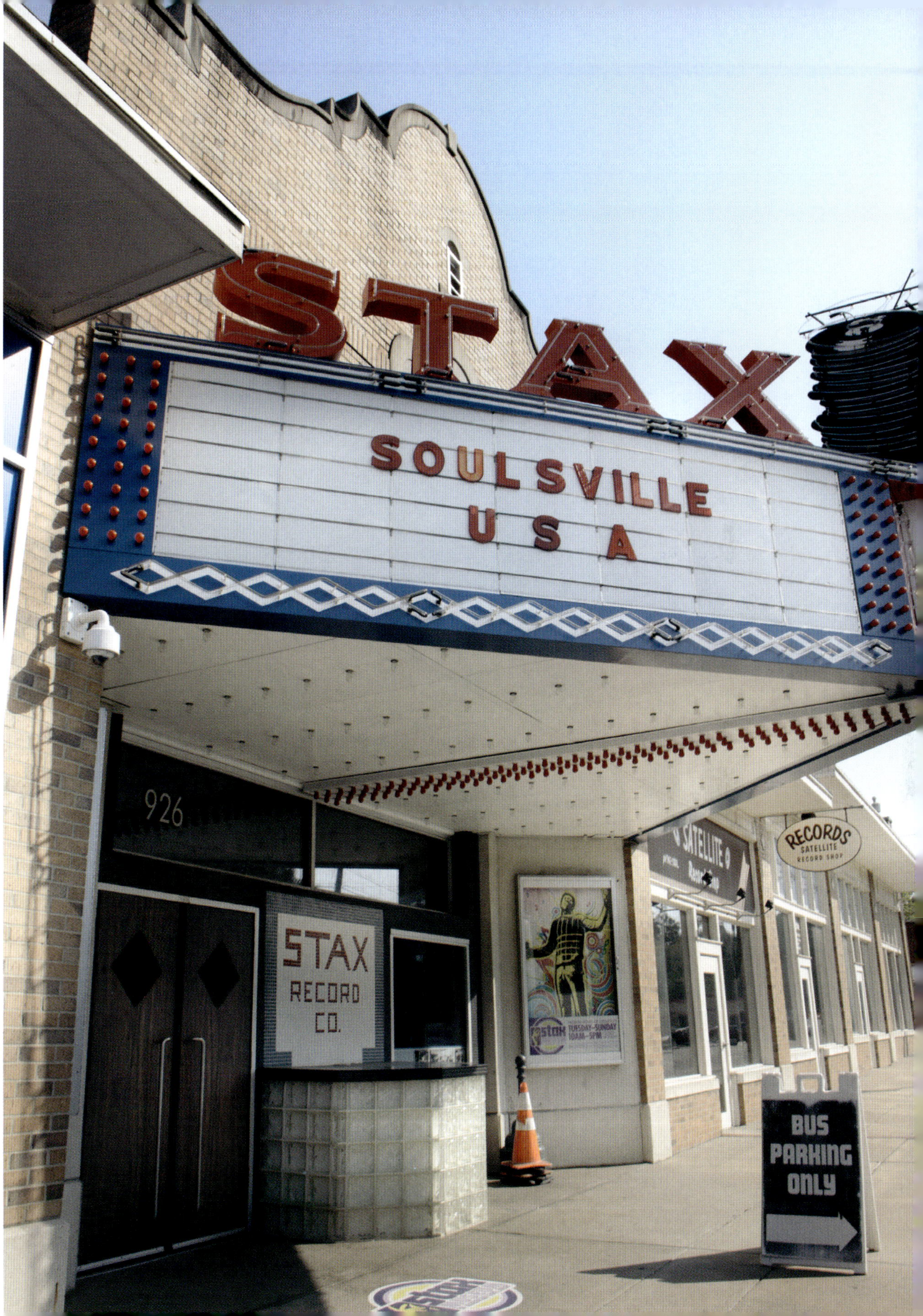

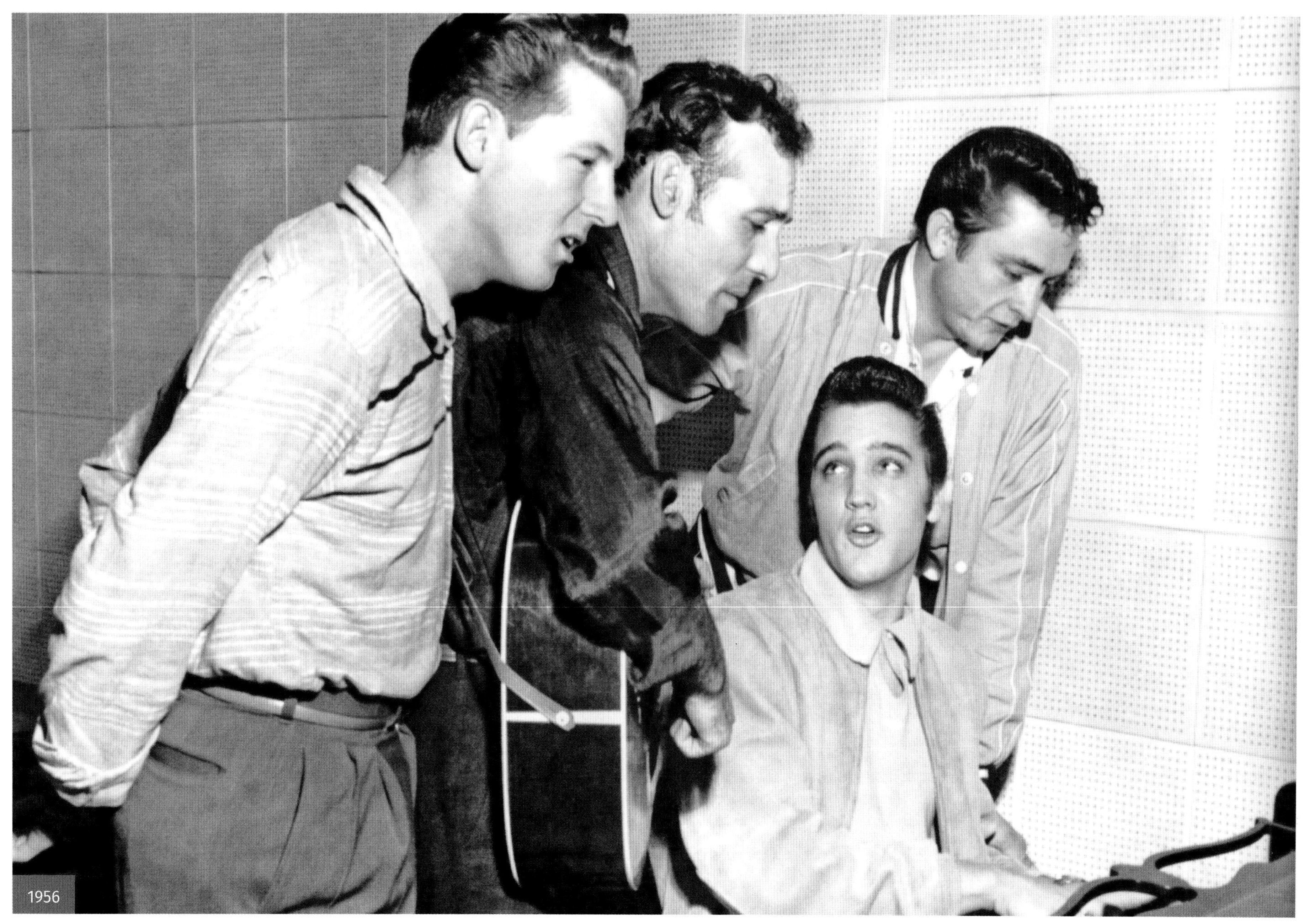

SUN RECORDS, MEMPHIS

The birthplace of rock 'n' roll

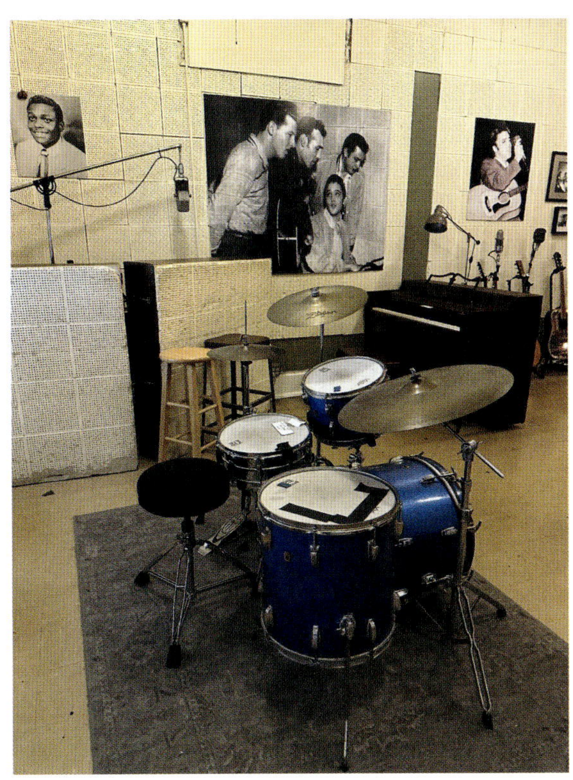

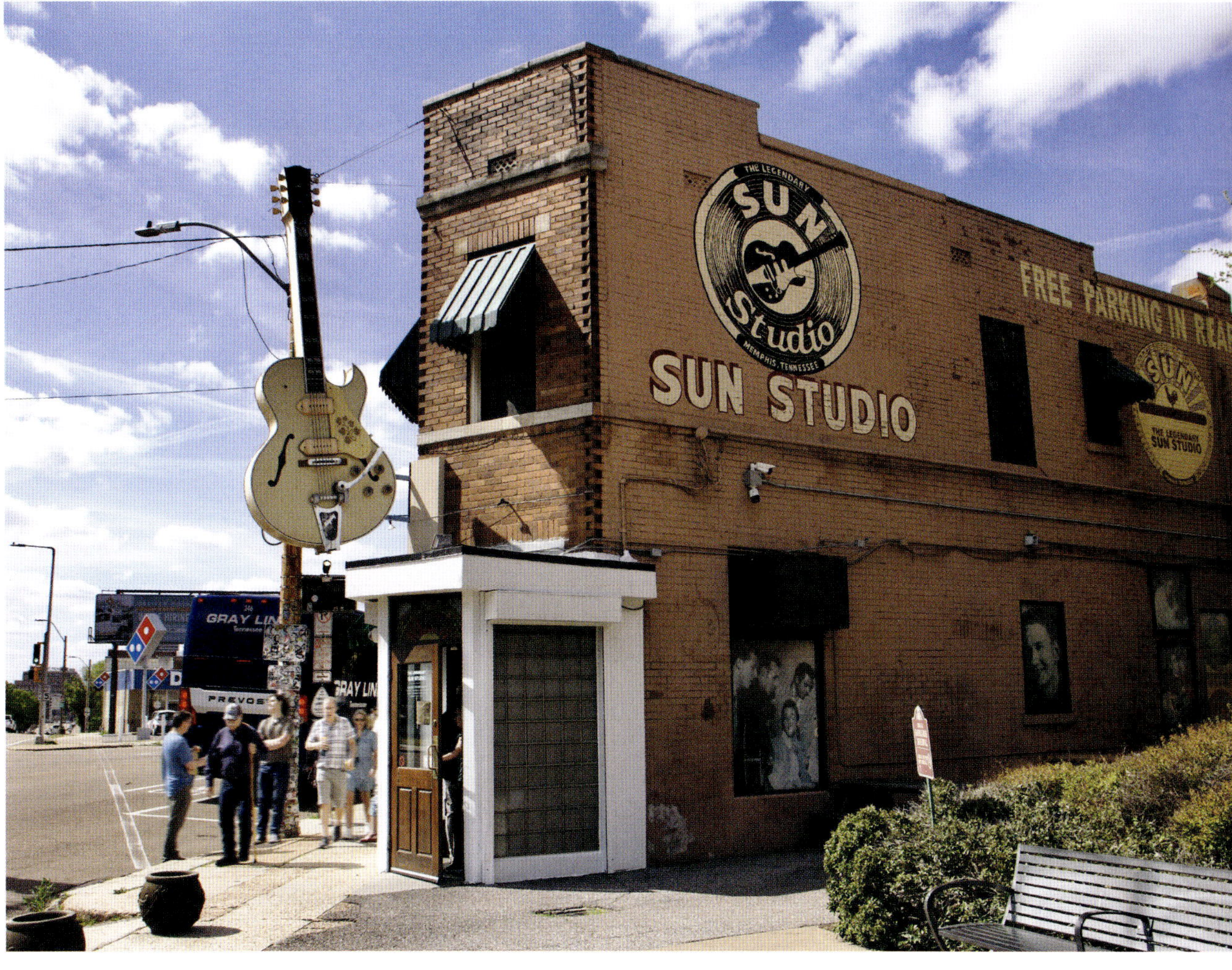

Founded in 1952 by Sam Phillips, Sun Records in Memphis, played a pivotal role in the birth of rock 'n' roll and served as the launching pad for artists like Elvis Presley, Johnny Cash, Jerry Lee Lewis, Carl Perkins, and Roy Orbison.

Sam Phillips, a former radio engineer and music enthusiast, had already opened the Memphis Recording Service in 1950, located at 706 Union Avenue. Initially, the studio catered to anyone who wanted to record music. Phillips then started up Sun Records. Its turning point came in 1954, when a young Elvis Presley walked into the studio to record a song as a gift for his mother. Intrigued by Elvis's voice and potential, Phillips paired him with guitarist Scotty Moore and bassist Bill Black. During a casual jam session, they recorded an energetic version of *That's All Right*—a blues song by Arthur Crudup—with a country twist. The song became a regional hit, and Elvis's unique sound—blending blues, country and gospel—caught on like wildfire. He released five singles on Sun, including *Blue Moon of Kentucky* and *Good Rockin' Tonight*, to help lay the foundation for rock 'n' roll as a genre.

Sun quickly became a magnet for talent. Johnny Cash arrived in 1955, followed by Carl Perkins, Jerry Lee Lewis, and Roy Orbison. In 1956, an impromptu jam session featuring Elvis, Cash, Lewis, and Perkins became known as the "Million Dollar Quartet," captured in a famous photograph and recording.

In 1955, Phillips sold Elvis's contract to RCA Records for $35,000, using the funds to invest in other artists. While Sun continued producing hits into the late 1950s, it gradually lost its artists to larger labels. By the 1960s, Sun had faded from prominence, and Phillips sold the label in 1969. The original studio still stands and operates today as Sun Studio, a working recording space and popular tourist destination.

RADIO CITY
Music Hall
RADIO CITY
Music Hall
Music Hall RADIO CITY
Music Hall
DORIS DAY, JAMES CAGNEY, CAMERON MITCHELL IN LOVE ME OR LEAVE ME
COMMERCIAL
DONT WALK
BUS STOP
1955

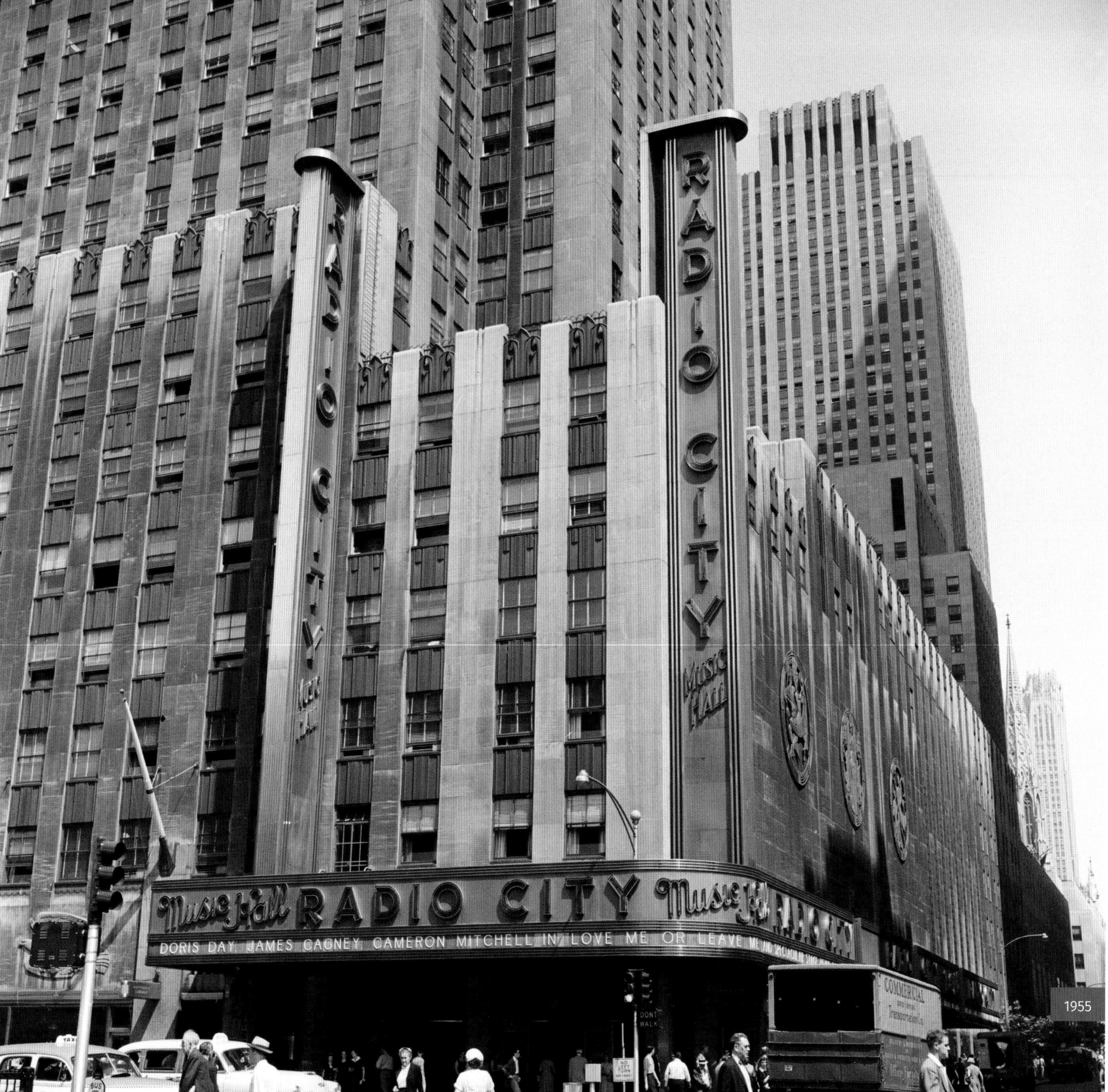

RADIO CITY MUSIC HALL, NEW YORK

An Art Deco gem that has resisted redevelopment and kept traditions alive

The Rockefeller Center was John D. Rockefeller Jr.'s ambitious plan to revitalize midtown Manhattan. The whole enterprise was going to be named Radio City and it included a spectacular music hall at Sixth Avenue and Fiftieth Street. The venue was a collaboration between Rockefeller, Radio Corporation of America (RCA), and theatrical producer Samuel "Roxy" Rothafel, whose vision was to create a "palace for the people."

With 6,200 seats, Radio City Music Hall was the largest theater in the world when it opened in 1932. Designed by architect Edward Durell Stone with interiors by Donald Deskey, the venue was a masterpiece of Art Deco architecture and furnishing. Its interior featured bold geometric patterns, luxurious materials, and striking murals. It began exclusively as a vaudeville stage, but lost tens of thousands of dollars in its first two weeks of operation. It soon switched to movies, premiering *King Kong* in 1933. The combination of popular movies with live musical productions by the dancing Rockettes—originally called the Roxyettes after their first manager, Rothafel—kept the theater going for decades.

By the 1970s, as the audience for family movies and stage shows declined, Radio City Music Hall was losing money again. In 1978, the city was shocked by an announcement that the theater, with its striking Art Deco interior and famous rising sun stage, would shut its doors forever and be torn down. Saved at the last moment by state support, it has been beautifully restored following a major restoration in 1999, which cost over $70 million.

Now managed by the operators of Madison Square Garden, it has switched back from movies to live concerts by a range of popular artists, from Cirque du Soleil to Lady Gaga. It has also hosted major events, including the Grammy Awards, Tony Awards, film premieres, and the NFL draft. The Rockettes also return annually for the "Christmas Spectacular," kicking up their heels in sync as the long-legged troupe has done since 1933.

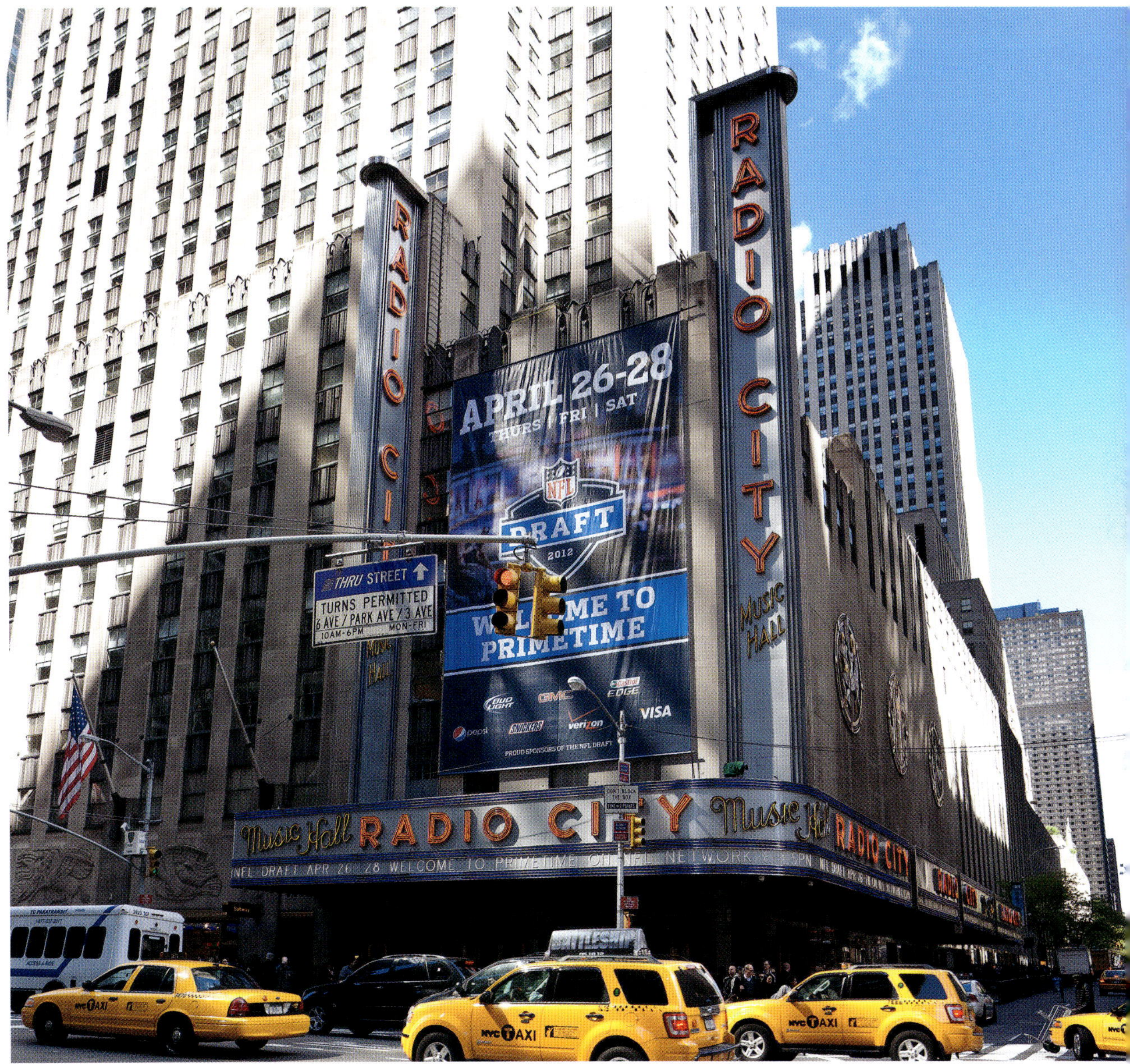

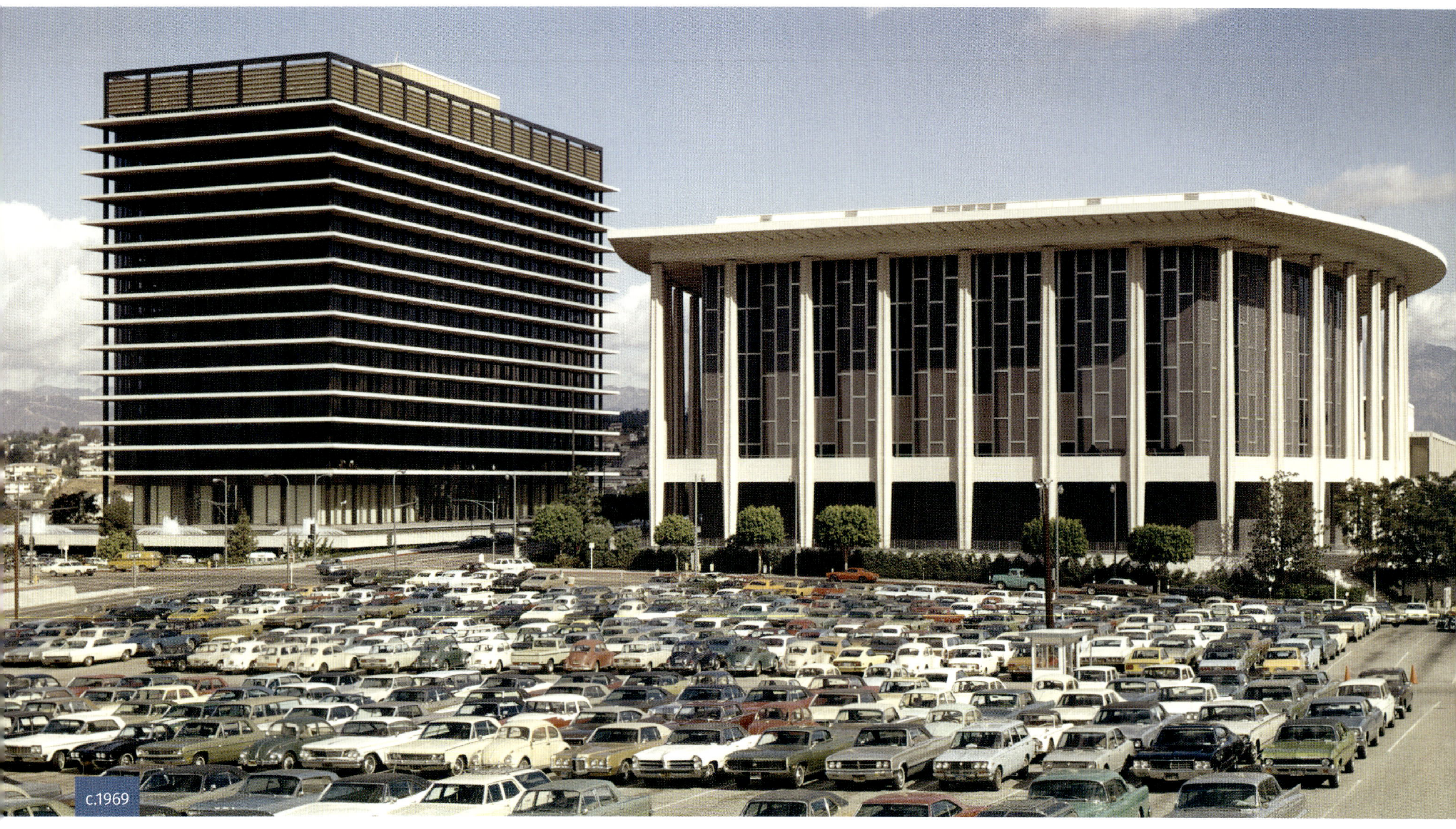

c.1969

LOS ANGELES MUSIC CENTER, CALIFORNIA

The city's Music Center has long been the home of innovative architecture

The 1964 Dorothy Chandler Pavilion was the first theater to be completed in the Los Angeles Music Center. It was named for Dorothy Buffum Chandler (wife of *Los Angeles Times* owner Norman Chandler), who was seeking a home for the Los Angeles Philharmonic. Designed by Welton Becket, it was the largest theater in the complex with 3,197 seats. A curved building with tall colonnades, the Pavilion has been home to the Christmas Eve Holiday Celebration since 1964. The Los Angeles Master Chorale resided here and the New York City Opera performed regularly. The smaller Ahmanson Theatre opened in 1967 with a production of *Man of La Mancha*. Two decades later,

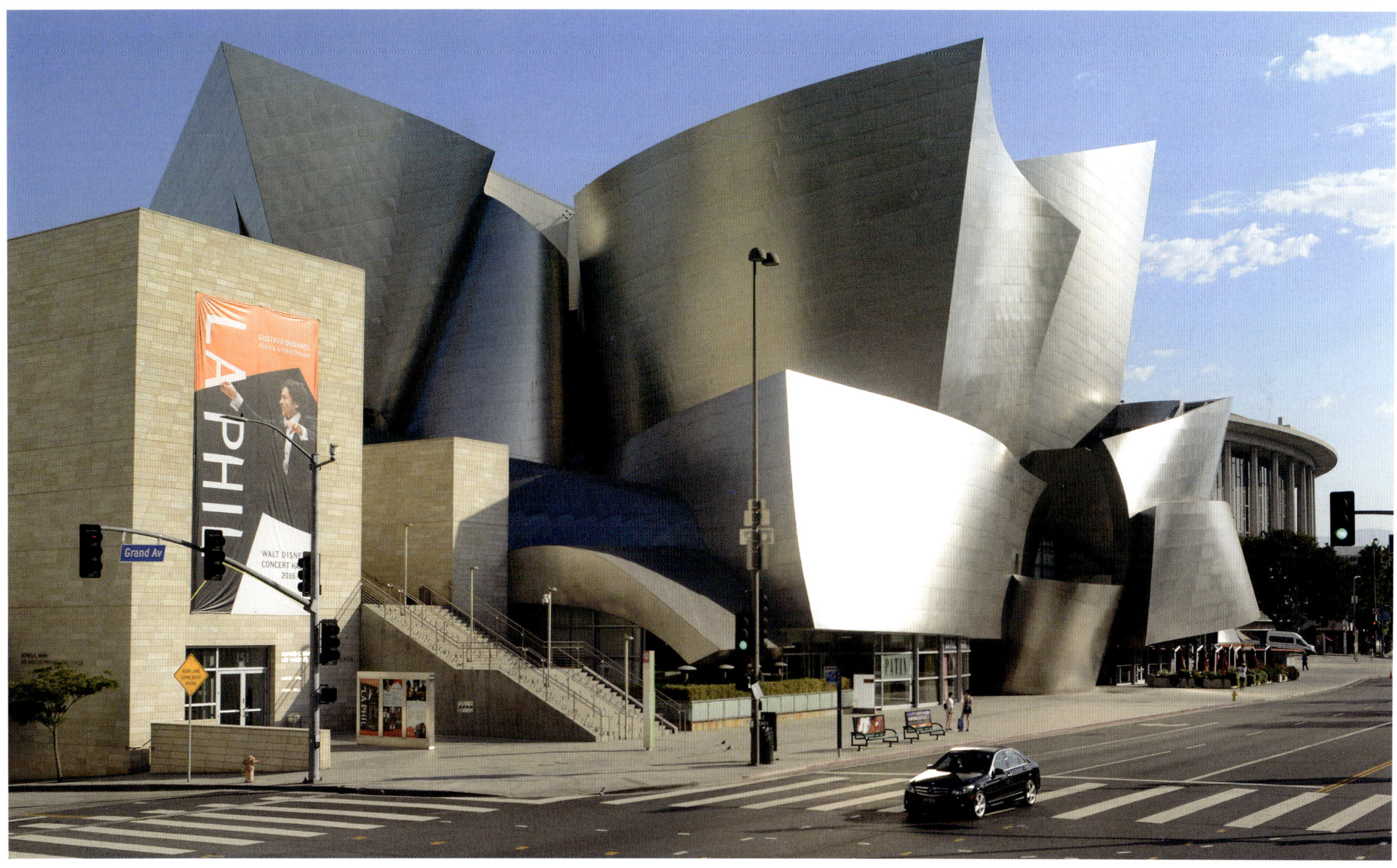

in 1989, *Phantom of the Opera* opened at the 2,000-seat Ahmanson with Michael Crawford in the title role. The smaller, 739-seat Mark Taper Forum—also constructed in 1967—welcomed more experimental productions like *Zoot Suit*, *Children of a Lesser God*, *Shadow Box*, and *Angels in America*.

The Los Angeles Music Center added the inspirational, Frank Gehry-designed Walt Disney Concert Hall in October 2003. It sits just outside the original 1960s complex and features 2,265 seats, including the 266-seat Roy Disney Cal Arts Theatre and the outdoor Keck Foundation's Children's Theatre. It is now home to the Los Angeles Philharmonic and Master Chorale. Today, a $30 million renovation of the county-owned Music Center Plaza is in the works. The plaza connects the theaters and restaurants and the plan is to improve the space for larger outdoor public events and create connections with the nearby Civic Center.

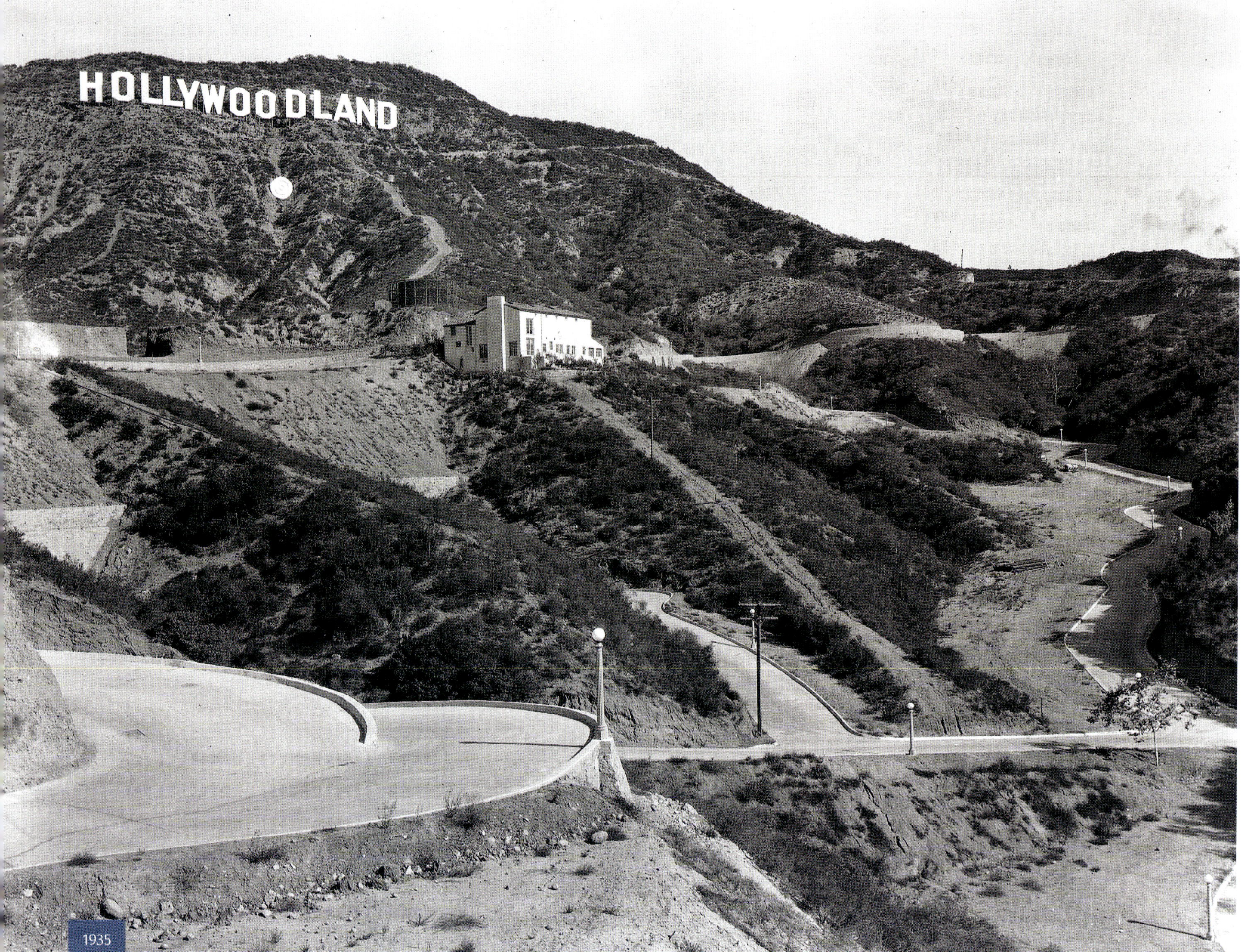

THE HOLLYWOOD SIGN, LOS ANGELES

The world's most famous sign almost got demolished...

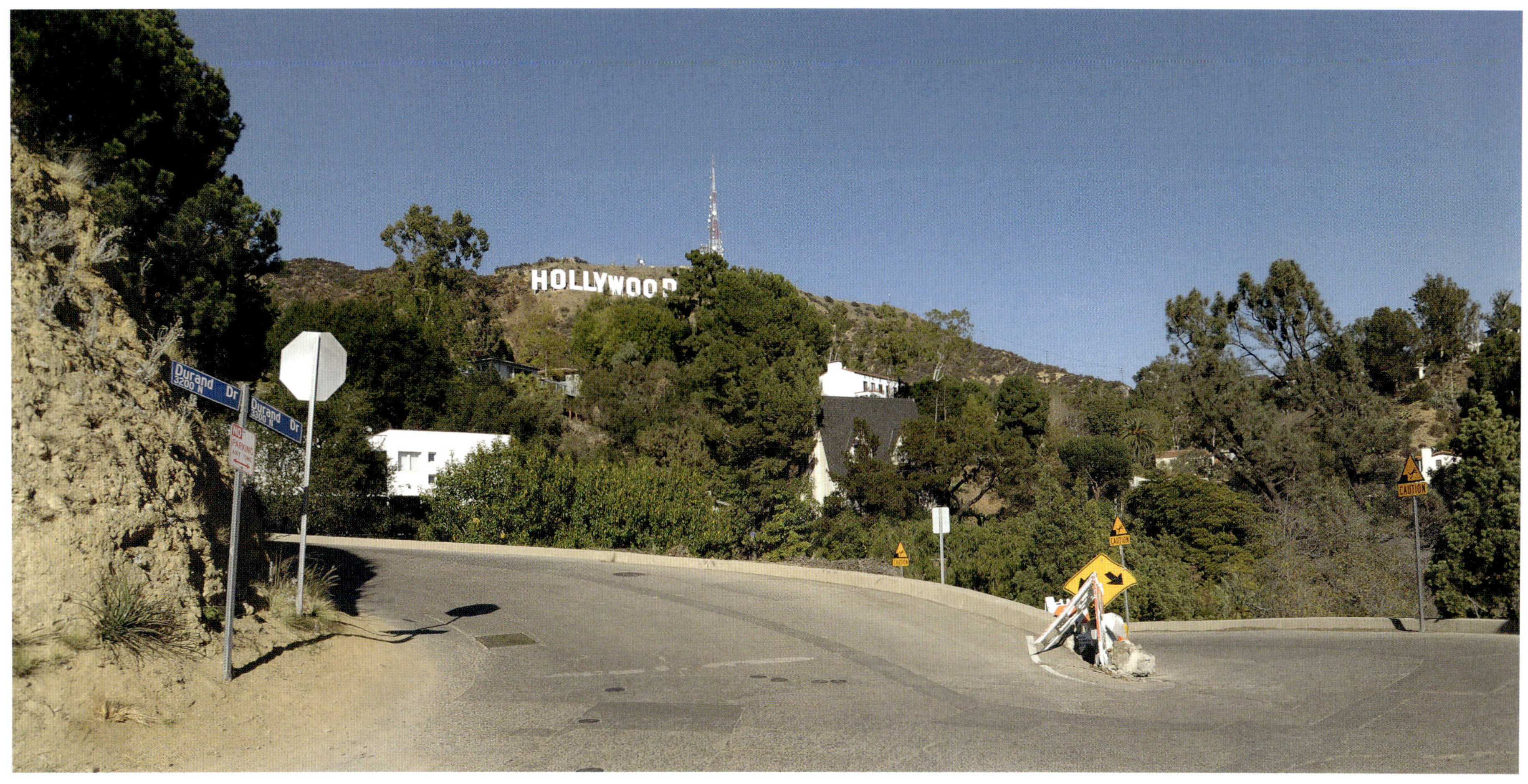

By the time this picture was taken, in 1935, the Hollywoodland sign had been gracing Mount Lee in the Santa Monica Mountains for twelve years. The original Hollywoodland sign was erected in 1923 by developers as an advertising gimmick. The letters were fifty feet tall and thirty feet wide, and were made of white-painted metal squares studded with 4,000 twenty-watt light bulbs; the sign cost $21,000 to build, and it was maintained by a caretaker who lived in a small house behind the sign.

A 35-foot, white-painted metal circle (seen as a small white dot from miles away) was put 200 feet below as an eye-catcher. While an inspiration to many, the Hollywoodland sign spelled shattered dreams for actress Peg Entwistle, who jumped from the letter H to her death fifty feet below in 1932. In the 1940s, Albert Kothe, the man entrusted with caring for the sign, got drunk, swerved off the road, and collided with the same H in his Model A Ford.

In 1944, the now bankrupt developer donated the sign to the city, which planned to tear it down; five years later, the Hollywood chamber of commerce decided to restore the "Hollywood," abandoning the "land." But it wasn't until 1974, when the sign was given landmark status, that a new era of preservation and recognition began. During the 1960s, the Hollywood Kiwanis Club had raised enough money to repair the sign, but soon after Kiwanis spent the last of their funds, one of the Os crumbled. In 1978 Alice Cooper spearheaded a public campaign to restore the landmark when he donated $27,000 to replace the missing O; Hugh Hefner and Andy Williams were among other celebrities who also donated to the cause. Today the chamber of commerce, the Hollywood Sign Trust, and the City of Los Angeles are the official stewards, and the sign is monitored 24 hours a day by City of Los Angeles security specialists.

In 2010, grants from The Tiffany & Co. Foundation and Aileen Getty, along with contributions from Hollywood leaders and fans around the world, ensured the sign will remain protected; however, residents living close by complain about the increasing number of tourists and tour buses seeking close access to the summit, and have been known to post placards reading "Tourists Go Away."

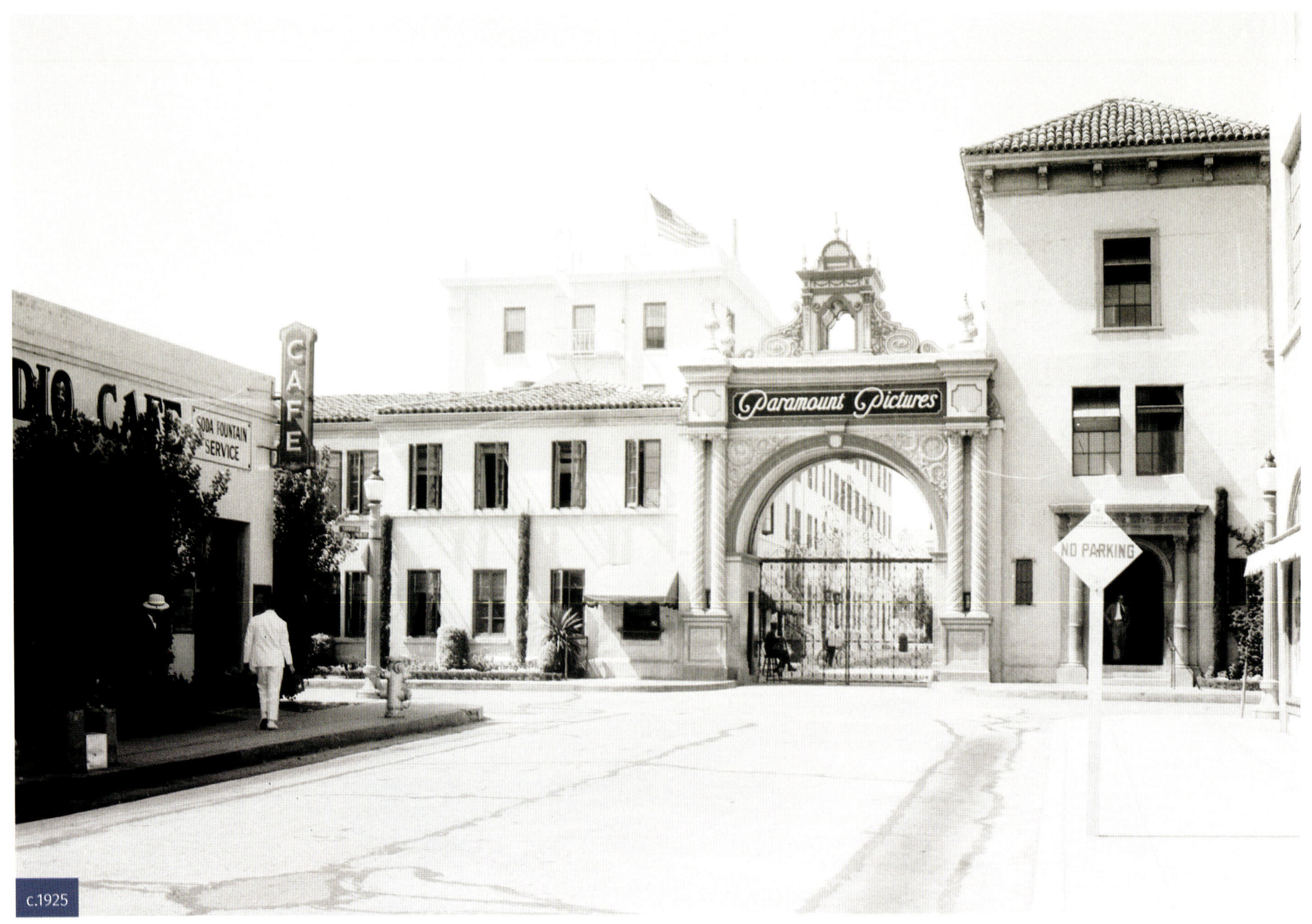

c.1925

PARAMOUNT STUDIOS, HOLLYWOOD

The last remaining studio from Hollywood's Golden Age

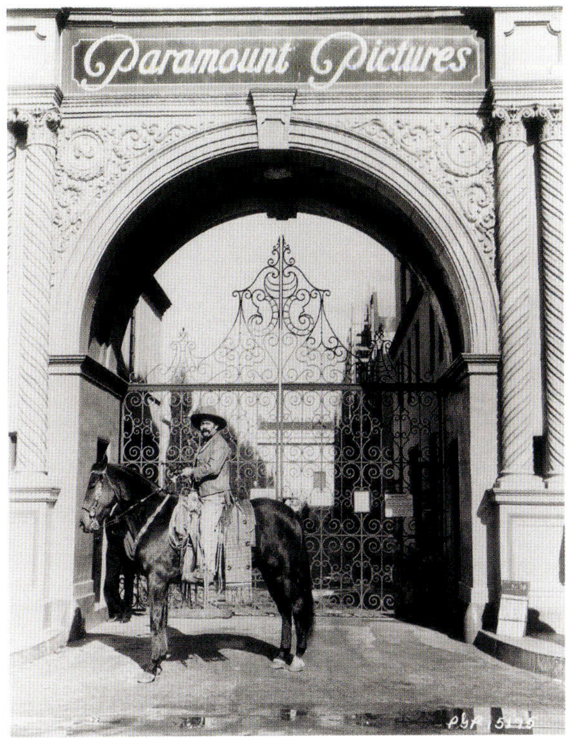

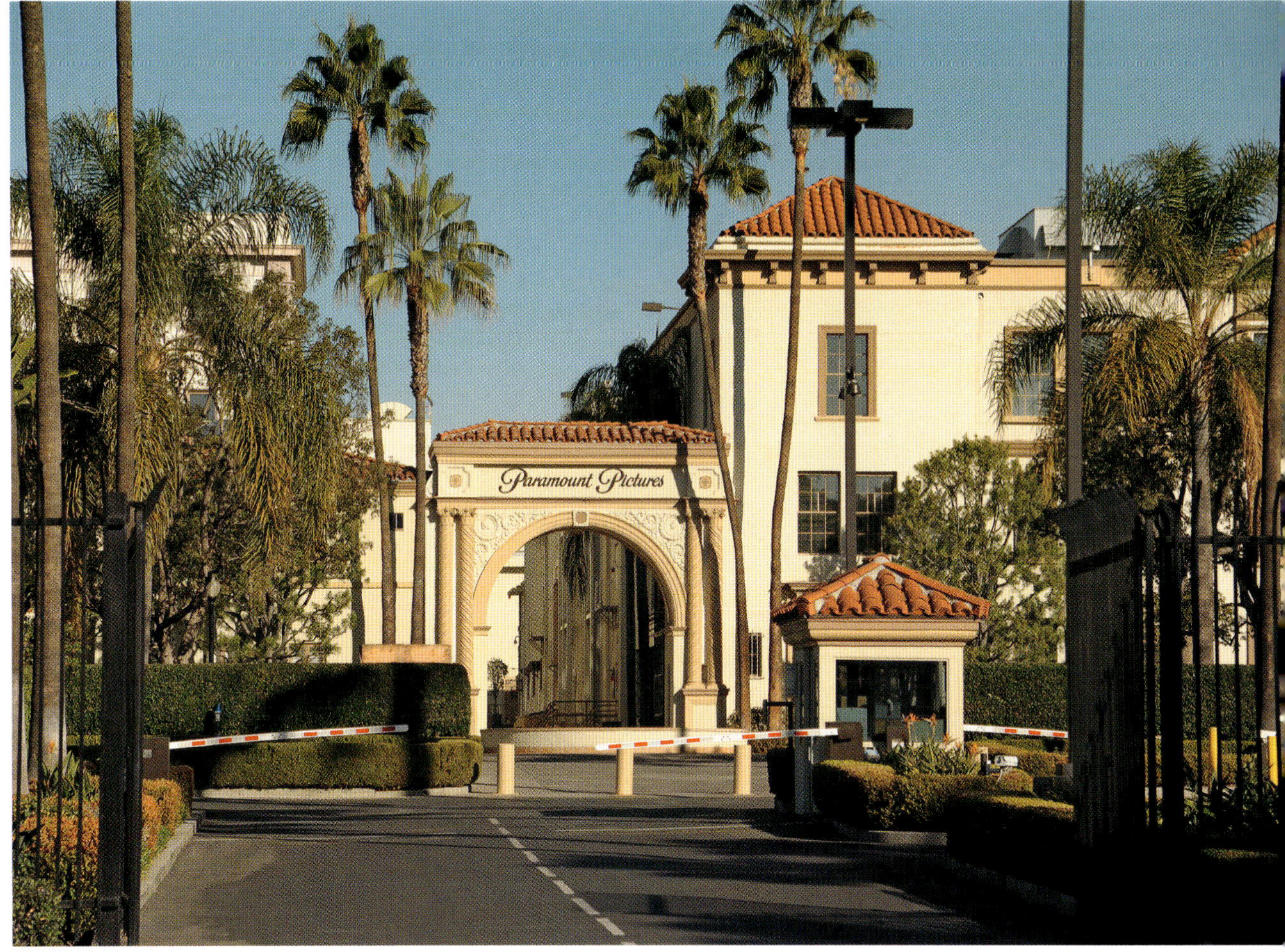

The Paramount Studio Building, located at 5555 Melrose Avenue in Hollywood is the longest operating major film studio in the United States. Founded by Adolph Zukor in 1912 as the Famous Players Film Company, Paramount evolved into a dominant force in Hollywood's Golden Age. The current studio lot was established in 1926. The studio's main building, often referred to as the Administration Building, was constructed in a classic Spanish Colonial Revival style, typical of Southern California architecture of the 1920s. The building housed executive offices, production departments, and post-production suites. One of the most recognized landmarks on the lot is the Bronson Gate, named after nearby Bronson Avenue. It was featured in *Sunset Boulevard*, starring William Holden and Gloria Swanson. This iconic, arched gate, adorned with wrought-iron filigree, has been featured in numerous films and television series. According to legend, it once bore a sign reading, "The public shall not pass," reflecting the exclusivity and mystery that surrounded early Hollywood film production. Today, the Bronson Gate symbolizes Paramount's long-standing legacy in global entertainment.

In 1948, the Supreme Court's Paramount Decree forced the studio to divest its theater chains, fundamentally changing its business model. In 1957 Desilu Productions (of the *I Love Lucy* series) took over RKO Studios on Gower, which eventually became part of the Paramount lot. In 1966 Paramount was taken over by Gulf and Western, then, diversifying its output, Paramount Television began in 1967 with series such as *Gunsmoke* and *Happy Days*.

Viacom bought the studio in 1994 for $10 billion. The *Indiana Jones*, *Star Trek*, *Mission: Impossible*, *Anchorman*, and *Jack Reacher* movies are among some of Paramount's great successes. Today, Paramount operates on a 62-acre lot that still includes the historic original structures and the studio remains active in film and television production.

ABOVE: The Bronson Gate was the main entrance to the studio until 1978. Today, the gate is well inside the Paramount estate.

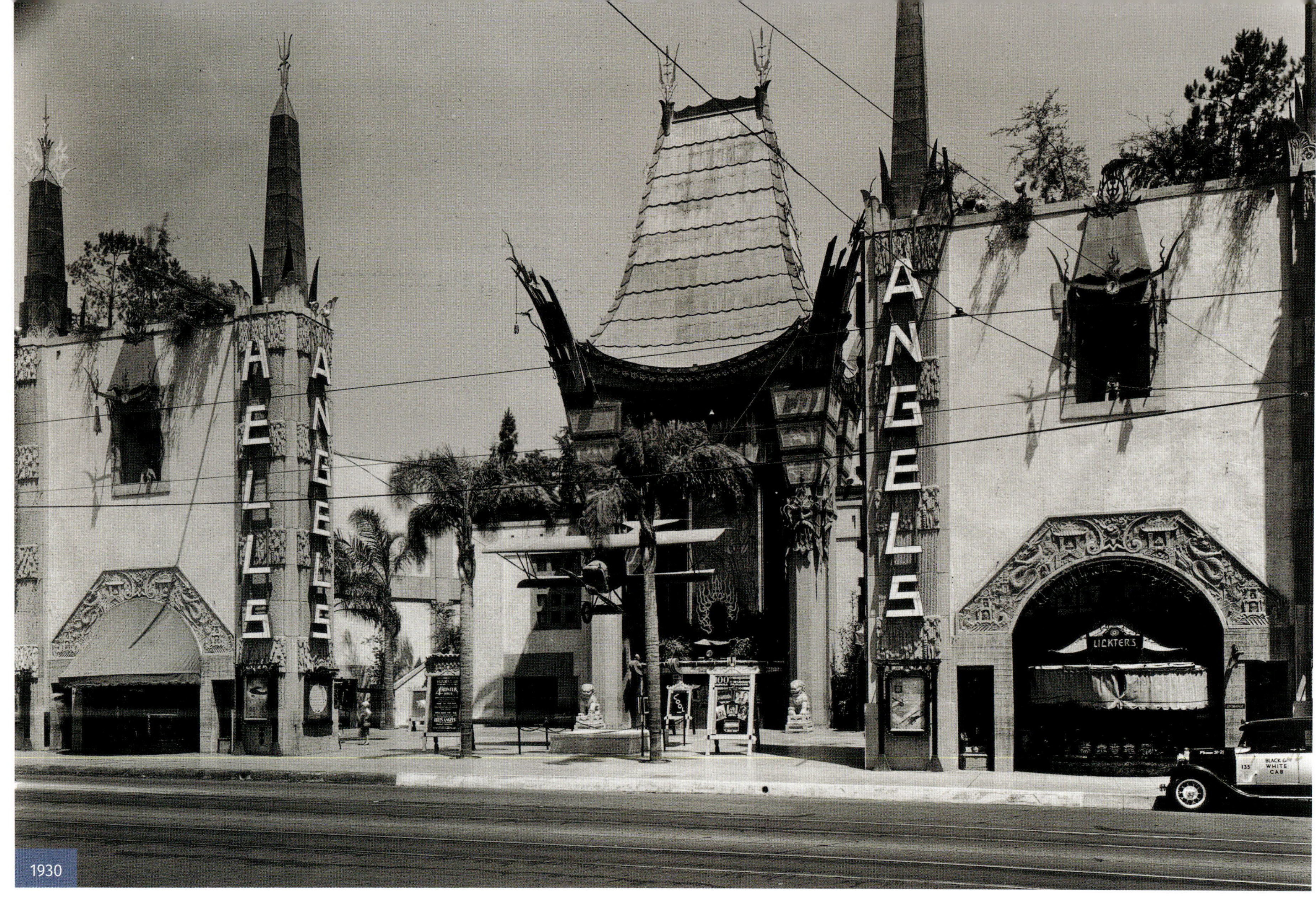

1930

GRAUMAN'S CHINESE THEATRE, LOS ANGELES

Sid Grauman's happy knack with publicity helped create the world's most famous cinema

Grauman's Chinese Theatre opened on May 18, 1927. It was commissioned following the success of the nearby Grauman's Egyptian Theatre, which had opened five years earlier. At a cost of $2 million, the theater was to be Sid Grauman's masterpiece. It opened with the premiere of Cecil B. DeMille's film *The King of Kings*. The opening attracted thousands of people, and the crowd became unruly as fans tried to catch a glimpse of arriving movie stars and celebrities. Grauman had spared no expense on the theater's decor. He imported temple bells, pagodas, and other genuine artifacts from China. The first footprint ceremony took place on April 30, 1927, when Mary Pickford and Douglas Fairbanks pressed their feet into squares of wet cement. Norma Talmadge had accidentally stepped into wet cement on the forecourt, giving showman Sid Grauman his famous idea. Ever since that sidewalk-shaping event in 1927, the stars of yesterday and today have left their footprints in the sidewalks near the theater.

Known for its gala premieres, the Chinese Theatre had over 10,000 spectators on the sidewalk for the 1939 opening of *The Wizard of Oz*. Little has changed at

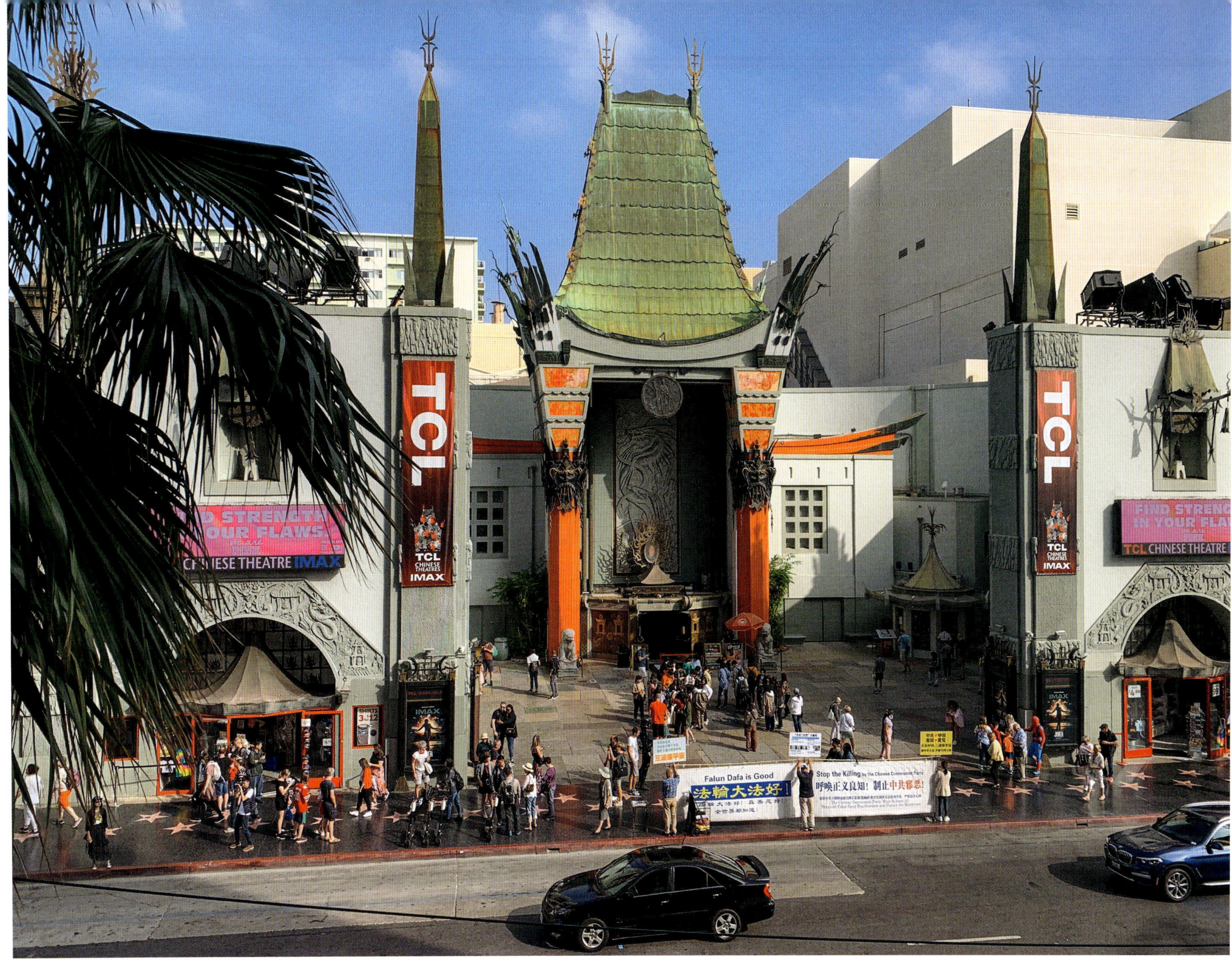

6925 Hollywood Boulevard. Grauman's Chinese Theatre remains a much sought-after venue for premieres, and more than four million tourists visit its cement handprints and footprints in the forecourt every year. The theater is steeped in Hollywood tradition, and the two original giant Foo Dogs brought from China still guard the theater's entryway.

Following the Northridge earthquake of 1994, an extensive retrofit was implemented. In 2013 the owners teamed up with Chinese electronics manufacturer TCL (The Creative Life) in a multimillion-dollar partnership that included naming rights. And so it is now officially known as the TCL Chinese Theatre. It was declared a Los Angeles Historical and Cultural Landmark in 1968.

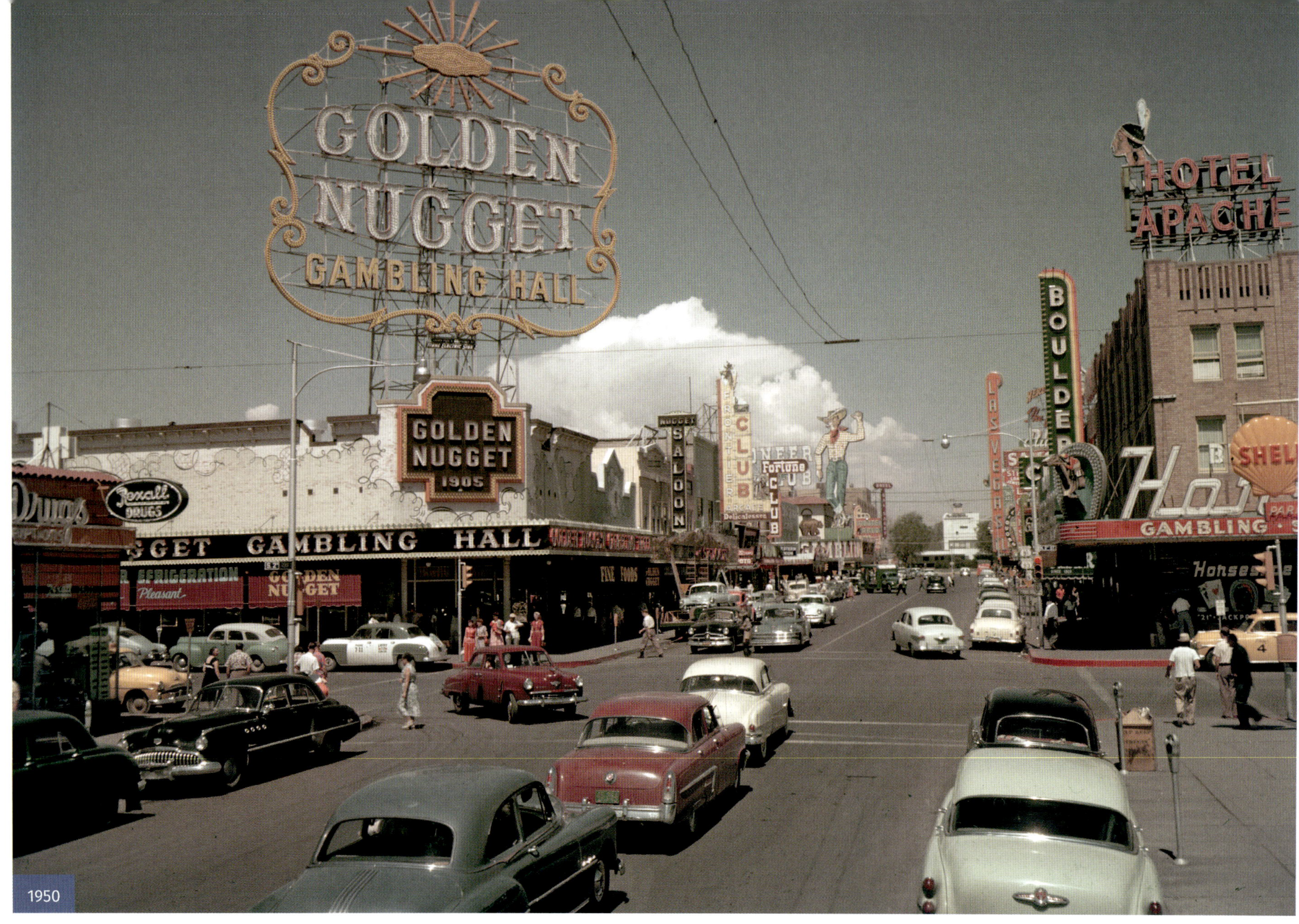

1950

FREMONT STREET, LAS VEGAS

The Golden Nugget and Vegas Vic welcomed early gamblers

In one lifetime Las Vegas has been transformed from a few casinos in a desert oasis to the world's greatest, glitziest center of entertainment. It all started in Fremont Street. Fremont Street in daytime took on a different atmosphere than the street at night, when it lived up to its "Glitter Gulch" nickname. The spectacular 48-foot-high open-frame neon sign atop the Golden Nugget was designed by Hermon Boernge of the Young Electric Sign Company and installed in 1948. The gold nugget at the top of the sign was 12 feet wide, and its "neon rays" spread 26 feet. The hotel opened in August 1945 and was owned by Guy McAfee, a former Los Angeles police captain and gambling operator. McAfee had left California under threat of prosecution for his gaming activities and moved to Las Vegas in 1939, where his expertise in casino operations was welcomed. It was McAfee who has been credited with giving the four-mile stretch of Highway 91 the moniker "the Strip," as it reminded him of Sunset Strip in Los Angeles.

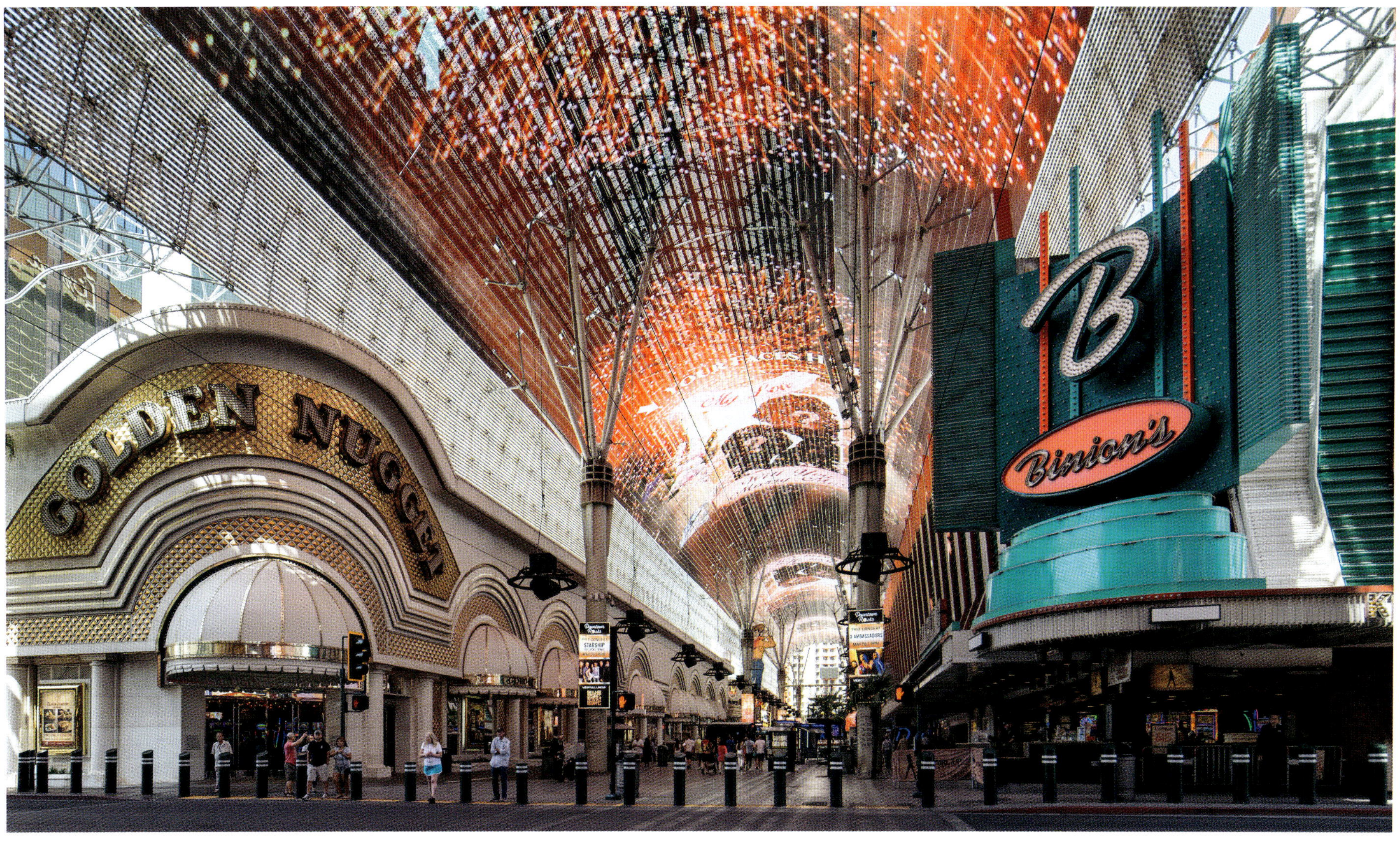

The Hotel Apache (at right in the 1950 photo) with its distinct neon sign first opened in March 1932, but it was not until 1946 that the Eldorado Club took over the first floor. Until the mid-1940s, the Hotel Apache also played an interesting role in Las Vegas policing, which was relatively unsophisticated in the city's early decades. Owing to the fact that early squad cars had no radios, the city's police would signal officers in the surrounding streets by flashing a large red light atop the hotel.

Over fifty years later, the Golden Nugget is still a vibrant part of Fremont Street but was transformed into an elegant resort by Steve Wynn in the mid 1980s. It contrasts sharply with the vibrant blue and coral neon of Binion's Horseshoe, which replaced the Eldorado Club in 1951. The Golden Nugget has long been regarded as the most elegant of the downtown hotels. One of its most popular attractions is the award-winning Tank Pool and Jacuzzi which features a 200,000-gallon shark tank. In November 2009, a new 500-room hotel tower was added with an entrance accented by the dramatic vertical fish tank of the Chart House restaurant. The hotel maintains a connection to its mineral roots via the "Hand of Faith" on display in its lobby—the largest golden nugget in existence, and at 61 pounds, the second-heaviest ever discovered.

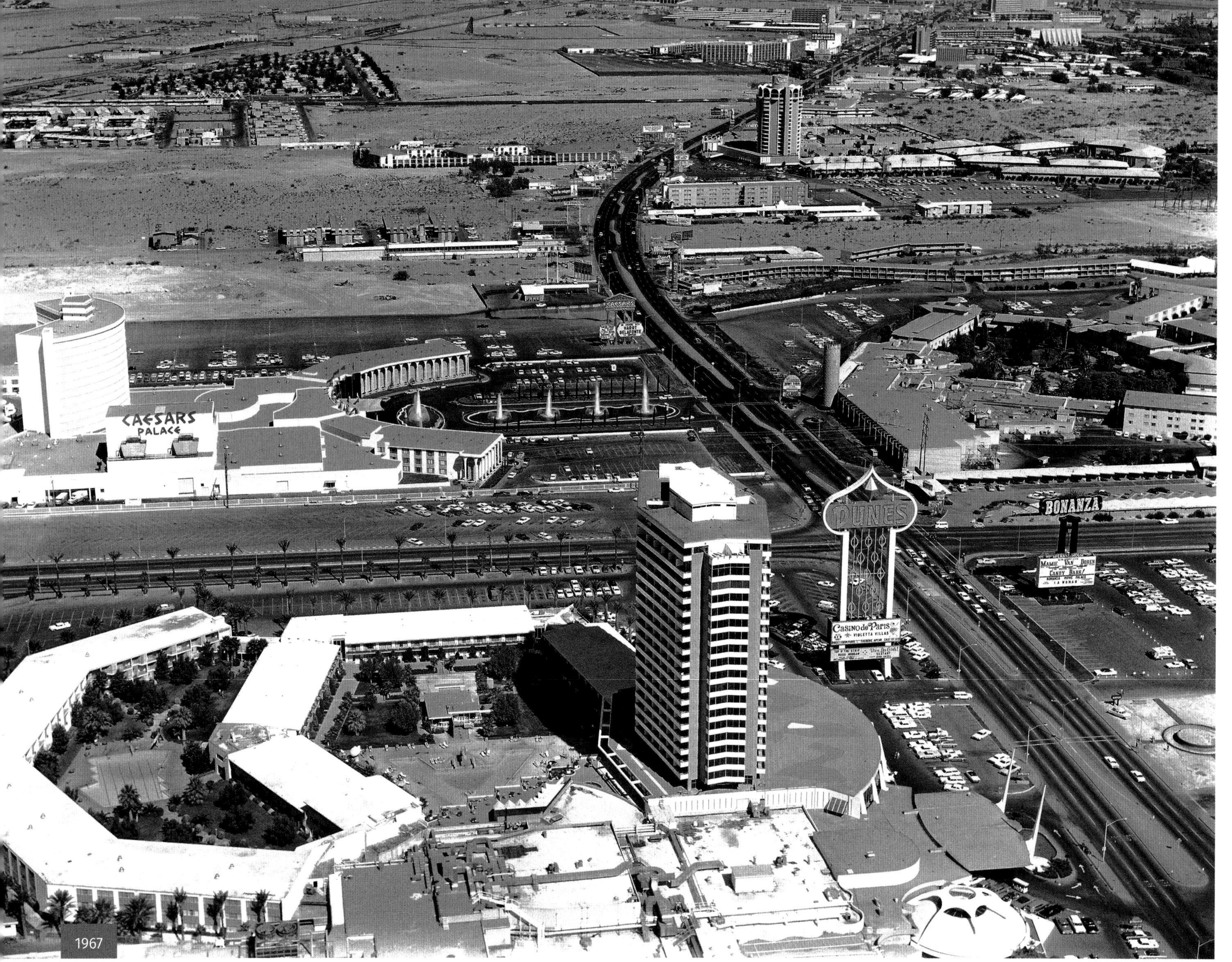

1967

DUNES HOTEL/BELLAGIO RESORT & CASINO, LAS VEGAS

In the city that never sleeps, the development never stops

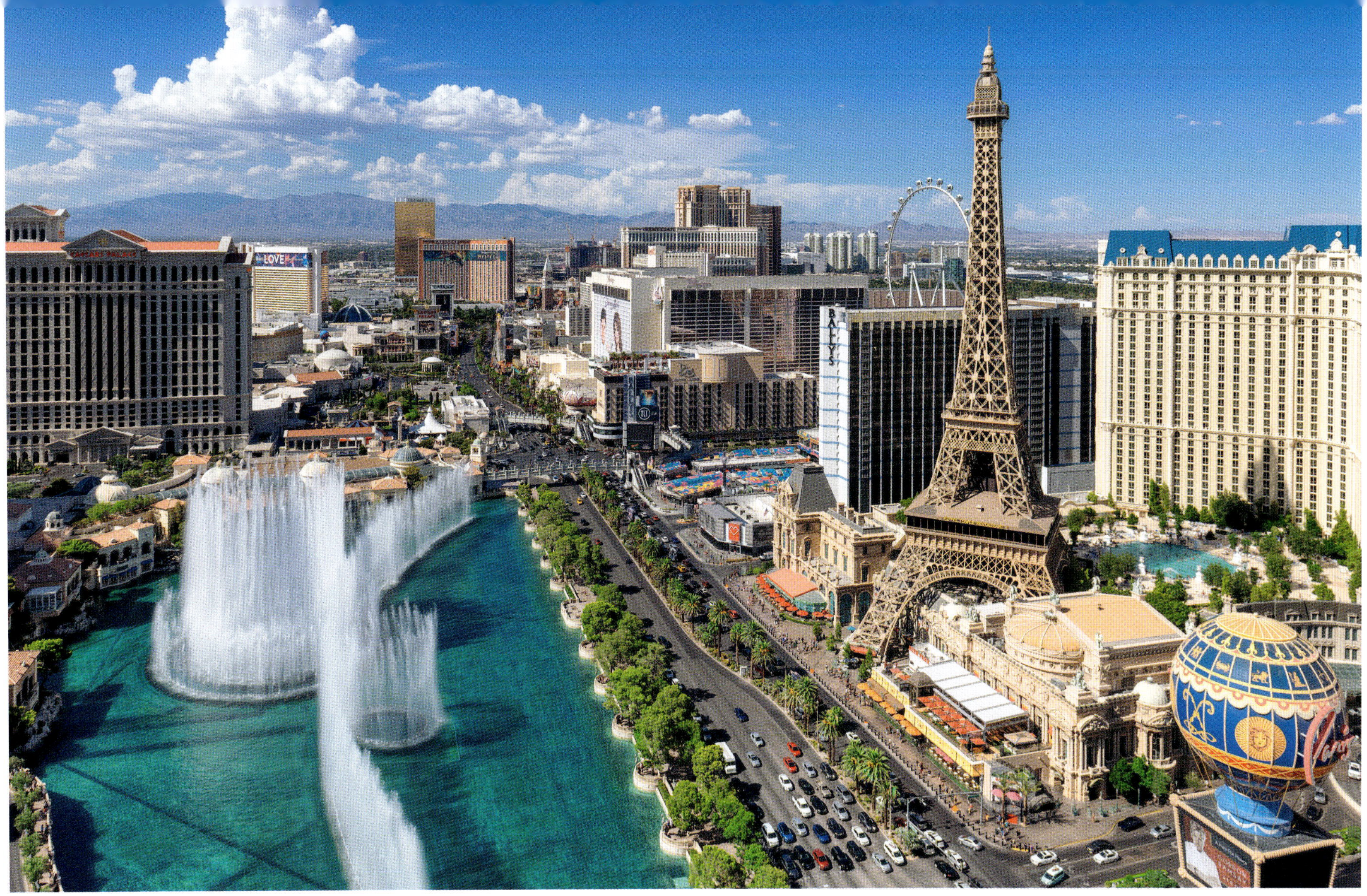

The vintage photo shows an aerial view of the Dunes hotel as it looked around 1967, just after the completion of Caesars Palace to the north, and prior to the destruction of the Flamingo's neon bubble tower in 1968.

The 180-foot neon pylon just in front of the hotel was added to the Dunes in 1964, and was the tallest freestanding sign in the world at the time. Designed by Lee Klay of Federal Sign in Los Angeles, the $500,000 sign provoked complaints from hotel guests who were disturbed by the red glow given off by the three miles of neon tubing. As a result, the hotel was forced to line the window drapes of those rooms that faced the sign. The 24-story high-rise, which opened on July 15, 1965, stands in stark contrast to the low-rise rooms in the background. Yet another innovation by Dunes general manager Major Riddle, the new tower added 250 rooms to the hotel's inventory, and was home to the Top O' the Strip restaurant, a nursery for the children of visiting guests, and a shopping arcade.

Today, the aerial view of the lake at the Bellagio shows the outline of the fountain mechanisms that can shoot water up to 500 feet in the air. More than a thousand fountains make up the display, which entertains millions of visitors each year. Spectators gather around the perimeter to watch the spectacle, and passing cars even stop Strip traffic in their quest to watch the display. The majestic water display spouts and sways to synchronized light and music, choreographed by the California-based design firm WET, and in the background a team of 30—including engineers, lake maintenance personnel, and divers to search out coins—work diligently to ensure that the popular attraction is maintained in tip-top shape.

In 2019 a collaboration with HBO resulted in a special four-minute show that combined pyrotechnics and water along with a custom *Game of Thrones* musical score. The NFL draft event in April 2022 also made use of the Bellagio lake and fountains as a backdrop for their spectacular red carpet opening program.

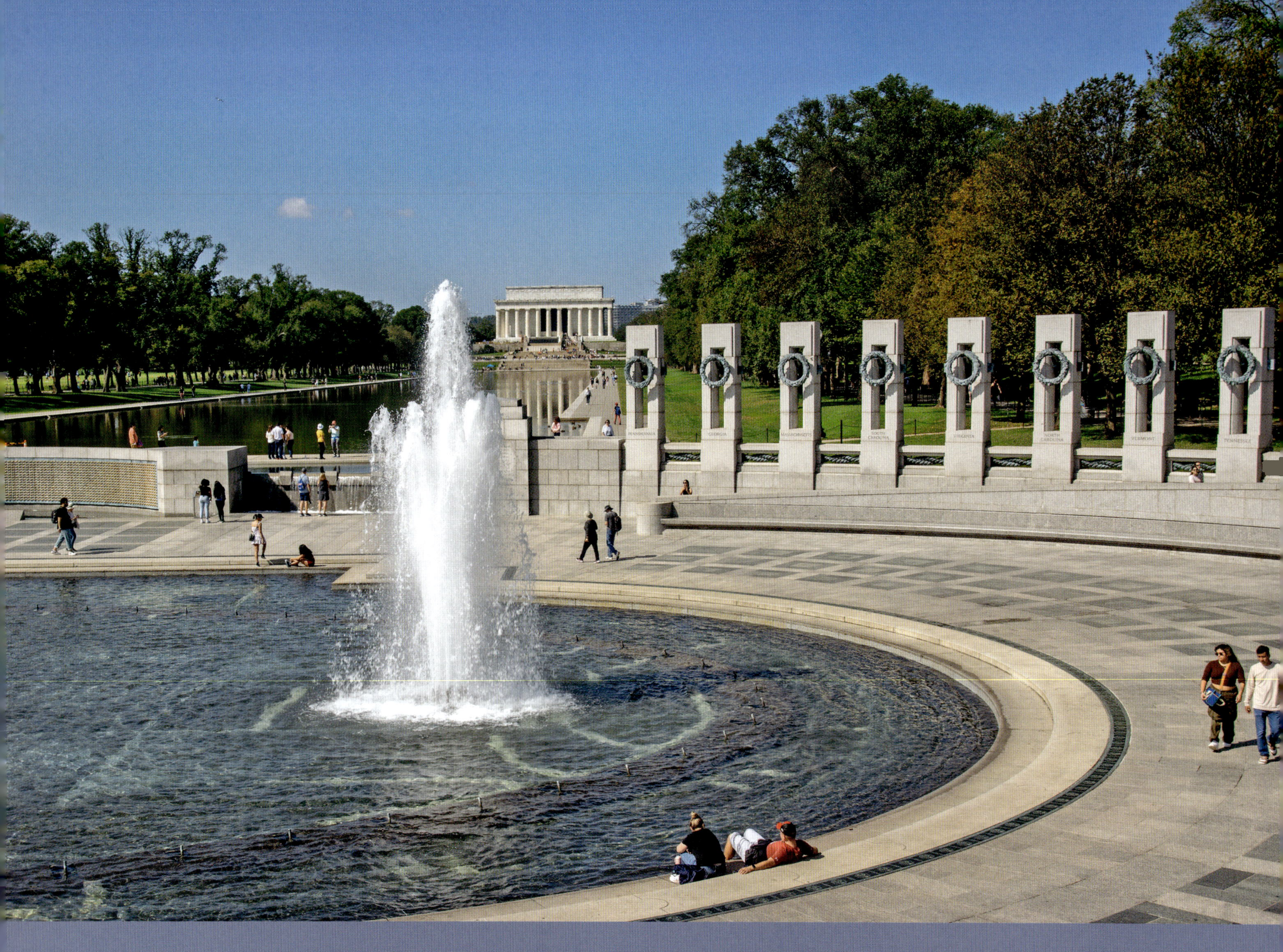

CARVED IN STONE: AMERICA’S GREAT MEMORIALS

Across the United States monuments and memorials stand as silent witnesses to the nation's greatest trials, triumphs, and ideals. These structures—carved in granite, cast in bronze, or etched into black marble—serve as enduring testaments to the people and events that have shaped the America we know today.

MOUNT RUSHMORE: FOUNDERS OF A NATION IN STONE

Perhaps the most iconic of American monuments is Mount Rushmore, carved into the granite face of the Black Hills of South Dakota. The colossal visages of George Washington, Thomas Jefferson, Theodore Roosevelt, and Abraham Lincoln look out over the landscape, each representing pivotal eras of America's development: the founding, expansion, conservation, and preservation of the Union.

Conceived by a South Dakota historian but changed in theme and taken in hand by sculptor Gutzon Borglum, the project began in 1927 and took 14 years to complete. Washington stands at the forefront, representing the birth of the nation. Jefferson symbolizes its expansion through the Louisiana Purchase. Teddy Roosevelt, who championed progressive reforms and the Panama Canal, embodies development, while Lincoln, preserver of the Union during the Civil War, stands for unity.

Controversially, Mount Rushmore was built on land sacred to the Lakota Sioux, and its legacy continues to spark dialogue about Indigenous rights and the meaning of national memory. Nonetheless, it remains a powerful symbol of American ambition and identity.

THE NATIONAL MALL: AMERICA'S CIVIC ALTAR

In the heart of Washington, DC, the National Mall functions as America's ceremonial stage—an open space lined with monuments that represent the nation's history, values, and sacrifices. Each structure has a story to tell.

At the western end of the Mall sits the Lincoln Memorial, an awe-inspiring Greek temple housing a 19-foot seated statue of Abraham Lincoln. Completed in 1922, it was designed to evoke permanence and reverence. The walls are inscribed with Lincoln's Gettysburg Address and Second Inaugural Address.

The memorial has become the site of major moments for democratic protest, particularly for the Civil Rights Movement. From this spot, Eleanor Roosevelt chided the Daughters of the American Revolution for excluding Black opera singer Marian Anderson, but more famously Martin Luther King Jr. delivered his "I Have a Dream" speech in 1963. In this way, Lincoln's legacy extends beyond the Civil War.

MARTIN LUTHER KING JR. MEMORIAL: A DREAM IN STONE

Unveiled in 2011, the Martin Luther King Jr. Memorial is the first to honor an African American on the National Mall. Located near the Tidal Basin, King is depicted emerging from a "stone of hope," a reference to a line from his famous speech: "Out of the mountain of despair, a stone of hope."

The statue's stern gaze faces the Jefferson Memorial across the Tidal Basin and is fittingly installed close to the more linear FDR memorial. Franklin Delano Roosevelt was a man of the greatest integrity who helped steer the nation through twelve years of Depression and war.

WAR MEMORIALS

While many Civil War memorials have come under scrutiny for the values they represent, there can be little debate over the significance of the Korean, Vietnam and World War II memorials along the National Mall.

Baltimore in Maryland was the first large city to erect a fitting tribute to George Washington, with the nation's capital lagging embarrassingly behind and eventually constructing a magnificent edifice, but with two different types of stone. Between the DC Washington Monument and the Lincoln Memorial lies the World War II Memorial completed in 2004. It honors the 16 million Americans who served and the over 400,000 who died in the conflict that redefined the twentieth century.

The memorial is circular, with 56 granite pillars representing the US states and territories, flanking two pavilions labeled "Atlantic" and "Pacific," denoting the two theaters of war. A central fountain and a field of gold stars (each one representing 100 fallen soldiers) form its emotional heart. It is a space of grandeur and solemnity, reminding visitors of the scale of the war and the unity of a nation at its most tested moment after the shock of Pearl Harbor.

Each memorial site is a space for reflection: on the past, on sacrifice, and on the responsibility of those who inherit democracy. And while the monuments may be made of stone and bronze, their true power lies in the emotions they stir and the conversations they spark about American values.

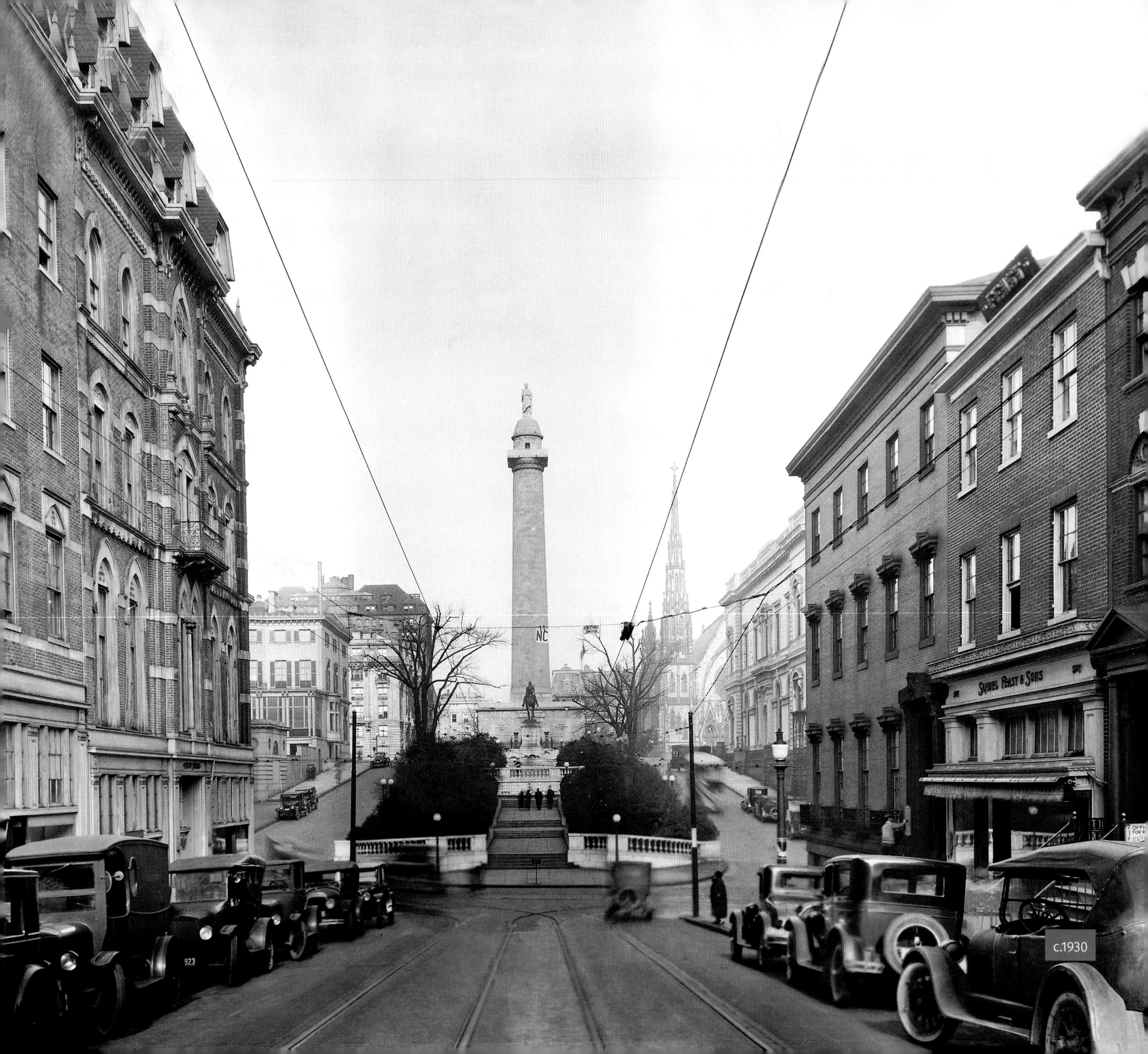

c.1930

GEORGE WASHINGTON MONUMENT, BALTIMORE

The first grand memorial to America's most important founding father

Baltimore's Washington Monument, located in the Mount Vernon neighborhood, holds the distinction of being the first major US monument dedicated to George Washington. Designed by architect Robert Mills, who would later design the larger, endlessly delayed Washington Monument in DC, Baltimore's tribute to the nation's first president began construction in 1815 and was completed in 1829.

The idea for a monument to Washington was proposed shortly after his death in 1799. Baltimore, a growing city with civic pride and national ambitions, raised funds through a public lottery authorized by the Maryland General Assembly in 1810. In 1813, the Washington Monument Society of Baltimore was formed to oversee the project.

Robert Mills, a prominent American architect won the design competition in 1815. His original plan called for a rotunda and elaborate colonnade (which he also proposed for his later Washington monument), but due to funding constraints the design was scaled back to a simpler 220-foot-tall Doric column made of white Maryland marble.

Construction began on July 4, 1815. The site chosen was then called Howard's Woods, land donated by John Eager Howard, a Revolutionary War hero and former Maryland governor. The location was later developed into Mount Vernon Place, which became a central and elegant urban square.

Atop the column stands a 15-foot statue of George Washington, also designed by Mills and carved by Italian sculptor Enrico Causici. The statue depicts Washington resigning his commission as commander-in-chief of the Continental Army—an act symbolizing his commitment to democracy and civilian leadership. A spiral staircase of 227 steps leads to a viewing platform just below the statue, providing panoramic views of Baltimore and its harbor, symbolizing both civic pride and the city's growing economic power.

Over the years, the structure experienced wear and required several restorations. A significant restoration project was completed in 2015, just in time for the monument's bicentennial. The $5.5 million renovation included structural repairs, cleaning of the marble, and restoration of the statue.

Almost sixty years before the towering obelisk in the nation's capital was completed (in 1888), Baltimore's Washington Monument stood as the first architectural tribute to the founding father.

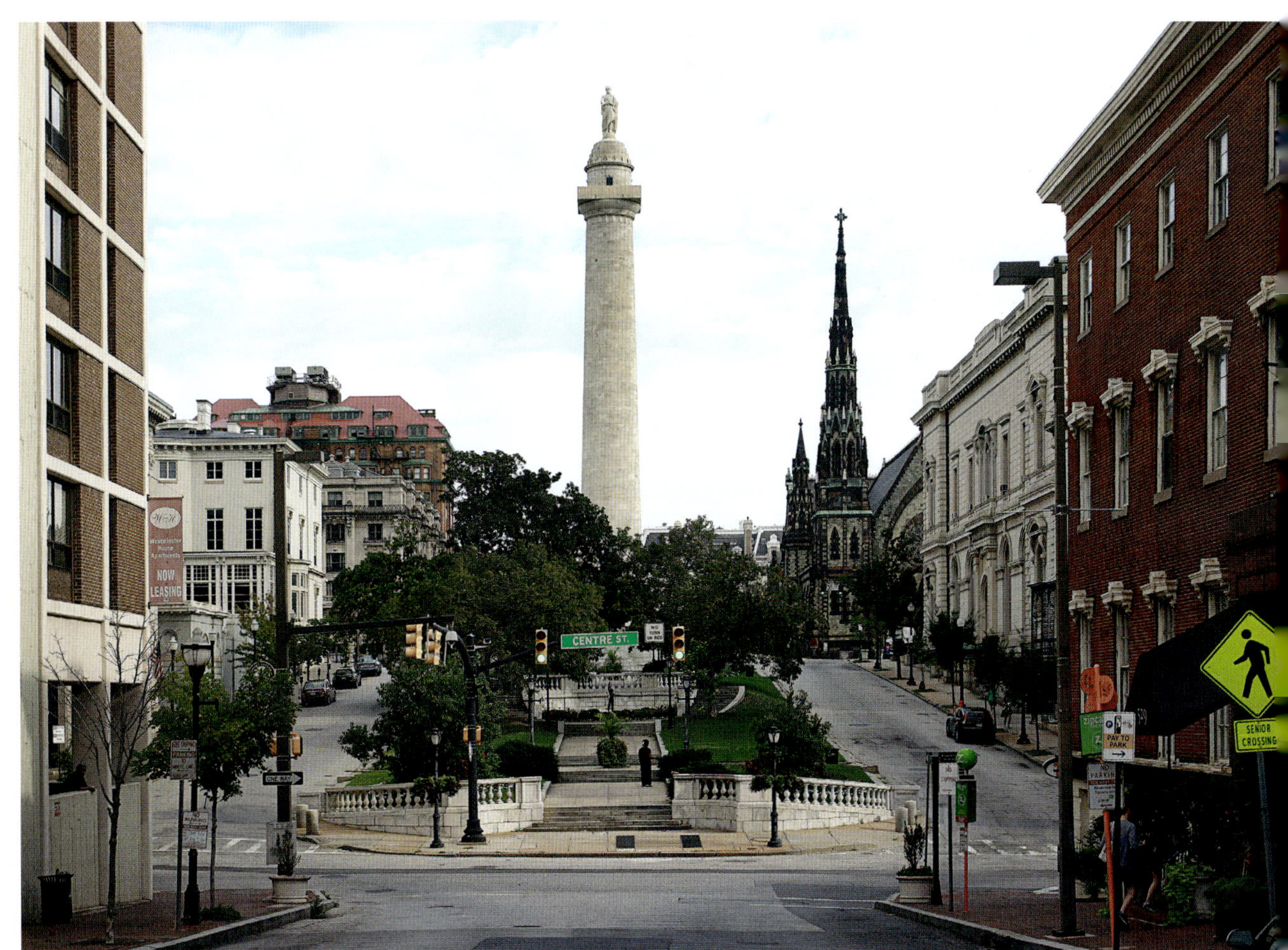

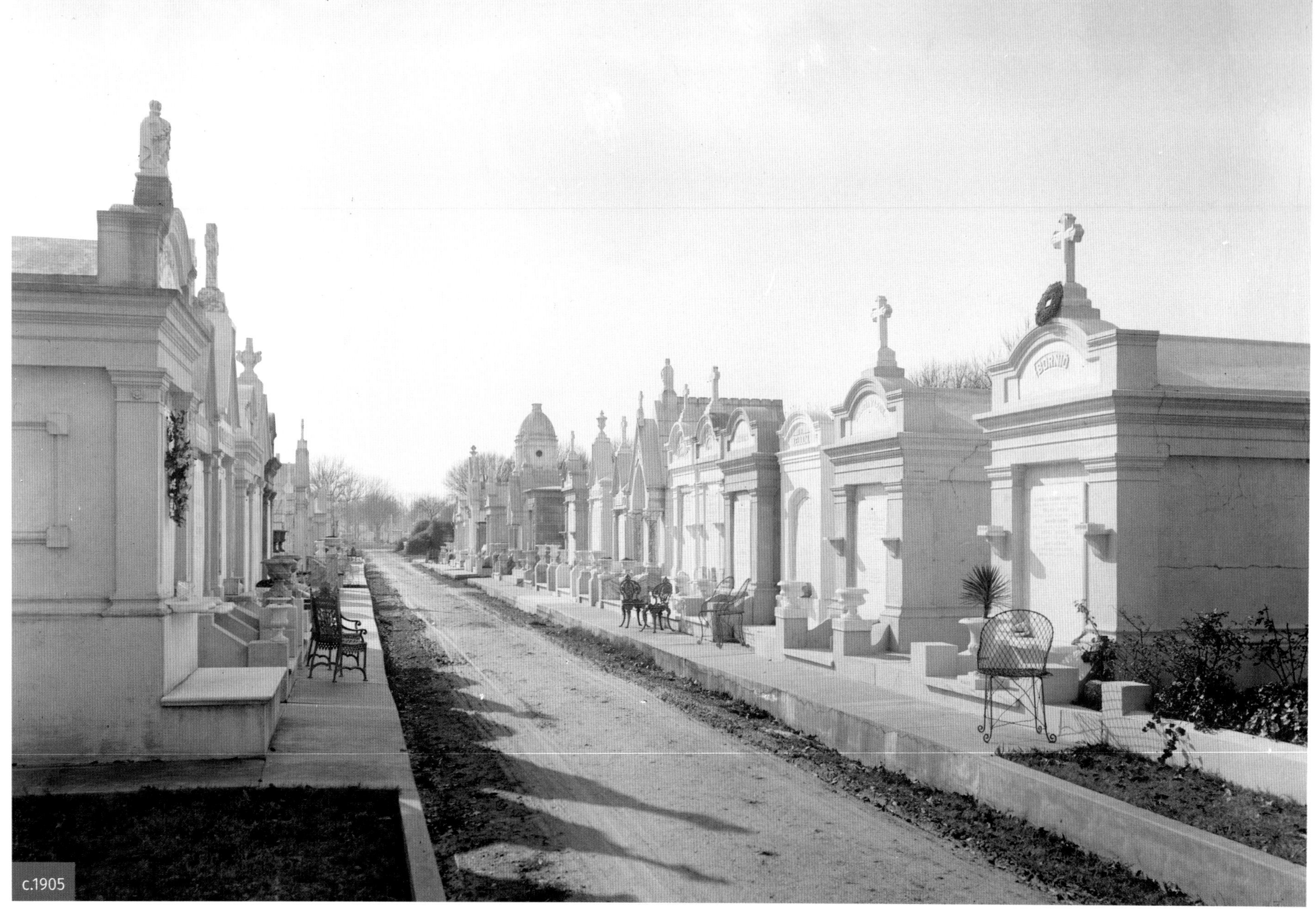
c.1905

METAIRIE CEMETERY, NEW ORLEANS

In its time, Metairie has witnessed both the quick and the dead...

Metairie Cemetery, located on the western edge of New Orleans, is one of the most historically and architecturally significant cemeteries in the United States. Known for its elaborate tombs, monuments, and mausoleums, the cemetery has an unusual origin. It was once the site of the Metairie Race Course, a prominent horse racing track established in 1838. It was owned by the Metairie Jockey Club, an elite social and sporting organization composed of the city's wealthiest citizens and the center of New Orleans society. Its oval layout was about one mile in circumference and located on the outskirts of the city at the time.

Charles T. Howard, a wealthy entrepreneur and lottery magnate, was snubbed by the exclusive Jockey Club when he applied for membership. He vowed that one day he would turn the racetrack into a cemetery. During the Civil War, horse racing was suspended, and the track fell into disuse. After the war, Howard still had the money to

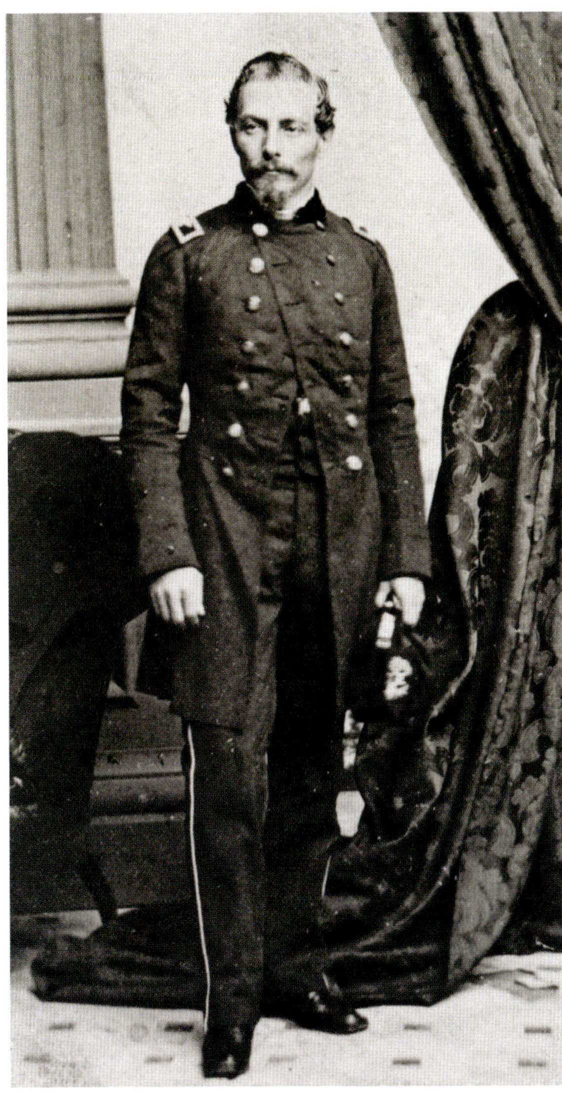

ABOVE: Pierre Gustave Toutant-Beauregard was an American military officer often regarded as the Confederate general who started the American Civil War by capturing Fort Sumter in Charleston Harbor. He died in New Orleans in 1893 at age 74.

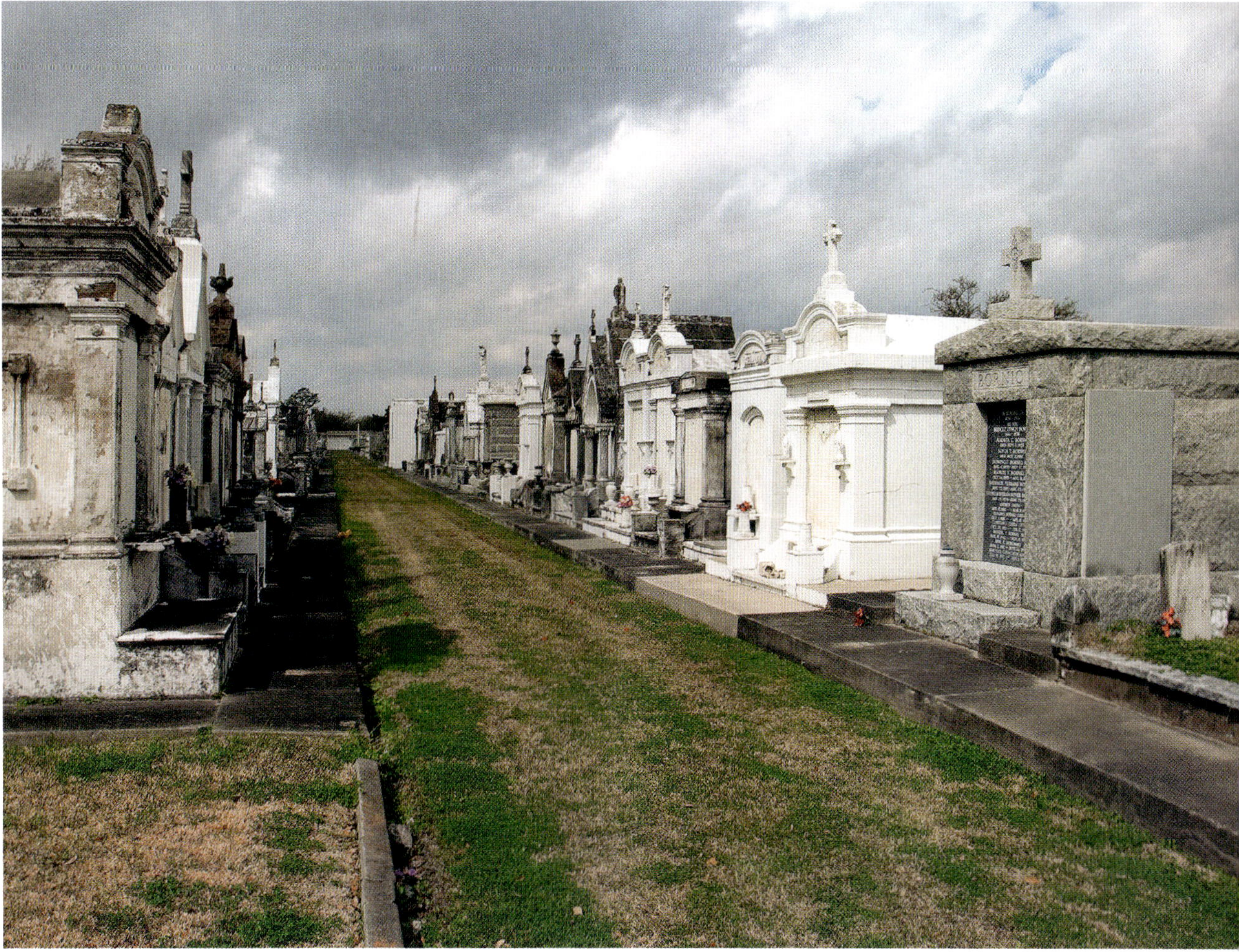

purchase the land and in 1872 fulfilled his promise and opened Metairie Cemetery. The track's oval shape was retained in the cemetery's design, forming the main road that still curves through the grounds today.

Howard spared no expense in developing the cemetery and, like the Jockey Club, it became a place to be seen by the New Orleans elite—but only *after* they had shuffled off this mortal coil.

Designed to reflect both classical and Gothic influences, many of the tombs in Metairie Cemetery resemble small chapels, cathedrals, or Greco-Roman temples. The cemetery also features an Army of Tennessee monument along with the tombs of important Confederate generals, P. G. T. Beauregard and John Bell Hood.

Charles T. Howard himself is interred in a grand tomb featuring a life-sized statue of him atop a pedestal, facing the entrance of the cemetery he founded. Ironically, given the former use of the site, he was killed after being thrown from a horse.

Today, it is open to the public and is recognized not only as a historic cemetery but also as a repository of New Orleans' influential figures.

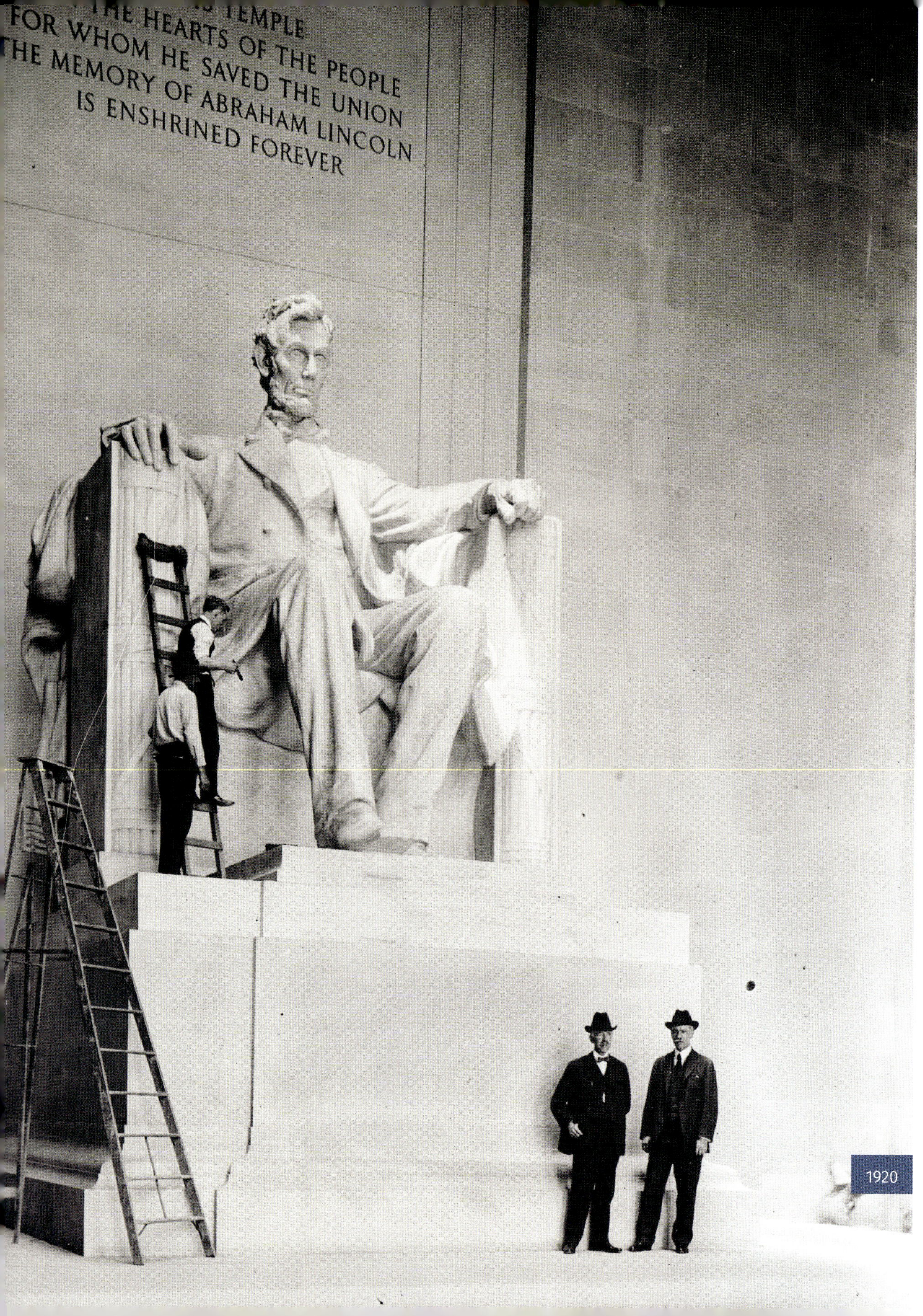

LINCOLN MEMORIAL, WASHINGTON, DC

Abraham Lincoln's monument has become the lodestone of political protest in Washington, DC

1920

As early as 1867, just two years after President Abraham Lincoln's assassination, Congress began introducing bills to create a memorial in honor of the famed leader. But it was not until 1911 that the Lincoln Memorial Commission was created by Congress. The creation of the Lincoln Memorial aligned with the implementation of the McMillan Plan to put the National Mall at the core of the city. The future Lincoln Memorial was intended to go at one end of a large park. Although a spot was chosen at the west end of the Mall, this was not the Lincoln Memorial Commission's first choice.

The western side of Washington near the National Mall and the Potomac River was not structurally sound, and had swamp-like ground. Despite structural challenges, construction began on the Lincoln

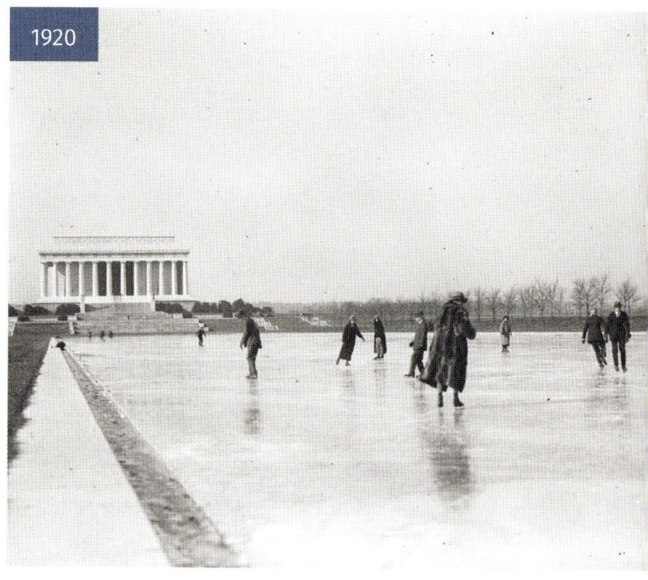

1920

Memorial. It was designed in a neoclassical style by architect Henry Bacon, and Daniel Chester French was commissioned to create the large statue of Lincoln. Building work started in 1914 and was a lumbering process from the start. Eight years later, on Memorial Day 1922, the Lincoln Memorial was finally completed, with President William Howard Taft proudly showcasing the new monument. Aside from the President there was another special guest at its opening: Robert Todd Lincoln, Abraham Lincoln's only surviving son.

The Lincoln Memorial's importance and involvement in Washington, DC does not end with its foundation nor its current status as a tourist attraction. In much the same way, Lincoln's representation in the fight to unite the country did not end with his assassination. Throughout the twentieth century, the Lincoln Memorial served as an important site for civil rights activism.

In 1939, Black musician Marian Anderson was prevented from performing in the Daughters of the American Revolution's Constitution Hall because of her race, and so with the support of the First Lady, Eleanor Roosevelt, the singer was able to perform on the steps of the Lincoln Memorial. The performance attracted a live audience of 75,000 people and nationwide radio listeners. On August 28, 1963, another landmark moment for the Civil Rights Movement happened on the steps of the Lincoln Memorial. As a result of the March on Washington for Jobs and Freedom, 250,000 people gathered around the Reflecting Pool, standing in front of the statue of the late President and author of the Emancipation Proclamation to hear Martin Luther King Jr. give his iconic "I Have a Dream" speech.

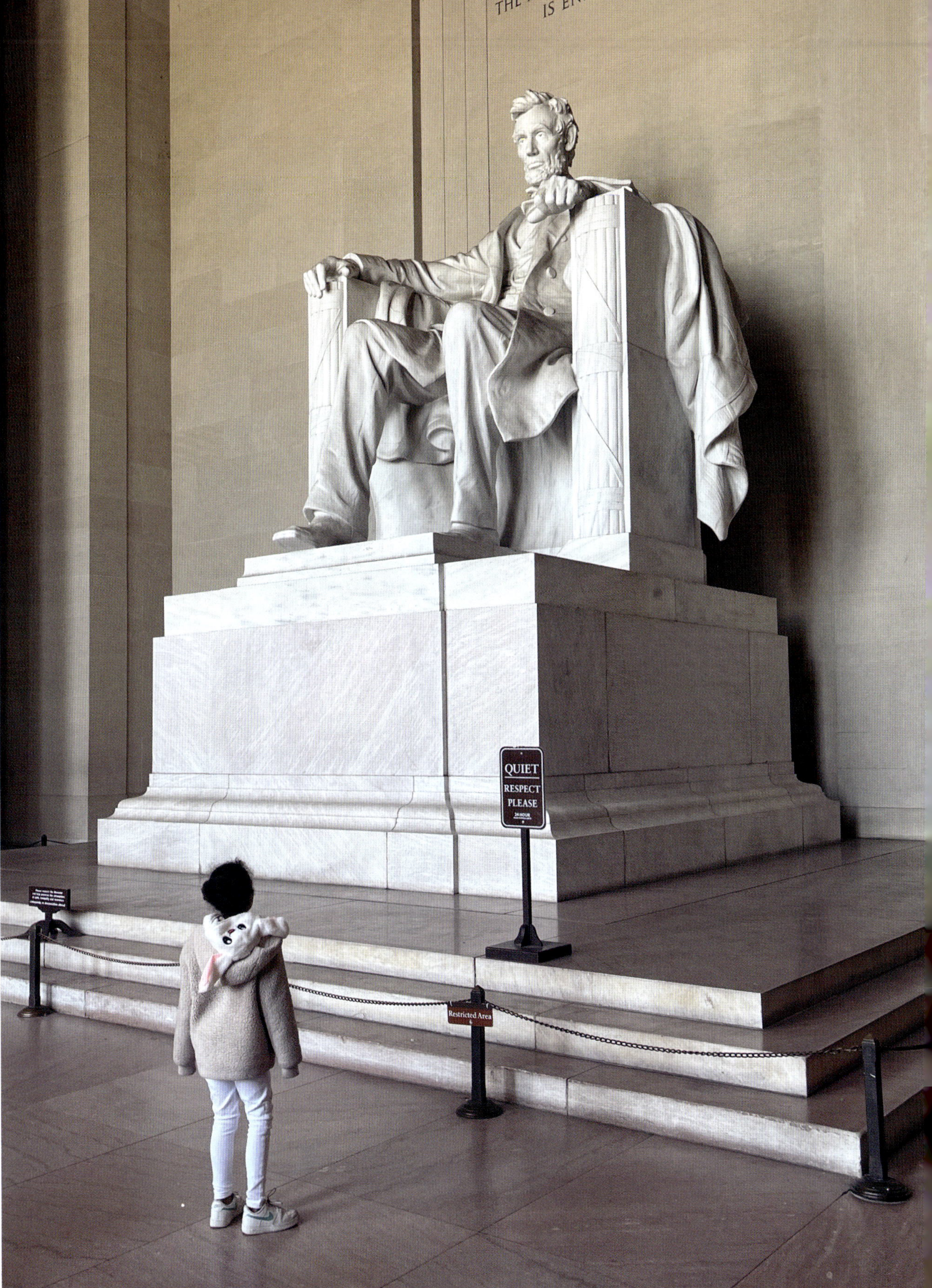

LEFT: The Reflecting Pool proved to be a popular ice-skating amenity in winter, and with the water only a matter of inches deep, there was no risk of fatal accidents.

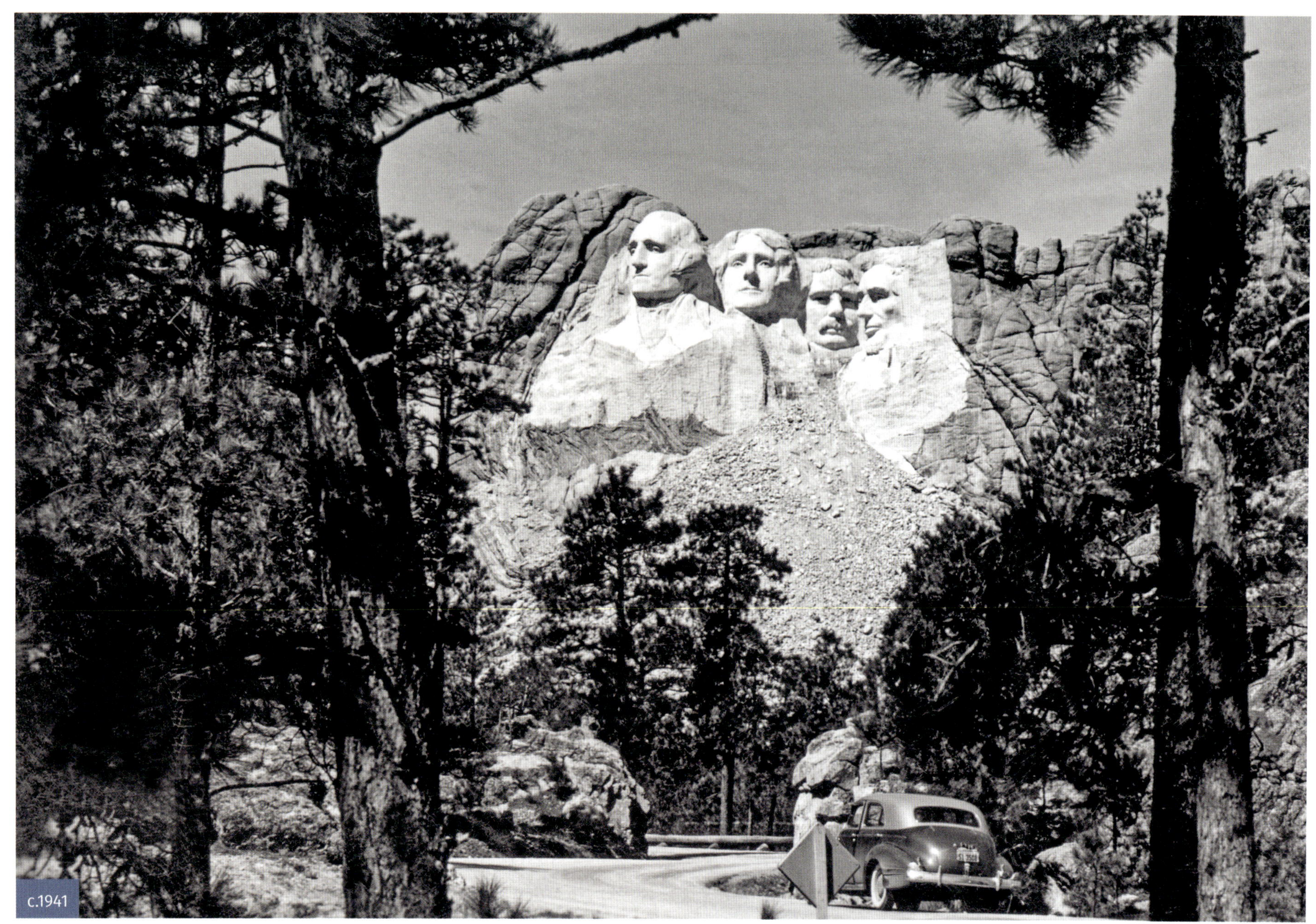

c.1941

MOUNT RUSHMORE, SOUTH DAKOTA

A monument to western pioneers was hijacked for a national celebration

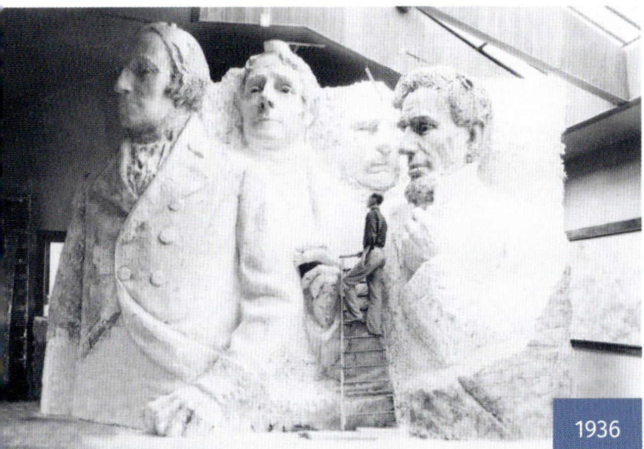

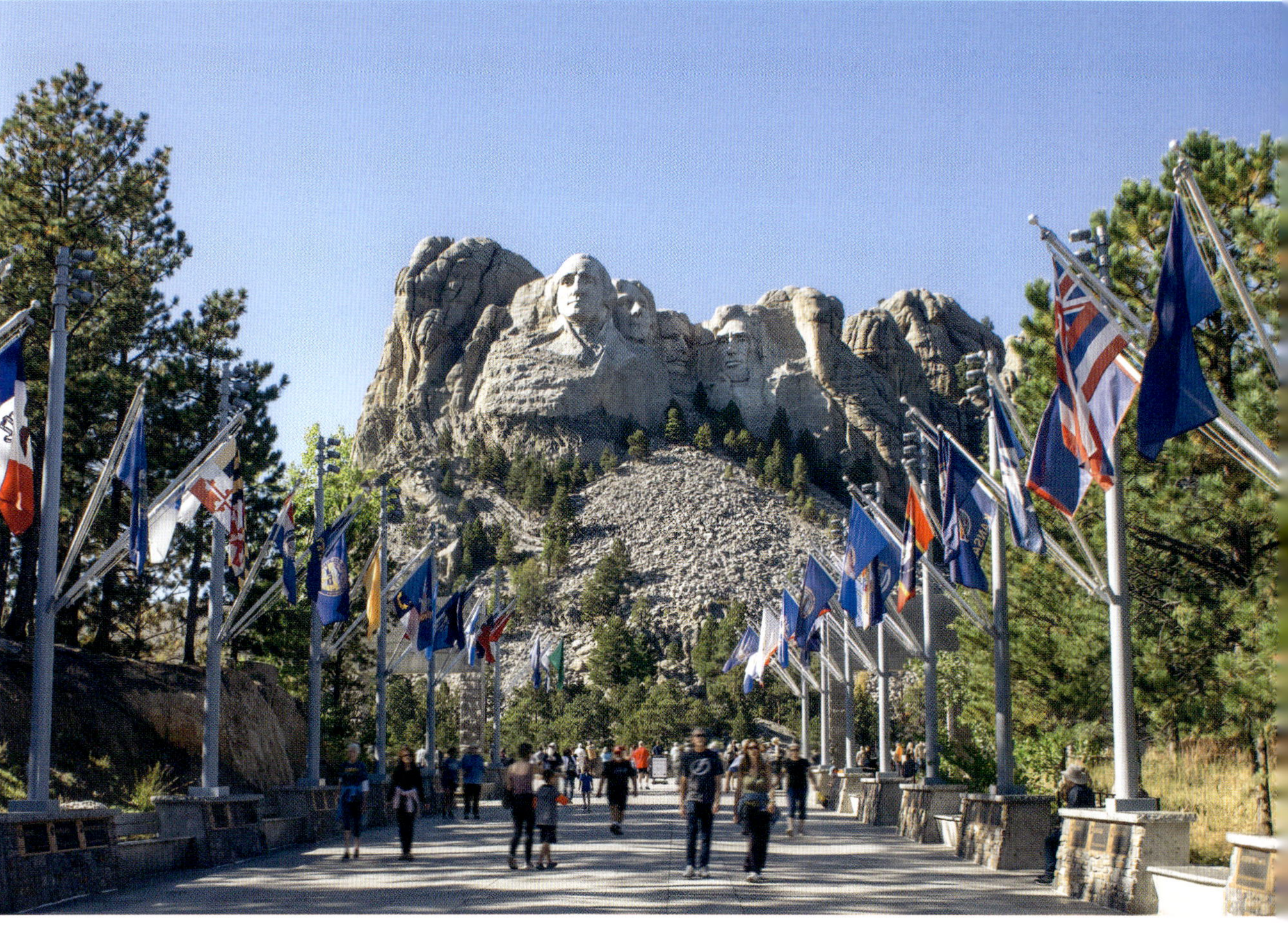

Mount Rushmore National Memorial, located in the Black Hills region of South Dakota, is one of the most recognizable landmarks in the United States. Featuring the 60-foot-tall faces of Presidents George Washington, Thomas Jefferson, Theodore Roosevelt, and Abraham Lincoln, the monument symbolizes the birth, growth, development, and preservation of the United States.

The origins of Mount Rushmore trace back to the early 1920s when Doane Robinson, a South Dakota state historian, envisioned carving giant sculptures into the Black Hills to promote tourism. His original idea was to sculpt famous figures of the American West, such as Lewis and Clark or Buffalo Bill Cody. However, renowned sculptor Gutzon Borglum, who was recruited for the project, proposed a more nationally unifying vision: depicting US presidents to represent foundational moments in American history.

Work on the monument began in 1927 after President Calvin Coolidge lent his support and Congress approved federal funding. Borglum chose the southeastern face of Mount Rushmore for its exposure to sunlight and the quality of the granite.

The four presidents chosen for the monument each represented a key aspect of American heritage: George Washington, as the nation's founding father and first president, symbolizes the birth of the United States. Thomas Jefferson represented expansion into the Indian territories of the west. Abraham Lincoln embodied the preservation of the Union during the Civil War. Theodore Roosevelt was selected for his role in the construction of the Panama Canal, signifying growth, but also his work on preservation.

Construction was a massive undertaking, involving over 400 workers using dynamite and jackhammers to carve the granite. Despite the risks, there were no fatalities during the 14 years of work. The Great Depression, World War II, and Borglum's death in 1941 all impacted the timeline and scale of the project. His son, Lincoln Borglum, took over and declared the monument complete in October 1941, though the original design had called for full busts rather than just heads.

Mount Rushmore has not been without controversy. The monument is located on land sacred to the Lakota Sioux, which was taken in violation of the 1868 Treaty of Fort Laramie. For many Indigenous people, Mount Rushmore is a painful symbol of colonization and broken promises. Despite these complexities, Mount Rushmore remains a powerful national symbol attracting two million visitors annually.

ABOVE: Gutzon Borglum's studio model of Mount Rushmore shows that the sculptor originally intended to extend the monumental figures.

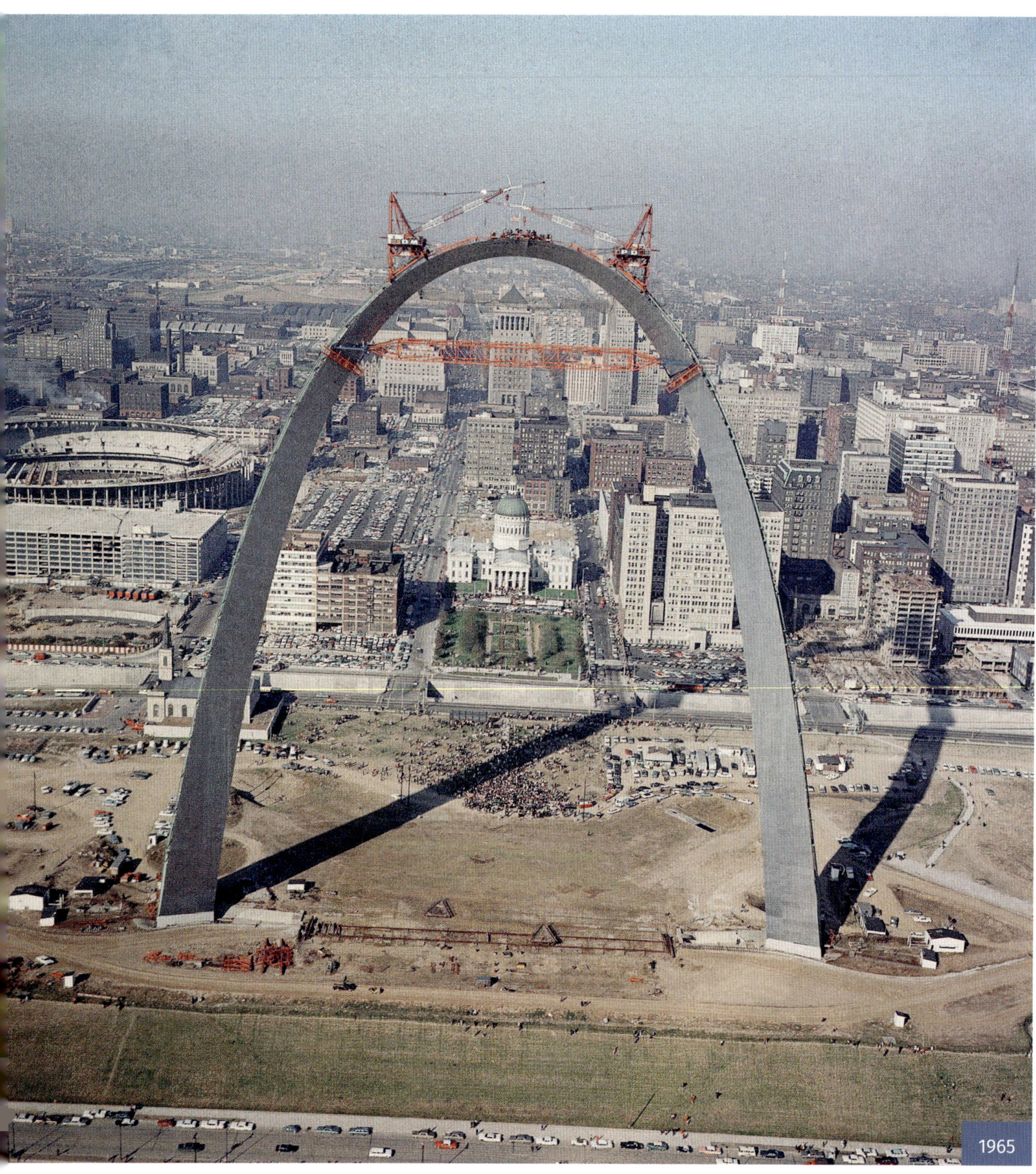

1965

THE GATEWAY ARCH, ST. LOUIS

A monumental tribute to the brave settlers heading out West

The Gateway Arch, rising 630 feet above the western bank of the Mississippi River in St. Louis, Missouri, is one of the most iconic landmarks in the United States if not the world. Known as "The Gateway to the West," the Arch commemorates the westward expansion of the United States and the pioneering spirit of nineteenth-century America.

The idea for a monument in St. Louis dates back to the 1930s. City leaders wanted to revitalize the riverfront and honor the city's historical significance as the starting point for many westward expeditions, most notably the Lewis and Clark Expedition of 1804. St. Louis had long been considered the launching point for settlers, who often arrived by riverboat, and traders heading into uncharted territories.

In 1935, President Franklin D. Roosevelt signed a bill establishing what was originally called the Jefferson National Expansion Memorial. To find a fitting monument, a national design competition was held in 1947–48. Out of 172 entries, the winning design was submitted by Finnish-American architect Eero Saarinen (TWA Building, Dulles Airport). The arch's shape—a perfect inverted catenary curve—was both striking and structurally sound.

Financial constraints, land clearance, and complex political delays pushed the ground breaking to 1959. The project finally began under the supervision of Saarinen (who tragically died of a brain tumor in 1961 before seeing the arch built). Work on the Arch itself was begun in 1963.

Building the Gateway Arch was a massive feat of engineering. Constructed using stainless steel and carbon steel, the arch consists of two hollow legs that rise separately and meet at the top. Each leg is triangular in cross-section, tapering as it ascends. The sections were built on the ground, hoisted into place by cranes, and welded together.

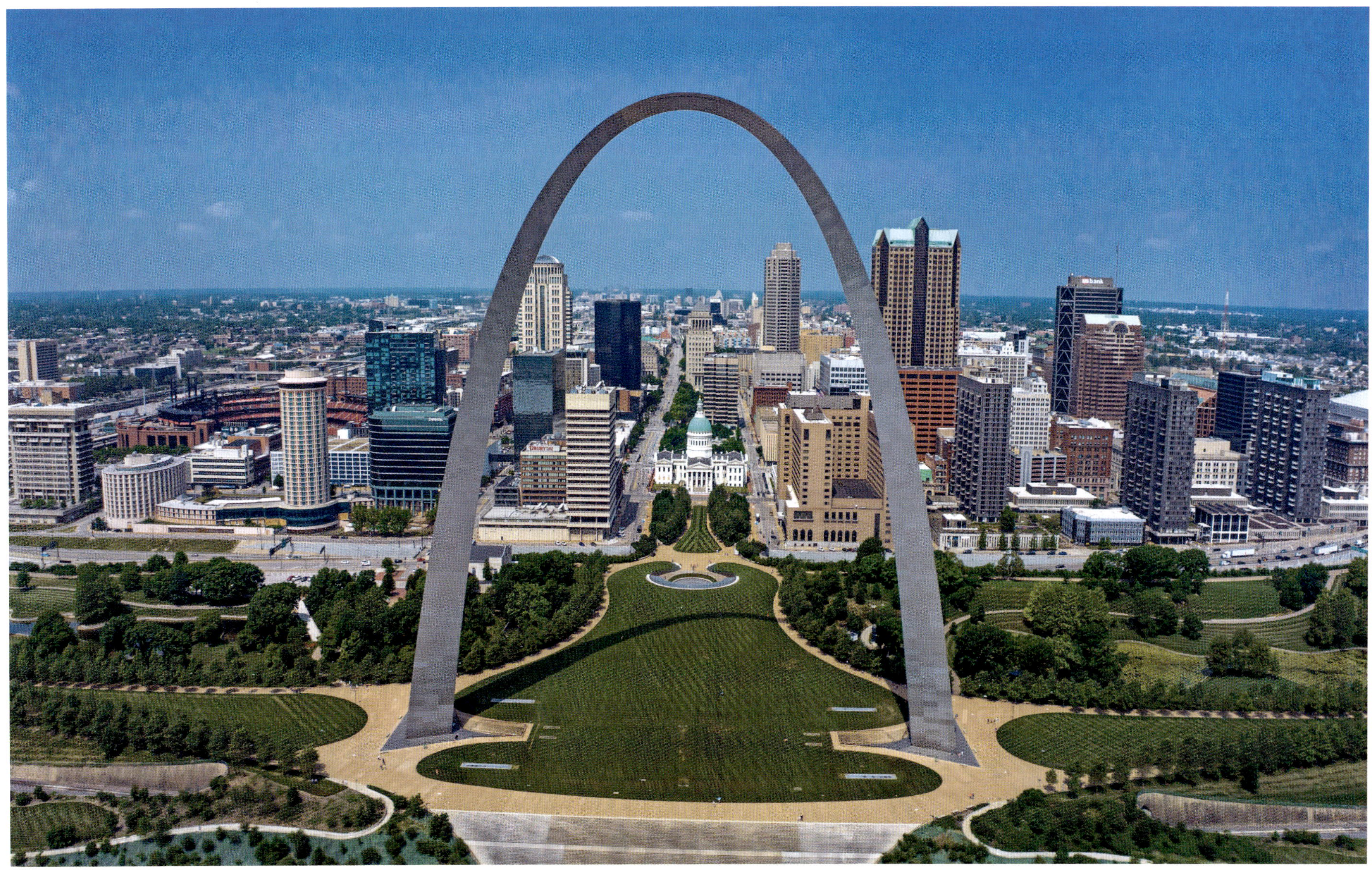

The final piece was inserted at the top on October 28, 1965, with only a narrow margin for error—any misalignment would have prevented the legs from joining. Fortunately, the engineering was flawless. The completed arch opened to the public in June 1967, offering an observation deck at the top, accessible via a unique tram system inside the legs.

At 630 feet high and 630 feet wide at the base, the Gateway Arch is the tallest man-made monument in the US and the world's tallest arch. It has since become a defining feature of the St. Louis skyline and a symbol of the city's historical importance and has repaid the labyrinthine negotiations to get it completed (something that Jefferson, the accomplished politician, would probably have enjoyed).

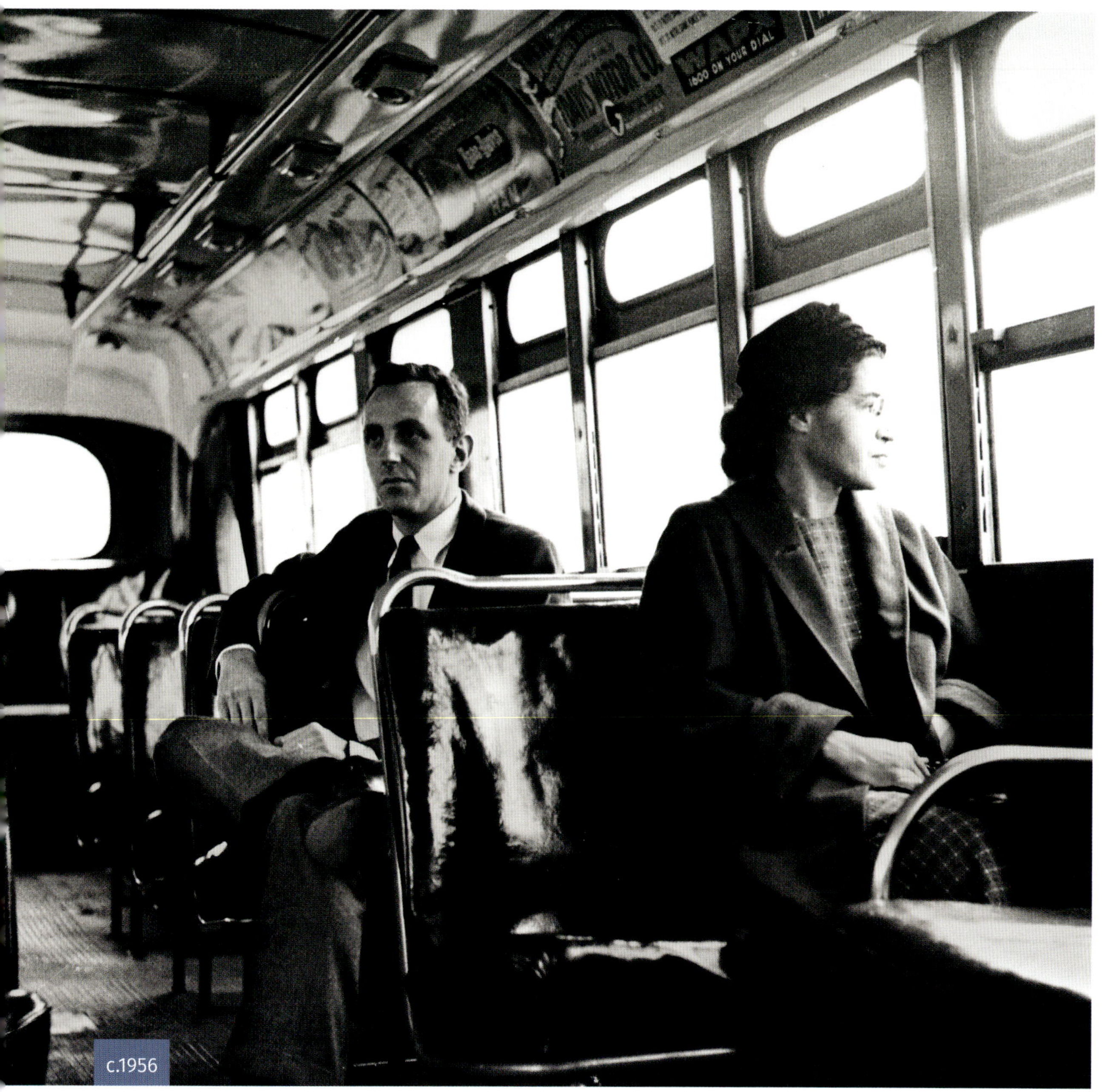

c.1956

MONTGOMERY BUS BOYCOTT, ALABAMA

Rosa Parks' quiet, dignified resistance helped change attitudes

The Montgomery Bus Boycott was a pivotal event in the American Civil Rights Movement. On December 1, 1955, Rosa Parks, a 42-year-old Black civil rights activist, boarded a segregated city bus in Montgomery. At the time, racial segregation laws—often called Jim Crow laws—required Black passengers to sit at the back of the bus and give up their seats to white passengers if the front was full.

When the bus driver ordered Parks to move from a Black-designated seat for a white man, she quietly refused. Her arrest that day was not spontaneous—Parks was an active member of the NAACP (National Association for the Advancement of Colored People) and had long been involved in civil rights issues. Nonetheless, her dignified stance and arrest became a rallying point for a community weary of injustice.

In response to Parks' arrest, local civil rights leaders quickly organized a boycott of the city's bus system. Flyers were distributed throughout the Black community urging people not to ride the buses on Monday, December 5. The turnout was overwhelming—thousands of Black residents walked, or used alternative transportation instead of taking the bus.

The success of the one-day boycott led to the formation of the Montgomery Improvement Association (MIA), led by the little-known Reverend Dr. Martin Luther King Jr., who was only 26 years old. The MIA continued the boycott, demanding courteous treatment for Black passengers, first-come-first-served seating in buses regardless of race, and the hiring of Black drivers.

The boycott lasted for over a year—381 days in total—during which participants endured regular harassment, threats, and violence. Many lost their jobs, and Dr. King's house was bombed. Despite these hardships, the Black community remained united and determined to see the dispute out.

On November 13, 1956, the US Supreme Court upheld a lower court ruling in Browder vs. Gayle, declaring that segregation on public buses was unconstitutional. The decision took effect on December 20, 1956, officially ending the boycott. Rosa Parks became an enduring symbol of resistance, and Dr. King emerged as a key leader of the Civil Rights Movement.

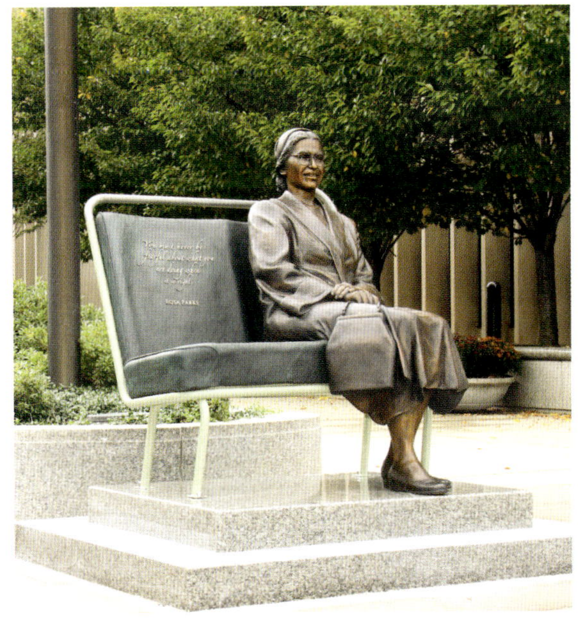

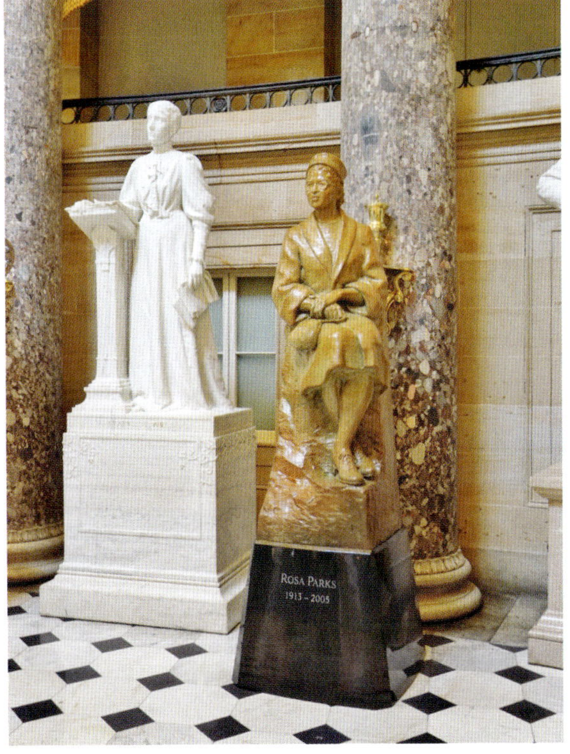

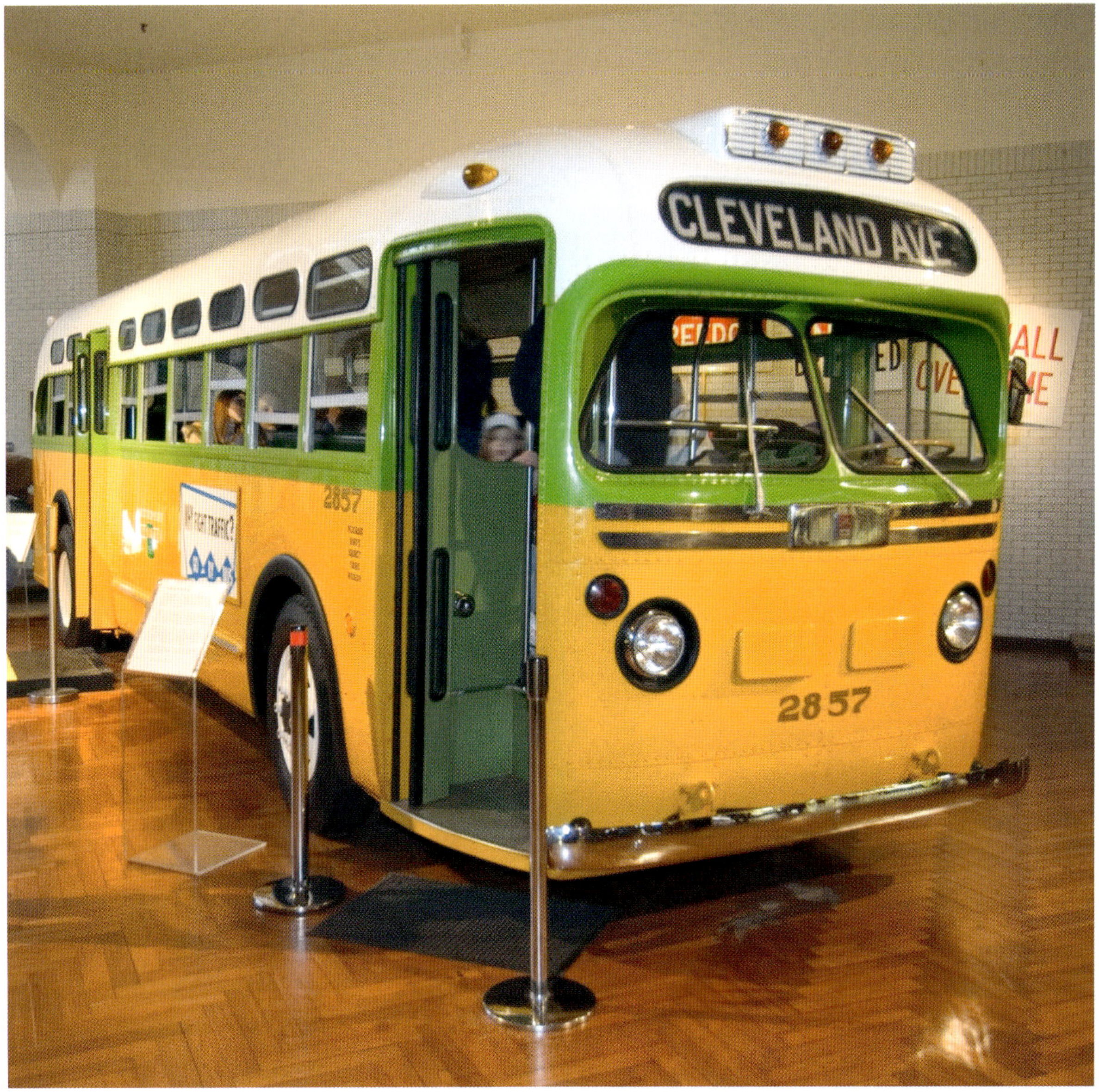

The Montgomery Bus Boycott proved that nonviolent protest could bring about meaningful change. It was a watershed moment that laid the groundwork for future actions like the Freedom Rides, sit-ins, and the March on Washington.

ABOVE: The Montgomery City Transportation bus that Rosa Parks rode when arrested is on display at the Henry Ford Museum at Greenfield Village, Dearborn, Michigan.

LEFT: President Barack Obama unveiled a statue of Rosa Parks at the United States Capitol in February 2013. There are many more across the nation, including the bronze bus seat in New Jersey.

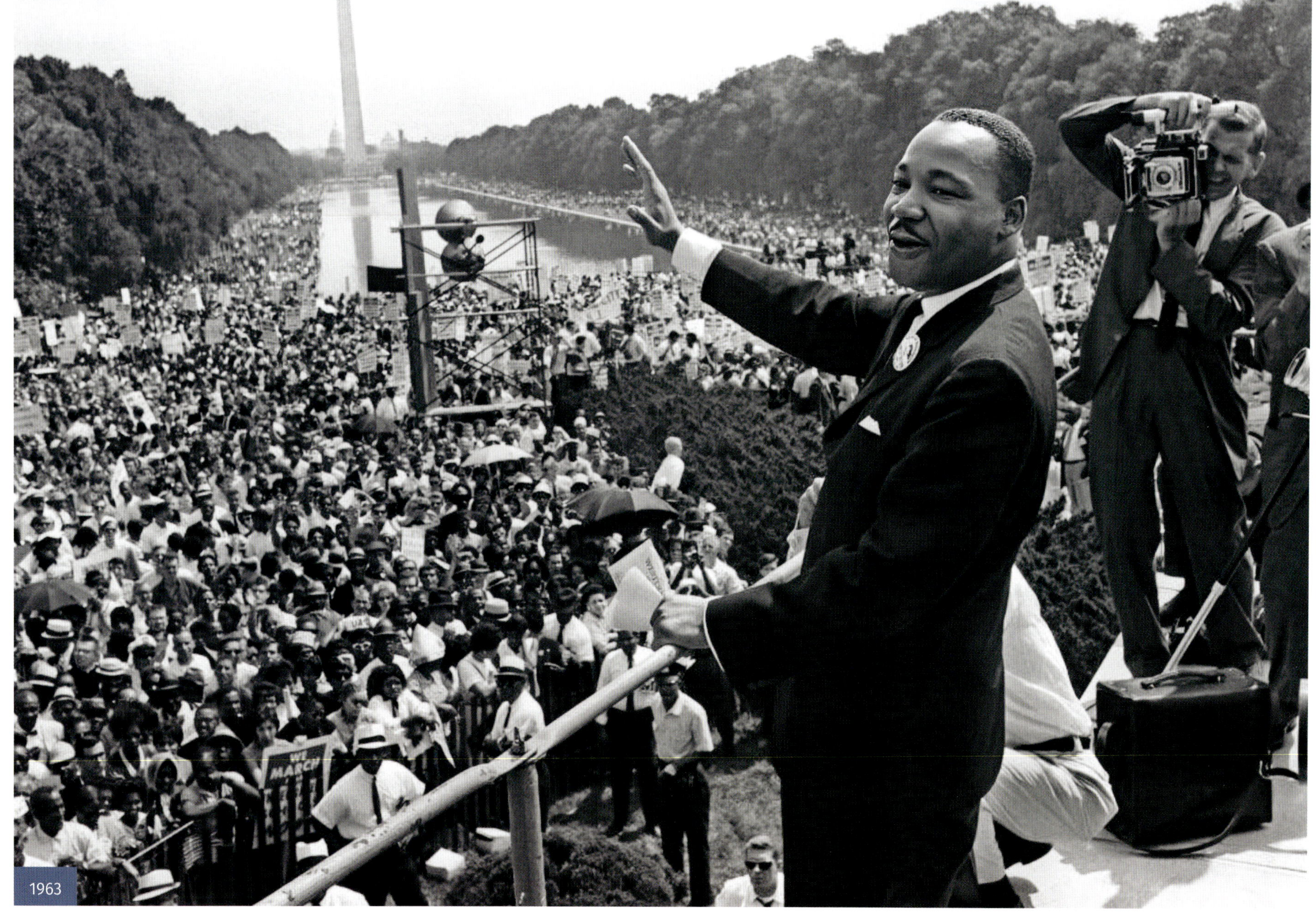

1963

DR. MARTIN LUTHER KING JR. MONUMENT, WASHINGTON, DC

The figurehead of the Civil Rights Movement delivered his key speech on the National Mall

Born on January 15, 1929, in Atlanta, Georgia, Martin Luther King Jr. rose to national prominence during the 1950s and 1960s as a powerful advocate for racial equality, justice, and peace. King earned a sociology degree from Morehouse College, a divinity degree from Crozer Theological Seminary, and a doctorate from Boston University. Influenced by the teachings of Mahatma Gandhi, King believed in achieving change through nonviolent protest and civil disobedience.

His leadership began in earnest with the Montgomery Bus Boycott. King's passionate speeches and steady resolve galvanized the African American community and attracted national attention. His most famous campaigns included the Birmingham Campaign (1963), which exposed the brutality of segregation, and the March on Washington in August 1963. It was during that march, in front of the Lincoln Memorial, that King delivered his most iconic speech—"I Have a Dream"—a call for a future in which people would “not be judged by the color of their skin but by the content of their character.” Over 250,000 people attended the rally, making it one of the largest civil rights gatherings in American history.

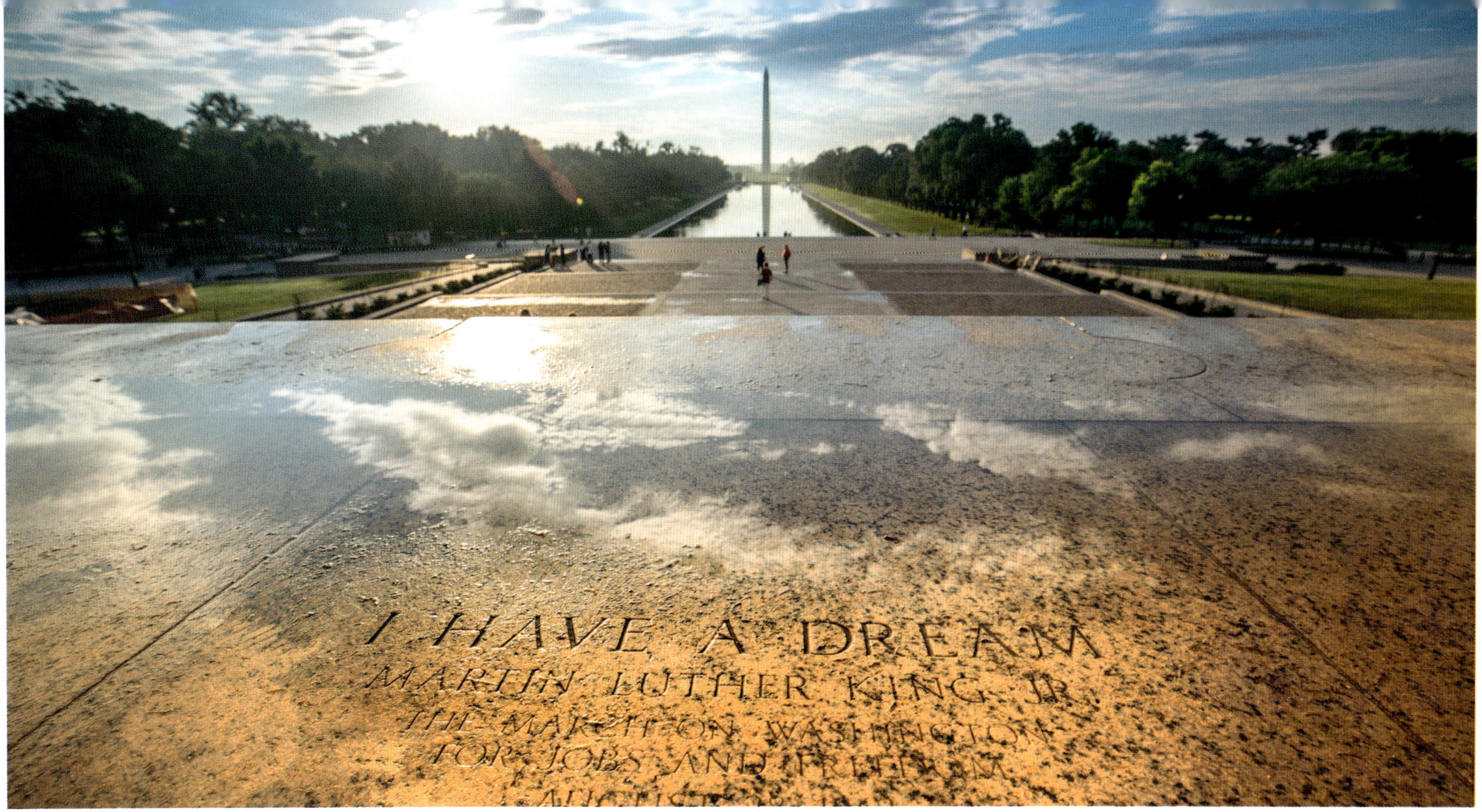

King’s leadership was instrumental in the passage of landmark civil rights legislation, including the Civil Rights Act of 1964 and the Voting Rights Act of 1965. In 1964, he became the youngest recipient of the Nobel Peace Prize. On April 4, 1968, King was assassinated in Memphis, Tennessee, where he had gone to support striking sanitation workers. His death was a devastating blow to the Civil Rights Movement but his legacy endured.

Decades after his death, the idea of honoring King with a national memorial began to take shape. In 1996, Congress authorized the creation of the Martin Luther King Jr. National Memorial on the National Mall in Washington, DC—the first major monument on the Mall dedicated to a Black American.

The memorial’s design was inspired by a line from King’s “I Have a Dream” speech: “Out of the mountain of despair, a stone of hope.” This phrase gave rise to the visual centerpiece of the memorial: a massive sculpture of King carved from white granite, emerging from a “stone of hope” set apart from a symbolic “mountain of despair.” The memorial was officially dedicated on October 16, 2011, with President Barack Obama officiating the ceremony.

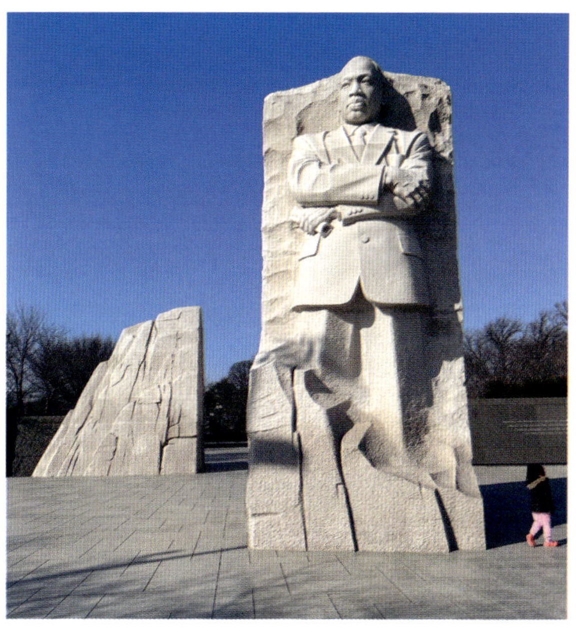

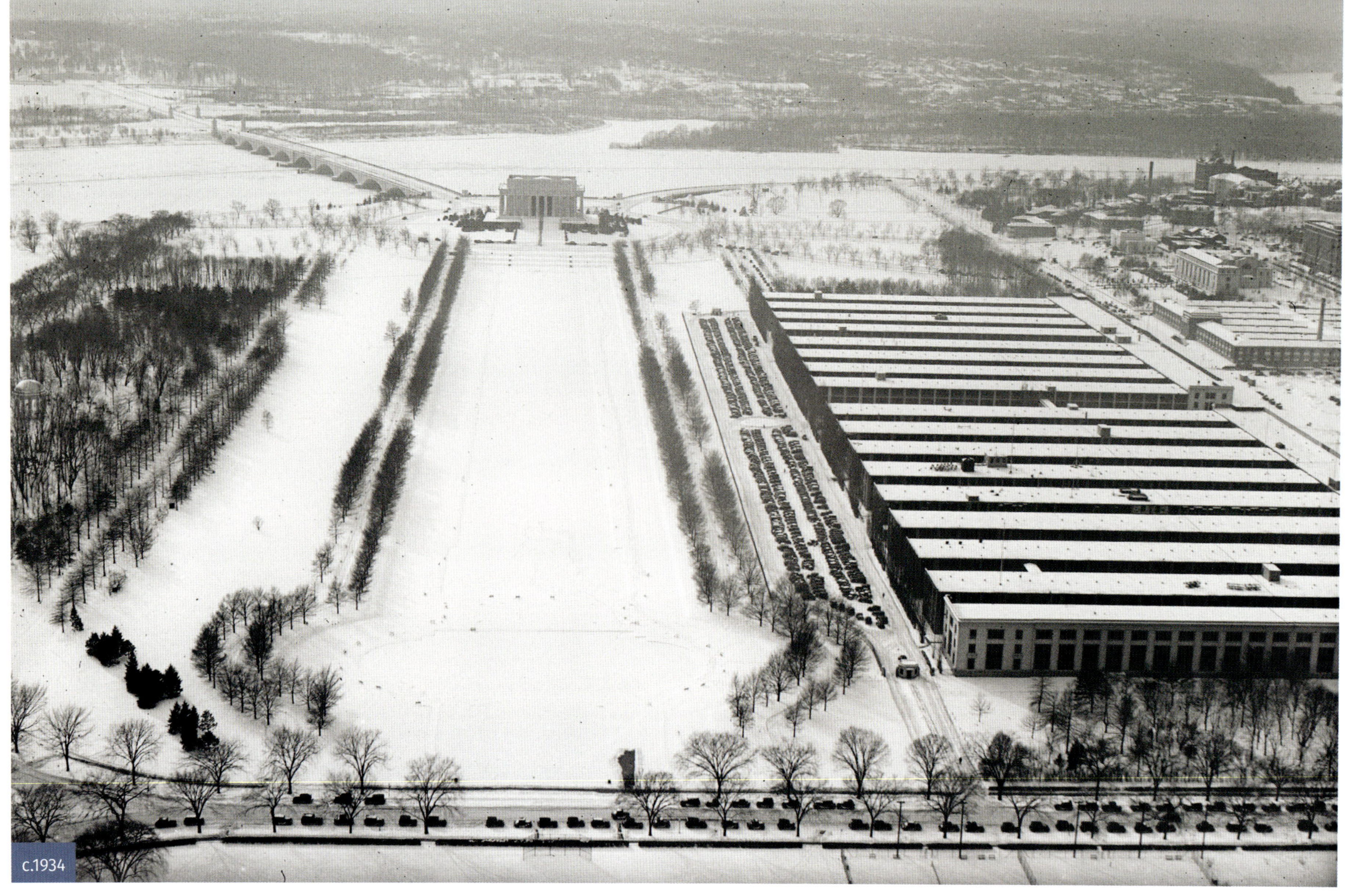

NATIONAL WWII MONUMENT, WASHINGTON, DC

A fitting monument to those who gave their lives fighting the Axis powers

The National World War II Memorial in Washington, DC, stands as a powerful tribute to the 16 million men and women who served in the US Armed Forces during World War II. The journey to its creation was long and, at times, controversial. Efforts to establish a national memorial began in the 1980s, largely due to the persistent advocacy of World War II veteran Roger Durbin, who proposed the idea to Congresswoman Marcy Kaptur of Ohio in 1987.

Recognizing the need to honor the sacrifices of an aging generation, Kaptur introduced legislation in 1989 to build the memorial. After several years of lobbying, Congress finally authorized the memorial in 1993, with President Bill Clinton signing the legislation into law. The American Battle Monuments Commission (ABMC) was appointed to manage the project. Fundraising efforts began soon after, with the memorial financed through a combination of private donations and federal funds. Actor Tom Hanks and Senator Bob Dole—himself a wounded World War II veteran—were among the most prominent supporters and fundraisers, helping to generate over $190 million.

Ultimately, a location was chosen on the National Mall, between the Lincoln Memorial and the Washington Monument. Some critics opposed this, arguing that the new structure would disrupt the Mall's open sightlines and historical layout. The design, by architect Friedrich St. Florian, was selected through a national competition. His vision incorporated classical elements symbolizing strength, unity, and sacrifice. The final design features a large plaza with a sunken pool, surrounded by 56 granite pillars representing the US states and territories of the time, and two arches symbolizing the Atlantic and Pacific theaters of war. Bronze relief panels illustrate scenes from the home front and combat zones, while the Freedom Wall displays 4,048 gold stars, each representing 100 American lives lost.

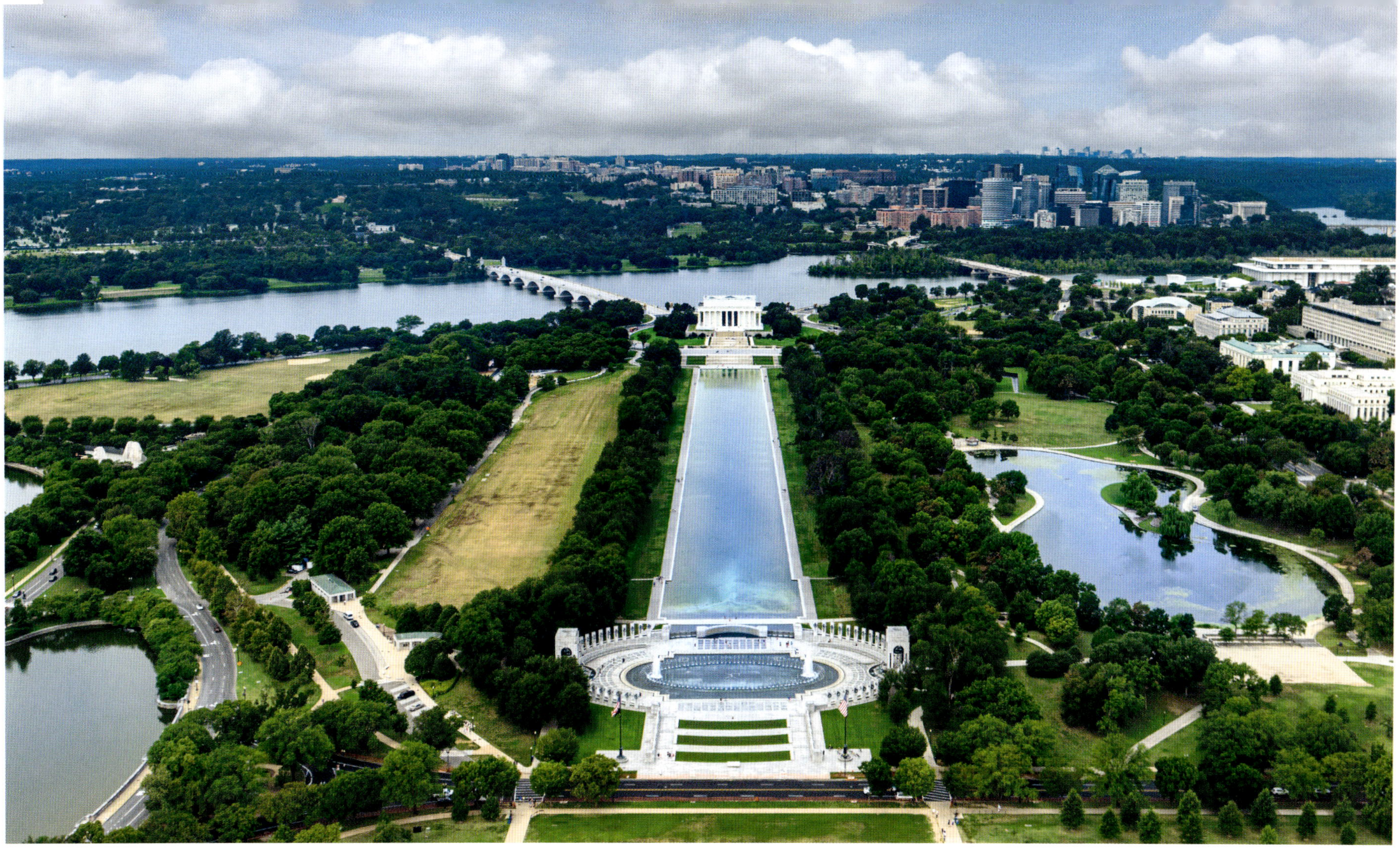

Construction began in September 2001 and concluded in April 2004. It was formally dedicated by President George W. Bush on May 29, 2004, in a ceremony attended by thousands of veterans and their families. Since its opening, the memorial has become one of the most visited sites in Washington, DC, drawing millions each year. As the number of living World War II veterans continues to decline, the memorial stands as a lasting reminder of their sacrifice and the enduring legacy of the "Greatest Generation."

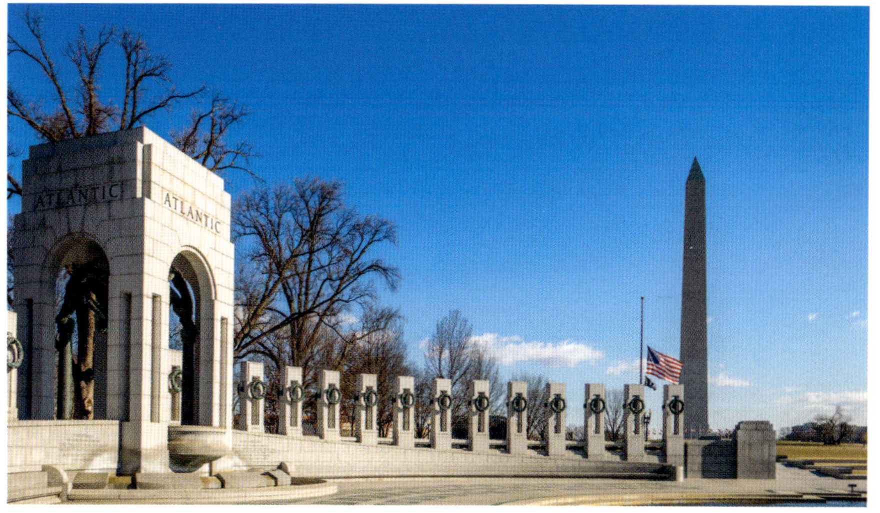

PICTURE CREDITS

Alamy: Pages 8, 23 (right), 24, 27, 33 (right), 51, 53 (top), 64, 65, 67, 81 (right). 85, 88, 89 (right), 96 (top), 135, 137 (right), 146, 148 (left), 148 (right), 157 (right), 161 (bottom), 171, 176, 185, 201, 203, 209, 222, 232, 233, 236, 237 (bottom), 239 (top), 240, 241 (top), 247 (top), 250, 260, 266, 267 (left), 267 (right), 269 (top left), 271, 273 (right), 290, 297, 306, 308, 309, 310, 312.
Sanjay Acharya: Page 261 (right).
Gert Boers/Unsplash: Page 196.
Mark Campi: Page 119.
James Campi Jr: Page 129 (top).
Andrew Carrotflower: Page 77 (bottom right).
Chicago Historical Society: Pages 168, 178.
Simon Clay/Pavilion Image Library: Page 179 (bottom).
Corbis: Pages 8, 165 (top), 296.
Ken Fitzgerald/Pavilion Image Library: Page 227 (bottom).
Ford Piquet Avenue Plant Museum: Page 177.
Free Library of Philadelphia: Page 56.
Getty Images: Front Cover and Pages 20, 28, 80, 84 (top), 220, 230 (bottom), 245 (left), 252, 254, 262, 268, 269 (right), 270, 276, 280, 282, 286, 294, 314.

Wally Gobetz: Page 125 (right).
Vaughan Grylls/Pavilion Image Library: Page 289.
Harley-Davidson Museum: Page 184.
Frank Hopkinson: Pages 75, 99, 213, 231, 277, 305, 313 (bottom).
Houston Metropolitan Research Center, Houston Public Library: Pages 226, 227 (top).
J.D. Iveson: Page 141 (right).
Jacobson Photo, San Antonio: Page 48.
Crystal Jo/Unsplash: Page 189
Evan Joseph/Pavilion Image Library: Pages 147 (bottom left), 147 (right), 167, 225 (top), 285.

Library of Congress: Pages 7, 10, 11 (Carol M. Highsmith), 12, 13 (Highsmith), 14, 15 (left), 18, 19 (top), 19 (bottom) (Highsmith), 22, 23 (top left), 23 (bottom) (Highsmith), 26, 29 (bottom left), 32, 33 (left), 34, 36, 38, 39 (left), 39 (right) (Highsmith), 40, 42, 44, 45 (left), 46 (left), 46 (top), 50, 52, 58, 60, 61 (top), 61 (right) (Highsmith), 62, 63 (left), 66, 68, 70, 71 (top), 72, 74, 76, 77 (top), 78, 82, 84 (bottom), 89 (left), 92, 94, 96 (bottom), 98 (left), 98 (right), 100, 101 (left), 102, 104, 106, 107 (left), 112, 113 (left), 114, 116, 117 (top left), 118, 119 (left), 120, 122, 124, 125 (top left), 125 (bottom left), 126, 127 (top), 128, 129 (bottom right), 130, 131 (top), 132, 133, 134, 136, 137 (left), 138 (top), 140, 141 (left), 142, 144, 146, 147 (top left), 150, 152 (top), 154, 156, 157 (left), 158, 160, 162, 163 (bottom), 166, 167, 170, 172, 174, 179 (top left), 180, 181 (left), 182, 183, 186, 187 (left), 188, 189 (left), 190, 191 (top left), 191 (top right), 192, 194, 198, 199 (top), 200, 202, 203 (left), 204, 206, 208, 210, 211 (left), 211 (right) (Highsmith), 212, 214, 216, 218, 224, 228, 235 (bottom), 237 (top), 238, 239 (bottom left), 242, 244, 246, 247 (bottom) (Highsmith), 249 (left), 251 (left), 253 (left), 264, 265 (top left), 265 (bottom left), 272, 273 (top left), 273 (top right), 274 (top right), 274 (bottom right), 278, 279 (left), 300, 302, 303 (left), 304, 307 (left).
Los Angeles Public Library: Page 208.
Ken Lund: Page 95.
Memphis and Shelby County Room/Memphis Public Library: Page 274 (left).
Missouri Historical Society: Page 86.

Alexander D. Mitchell IV: Page 127.
Karl Mondon/Pavilion Image Library: Pages 59, 79, 87, 145, 151, 153, 169, 175 (right), 187 (right), 195, 207,215, 229, 239 (right), 255, 287, 291 (right), 295, 298, 301.
NASA: Pages 256, 258, 259 (left), 261 (left).
Rembrandt Peale: Page 77 (bottom left).
Robert Price: Page 111.
Pullman Historic Site: Page 179 (top right).
Mark Riley: Page 163 (top).
San Antonio International Airport: Page 248.
San Diego Historical Society: Pages 16, 164.
Shutterstock: Pages 15 (right), 21 (right), 25, 29 (top), 30, 35, 46 (bottom), 47, 53 (bottom), 54, 69, 71 (bottom), 90, 97, 101 (right), 131 (bottom), 155, 161 (top), 165 (bottom), 173, 175 (left), 181 (right), 191 (bottom), 193, 205, 217, 219, 221, 225 (bottom), 241 (bottom), 243, 245 (right), 253 (right), 257 (left), 273 (bottom left), 279 (right), 281, 283, 284, 293, 307 (right), 311, 313 (top), 315.
Society of California Pioneers: Page 152 (bottom).

Joe Sonderman Collection: Pages 230 (top), 234, 235 (top).
State Library of Florida: Page 138 (bottom).
Bruce Torrance Historic Hollywood Collection: Pages 291 (left), 292.
United States National Park Service: Page 251 (right).
David Veasey/Pavilion Image Library: Pages 45 (right), 57, 63 (right), 83, 159.
VTS Marketplace: Page 149.
David Watts/Pavilion Image Library: Pages 17, 29 (bottom right), 37, 41, 43, 45, 49, 73, 93, 108, 115, 117 (right), 117 (bottom), 121, 265 (right), 303 (right).
Ben Whittick: Page 139 (left).
Wikimedia Commons: Pages 199 (bottom), 249 (right).
Billy Wilson: Page 113.

INDEX

INDEX

INDEX